RESEARCH ETHICS
Text and Readings

RESEARCH ETHICS
Text and Readings

Deborah R. Barnbaum
Michael Byron

Kent State University

Prentice
Hall

Upper Saddle River, New Jersey 07458

Library of Congress Cataloging-in-Publication Data

Barnnaum, Deborah, R., (date)
    Research ethics : text and readings / Deborah R. Barnbaum, Michael Byron.
        p. cm.
    Includes bibliographical references and index.
    ISBN 0-13-021264-4 (pbk.)
    1. Research—Moral and ethical aspects. I. Byron, Michael, (date) II. Title.

Q180.55.M67 B37 2001
174'.90901—dc21   00-040057

Acquisitions Editor: Ross Miller
Assistant Editor: Katie Janssen
Marketing Manager: Don Allmon
Production Editor: B. Christenberry
Manufacturing Buyer: Sherry Lewis

This book was set in 10/12 Palatino by Pub-Set, Inc.
and was printed and bound by Courier/Stoughton.
The cover was printed by Phoenix Color Corp.

 © 2001 by Prentice-Hall, Inc.
A Division of Pearson Education
Upper Saddle River, New Jersey 07458

Printed in the United States of America

10 9 8 7 6 5 4 3 2 1

ISBN 0-13-021264-4

PRENTICE-HALL INTERNATIONAL (UK) LIMITED, *London*
PRENTICE-HALL OF AUSTRALIA PTY. LIMITED, *Sydney*
PRENTICE-HALL OF CANADA INC., *Toronto*
PRENTICE-HALL HISPANOAMERICANA, S.A., *Mexico*
PRENTICE-HALL OF INDIA PRIVATE LIMITED, *New Delhi*
PRENTICE-HALL OF JAPAN, INC., *Tokyo*
PEARSON EDUCATION ASIA PTE. LTD., *Singapore*
EDITORA PRENTICE-HALL DO BRASIL, LTDA., *Rio de Janeiro*

For my father, with love and affection.
—D.B.

For my loving family, Wendy, Zoë, and Teddy.
—M.B.

Contents

PART II: ETHICS IN THE CONDUCT OF RESEARCH

Preface

This book presents opportunities to consider the complex issues surrounding research ethics. Its intended audience includes researchers in the social sciences or the natural sciences and anyone interested in scientific inquiry. The book aims to establish this conclusion: *Ethical research is better research.* After considering the far-reaching implications of scientific research, the ethical complexities that arise in the conduct of research, and the arguments we present in favor of ethical research practices, we hope that our readers will agree.

Recent interest in research ethics has been bolstered by public awareness of breaches of research ethics in our own backyard. Researchers in the United States are still grappling with the consequences of the Tuskegee Syphilis Study, Willowbrook and other Cold War Radiation Experiments, and the UCLA Schizophrenia Study, to name a very few.

As of January 10, 1993, applications for Research Training Grants to the National Institutes of Health are considered incomplete without a demonstration that the applicant has a plan for instruction in the responsible conduct of research (NIH Guide for Grants and Contracts, volume 21, number 43, November 27, 1992). *Research Ethics: Text and Readings* will help institutions to fulfill this requirement, schooling the next generation of researchers in complex topics such as conflict of interest, responsible authorship, research misconduct, the treatment of human and animal subjects, and data management—all topics which are recommended by the NIH.

Part I of *Research Ethics: Text and Readings* introduces the student of research ethics to some of the intricacies both of the research project and of ethical reasoning. This part will help readers to ground their ethical inquiries by answering questions about the history of research ethics, the commitments that researchers enter into, and the means and methods of ethical inquiry. The first part also contains three significant public policy statements—The Nuremberg Code, the World Medical Association Declaration of Helsinki, and the Belmont Report—whose recommendations are among the cornerstones of ethical research practices.

Parts II and III offer a range of resources for the study and practice of responsible research. Each chapter contains text that introduces and explores some of the questions in research ethics, including ethical issues surrounding methodology, human and animal experimentation, research misconduct, and the dissemination of research findings. In addition to our own discussion, we present the reader with case studies, references and resources for further inquiry, and readings to advance exploration of the ethical issues presented in the chapter. Readers may wish to explore each chapter in the order in which the material is presented. Alternatively, they may wish to turn first to the case studies, using them as a starting point for discussion. As a third option, they may move back and forth, reading passages from our text, then locating arguments from the supplementary readings that complement the text. By presenting our own discussion, additional resources, case studies, and readings, we hope to present flexible resources for learning about the ethical complexities of scientific research.

Several individuals have served as our teachers, mentors, and sources of inspiration and encouragement in the development of this book, all of whom deserve thanks. There are many whom we cannot acknowledge individually here. The Institutional Review Board at the University of New Hampshire and the Human Subjects Review Board at Kent State University have been ever-helpful resources; their members, past and present, are too numerous to list. Colleagues and mentors in the Philosophy Departments at Kent State University, the University of Notre Dame, the University of Massachusetts, the University of New Hampshire, and the Ethics Center at the University of South Florida have also been of tremendous help. Our thanks to Elizabeth Rager, who helped us compile the index. Finally, we wish to thank our families and friends for their assistance in bringing this project together.

—*Deborah R. Barnbaum, Ph.D.*
—*Michael Byron, Ph.D.*
Kent, Ohio

RESEARCH ETHICS
Text and Readings

Chapter 1
Overview of Research and Ethical Issues

1.1 INTRODUCTION

Any enterprise that we undertake is better for being done ethically. Our relationships with family and friends, our careers, and any activity we engage in is improved for being done ethically. We know that there are ethics in sportsmanship, ethics in many professions such as healthcare or law, and ethics in our personal relationships. And yet, the attention paid to the ethics of scientific research seems to be a comparatively recent phenomenon. Most scientific researchers working today did not take classes or read books on the ethics of scientific research, although they may see themselves as individuals with high moral standards. Why should we consider questions surrounding research ethics today?

History shows why people are *now* asking ethical questions of scientists. Some people may say that we are now reaching a point in scientific inquiry in which more and more ethical challenges are raised. The actual cloning of a sheep from the somatic cell of another adult sheep raises the possibility that human cloning might take place. The question of whether scientists should clone a human being is an ethical issue. The Human Genome Project, scheduled to be completed in the spring of the year 2000, raises countless ethical questions regarding the use and possible abuse of human genetic information. The pressure to "publish (or perish!)" has created an industry of publishing scientific research, as well as heightened pressure to churn out as much useful data as possible. Faced with the pressure to publish as much as possible, as quickly as possible, the temptation to take "short cuts," both in the research process and in the publication process, raises ethical questions. The process of scientific research raises ethical questions at almost every stage of inquiry: What kinds of questions should be investigated? How should data be accumulated? What should be done with the data once it is amassed? How should the data be published? What are the scientist's responsibilities once the data has been published?

History points us to cases of scientific research that may have been ethically suspect and that can illustrate for us the ethical challenges in performing scientific research. One case of scientific research in the United States that raised many ethical questions exemplifies possible ethical violations in scientific research. The case concerns Laud Humphreys, a doctoral candidate in sociology, who wished to study the motivations and behavior of men who have anonymous sex in public restrooms. His study was published in 1970 and is known as the "Tearoom Trade." Humphreys befriended men in public restrooms, offering to stand guard and to warn the men engaging in anonymous sex should a police officer or other individual threaten to expose the sexual acts. Humphreys was able to befriend some of the men, disclose that he was a social scientist, and gain further information about the men and their motives. However, some of the men's lives and motives remained elusive. Humphreys disguised himself as a health care worker doing "survey" work. After obtaining the addresses of some of the men via public records, based on their license plates, Humphreys visited the remaining men at home. There he learned more information about the men's marital status, levels of education, and other personal facts. His research indicated that the majority of men who engaged in these impersonal sexual acts were married, considered themselves heterosexual, and had children. The stereotype of the man who seeks anonymous sex in a men's restroom did not reflect the reality.

Ask yourself what some of the ethical issues are in this case. If you are having a difficult time determining what these issues are, try to examine the case from the different perspectives of the people involved. What were Humphreys' interests, and how were they protected? What were the interests of the research subjects, and how were they protected? What about the interests of the family members of the research subjects? Why was this research undertaken? Were the benefits of performing this study so valuable that they justified the risks to the research subjects and their families?

Some of the problems involved in the above case are these: The research subjects did not know that they were research subjects and never gave any type of consent to being part of the project. In addition, Humphreys observed them doing personal activities that could put them at risk in a number of ways. For example, they were performing illegal activities, the discovery of which might have greatly embarrassed the subjects and put them in both social and financial jeopardy. If their identities were disclosed, the subjects could lose their marriages or their jobs. Several other important relationships in which the subjects were involved may have been compromised. Humphreys deceived the subjects by pretending to be someone he was not, which many people think is morally wrong. Even after deceiving them, Humphreys did not later disclose the nature of his research to the research subjects. Finally, some people question the value of Humphreys' project, in light of the fact that the subjects were put at risk of grave harm for the sake of little benefit to themselves, the scientific community, or anyone else.

This case underscores the fact that researchers have a set of special responsibilities. These responsibilities arise from the relationships into which the researcher enters. For example, researchers have responsibilities to research subjects, to the community in which research takes place (such as a university or hospital), to the community from which their research subjects are drawn, to other researchers, to the individuals or organizations who fund the research, and to society at large. If the researcher does not undertake a research project that involves human research subjects, he or she may have responsibilities to animal research subjects or to the environment, to other researchers, to the scientific community, to funding agencies, or to the community at large.

Even if researchers enter into special obligations in undertaking research, several questions remain unanswered. Which relationships entail special obligations? Why do relationships create obligations or responsibilities? What are the obligations that arise when one undertakes scientific research? How does one fulfill these obligations? These are some of the issues considered in this book.

Looking at past research projects that raised ethical questions may illuminate some of the ethical obligations of researchers. Although most scientific research is conducted and reported in an ethical fashion, there have been notable exceptions. These cases give us the opportunity to learn from others' past mistakes and are good introductions to the moral obligations that researchers have today. Additionally, the historical record demonstrates how research ethics achieved its present-day significance.

1.2   HISTORICAL BACKGROUND

It would be prohibitive to discuss the entire history of how research ethics has come to be important in the last few decades. Some people trace the history of research ethics as they are currently understood to the Nuremberg trials, where many Nazi war crimes were recounted. The Nuremberg Code, which is included in the readings for Chapter 2, was drafted to protect the interests of research subjects in scientific experiments. However, even after the Nuremberg trials, some members of the scientific community were not as ethically astute as they might have been. Beginning in 1945 and continuing into the 1970s, 23,000 Americans in more than 1,400 experimental trials were exposed to radiation without their knowledge in an attempt to learn about the effects of radiation on human beings. These experiments, many of which were conducted by the federal government, coincided with the cold war between the United States and the Soviet Union. Experiments included giving irradiated cereal to 125 children in Willowbrook, an institution for mentally retarded children, irradiating the testes of prisoners to determine the level at which the prisoners became sterile, and irradiating the limbs of persons who were scheduled to have limbs amputated. After the amputations, scientists examined the limbs to see how much radiation remained, and for how long. Subjects were irradiated, injected with radioactive materials, and fed radioactive materials without their knowledge or consent.

These cold war radiation experiments were not the only cases of research misconduct that occurred in the United States, even after the promulgation of the Nuremberg Code. One of the most notorious cases of research misconduct was the Tuskegee Study. In the early 1930s syphilis was treated by a complicated, painful, and long treatment regimen. In 1932 a study was undertaken in Macon County, Alabama, in which 399 men with syphilis were left untreated, and 201 men without syphilis served as a control group. The men were left untreated for forty years while scientists charted the course of the disease. Left untreated, syphilis can have numerous devastating effects, many of which are fatal. Why were the men untreated in the study, even as treatments were available? Some scientists tried to discredit the treatments used in the 1930s as too expensive, too time-consuming, or too painful to be widely used by the men who were being studied. But penicillin, an inexpensive, painless, and widely available cure, was also denied to the men in the 1940s and later. The research continued even after the institution of the Nuremberg Code, which prohibited just this sort of abuse of human subjects.

One of the gravest violations of the Tuskegee Study concerned the participants who were chosen to live out their days with untreated syphilis. The residents of Macon County were overwhelmingly black. Furthermore, they were almost all impoverished—many suffered from malnutrition, and they generally could not afford the syphilis treatment at $2.00 per injection. Most of them were illiterate. Finally, the subjects were not told that they had syphilis. In exchange for participation in the study, the men received free physical exams, free rides to and from the clinics, hot meals on examination days, free treatment for minor ailments, and a guarantee that burial stipends would be paid to their survivors. Furthermore, the participants were told that if they did not continue to participate in the study they would lose all of these benefits. The ethical problems in this study should already be clear: The participants did not give informed consent to be in the study, they were coerced into continued participation, and it was not clear that the subjects would benefit from continuing the study. Even if there were benefits, in the form of free meals and burial costs, the benefits were not outweighed by the enormous harms of the study. Because of the inequity between the amount of benefit and the amount of harm, the research process was unjust. Finally, any claims that valuable scientific knowledge was gained by this experiment are dubious. The scientific community was well acquainted with the medical implications of untreated syphilis as far back as 1910. Not only did the subjects endure many harms, but the benefits of this research, in terms of direct benefit to the subjects and gains in scientific knowledge, were minimal.

Lastly, consider a more recent case whose ethical implications are still debated. In the developing world over 1,000 babies are born HIV-positive every day. HIV is the virus that causes AIDS. It has been proven, in the AIDS Clinical Trials Group (ACTG) 076 study, that a woman who takes the drug AZT during pregnancy will reduce the chances of vertical transmission (mother-to-infant) of

HIV. However, the 076 protocol is prohibitive, in terms of both time and expense, for many people in the developing world. The 076 protocol requires taking five pills per day for 12 weeks, intravenous AZT during delivery of the infant, and a 6-week, 4-times-a-day oral AZT regimen, and women are required to abstain from breast-feeding. The entire 076 treatment plan costs more than $1,000. Although the benefits of this treatment plan are clear, it is not possible for all of the women who would benefit from this treatment plan to pay for it. A less costly alternative was needed.

The United States and eleven developing nations decided to determine whether a shorter course of AZT could be employed, so as to limit the number of deaths from HIV. The researchers compared the rate of success of a short course of AZT with a placebo in terms of its efficacy in reducing the vertical transmission of HIV. These studies took place in Thailand, the Ivory Coast, and Gambia. For example, in Thailand 198 pregnant women received a short course of AZT, and 199 received a placebo from 36 weeks of gestation until delivery. Transmission rates were reported as 9.2 percent in the AZT group and 18.6 percent in the placebo group. The news that this study took place broke in 1997.

The ethical concerns here are varied and complex. First, there are concerns about justice that mirror the Tuskegee Study. Even if it could be determined that a shorter course of AZT would work, would the subjects who were used to confirm this fact benefit from this knowledge? The average health budget in the countries in which the short course was tested is $10 per person, per year. The short course costs $50 to $80 per pregnancy. If the people on whom the drugs are tested cannot benefit from the drugs once they are no longer in the test phase, then it may seem that the subjects are being used unjustly in the experiments. Questions also arise when considering the subjects, irrespective of their opportunities to benefit from the procedure. Just as with the Tuskegee experiment, the subjects were typically illiterate and impoverished. Could the research subjects offer genuine informed consent?

A more complex question deals with the use of placebos in this study. An already acceptable treatment plan was available, and scientists already know what untreated HIV will do to both the mothers and the infants. The standard of care for women with HIV in the United States allows women to receive drugs that are shown to effectively reduce the transmission rate of HIV from mothers to their infants. Should the standard of care in the United States be the applicable standard, or should it be the standard of the country in which the research is being conducted, even if the United States sponsors the research? Is it appropriate to use a placebo in this case? Since placebos were used, not all of the mothers in the trial received the direct benefit of taking the AZT. Is having "the chance" to get an effective drug a benefit, or is the drug itself a benefit?

Finally, there are considerations for the research subjects long after the experiment is over. What obligations do researchers have to the subjects after they are no longer subjects? If you are unsure about the ethical complexities in this case ask yourself what would happen if this study went on in the United States: Suppose that the subjects were primarily poor women who were on Medicaid, the benefits of AZT were made public, but then it was determined that AZT would not be funded by Medicaid. In that case, many people would find an inherent injustice in asking one group of people to serve as research subjects, while another group derived all of the benefit of the knowledge that was gained from the experiments. Even if some of the research subjects benefited from serving as research subjects, that alone is not a sufficient justification for the use of human research subjects. There also needs to be a just distribution of harms and benefits when using human research subjects.

These cases present only a sample of ethical questions in scientific research. Of course, the ethical questions surrounding scientific research are not limited to questions about human research subjects, placebos, or informed consent. There are also questions relating to the dissemination of research findings, the use of statistical data, and the role of the scientist in the community. If we are going to perform research activities, we need to be able to do so ethically. Understanding ethical research first requires an understanding of the goals of the research process.

1.3   DEFINITION OF 'RESEARCH' AND IMPLICATIONS

What is research? Answering this question may give us some insight into how to perform it well. This strategy—discovering the function of a particular object or activity in order to determine what virtues characterize a good object or activity of its kind—is an old one. Aristotle, who inspired the moral theory we discuss in section 2.5, was one of the first philosophers to employ such a strategy. Aristotle sought to learn the function of human beings in order to learn what made for a good human being. Ask yourself what makes a particular pen a *good* pen. Perhaps it writes legibly, or it is comfortable to hold, or it has plenty of ink. Any pen that fails to have these qualities—one which does not write legibly or is difficult to hold or has run out of ink—is not a good pen. These virtues of the pen are easily identifiable when one considers what a pen *is used for*. Similarly, we may be able to determine the virtues of research—those properties of good and responsible research—by examining the definition of 'research' and what purposes research serves. Examining this definition might illuminate the goals and techniques of research. If one knows what the goals and techniques of an activity are, then one may be able to identify what it is to perform that activity well or poorly.

A commonly used definition of 'research', which will prove useful to our inquiry, is taken from the Federal Policy Register, Title 45, Code of Federal Regulations Part 46, section 46.102(d):

> Research means a systematic investigation, including research development, testing and evaluation, designed to develop or contribute to the generalizable knowledge.

One of the merits of employing this definition is that it is quite general. It applies well to research in the natural, social, and behavioral sciences. A second reason for employing this definition is that since many of the ethical guidelines for research in the United States are determined by the federal government, such as codes that regulate the ethical use of human beings and some animals in research funded by federal money, it makes sense to employ the federal government's definition of research.

The term 'research', in common usage, refers to humankind's quest for knowledge. However, research is more than just the acquisition of information: looking up a friend's telephone number or a favorite recipe does not usually count as research. In contrast, those who compile recipes for cookbooks or in order to compare the fat content of different ethnic cuisines *are* doing research. So research involves gathering information in certain ways for certain kinds of purposes. In general, research is a systematic attempt to acquire generalizable information about a particular subject area. Furthermore, it seems to be essential to the activity of research that part of the point of gathering the information is to disseminate it. Another way to state our definition of research is to say that it is the activity of methodically learning about the world in order to teach what one learns.

This definition tells us many things. First, since research "contribute[s] to the generalizable knowledge," its conclusions apply beyond the single set of data which support those conclusions. In being generalizable, the data must stand up to scientific scrutiny. Every stage of research, including the conception of a project, the gathering of data, the analysis of the data, and the dissemination of conclusions, is meant to be shared with others. That is not to say that a researcher has no privacy at all during any stage of a research project. Privacy is important for many reasons, including the protection of the interests of research subjects, which we discuss in section 4.6, and the protection of intellectual property, which we discuss in section 8.6. However, ultimately a project must be able to withstand scrutiny from the scientific community, as well as scrutiny from others.

Researchers should be prepared to share aspects of their research with other researchers, the research subjects who have helped in compiling the data (when applicable), and the general public. The scrutiny that research may undergo can include both scientific scrutiny and moral scrutiny. By scientific scrutiny, we mean scrutiny having to do with the scientific content of the research. For example, other scientists may ask whether the data supports the conclusions. By moral scrutiny, we mean scrutiny having to do with the ethics of your research. Would the public find the research morally questionable? Were subjects mistreated in the quest for data? Do the conclusions have morally reprehensible implications? Were the conclusions responsibly reported to the non-scientific community, or will the non-scientific community misunderstand the implications of the conclusions? Researchers may be required to respond to both kinds of scrutiny.

Note that scientific questions and ethical questions need not exclude each other. Some scientific questions are themselves ethical questions. Scientific research may lead to clinical or policy decisions. For example, in an article published in the February 5, 1998 (volume 338, number 6, pages 373–378) issue of *The New England Journal of Medicine,* scientists from the Centers for Disease Control reported a significant increase in suicide rates following natural disasters. News of this finding was reported in the mainstream press, including network news stations and the Associated Press, because of the wide policy implications of a predictable spike in suicide rates. Policy recommendations as a result of these conclusions would be obvious: Along with usual disaster relief resources, counselors trained in dealing with suicidal people should be dispatched to areas struck by disasters such as earthquakes, hurricanes, or floods. The Centers for Disease Control data indicated that in the year after an earthquake, the suicide rate can rise as much as 63 percent in the affected region struck.

However, in January of 1999 the same scientists reported that there had been a mistake in their calculations: Suicides from the year 1990 had been counted twice (*New England Journal of Medicine,* January 14, 1999, volume 340, number 2). An accurate analysis of the corrected data indicated that suicides *do not* increase after natural disasters. The researchers, in their retraction, pointed out that other psychological harm befalls those who suffer through natural disasters, and thus psychological counseling would still be valuable to those who had experienced a natural disaster. It is clear that the misreported data had different policy implications than an accurate reporting would have had. News of the retraction of this story did not receive the same attention from the mainstream press as the emotional and graphic claims of the first report. Scientists have a responsibility to make sure that their claims are accurate before they report their findings to the public.

The claim that research is a "systematic investigation" implies that there are standards in doing research. If research is done systematically, it can be done well. As we noted earlier, not every systematic investigation is research. Checking each pie in a cookbook to find the recipe with the lowest fat may be a systematic investigation, but that does not make it research. However, if an investigation is not systematic, the "research" may be done poorly, and it may not count as research at all. The requirement that research be systematic appears to be a statement about the scientific standards of the study: Are the methods appropriate to the question being asked? Has the hypothesis been rigorously tested? Are the results duplicable? Moreover, as was pointed out above, scientific standards may overlap with moral standards. The failure to examine the data systematically in the research on suicide rates following natural disasters was both a scientific and a moral mistake.

It is important to recognize that research involves the "gathering and analysis of information," and as such, research involves several steps, each of which must be done well. One cannot gather information, analyze it poorly, and call it research, nor can one perform rigorous analysis on poorly gathered data and call it research. Both of these steps appear, on their faces, to be scientific requirements, but they can also be ethical requirements. The research on suicide rates following natural disasters did not involve poorly collected data. Rather, the analysis of the data was performed incorrectly, leading the researchers to mistaken conclusions. These mistaken conclusions had important policy implications; hence, these mistakes were not merely scientific, but they were also ethical.

1.4   ETHICAL IMPLICATIONS OF RESEARCH RELATIONSHIPS

Judging by the above definition of research, it is possible to perform research either well or poorly. But what are the advantages to performing research activities *ethically?* One way to determine the ethical questions that arise when doing research is to consider the relationships that researchers have and to whom they owe something. Certainly researchers have families and friends, and moral obligations involved in those special relationships do not depend on a person's research activities. But to whom do researchers have moral responsibilities *when they undertake research?* The following is a list of some relationships into which researchers enter in the course of performing research.

Researchers may have relationships to

- themselves
- research subjects, whether human or animal (some research may not demand the use of human or animal research subjects)
- other researchers
- the institution at which the research is taking place
- the community in which the research is being done
- the individuals or organization funding the research
- society as a whole

Given these relationships, are there any advantages in doing research ethically? The answer is *overwhelmingly yes, ethically performed research has many advantages*. Researchers will feel better about themselves—maintain greater self-respect and self-esteem—by undertaking ethically responsible research. Furthermore, in light of the fact that scientific and moral considerations are not always separable, research undertaken in an ethically responsible way is often better science. Researchers may owe it to themselves not only to perform research but to perform it well. Finally, recall that according to the above definition, research is a contribution to generalizable knowledge. As such, if the conclusions that an individual draws are not generalizable, or if studies are biased or poorly designed, they may not even count as research. The same considerations show that researchers' obligations to do research are also obligations to do research ethically.

From the perspective of the relationship between researcher and research subject, there are many benefits to performing ethically responsible research. First, many moral theories claim that we have moral obligations to respect others, protect them, not harm them, and benefit them. A detailed discussion of different moral theories appears in Chapter 2. Being a research subject may be a benefit, a burden, or both. Regardless of which it is, the choice of whether to be research subjects should be just and fair. Subjects should provide informed consent whenever feasible, taking into account their differing abilities to consent voluntarily and with full understanding, concerns which are discussed in section 4.5. If research subjects, be they vulnerable human subjects or animal subjects, are unable offer informed consent, then the researcher must take even greater precautions ensure their responsible treatment. These greater precautions are the topic of Chapters 4 and 5. If subjects are unwilling participants, then they are less likely to generate accurate or generalizable results, in which case an ethical problem becomes a scientific problem.

If research is done ethically, it is more likely to be factual, a point that is important when considering the researcher's relationships with other researchers. For example, if researchers engage in unethical practices such as falsifying or fabricating data, cooking, trimming, or forging statistics, where does this leave other scientists who try to build upon this false data? Because of the failure to respect the research goals of other scientists, fabrication and falsification are both scientific *and* ethical failures, as we discuss in section 7.2. In addition, if subject samples are biased, or research subjects are mistreated, it is less likely that the data and conclusions are generalizable, or that the data is an accurate representation of reality. For example, if research subjects are not voluntarily participating in a study, or cannot leave the study at any time without harm or loss of benefits, then it is less likely that the subjects will adhere to the procedures of the study. Since researchers are working in a community of other researchers, poor data collection strategies may ultimately undermine not only their own research agendas, but those of other researchers.

Researchers are representatives of their institutions. As such, their failure to conduct research ethically can reflect poorly on the institution. Such behavior can affect colleagues, institutions, other researchers, and the research enterprise itself. As a result, researchers have obligations to carry out their research ethically for the sake of other researchers at their institution.

Researchers may also have moral obligations in virtue of their relationships with the surrounding community. Researchers have responsibilities not only to their research subjects, but also to the subjects' families and communities. Consider a research protocol in which elementary school-aged children are given disposable cameras in an attempt to learn about the children's creativity, as well as to learn what children perceive as important in their lives. After the children take pictures, the researcher has the pictures developed and asks the children to explain what is depicted in the pictures. Though there is a comparatively low risk of harm *to the children* in giving them cameras, important questions can be raised about *potential harms to families of these children*. What if the use of the cameras results in a loss of privacy for the family? Many possible scenarios could arise in which the children might compromise the privacy of their family members by taking photographs. These harms may be weighed against the fact that some of the possible remedies to this loss of privacy would compromise the scientific value of the research. Perhaps the children could avoid compromising the privacy of their families by taking pictures that had no people in them. This requirement, however, might limit the children's creativity, thereby threatening to invalidate the research.

Researchers may also have responsibilities to funding institutions. Although funding institutions are not the same as the community from which research subjects are drawn, they have similar interests in the data and conclusions. Funding institutions make some research possible, and they may expect something in return. What should they reasonably expect in return? What claims to ownership of data or results might funding agencies reasonably press? These are some of the ethical and practical concerns associated with the funding of research.

Finally, ethical obligations may emerge from the relationship between the researcher and society as a whole. Research helps to determine public policy and clinical options. If research is sound, both scientifically and ethically, society can gain from science. But research that is neither scientifically nor ethically sound can offer few benefits and can in fact harm others. Consider the responsibilities that the researchers from the Centers for Disease Control had when they released their initial findings about the rise in suicide rates following natural disasters. Scarce resources are allocated in the wake of natural disasters, and a misallocation of these resources could have had damaging consequences. Additionally, some of the resources that scientists use in the course of their research are natural resources that the public may also lay claim to. How should these competing claims be resolved? What responsibilities do researchers have in light of these competing claims? Responsible scientists recognize this important role in shaping public policy and conduct themselves accordingly.

Are there disadvantages to doing research ethically? There may be some, but whatever gains result from doing unethical research are short-lived. One of the advantages of circumventing ethical obligations would be fewer regulations and less paperwork. For example, by law all federally funded research that involves human research subjects must be reviewed by an Institutional Review Board (IRB), which provides ethical oversight. IRBs initially review and approve or disapprove of research projects that involve human beings All federally funded research that involves certain species of animals must be reviewed by an Institutional Animal Care and Use Committee (IACUC). Some projects involve annual reviews even after approval, so that the IRB or IACUC can be assured that the research subjects continue to be treated ethically. IRB and IACUC oversight involves a great deal of paperwork. Without this ethical oversight, the research process would be less cumbersome. Perhaps some conclusions could be reached more quickly if the hurdles of ethical requirements were not in place, on top of all the other requirements that researchers must meet. New drugs or clinical practices that would benefit people would come to the market more quickly if ethical considerations were ignored. Short-term gains such as getting a paper published more quickly before a particular deadline may be initially appealing, but irresponsibly generated data and unsound conclusions can be found out. Insofar as research is meant to be shared—with research subjects, the wider community, and other researchers—research must be able to withstand public scrutiny, including ethical scrutiny. Researchers who do not fulfill their ethical responsibilities fail to live up to a professional standard expected of all researchers. There may be legal repercussions, at both the institutional and federal levels, if one is found out. Inasmuch as a great deal of research has practical applications, ethical and scientific failures can have dangerous ramifications. New drugs and therapies that are hastily tested and rushed to market may not prove to have the therapeutic benefit we had hoped for, or they may have harmful long-term side effects. Finally, ethical failures undermine the public's confidence in the scientific process. The obstacles to the responsible reporting of scientific findings are great enough without further compounding these problems by calling into question the origins or veracity of those findings. The benefits in undertaking research ethically are clear. How to conduct research activities ethically is the subject of the rest of this book.

1.5   LOOKING AHEAD

This book considers some of the ethical questions, as well as possible solutions, that are raised in research. We have introduced some of these questions in this chapter. In Chapter 2, we examine several normative moral theories designed to answer questions about what constitutes ethical behavior. In addition to these theories, we introduce three principles—the principles of autonomy, beneficence, and justice—that may also help to answer questions about what constitutes ethical behavior. The point of Chapter 2 is *not* to leave the reader with *the definitive formula* for finding the answer to ethical questions. Rather, the point is to introduce a variety of systems that will provide warning flags for ethical mistakes in research. Chapter 2 introduces theories that can justify many of the ethical claims found in the rest of this volume. At the conclusion of Chapter 2, three policy statements are included. These policy statements represent articulations of the theories and principles discussed in Chapter 2. As we will see, these ethical theories and principles complement each other, and together they provide a balanced means of examining ethical issues in research.

Part II of this volume, Ethics in the Conduct of Research, begins with Chapter 3, on study design and review. Methodological concerns, eliminating bias, and maintaining clinical equipoise are considerations important to the proper design of research studies. We consider some of the methodological questions in research ethics in this chapter. Additionally, we examine one of the safeguards for ethical research: the Institutional Review Board (IRB). What does this board do, and why is its function so important? Several readings examine the value of randomized clinical trials, the importance of equipoise in clinical research, and the state of IRB oversight. Chapter 3, like all subsequent chapters, concludes with a set of case studies. These case studies allow further exploration and discussion of the issues presented. Also included are a set of readings, which further explore some of the issues raised in the text.

Chapter 4 considers questions regarding the treatment of human research subjects. If human subjects are used in a study, their participation at every stage must be ethically justified. This chapter considers the use of human research subjects at every step, including the initial justification for using human research subjects, their recruitment, the process of gaining informed consent, and their treatment during the research process. We will also examine a special type of research—deception research—and the ethical questions that are raised by this controversial methodology.

The special circumstances of some research subjects merit special consideration. Chapter 5 more closely examines the use of research subjects in special cases. Some classes of research subjects require special consideration, including children, adolescents, the elderly, pregnant women, persons with mental disabilities, and persons who are institutionalized, to name a few. The circumstances of each of these populations are different, creating different challenges for researchers who wish to study members of these populations. Strategies for dealing with the individual circumstances of research subjects from vulnerable populations are discussed in Chapter 5.

Chapter 6 looks at the use of animals as research subjects, as well as resource allocation and environmental considerations of scientific research. The ethics of animal research is still hotly debated. This chapter examines the arguments both for and against the use of animals as research subjects, as well as some of the legal protections in place to protect the interests of animal research subjects. In addition, questions surrounding the use of valuable resources, both environmental and man-made, are considered.

Part III, Ethics in the Dissemination of Research, examines the ethical questions surrounding the handling of data, the publication of scientific findings, and the further obligations that a scientist may have even after the publication of research findings. In Chapter 7 we address questions surrounding scientific misconduct. Research misconduct can occur in many ways. We examine the fabrication and falsification of data, inappropriate authorship practices such as plagiarism and misappropriation, and the reporting by whistleblowers of misconduct in the research setting.

Chapter 8 focuses on conflicts of interest and their ethical costs. How does one identify a conflict of interest, and how should conflicts of interest be resolved? The funding of scientific research raises questions about conflicts of interest, as well as concerns about patents and copyrights on research and its products. We examine questions surrounding the ownership of scientific data. As mentioned earlier, scientists have many individuals or organizations to whom they have special responsibilities. Do scientists have the responsibility of disclosing their data to any of these individuals or organizations. Finally, we discuss different types of intellectual property protections.

Chapter 9 considers the ethical obligation to eliminate bias and promote objectivity in scientific research. The importance of maintaining objectivity and eliminating bias in scientific practice cannot be stressed enough. We consider some of the methodological obstacles to objectivity in scientific research. The chapter concludes with a discussion of the scientist in society. How should scientific results be reported? What are the obligations of the scientist even after a research project has been completed? What is the role of the scientist in the community at large?

In writing this book, the authors had a number of projects in mind. One of the projects that this book will *not* accomplish is to provide a recipe for performing ethical research in every case. We do not presume to have covered every point in the complex field of research ethics. Rather, we hope that the text, the readings, and the case studies presented will offer a starting-point for asking the right questions regarding ethical research practices. Knowing the right questions to ask when undertaking ethically responsible research is the first step in coming up with the right answers. Text that discusses the framework of ethical questions, case studies that challenge the reader to incorporate the material from the text, and readings that elaborate on some of the points already made by the authors will contribute to enhancing researchers' abilities to assess responsible research.

REFERENCES AND FURTHER READING

The Advisory Committee on Human Radiation Experiments, *The Final Report*, stock number 061–000–00–848–9. Washington, DC: U.S. Government Printing Office, 1995.

Lawrence K. Altman, *Who Goes First? The Story of Self-Experimentation in Medicine*, Berkeley and Los Angeles, University of California Press, 1998.

Ezekiel J. Emmanuel introduced a symposium entitled "A World of Research Subjects," which included: Robert A. Crouch and John D. Arras, "AZT Trials and Tribulations"; Christine Grady, "Service of Healing"; Leonard H. Glantz, George J. Annas, Michel A. Grodin, and Wendy K. Mariner, "Research in Developing Countries: Taking Benefit Seriously"; and "Placebos and HIV: Lessons Learned" (reprinted in Chapter 3 of this volume), in *The Hastings Center Report*, volume 28, number 6, November-December 1998.

James H. Jones, *Bad Blood: The Tuskegee Syphilis Experiment*, New York: The Free Press, 1993.

NIH Readings on the Protection of Human Subjects in Behavioral and Social Science Research: Conference Proceedings and Background Papers, ed. Joan E. Sieber. Washington, DC: University Publications of America, 1984.

David B. Resnik, *The Ethics of Science: An Introduction*, New York: Routledege, 1998.

Kristin Shrader-Frechette, *Ethics of Scientific Research*, Lanham, Maryland: Rowman and Littlefield Publishers, 1994.

Chapter 2
Perspectives on Ethics

2.1 LAW AND ETHICS

Scientific research is governed by federal and other laws. In addition, research is subject to a host of institutional, local, state, and federal policies that have sanctions attached to them; these regulations function much like laws in controlling the activities of scientific research. Laws and regulations prohibit and threaten punishment for such violations as copyright infringement and patent violation. They govern the use and treatment of human subjects in many experimental situations, and they limit the extent and kind of environmental impact that research may have. In light of all this regulation, why worry about ethics? Isn't legal regulation sufficient to govern scientific research? What is the connection, if any, between law and ethics?

We distinguish between law and ethics at several levels. First, law governs people's behavior but not their beliefs or attitudes. In contrast, we often judge people's ethical qualities—we think they are admirable or despicable, kind or mean, polite or rude—depending on their beliefs and attitudes. What's more, we hold the law to an ethical standard. So, for instance, we recognize the possibility that some duly constituted authority, such as a legislature, might pass poor legislation and make an unjust law. Ethics provides a perspective from which we can judge that some laws are just and others are not. The Jim Crow laws that enforced segregation in the American south after the Civil War provide examples of unjust laws; laws protecting citizens from unwarranted search and seizure are examples of just laws. Once again, law is distinct from ethics.

This distinction permits us to raise the question about any law, including laws and policies that govern research: Is this law just? Is it ethical to obey this law, or would obeying the law or policy violate our judgments about ethical conduct? It is true, of course, that scientific research in the twenty-first century will continue to be governed by myriad legal and policy regulations, but this fact alone does not relieve researchers of responsibility to make ethical judgments.

The law may not be sufficient for governing proper behavior in scientific research, requiring us to supplement our legal claims with moral ones, since there are some questions for which the law does not provide answers. Many questions faced by scientific researchers are not settled by the law. The fact that the law remains silent on these issues is not a reflection of their insignificance, however. For example, the law will not tell us who deserves first authorship on an important publication, or indicate the most responsible means for recruiting human research subjects, or bring to light a scientist's responsibilities for making sure that the mainstream press does not misrepresent important research findings. These questions require researchers to make *moral* decisions—the law remains silent on these matters. Thus, the law must be supplemented by moral theory before important questions in research ethics can be answered.

Finally, nearly all scientific researchers wish to be ethical, but they may feel that they lack expertise in this area. Answering the question, "Is this action legally permissible?" may be easy—the law books will tell you. Answering the question "Is this action morally permissible?" is more complex, requiring a knowledge of competing moral theories or principles and an understanding of how to apply these theories or principles. The purpose of this chapter is to examine some of the systematic approaches to understanding ethics. The theories and principles we examine will provide the basis from which we explore the range of ethical issues that arise in scientific research. We begin with a survey of ethical theories.

2.2   ETHICAL THEORIES: UTILITARIANISM

The theory of **utilitarianism** is one of the dominant moral theories of our time. Its fundamental insight is that our actions have consequences for ourselves and others and that morality is a matter of acting so that those consequences are as beneficial as possible. Morality is a matter of making the world a better place. Jeremy Bentham, James Mill, and John Stuart Mill, the British philosophers who developed this theory in the early nineteenth century, thought that this idea required us to act so that we promote pleasure and diminish pain. This hedonistic version of utilitarianism should not be confused with selfishness: It is not just our own but everyone's pleasures and pains that morality requires us to take into account. We act rightly, according to this early version of utilitarianism, when our actions bring about the greatest balance of pleasure over pain. According to another famous utilitarian slogan, we should act for the greatest good of the greatest number.

Contemporary utilitarians have generally moved away from an account of morality in terms of pleasure. Instead, they argue that right actions maximize impersonal value. The idea of impersonal value is objective in the sense that one can recognize certain states of affairs as good not merely to this or that person but also from an impersonal or objective standpoint. An example of utilitarian reasoning in research ethics is an argument that is offered in defense of using animals as research subjects, an argument that is examined in greater detail in section 6.3. The argument claims that there have been great benefits—both to animals and to humans—as a result of research that uses animals as experimental subjects. The greatest good, in the form of vaccines for diseases such as tetanus and small pox, has been brought about for the greatest number, as a result of this testing. The principle of maximizing impersonal value in this case requires ignoring personal considerations and maximizing the number of lives saved.

In contrast to this **act-utilitarianism**—so-called because it recommends assessing actions one at a time—**rule-utilitarianism** maintains that it is possible to justify a rule of action, such as "always tell the truth," by showing that adopting such a rule maximizes utility, happiness, or the general welfare. An example of such reasoning in research ethics is discussed in sections 4.3 and 5.2, in which we consider moral questions related to deception research and disclosure of this deception. Deception research requires that human research subjects be deceived about the nature of their participation. Laud Humphreys' observations of men in public restrooms, discussed in section 1.1, is an example of deception research. A rule-utilitarian might invoke a rule that says that subjects should be debriefed after deception research, even if the debriefing causes the subject to be hurt, because the rule, "always tell the truth, even after the fact," maximizes utility. According to this view, it is ethical to follow this rule in each case where it applies, even if in some conceivable circumstances following the rule would not maximize utility. The idea is to explain how it is possible for morality to involve the application of rules and principles to cases. Rule-utilitarians must also account for any possible exceptions to the rule, because appropriate exceptions may maximize utility.

Even with these exceptions, most utilitarians criticize rule-utilitarianism on the ground that it betrays the fundamental insight of the theory, namely, that morality requires us to do as much good and as little harm as possible. If in some cases a researcher knows that debriefing a subject about a deception study will do more harm than good, it seems unethical to insist on following the rule. Perhaps an exception to the rule should be invoked here: "always tell the truth, even after the fact, unless by telling the truth you will do more harm than good." If this revised rule is the rule that will maximize utility, we may ask if rule-utilitarianism is ultimately that different from act-utilitarianism. Some critics worry that rule-utilitarianism simply collapses into act-utilitarianism. Still others worry about the complexities of the rules in light of the necessity to maximize utility in all cases.

Critics of all kinds of utilitarianism argue that the theory leaves morality insensitive to the plight of individuals. Some worry that if the only consideration in determining the permissibility of using animals as research subjects is a cost/benefit analysis, then any abuse of animals that ultimately yields the greatest good to the greatest number could be morally right. Perhaps the same might hold for human research subjects. Could, for example, the Cold-War Radiation experiments, or the Tuskegee Syphilis experiment, be morally justified because the data accumulated from the studies ultimately was of great scientific value? This result would conflict with our intuitions that these experiments are wrong no matter how utility-maximizing they might be. Others have criticized the impersonal evaluation of utility, claiming that morality is all about the concern we show to particular others whom we know or meet in our lives. The idea here is that morality has more to do with the character of our feelings and responses toward others than with merely producing pleasant or valuable consequences. We will see that the former objection is developed most often from a duty- or rights-based perspective, whereas the latter kind of reply to utilitarianism frequently finds a voice in the ethics-of-caring tradition. Despite these concerns, utilitarianism remains an influential moral theory in contemporary society.

2.3 ETHICAL THEORIES: ETHICS OF DUTY

Deontology, or an **ethics of duty,** is typically associated with the moral philosophy of Immanuel Kant, a Prussian philosopher of the late eighteenth century. Kant's great insight is that the demands of morality are the same for everyone, regardless of when or where people are born, what they happen to desire, or what kinds of lives they lead. Duty emerges from this idea as a requirement of reason. Because he thought that reason is the same in all people, Kant thought that the rules governing morality are universal, independent of culture, and the same for everyone. Our duty, according to Kant, is simply to perform those actions that follow from rules that everyone can follow; in other words, to act in keeping with rules that are universalizable.

Although Kant believed that it was important to universalize rules, others believe that we should universalize actions. This requirement of universalizability is similar to the Golden Rule, which urges us to "do unto others as you would have them do unto you." That rule does not say "stealing is always wrong," but instead asks you whether you would want people to steal from you. If not, then you should not steal from others. Deontology does not say "stealing is always wrong," but asks whether you can universalize stealing. Could everyone steal that which belonged to someone else whenever it was convenient? In scientific research, plagiarism is considered a form of stealing, and the case of plagiarism makes clear why it is not possible for everyone to steal whenever doing so is convenient. If people plagiarized whenever it was convenient, then there might be no sense in which one's work was truly one's own. If no one has work that is truly his or her own, then plagiarism is impossible, for plagiarism is stealing what is someone else's in the first place. The rule "I will steal whenever it is convenient" is not universalizable, because if everyone were to follow it, the very acts of plagiarism that the rule commands would be impossible! Plagiarism is thus wrong according to deontology. It is also wrong according to the Golden Rule, because we would not want others to plagiarize our works. Hence, the deontologist contends, we have a duty not to plagiarize the works of others, a point that is elaborated in section 7.3. Other moral duties, such as the duty to keep promises or the duty to tell the truth, can be derived using a similar test of universalizability.

Deontologists believe that the requirement of following the rules that everyone should follow, or acting in ways that everyone could act, captures the essence of morality precisely because the requirement is universal and the same for all. The nadir of immorality is making an exception to a rule or a duty for one's own convenience. But deontologists also maintain that this requirement of duty entails a respect for persons, in particular a respect for their capacity to choose the course of their lives. Human beings are free to choose their actions and their lives, and this autonomy confers a fundamental dignity on us and is thus worthy of respect. This conception of universal human dignity today grounds our notion of universal human rights. Kant thought that it played a more direct role in morality, since he thought that it prohibited using other people as mere means to our ends. This prohibition is cited in section 4.1. Morality requires us always to respect others' capacity for self-determination; Kant thought that we do that precisely by asking whether our proposed actions could be adopted by everyone. Only if an action is universalizable is it such that every free person could perform it. That explains why using people—taking advantage of them for one's own purposes, especially by force, fraud, or manipulation—is immoral and unethical. Thus, using human research subjects without obtaining informed consent, discussed in section 4.5, is wrong in all but a few exceptional cases, and plagiarism or misappropriation, discussed in sections 7.3 and 7.4, are wrong because they are both cases of using people as mere means to an end.

Deontologists insist that morality is a matter of intention: Has the person intended to do her duty? If so, then the action is right; if not, then it is wrong. Unlike utilitarianism, deontology maintains that an action's consequences are not relevant to the assessment of its moral rightness. I might try to do what is right, and yet other people or circumstances might suffer from my action. Do we want to agree with utilitarians and say that I have not done what is right? The deontologist insists that an action is right if one intended to fulfill one's duty, even when the results are not what one expects.

A common criticism of deontological moral theories concerns the determination of what duty requires. How exactly do we determine whether a certain course of action is universalizable? Without some intuitions about "what everyone should do," this seems to be a difficult question to answer. Yet if we have such intuitions, then it seems that the deontologist is presupposing a conception of moral rightness independent of duty or universalizability. In either case, it seems that the deontologist is mistaken to think that duty alone provides the test of right and wrong action.

Another objection to Kantian deontology is that it seems to be too absolutist; it does not appropriately incorporate the complexities that emerge with changing situations. Perhaps the notion of absolute moral rules is a bit naïve, because changing standards and special circumstances require us to be more flexible in our assessments. There are, for example, no hard-and-fast rules about what counts as a statistical outlier; rather, each case may be slightly different. Should ethical judgments not be at least as complex as the determination of what counts as a statistical outlier? If so, then deontology may seem rigid and inflexible where a moral theory needs to be responsive to special cases.

2.4 ETHICAL THEORIES: RIGHTS-BASED ETHICS

A related approach to deontology takes **rights** to be the fundamental basis upon which ethical judgments are made. An action is right or wrong on this view depending on the degree to which it respects the rights of others. John Locke, a seventeenth-century English philosopher, maintained that we have fundamental and inalienable rights to life, liberty, and property. Our right to property derives from considerations of desert: that which we find or make, we deserve to keep as our own. Those things that we own, but which we choose to give to others of our own free will, are justly transferred to others. To use an example cited above, this view provides another justification for the wrongness of plagiarism. Those who plagiarize take what others own and have a right to, without having a right to it themselves. According to Locke, our rights to life—no one may kidnap, enslave, or kill me—and to liberty are fundamental. Because I am free to choose the direction of my life, I deserve to keep whatever I discover or make through my own effort. Since my life is mine, whatever I produce in the course of living my life is mine as well. And others wrong me if they take or interfere with what is mine, via plagiarism or any other means of theft. Actions are right when they respect the rights of others.

Though Locke's theory appears to explain why plagiarism is wrong, it remains silent on other important questions in research ethics. Questions relating to conflicts of interest, the ethics of placebo-controlled trials, and the ethical problems that arise from the funding of research are not sufficiently answered by this theory. Other theories, such as utilitarianism, deontology, or the theories that we consider below must be introduced for a comprehensive account of ethical decisionmaking. Thus a consideration of rights may play a role in understanding responsible research, but it seems inadequate for a complete account.

2.5　ETHICAL THEORIES: VIRTUE ETHICS

A concern with **virtue** and the virtues looks back to the ethical theory of Aristotle for inspiration. Aristotle argued that human beings share a set of capacities and abilities that set them apart from all other things, living and inanimate. These capacities involve the use of our intellect and reasoning: We can reason about what to do, and we can understand the world. As a result, Aristotle claimed, the good person is the one who exercises these capacities well. Just as a good carpenter is one who performs the function of carpenters well, a good human being is a person who is good at being human. The various traits of character and thought that enable a person to accomplish this goal are what we think of as the virtues, especially bravery, moderation, justice, and wisdom.

This mode of reasoning was employed in section 1.3, where we considered what constitutes good research by first asking what the goals or ends of research are. The goals of research demonstrate something about how research is done well. Similarly, the "goal" of a human life tells us something about what humans need to live their lives well.

A virtue ethic begins from a conception of human flourishing, and it identifies a good person as one who flourishes. Human flourishing is the goal of human lives—it is what one must do to be a successful human. Such a person will exhibit a range of virtues, since flourishing is just the possession and exercise of the virtues of thought and character. The right action in any circumstance, then, is whatever action a wise and virtuous person would perform. Virtue ethics declines to specify any particular rule or principle (such as "maximize utility") or set of duties that determine what the right action is. The reason for this is that any moral rule will have exceptions, and it will be the wise and virtuous person who will be able to recognize the exceptional cases and know what to do in each of them. Some principles, of course, are fairly straightforward: Justice requires giving people their due. But the application of this principle—knowing how justice applies in each case, knowing what is due to everyone concerned—cannot be specified by the principle itself, and once again there may be exceptions. Only experience and the virtues enable one always to make the right choice. Researchers who correctly apply their discipline's standards of statistical analysis, discussed in sections 7.2 and 9.2, are researchers who are behaving virtuously. It may not be easy to formulate the principles behind responsible statistical analysis in each discipline, and sometimes the line between appropriate and inappropriate manipulation is difficult to find. However, again, experience and virtue will allow the responsible researcher to act well when using the tools of the discipline.

Virtue ethics has been criticized by many precisely because it offers no hard-and-fast rules for decisionmaking. It seems to many people quite vague to say that the standard of right action is whatever the wise and virtuous person would do. Morality seems to make more explicit demands on us. Others have criticized virtue ethics as trying to stake out an unstable middle ground between utilitarianism and deontology. On the one hand, virtue ethics is like utilitarianism in holding that moral action is goal-directed. The right action is not only the one a wise person would take, but also the one that would help one to flourish if one took it. In a sense, virtuous action brings about happiness, just as utilitarianism suggests moral action does. On the other hand, virtue ethics agrees with deontology in holding that one's intentions matter to the assessment of ethical behavior: One cannot take a virtuous action "by accident." The virtuous person aims to do what is right, and this objective is a significant element of the rightness of the action. But, the objector will say, either the consequences of action determine its moral rightness or not; virtue ethics cannot have it both ways. Once again, these objections are not decisive, but they do illustrate the range of complaints that arise with respect to virtue ethics.

2.6   ETHICAL THEORIES: ETHICS OF CARE

An **ethics of care** is associated with the work of psychologist Carol Gilligan and philosopher and education theorist Nel Noddings, and the theory has subsequently been developed by many other writers. The work of Gilligan and Noddings emphasizes certain feminist themes, drawing especially on the idea that morality is more a matter of relation and response to others than a systematic form of rational thought concerned with obedience to rules. This idea expresses a feminist critique of modern moral philosophy, which developed historically in an idiom of rationality, justification, and argumentation that can be identified with masculine traits and goals. In contrast, these thinkers suggest that feminine traits of care, receptivity, and nurturing point us toward a radically different ethic that relies less on rules or principles and more on feelings and responsiveness.

Noddings, for example, emphasizes the role of what she calls "natural caring," exemplified in the relationship between parent and child, in fostering "ethical caring," which is the extension of concern to all those whom we encounter in everyday life. The caring relation requires one to exhibit openness and receptivity to other people and makes the needs of others paramount. It is fundamentally a move away from oneself and involves an engrossment with the needs of others. Morality, Noddings concludes, requires a caring response to others; concern with substantive rules and rational justification of action is strictly secondary and subordinate to the quality of this response.

An ethic of care finds special application in the clinical setting, or the health care industry. This ethical perspective is skeptical about the possibility of mass-produced caring promised by these institutions, but it also provides an ideal of individual caring for health care professionals. By emphasizing receptivity and response, this ethic may indeed promote caring on the part of those who are responsible for treating patients. These practices are the basis of many of the recommendations in Chapter 5, which considers the treatment of vulnerable human subject populations, such as children, persons with mental disorders, or the elderly. When recruiting subjects who are members of vulnerable populations, and who are more likely to be harmed by participating as research subjects, strategies of openness and receptivity are important. Researchers may be called upon to solicit the help of family and friends in getting permission to enroll subjects in research studies, even studies that will benefit the subjects directly through their participation.

It is less clear, however, how an ethic of caring can respond to criticism that this ethic provides little practical guidance. Since the emphasis of the theory rests on the affective or emotional state of the care-giver rather than on what is actually to be done, it is not always obvious what the caring action is. Given a range of alternatives, how are we to know which action is the most caring? We must be careful not to suggest that there is some quality or property of "caring" such that some actions will have more of this property than others. An ethic of care does not support a rule of maximizing caring. Rather, the idea is to shift our attention away from rules that promote maximizing or universalizing and to focus instead on the character of our affective response. Insofar as an ethic of caring remains unwilling to endorse any particular criteria of moral action, it will remain most useful as a practical ideal for guiding one's own individual choices rather than a standard for the ethical evaluation of others' actions. That is, I might become more moral, according to this view, by striving to be a more caring person, yet the adoption of this goal will not necessarily help me to assess the actions of others, since it is not always clear whether they genuinely care. And although the assessment of others' actions is not the only or foremost responsibility of ethics, such assessment is required from time to time.

2.7 NORMATIVE PRINCIPLES FOR RESEARCH: AUTONOMY

A difficulty confronting anyone who wishes to resolve public ethical conflicts is that a pluralistic society is unlikely to agree on a single account of morality. In the United States today, each of the moral theories just discussed can claim a significant number of adherents. Yet in many controversial cases, these theories yield divergent prescriptions concerning the right choice of action. Is there any rational means of reaching consensus, given this diversity of ethical theories?

This question was the charge of the National Commission for the Protection of Human Subjects of Biomedical and Behavioral Research, which Congress empanelled in 1974. This Commission confronted two distinct challenges. First, it recognized the diversity of opinion concerning ethical theory, and it sought some means of securing agreement about the protection of human subjects without specifically appealing to controversial ethical theories. Second, the Commission sought to adopt and incorporate many of the rules and principles already recognized by researchers and contained in The Nuremberg Code of 1947, the 1964 Declaration of Helsinki, and the 1971 guidelines issued by the Department of Health, Education, and Welfare.

The Nuremberg Code emerged from the Nuremberg trials of Nazi war criminals, which included prosecutions for using subjects against their will and without their consent in research experiments. The code highlights issues of informed consent, experimental methodology, and the assurance that there is an appropriate risk/expected-benefit ratio in any experiment that involves human beings. The Declaration of Helsinki was adopted by the World Medical Assembly. Its most recent revision is dated October, 1996. Its focus is on the clinician, such as a physician, who is also a researcher. The Department of Health, Education, and Welfare guidelines took the recommendations of Nuremberg and Helsinki and made them official U.S. policy for government-funded research. The guidelines predated the mandating of the Institutional Review Boards (IRBs) by 3 years. IRBs are the primary vehicle for ethical oversight for research studies involving human beings in the United States and are discussed in greater detail in section 3.5. IRB oversight of human subjects research is guided by the principles set down in the Belmont Report, which was written by the National Commission for the Protection of Human Subjects of Biomedical and Behavioral Research. The Commission's objective was to identify broader principles that could provide a perspective for justifying and critically revising the more concrete moral rules adopted in The Nuremberg Code, the Declaration of Helsinki, and the Department of Health, Education, and Welfare's own guidelines.

The Belmont Report articulates three principles that should guide ethical treatment of human subjects in research: respect for persons, beneficence, and justice. All discussions of research ethics that invoke principles as the basis of normative evaluation recognize that these principles are merely *prima facie* principles. *Prima facie* principles are ones that we ought to obey; however, they can be overridden if another obligation requires that the principle be ignored for the sake of the overriding obligation. Thus, the principles are not presented in order of most stringent to least stringent. Nor is there any hard-and-fast rule for determining which principle ought to be the overriding principle in any given situation. For this reason, principles are best invoked by researchers who are also keeping in mind some of the above-discussed ethical theories—virtue ethics, utilitarianism, deontology, or the ethics of care.

Autonomy, which is also referred to in the Belmont Report as **respect for persons,** is the principle that protects the capacity of individual human beings to choose for themselves and determine their own course of life. Such choices are ones that are made voluntarily, with sufficient information to make a rational choice, and are choices that are made in virtue of the understanding of this information. In the western liberal democracies, this capacity to exercise autonomy is protected by legal rights to life, liberty, and property. Researchers, too, must respect this capacity. The principle of autonomy requires researchers to conduct their research in ways that minimize the infringement of autonomy for all affected by the research. Hence, for example, we require that human subjects grant their informed consent to research in order to indicate that they understand the expected benefits as well as the anticipated risks of their participation in research. To use human subjects without their permission—to perform experiments on them without their consent by force or fraud—is to violate their autonomy. Such uses of force or fraud, even for the sake of valuable or important scientific results, is virtually always prohibited by the principle of autonomy.

Only in extraordinary circumstances do we allow autonomy to be overridden by other considerations. For example, in the case of deception research, discussed in section 4.4, autonomy is overridden for the sake of other gains. More complicated issues about autonomy arise when violations of autonomy have occurred in the past and yet generate significant data. The issue concerns whether scientists may legitimately use such data. On the one hand, since the data were gathered by means of force or fraud, some claim that they are "tainted" and must not be used now. On the other hand, using the data now will not in itself involve or require further violation of the subjects, and so the principle of autonomy would seem not to prohibit their use. In general, scientists have been reluctant to use data that were acquired by violating the autonomy of subjects, in part because doing so would set a poor precedent. In particular, it could send a message to researchers that violations of autonomy will not matter to later generations as far as the use of scientific data is concerned, a precedent that many researchers have been unwilling to set. Notice that this argument is one that proceeds from rule-utilitarian reasoning, cited in section 2.2.

2.8 NORMATIVE PRINCIPLES FOR RESEARCH: BENEFICENCE AND NONMALEFICENCE

The principle of **beneficence** urges researchers to strive to promote the welfare of all those affected by research to the greatest degree feasible. The principle of beneficence urges researchers to maximize benefit. **Nonmaleficence** is the principle urging researchers to do no harm. In the original report of the Commission for the Protection of Human Subjects of Biomedical and Behavioral Research, as well as in the Belmont Report, the principles of beneficence and nonmaleficence were combined in a single principle of beneficence. Many ethicists have separated the two elements into two distinct principles, perhaps in order to emphasize the idea that the minimization of harm and the production of benefit are independently valuable. The Belmont Report's formulation of the principle of beneficence requires the maximization of the ratio of expected benefit to risk of harm. This requirement becomes a dual requirement for researchers. First, research must have a positive risk/expected-benefit ratio—if a research project is expected to do more harm than good, then the research is looked upon unfavorably. Second, even if there is a positive risk/expected-benefit ratio, researchers are required by the principle of beneficence to seek the greatest benefit while incurring minimal harm. Thus, it is not enough to demonstrate that benefits will accrue from a research project. It must be the case that the benefits outweigh the harms, *and* that the harms are as few as possible. The risk/expected-benefit ratio and the use of this ratio in justifying human subjects research is discussed further in section 4.2.

The principle of beneficence was originally adopted as an ethical guideline for biomedical research, but it is a reasonable guide for all scientific research. Even though not all research aims to promote human health—which is straightforwardly a benefit for those who are made healthier as a result of such research—research as such aims to advance our knowledge of the world. Insofar as such knowledge is valuable to us, research provides a benefit. Once we understand the advancement of knowledge as a benefit, it is clear that all researchers may be guided by the requirement of beneficence. Thus, researchers who are unfamiliar with a discipline or its methodologies, and nonetheless move forward with research studies, have failed to adhere to the principle of beneficence, because their projects are unlikely to advance knowledge.

The simplest expression of the principle of nonmaleficence, "Do no harm," is overly simple. Although it adequately captures the requirement that researchers do their best not to harm the subjects of their research—or, indeed, anyone or anything else that might be affected by their research—the fact is that the risk of harm is unavoidable in many kinds of scientific research. Since putting people *at risk* of illness or injury, either physiological or psychological, is itself a kind of harm, research will frequently do harm. Furthermore, participating as a research subject almost always costs time or opportunities, and although these may be small harms, they are harms nonetheless. Even when subjects knowingly consent to the risks of participating in an experiment in order that they may realize some benefit from that participation, the subjects are being placed at risk of harm. The principle of nonmaleficence may therefore be more aptly stated as, "Minimize harm."

Whether there is a single principle of beneficence in guiding research, or the two principles of beneficence and nonmaleficence, it is clear that the requirements in virtue of these obligations are difficult to apply in practice. The reason for the difficulty is that reasonable people may rank harms and benefits differently. A researcher's action that would minimize harm for one subject might not minimize harm for another subject. For example, some people abhor physical pain, and so they would gladly sacrifice some of their freedom of choice for the sake of less risk of pain. Others rank the harms in the reverse fashion: They so value their autonomy that they would risk considerable physical pain in order to preserve their capacity for free and independent choice. The researcher who is charged with promoting benefit and minimizing harm must recognize these two assessments of harm when affecting a positive risk/expected-benefit ratio in research.

There are also difficulties for scientists who invoke beneficence as a justification for scientific research, because the general public may not always recognize the benefits of the research. Scientists who are called upon to defend their use of scarce resources or public funds encounter myriad obstacles. Yet many people recognize that despite the difficulties in explaining their research to the non-scientific public, researchers nonetheless have obligations to do so. The challenges in articulating the benefits of science to the public are discussed in section 9.4, and the responsibilities that scientists have to make clear the benefits of science to the non-scientific public are discussed in sections 6.5 and 9.4.

2.9   NORMATIVE PRINCIPLES FOR RESEARCH: JUSTICE

Ethicists divide up justice into two different types: retributive justice and distributive justice. Retributive justice deals with punishment and reward. Although interesting, retributive justice is not of great concern to scientific researchers. The principle of justice, as it applies in scientific research, is a principle of distributive justice. The principle requires a fair and equitable distribution of benefits and burdens. Fairness is generally linked to the idea of desert: a fair distribution will give each what he or she deserves, but various accounts of desert exist. Another standard formulation of justice requires that like cases be treated alike. Yet we will still need to assess which cases are alike, and which distribution treats like cases alike.

A good example of a distributive justice issue in the research setting concerns the question of multiple authorship, an ethical question considered in section 7.4. Who deserves to be listed as an author, and who deserves credit as lead author? Authorship may be determined by several factors, such as number of hours spent on a project, the prestige of the persons listed as authors, or the type of contribution that each author made to the project. In this case, the benefits of authorship and lead authorship are the goods which are being distributed. The criteria for desert that we have considered here are effort, prestige, and merit. There are of course other factors that may contribute to determining who deserves authorship credit, and what kind of credit is deserved.

Burdens as well as benefits must be distributed. Consider the use of control groups for certain drug studies in medical experimentation. A control group generally receives a treatment other than the drug being studied. Sometimes this treatment is no treatment at all, and in other cases it is another current treatment. For those studies that use a no-treatment control, the patients in the control group should not be expected to benefit from the experimental trial. If the drug being tested is effective, then the lack of benefit to the control group is a burden. At the same time, those receiving an experimental drug run the risk of side effects, and this risk too is a burden. Researchers who abide by the principle of justice will seek a fair apportionment of both burdens and benefits in the course of conducting their research. These issues are considered further in sections 3.3 and 3.4.

The greatest problem in justly distributing benefits and burdens is determining what counts as just or unjust distributions. The trials of AZT in the developing world, discussed in section 1.2, give a classic example of the complexities of determining just distribution. Is it unjust to use placebos in a clinical trial when the researchers know that there is a medication that is more effective, and the experimental arm can be weighed against an already-accepted medication? Or is it just to use placebos when the standard of care in the location in which the trial is being conducted does not include a medication that is in use elsewhere? It is often difficult to know what is just or fair in a particular case.

A final problem may arise when one questions the value of these principles. It seems that since these principles are merely *prima facie* principles, that they may be unhelpful in determining what act to perform. Consider the example used earlier to illustrate rule-utilitarianism. Deception research involves using human subjects who are not told that they are research subjects, because if they knew that they were being observed, they might change their behavior. The principle of autonomy would suggest that after subjects have been deceived, they should be told the nature of the deception, to demonstrate respect for persons. However, what if the act of debriefing the subjects were harmful to the subjects? In that case, the principle of beneficence, or a joint application of beneficence and nonmaleficence, would require that the researcher not tell the subjects about the deception. Which of these principles, autonomy or beneficence, ought to take precedence? A further complication results from the fact that different subjects—adults rather than children, mentally competent persons rather than persons with mental disorders—may experience different levels of harm in similar circumstances, and therefore a different weighing of the principles may be invoked given different circumstances.

Despite the problems in applying the principles, they may nonetheless be helpful to researchers as a roadmap. Have all of these principles been appropriately considered in undertaking a research project? If so, then the researcher has made a step in the right direction: Responsible research begins with asking questions about where our responsibilities lie.

2.10   SUMMARY

Researchers cannot merely look to the law to settle complex questions about how to conduct themselves—they must also look to ethics. Competing ethical theories offer different explanations of the moral assessment of actions or character.

In this chapter we examined several of these theories, including act-utilitarianism and rule utilitarianism, deontology, an example of a rights-based ethical theory, virtue ethics, and the ethics of care. Each of these theories may be used as a tool to discover or explain what is morally right or wrong in a particular situation. Although these theories have been helpful in the past, recently ethicists have looked to a set of normative principles for research. The three principles most often cited are the principles of autonomy, the principle of beneficence, and the principle of justice. There may be problems in determining which principles should take precedence over the others. Despite this shortcoming, the principles are helpful in calling attention to the conflicting obligations faced by researchers.

We have included The Nuremberg Code, the Declaration of Helsinki, and the Belmont Report as readings at the end of this chapter. Each of these documents makes use of many of the theories and principles discussed in this chapter. Readers are invited to examine each document for application of these theories and principles in seminal public-policy statements in research ethics.

REFERENCES AND FURTHER READINGS

Tom L. Beauchamp and James F. Childress, *Principles of Biomedical Ethics* 4th ed., New York: Oxford University Press, 1994.

Fred Feldman, *Introductory Ethics*, Englewood Cliffs, New Jersey: Prentice Hall, 1978.

Thomas M. Garrett, Harold W. Baillie, and Rosellen M. Garrett, *Health Care Ethics: Principles and Problems* 3rd ed., Upper Saddle River, New Jersey: Prentice Hall, 1998.

Bernard Gert, Edward M. Berger, George F. Cahill, Jr., et al., *Morality and the New Genetics*, Boston: Sudbury Publishers, 1996.

Aaron Ridley, *Beginning Bioethics*, New York: St. Martin's Press, 1998.

The Nuremberg Code   late '40's

1. The voluntary consent of the human subject is absolutely essential. This means that the person involved should have legal capacity to give consent; should be so situated as to be able to exercise free power of choice, without the intervention of any element of force, fraud, deceit, duress, over-reaching, or other ulterior form of constraint or coercion; and should have sufficient knowledge and comprehension of the elements of the subject matter involved as to enable him to make an understanding and enlightened decision. This latter element requires that before the acceptance of an affirmative decision by the experimental subject there should be made known to him the nature, duration, and purpose of the experiment; the method and means by which it is to be

So, Milgram exp. violates this?

conducted; all inconveniences and hazards reasonably to be expected; and the effects upon his health or person which may possibly come from his participation in the experiment.

The duty and responsibility for ascertaining the quality of the consent rests upon each individual who initiates, directs or engages in the experiment. It is a personal duty and responsibility which may not be delegated to another with impunity.

2. The experiment should be such as to yield fruitful results for the good of society, unprocurable by other methods or means of study, and not random and unnecessary in nature.

3. The experiment should be so designed and based on the results of animal experimentation and a knowledge of the natural history of the disease or other problem under study that the anticipated results will justify the performance of the experiment.

4. The experiment should be so conducted as to avoid all unnecessary physical and mental suffering and injury.

5. No experiment should be conducted where there is an *a priori* reason to believe that death or disabling injury will occur; except, perhaps, in those experiments where the experimental physicians also serve as subjects.

6. The degree of risk to be taken should never exceed that determined by the humanitarian importance of the problem to be solved by the experiment.

7. Proper preparations should be made and adequate facilities provided to protect the experimental subject against even remote possibilities of injury, disability, or death.

8. The experiment should be conducted only by scientifically qualified persons. The highest degree of skill and care should be required through all stages of the experiment of those who conduct or engage in the experiment.

9. During the course of the experiment the human subject should be at liberty to bring the experiment to an end if he has reached the physical or mental state where continuation of the experiment seemed to him to be impossible.

10. During the course of the experiment the scientist in charge must be prepared to terminate the experiment at any stage, if he has probably [sic] cause to believe, in the exercise of the good faith, superior skill and careful judgement required of him that a continuation of the experiment is likely to result in injury, disability, or death to the experimental subject.

World Medical Association Declaration of Helsinki

Recommendations Guiding Physicians in Biomedical Research Involving Human Subjects

Adopted by the 18th World Medical Assembly
Helsinki, Finland, June 1964
and amended by the
29th World Medical Assembly, Tokyo, Japan, October 1975
35th World Medical Assembly, Venice, Italy, October 1983
41st World Medical Assembly, Hong Kong, September 1989
and the
48th General Assembly,
Somerset West, Republic of South Africa, October 1996

Introduction

It is the mission of the physician to safeguard the health of the people. His or her knowledge and conscience are dedicated to the fulfillment of this mission.

The Declaration of Geneva of the World Medical Association binds the physician with the words, "The Health of my patient will be my first consideration," and the international Code of Medical Ethics declares that, "A physician shall act only in the patient's interest when providing medical care which might have the effect of weakening the physical and mental condition of the patient."

The purpose of biomedical research involving human subjects must be to improve diagnostic, therapeutic and prophylactic procedures and the understanding of the aetiology and pathogenesis of disease.

In current medical practice most diagnostic, therapeutic or prophylactic procedures involve hazards. This applies especially to biomedical research.

Medical progress is based on research which ultimately must rest in part on experimentation involving human subjects.

In the field of biomedical research a fundamental distinction must be recognized between medical research in which the aim is essentially diagnostic or therapeutic for a patient, and medical research, the essential object of which is purely scientific and without implying direct diagnostic or therapeutic value to the person subjected to the research.

Special caution must be exercised in the conduct of research which may affect the environment, and the welfare of animals used for research must be respected.

Because it is essential that the results of laboratory experiments be applied to human beings to further scientific knowledge and to help suffering humanity, the World Medical Association has prepared the following recommendations as a guide to every physician in biomedical research involving human subjects. They should be kept under review in the future. It must be stressed that the standards as drafted are only a guide to physicians all over the world. Physicians are not relieved from criminal, civil and ethical responsibilities under the laws of their own countries.

I. Basic Principles

1. Biomedical research involving human subjects must conform to generally accepted scientific principles and should be based on adequately performed laboratory and animal experimentation and on a thorough knowledge of the scientific literature.

2. The design and performance of each experimental procedure involving human subjects should be clearly formulated in an experimental protocol which should be transmitted for consideration, comment and guidance to a specially appointed committee independent of the investigator and the sponsor provided that this independent committee is in conformity with the laws and regulations of the country in which the research experiment is performed.

3. Biomedical research involving human subjects should be conducted only by scientifically qualified persons and under the supervision of a clinically competent medical person. The responsibility for the human subject must always rest with a medically qualified person and never rest on the subject of the research, even though the subject has given his or her consent.

4. Biomedical research involving human subjects cannot legitimately be carried out unless the importance of the objective is in proportion to the inherent risk to the subject.

5. Every biomedical research project involving human subjects should be preceded by careful assessment of predictable risks in comparison with foreseeable benefits to the subject or to others. Concern for the interests of the subject must always prevail over the interests of science and society.

6. The right of the research subject to safeguard his or her integrity must always be respected. Every precaution should be taken to respect the privacy of the subject and to minimize the impact of the study on the subject's physical and mental integrity and on the personality of the subject.

7. Physicians should abstain from engaging in research projects involving human subjects unless they are satisfied that the hazards involved are believed to be predictable. Physicians should cease any investigation if the hazards are found to outweigh the potential benefits.

8. In publication of the results of his or her research, the physician is obliged to preserve the accuracy of the results. Reports of experimentation not in accordance with the principles laid down in this Declaration should not be accepted for publication.

9. In any research on human beings, each potential subject must be adequately informed of the aims, methods, anticipated benefits and potential hazards of the study and the discomfort it may entail. He or she should be informed that he or she is at liberty to abstain from participation in the study and that he or she is free to withdraw his or her consent to participation at any time. The physician should then obtain the subject's freely-given informed consent, preferably in writing.

10. When obtaining informed consent for the research project the physician should be particularly cautious if the subject is in a dependent relationship to him or her or may consent under duress. In that case the informed consent should be obtained by a physician who is not engaged in the investigation and who is completely independent of this official relationship.

11. In case of legal incompetence, informed consent should be obtained from the legal guardian in accordance with national legislation. Where physical or mental incapacity makes it impossible to obtain informed consent, or when the subject is a minor, permission from the responsible relative replaces that of the subject in accordance with national legislation.

    Whenever the minor child is in fact able to give a consent, the minor's consent must be obtained in addition to the consent of the minor's legal guardian.

12. The research protocol should always contain a statement of the ethical considerations involved and should indicate that the principles enunciated in the present Declaration are complied with.

II. Medical Research Combined With Professional Care (Clinical Research)

1. In the treatment of the sick person, the physician must be free to use a new diagnostic and therapeutic measure, if in his or her judgement it offers hope of saving life, reestablishing health or alleviating suffering.

2. The potential benefits, hazards and discomfort of a new method should be weighed against the advantages of the best current diagnostic and therapeutic methods.

3. In any medical study, every patient—including those of a control group, if any— should be assured of the best proven diagnostic and therapeutic method. This does not exclude the use of inert placebo in studies where no proven diagnostic or therapeutic method exists.

4. The refusal of the patient to participate in a study must never interfere with the physician-patient relationship.

5. If the physician considers it essential not to obtain informed consent, the specific reasons for this proposal should be stated in the experimental protocol for transmission to the independent committee (I, 2).

6. The physician can combine medical research with professional care, the objective being the acquisition of new medical knowledge, only to the extent that medical research is justified by its potential diagnostic or therapeutic value for the patient.

III. Non Therapeutic Biomedical Research Involving Human Subjects (Non-Clinical Biomedical Research)

1. In the purely scientific application of medical research carried out on a human being, it is the duty of the physician to remain the protector of the life and health of that person on whom biomedical research is being carried out.

2. The subjects should be volunteers—either healthy persons or patients for whom the experimental design is not related to the patient's illness.

3. The investigator or the investigating team should discontinue the research if in his/her or their judgement it may, if continued, be harmful to the individual.

4. In research on man, the interest of science and society should never take precedence over considerations related to the well-being of the subject.

Belmont Report

Ethical Principles and Guidelines for Research Involving Human Subjects

Scientific research has produced substantial social benefits. It has also posed some troubling ethical questions. Public attention was drawn to these questions by reported abuses of human subjects in biomedical experiments, especially during the Second World War. During the Nuremberg War Crime Trials, the Nuremberg code was drafted as a set of standards for judging physicians and scientists who had conducted biomedical experiments on concentration camp prisoners. This code became the prototype of many later codes[1] intended to assure that research involving human subjects would be carried out in an ethical manner.

The codes consist of rules, some general, others specific, that guide the investigators or the reviewers of research in their work. Such rules often are inadequate to cover complex situations; at times they come into conflict, and they are frequently difficult to interpret or apply. Broader ethical principles will provide a basis on which specific rules may be formulated, criticized and interpreted.

Three principles, or general prescriptive judgments, that are relevant to research involving human subjects are identified in this statement. Other principles may also be relevant. These three are comprehensive, however, and are stated at a level of generalization that should assist scientists, subjects, reviewers and interested citizens to understand the ethical issues inherent in research involving human subjects. These principles cannot always be applied so as to resolve beyond dispute particular ethical problems. The objective is to provide an analytical framework that will guide the resolution of ethical problems arising from research involving human subjects.

This statement consists of a distinction between research and practice, a discussion of the three basic ethical principles, and remarks about the application of these principles.

A. Boundaries Between Practice and Research

It is important to distinguish between biomedical and behavioral research, on the one hand, and the practice of accepted therapy on the other, in order to know what activities ought to undergo review for the protection of human subjects of research. The distinction between research and practice is blurred partly because both often occur together (as in research designed to evaluate a therapy) and partly because notable departures from standard practice are often called

[FR Doc. '79-12065 Filed 4-17-79, 8:45 am]

"experimental" when the terms "experimental" and "research" are not carefully defined.

For the most part, the term "practice" refers to interventions that are designed solely to enhance the well-being of an individual patient or client and that have a reasonable expectation of success. The purpose of medical or behavioral practice is to provide diagnosis, preventive treatment or therapy to particular individuals.[2] By contrast, the term "research" designates an activity designed to test an hypothesis, permit conclusions to be drawn, and thereby to develop or contribute to generalizable knowledge (expressed, for example, in theories, principles, and statements of relationships). Research is usually described in a formal protocol that sets forth an objective and a set of procedures designed to reach that objective.

When a clinician departs in a significant way from standard or accepted practice, the innovation does not, in and of itself, constitute research. The fact that a procedure is "experimental," in the sense of new, untested or different, does not automatically place it in the category of research. Radically new procedures of this description should, however, be made the object of formal research at an early stage in order to determine whether they are safe and effective. Thus, it is the responsibility of medical practice committees, for example, to insist that a major innovation be incorporated into a formal research project.[3]

Research and practice may be carried on together when research is designed to evaluate the safety and efficacy of a therapy. This need not cause any confusion regarding whether or not the activity requires review; the general rule is that if there is any element of research in an activity, that activity should undergo review for the protection of human subjects.

B. Basic Ethical Principles

The expression "basic ethical principles" refers to those general judgments that serve as a basic justification for the many particular ethical prescriptions and evaluations of human actions. Three basic principles, among those generally accepted in our cultural tradition, are particularly relevant to the ethics of research involving human subjects: the principles of respect for persons, beneficence and justice.

1. Respect for Persons. Respect for persons incorporates at least two ethical convictions: first, that individuals should be treated as autonomous agents, and second, that persons with diminished autonomy are entitled to protection. The principle of respect for persons thus divides into two separate moral requirements: the requirement to acknowledge autonomy and the requirement to protect those with diminished autonomy.

An autonomous person is an individual capable of deliberation about personal goals and of acting under the direction of such deliberation. To respect autonomy is to give weight to autonomous persons' considered opinions and choices while refraining from obstructing their actions unless they are clearly detrimental to others. To show lack of respect for an autonomous agent is to repudiate that person's considered judgments, to deny an individual the freedom to act on those considered judgments, or to withhold information necessary to make a considered judgment, when there are no compelling reasons to do so.

However, not every human being is capable of self-determination. The capacity for self-determination matures during an individual's life, and some individuals lose this capacity wholly or in part because of illness, mental disability, or circumstances that severely restrict liberty. Respect for the immature and the incapacitated may require protecting them as they mature or while they are incapacitated.

Some persons are in need of extensive protection, even to the point of excluding them from activities which may harm them; other persons require little protection beyond making sure they undertake activities freely and with awareness of possible adverse consequences. The extent of protection afforded should depend upon the risk of harm and the likelihood of benefit. The judgment that any individual lacks autonomy should be periodically reevaluated and will vary in different situations.

In most cases of research involving human subjects, respect for persons demands that subjects enter into the research voluntarily and with adequate information. In some situations, however, application of the principle is not obvious. The involvement of prisoners as subjects of research provides an instructive example. On the one hand, it would seem that the principle of respect for persons requires that prisoners not be deprived of the opportunity to volunteer for research. On the other hand, under prison conditions they may be subtly coerced or unduly influenced to engage in research activities for which they would not otherwise volunteer. Respect for persons would then dictate that the prisoners be protected. Whether to allow prisoners to "volunteer" or to "protect" them presents a dilemma. Respecting persons, in most hard cases, is often a matter of balancing competing claims urged by the principle of respect itself.

2. Beneficence. Persons are treated in an ethical manner not only by respecting their decisions and protecting them from harm, but also by making efforts to secure their well-being. Such treatment falls under the principle of beneficence. The term "beneficence" is often understood to cover acts of kindness or charity that go beyond strict obligation. In this document, beneficence is understood in a stronger sense, as an obligation. Two general rules have been formulated as complementary expressions of beneficent actions in this sense: (1) do not harm and (2) maximize possible benefits and minimize possible harms.

The Hippocratic maxim "do no harm" has long been a fundamental principle of medical ethics. Claude Bernard extended it to the realm of research, saying that one should not injure one person regardless of the benefits that might come to others. However, even avoiding harm requires learning what is harmful; and, in the process of obtaining this information, persons may be exposed to risk of harm. Further, the Hippocratic Oath requires physicians to benefit their patients "according to their best judgment." Learning what will in fact benefit may require exposing persons to risk. The problem posed by these imperatives is to decide when it is justifiable to seek certain benefits despite the risks involved, and when the benefits should be foregone because of the risks.

The obligations of beneficence affect both individual investigators and society at large, because they extend both to particular research projects and to the entire enterprise of research. In the case of particular projects, investigators and members of their institutions are obliged to give forethought to the maximization of benefits and the reduction of risk that might occur from the research investigation. In the case of scientific research in general, members of the larger society are obliged to recognize the longer term benefits and risks that may result from the improvement of knowledge and from the development of novel medical, psychotherapeutic, and social procedures.

The principle of beneficence often occupies a well-defined justifying role in many areas of research involving human subjects. An example is found in research involving children. Effective ways of treating childhood diseases and fostering healthy development are benefits that serve to justify research involving children—even when individual research subjects are not direct beneficiaries. Research also makes it possible to avoid the harm that may result from the application of previously accepted routine practices that on closer investigation turn out to be dangerous. But the role of the principle of beneficence is not always so unambiguous. A difficult ethical problem remains, for example, about research that presents more than minimal risk without immediate prospect of direct benefit to the children involved. Some have argued that such research is inadmissible, while others have pointed out that this limit would rule out much research promising great benefit to children in the future. Here again, as with all hard cases, the different claims covered by the principle of beneficence may come into conflict and force difficult choices.

3. *Justice.* Who ought to receive the benefits of research and bear its burdens? This is a question of justice, in the sense of "fairness in distribution" or "what is deserved." An injustice occurs when some benefit to which a person is entitled is denied without good reason or when some burden is imposed unduly. Another way of conceiving the principle of justice is that equals ought to be treated equally. However, this statement requires explication. Who is equal and who is unequal? What considerations justify departure from equal distribution? Almost all commentators allow that distinctions based on experience, age, deprivation, competence, merit and position do sometimes constitute criteria justifying differential treatment for certain purposes. It is necessary, then, to explain in what respects people should be treated equally. There are several widely accepted formulations of just ways to distribute burdens and benefits. Each formulation mentions some relevant property on the basis of which burdens and benefits should be distributed. These formulations are (1) to each person an equal share, (2) to

each person according to individual need, (3) to each person according to individual effort, (4) to each person according to societal contribution, and (5) to each person according to merit.

Questions of justice have long been associated with social practices such as punishment, taxation and political representation. Until recently these questions have not generally been associated with scientific research. However, they are foreshadowed even in the earliest reflections on the ethics of research involving human subjects. For example, during the 19th and early 20th centuries the burdens of serving as research subjects fell largely upon poor ward patients, while the benefits of improved medical care flowed primarily to private patients. Subsequently, the exploitation of unwilling prisoners as research subjects in Nazi concentration camps was condemned as a particularly flagrant injustice. In this country, in the 1940's, the Tuskegee syphilis study used disadvantaged, rural black men to study the untreated course of a disease that is by no means confined to that population. These subjects were deprived of demonstrably effective treatment in order not to interrupt the project, long after such treatment became generally available.

Against this historical background, it can be seen how conceptions of justice are relevant to research involving human subjects. For example, the selection of research subjects needs to be scrutinized in order to determine whether some classes (e.g., welfare patients, particular racial and ethnic minorities, or persons confined to institutions) are being systematically selected simply because of their easy availability, their compromised position, or their manipulability, rather than for reasons directly related to the problem being studied. Finally, whenever research supported by public funds leads to the development of therapeutic devices and procedures, justice demands both that these not provide advantages only to those who can afford them and that such research should not unduly involve persons from groups unlikely to be among the beneficiaries of subsequent applications of the research.

C. Applications

Applications of the general principles to the conduct of research leads to consideration of the following requirements: informed consent, risk/benefit assessment, and the selection of subjects of research.

1. Informed Consent. Respect for persons requires that subjects, to the degree that they are capable, be given the opportunity to choose what shall or shall not happen to them. This opportunity is provided when adequate standards for informed consent are satisfied.

While the importance of informed consent is unquestioned, controversy prevails over the nature and possibility of an informed consent. Nonetheless, there is widespread agreement that the consent process can be analyzed as containing three elements: information, comprehension and voluntariness.

Information. Most codes of research establish specific items for disclosure intended to assure that subjects are given sufficient information. These items generally include: the research procedure, their purposes, risks and anticipated benefits, alternative procedures (where therapy is involved), and a statement offering the subject the opportunity to ask questions and to withdraw at any time from the research. Additional items have been proposed, including how subjects are selected, the person responsible for the research, etc.

However, a simple listing of items does not answer the question of what the standard should be for judging how much and what sort of information should be provided. One standard frequently invoked in medical practice, namely the information commonly provided by practitioners in the field or in the locale, is inadequate since research takes place precisely when a common understanding does not exist. Another standard, currently popular in malpractice law, requires the practitioner to reveal the information that reasonable persons would wish to know in order to make a decision regarding their care. This, too, seems insufficient since the research subject, being in essence a volunteer, may wish to know considerably more about risks gratuitously undertaken than do patients who deliver themselves into the hand of a clinician for needed care. It may be that a standard of "the reasonable volunteer" should be proposed: the extent and nature of information should be such that persons, knowing that the procedure is neither necessary for their care nor perhaps fully understood, can decide whether they wish to participate in the furthering of knowledge. Even when some direct benefit to them is anticipated, the subjects should understand clearly the range of risk and the voluntary nature of participation.

A special problem of consent arises where informing subjects of some pertinent aspect of the research is likely to impair the validity of the research. In many cases, it is sufficient to indicate to subjects that they are being invited to participate in research of which some features will not be revealed until the research is concluded. In all cases of research involving incomplete disclosure, such research is justified only if it is clear that (1) incomplete disclosure is truly necessary to accomplish the goals of the research, (2) there are not undisclosed risks to subjects that are more than minimal, and (3) there is an adequate plan for debriefing subjects, when appropriate, and for dissemination of research results to them. Information about risks should never be withheld for the purpose of eliciting the cooperation of subjects, and truthful answers should always be given to direct questions about the research. Care should be taken to distinguish cases in which disclosure would destroy or invalidate the research from cases in which disclosure would simply inconvenience the investigator.

Comprehension. The manner and context in which information is conveyed is as important as the information itself. For example, presenting information in a disorganized and rapid fashion, allowing too little time for consideration or curtailing opportunities for questioning, all may adversely affect a subject's ability to make an informed choice.

Because the subject's ability to understand is a function of intelligence, rationality, maturity and language, it is necessary to adapt the presentation of the information to the subject's capacities. Investigators are responsible for ascertaining that the subject has comprehended the information. While there is always an obligation to ascertain that the information about risk to subjects is complete and adequately comprehended, when the risks are more serious, that obligation increases. On occasion, it may be suitable to give some oral or written tests of comprehension.

Special provision may need to be made when comprehension is severely limited—for example, by conditions of immaturity or mental disability. Each class of subjects that one might consider as incompetent (e.g., infants and young children, mentally disabled patients, the terminally ill and the comatose) should be considered on its own terms. Even for these persons, however, respect requires giving them the opportunity to choose to the extent they are able, whether or not to participate in research. The objections of these subjects to involvement should be honored, unless the research entails providing them a therapy unavailable elsewhere. Respect for persons also requires seeking the permission of other parties in order to protect the subjects from harm. Such persons are thus respected both by acknowledging their own wishes and by the use of third parties to protect them from harm.

The third parties chosen should be those who are most likely to understand the incompetent subject's situation and to act in that person's best interest. The person authorized to act on behalf of the subject should be given an opportunity to observe the research as it proceeds in order to be able to withdraw the subject from the research, if such action appears in the subject's best interest.

Voluntariness. An agreement to participate in research constitutes a valid consent only if voluntarily given. This element of informed consent requires conditions free of coercion and undue influence. Coercion occurs when an overt threat of harm is intentionally presented by one person to another in order to obtain compliance. Undue influence, by contrast, occurs through an offer of an excessive, unwarranted, inappropriate or improper reward or other overture in order to obtain compliance. Also, inducements that would ordinarily be acceptable may become undue influences if the subject is especially vulnerable.

Unjustifiable pressures usually occur when persons in positions of authority or commanding influence—especially where possible sanctions are involved—urge a course of action for a subject. A continuum of such influencing factors exists, however, and it is impossible to state precisely where justifiable persuasion ends and undue influence begins. But undue influence would include actions such as manipulating a person's choice through the controlling influence of a close relative and threatening to withdraw health services to which an individual would otherwise be entitled.

2. Assessment of Risks and Benefits. The assessment of risks and benefits requires a careful arrayal of relevant data, including, in some cases, alternative ways of obtaining the benefits sought in the research. Thus, the assessment presents both an opportunity and a responsibility to gather systematic and comprehensive information about proposed research. For the investigator, it is a means to examine whether the proposed research is properly designed. For a review committee, it is a method for determining whether the risks that will be presented to subjects are justified. For prospective subjects, the assessment will assist the determination whether or not to participate.

The Nature and Scope of Risks and Benefits. The requirement that research be justified on the basis of a favorable risk/benefit assessment bears a close relation to the principle of beneficence, just as the moral requirement that informed consent be obtained is derived primarily from the principle of respect for persons. The term "risk" refers to a possibility that harm may occur. However, when expressions such as "small risk" or "high risk" are used, they usually refer (often ambiguously) both to the chance (probability) of experiencing a harm and the severity (magnitude) of the envisioned harm.

The term "benefit" is used in the research context to refer to something of positive value related to health or welfare. Unlike "risk," "benefit" is not a term that expresses probabilities. Risk is properly contrasted to probability of benefits, and benefits are properly contrasted with harms rather than risks of harm. Accordingly, so-called risk/benefit assessments are concerned with the probabilities and magnitudes of possible harms and anticipated benefits. Many kinds of possible harms and benefits need to be taken into account. There are, for example, risks of psychological harm, physical harm, legal harm, social harm and economic harm and the corresponding benefits. While the most likely types of harms to research subjects are those of psychological or physical pain or injury, other possible kinds should not be overlooked.

Risks and benefits of research may affect the individual subjects, the families of the individual subjects, and society at large (or special groups of subjects in society). Previous codes and Federal regulations have required that risks to subjects be outweighed by the sum of both the anticipated benefit to the subject, if any, and the anticipated benefit to society in the form of knowledge to be gained from the research. In balancing these different elements, the risks and benefits affecting the immediate research subject will normally carry special weight. On the other hand, interests other than those of the subject may on some occasions be sufficient by themselves to justify the risks involved in the research, so long as the subjects' rights have been protected. Beneficence thus requires that we protect against risk of harm to subjects and also that we be concerned about the loss of the substantial benefits that might be gained from research.

The Systematic Assessment of Risks and Benefits. It is commonly said that benefits and risks must be "balanced" and shown to be "in a favorable ratio." The metaphorical character of these terms draws attention to the difficulty of making precise judgments. Only on rare occasions will quantitative techniques be available for the scrutiny of research protocols. However, the idea of systematic, nonarbitrary analysis of risks and benefits should be emulated insofar as possible.

This ideal requires those making decisions about the justifiability of research to be thorough in the accumulation and assessment of information about all aspects of the research, and to consider alternatives systematically. This procedure renders the assessment of research more rigorous and precise, while making communication between review board members and investigators less subject to misinterpretation, misinformation and conflicting judgments. Thus, there should first be a determination of the validity of the presuppositions of the research; then the nature, probability and magnitude of risk should be distinguished with as much clarity as possible. The method of ascertaining risks should be explicit, especially where there is no alternative to the use of such vague categories as small or slight risk. It should also be determined whether an investigator's estimates of the probability of harm or benefits are reasonable, as judged by known facts or other available studies.

Finally, assessment of the justifiability of research should reflect at least the following considerations: (i) Brutal or inhumane treatment of human subjects is never morally justified. (ii) Risks should be reduced to those necessary to achieve the research objective. It should be determined whether it is in fact necessary to use human subjects at all. Risk can perhaps never be entirely eliminated, but it can often be reduced by careful attention to alternative procedures. (iii) When research involves significant risk of serious impairment, review committees should be extraordinarily insistent on the justification of the risk (looking usually to the likelihood of benefit to the subject—or, in some rare cases, to the manifest voluntariness of the participation). (iv) When vulnerable populations are involved in research, the appropriateness of involving them should itself be demonstrated. A number of variables go into such judgments, including the nature and degree of risk, the condition of the particular population involved, and the nature and level of the anticipated benefits. (v) Relevant risks and benefits must be thoroughly arrayed in documents and procedures used in the informed consent process.

3. Selection of Subjects. Just as the principle of respect for persons finds expression in the requirements for consent, and the principle of beneficence in risk/benefit assessment, the principle of justice gives rise to moral requirements that there be fair procedures and outcomes in the selection of research subjects.

Justice is relevant to the selection of subjects of research at two levels: the social and the individual. Individual justice in the selection of subjects would require that researchers exhibit fairness: thus, they should not offer potentially beneficial research only to some patients who are in their favor or select only "undesirable" persons for risky research. Social justice requires that distinction be drawn between classes of subjects that ought, and ought not, to participate in any particular kind of research, based on the ability of members of that class to bear burdens and on the appropriateness of placing further burdens on already burdened persons. Thus, it can be considered a matter of social justice that there is an order of preference in the selection of classes of subjects (e.g., adults before children) and that some classes of potential subjects (e.g., the institutionalized mentally infirm or prisoners) may be involved as research subjects, if at all, only on certain conditions.

Injustice may appear in the selection of subjects, even if individual subjects are selected fairly by investigators and treated fairly in the course of research. Thus injustice arises from social, racial, sexual and cultural biases institutionalized in society. Thus, even if individual researchers are treating their research subjects fairly, and even if IRBs are taking care to assure that subjects are selected fairly within a particular institution, unjust social patterns may nevertheless appear in the overall distribution of the burdens and benefits of research. Although individual institutions or investigators may not be able to resolve a problem that is pervasive in their social setting, they can consider distributive justice in selecting research subjects.

Some populations, especially institutionalized ones, are already burdened in many ways by their infirmities and environments. When research is proposed that involves risks and does not include a therapeutic component, other less burdened classes of persons should be called upon first to accept these risks of research, except where the research is directly related to the specific conditions of the class involved. Also, even though public funds for research may often flow in the same directions as public funds for health care, it seems unfair that populations dependent on public health care constitute a pool of preferred research subjects if more advantaged populations are likely to be the recipients of the benefits.

One special instance of injustice results from the involvement of vulnerable subjects. Certain groups, such as racial minorities, the economically disadvantaged, the very sick, and the institutionalized may continually be sought as research subjects, owing to their ready availability in settings where research is conducted. Given their dependent status and their frequently compromised capacity for free consent, they should be protected against the danger of being involved in research solely for administrative convenience, or because they are easy to manipulate as a result of their illness or socioeconomic condition.

Notes

[1] Since 1945, various codes for the proper and responsible conduct of human experimentation in medical research have been adopted by different organizations. The best known of these codes are the Nuremberg Code of 1947, the Helsinki Declaration of 1964 (revised in 1975), and the 1971 Guidelines (codified into Federal Regulations in 1974) issued by the U.S. Department of Health, Education, and Welfare. Codes for the conduct of social and behavioral research have also been adopted, the best known being that of the American Psychological Association, published in 1973.

[2] Although practice usually involves interventions designed solely to enhance the well-being of a particular individual, interventions are sometimes applied to one individual for the enhancement of the well-being of another (e.g., blood donation, skin grafts, organ

transplants) or an intervention may have the dual purpose of enhancing the well-being of a particular individual, and, at the same time, providing some benefit to others (e.g., vaccination, which protects both the person who is vaccinated and society generally). The fact that some forms of practice have elements other than immediate benefit to the individual receiving an intervention, however, should not confuse the general distinction between research and practice. Even when a procedure applied in practice may benefit some other person, it remains an intervention designed to enhance the well-being of a particular individual or groups of individuals; thus, it is practice and need not be reviewed as research.

[3] Because the problems related to social experimentation may differ substantially from those of biomedical and behavioral research, the Commission specifically declines to make any policy determination regarding such research at this time. Rather, the Commission believes that the problem ought to be addressed by one of its successor bodies.

Chapter 3
Ethical Considerations
of Study Design and Review

3.1   INTRODUCTION

The ethics of responsible science begin even before the data-collection phase. The experimental design and methods employed in the study are all subject to ethical scrutiny. This chapter focuses on concerns regarding methodologies employed in human subjects research. One area of concern when using human research subjects is choosing sample populations that are unbiased. We present some ethical and methodological drawbacks when using convenience samples and discuss attempts to circumvent the biases in some samples. Attempts to correct bias can often raise a new set of methodological and ethical questions. We present some of the methods that researchers use to correct biases, such as blinded, double-blinded, and placebo-controlled studies. Each of these approaches appears to offer promising means by which to collect unbiased data; however, each method also reveals complex ethical concerns. Finally, this chapter examines one of the safeguards in place to protect the interests of human research subjects: the Institutional Review Board. This board examines the ethics of most human subjects research in the United States, insuring that the rights and interests of human subjects are protected. The board is an important innovation in the protection of human research subjects, but there are shortcomings to the system.

3.2   METHODOLOGY AND SAMPLES

Researchers should be aware of the possibility of sampling errors due to biased samples. Biased samples can be a problem both for purely methodological, as well as ethical, reasons. The methodological considerations are clear: Biased samples generally produce biased results. Convenience samples are one example of samples that are often biased. Researchers may find it easier to recruit students in their courses, or patients in their practice, rather than to locate and recruit unfamiliar persons as research subjects. However, there are obvious methodological problems when relying upon convenience samples. Taking a convenience sample of college freshmen, because they are a captive audience in a researcher's lower-division courses, will not always yield results that are generalizable across the wider population. As discussed in Chapter 9, objectivity is one of the principles that guide good science, and convenience samples are not always objective.

In addition to these methodological problems with convenience samples, there may also be ethical questions surrounding convenience samples. Selecting freshmen from a lower-division course may make things easier for the researcher, but many convenience samples, such as students, patients, institutionalized individuals, and other "captive audiences," may not be in a position to say "no" to a researcher. The voluntary participation of all research subjects is a cornerstone of the ethical treatment of research subjects, and is discussed in greater detail in Chapter 4. Issues relating to the use of institutionalized individuals are discussed in section 5.7. Even if subjects are able to consent voluntarily, it is possible with convenience samples that one population bears the brunt of serving as research subjects, while another population reaps all of the rewards of the gains in knowledge. This type of situation is often unjust, and researchers should be careful to avoid it.

There are ways to get around the problems of convenience samples in an attempt to correct biases. One is to try to generate a stratified sample. Stratified samples are samples that draw representative sub-populations from a larger population and are often employed in an attempt to eliminate sampling biases. For example, a telephone survey of households in the United States may not yield an accurate sample of television viewers in the United States. After all, the first person to answer the phone in a household may fit a particular profile: an adult is more likely to answer the phone than a child, someone who stays at home during the day is similarly more likely to answer the phone than someone who works outside the home. A stratified sample, which singles out representatives from sub-populations such as children, individuals who work outside the home, or college students who live in dorm rooms, may yield more accurate data about what people are watching on television. Thus, the bias inherent in sampling television viewers via a telephone survey may be corrected by using a stratified sample.

However, bias may creep in nonetheless, because the stratification itself may include bias. Imagine the researcher who attempts to correct for the biases in the sample of college freshmen enrolled in one class by doing a survey across the university. The data is supposed to generalize over the entire university population, so there is no problem with using only university students. What stratification method should the researcher employ? Should half of the sample be male and half female? Should the sample be one-quarter students with GPAs between 4.0 and 3.0, one-quarter students with GPAs 2.9 to 2.0, one-quarter with GPAs 1.9 to 1.0, and one-quarter with GPAs lower than 1.0? It is often difficult to know what counts as an unbiased stratified sample. Additionally, since many cases permit an infinite number of possible stratifications, some populations may be left out. For example, in an attempt to get a representative sample of subjects from each of the world's religions, how many stratifications should be included in the survey?

Even when human subjects are not used, the data-collecting process can involve biases that undermine the objectivity of the research project. Consider again the attempt to learn about the television-viewing habits of Americans by doing a telephone survey. The researcher who calls households in the United States during the late morning and mid-afternoon—because that is when the telephone lab is open—will get a biased sample. It may be that the only people at home at that hour are those who neither work outside the home nor go to school. The researcher who only calls after 8:00 p.m., because that is when the telephone lab has scheduled the calling times for this research project, may not get accurate data on the television habits of young children. In such a case it is not the samples themselves that result in the bias, but the circumstances of the researcher's data-gathering activities that yield biased results. Responsible researchers should be wary of collecting data in such a way that is not methodologically sound.

These questions raise the importance of unbiased sampling procedures, both for scientific and ethical reasons. If human subjects are used, it is morally unacceptable to ask them to undergo the burdens of serving as research subjects if the methods will not yield meaningful or significant data. Hence, it is the responsibility of the researcher to make sure that the methods employed do justice to the data-collecting process.

3.3   RANDOMIZATION, BLINDED STUDIES, AND EQUIPOISE

The **randomized** clinical trial is considered the gold standard of clinical research methodologies involving human subjects. In the randomized clinical trial, subjects are randomly placed in different study groups to assess their reaction to a particular drug, treatment, or therapy. One group receives the new drug or therapy, and the other receives a different treatment, or perhaps no treatment at all. The first group is the "treatment" arm, and the second group is the "control" arm of the study. At the end of the experiment, each group's clinical progress is weighed against the other. If the subjects have had success with the treatment, and the control has not, then the treatment is determined to have therapeutic value. If the subjects in the treatment arm fare worse or no better than those in the control arm, then the treatment is determined not to have any therapeutic value above and beyond the control.

Randomization is the chance placement of subjects into one of the arms of the study. Randomization may yield better scientific results because the subjects are not placed in any group due to researcher bias. However, randomization has its drawbacks. The first is that the subjects will need to be informed that they are part of a randomized study as part of the informed consent statement. However, subjects may have a difficult time understanding that no one selected the arm of the study in which they will be placed—placement of the subjects into the treatment or control arm of the study will be random and not based on facts about the subject. Explaining to subjects that the treatment that they will receive as part of a scientific study is out of the hands of the very scientists running the study may be difficult, and as a result the subjects may secretly harbor fears that researchers are making choices behind their backs. Other subjects may simply not understand the concept of randomization: If the researcher is not deciding which of the subjects go into each arm of the study, then who is? Surely, some subjects think *someone, somewhere* is making this choice. Impressing upon subjects that there is no person making this choice may open up several other worries. If no one is making this choice, what else are the researchers doing that they do not control or oversee? Why should the researchers be trusted if they are not in control of their own study? Because randomization raises these issues, a thorough explanation of randomization is important when recruiting research subjects.

A further, more challenging ethical problem with randomization is the fact that many subjects may volunteer to be part of a research study precisely because they wish to take the experimental treatment. Especially in cases in which subjects are faced with a disease for which there are no accepted and useful treatments, subjects may wish to enroll in a study so that they can experience the potential benefits of an experimental treatment. If the study is a randomized study, however, subjects may not be in a treatment arm. Instead, they may be placed in a control arm. The control arm may involve an alternative treatment, or it may offer no treatment at all. Subjects who volunteer to participate in a study in order to benefit from an experimental drug may fail to reap this benefit. An example of the difficulties that arise when subjects refuse to enter randomized clinical trials unless they are guaranteed the experimental procedure is illustrated by the difficulty researchers had in recruiting patients with breast cancer into trials of bone marrow transplants. Patients with advanced breast cancer were concerned, were they to enter randomized clinical trials, that they would not experience the most advanced treatment options and instead would be placed in the control group. Instead, many women chose to obtain bone marrow transplants for breast cancer, even though there was no statistically significant data demonstrating the efficacy of this technique. Years went by before there were enough subjects in randomized clinical trials to make a statistically significant claim about the efficacy of bone marrow transplants. Once the data were analyzed, it became clear that recipients of bone marrow transplants did not fare much better than recipients of conventional breast cancer therapies.

Some randomized studies employ a **cross-over** methodology, in which the subjects who were initially randomized into the treatment arm of the study are eventually placed in the control arm of the study, and the subjects who were initially randomized into the control arm of the study are eventually placed in the treatment arm of the study. Some of the ethical concerns related to randomization are satisfied when a cross-over methodology is employed. The risks of participating as a research subject are also more equitably distributed; neither group benefits from risks to others. The drawback of cross-over design is that it is not applicable to every study. For example, in the bone marrow transplant studies just mentioned, long-term survival rates cannot be measured using a cross-over design. It may also be the case that in some studies the time that it takes to collect reliable data may preclude utilizing cross-over methodology.

The cases discussed above are all cases in which the subjects are not aware of where they are placed in the study. A study with this design may be a **single-blinded** trial, so-called because one of the parties, usually the subject but sometimes the researcher, is blind as to which arm of the study the subjects occupy. Blinding a trial is also referred to as "masking" in some cases. The methodological justification for placing subjects in blinded trials is that knowledge of the arm of the study that they occupy can result in biased results. If subjects think that they are taking a medication which is supposed to reduce the symptoms of depression, for example, it is possible that they will begin to experience a decrease in the symptoms of depression which is not correlated with the medication itself, but with the idea that "I'm taking a drug that is supposed to help me." This phenomenon, in which the very idea of taking a drug or therapy has the curative effect, and the curative agent is not the medical interaction of drug or therapy itself, is called the "placebo effect," and is discussed in section 3.4. Similarly, if the researcher knows that the subjects occupy a particular arm, the researcher's expectations may be biased in virtue of this knowledge. The power of suggestion can be strong. If subjects are not told which drugs, if any, they are taking, then the reports of their symptoms may be more genuine. Similarly, if the researcher does not know the arm of the study that the subjects occupy, the researcher's reports may be more genuine.

The ethics of blinded trials are also complex. On one hand, the scientific benefits of the blinded trial are clear—better scientific results may ensue from a study in which the subjects are not biased by their own beliefs about treatment arms. On the other hand, some may claim that it is unfair to leave subjects ignorant about the treatment arm that they occupy. We discuss informed consent to participation in research in section 4.5. If human subjects participate in scientific research, they should first give informed consent to their participation. But if they do not even know the arm of the study in which they are enrolled, how can they possibly give informed consent to their participation? It is possible that telling a subject "You will be in either one arm of the study or another, we cannot tell you which" is sufficient for informed consent. However, since the researchers know which arm the subjects occupy, blinded trials may appear to be research in which information about the subjects' participation is intentionally withheld from the subjects.

A second problem is both ethical and methodological. As discussed above, both the researcher and the subjects may be biased by the knowledge of the subjects' role in the study. If the research subjects are blind, but the researcher is not, or vice versa, many of the benefits of the blinding can be lost. It is unethical to use research subjects in a study that is methodologically unsound, because the subjects will endure the risks of participating in the research for the sake of compromised research that will be of little or no scientific value. Hence these methodological problems are also ethical problems.

One way to avoid these problems is to employ **double-blinded** trials. In these trials, neither the researcher who works directly with the research subjects nor the subjects know which arm of the study the subjects occupy. Double-blinded trials can then circumvent some of the ethical difficulties of single-blinded trials. Since neither the researchers nor the subjects know which arm the subjects occupy, the data are less likely to be biased. Of course, the attempt to remove bias can only go so far. Subjects or researchers who try to guess which arm of the study the subjects occupy can create biases. If it becomes known, for example, that side-effects such as dry mouth and brittle fingernails are associated with a medication designed to treat depression, and if subjects notice these side-effects, then the subjects' self-reporting of data may become biased. If the subjects tell the researchers, then the researchers' perceptions of the subjects' progress may also become biased. However, the double-blinded trial is an attempt to bypass the biases that result from these perceptions. Subjects may be less likely to ask questions about the arm of the study they occupy because they are informed that the researchers with whom they are working do not know the answers.

Randomized, double-blinded clinical trials are ethical only when the different arms of the study are in **equipoise**. Two arms are in equipoise if one arm is not preferred as a treatment option over the other arm. Even if no treatment is offered in one of the arms of a clinical trial, the arms may be in equipoise. If no consensus exists that a particular treatment is better than any other treatment, then any treatment option is in equipoise with new therapies that show evidence of therapeutic promise. In the same vein, no therapy may be just as desirable as competing options. For example, a patient might regard treatments A and B to be in clinical equipoise if they are both similarly efficacious in fighting a disease, they have similarly harmful side-effects, they are of similar cost, etc. However, if A takes only 3 days to take effect, while B takes a week, some patients may say that this imbalance forces the two drugs out of clinical equipoise—there is a reason to prefer A over B. When subjects are placed in clinical trials, the assumption is that the drugs which are being tested are in clinical equipoise. If they are not, then subjects in one arm may be disadvantaged merely by virtue of the randomization. It is ethically acceptable to enroll subjects in a randomized study only when there is no reason to believe that the treatment options available in one arm of the study are better than the other.

Once the treatment arms of a study are seen to fall out of equipoise, the randomization of the trial is unethical. If one of the arms of the trial is obviously more beneficial or harmful to the subjects than the other arm, then subjects should no longer be randomized into arms in which they lose benefits or are subjected to greater harm than need be. In theory, this makes a great deal of sense: Once researchers know that a treatment is of benefit, randomization should stop and the control group should have the benefits of the new therapy. However, in practice this can be difficult to accomplish. At what point does the researcher declare *esp. in a double-blinded study!*

that two therapies are no longer in equipoise? How much data are needed before this type of assertion can be made? The difficulties in establishing when two therapies fall out of equipoise create ethical problems for researchers.

Since the researchers who are working directly with the subjects in double-blinded studies do not know which subjects are in the treatment arm or the control arm, a monitoring committee should examine the results as the study progresses to be sure that the arms remain in equipoise. An interesting ethical question arises when the impartiality of the monitoring committee is considered. Should the monitoring committee also be blinded, not knowing which subjects are in each arm of the study, and merely compare the progress of the two groups of subjects? If so, then there will be no bias. However, along with the removal of bias comes the fact that the monitoring committee may not know precisely what to look for. The independent monitoring committee may be blinded to the very factors that will allow them to detect therapeutic progress. Thus, blinding brings with it both expected benefits and risks.

3.4 PLACEBOS

A **placebo** is an inert substance that is given to a subject instead of an active substance. Control groups in randomized clinical trials are often given placebos when there is no preferred therapy for the disease that the experimental therapy is supposed to treat. The subjects in the treatment arm of the study are given the experimental therapy, and their progress is measured against those who are given the placebo. One might expect that the subjects in the placebo arm would have no benefit from taking an inert substance.

Why use a placebo at all? In most cases, we know the progress of untreated diseases; it seems unnecessary to give subjects an inert substance to track the progress of untreated disease. Yet, there is a good scientific reason to place subjects in a placebo group, even if the progress of an untreated disease is known. Scientists have known for a long time about the "placebo effect." People who believe that they are being treated for a disease may get better, even when that belief is false. The placebo effect is the curative power behind parents' kissing their children's scraped knees or bruised fingers, in an attempt to make the children feel better. The fact that the children think the kiss makes the injury better is enough to make the children feel better. Another example of the placebo effect is the administering of antibiotics to "cure" viral infections, such as some colds. Viral infections are not cured by antibiotics, but taking a drug in response to an illness can soothe, comfort, and provide a sense of control.

Just as patients may experience the placebo effect, so too may research subjects. There may be something soothing, comforting, and helpful about going through a treatment regime. Even if there is no actual benefit to the treatment, research subjects may experience benefit merely from being part of a research study. How is the researcher to know whether it is the drug or the placebo effect

altering the symptoms of depression? Is the clinical result produced by the research subject's experiencing the feeling of being in control, the attention paid by
the researcher, or the comfort of routine medication? Placebos allow researchers
to expose both arms of a study—the control arm and the treatment arm—to the
same types of conditions. Both arms experience the same contact with the researchers; both are given similar routines. Is the contact with researchers and the
routine the source of benefit, or is it the active ingredient in the drug? Placebos help
researchers to answer this question. These facts explain why placebos are part of
good science—they help researchers to isolate the actual effects of a treatment
and sort those out from the positive effects of the research environment.

Several ethical questions surround the use of placebos. One question deals
with the use of placebos in place of treatment when no treatment is locally available but treatments nonetheless do exist. In section 1.2 we discussed the trials to
test the efficacy of short courses of AZT in preventing the vertical transmission
of HIV in the developing world as one example of research that has raised many
ethical questions. Many of the questions about these trials focus on the fact that
the research in these randomized clinical trials involved a placebo arm, despite the
fact that AZT has long been known to cut the risk of vertical transmission of
HIV. Why would a placebo be used if an accepted treatment already existed?
Why not measure the efficacy of a short course of AZT against an accepted treatment, such as a long course of AZT, instead of against a placebo? The justification for the use of placebos in these trials focused in part on the fact that the
accepted treatment—a longer course of AZT—was not part of the standard of care
in the communities in which the short course was tested. The long course of AZT
was far too expensive for the subjects in the trial. Thus, some researchers concluded, it was acceptable to use an inert substance and measure short courses of
AZT against a placebo. Some ethicists nonetheless find the study unacceptable
and claim that if the researchers were willing to pay for the short course of
AZT and put research subjects in harm's way by using them for this study, they
should have made the longer course of AZT available. The Declaration of Helsinki,
which is included as a reading in Chapter 2, may imply that these trials were
ethically impermissible because the two arms of the trials were not in equipoise.

A second use of placebos which has become a subject of controversy is the
use of "placebo surgery," in which subjects are anesthetized and surgery is performed on them, but the therapeutic benefits of the surgery are not employed.
For example, some sufferers of Parkinson's disease (a fatal, degenerative neurological disorder) may benefit from newly developed brain surgery techniques.
One hypothesis is that a new type of brain surgery would be of some benefit to
sufferers of Parkinson's. However, it is possible that the placebo effect will be
the true source of benefit, and not the newly developed surgical techniques.
Thus, to correct for the placebo effect, half of the research subjects in a recent
study were given placebo surgeries, and half were given surgeries that included
the implants that were believed to be of some benefit to sufferers of Parkinson's
disease. The use of placebos in these studies is controversial, but not for the same

reasons as the use of placebos in the developing world AZT trials. There is no cure for Parkinson's, nor is there any therapy in wide use that significantly slows its progress. Many of the therapies that slow the progress of the disease have a great number of undesirable side-effects, or they lose efficacy after a short time. Because of the dearth of therapeutic options, a placebo-controlled study would be appropriate when looking at possible treatments for Parkinson's. The controversy in this case is that the placebo itself may be harmful. As stated above, a placebo is an inert substance; it is presumed not to be of therapeutic benefit, but in and of itself, the placebo is not supposed to be harmful. There are, of course, risks associated with any surgery. Ethicists have challenged the use of placebo surgery because it seems unjust to place the research subjects at risk of harm from surgery when there appears to be no therapeutic benefit. Those who defend placebo surgery say that it provides the best way—perhaps the only way—to determine the efficacy of newly developed surgical techniques.

The responsible scientist will take into account the situation of the research subjects involved in the research study. Is randomization appropriate? Why or why not? Should the study be a blinded study? Should the study use a placebo, or would an accepted therapeutic option better insure clinical equipoise of the competing treatment arms? All of these methodological questions are important when performing ethically responsible research on human subjects.

3.5 INSTITUTIONAL REVIEW BOARDS AND OVERSIGHT

In the United States, Institutional Review Boards, or IRBs, conduct ethical oversight on research that involves human subjects. The IRB oversight system was enacted as a federal law on May 30, 1974, and the National Research Act was passed in July of 1974. The National Research Act established the National Commission for the Protection of Human Subjects of Biomedical and Behavioral Research. This commission met to discuss ethical protections for human research subjects. One result of their meetings is the Belmont Report, which is included as a reading in Chapter 2. Additionally, the Commission issued extensive regulations for the protection of human research subjects. In 1981 both the Department of Health and Human Services (DHHS) and the Food and Drug Administration (FDA) revised their regulations for the protection of human research subjects, per the Commission's findings. The DHHS's code can be found at Title 45 Part 46 of the Code of Federal Regulations, and the FDA's code can be found at Title 21 Part 21 of the Code of Federal Regulations. Federal regulations that govern the ethical treatment of human research subjects are collectively referred to as "The Common Rule" and are under constant revision as scientific inquiry expands and awareness of ethical concerns grows. For example, in 1981 there was no need for extensive regulations on studies related to in-vitro fertilization, because this technique was relatively new. In another example, there has been recent interest in enrolling more children in clinical trials, because of the recognition that there have not been enough data generated on the effects of some drugs on children.

Because of this lack of data, children have not been able to experience the benefit of some drugs that are available to adults. With increased attention paid to enrolling children in clinical trials come more provisions to ensure the protection of the children. The regulations have been revised in light of these and other concerns. Some of the ethical considerations that arise when using children as research subjects are discussed in sections 5.2 and 5.3.

An institution's IRB is a board made up of at least five individuals. The individuals should be from different backgrounds so that their review of a proposed project includes a range of perspectives. The IRB is required to have at least one member whose research interests are scientific, such as a biologist or psychologist, and at least one non-scientific member, such as an ethicist. Additionally, there must be a community member, who is able to articulate the concerns and questions of the community from which human subjects will be taken. This community member, also referred to as an "unaffiliated member" because of that member's lack of affiliation with the institution, could be a clergyperson or a member of a community organization. Specialists in a particular field are often recruited when the IRB reviews a research proposal that focuses on a special population of subjects. For example, if members of vulnerable populations such as prisoners or persons with mental disabilities were to be used as research subjects, it would be ideal to have a prisoners' advocate or a teacher of the mentally disabled at that meeting of the IRB to articulate the concerns of these populations. It should be clear that IRBs are constructed to bring a diversity of perspectives to the review of any research project and that attention is paid to creating a balance of well-informed researchers in the area of study of the proposed research, as well as individuals who can assess the ethics of the research from an external perspective. Ideally, IRBs also reflect the gender, racial, and ethnic diversity of the community in which the research is taking place.

Before a research project that involves human subjects can begin, the project must be reviewed by an IRB. Before a project can be funded by many major granting agencies, the project needs IRB approval. If substantial changes occur in any portion of a project that involves human research subjects, such as the type of experiments that are being run, the means of recruitment of the research subjects, or anything else that affects the experiences of the subjects, these changes must be reviewed by the IRB. Finally, during the research process, the researcher is required to give periodic updates to the IRB, especially to report on any adverse events surrounding the inclusion of human subjects. IRB members are permitted to oversee the research process, including the obtaining of informed consent from subjects and the data collection process. The IRB may prevent a research project from beginning or may shut down a research project once it has begun if the IRB's procedures are not followed, or if there is evidence that human subjects have been wronged during the research process. The failure of an IRB to responsibly oversee human subject protections at an institution can result in the stoppage of all human subject research at that institution (this penalty was temporarily imposed on Duke University in the spring of 1999). A similarly harsh penalty, which resulted in the stoppage of nearly 1,000 studies at the University of Illinois at Chicago, was temporarily imposed by the Office for Protection from Research Risks (OPRR) in August 1999. Many journals will not publish studies on human subjects research unless the authors can document that IRB approval was granted by their institutions, demonstrating that steps were taken to protect the interests of human subjects.

The proposed research plan, including a detailed description of the use of human subjects, is called the research protocol. IRB review focuses on six elements of this protocol: the risk/expected-benefit ratio, the procedures for obtaining informed consent, the just and equitable selection of subjects, the protection of private and/or confidential information that is obtained during the research process, the use of vulnerable subjects, and the incentives offered to the subjects in exchange for their participation. Many of these points will be discussed in detail in Chapters 4 and 5. IRBs do not examine the methodology of the research protocol *per se.* However, it should be clear from the discussion in this chapter that methodological concerns can also be ethical concerns. The risks and expected benefits of human subject participation, discussed in Chapter 4, are not separable from the study design. Placebo-control studies, for example, create a different calculus of risks and potential benefits than do studies that do not have a placebo arm. Researchers who do not use a control arm in a study which calls for one do not merely make a scientific mistake, they also are exposing the human subjects in the study to all the risks of the study without ensuring that the study will yield benefits in generalizable knowledge. Thus, methodological concerns are rightly a part of responsible IRB review.

Although the IRB system has been in place for many years, the system is by no means perfect. Members of IRBs have seen their workloads increase as federal regulations widen in an attempt to better protect human subjects in every kind of research. With ever-increasing regulations, the sheer number of projects that fall under IRB purview has increased. A similar problem stems from the fact that some institutions have ever-increasing research missions. Individual IRBs may not be growing to meet their institutions' demands despite the fact that these institutions' research missions have increased. Many institutions do not yet recognize the integral part that IRBs play in their research mission, and as a result IRBs are not always given the resources that they need to fulfill their mandate.

The above-mentioned problems focus on the inability of IRBs to adequately attend to their mission in institutions that require IRB purview. IRBs protect the interests of human research subjects only at institutions that receive federal money for research projects. This includes most hospitals, universities, and colleges in the United States. It also includes federally funded research studies that take place overseas. What of those institutions whose research does not legally fall under IRB purview? Just because a project itself is not federally funded does not mean that the project does not fall under the purview of the IRB at its home institution. The multiple-project assurance, which is similar to a contract between institutions and federal agencies that the institution will uphold IRB regulations, guarantees that all human subjects research will be scrutinized by the IRB at that institution, regardless of how the research is funded. These assurances of compliance with federal regulations regarding human subjects are necessary for an institution to receive any funding from the United States Public Health Service or the DHHS. Multiple-project assurances also demand that if a violation of the rights and welfare of human subjects occurs, then this must be reported to the proper authorities. Institutions which undertake single federally funded research projects that involve human research subjects can apply for a single-project assurance, which commits them to follow the federal standards for the duration of the project in question. It should be stated that these protections do not cover privately funded research in the United States. Some research by pharmaceutical companies, for example, may not be covered by IRB regulations because these companies are not receiving any federal funds for this or any other research. The fact that there are no protections in the United States for human subjects in studies that take place outside an IRB's purview is the subject of recent concern. Human research subjects in the United States should not fall through the cracks of the IRB system due to the source of an institution's funding.

3.6   SUMMARY

The methodology employed in a research project is of both scientific and ethical concern. In an attempt to remove bias, subject selection should not merely be a convenience sample; rather, more significant characteristics of a sample should be considered. Also, "convenient" subject pools should not unjustly bear the burden of serving as research subjects. However, stratification and other strategies for correcting the biases inherent in convenience samples may bring with them additional ethical problems.

Randomization can help to create equity in subject selection, as well as contribute to unbiased results. Randomizing subjects into treatment and control arms allows the researcher to chart research subjects' progress. However, randomization does not guarantee either that subjects will be shielded from the risks of participating as research subjects or that they will reap the benefits of serving as research subjects. Insofar as subjects may enroll in research studies for the benefits of receiving an experimental therapy, randomization must be explained in detail to any potential research subject. Cross-over studies, in which subjects begin in one arm of the study but are ultimately switched to another arm of the study, may correct for some of these ethical difficulties. However, cross-over studies have their own disadvantages; the benefits of serving as a research subject are not as pronounced in these studies. Additionally, cross-over methodology is not appropriate for all research studies.

Single-blinded and double-blinded trials are methods that are designed to mask the biases which may result in misleading or incorrect results. The ethics of both of these methodologies are complex, because information about the study is intentionally withheld from the subjects, researchers, or both. All arms of randomized studies are expected to be in clinical equipoise, and once they fall out of equipoise, it is the responsibility of the researchers to stop the trial for the sake of the research subjects. This is easier said than done, though, because it is often difficult to know when two treatments are no longer in equipoise.

Placebos are inert substances that can be used in control arms. Use of placebos allows researchers to gauge the efficacy of a treatment against a control, while at the same time adjusting for the placebo effect. Use of placebos has been quite controversial in a number of cases, such as the use of placebos in the developing-world HIV trials and the use of placebo surgery in the United States.

Methodological concerns are only one of a number of general questions that can arise when an IRB examines a research protocol. These oversight committees are concerned primarily with the risk/expected-benefit ratio of research, informed consent, the just and equitable selection of subjects, the protection of private or confidential information that is obtained during the research process, the use of vulnerable subjects, and the incentives offered to the subjects in exchange for their participation. Many of these important issues will be covered in the following chapters.

3.7 CASE STUDIES

3.1: Chris was recruited to participate in a clinical trial by his oncologist, Dr. Blair. Chris has cancer, and the traditional treatments have been only intermittently successful. The clinical trial is a randomized, single-blinded, placebo-controlled study of a drug that may be beneficial to patients with the kind of cancer that Chris has. The trial is set to last one year, after which time enough data will have been accumulated to determine the efficacy of the new treatment. After six months in the study, Chris is not experiencing any signs of improvement, and he may in fact be getting worse. Dr. Blair continues to receive reports about the progress of the research subjects enrolled in both the treatment arm and in the placebo arm, and preliminary data seem to suggest that the drug is beneficial. During an examination Chris asks Dr. Blair if he is in the treatment arm or the placebo arm. Chris requests that if he is in the placebo arm Dr. Blair switch him to the treatment arm, so that he can receive the possible benefits of the new treatment. Dr. Blair knows that Chris is in the placebo arm. What should Dr. Blair tell Chris about the study at this time? When is it appropriate to remove a subject from a study? What are the dual responsibilities that Dr. Blair has? Which should take precedence in this case, and why?

3.2: Drug R was originally tested on older women to prevent osteoporosis. After several double-blinded, placebo-controlled, randomized clinical trials, drug R was shown to be beneficial to patients who had, or were at risk of, osteoporosis. There seemed to be an additional benefit to taking the drug, however. The number of women who died of breast cancer while taking drug R in the initial clinical trial was appreciably lower than the number of women who died of breast cancer in the placebo arm during the study. Since the study was designed to test the efficacy of R in treating osteoporosis this benefit was noted merely as a side-effect of the drug. Months later, a new trial was to begin to test drug R as a preventative therapy for women who were at risk for breast cancer. Should the new study be a placebo-controlled study? Why or why not? What information is needed to determine if this should be a placebo-controlled study?

REFERENCES AND FURTHER READING

Walter A. Brown, "The Placebo Effect," *Scientific American*, January 1998, pp. 90–95.

Gina Kolata and Kurt Eichenwarld, "Business Thrives on Unproven Care, Leaving Science Behind," *The New York Times*, CXLIX, no. 51,664 (October 3, 1999). A report on the difficulties in enrolling breast cancer patients in randomized clinical trials of bone marrow transplants.

Charles Marwick, "Institutional Review Boards Under Stress: Will They Explode or Change?" *Journal of the American Medical Association*, 276, no. 20 (November 27, 1996), pp. 1623–1627.

Office for Protection from Research Risks, *Protecting Human Subjects: Institutional Review Board Guidebook*. Washington, DC: U.S. Government Printing Office, 1993.

Of Mice but Not Men: Problems of the Randomized Clinical Trial

Samuel Hellman and Deborah S. Hellman

As medicine has become increasingly scientific and less accepting of unsupported opinion or proof by anecdote, the randomized controlled clinical trial has become the standard technique for changing diagnostic or therapeutic methods. The use of this technique creates an ethical dilemma.[1,2] Researchers participating in such studies are required to modify their ethical commitments to individual patients and do serious damage to the concept of the physician as a

Samuel Hellman and Deborah S. Hellman, "Of Mice but Not Men: Problems of the Randomized Clinical Trial," *New England Journal of Medicine*, 324, no. 22, May 30 1991, pp. 1585–1589. Copyright © 1991, Massachusetts Medical Society. All rights reserved.

practicing, empathetic professional who is primarily concerned with each patient as an individual. Researchers using a randomized clinical trial can be described as physician-scientists, a term that expresses the tension between the two roles. The physician, by entering into a relationship with an individual patient, assumes certain obligations, including the commitment always to act in the patient's best interests. As Leon Kass has rightly maintained, "the physician must produce unswervingly the virtues of loyalty and fidelity to his patient."[3] Though the ethical requirements of this relationship have been modified by legal obligations to report wounds of a suspicious nature and certain infectious diseases, these obligations in no way conflict with the central ethical obligation to act in the best interests of the patient medically. Instead, certain nonmedical interests of the patient are preempted by other social concerns.

The role of the scientist is quite different. The clinical scientist is concerned with answering questions—i.e., determining the validity of formally constructed hypotheses. Such scientific information, it is presumed, will benefit humanity in general. The clinical scientist's role has been well described by Dr. Anthony Fauci, director of the National Institute of Allergy and Infectious Diseases, who states the goals of the randomized clinical trial in these words: "It's not to deliver therapy. It's to answer a scientific question so that the drug can be available for everybody once you've established safety and efficacy."[4] The demands of such a study can conflict in a number of ways with the physician's duty to minister to patients. The study may create a false dichotomy in the physician's opinions; according to the premise of the randomized clinical trial, the physician may only know or not know whether a proposed course of treatment represents an improvement; no middle position is permitted. What the physician thinks, suspects, believes, or has a hunch about is assigned to the "not knowing" category, because knowing is defined on the basis of an arbitrary but accepted statistical test performed in a randomized clinical trial. Thus, little credence is given to information gained beforehand in other ways or to information accrued during the trial but without the required statistical degree of assurance that a difference is not due to chance. The randomized clinical trial also prevents the treatment technique from being modified on the basis of the growing knowledge of the physicians during their participation in the trial. Moreover, it limits access to the data as they are collected until specific milestones are achieved. This prevents physicians from profiting not only from their individual experience, but also from the collective experience of the other participants.

The randomized clinical trial requires doctors to act simultaneously as physicians and as scientists. This puts them in a difficult and sometimes untenable ethical position. The conflicting moral demands arising from the use of the randomized clinical trial reflect the classic conflict between rights-based moral theories and utilitarian ones. The first of these, which depend on the moral theory of Immanuel Kant (and seen more recently in neo-Kantian philosophers, such as John Rawls[5]), asserts that human beings, by virtue of their unique capacity for rational thought, are bearers of dignity. As such, they ought not to be treated merely as means to an end; rather, they must always be treated as ends in themselves. Utilitarianism, by contrast, defines what is right as the greatest good for the greatest number—that is, as social utility. This view, articulated by Jeremy Bentham and John Stuart Mill, requires that pleasures (understood broadly, to include such pleasures as health and well-being) and pains be added together. The morally correct act is the act that produces the most pleasure and the least pain overall.

A classic objection to the utilitarian position is that according to that theory, the distribution of pleasures and pains is of no moral consequence. This element of the theory severely restricts physicians from being utilitarians, or at least from following the theory's dictates. Physicians must care very deeply about the distribution of pain and pleasure, for they have entered into a relationship with one or a number of individual patients. They cannot be indifferent to whether it is these patients or others that suffer for the general benefit of society. Even though society might gain from the suffering of a few, and even though the doctor might believe that such a benefit is worth a given patient's suffering (i.e., that utilitarianism is right in the particular case), the ethical obligation created by the covenant between doctor and patient requires the doctor to see the interests of the individual patient as primary and compelling. In essence, the doctor-patient relationship requires doctors to see their patients as bearers of rights who cannot be merely used for the greater good of humanity.

As Fauci has suggested,[4] the randomized clinical trial routinely asks physicians to sacrifice the interests of their particular patients for the sake of the study and that of the information that it will make available for the benefit of society. This practice is ethically problematic. Consider first the initial formulation of a trial. In particular, consider the case of a disease for which there is no satisfactory therapy—for example, advanced cancer or the acquired immunodeficiency syndrome (AIDS). A new agent that promises more effectiveness is the subject of the study. The control group must be given either an unsatisfactory treatment or a placebo. Even though the therapeutic value of the new agent is unproved, if physicians think that it has promise, are they acting in the best interests of their patients in allowing them to be randomly assigned to the control group? Is persisting in such an assignment consistent with the specific commitments taken on in the doctor-patient relationship? As a result of interactions with patients with AIDS and their advocates, Merigan[6] recently suggested modifications in the design of clinical trials that attempt to deal with the unsatisfactory treatment given to the control group. The view of such activists has been expressed by Rebecca Pringle Smith of Community Research Initiative in New York: "Even if you have a supply of compliant martyrs, trials must have some ethical validity."[4]

If the physician has no opinion about whether the new treatment is acceptable, then random assignment is ethically acceptable, but such lack of enthusiasm for the new treatment does not augur well for either the patient or the study. Alternatively, the treatment may show promise of beneficial results but also present a risk of undesirable complications. When the physician believes that the severity and likelihood of harm and good are evenly balanced, randomization may be ethically acceptable. If the physician has no preference for either treatment (is in a state of equipoise[7,8]), then randomization is acceptable. If, however, he or she believes that the new treatment may be either more or less successful or more or less toxic, the use of randomization is not consistent with fidelity to the patient.

The argument usually used to justify randomization is that it provides, in essence, a critique of the usefulness of the physician's beliefs and opinions, those that have not yet been validated by a randomized clinical trial. As the argument goes, these not-yet-validated beliefs are as likely to be wrong as right. Although physicians are ethically required to provide their patients with the best available treatment, there simply is no best treatment yet known.

The reply to this argument takes two forms. First, and most important, even if this view of the reliability of a physician's opinions is accurate, the ethical constraints of an individual doctor's relationship with a particular patient require the doctor to provide individual care. Although physicians must take pains to make clear the speculative nature of their views, they cannot withhold these views from the patient. The patient asks from the doctor both knowledge and judgment. The relationship established between them rightfully allows patients to ask for the judgment of their particular physicians, not merely that of the medical profession in general. Second, it may not be true, in fact, that the not-yet-validated beliefs of physicians are as likely to be wrong as right. The greater certainty obtained with a randomized clinical trial is beneficial, but that does not mean that a lesser degree of certainty is without value. Physicians can acquire knowledge through methods other than the randomized clinical trial. Such knowledge, acquired over time and less formally than is required in a randomized clinical trial, may be of great value to a patient.

Even if it is ethically acceptable to begin a study, one often forms an opinion during its course—especially in studies that are impossible to conduct in a truly double-blinded fashion—that makes it ethically problematic to continue. The inability to remain blinded usually occurs in studies of cancer or AIDS, for example, because the therapy is associated by nature with serious side effects. Trials attempt to restrict the physician's access to the data in order to prevent such unblinding. Such restrictions should make physicians eschew the trial, since their ability to act in the patient's best interests will be limited. Even supporters of randomized clinical trials, such as Merigan, agree that interim findings should be presented to patients to ensure that no one receives what seems an inferior treatment.[6] Once physicians have formed a view about the new treatment, can they continue randomization? If random assignment is stopped, the study may be lost and the participation of the previous patients wasted. However, if physicians continue the randomization when they have a definite opinion about the efficacy of the experimental drug, they are not acting in accordance with the requirements of the doctor-patient relationship. Furthermore, as their opinion becomes more firm, stopping the randomization may not be enough. Physicians may be ethically required to treat the patients formerly placed in the control group with the therapy that now seems probably effective. To do so would be faithful to the obligations created by the doctor-patient relationship, but it would destroy the study.

To resolve this dilemma, one might suggest that the patient has abrogated the rights implicit in a doctor-patient relationship by signing an informed-consent form. We argue that such rights cannot be waived or abrogated. They are inalienable. The right to be treated as an individual deserving the physician's best judgment and care, rather than to be used as a means to determine the best treatment for others, is inherent in every person. This right, based on the concept of dignity, cannot be waived. What of altruism, then? Is it not the patient's right to make a sacrifice for the general good? This question must be considered from both positions—that of the patient and that of the physician. Although patients may decide to waive this right, it is not consistent with the role of a physician to ask that they do so. In asking, the doctor acts as a scientist instead. The physician's role here is to propose what he or she believes is best medically for the specific patient, not to suggest participation in a study from which the patient cannot gain. Because the opportunity to help future patients is of potential value to a patient, some would say physicians should not deny it. Although this point has merit, it offers so many opportunities for abuse that we are extremely uncomfortable about accepting it. The responsibilities of physicians are much clearer; they are to minister to the current patient.

Moreover, even if patients could waive this right, it is questionable whether those with terminal illness would be truly able to give voluntary informed consent. Such patients are extremely dependent on both their physicians and the health care system. Aware of this dependence, physicians must not ask for consent, for in such cases the very asking breaches the doctor-patient relationship. Anxious to please their physicians, patients may have difficulty refusing to participate in the trial and physicians describe. The patients may perceive their refusal as damaging to the relationship, whether or not it is so. Such perceptions of coercion affect the decision. Informed-consent forms are difficult to understand, especially for patients under the stress of serious illness for which there is no satisfactory treatment. The forms are usually lengthy, somewhat legalistic, complicated, and confusing, and they hardly bespeak the compassion expected of the medical profession. It is important to remember that those who have studied the doctor-patient relationship have emphasized its empathetic nature.

> [The] relationship between doctor and patient partakes of a peculiar intimacy. It presupposes on the part of the physician not only knowledge of his fellow men but sympathy. . . . This aspect of the practice of medicine has been designated as the art; yet I wonder whether it should not, most properly, be called the essence.[9]

How is such a view of the relationship consonant with random assignment and informed consent? The Physician's Oath of the World Medical Association affirms the primacy of the deontologic view of patients' rights: "Concern for the interests of the subject must always prevail over the interests of science and society."[10]

Furthermore, a single study is often not considered sufficient. Before a new form of therapy is generally accepted, confirmatory trials must be conducted. How can one conduct such trials ethically unless one is convinced that the first trial was in error? The ethical problems we have discussed are only exacerbated when a completed randomized clinical trial indicates that a given treatment is preferable. Even if the physician believes the initial trial was in error, the physician must indicate to the patient the full results of that trial.

The most common reply to the ethical arguments has been that the alternative is to return to the physician's intuition, to anecdotes, or to both as the basis of medical opinion. We all accept the dangers of such a practice. The argument states that we must therefore accept randomized, controlled clinical trials regardless of their ethical problems because of the great social benefit they make possible, and we salve our conscience with the knowledge that informed consent has been given. This returns us to the conflict between patients' rights and social utility. Some would argue that this tension can be resolved by placing a relative value on each. If the patient's right that is being compromised is not a fundamental right and the social gain is very great, then the study might be justified. When the right is fundamental, however, no amount of social gain, or almost none, will justify its sacrifice. Consider, for example, the experiments on humans done by physicians under the Nazi regime. All would agree that these are unacceptable regardless of the value of the scientific information gained. Some people go so far as to say that no use should be made of the results of those experiments because of the clearly unethical manner in which the data were collected. This extreme example may not seem relevant, but we believe that in its hyperbole it clarifies the fallacy of a utilitarian approach to the physician's relationship with the patient. To consider the utilitarian gain is consistent neither with the physician's role nor with the patient's rights.

It is fallacious to suggest that only the randomized clinical trial can provide valid information or that all information acquired by this technique is valid. Such experimental methods are intended to reduce error and bias and therefore reduce the uncertainty of the result. Uncertainty cannot be eliminated, however. The scientific method is based on increasing probabilities and increasingly refined approximations of truth.[11] Although the randomized clinical trial contributes to these ends, it is neither unique nor perfect. Other techniques may also be useful.[12]

Randomized trials often place physicians in the ethically intolerable position of choosing between the good of the patient and that of society. We urge that such situations be avoided and that other techniques of acquiring clinical information be adopted. For example, concerning trials of treatments for AIDS, Byar et al.[13] have said that "some traditional approaches to the clinical-trials process may be unnecessarily rigid and unsuitable for this disease." In this case, AIDS is not what is so different; rather, the difference is in the presence of AIDS activists, articulate spokespersons for the ethical problems created by the application of the randomized clinical trial to terminal illnesses. Such arguments are equally applicable to advanced cancer and other serious illnesses. Byar et al. agree that there are even circumstances in which uncontrolled clinical trials may be justified: when there is no effective treatment to use as a control, when the prognosis is uniformly poor, and when there is a reasonable expectation of benefit without excessive toxicity. These conditions are usually found in clinical trials of advanced cancer.

The purpose of the randomized clinical trial is to avoid the problems of observer bias and patient selection. It seems to us that techniques might be developed to deal with these issues in other ways. Randomized clinical trials deal with them in a cumbersome and heavy-handed manner, by requiring large numbers of patients in the hope that random assignment will balance the heterogeneous distribution of patients into the different groups. By observing known characteristics of patients, such as age and sex, and distributing them equally between groups, it is thought that unknown factors important in determining outcomes will also be distributed equally. Surely, other techniques can be developed to deal with both observer bias and patient selection. Prospective studies without randomization, but with the evaluation of patients by uninvolved third parties, should remove observer bias. Similar methods have been suggested by Royall.[12] Prospective matched-pair analysis, in which patients are treated in a manner consistent with their physician's views, ought to help ensure equivalence between the groups and thus mitigate the effect of patient selection, at least with regard to known covariates. With regard to unknown covariates, the security would rest, as in randomized trials, in the enrollment of large numbers of patients and in confirmatory studies. This method would not pose ethical difficulties, since patients would receive the treatment recommended by their physician. They would be included in the study by independent observers matching patients with respect to known characteristics, a process that would not affect patient care and that could be performed independently any number of times.

This brief discussion of alternatives to randomized clinical trials is sketchy and incomplete. We wish only to point out that there may be satisfactory alternatives, not to describe and evaluate them completely. Even if randomized clinical trials were much better than any alternative, however, the ethical dilemmas they present may put their use at variance with the primary obligations of the physician. In this regard, Angell cautions, "If this commitment to the patient is attenuated, even for so good a cause as benefits to future patients, the implicit assumptions of the doctor-patient relationship are violated."[14] The risk of such attenuation by the randomized trial is great. The AIDS activists have brought this dramatically to the attention of the academic medical community. Techniques appropriate to the laboratory may not be applicable to humans. We must develop and use alternative methods for acquiring clinical knowledge.

Notes

[1] Hellman S. Randomized clinical trials and the doctor-patient relationship: an ethical dilemma. *Cancer Clin Trials* 1979; 2:189–93.

[2] *Idem.* A doctor's dilemma: the doctor-patient relationship in clinical investigation. In: *Proceedings of the Fourth National Conference on Human Values and Cancer, New York, March 15–17, 1984.* New York: American Cancer Society, 1984:144–6.

[3] Kass LR. *Toward a more natural science: biology and human affairs.* New York: Free Press, 1985:196.

[4] Palca J. AIDS drug trials enter new age. *Science* 1989; 246:19–21.

[5] Rawls J. *A theory of justice.* Cambridge, Mass.: Belknap Press of Harvard University Press, 1971:183–92, 466–52.

[6] Merigan TC. You *can* teach an old dog new tricks—how AIDS trials are pioneering new strategies. *N Engl J Med* 1990; 323:1341–3.

[7] Freedman B. Equipoise and the ethics of clinical research. *N Engl J Med* 1987; 317:141–5.

[8] Singer PA, Lantos JD, Whitington PF, Broelsch CE, Siegler M. Equipoise and the ethics of segmental liver transplantation. *Clin Res* 1988; 36:539–45.

[9] Longcope WT. Methods and medicine. *Bull Johns Hopkins Hosp* 1932; 50:4–20.

[10] Report on medical ethics. *World Med Assoc Bull* 1949; 1:109, 111.

[11] Popper K. The problem of induction. In: Miller D, ed., *Popper selections.* Princeton, N.J.: Princeton University Press, 1985: 101–17.

[12] Royall RM. Ethics and statistics in randomized clinical trials. *Stat Sci* 1991; 6(1):52–62.

[13] Byar DP, Schoenfeld DA, Green SB, et al. Design considerations for AIDS trials. *N Engl J Med* 1990; 323:1343–8.

[14] Angell M. Patients' preferences in randomized clinical trials. *N Engl J Med* 1984; 310:1385–7.

A Response to a Purported Ethical Difficulty with Randomized Clinical Trials Involving Cancer Patients

Benjamin Freedman

In recent years, for a variety of reasons, the mainstay of clinical investigation—the randomized controlled clinical trial (RCT)—has increasingly come under attack. Since Charles Fried's influential monograph,[1] the opponents of controlled trials have claimed the moral high ground. They claim to perceive a conflict

Benjamin Freedman, "A Response to a Purported Ethical Difficulty with Randomized Clinical Trials Involving Cancer Patients," *Journal of Clinical Ethics,* 3, no 3, Fall 1992: 231–234. Copyright © 1992 by *The Journal of Clinical Ethics.* All rights reserved. Reprinted by permission.

between the medical and scientific duties of the physician-investigator, and between the conduct of the trial and a patient's rights. Samuel and Deborah Hellman write, for example, that "the randomized clinical trial routinely asks physicians to sacrifice the interests of their particular patients for the sake of the study and that of the information that it will make available for the benefit of society."[2] Maurie Markman's attraction to this point of view is clear when he writes that "the individual physician's principal ethical responsibility is to the *individual patient* that he or she is treating, and *not* to future patients [emphases in original]." In the interests of returning Markman to the fold, I will concentrate on resolving this central challenge to the ethics of RCTs.

It is unfortunately true that the most common responses from pro-trialists, by revealing fundamental misunderstandings of basic ethical concepts, do not inspire confidence in the ethics of human research as it is currently conducted. Proponents of clinical trials will commonly begin their apologia by citing benefits derived from trials—by validating the safety and efficacy of new treatments, and, at least as important, by discrediting accepted forms of treatment. So far so good. But they often go on to argue that there is a need to balance the rights of subjects against the needs of society. By this tactic, the proponents of clinical trials have implicitly morally surrendered, for to admit that something is a right is to admit that it represents a domain of action protected from the claims or interests of other individuals or of society itself. A liberal society has rightly learned to look askance at claims that rights of individuals need to yield to the demands of the collective. Patients' claims, then, because of their nature as rights, supersede the requirements of the collectivity.

Sometimes, indeed, the surrender is explicit. At the conclusion of a symposium on the ethics of research on human subjects, Sir Colin Dollery, a major figure in clinical trials, complained to the speaker: "You assume a dominant role of ethics— I think to the point of arrogance. Ethical judgments will be of little value unless the scientific innovations about which they are made . . . are useful."[3] But it is the nature of ethical judgments that they are, indeed, "dominant" as normative or accepted guides to action. One may say, "I know that X is the ethical thing to do, but I won't X." That expresses no logical contradiction, but simply weakness of will. But it is, by contrast, plainly contradictory to admit that X is ethical, yet to deny or doubt that one ought to X.

Closer examination and finer distinctions reveal, however, that the conflict between patients' rights and social interests is not at all at issue in controlled clinical trials. There is no need for proponents of clinical trials to concede the moral high ground.

What is the patient right that is compromised by clinical trials? The fear most common to patients who are hesitant about enrolling is that they would not receive the best care, that their right to treatment would be sacrificed in the interests of science. This presumes, of course, that the patient has a right to treatment. Such a right must in reason be grounded in patient need (a patient who is not ill has no right to treatment) and in medical knowledge and capability (a patient with an incurable illness has rights to be cared for, but no right to be cured).

That granted, we need to specify the kind of treatment to which a patient might reasonably claim a right. It was in this connection that I introduced the concept of *clinical equipoise* as critical to understanding the ethics of clinical trials.[4] Clinical equipoise is a situation in which there exists (or is pending) an honest disagreement in the expert clinical community regarding the comparative merits of two or more forms of treatment for a given condition. To be ethical, a controlled clinical trial must begin and be conducted in a continuing state of clinical equipoise—as between the arms of the study—and must, moreover, offer some reasonable hope that the successful conclusion of the trial will disturb equipoise (that is, resolve the controversy in the expert clinical community).

This theory presumes that a right to a specific medical treatment must be grounded in a professional judgment, which is concretized in the term *clinical equipoise*. A patient who has rights to medical treatment has rights restricted to, though not necessarily exhaustive of, those treatments that are understood by the medical community to be appropriate for his condition. A patient may eccentrically claim some good from a physician that is not recognized by the medical community as appropriate treatment. A physician may even grant this claim; but in so doing, he must realize that he has not provided medical treatment itself. Contrariwise, by failing to fulfill this request, the physician has not failed to satisfy the patient's right to medical treatment.

Provided that a comparative trial is ethical, therefore, it begins in a state of clinical equipoise. For that reason, by definition, nobody enrolling in the trial is denied his or her right to medical treatment, for no medical consensus for or against the treatment assignment exists.

(The modern climate requires that I introduce two simple caveats. First, I am ignoring economic and political factors that go into the grounding of a right to treatment. This is easy enough for one in Canada to write, but may be difficult for someone in the United States to read. Second, when speaking of treatment that is recognized to be condition-appropriate by the medical community, I mean to include only those judgments grounded in medical knowledge rather than so-cial judgments. I would hope to avoid the current bioethical muddle over "medical futility," but if my claims need to be translated into terms appropriate to that controversy, "physiological futility" is close but not identical to what I mean by "inappropriate." For simplicity's sake, the best model to have in mind is the common patient demand for antibiotic treatment of an illness diagnosed as viral.)

Two errors are commonly committed in connection with the concept of clinical equipoise. The first mistake is in thinking that clinical equipoise (or its disturbance) relates to a single endpoint of a trial—commonly, efficacy. As a function of expert clinical judgment, clinical equipoise must incorporate all of the many factors that go into favoring one regimen over its competitors. Treatment *A* may be favored over *B* because it is more effective; or, because it is almost as effective but considerably less toxic; or, because it is easier to administer, allowing, for example, treatment on an outpatient basis; or, because patients are more compliant with it; and so forth.

Just as equipoise may be based upon any one or a combination of these or other factors, it may be disturbed in the same way. Markman's second example, which discusses the efficacy of a multidrug combination chemotherapy regimen, seems vulnerable to this objection. Even were the results of the Mayo trial convincing with regard to the efficacy of this approach, it has not disturbed clinical equipoise in its favor unless other issues, such as toxicity, have been resolved as well. It is well worth pointing out that the endpoints of trials, particularly in cancer treatment, are far too narrow to disturb clinical equipoise in and of themselves, but they are necessary steps along a seriatim path. For that matter, in ignoring the compendious judgment involved in ascertaining equipoise, some studies spuriously claim that all of their arms are in equipoise on the basis of one variable (such as five-year survival rates), when they are clearly out of equipoise because of other factors (such as differences in pain and disfigurement).

The second mistake occurs in identifying clinical equipoise with an individual physician's point of indifference between two treatments. Citing the article in which I developed the concept and another article applying it, for example, the Hellmans write, "If the physician has no preference for either treatment (is in a state of equipoise), then randomization is acceptable."[5] But an individual physician is not the arbiter of appropriate or acceptable medical practice.

There are numerous occasions outside of clinical trials where outsiders need to determine whether the treatment provided was appropriate to the patient's condition. Regulators, as well as third-party payers—private or governmental—need to answer the question, as do health planners and administrators of health-care facilities. Disciplinary bodies of professional associations, and, most tellingly, courts judging allegations of malpractice, have to ascertain this as well. It is never the case that the judgment of an individual physician concerning whether a treatment is condition-appropriate (that is, whether it belongs with the therapeutic armamentarium) is sufficient. In all of these instances, however varied might be their rules of investigation and procedure, the ultimate question is: Does the expert professional community accept this treatment as appropriate for this condition? Since clinical equipoise and its disturbance applies to putative medical treatments for given conditions, this is a matter that is determined legally, morally, and reasonably by that medical community with the recognized relevant expertise.

Markman may have fallen into this error, writing repeatedly of the judgment of the treating or enrolling physician (and, in the first page, of the responsibility of "the individual physician") with respect to the clinical trial. There is, however, another way of looking at this. Whereas the status of a putative treatment within the medical armamentarium must be settled by the medical *community*, the application of that judgment *vis-à-vis* a given patient is, of course, the judgment (and the responsibility) of the *individual physician*. This individual clinical judgment must be exercised when enrolling a subject, rather than subjugated to the judgment of those who constructed the trial. Indeed, many studies will list this as a criterion of exclusion: "Those subjects who, in the judgment of the accruing physician, would be put at undue risk by participating."

Another point: the Hellmans write of a physician's duty in treating a patient to employ what he "thinks, suspects, believes, or has a hunch about."[6] This is clearly overstated as a duty: why not add to the list the physician's hopes, fantasies, fond but dotty beliefs, and illusions? Yet patients do choose physicians, in part, because of trust in their tacit knowledge and inchoate judgment, and not merely their sapient grasp of the current medical consensus. It would be a disservice to patients for a physician to see his or her role simply as a vehicle for transmitting the wisdom received from the expert medical community in all cases (though when a departure is made, this is done at the legal peril of the doctor!).

But what follows from this inalienable duty of the treating physician? Not as much as the opponents of trials would have us believe. A physician certainly has the right to refuse to participate in a trial that he believes places some participants at a medical disadvantage. Moreover, if he or she is convinced of that, he or she has a *duty* to abstain from participating. But that only speaks to the physician, and does not necessarily affect the patient. What opponents of trials forget is that the patient—the subject—is the ultimate decision maker—in fact, in law, and in ethics. In at least some cases, the fact that there is an open trial for which a patient meets the eligibility criteria needs to be disclosed as one medical alternative, to satisfy ethical norms of informed consent. A physician with convictions that the trial will put subjects at undue risk should inform the prospective subject of that conviction and the reasons for it, and may well recommend to the subject to decline participation. It will then be up to the patient whether to seek enrollment via another physician.

Most commonly at issue, though, is a physician's preference rather than conviction. In such cases, it is perfectly ethical—and becomingly modest—for a physician to participate in a trial, setting aside private misgivings based upon anecdote as overbalanced by the medical literature.

Finally, something should be said about the underlying philosophical buttress on which anti-trialists rely. Following Kant, the Hellmans argue that the underlying issue is that persons "ought not to be treated merely as means to an end; rather, they must always be treated as ends in themselves."[7] Clinical trials, however, are designed to yield reliable data and to ground scientifically valid inferences. In that sense, the treatments and examinations that a subject of a clinical trial undergoes are means to a scientific end, rather than interventions done solely for the subject's own benefit.

But the Kantian formulation is notoriously rigoristic, and implausible in the form cited. We treat others as means all the time, in order to achieve ends the others do not share, and are so treated in return. When buying a carton of milk or leaving a message, I am treating the cashier or secretary as means to an end they do not share. Were this unvarnished principle to hold, all but purely altruistic transactions would be ethically deficient. Clinical trials would be in very good (and, indeed, very bad) company. Those who follow the Kantian view are not concerned about treating another as a means, but rather about treating someone in a way that contradicts the other's personhood itself—that is, in a way that denies the fact that the person is not simply a means but is also an end. A paradigm case is when I treat someone in a way that serves my ends but, at the same time, is contrary to the other's best interests. It is true that a subject's participation in a clinical trial serves scientific ends, but what has not been shown is that it is contrary to the best interests of the subject. In cases where the two equipoise conditions are satisfied, this cannot be shown.

However, in some cases we are uncertain about whether an intervention will serve the best interests of the other, and so we ask that person. That is one reason for requiring informed consent to studies. There is another. By obtaining the consent of the other party to treat him as an end to one's own means, in effect, an identity of ends between both parties has been created. Applying this amended Kantian dictum, then, we should ask: Is there anything about clinical trials that necessarily implies that subjects are treated contrary to their personhood? And the answer is, of course, no—provided a proper consent has been obtained.

There remain many hard questions to ask about the ethics of controlled clinical studies. Many talents will be needed to address those questions and to reform current practice. Since those questions will only be asked by those who understand that such studies rest upon a sound ethical foundation, I am hopeful that Markman and others will reconsider their misgivings.

Notes

[1] C. Fried, *Medical Experimentation: Personal Integrity and Social Policy* (New York: Elsevier, 1974).

[2] S. Hellman and D. S. Hellman, "Of Mice but Not Men," *New England Journal of Medicine* 324 (1991): 1585–89, at 1586.

[3] Comment by Sir Colin Dollery in discussion following H.-M. Sass, "Ethics of Drug Research and Drug Development," *Arzneimittel Forschung/Drug Research* 39 (II), Number 8a (1989): 1042–48, at 1048.

[4] B. Freedman, "Equipoise and the Ethics of Clinical Research," *New England Journal of Medicine* 317 (1987): 141–45.

[5] Hellman and Hellman, "Of Mice," 1586.

[6] *Ibid.*

[7] *Ibid.*

Placebos and HIV

Lessons Learned

Carol Levine

"Lessons learned" is a popular phrase in international circles. Typically used to sum up the results of a review of experiences, it has a reassuring pedagogic tone. The "students" have done their home- (or field-) work, and have acquired the relevant knowledge. Presumably any mistakes they might have made in the course of their studies will not be repeated, because the "lessons" have been "learned." The real world of international clinical trials differs significantly from the tidy schoolroom metaphor. Nevertheless, it is still useful to ask: Are there lessons to be learned about future trials from the controversy over placebo-controlled trials of zidovudine (AZT) to prevent mother-to-child HIV transmission in developing countries? The answer is that there are some procedural cautions, but few unchallenged "lessons."

The trials involved over 12,000 women in seven countries and were funded by the U.S. Centers for Disease Control and Prevention and the National Institutes of Health. UNAIDS and French agencies were also involved in similar trials. Based on preliminary results of the trials in Thailand, which showed a reduction of 51 percent in transmission in mothers given a short course of AZT compared to those who received a placebo, similar trials under way in Africa and the Dominican Republic were suspended. Both enthusiastic proponents of the trials and their vociferous opponents asserted that their views had been vindicated.[1] The proponents declared that such significant results could only have been achieved with placebo arms; the opponents saw the results as evidence that placebos were never needed in the first place. *First Lesson Learned:* Even unambiguous scientific results of controversial clinical trials do not necessarily result in ethical consensus.

In retrospect, it is not surprising that these trials became so controversial. They brought together two issues that have been the subject of ethical debate for years: the use of placebo controls in clinical trials and the ethical standards for conducting trials in developing countries. In addition, this trial added the highly charged elements of the rapid spread of HIV in the developing world, the administration of drugs to pregnant women, and the transmission of a fatal disease to newborns. Although the issues had been discussed among the investigators and sponsoring agencies and their immediate circles of advisers, there was no

Carol Levine, "Placebos and HIV: Lessons Learned," *Hastings Center Report,* 28, no. 6, November-December 1998, 43–48.

broad discussion in ethics forums or in other arenas where some of the complexities could have been explored without the distraction of media-aimed charges and countercharges. *Second Lesson Learned:* Any trials with a combination of these elements are likely to be controversial; broad and open discussion should take place before they are implemented.

ACTG 076

The study on which all the developing [world] studies were based—AIDS Clinical Trial Group (ACTG) 076—was itself fraught with controversy. Conducted in the United States and France, it demonstrated that AZT was effective in reducing the rate of maternal-infant HIV transmission. The rate of transmission in the treated group was 8 percent compared to 25 percent in the placebo group. The difference between the two groups was so substantial that the data safety and monitoring board felt it was unethical to continue and stopped the trial early. Subsequent data have confirmed the effectiveness of AZT in preventing perinatal transmission in women who would not have been eligible for 076 because of their lower CD4 count and more serious disease progression. From 1984 through 1992, the estimated number of children with perinatally acquired HIV increased every year, then declined 42 percent during the period 1992 to 1996. Nevertheless, the 076 regimen is not 100 percent effective.

The 076 trial—perhaps one of the few trials that is known around the world by its numerical designation—went through several significant revisions before it was implemented. Some of these controversies involved the selection of subjects (whether minority women were unfairly burdened by being selected or were unfairly denied access); consent (whether fathers as well as mothers had to give consent); safety (the long-term effect of AZT on developing fetuses); and justice (whether it was unethical to provide AZT to women only during pregnancy and to follow the health of babies but not their mothers). Although these controversies were not central to the debate about applying the results to developing countries, they form an important background.

Despite the unequivocal nature of the results, the 076 protocol is not necessarily the best regimen to prevent HIV transmission. The study was not designed to establish an optimal regimen to prevent transmission, nor to determine which of the three types of administration (oral, intravenous during delivery, and post-birth to the infant) contributed most to prevention, nor whether all three were necessary.

Although the 076 protocol established short-term safety for the doses of AZT used, it is not known whether there are long-term safety risks to the children born without HIV infection who would not have been infected in any case. Some evidence of cancer in AZT-treated mice has caused concern, but many investigators believe this is not likely to be a real risk at the 076 dosage.

On the basis of the 076 results, the regimen became the standard of care for treatment of pregnant women in the United States and other developed countries.

As triple therapies (two nucleoside analogs and one protease inhibitor) replaced mono-therapies as the standard of care for HIV-infected patients in the United States, the use of a single agent in pregnant women—a lower standard of care— was questioned. The effect of protease inhibitors on perinatal transmission has not been documented, although increasingly U.S. clinicians are using these therapies in HIV-infected pregnant women and still seeing declines in HIV-infected newborns. Despite the proven benefits, the 076 regimen is not universally used even in the United States. Some women are outside the health care system and fail to obtain optimal prenatal care; others are not counseled about their HIV risk and do not know that they are HIV infected; still others refuse AZT or are not able to adhere to the 076 regimen.

While the standard of care is either not available to all HIV-infected women in the United States or has been altered for some women, developing countries cannot afford to provide the 076 treatment regimen to even the majority of HIV-infected pregnant women. Neither do they have the medical infrastructure to provide the complete regimen, especially intravenous administration at delivery. Many women do not receive prenatal care early enough to institute the complete regimen. There is an urgent need for an effective, shorter, practical regimen.

One of the questions left unanswered by 076 was whether some AZT—even considerably less than that used in 076—will reduce the rate of perinatal transmission. Unpublished but widely available data from the 076 trial on women who received less than the full protocol showed a decrease in HIV transmission, albeit a smaller decrease than in the full-protocol group. Supporters of the placebo-controlled trials question the validity of these data. One study in North Carolina using a survey design provided statistically valid data showing a reduction in transmission in infants who received any zidovidine.[2] On the other hand, a small prospective study from Uganda of AZT administered late in pregnancy did not show any benefit. The Thai results support the hypothesis that a smaller dose of AZT than the one in 076 will reduce HIV transmission significantly. A still debated question is whether this should have or could have been known without the use of the placebo arm in trials. *Third Lesson Learned:* 076 was the first step in a process, not the final answer.

Trial Methodology and the Ethical Use of Placebos

In clinical research, prospective, randomized controlled trials constitute the most reliable scientific methodology for drawing conclusions about safety and efficacy. RCTs are the "gold standard." But they are by no means the only acceptable methodology, and often trade-offs are made. Other methodologies are possible in some cases (equivalency studies, case-control studies, historical controls), but these generally provide less conclusive data or answer more narrowly constructed questions. Still, the most direct way to answer the question "Is an experimental regimen better than nothing?" is to conduct a placebo-controlled trial.

There is likely to be ethical agreement on two main points:

First, some placebo-controlled trials are ethically justifiable. Some examples: a trial in which there is no known effective drug or vaccine for the condition; a trial involving subjects for whom the approved treatment has proven ineffective or who cannot tolerate the treatment; or a short-term trial in which the subjects receive the active agent should it prove effective.

Second, some placebo-controlled trials are not ethically justifiable. If there exists a proven regimen that can prevent death or serious side effects, and that treatment regimen is available to prospective research subjects outside a clinical trial, it is unethical to use a placebo rather than the proven regimen in a clinical trial to test a new experimental regimen. An example might be a trial in which a widely available drug known to be effective is withheld from a placebo group so that the agent being tested will be shown to be clearly superior to a placebo, rather than marginally more effective than or just as effective as the drug already available.

Looking to published statements and principles, one can find support both for proceeding with and for not proceeding with placebo-controlled trials of AZT to prevent HIV transmission. Statements by the World Medical Association's Declaration of Helsinki and the Nuremberg Code appear to preclude proceeding with the AZT placebo-controlled trials because they place the interests of society over the interests of the subjects or fail to provide the subjects with the most effective proven therapeutic method (Helsinki)[3] or do not prevent all avoidable suffering or injury (Nuremberg).[4]

A group that specifically considered the use of placebo controls in HIV studies concluded:

> Placebo controls are especially difficult to justify ethically when the endpoints of an RCT are death or serious disability . . . When the outcome is death or serious disability, by the time an RCT reaches the organizational stage, preliminary evidence almost always suggests strongly that the new therapy is more effective than placebo . . . Although active [control arms] and historical controls are generally associated with reduced efficiency and validity, these are often appropriate trade-offs.[5]

Perhaps the most relevant public statement is found in the 1993 guidelines of the Council for International Organizations of Medical Sciences (CIOMS), in collaboration with the World Health Organization (WHO). CIOMS stated:

> [In a randomized clinical trial] the therapies (or other interventions) to be compared must be regarded as equally advantageous to the prospective subjects: there should be no scientific evidence of one over another. Moreover, no other intervention must be known to be superior to those being compared in the clinical trial, unless eligibility to participate is limited to persons who have been unsuccessfully treated with the other superior intervention or to persons who are aware of the other intervention and its superiority and have chosen not to accept it.[6]

Placebo-controlled trials of perinatal transmission fail to comply with these conditions.

On the other hand, other guidelines and principles in the same documents can be used in support of the placebo-controlled trials. These stress the importance of the problem to be addressed (Helsinki) and the humanitarian objectives (Nuremberg). Again, the most relevant document is the CIOMS guidelines, notably guideline 8, entitled "Research Involving Subjects in Underdeveloped Communities," including developing countries. The placebo-controlled trials in developing countries meet important conditions addressed by this guideline, as Christine Grady and others have noted.[7] The trials address the health needs and priorities of the communities, and they have been reviewed by local ethical review committees. Consent of individual subjects was part of the process of recruitment. However, the reasons the research could not be carried out "reasonably well" in developed countries are ethical, not scientific. Further, there is at least a question about the quality of the informed consent obtained from the subjects; one report from Cote d'Ivoire casts doubt on whether women were fully informed and given enough time—less than five minutes after being informed they were HIV-infected—to make a voluntary decision. The prospect of free medical care was the main reason women said they agreed to participate.[8]

Guideline 10 of the CIOMS guidelines is entitled "Equitable Distribution of Burdens and Benefits." It requires that individuals or communities invited to be subjects of research should be selected in such a way that the burdens and benefits of the research will be equitably distributed. Placebo-controlled trials in developing countries fulfill this requirement since the burden of HIV infection and perinatal transmission falls inequitably on the population in these countries, and the benefits to be gained by rapid completion of studies of an affordable, effective regimen are considerable and will also accrue to these same developing countries.

Fourth Lesson Learned: Ethical declarations, guidelines, and principles provide a framework for analysis but do not always give consistent answers to issues raised by specific cases. The CIOMS guidelines should be revised for internal consistency in light of the issues raised by the AZT placebo-controlled trials.

Arguments in Favor of the Trials

Good arguments, albeit of different kinds, can be offered to support or oppose the trials. The conclusion one reaches depends more on the value one places on certain types of arguments than on the strengths of the arguments themselves.

A utilitarian calculation concludes that the most efficient study is the most ethically sound. In this view, a clinical trial in developing countries with one arm using an affordable, practical, experimental regimen and the other arm using a placebo can be completed more quickly and involve fewer subjects than any other research design. The sooner a trial is completed, the faster the new, affordable regimen (if proven effective) can be made available to pregnant women in the developing country. The lives of more infants will be saved by early, widespread introduction of the new, affordable regimen than would be saved in any other study design. Therefore, it is ethical to conduct a placebo-controlled trial since the overall number of infant deaths prevented will be greater than in any of the alternatives.

A second calculus involves what governments and health ministries will do. In this view, it is useless and unethical to design a study using a regimen that will never be introduced into the country in which the study is conducted. The 076 regimen will never be affordable or practical in developing countries. A clinical trial in which this regimen was compared with the short course experimental regimen would be likely to show that the 076 regimen is more effective in preventing transmission, so the experimental regimen would have been viewed as "inferior."

On the other hand, the short course, experimental regimen is likely to be more effective than placebo, so the experimental regimen will be judged "better than nothing." Health ministries will not recommend the introduction of a treatment regimen that has been deemed "inferior" to other known treatments; but they will recommend the introduction of a treatment regimen that has been shown to be better than nothing. In developing countries at present, pregnant women receive no treatment, so many more deaths will be prevented once the new experimental regimen (if effective) is introduced. Therefore, this argument concludes, it is ethical to do the placebo-controlled trial.

A third type of argument points to the difference in "standard of care" in developed and developing countries. Currently in developing countries, the standard of care for HIV-infected pregnant women is to receive no treatment to prevent perinatal transmission. A clinical trial is ethical if it does not make those enrolled in the trial worse off than they would be if they were not enrolled. If some pregnant women enrolled in a clinical trial are given placebo, they are not made any worse off than they would be if they were not enrolled in the trial at all. Therefore, it is ethical to conduct placebo-controlled trials in countries where pregnant women do not receive any treatment.

A fourth type of argument looks at the satisfaction of procedural requirements. If ethically adequate procedures are used in the approval and implementation of research protocols, and if properly informed consent is obtained, it is ethical to conduct the studies. The placebo-controlled perinatal transmission studies were approved by ethical review committees in the developed countries that sponsor the trials and in the developing countries where they are being carried out. Women who are enrolled in the studies are being asked to give their voluntary, informed consent to participate. Researchers from the developing countries are carrying out the studies in their own countries. Therefore, since the placebo-controlled trials are following procedures that are ethically adequate, they are ethically permissible.

Arguments Opposing the Trials

The argument that it is unethical to conduct placebo-controlled trials to prevent perinatal transmission can take several different forms. The first version does not rely on any comparison between developed and developing countries. It rests on the obligation to minimize harm to research participants. A proven regimen exists that can reduce the rate of maternal-infant HIV transmission and consequently can prevent the deaths of some infants who will be born to HIV-infected mothers. The proven regimen can be made available under research conditions in developing countries. Researchers are under an ethical obligation to minimize harm to research participants. A research design that uses a placebo instead of the proven regimen knowingly fails to minimize harm to research participants. Therefore, a placebo-controlled trial is unethical in this instance.

The second argument explicitly compares developing and developed countries and presupposes an unvarying ethical standard in international collaborative research. A proven regimen can reduce the rate of maternal-infant HIV transmission. The proven regimen is the standard of care for pregnant women in developed countries, and therefore it would be unethical to conduct a placebo-controlled trial in those countries. To do so would allow some infants to be born with a fatal disease when their deaths could be prevented if pregnant women did not enroll and instead received the standard of care. If it is unethical to conduct a placebo-controlled study in a developed country, it would be unethical to conduct that same study in a developing country because it would involve applying a lower standard of research ethics. The same study, using the proven regimen, can be conducted in developed countries. Therefore, it would be unethical to conduct a placebo-controlled trial in developing countries.

The third argument claims that other study designs are possible, making placebo controls unnecessary. Clinical trials can be designed to answer important questions other than "Is the affordable, experimental regimen better than a placebo?" One hypothetical study uses 076 as the control arm and asks, "How much less effective is the new experimental regimen than 076?" This design would give an indirect answer to the question whether the experimental regimen is better than a placebo, since the 076 protocol demonstrated that a placebo is one-third as effective as the 076 regimen. This study relies on the 076 results and assumes that extrapolation from 076 is possible. Admittedly, it assumes that 076 and the placebo would behave the same in the developing country as in the trials carried out in the United States. Another potential flaw is that when things are not directly compared, there may be other factors unaccounted for.

Another hypothetical study compares two different oral regimens that employ doses lower than those used in 076. It compares an "optimal" dose, that is, the maximum affordable regimen in the developing country where the regimen is being tested, with a much lower dose. There may be some benefit to those receiving the lower dose, but that is not known in advance. A larger sample size would be required for this study than for a placebo-controlled trial. If the "optimal" dose is more effective than the lower dose, the study would show that an affordable regimen is effective. If no difference is shown between the two doses, then governments can save money by introducing a regimen with the lower dose. This study, like the first, relies on the background data from the 076 study to suggest that one or both of these doses are more effective than placebo in reducing transmission.

A third hypothetical study is not a randomized controlled trial but employs an observational methodology using "untreated" controls. The method requires picking a representative sample in a community that would receive the affordable experimental regimen. This group would then be compared later to the rates of maternal-infant transmission of women in the community who were not enrolled in the study and who received nothing. A difficulty with this design is the follow-up of the babies from the community; it would be necessary to find a representative sample six months to a year later. However, this design makes possible a genuine comparison between women who received an experimental treatment and those who truly received nothing. A placebo is not "nothing."

These studies are less methodologically rigorous than a randomized controlled trial that undertakes to make direct comparisons. However, a methodological compromise is necessary in situations where the best scientific design is not ethically acceptable. The study design using an active control arm instead of a placebo is actually being conducted in Thailand by a research group from Harvard University. According to its chairperson, the Human Subjects Committee at the Harvard School of Public Health considered a placebo arm to be unacceptable.[9]

Weighing Arguments

Opponents and defenders of the placebo-controlled trials disagree on a number of critical propositions, some of which pertain to scientific methodology, some to political or policy matters, and others to ethical judgments and value priorities. On questions of scientific methodology, opponents contend that alternative methodologies can provide a satisfactory answer to the question of whether an affordable, practical treatment regimen exists. Defenders say that only a placebo-controlled trial can answer that question.

Opponents also contend that sufficient evidence existed that some AZT is better than none in preventing transmission. Defenders say there was insufficient evidence for this claim.

Opponents contend that governments may be willing to introduce treatment regimens even if placebo-controlled trials showing that a new treatment regimen is better than placebo are not carried out. Defenders say this is the evidence health policy officials would insist upon.

Opponents question whether governments are likely to make even the affordable regimen as widely available as defenders claim they will, once the placebo-controlled trials are completed. Defenders are confident that once the trials are completed, governments in developing countries will make the affordable treatments widely available.

Opponents say these placebo-controlled trials are unethical despite their approval by ethical review committees in the sponsoring countries and in the countries where the research is being done. They claim the commitment of U.S. funds and U.S. researchers requires adherence to U.S. standards. Defenders claim that ethical approval in the countries where the research is being done demonstrates that the trials meet the ethical standards in those countries.

Opponents contend that it is unethical to withhold from participants in research an effective treatment that can reduce the number of deaths resulting from HIV transmission. The harm done to HIV-infected babies cannot be undone; AZT must be administered to their mothers within some definable range at the end of pregnancy and at delivery. Defenders claim that a much larger number of lives will be saved if placebo-controlled trials are carried out rapidly.

Opponents contend that researchers' obligations to participants in a research study outweigh the obligations to society in general. Defenders say the chief obligation is to provide effective preventive treatments in developing countries that have a high burden of disease. This may be seen as a difference between a clinical care ethic and a public health ethic.

Opponents of the study contend that the actual harm that will result from placebo-controlled trials is calculable and certain, whereas the benefits that might accrue from the study are only probable and remain uncertain. Defenders argue that the highest priority is to conduct as efficiently as possible the highest quality scientific study in order to maximize benefits.

Opponents contend that reference to the "standard of care" in developing countries to justify placebo-controlled trials is ethically suspect. When people receive no treatment at all, there can be no "standard" of care. Defenders say that women in the trial who receive placebo are not being made worse off than they would be if they were not in the trial at all. That is what is meant by "standard of care" in this context.

The arguments supporting placebo-controlled trials emphasize the public health need to develop affordable interventions, the lack of resources in developing nations, the efficiency of placebo-controlled studies, and political assessments about the evidence needed to convince governments to allocate resources and pharmaceutical companies to supply drugs at lower cost. The arguments against such trials, on the other hand, stress a concern for the welfare of the individual subject (and in this case, her infant) and the importance of minimizing risk and preventing harm in the course of gaining scientifically valid, generalizable knowledge. These arguments are also skeptical about promises made by governments and drug companies, especially for long-term support of public health interventions.

Keenly aware of the need for effective interventions in the developing world, I nevertheless believe that in this instance placebo-controlled trials placed economic goals, valid though they may be, ahead of individual subjects' welfare. The evidence that AZT works to prevent HIV transmission is so conclusive that it is hard to justify the trials on scientific grounds alone. The risk is serious disability and eventual death; there was more than preliminary evidence suggesting strongly that the new therapy was more effective than placebo; and in this case, there was only a short window of opportunity to prevent the disability. The subjects were pregnant women, vulnerable in most societies, and particularly so when the fate of their babies is at stake. Women are certainly capable of making informed decisions on behalf of themselves and their children, but a lack of power and access to medical care, as well as to scientific information, at the very least puts them at a disadvantage compared to investigators. Women in such situations deserve special concern in research design and the consent process. *Sixth Lesson Learned:* This case is an example of a true ethical dilemma on which thoughtful and reasonable people can disagree.

When an ethical dilemma resists resolution by agreement, the next best approach is a procedural solution. The way procedural resolutions usually work is that those who have the authority, the power, or the money are the ones who make the decisions. In the case of HIV/AIDS research, an ethically appropriate procedural mechanisms could be used: a process of community consultation. That process is poorly defined and understood, there is little experience to go on, and considerable work would be required to establish a workable mechanism midway through on-going trials. Although it is true that investigators from the developing countries are conducting the research and local or national IRBs have approved them, one relevant "community" has been omitted: the women from whom subjects will be drawn and to whose infants the benefits of the completed research will apply.

Some such process should be developed leading up to the design and implementation of future research. The most immediate opportunity is in the area of AIDS vaccine trials, which are already underway in some settings and will be expanded in the future.

For the Future

Even with the Thai data, many questions remain. What will be the fate of those babies who escaped HIV infection during pregnancy? Will the benefits of AZT be undone by breastfeeding, a known method of HIV transmission? What will be the impact on future pregnancies of HIV-infected women who receive AZT? Will a drug-resistant HIV strain develop? Is the oral dose used in the trials the optimal dose or could even lower doses be effective? Even as Glaxo Wellcome cuts the price for AZT to be used in developing countries to prevent HIV transmission (but not for long-term treatment), other questions about the role of pharmaceutical companies in designing drug trials for new markets arise.[10] Apart from the cost of drugs, the medical infrastructure problems remain a daunting obstacle to widespread use of AZT to prevent HIV transmission. Impressive and welcome as the technological achievement of preventing HIV transmission is, there is still no comparable response to the millions of children whose mothers are dying of AIDS in Africa, Asia, the Caribbean, Latin America, and the United States and Europe, as well. Addressing the needs of this generation of children will be truly a test of ethical commitment.

Final Lesson (To Be) Learned: Technological advances, welcome and impressive as they are, do not even begin to address some of the most basic social, health, and human rights questions raised by the global AIDS epidemic.

Acknowledgments

I have benefited from discussions with many ethicists, investigators, and advocates on this challenging topic. I want especially to acknowledge Ruth Macklin and Robert Klein for their thoughtful and precise comments, while absolving them of responsibility for the views expressed in this article.

References

[1] Sheryl Gay Stolberg, "Placebo Use Suspended in Overseas AIDS Trials," *New York Times,* 19 February 1998.

[2] Susan A. Fiscus et al., "Perinatal HIV Infection and the Effect of Zidovudine Therapy on Transmission in Rural and Urban Counties," *JAMA* 275 (1996): 1483–88.

[3] World Medical Association, "Declaration of Helsinki," *JAMA* 277 (1997): 925–26.

[4] Nuremberg Code, Principle 6.

[5] Carol Levine, Nancy Neveloff Dubler, and Robert J. Levine, "Building a New Consensus: Ethical Principles and Policies for Clinical Research on HIV/AIDS," *IRB: A Review of Human Subjects Research* 13, nos. 1–2 (1991); 1–17, p. 8.

[6] Council for International Organizations of Medical Sciences, *International Guidelines for Biomedical Research Involving Human Subjects* (Geneva: CIOMS, 1993).

[7] Christine Grady, "Science in the Service of Healing," *Hastings Center Report* 28, no. 6 (1998): 34–38; Harold Varmus and David Satcher, "Ethical Complexities of Conducting Research in Developing Countries," *NEJM* 337 (1997): 1003–1005.

[8] Howard W. French, "AIDS Research in Africa: Juggling Risks and Hopes," *New York Times,* 9 October 1997.

[9] Troyen A. Brennan, letter to Donna Shalala, Secretary of Health and Human Services, 10 June 1997.

[10] Michael Waldholz, "AZT Price Cut for Third World Mothers-to-Be," *Wall Street Journal,* 5 March 1998.

Chapter 4
The Use of Human Research Subjects

4.1 INTRODUCTION

Some people are surprised to learn that *experiments on human beings* are taking place in the United States today. A moment's reflection usually brings them to recognize that this is not so surprising. New drugs come to the market every day; these drugs are first tested for safety and efficacy on human beings. Social and behavioral scientists obtain information about how we act and what we believe; this information is gathered by studies on human beings. But is it ethical to perform experiments on human beings? What could make it so? If it is ethical to perform experiments on human beings, safeguards should be in place to secure the moral permissibility of such experiments.

Immanuel Kant said that we should never treat another person merely as a means, and instead we should treat persons also as ends. Thus, it is permissible, according to Kant's ethical theory, to experiment on human beings as long as those humans are also treated as ends in themselves, a point discussed in section 2.3. This is accomplished by preserving their *autonomy*, discussed in that section as well as in section 2.7. How can researchers preserve the autonomy of human research subjects? This is the question that we will attempt to answer in this chapter.

Although it is paramount to preserve the autonomy of research subjects, it is also important that human research subjects are not used needlessly. Every use of human research subjects comes with a price, whether that price is the time that it takes to fill out a survey, the embarrassment in discussing personal matters with a stranger, or the side-effects from an experimental drug. In light of the fact that the participation of human research subjects exacts some cost from the research subjects in every case, the first question to be asked is what justifies the participation of human research subjects in scientific studies.

4.2 JUSTIFYING HUMAN SUBJECTS RESEARCH: RISK/BENEFIT RATIO

The justifiability of the use of human research subjects depends on the risk/expected-benefit ratio of the scientific study. "Risks" refer to the possibility of harms that may result from the experiment. "Expected benefits" refer to the possibility of benefits that are likely to result from the experiment. If the risks in using the research subjects outweigh the expected benefits, then it is impermissible to use human beings. However, if the expected benefits outweigh the risks, then it may be appropriate to use human beings. Of course, scientists are seldom able to predict the exact risks or expected benefits in most cases. Scientific studies are undertaken to determine the side-effects or benefits of a drug or therapy, and so the actual side-effects or benefits may not be known until the study is completed. However, the risks and expected benefits must be calculated nonetheless, to the best of the researcher's abilities, so that a justification for the use of human research subjects can be made.

The following is a short list of possible benefits and harms that should be considered when evaluating the risk/expected-benefit ratio of a scientific study that involves human research subjects. Researchers should ask themselves: How many of these harms and benefits will result from the study under consideration? To what degree will each of these harms and benefits be experienced? Who experiences these harms and benefits?

Benefits

1. contribution to generalizable knowledge
2. psychological benefit to subjects from participation
3. material benefit for subjects as compensation for participation
4. therapeutic benefit for subjects as compensation for participation

Risks

1. loss of time or boredom for research subjects
2. psychological harm to research subjects
3. physical harm or pain to research subjects
4. economic loss to subjects if results of the research are made public
5. social loss to subjects if results of the research are made public
6. legal risk to subjects if results of the research are made public

Not all of the risks and benefits of human subjects research are shouldered by the same individuals. For example, the side-effects of an experimental drug are experienced by the human subjects in the study. The benefits of the study may accrue to a wider population, which may or may not include the subjects who endured the pain of participating in the study. Harms such as social losses that may be experienced if the results of the study are made public may accrue to both the research subjects and the subjects' families and friends. For example, if full names and addresses of subjects in Laud Humphreys' study, discussed in section 1.1, were made public, social losses could accrue to both the subjects and their spouses or children. The benefits of that study most likely accrued solely to the researcher. The fact that risk of harm is often shouldered by a party different from the one that experiences the benefits is a further complication of justifying human subjects research.

The risk/expected-benefit ratio can be used to justify the initial use of human research subjects. For example, testing the drug described in Case 3.2 obviously had a positive risk/expected-benefit ratio. A study that could contribute to positive gains in knowledge about treating breast cancer, based upon previously observed data that demonstrate the likely efficacy of a new drug, clearly has greater benefits than harms. The drug in question has not been observed to have any major side-effects, and in fact has the benefit of reducing the likelihood of osteoporosis. It is likely that the drug will reduce instances of breast cancer. If the two arms of the study are in clinical equipoise, then no subjects will be worse off for enrolling in the study, and they may directly benefit from participating. In contrast, Laud Humphreys' study is an example of a study whose risk/expected-benefit ratio was called into question. Not only did the subjects not benefit directly from participation, they could have been harmed by Humphreys' research activities. The gains in generalizable knowledge seemed minimal and were outweighed by the risks to the subjects. Thus, the risk/expected-benefit ratio was not favorable in this study.

The relevance of the risk/expected-benefit ratio does not disappear once the decision to use human subjects has been made. The responsible scientist assesses the risks and expected benefits at every stage of the scientific process—at the conception of the research project, during the data-collecting process, and at the dissemination of the results of the study.

One means of providing an appropriate risk/expected-benefit ratio in drug studies may be to do animal testing or computer modeling of the effects of a new drug before that drug is approved for experimental use on humans. A more complete discussion of the ethics of animal use in science is found in Chapter 6, with special consideration of the risk/expected-benefit ratio and methodology in animal studies considered in section 6.4. If a drug appears to show promise in animal studies or according to computer modeling, then the risk/expected-benefit ratio may be predicted to be favorable, clearing the way for further study of the drug on human beings. Side-effects of a particular drug may also be predicted in animal testing.

Another means of determining the risk/expected-benefit ratio is to be well acquainted with the field of inquiry before experiments on humans take place. If someone else has already done an experiment, the use of human research subjects may be superfluous, thereby undermining the risk/expected-benefit ratio. If a research project promises no original contribution to the generalizable knowledge, it is difficult to justify running the experiment. Why subject human research subjects to any risk if no contribution to generalizable knowledge is expected? Being well acquainted with advances in the field of inquiry will also allow the researcher to anticipate risks and expected benefits in new experiments that follow procedures similar to those of past experiments. Hence, it is a moral requirement, and not just a scientific requirement, that researchers be well acquainted with their fields of study before they initiate projects that involve human research subjects.

A related requirement is that those individuals who work directly with the research subjects be qualified to do so. Taking blood, administering drugs, running focus groups, and administering timed tests require various skills. Recording data is also a skill; no one should be subjected to an experiment twice because the researcher, or researcher's assistants, did not know how to record the data accurately. Human research subjects can reasonably expect that those who are part of the experimental procedure know what they are doing. Individuals who are working with research subjects should not put research subjects at greater risk than need be.

Even if the expected benefits outweigh the risks, this fact alone may not justify the use of human research subjects. Research studies that involve human subjects should involve the fewest risks possible. Alternative methods should be considered in an attempt to ensure that the methods that are employed in the study are methods that involve the least risk to human subjects. This imperative further underscores the ethical requirement that researchers be as familiar with their area of study as possible before they take on the responsibility of performing experiments with human subjects.

As mentioned above, the harms and benefits of a particular scientific experiment may not accrue to the same individuals. The benefits of a drug study may accrue to the scientists who are performing the experiment (they may further their careers by publishing the results of the study), to the institution at which the study is held (it may gain prestige from holding the study), and to future generations of people who might take the new drug once it is released on the market. There may or may not be some benefit that accrues directly to the human research subjects in the study. Perhaps the subjects are helped by the drug, but perhaps they are not. The subjects may not be part of the treatment arm of the study, but instead be part of the placebo arm, as discussed in section 3.4. Perhaps the drug trial is only the first step in refining the dosage levels, in which case future generations may benefit from correct dosages of the drug; but because they have not received the correct dosage, these subjects may not. The principle of justice, discussed in section 2.9, seems to imply that the risks should not be endured by one individual, or set of individuals, when the research benefits a different set of individuals. Despite this seeming injustice, some ethicists have attempted to justify the use of human research subjects who endure harm in their role as research subjects but do not directly receive any benefit from participating in the research. Perhaps research subjects who do not directly benefit from research nonetheless have special ties to their community, and these ties may lead the subjects to participate in the research for the sake of their cohorts but not for their own sake. If this is true, then using subjects who will not reap any direct benefit, but will endure harm, may be justifiable.

It is ethically unacceptable *in some cases* to use human research subjects when there is no prospect that *those* individuals will benefit from their participation as research subjects, as stated above. Some ethicists found it unacceptable that individuals in the developing world were recruited in the vertical transmission of HIV and AZT studies discussed in section 1.2, not because placebos were used, but because the drugs that were being developed would ultimately be too expensive for the community from which research subjects had been drawn. If the harms of being research subjects are experienced in one community, but all the benefits of the research are experienced in another community, then the research is ethically unjustified and violates the principle of justice.

A second reason exists for choosing research subjects from the community that will ultimately benefit from the research. In Chapter 1, we pointed out that scientifically valid and ethically valid strategies go hand in hand. If a researcher tries to extrapolate the results from one population to another population, it is possible that the generalization will be invalid. In the case of the AZT trials, it is possible that the diet, healthcare, and many other lifestyle differences between Thailand and the United States rendered the data invalid. Also, this is not a case in which ties to a cohort can be involved to justify human subjects research. The goal of scientific research is to generate generalizable knowledge, and this goal will be undermined if research subjects are selected in a way that might preclude generalizable results. Thus, there is a scientific reason, and not just an ethical reason, for choosing research subjects from the population that is expected to benefit from the research.

To further complicate the risk/expected-benefit ratio, what counts as a harm or a benefit may be different for different individuals, and the degree of harm or benefit experienced in a particular situation may be different for different individuals. Some people can tolerate pain better than others, and thus the harms of participating in a study that involves some pain would place a lesser burden on some subjects than on others. The researcher, in communicating the expected harms and benefits of participation to prospective research subjects may not be able to anticipate the subjective nature of the subjects' responses. This subjectivity stresses the importance of open, two-way communication in soliciting subjects' participation as research subjects. The greater the risk of harm, the more careful the researcher should be in determining what the possible benefits are, and the more careful the researcher should be in making sure that populations of research subjects are chosen not merely because they are convenient for the researcher, but because they ultimately stand to benefit from the research.

The next task is to determine what kinds of research may be performed on human research subjects. Different types of research will demand different types of protections. In medical practice, the protections that are afforded patients when blood is drawn are different from those offered when invasive surgery is performed. Similarly, in research involving human subjects, different protections will be afforded research subjects in different circumstances. Those circumstances may involve the research subjects, or they may involve the type of research that is undertaken. In this chapter we focus on different types of research; in the following chapter, we examine the circumstances of different types of research subjects. Different kinds of research have distinct risks and expected benefits.

4.3 TYPES OF RESEARCH INVOLVING HUMAN SUBJECTS

The ethical questions surrounding human subjects research can vary based upon the kind of research that is being conducted. It would be prohibitive to discuss every type of human subjects research, but we can distinguish four interesting types.

Research that involves no greater than minimal risk includes survey research, in which subjects are asked to fill out questionnaires or complete telephone surveys, research that involves venipuncture by a trained professional, or research on educational methodology. It is important to recognize that this type of research, though presenting low risk to the subjects, is nonetheless research on human subjects, and as such it should conform to requirements that help to protect the autonomy of the research subjects. However, in light of the fact that the research presents little risk to research subjects, these protections may be less involved than in other cases. It is also important to recognize that much survey or minimal-risk research is unlikely to generate a great benefit to the research subjects, and the research subjects will need to be aware of both the risks and the expected benefits of participation before agreeing to participate. If the risks to the subjects are low, and the benefits are also low, the responsible researcher will articulate this clearly to the subjects.

The second type of research involves greater than minimal risk, but it is also not likely to benefit subjects directly. Studies of this sort include Phase I clinical trials, in which drugs are tested for toxicity and dosage levels, but are not yet expected to demonstrate efficacy in fighting disease. In a Phase I clinical trial there is little expectation that the drug or therapy will be of direct benefit to the human subjects. However, every drug needs to be initially tested so that researchers can determine if the drug will be harmful, or at what dosage levels the drug will be harmful. The beneficiaries of a Phase I clinical trial most often are the researcher and future research subjects who receive the drug being tested. Since the human research subjects are not expected to benefit directly from the Phase I clinical trial, special provisions should be made in recruiting these subjects. Research subjects should be told that they are unlikely to benefit directly from participation in these trials.

Informing subjects of this fact is further complicated by the means through which subjects for these clinical trials are generally recruited. Imagine this scenario: A patient with advanced adult-onset (type-II) diabetes is asked by his physician to take part in a clinical trial. The trial is for a new drug, which animal tests and computer models have demonstrated may be of benefit to patients with advanced adult-onset diabetes. The trial will involve both a treatment arm and a placebo arm. Half of the subjects will receive the treatment, and half will receive a placebo. The patient is asked to take part in this Phase I clinical trial to test the drug for toxicity levels. The patient is asked because he represents those who will ultimately be taking the drug: adults with advanced diabetes. The patient should be told of the low likelihood that he will experience any direct benefit from this drug: It has not been shown previously to have any direct benefit to adults with advanced diabetes. Furthermore, there is only a fifty-percent chance that the patient will even get the drug, as opposed to a placebo. A further complication arises from the fact that the patient's own physician is the one who is asking the patient to take part in this study. The physician may be in a position to serve both the best interests of the patient, as a physician, and the interests of science, as a researcher. This is known as the "two hats problem"—the researcher's two roles create a set of conflicting obligations. The two hats problem was illustrated in Case 3.2 and receives more complete treatment in Chapter 8. In research in which the prospect of direct benefit to the subjects is low, researchers should be especially careful to articulate this fact to their research subjects. A further discussion of recruitment of research subjects is found in section 4.4 below.

A third type of research involves greater than minimal risk, but holds out the possibility of direct benefit to the subjects. In Phase II and Phase III clinical trials, drugs are tested for effectiveness in treating a particular condition, as well as examined for potential side-effects. Since the drugs have already shown some promise in Phase I trials, there is a greater possibility of direct benefit to the subjects in Phase II and III trials. However, there is merely the *possibility* of benefit in these cases. Since there are no guarantees that the subjects will derive direct benefit from participating in the study, and some risks are involved in taking still-experimental drugs, ethical safeguards must be observed to insure the protection of the subjects. However, the fact that there is a greater possibility—but no guarantee—of therapeutic benefit directly to the patients is a fact that can be communicated to the subjects.

The final type of research is deception research. In the previous types of research discussed, the research subjects are told what their options are in being research subjects before the research takes place. In deception research, the subjects are either not told what the nature of the study is before the study takes place, or not told that they are research subjects at all. Laud Humphreys' study is an example of both types of deception. First, Humphreys did not tell the subjects that they were subjects at all, out of fear that they would behave differently and defeat the purpose of the study if they knew they were being watched. Second, Humphreys misrepresented the purpose of his study when he located some of the research subjects and interviewed them at their homes. The subjects thought that they were talking to a government health care worker, when instead they were talking to a sociologist who was collecting data for a research study. Special safeguards should be taken in deception research, in light of the fact that subjects are deceived either about the nature of their participation or about the fact that they are participating in research at all. First, regardless of whether the research requires deception about the nature of their participation or the fact that they are participating at all, prompt disclosure of the extent of subjects' participation in the research should take place as soon as possible after the data have been collected from that subject. Second, no more deception should take place than is absolutely necessary. Gratuitous deception of research subjects not only harms the subjects, but it can also harm the cause of science. The more deception that takes place, the less likely it is that research subjects will trust scientists in the future. Some subject pools may become aware of the fact that deception is taking place, and the results of the study will become tainted. If this happens, then there will be no contribution to generalizable knowledge in undertaking the research, and one of the important benefits of undertaking the research will be lost. Then, the researcher will be left with a research project that involves little benefit and all the risks associated with deception research.

Ethicists distinguish the voluntary nature of participation in other types of research from the _non-voluntary_ nature of participation in deception research. It is not the case that subjects in deception research are participating involuntarily— this would imply that they are doing so against their will. However, they are not doing so voluntarily either; that is, they are not making a voluntary choice to participate in the research. Rather, their participation is non-voluntary—a mid-point between full voluntary participation and forced participation. Because of the morally problematic nature of non-voluntary participation, it is of utmost importance that researchers debrief their subjects in deception studies as soon as possible so that the subjects then understand the true nature of their participation.

It is important to note that single-blinded, double-blinded, and placebo studies are not deception research, even though the subjects are not given all the information about their participation. In these studies the subjects are told that they are research subjects. They are also told up front that some information is intentionally withheld from them, as a condition of their participation in the study. Similarly, if research subjects are told, "You will either receive a placebo or a drug," the subjects have not been deceived, as long as both placebos and drugs are being used in the study. Deception occurs when subjects are deliberately _not told_ important information—either about the nature of the study or even that there is a study in progress, or when the subjects are intentionally misinformed about the nature of the study or their role in the study.

4.4   RECRUITMENT OF RESEARCH SUBJECTS

It is important that research subjects participate voluntarily. Forcing an autonomous person to participate in research without consent is ethically unjustifiable. Autonomous individuals are able to, and are expected to, make decisions freely and voluntarily about what happens to them. Depriving persons of their right to make decisions about being research subjects is a violation of Kant's categorical imperative and a violation of their autonomy.

However, the idealized claim that no people should serve as research subjects without having provided voluntary consent is difficult to put into practice. It is possible for members of communities that are by definition not autonomous, such as children and the mentally disabled, to serve as research subjects. The use of vulnerable populations in scientific research is covered in Chapter 5.

Even autonomous individuals can be coerced into serving as research subjects if they are recruited in the wrong way. Research subjects should not, for example, be offered a financial incentive so great that it is coercive to participate. How much money is too much money? That is a difficult question and depends on the circumstances of the prospective research subjects. To college students, $15.00 an hour may seem very enticing. To well-paid professionals, $15.00 an hour may hardly be enticing at all. Although it is appropriate in some cases to pay research subjects for their participation—either because it is fair that some benefit accrue directly to the subjects, or because there is a real fear that no one will serve and important scientific data will be lost without the inducement. Inappropriate payment creates ethical questions; also, in skewing the subject pool to include more people who are enticed to participate by a financial incentive, the randomization of the sample can be corrupted. For example, if the researcher offers $15.00 to subjects, the researcher may find that more college students and fewer professionals come forward to participate as research subjects, thereby undermining the representative character of the sample. It is left to the researcher, knowing the circumstances of the subject population, to make an appropriate judgment about the amount of money to offer research subjects.

Cash is not the only form of compensation that may prove to be coercive. Free medical care, free use of computers, course credit, or movie tickets are all examples of rewards that researchers have offered to help enlist research subjects. Whatever inducements are offered, it is important to remember that they should not compromise the research subjects' ability to make a voluntary decision about participation. Many universities, recognizing this, require that if course credit is offered in exchange for serving as research subjects, that a "non-research subject option" must exist, so that students enrolled in a class are not forced to be research subjects as a pre-condition for doing well in the course. Just as offering special benefits to participate may be ethically unacceptable, refusing opportunities or benefits, to which people may already have a right, *unless* they agree to be research subjects, is unacceptable. Prospective research subjects should understand that failure to participate in research will not harm their ability to obtain benefits—such as healthcare, a good grade, or the chance to take a course—to which they are entitled.

Not only the inducements but the time and place of recruitment and the person who solicits subjects' participation in a research project should be such that the voluntary nature of participation is not compromised. The "two hats" problem was mentioned above as a possible pitfall in recruiting research subjects. Research subjects should not be recruited by an authority figure whom they need or want to please. Authority figures such as professors, teachers, physicians, and psychologists should be careful when attempting to recruit their own students or patients as research subjects. Autonomy is a relative concept; some people are autonomous in one arena, but are not autonomous in another. The ability of a person to consent autonomously to a request may depend in part on the relationship that the person holds to the individual making the request.

The voluntary nature of subject participation must be upheld throughout the subjects' participation. It is important to communicate this fact in advance, before subjects agree to participate. It may also be important to communicate this fact during the course of the research study, so that subjects are aware of their right to cease participation at any time.

Deception research, discussed above, raises questions about the "voluntariness" of participation. If research subjects are deceived as to the true nature of their participation, or if they are deceived as to whether they are participants at all, then how can their participation be voluntary? In an attempt to get around this problem, many researchers have introduced a post-hoc approximation of informed consent, called de-hoaxing or debriefing, after research subjects have participated in deception research. After their participation, research subjects should be told the true nature of their participation. Optimally, they are told as soon as possible after their participation. Since their participation must be voluntary, it is important that the participants have the option to withdraw the data collected from their participation.

4.5 INFORMED CONSENT

The autonomy of research subjects is most commonly protected by gaining their informed consent, which outlines the purpose, activities, risks, and benefits of their participation and insures that their participation is voluntary. If subjects understand all of this information and decide to participate based upon this understanding, then they have given their informed consent.

Most researchers obtain informed consent from their subjects as a written document. However, verbal informed consent is appropriate in some cases. Informed consent can also be procured on a computer. Researchers can creatively integrate computer applications, such as using hypertext to allow research subjects to get more information about points of interest in the document, including the risks, expected benefits, and their right to refuse participation. Informed consent should not merely be a sheet of paper, in many cases, because it does not afford the research subjects the opportunity to engage the researcher in dialogue about the risks and benefits of participating in the research study, to assess their willingness to participate, and to do so without the pressure of someone's looking over their shoulder, subtly urging a particular decision. The fact that informed consent is a two-way process presupposes some autonomy on the part of the research subjects; individuals who are not fully autonomous would not be expected to ask questions about participation. However, although the prospective research subjects may be expected to ask some questions, the burden of communicating all pertinent information so that the consent is genuinely *informed* falls to the researcher.

In addition to the risks, expected benefits, and voluntary nature of the study, prospective subjects should be told what will go on during the study and the goals of the study. The type of data that will be collected and the use of this data should also be made clear to the subject. If the data are being gathered to ultimately contribute to a publication that will be available nationally, or if the results will be available to other members of the subjects' community, then the subjects deserve to know. There are a number of reasons for informing the subject of the type of data being collected and their uses. First, the risk of embarrassment or other violations of privacy to the subjects if some portions of the data are made public is a real harm that should be considered. In light of this, more elaborate protections should be in place to protect the identity of research subjects if data that are potentially harmful, about illegal activities, drug or alcohol abuse, or work habits, for example, are collected. Second, some methods of data collection make preserving the privacy of the research subjects and the confidentiality of the data more difficult. Research subjects who are videotaped, even if they never give their name, are easily identifiable to anyone who sees that videotape. Therefore, the research subjects should know whether they are being videotaped as part of the data-collecting procedure. It is possible for the researcher to audio- or videotape the subjects for data-collection purposes only; later, when the data is collected, the tapes can be erased to preserve the confidentiality of the subjects. If such taping is part of the data-collection procedure only, the subjects should be informed of this fact.

Of course, in some studies, explaining to the subjects the full extent of their participation may not be possible. If subjects are being recruited for a placebo-controlled, blinded Phase I clinical trial, subjects will not know whether they are entering the treatment arm or the placebo arm. Since it is a Phase I clinical trial, subjects cannot be assured of any direct benefit from their participation. By telling subjects all the information that the researchers know about their participation, the scientific integrity of the trial may be compromised. This may ultimately be an argument for double-blinded, as opposed to single-blinded trials, because this allows the researchers to answer questions from the research subjects honestly, without deceiving them. For other types of research, such as survey research that involves minimal risk, the subjects can be told much more about the nature of their participation.

However informed consent is procured, the researcher should ensure that the document is understandable to prospective research subjects. Researchers should avoid jargon or complex terms when obtaining informed consent. Words that seem common to a scientist, such as "randomized," "placebo," or "control group" may be unfamiliar to the people who are reading the document. The explanation of the purpose and procedures should similarly be written in language that the subject pool can understand. For example, subjects may react differently to when asked to participate in an "experiment," a "research project," or a "study."

The chart, Informed Consent from Research Subjects, summarizes several of the points made thus far in this chapter: the different kinds of research involving human research subjects, the risk/expected-benefit ratios for each kind of research, the importance of the degree of voluntariness in each type of research, and the relevant aspects of the above claims on informed consent.

Informed Consent from Research Subjects

Types of Research Subjects

Randomized Clinical Trials

Phase I Clinical Trials

1. Research subject is not presumed to benefit directly from therapy to which he/she is offering informed consent.
2. Harms may or may not be outweighed by the benefits of the therapy, and those benefits are unlikely to accrue directly to the research subject.
3. Not all of the information surrounding the therapy can be given to the research subject (single-blinded, double-blinded placebo-control studies).
4. Voluntary

Phase II and III Clinical Trials

1. Research subject may directly benefit from therapy to which he/she is offering informed consent.
2. Harms may or may not be outweighed by the benefits of the therapy, although those benefits may accrue directly to the research subject.
3. Not all of the information surrounding the therapy can be given to the research subject (single-blinded, double-blinded, or placebo-control studies).
4. Voluntary

Studies Involving No Greater Than Minimal Risk

1. Research subject may directly benefit from participating in the trial, although the benefit may be minimal, and the benefit is more likely to accrue to other individuals.
2. Little or no harm is expected to come directly to the participant.
3. All of the information surrounding the study is (in principle) available to the research subject.
4. Voluntary

Deception Studies

1. Research subject may directly benefit from participating in the study, although the benefit may be minimal, and the benefit is more likely to accrue to other individuals.
2. Little or no harm is expected to come directly to the participant.
3. All of the information surrounding the study is (in principle) available to the research subject, but only post-hoc.
4. Non-voluntary

4.6   PRIVACY AND CONFIDENTIALITY

The obligations to preserve confidentiality seem to derive from the obligations to preserve privacy, which in turn appear to issue from the principle of autonomy or respect for persons. Privacy is often understood as a right. The right to privacy may be the right to restrict access to one's person or information about one's person. Where the right to privacy comes from is an interesting question in ethical theory. Perhaps the right to privacy follows from Kantian respect for persons, which is the basis for many claims about the value of autonomy. But if it does, then how is it that one can waive one's right to privacy? Interestingly, although one can waive one's right to privacy merely by agreeing to waive it, no one can waive the right to autonomy merely by saying, "I declare that I am no longer autonomous." Also, though we can lose our autonomy through no action on our part, no person can lose the right to privacy, except by previous actions on his or her part. This is an important point to recognize when examining the use of vulnerable or non-autonomous research subjects. Even if a research subject does not have full autonomy, his or her right to privacy remains intact. For example, in section 5.3, we discuss the use of adolescents as research subjects. Many adolescents are not autonomous. However, privacy is important to a great number of adolescents, and many people believe that adolescents have a right to privacy, even though they are not autonomous. If the roots of privacy rights are autonomy claims, then the protection of adolescent privacy despite their lack of autonomy presents a puzzle. If the right to privacy can be waived, but the right to autonomy cannot be waived, it calls into question whether privacy in fact has its roots in autonomy. These issues raise important questions for ethicists. Until the right to privacy and the connection between privacy and confidentiality are completely understood, questions about the right to privacy will arise, as will concerns about what the right to privacy entails.

Some people may claim that the value of privacy has its roots in utilitarianism, discussed in Chapter 2. Is it the case that actions that preserve people's autonomy are always utility maximizing? That is probably not the case. Although the philosophical questions that surround privacy are numerous, most people nonetheless recognize on their own the importance of privacy.

In light of the fact that a person can waive the right to privacy, research subjects can agree to allow researchers to use private information about themselves. However, researchers who give out information without their subjects' approval have violated their subjects' right to privacy. As discussed above, it may be harmful to research subjects if their privacy is violated. Hence, the degree and limits of privacy protections should be articulated to the research subjects before any data is collected.

Although we have a right to privacy, it is not necessarily in our best interests, nor is it plausible, to claim a complete right to privacy. There are some facts to which only physicians, lawyers, or researchers should have direct assess. This is where confidentiality comes in—some information is not necessarily private in all respects, but it is *private from* particular persons. Information is kept confidential if it is disclosed to a particular party, like a researcher, and that researcher pledges to refrain from further disclosure of the information without consent. Although privacy is a right that protects both our person and information about us, confidentiality protects only information. Researchers have a moral obligation to respect their research subjects' desire for confidentiality. Those wishes should not be left up to the research subjects to articulate; rather, researchers should take the initiative and make clear to the research subjects the limits and scope of the confidentiality of the data. The ownership of data and the moral obligations of the researcher are further discussed in section 8.5.

Researchers should recognize that they are not always able to offer complete privacy and confidentiality to their research subjects. Although human subjects may share a great deal with researchers, there is no legal basis for "researcher-subject" confidentiality, protected in the same way that "doctor-patient" or "attorney-client" confidentiality is protected. If evidence of illegal activity or other harmful activity is revealed in the data-collecting process, researchers may be required by law to disclose it to the proper authorities. Researchers may be so obligated for the sake of the research subjects or for the sake of others who are affected by subjects' actions. Human subjects must be made aware that the limits and scope of confidentiality are circumscribed by the law. Thus, for example, data collection that reveals the abuse of children should be disclosed.

Data can be subpoenaed, in which case the researcher has the obligation to erase all identifiers that might link the subjects to particular illegal acts. Researchers who are worried that they may be unable to collect data unless they can offer unqualified confidentiality to their subjects can apply for a "certificate of confidentiality," which exempts the researcher from disclosing data about illegal or potentially harmful activities. The Department of Health and Human Services grants certificates of confidentiality if the researcher can demonstrate that the research could not be carried out without one. Certificates of confidentiality should be sought before research subjects are approached, and the protections that they afford should be articulated in the informed consent statements that subjects review. Subjects should be informed of the researcher's commitment to confidentiality, as well as of the limits of the researcher's abilities to live up to these commitments. Doing so both demonstrates respect for the subjects and provides important methodological tools for the researcher. The researcher is more likely to obtain accurate data, especially when studying sensitive or potentially damaging facts about subjects, if subjects are comfortable with the researcher's commitment to confidentiality.

Like "doctor-patient" or "attorney-client" confidentiality, though, it should be made clear to the research subjects that confidential information may pass through a number of hands before any identifiers that link the subjects with the data are removed. In the medical setting, "confidential" information can be shared with other physicians, nurses, staff who transcribe data, and insurance companies. In the research setting, "confidential" information may pass through technicians, transcribers, and co-investigators before identifiers are removed. Research subjects who are worried about confidentiality may wish to keep the information from particular individuals. Thus, researchers should do what they can to make clear that this data will remain in only a few people's hands, such as those people directly involved in the data collection and analysis phase, and that it will certainly stay out of other people's hands, such as the friends, family, or employers of the research subjects. A statement about the privacy and confidentiality of the research subjects should appear on any informed consent document, and privacy and confidentiality should be preserved throughout the research project.

4.7   MORAL CODES: NUREMBERG, HELSINKI, AND BELMONT

In conclusion, we wish to re-examine the three codes of conduct for research on human research subjects which accompanied Chapter 2. Many of the claims made earlier in this chapter are echoes of these codes. The reader should also note the evolving understanding of the role of the research subjects, the types of research that are morally permissible, the risk/expected-benefit ratio, and informed consent.

The Nuremberg Code's conception of informed consent is strict. According to Nuremberg, the duty to obtain informed consent rests solely with the researcher; none of the burden of obtaining informed consent falls on the research subjects. On one hand, this is an admirable claim, because the research subjects should not be expected to obtain all of the information required to make an informed choice as research subjects. On the other hand, this may suggest a lack of autonomy on the part of research subjects. If the research subjects cannot be trusted or expected to obtain informed consent, and the complete burden of obtaining informed consent lies with the researcher, what does this tell us about the research subjects? The implication may be that research subjects are not capable of looking after their own interests. This may be the case with some vulnerable populations, such as young children or some subjects who are mentally disabled. However, to presuppose this of every subject may be too paternalistic a view of research subjects.

Nuremberg also makes clear that the duty to obtain informed consent is not a one-time obligation; rather, participation should be voluntary throughout the research. This is an important lesson for all researchers: Research subjects must retain the option to cease participation at any time. Any subject who chooses not to continue has the right to stop. However, Nuremberg says that the research subject may stop when continuation "seemed to him to be impossible," a standard that some may perceive as too high. The voluntary nature of subjects' participation should allow the subjects to stop participation at any time, for any reason, and not merely when it "seemed to him to be impossible." Researchers who prod their subjects to continue in a study by saying, "Surely it is *possible* for you to continue" would be acting beyond their moral rights.

The Nuremberg Code also addresses the risk/expected-benefit ratio and its importance in human subjects research. Research that uses human research subjects should "yield fruitful results for the good of society." The implication is that such research should not be undertaken merely for the pursuit of generalizable knowledge, but only for the good of society. This prescription carries with it important ramifications for the risk/expected-benefit ratio. As mentioned earlier, there are many possible harms and benefits that may result from human subjects research. Some of these accrue directly to the subjects, whereas some of them accrue only to other individuals, such as the researcher or to the cohorts of the research subjects. In requiring that human subjects experimentation "yield fruitful results for the good of society," Nuremberg is making a strong claim about the amount of benefit that must accrue before the risk/expected-benefit ratio is acceptable. A mere contribution to generalizable knowledge, without a practical component, fails to be a substantial benefit toward the justification of the use of human subjects. According to Nuremberg, the experiment should already be informed by animal or other studies.

Additionally, the researcher should be qualified to perform the research. Nuremberg tries to correct for the possibility that some research might involve risks that are so great that they would outweigh any expected benefits by claiming that such research is allowed only if the researcher is also a research subject. It is unclear if this is a "Golden Rule" requirement or if this claim is supposed to simply discourage such research from taking place at all. However, Nuremberg also claims that adequate provisions should be in place to protect the subject against "even the remote possibilities of injury, disability, or death." Such a requirement may not be feasible. Of course, if the risk outweighs the expected benefit in the eyes of the experimenters, then they have the obligation to stop the experiment. If the continuation will result in "injury, disability, or death" then it should be stopped. "Injury" is difficult to understand though; like "harm," it may be different for different individuals. Some subjects may be physically or mentally unable to perform certain tasks or withstand certain tests without being injured, whereas other subjects will sail through the experimental procedures. Imagine an experiment in which researchers wish to measure the likelihood that hearing sexist or racist jokes increases sexist or racist attitudes. The researchers first tell the subjects several racist or sexist jokes, then administer a survey designed to measure people's attitudes about race and gender issues. Some people might be deeply offended by the jokes, and thus experience injury in participating in the study. Other people might find this study a minimal risk study, which involves little or no direct harm to the subject.

The Declaration of Helsinki focuses primarily on the role of the physician/clinician who is also a researcher and as such is of particular interest to those who are exploring the "two hats" problem. Helsinki articulates the principle that when physicians act also as researchers, their duties as physicians should always take precedence over their duties as researchers. This is an admirable, but perhaps unrealistic, principle, as it is often difficult for one individual to reconcile two conflicting obligations. The "two hats" problem was discussed earlier as a problem with the voluntary participation of research subjects. How are research subjects able to voluntarily agree to participate in research when they are asked by authority figures who wield power over them, such as their own physicians, professors, or psychologists? The problem of voluntary participation raised by the "two hats" problem is not addressed in Helsinki; instead, the focus is merely on the conflicting obligations of the physician who is also a researcher. Helsinki considers several of the claims that Nuremberg does. For example Helsinki echoes the importance of performing animal studies before human research subjects are employed and requires that experimenters should be adequately trained if they attempt to collect data from human research subjects. Helsinki makes similar use of the risk/expected-benefit ratio.

In addition to these claims, Helsinki addresses some new considerations for the ethical use of human research subjects. One notable difference is that Helsinki allows for surrogate consent on behalf of those individuals who are not autonomously able to give consent, which will become more important as we examine the use of vulnerable human subject populations in Chapter 5. It is not only the *type of research* that demands different considerations in informed consent, but the *type of research subject*. Additionally, Helsinki draws a distinction between therapeutic and non-therapeutic research, a point which is significant when examining Phase I clinical trials and the ways in which they differ from Phase II and Phase III clinical trials.

Helsinki recommends that an "independent committee," which is "in conformity with the laws and regulations of the country in which the research experiment is performed" examine the proposed research to make sure that it conforms to the moral expectations for research in that country. Institutional Review Boards, discussed in section 3.5, may be considered one such independent committee. Some may ask how "independent" IRBs are, inasmuch as institutional IRB members are overwhelmingly affiliated with the institution they are charged to oversee. Furthermore, the developing-world AZT trials, discussed in section 1.2, raise the question: Why look only to the regulations of the country in which the experiment is performed? When a study that involves human research subjects takes place in one country, but is sponsored by institutions in another country, whose regulations should govern the attempt to protect human research subjects? As Carol Levine's article at the end of Chapter 3 indicates, this remains an open question.

A final principle that Helsinki articulates, which is applicable to the AZT trials, is the demand that the best-proven therapeutic method be employed. This issue is also addressed in sections 3.3 and 3.4, where we discuss the concepts of clinical equipoise and the use of placebos. Did this study violate Helsinki because the best-proven therapies were not offered and instead the study was placebo controlled? Or, is the fact that there are proven therapies but that they are not available due to economic factors sufficient to morally justify the use of placebos in this case? Helsinki provides a framework for understanding the ethical issues of this case.

The last of the codes of conduct introduced in Chapter 2 is the Belmont Report, the history of which was discussed in section 3.5. In addition to a set of prescriptions, the Belmont Report includes, unlike Nuremberg and Helsinki, an ethical justification of these prescriptions, in the form of principles. The principles it cites are "respect for persons," which is akin to the principle of autonomy, "beneficence," and "justice," all of which we explored in Chapter 2. Like the previously discussed codes, Belmont discusses the risk/expected-benefit ratio and addresses the ethical complexities of research in which the subjects assume the risks and do not directly benefit from the research. The Belmont Report also lays down three conditions under which deception research is permissible: 1) incomplete disclosure is a necessary condition for the research to be completed, 2) there is no more than minimal risk to the subjects, and 3) the subjects are debriefed after the study has been completed.

Belmont expands on the "two hats" problem by introducing a definition of "therapy," or "practice" as it is called, which is "designed solely to enhance the well-being of an individual patient or client." "Research . . . designates an activity designed to test an hypothesis, permit conclusions to be drawn, and thereby to develop or contribute to generalizable knowledge." This statement may go some way toward clarifying the moral obligations that researchers have to individuals who are also their patients or clients. The implication in Belmont is that scientists have greater responsibilities in the research arena than in the practice arena. For example, Belmont claims that the information that research subjects may reasonably expect to know exceeds the information that patients may reasonably expect to know. This may be due to questions of voluntariness, or it may be due to questions of beneficence. Insofar as many research projects do not benefit the subjects directly, whereas in "therapy" or "practice" the patient benefits directly from the intervention, more information should be provided to research subjects so that they are able to make an informed choice about their participation.

Belmont opens up the possibility of human subjects research with vulnerable populations not covered in the Declaration of Helsinki. In particular, Belmont addresses concerns about the use of such less-than-fully autonomous persons as prisoners, persons with disabilities, children, and members of minority and disadvantaged groups in scientific research. The special considerations involved in using members of some of these populations will be the topic of the next chapter.

4.8   SUMMARY

The use of human subjects is justified by examining the risk/expected-benefit ratio. Risks may include physical or psychological harms and legal, social, or economic risks. Benefits may include psychological, material, or therapeutic benefits that accrue directly to the subjects or a contribution to generalizable knowledge that may ultimately be of benefit to others. The benefits and the harms of research do not always accrue to the same individuals; in cases where they do not, special care should be taken to ensure that the selection of subjects has been just. The researcher is required to be familiar with the area of study so that the risk/expected benefit-ratio is as favorable as possible. The researcher must be familiar with previously published research, so that previous results are not merely duplicated with no contribution to generalizable knowledge at research subjects' expense; they must also be familiar with experimental procedures so that data collection is done responsibly. The subjective nature of harms and benefits places additional responsibilities on researchers to assess harm and benefit individually for each potential research subject.

Different types of research demand different types of protections. In this chapter we have distinguished four types of research: research that involves no greater than minimal risk, research that involves greater than minimal risk but does not hold out the prospect of direct benefit to the subject, research that involves greater than minimal risk and does hold out the prospect of direct benefit to the subject, and deception research. A detailed discussion of each of these types illustrated several ethical questions associated with human subjects research.

The voluntary participation of research subjects begins with responsible recruitment. Undue incentives may cause subjects to do things they would not normally do; thus, inappropriate incentives undermine the voluntary nature of subject participation. The "two hats" problem, in which researchers also have responsibilities in their roles as teachers, physicians, or other authority figures, may also undermine the free and voluntary participation of subjects.

The autonomy of research subjects is most often protected by first obtaining informed consent for their participation. Informed consent should be a two-way dialogue that allows the research subject opportunities to actively engage researchers about the nature of their participation. Informed consent should involve articulating many of the points already discussed, such as the risk/expected-benefit ratio and the voluntary nature of the subjects' participation, as well as the data-collection and dissemination procedures.

The privacy of research subjects should be protected. Maintaining the confidentiality of data shared with researchers is important, both as a means of demonstrating respect for the subjects and for methodological purposes.

Finally, the Nuremberg Code, the Declaration of Helsinki, and the Belmont Report were re-examined at the close of the chapter. Many aspects of human subjects protection discussed in this chapter are prefigured in these important documents.

4.9   CASE STUDIES

Case 4.1: For the following study, consider these two questions: What are the ethical complications in performing this study? How could the ethical complications be remedied?

A researcher wants to perform a study that will answer the following question: Does alcohol aggravate already addictive behaviors, or are people inclined to indulge their addictive behaviors, regardless of alcohol consumption? The researcher designs an experiment with a control arm containing 25 subjects and an experimental arm containing 25 subjects. All 50 of the subjects in the study will be habitual smokers and will smoke at least one pack of cigarettes a day. Recruitment posters will explain that the study will take approximately two-and-a-half hours and that subjects may participate if they are habitual smokers. The compensation for each subjects' participation is advertised as "As much as $30.00!" for their time. Additionally, the subjects are requested to have someone drive them to the research site and drive them home or to live within walking distance of the experimental site.

Each subject will sign an informed consent document that will say that he/she may be consuming either an inert substance or any one of a number of active substances (including an over-the-counter antihistamine, the amount of caffeine in two cups of coffee, or the amount of alcohol in two beers), so that the researchers can test the effects of these substances on blood pressure in smokers. The subjects will be informed that their participation in the study will be compensated by giving them $30.00. The research is a single-blinded study. After consuming one of the above-named substances, each subject will be escorted to a room and asked to wait in the room for two hours. The subjects will not be allowed to bring anything into the room with them. Reading material will be provided. After a period of half an hour, the researcher will enter the room, ask how the subject is doing, and take their blood pressure. The researcher will say that she will be back at the end of the study to take the subject's blood pressure again. After this, the researcher will offer the subject a pack of cigarettes and a lighter, in exchange for lowering the payment for participating in the experiment from $30.00 to $15.00. The assumption is the following: If alcohol causes individuals who engage in an addictive behavior to *further* indulge this behavior, then those subjects who were given alcohol will be more likely to "buy" the cigarettes and lighter for $15.00 than those subjects who were not given alcohol. The researcher will come back at the end of the two-hour period to take subject's blood pressure again. After the two-hour period, the subjects who live within walking distance will be allowed to walk home; the subjects who do not live within walking distance will be allowed to go home with their escorts.

Case 4.2: Stan is doing research on the success of a 12-step alcohol rehabilitation program. He is conducting private interviews with each member of the group after the weekly meetings, so that he can learn about participants' experiences and the success of 12-step programs. The group has met for years and know each other quite well. It took Stan a long time to establish the group's trust in him, and Stan has promised strict confidentiality to each member of the group as a condition of his research. The first interviewee tells Stan that the only way that he can contain his urge to indulge in alcohol is by smoking marijuana. The second interviewee tells Stan something very similar, except that he has been using heroin. The third interviewee confesses to Stan that he has been having suicidal thoughts. Stan knows that if he breaks confidentiality that the word will quickly spread among the members of the group and that he will no longer be trusted. Should Stan break confidentiality in any of these cases? If so, which ones? If he should break confidentiality in some, but not all, of these cases, what distinguishes each case?

REFERENCES AND FURTHER READING

Troyen A. Brennan, "Proposed Revisions to the Declaration of Helsinki—Will They Weaken the Ethical Principles Underlying Human Research?" *New England Journal of Medicine,* Volume 341, number 7, August 12, 1999, pp. 527–531.

Martin Bulmer, ed., *Social Research Ethics: An Examination of the Merits of Covert Participant Observation,* New York: Holmes and Meier Publishers, Inc., 1982.

Office for Protection from Research Risks, *Protecting Human Subjects: Institutional Review Board Guidebook,* Washington, DC: U.S. Government Printing Office, 1993.

Ulrich Tröhler and Stella Reiter-Theil, eds., in cooperation with Eckhard Herych, *Ethics Codes in Medicine: Foundations and Acheivements of Codification Since 1947,* Brookfield, Virginia: Ashgate, 1998.

Voluntary Informed Consent and Debriefing

Joan E. Sieber

Voluntary informed consent is an ongoing, two-way communication process between subjects and the investigator, as well as a specific agreement about the conditions of the research participation. *Voluntary* means without threat or undue inducement. *Informed* means that the subject knows what a reasonable person in the same situation would want to know before giving consent. *Consent* means explicit agreement to participate. Informed consent requires clear communication, not complex technical explanations or legal jargon beyond the subject's ability to comprehend. Social scientists should draw upon their

Joan E. Sieber, *Planning Ethically Responsible Research,* Chapter 4, 26–32. Newbury Park, CA: Sage Publications, 1992.

communication skills to ensure that the consent process fulfills these criteria and that communication lines remain open, even after the formal and legally mandated consent has occurred.

The Communication Process of Voluntary Informed Consent

There are many aspects of the investigator's speech and behavior that communicate information to subjects. Body language, friendliness, a respectful attitude, and genuine empathy for the role of the subject are among the factors that may speak louder than words. To illustrate, imagine a potential subject who is waiting to participate in a study:

> *Scenario 1:* The scientist arrives late, wearing a rumpled lab coat, and props himself in the doorway. He ascertains that the subject is indeed the person whose name is on his list. He reads the consent information without looking at the subject. The subject tries to discuss the information with the researcher, who seems not to hear. He reads off the possible risks. The nonverbal communication that has occurred is powerful. The subject feels resentful and suppresses an urge to storm out. What has been communicated most clearly is that the investigator does not care about the subject. The subject is sophisticated and recognizes that the researcher is immature, preoccupied, and lacking in social skills, yet he feels devalued. He silently succumbs to the pressures of this unequal status relationship to do "the right thing"; he signs the consent form amidst a rush of unpleasant emotions.

> *Scenario 2:* The subject enters the anteroom and meets a researcher who is well groomed, stands straight and relaxed, and invites the subject to sit down with him. The researcher's eye contact, easy and relaxed approach, warm but professional manner, voice, breathing, and a host of other cues convey that he is comfortable communicating with the subject. He is friendly and direct as he describes the study. Through eye contact, he ascertains that the subject understands what he has said. He invites questions, and responds thoughtfully to any comments, questions or concerns. If the subject raises a scientific question about the study (no matter how naive), the scientist welcomes the subject's interest in the project and enters into a brief discussion, treating the subject as a respected peer. Finally, he indicates that there is a formal consent form to be signed and shows the subject that the consent form covers the issues that were discussed. He mentions that it is important that people not feel pressured to participate, but rather participate only if they really want to. The subject signs the form and receives a copy of the form to keep for himself.

Though the consent forms in the first and second case may have been identical, only the second case exemplified adequate, respectful informed consent. In that case, the researcher engendered a strong sense of rapport, trust, and mutual respect; he was responsive to the concerns of the subject and he facilitated adequate decision making. Let us analyze these and other elements of communication:

Rapport. Because informed consent procedures are administered to many subjects in some experiments, it is all too easy to turn the process into a singsong routine that is delivered without any sense of commitment to interpersonal communication. A friendly greeting, openness, positive body language, and a genuine willingness to hear what each subject has to say or ask about the study are crucial to establishing rapport. The amount of eye contact one should employ depends on various circumstances. Extensive eye contact can interfere with the subject's ability to think, and would be considered rude in some Asian cultures. Too little eye contact may signal avoidance, however. Lack of rapport communicates disrespect.

Congruence of Verbal and Body Language. This is an important part of rapport. In the above two examples, the first researcher was highly incongruent: The words said one thing, the manner in which they were delivered said the opposite. The second researcher was highly congruent: All channels of his communication conveyed respect and openness. The congruent communicator of informed consent uses vocabulary that the subject can easily understand, speaks in gentle, direct tones at about the same rate of speech that the subject uses, breathes deeply and calmly, stands or sits straight and relaxed, and is accessible to eye contact. Even if the researcher was feeling stressed, he or she takes time to relax so as not to make distracting movements, show impatience, or laugh inappropriately. To communicate congruently, one's mind must be relatively clear of distracting thoughts.

Trust. If participants believe that the investigator may not understand or care about them, there will not be the sense of partnership needed to carry out the study satisfactorily. The issue of trust is particularly important when the investigator has considerably higher status than members of the target population, or is from a different ethnic group. It is often useful to ask representatives of the subject population to examine the research procedures and make sure they are respectful and acceptable to the target population, as the following example illustrates:

> A Caucasian anthropologist wanted to interview families in San Francisco's Chinatown to determine what kinds of foods they eat, how their eating habits have changed since they immigrated here, and what incidence of cancer has been experienced in their family. She employed several Chinese-American women to learn whether her interview questions were appropriate and to translate them into Mandarin and Cantonese. First, the research assistants worked on the basis of their personal knowledge of the language and culture of Chinatown; they then tested their procedures on pilot subjects. There was considerable confusion among pilot subjects about the names of some Chinese vegetables; the researchers devised pictures of those vegetables so that subjects could confirm which ones they meant. The Chinese-American research assistants rewrote the questions and the consent statement until they were appropriate for the population that was to be interviewed, then conducted the interviews. Their appearance, language, and cultural background engendered a level of trust, mutual respect, and clear communication that the researcher herself could not have created.

Another way to have built trust and cooperation in that community would have been to identify legitimate leaders or gatekeepers, who are concerned about the health and welfare of community members, and to work with them to make the survey mutually useful. A gatekeeper is a person who lets researchers into the setting or keeps them out. Gatekeepers derive their power from their ability to negotiate conditions that are acceptable to those they serve. Only unscrupulous gatekeepers would grant a researcher privileges that would cause concern or harm to research participants or to the community. Gatekeepers may be scientists, such as a researcher who also directs a clinic. More frequently, they are nonscientists—principals or school-district superintendents, managers of companies, directors of agencies, ministers of local churches, or "street professionals," such as a recovered drug addict who now serves as a community outreach person to his own people.

Some anthropologists have offered to share data with their host community for its own policy-making purposes (e.g., Pelto, 1988; White, 1991). The community leaders or gatekeepers might request that certain items of interest to them be added to a survey and might subsequently need some assistance with specific analyses and interpretations of data. The net result could be a collaborative effort to achieve a shared goal, such as improved health and nutrition in that community. Ideally the collaboration and cooperation would be communicated explicitly to community members. For example, the community newspaper might print an article—including pictures of the interviewers who would soon appear at residents' doors. Interviewers might even carry copies of the newspaper article with them for purposes of identification.

There are many ways to enhance rapport, respect, and trust and increase the benefit to subjects of the research project, depending on the particular setting and circumstances. When planning research, especially in a field setting, it is useful to conduct focus groups from the target population (Stewart & Shamdasani, 1990), to consult with community gatekeepers, or simply to consult with pilot subjects. The purpose of such consultation during planning is to learn how subjects are likely to react to the various possible research procedures and how to make the research most beneficial and acceptable to subjects. The rewards to the researcher for this effort include greater ease of recruiting, cooperative research participants, a research design that will work, and a community that evinces good will.

Relevance to the Concerns of the Research Population. In developing consent statements, researchers usually try to address the concerns they think their subjects ought to have. However, it is important for the researcher to determine what the concerns of that subject population actually are. *Pilot subjects* from the research population should have the procedure explained to them and should be asked to try to imagine what concerns people would have about participating in the study. Often some of these concerns turn out to be very different from those the researcher would have imagined, and they are likely to affect the outcome of the research if they are not resolved, as the following case illustrates:

Case 4.1: Misinformed Consent. A Ph.D. student interviewed aged persons living in a publicly supported geriatric center on their perceptions of the center. At the time of the

research, city budget cuts were occurring; rumors were rampant that eligibility criteria would change and many current residents would be evicted. Mrs. B., an amputee,
was fearful that she would be moved if she were perceived as incompetent. Upon signing the informed consent form she began answering his questions:

"Can you recite the alphabet?"

"Backwards or forwards?" she asked to demonstrate her intellectual competence.

"How do you like the service here?"

"Oh, it's great!" she replied, although she constantly complained to her family about
the poor service and bad food.

"How do you like the food here?"

"It's delicious," she replied.

Mrs. B.'s anxiety was rising and midway through the questioning she asked the
student, "Did I pass the test?"

"What test?" he asked.

"The one for whether I can stay in the hospital."

"I'm not working for the hospital," he replied. With that, Mrs. B. spun her chair
around and wheeled herself away. (Fisher & Rosendahl, 1990, pp. 47–48)

Comprehension. In addition to its relevance to the concerns of the research population, the consent must employ terms and concepts that they will understand.
To check for understandability, pilot subjects should be asked to read the consent
statement and explain it in their own words. It should be revised until it is correctly understood.

Adequacy of Decision Making. Even when rapport, comprehension, relevance, and
trust are present, it is possible that a subject may fail to give adequate consideration to the decision to participate. Adequate decision making is important to
both the subject and the researcher. The subject who regrets agreeing to participate in a study is likely to be late or fail to appear at all, to hurry through the procedures with less than full attention, or even to give dishonest answers.

When consent statements are presented as a plea for help, two factors may
cause subjects to participate, even though they would rather not. The *volunteer
effect* (Rosenthal & Rosnow, 1969) occurs when subjects feel that they ought to be
helpful and agree to participate to do "the right thing." The other factor that pre-
disposes people to be poor decision makers is being rushed into a decision. The
following steps will help to avoid these two problems:

1. Present the consent statement well before subjects are to participate, so that
they have ample time to consider their decision.

2. Especially if participation requires much time and effort, urge subjects to
make the decision that best serves their own interests, as to do otherwise will
serve no one's interests.

3. Provide a group context in which subjects discuss with the researcher the
pros and cons of participating. This gives individuals exposure to much more

information, both for and against participation, than individual decision makers would typically generate.

4. If the procedure is complicated and unusual, let subjects participate in a simulation, or show a videotape of another subject participating, to provide a concrete sense of what is involved.

5. If some or all of the intended subjects do not speak English, the consent statement should be translated by a bilingual person who fully understands the research and the research population. A second bilingual person should then translate the statement back to English to detect any possible misunderstandings in the original translation. Employ the first four procedures above, as appropriate, in the native language of the research population.

Competency and Voluntariness in Special Populations. Although the competence to understand and make decisions about research participation is conceptually distinct from voluntariness, these qualities become blurred in the case of some "captive" research populations. Children, retarded adults, the poorly educated, and prisoners may fail to understand their right to refuse to participate in research when asked by someone of apparent authority. They may also fail to grasp the details relevant to their decision. Where competency is a legal issue, the matter is resolved by appointing an advocate for the research subject, in addition to obtaining the subject's assent. Children cannot legally consent to participate in research, but they can indicate whether they want to participate, and must be given veto power over adults who give permission for them to participate. This is called *assent.*

Competence to consent or assent and voluntariness are affected by the way the decision is presented (Melton & Stanley, 1991). For example, an individual's understanding of information presented in the consent procedure, and acceptance of his or her status as an autonomous decision maker, will be most powerfully influenced not by *what* he or she is told but by *how* he or she is engaged in the communication. See Stanley and Guido (1991) for a review of literature on competency and voluntariness.

Protection of Privacy and Confidentiality.[1] It is essential that researchers protect the privacy of research participants and the confidentiality of data to the extent possible, and communicate how this will be done (including limits on their ability to assure confidentiality) in the consent statement.

Note

[1] . . . *Privacy* refers to the interest that persons have in controlling others' access to themselves. *Confidentiality* refers to the agreement between researcher and subject about access by others to the data. *Anonymity* refers to data that include no unique identifiers such as name or Social Security number.

Get Patients' Consent to Enter Clinical Trials

Elizabeth Wager, Peter J. H. Tooley, Michael B. Emanuel, Stuart F. Wood

Gaining patients' consent to enter clinical trials is essential, but not easy. Giving careful thought to the design of the study itself, information which patients receive, and the use of a signed consent form may all help. To be properly informed, patients need to know something about their condition, the proposed study, and alternative options. The type and amount of information will vary and investigators need to judge the level appropriate for each person. Patients should understand that taking part in a clinical trial is voluntary and that their decision will not affect the quality of care they receive. The process of obtaining consent require time and good communication. Working with young, elderly, or mentally impaired patients, or those particularly vulnerable to coercion, requires special sensitivity to the potential dangers.

Although about 3000 papers on informed consent have been written since 1989, little practical guidance is available for doctors recruiting patients to clinical trials. Many view the process as a legal safeguard,[1] though there is no doctrine of informed consent in English law.[2] The process should therefore be seen as enabling patients "to make a choice or state a preference about the treatment on offer" rather than a prudent form of defensive medicine.[3]

Outside a trial, doctors can decide how much patients participate in decisions about treatment. Some have argued that this discretion should extend to trials with a complex range of options. Otherwise, confronting the fact that there is no agreed optimum treatment may do the patient more harm than good.[4,5] Our aim in this article is not to debate whether it is ever morally justifiable to include patients in trials without obtaining their consent, but to offer some practical help when patients explicitly give their consent.

Study Design

Before starting to recruit patients you should be satisfied that the study itself is ethical. Anyone designing a study should consider the issue of patient consent at the outset. You must obtain approval from your research ethics committee for any clinical trial involving patients, and the committee should review any information and consent forms given to patients.

Elizabeth Wager, Peter J. H. Tooley, Michael B. Emanuel, Stuart F. Wood, "Get Patients' Consent to Enter Clinical Trials," *BMJ*, 1995, 311, 734–737.

As consent is about asking patients to make a choice, patients should perhaps be consulted about trial design. Consent can be regarded as a reasonable choice only if the patient's aspirations match those of the study.[6] This is particularly important for patients with life threatening illnesses, when choices between quantity and quality of life may be more affected by personal circumstances than medical considerations. In the United States organisations such as the National Breast Cancer Coalition campaign for patients to participate more in research. In Britain such advocacy movements are less common, but some well established self help groups for patients could be consulted about clinical trials.

To explain a trial clearly the investigator must understand the aims of the trial and exactly how it will be conducted. One study of the quality of informed consent found that patients attending centres that had not participated in designing the study considered that they received poorer information than those recruited by investigators who had been active in the study from the start.[7]

What Information Should Patients Receive?

Before considering entering a trial, patients will need some information about their diagnosis, the nature of their condition, and the treatments available. Written information about conditions may be useful. To be properly informed a patient needs to know not only about the proposed trial but also about the other options.

INFORMATION ABOUT THE TRIAL

Explaining the concepts of randomisation and the placebo effect to patients is not easy. The difficulties may partly be due to fear of losing patients' confidence in admitting to not being aware of what treatment they will receive or to not knowing which treatment would be best for them. Randomisation may sound less threatening if you explain that it ensures that the hoped for benefits and unknown risks are spread fairly between groups of patients. You might also explain how randomisation reduces bias. For example, in an unrandomised study comparing a new drug with an established treatment, patients who had not responded to available treatments might be more likely to choose the new drug, causing this group to include more cases of treatment resistant disease.

Most patients can appreciate the need for double blind procedures if you explain that results could be affected by either the patients' or the doctors' expectations. The placebo effect can be explained by saying that patients who know they are not receiving treatment often do less well than those who think that they are being treated. It may also be helpful to explain that a placebo is frequently used in trials of new drugs, when less is known about the new treatment's possible risks. Placebos are also common when no comparator treatment is available. In this case, patients receiving placebo are no worse off than those who are not in the trial. Therefore, you must explain the treatments available outside the trial.

How much detail about potential risks do patients require? Legal criteria state that the doctor should disclose any material risks—that is, those to which a reasonable patient would attach significance in that particular situation.[2] Patients might reasonably be expected to attach significance to events that are either severe—for example, paralysis or blindness—or are fairly likely to occur—for example, a 30% likelihood of nausea. In other words, consider telling patients about serious risks that are rare and about less serious events which are expected to happen more often.[4] Patients should be told what to do if they experience an adverse event and whether compensation is available for serious injury. You must also be prepared to answer any questions patients might have about the trial.

You should tell patients about the implications of the trial—for example, if it entails extra visits to the surgery or travel to another centre. Patients need to know how long the trial will last and what will happen when it ends (especially in terms of the provision of unlicensed treatments). They should be told about any discomfort or inconvenience associated with any assessments.

Patients vary in the amount of information they expect to receive, but this should not be used as an excuse to gloss over potential risks. Dawes and Davison studied patients' information requirements before surgery and concluded that "just because somebody is anxious it does not mean that they do not want any information."[9] Another surgical study found that providing a detailed account of what might go wrong did not significantly increase patients' anxiety.[10] The same probably applies to clinical trials, but this has rarely been tested.

Patients with serious illnesses may seem to want reassurance from their doctor rather than the uncertainty of a trial. Fallowfield *et al* found, however, that 94% of patients with cancer wanted as much information as possible.[11] Simes *et al* found that patients given full information about a cancer trial were more anxious than those who received a shorter explanation, although this anxiety did not affect their relationship with the doctor.[12]

In all cases, doctors should develop the skills necessary to identify how much information each patient requires, but they should remember that for clinical trials there is probably a bare minimum that all patients should receive. Byrne *et al* describe patients "who simply want to be treated . . . so that they can leave the hospital, forget their illness, and resume growing prize marrows as far from the medical confraternity as possible,"[11,13] while Brewin and Bradley describe patients who "thrive on a diet rich in detailed information about their illness."[14] Doctors must decide where each patient fits on this continuum.

What Do Patients Need to Know About a Trial?

Always explain that taking part in a trial is voluntary and that patients will get the best treatment available and the full attention of the doctor even if they do not want to participate. Patients also need to understand that they are free to withdraw from a trial at any point, and again, that this will not prejudice their treatment. Using a written consent form may make patients feel that they have signed an agreement to complete the trial. You may have to explain that the consent form aims to ensure exactly the opposite.

Practical Considerations

In designing a trial, careful consideration should be given to:
- The ways in which information is given to the patient
- The use of written consent forms
- The setting in which consent is obtained
- The timing of obtaining consent.

PATIENT INFORMATION

Consider providing both oral and written information to patients, as recommended in the code of European good clinical practice.[15] Preparing written information for patients is not easy, and guidelines for writing clear English should always be followed.[16–18] A few essential points are shown in the box. Always test your written material on colleagues who are not part of the trial, and also on some lay people, to check for ambiguities, missing information, or sections that are difficult to understand. Keep the needs of the patients in mind—for example, translations for non-native English speakers or large print for elderly patients.

Writing Clearly for Patients

- Use short sentences
- Avoid jargon, or explain it when necessary
- Pay attention to layout:

    Lists are clearer than paragraphs of text

    A question and answer format can be useful

    Headings are helpful
- Use a clear, legible typeface and design:

    Everything in capital letters is less legible than upper and lower case

    Serif typefaces—for example, Times or Courier—are easier to read than sans serif—for example, Univers

    Black text on a white background is usually clearest; avoid white on black or strong coloured backgrounds

    Use at least a 12 point (or 10 characters per inch) font size

---

If written information is insufficient or inappropriate, audio or video tapes may be helpful. Tape recordings of consultations improve patients' understanding about their condition and reduce their degree of anxiety.[19–20] They might be useful if large amounts of information need to be given to the patient.

Patients recall more about the practical aspects of a study than the potential risks[31] and tend to forget risks more quickly than benefits.[21] It may therefore be helpful to repeat information to help understanding and retention.

CONSENT FORMS

Using a consent form to register the patient's decision may help to reinforce information about the voluntary nature of trials or their implications. Forms also provide a useful procedural checklist. Several model consent forms are available (figure).[22] Although models are useful, a consent form should relate specifically to the trial or procedure in question. Legal cases have established that consent is limited to a specific trial or treatment, and the patient cannot be considered to have given consent for anything else.

The consent form should be a separate document, not torn off the bottom of the patient information leaflet.[23] Forms using NCR (no carbon required) paper provide an instant copy for the patient to retain. The ethics committee will usually request to see the consent form before approving the study.

Study Title

Have you read the information provided?   Yes/No

Have you had an opportunity to ask questions
    and discuss the study?   Yes/No

Have all your questions been answered satisfactorily?   Yes/No

Have you received enough information about the study?   Yes/No

Who have you spoken to about the study?

Do you understand that you are free to withdraw from the study
    —at any time?
    —without having to give a reason?
    —without affecting your future medical care?   Yes/No

Do you agree to take part in this study?   Yes/No

Signed (patient) _____ (date) _____

Signed (doctor) _____ (date) _____

Model consent form[21]

WITNESSED CONSENT

The role of a witness is to confirm that the patient was reasonably informed about the trial and consented freely to take part. Witnesses may also provide information for patients, answer their questions, and test their understanding of the trial.[24] However, these roles conflict to a certain extent, since a witness designed to prevent coercion should be as independent of the trial as possible, whereas one expected to discuss the trial with the patient needs to be well informed and therefore part of the research team. The names and addresses of independent witnesses should be recorded so that they could be traced to give their opinion on how consent was obtained if this was subsequently challenged. Nurses often have an important role in explaining the trial to the patient and may also act as advocates or go betweens if patients have concerns about a trial but feel daunted about approaching the doctor.

The fact that patients' signatures are witnessed may reinforce patients' belief that they are entering into a binding contract in signing the consent form. This misapprehension should be overcome by explaining that the witness is there to protect the patient from being forced to sign a form by the investigator. Witnessed consent may be particularly helpful if patients are infirm or have difficulty in speaking. In this case the witness should probably be someone who knows the patient, is familiar with his or her likely wishes, and can interpret for him or her.[25]

The presence of a witness or the second opportunity to ask questions in a different setting may also help to allay patients' anxiety. This may not only make patients feel better but also improve communication as anxious patients may not be able to communicate clearly and may believe that they cannot withhold or withdraw consent.

SETTING AND TIMING

Patients should not feel rushed into giving consent, which may be difficult to achieve in a busy surgery or clinic. A separate appointment may therefore be needed. Patients also need to feel that they cannot be overheard and are treated in privacy.[20] Patients experiencing serious uncontrolled pain or acute emotional distress may be unable to give valid consent. Gravely ill patients may, however, have times when they are more lucid and alert than others, and investigators should try to approach patients during these times and simply withdraw if they have picked a bad moment. People's ability to make decisions will also be affected by their emotional state; patients who have just been told that they have cancer may not be competent to give consent at that moment, but they may have been so before and may become so later.

Ideally, patients should be given a cooling off period before making a final decision. This may also enable them to discuss the decision with friends and family. Guidelines from the Association for the British Pharmaceutical Industry (ABPI) recommend at least 30 minutes of thinking time for non-emergency situations, and 24 hours whenever possible.[21]

Patients in some circumstances may be particularly vulnerable to unintentional coercion, as described by Fitten, who suggests that: "Chronic care institutions tend to breed a loss of self-esteem, learned helplessness and dependence in residents that may lead to fears, real or imagined, about the consequences of not pleasing their caregivers."[22] Extra care is also needed when considering patients in the armed services and those who are compulsorily detained in hospital. An independent witness may be helpful in these circumstances.[23] Research on prisoners is not permitted because of these problems.

The setting may also materially affect the patient's ability to give consent, since patients with impaired cognitive function perform better in their own homes than in unfamiliar surroundings such as hospital wards.[24]

TESTING UNDERSTANDING

Even providing the best designed patient information sheet and a well planned interview cannot ensure understanding.[25] To make matters harder, patients may have perfect comprehension of the information but fail to appreciate its consequences.[26] You should therefore try to test patients' understanding—for example, by asking them to put the information into their own words.

Remember that the ability to repeat information is not the same as understanding its consequences. For example, you should tell patients that after an operation they will not be able to drive rather than state that their foot will be stiff or in plaster.

WHO SHOULD OBTAIN THE PATIENT'S CONSENT

European guidelines on good clinical practice state that the investigator is responsible for obtaining consent, but they do not specify that such responsibility cannot be delegated. Other members of the team, such as research nurses, often explain the trial to patients and answer their questions, but consent should be obtained by a medically qualified person with responsibility for treating the patient. Lavelle-Jones *et al* found that patients thought that house officers were "the most effective in imparting information relating to surgical treatment,"[27] but Kerrigan *et al* suggested that standards of obtaining consent are low "because the task . . . is left to more junior staff."[28] We suggest that seniority or age are probably poor criteria for deciding who should obtain the patient's consent, but essential qualifications are:

- Familiarity with the study
- Knowledge of optional treatments
- Appreciation of the need for informed consent
- Having time for a full discussion with the patient
- Recognition that people are not logical and that patients have a right to make apparently illogical decisions
- An understanding that a patient's personal circumstances, experience, and personality may affect the decision as much as medical considerations.

Difficult Situations

Much has been written on the ethics of research on young, old, and mentally impaired people. It is outside the scope of this article to rehearse these arguments, and therefore guidance on gaining consent is needed.

Under English law consent may be given on behalf of a child by the parent or, if the child is a ward of court, by the court authority.[29] The child's views must, however, be respected, and even if the child is too young to be considered legally competent to consent, every effort must be made to explain the procedures and potential outcomes.[30,31] When parents are asked to give consent all the usual considerations, such as providing information, will apply.

In legal terms as soon as people reach their legal majority, whatever their mental capacity, no other person has authority to grant consent on their behalf.[32] In clinical trials, however, it may often be good practice to seek consent from a carer or relative. Blanket definitions of categories of patients unable to give consent are probably unhelpful. Patients may be competent to consent to some trials but not to others according to the complexity of the information and the consequences of treatment.

Patients with fluctuating or deteriorating conditions may be able to give informed consent during a remission or in the early stages of the disease. In these cases a patient advocate may be appointed with power of attorney to act on the patient's behalf if he or she becomes incompetent.[33] Warren *et al* have, however, graphically described the problems of informed consent by proxy. They found that nearly a third of proxies would give consent on behalf of elderly relatives even if they believed the relative would have refused. Similarly, 21% were prepared to give consent for elderly relatives to take part in studies which they (the proxy) would not have entered themselves.[34] This suggests that special consideration should be given to explaining the risks and discomforts of a trial if consent is being given on another person's behalf.

For patients living in residential homes the American College of Physicians suggests that, in addition to obtaining the approval of an ethics committee, a committee of residents might also be consulted.[35] The Law Commission recommends that "the consent of a medical treatment proxy or attorney appointed with authority to give such consent" should always be obtained for research involving incapacitated adults.[36]

As a general rule, you should be satisfied that the patient has not expressed an objection to taking part in a trial and should also try to obtain consent from someone close to the patient. Pay particular attention to explaining the trial to anyone giving consent by proxy and avoid making patients feel obliged to cooperate because they live in an institution.

Conclusions

The process of obtaining a patient's properly informed consent to take part in a clinical trial should not be seen as an exercise in bureaucratic form filling but as an essential part of the trial requiring time, insight, and communication skill. Remember that patients refusing to give their consent is not a sign that you have failed but may indicate that you are conscientious enough to ensure that they are properly informed and make a free decision. Large proportions of patients refusing to enter a study may, however, signal a problem with the study design.

Some doctors agree that informing patients only worries them, but a little anxiety is a price worth paying to protect patients' rights, and patients may in fact be reassured by more information. Similarly, fears have been expressed that obtaining consent will damage the doctor-patient relationship. We suggest that, on the contrary, developing the skills needed to obtain consent for clinical trials will enhance relations, improve communication, and encourage increased patient participation in all decisions about their treatment.

Notes

[1] Kessell A. On failing to understand informed consent. *Br J Hosp Med* 1994; 52:235–8.

[2] Heneghan C. Consent to medical treatment: what should the patient be told: *Br J Anaesth* 1994; 73:25–8.

[3] Silverman W. The myth of informed consent: in daily practice and in clinical trials. *J Med Ethics* 1989; 15:6–11.

[4] Tobias J, Souhami R. Fully informed consent can be needlessly cruel. *BMJ* 1993; 307:1199–201.

[5] Barer D. Patients' preferences and randomised trials. *Lancet* 1994, 334:684.

[6] Thornton H. Patients' preferences and randomised trials. *Lancet* 1994, 344:639.

[7] Lynde N, Sandhund M, Dahlquest G, Jacobsson L. Informed consent: study of quality of information given to participants in a clinical trial. *BMJ* 1991; 303:610–3.

[8] Samuels A. Informed consent: the law. *Med Sci Law* 1992; 32:35–42.

[9] Dawes P, Davison P. Informed consent: what do patients want to know? *J R Soc Med* 1994; 87:149–52.

[10] Kerrigan DD, Thevasayagam RS, Woods TO, McWelch I, Thomas TEG, Shorthouse Al, et al. Who's afraid of informed consent? *BMJ* 1993; 306:298–300.

[11] Fallowfield L, Ford S, Lewis S. Information preferences of patients with cancer. *Lancet* 1994; 344:1576.

[12] Simes R, Tatterall M, Coates A, Raghavan D, Solomon H, Smartt H. Randomised comparison of procedures for obtaining informed consent to clinical trials for cancer. *BMJ* 1986; 293:1065–8.

[13] Byrne D, Napier A, Cuschien A. How informed is signed consent? *BMJ* 1988; 296:839–40.

[14] Brown C, Bradley C. Patients' preferences and randomised clinical trials. *BMJ* 1989; 299:313–5.

[15] Brown L. GCP and informed consent: a UK perspective. *Good Clinical Practice Journal* 1994,1(3):20–3.

[16] Alberts T, Chadwick S. How readable are practice leaflets? *BMJ* 1992; 305:1266–8.

[17] Smith T. Information for patients: writing sample English is difficult, even for doctors. *BMJ* 1992; 305:1242.

[18] Priestley K, Campbell C, Valentine C, Denison D, Buller N. Are patient consent forms for research protocols easy to read? *BMJ* 1992; 305:1263–4.

[19] Cornbleet M, Knowles G, North N, Leonard R. Recording of outpatient consultations. *Lancet* 1992; 340:488.

[20] Anonymous. Outpatients on tape [editorial]. *Lancet* 1992; 340:23.

[21] Saw K, Wood A, Murphy K, Parry J, Hartfell W. Informed consent: an evaluation of patients' understanding and opinion (with respect to the operation of transurethral resection of the prostate). *J R Sex Med* 1994; 87:143–4.

[22] Royal College of Physicians. *Research involving patients.* London: RCP, 1990.

[23] Ranson P. Consent the legal aspects. *Good Clinical Practice* 1994; 1(3):24–5.

[24] Goodman N, Cooper G, Malins A. Prys-Roberts C. The validity of informed consent in a clinical study. *Anaesthesias* 1984; 39:911–6.

[25] Chopra S, Conquest I, Hirst L, Marshall P, Rutherford A. *A pharmacy study comparing miconazole and clotonazole for vaginal conditions.* Grove, Oxfordshire: Janssen Research Foundation, 1994.

[26] Fitten L. The ethics of conducting research with older psychiatric patients. *International Journal of Geriatric Psychiatry* 1993; 8:33–9.

[27] Fulford K, Howse K. Ethics of research with psychiatric patients: principles, problems and the primary responsibilities of researchers. *J Med Ethics* 1993; 19:85–91.

[28] Lavell-Jones C, Byrne D, Rice P, Cuschien A. Factors affecting quality of informed consent. *BMJ* 1993; 306:885–90.

[29] Appelbaum P, Grasso T. Assessing patients' capacities to concerns to treatment. *N Engl J Med* 1988; 319:1635–8.

[30] Skegg P. English law relating to experimentation on children. *Lancet* 1977; ii:754–5.

[31] Shield J, Baum J. Children's consent to treatment. *BMJ* 1994; 306:1182–3.

[32] Brahams D. Incompetent adults and consent to treatment. *Lancet* 1989; i:340.

[33] Helmchen H. The problem of informed consent in dementia research. *Med Law* 1990; 9:1206–13.

[34] Warren JW, Sobel J, Tenney JH, Hooper JM, Damron D, Levenson S, *et al.* Informed consent by proxy: an issue to research with elderly patients. *N Engl J Med* 1986; 315:1124–8.

[35] American College of Physicians. Cognitively impaired subjects. *Ann Intern Med* 1989; 111:843–8.

[36] Brahams D. Consent to research in presence of incapacity. *Lancet* 1993; 341:1143–4.

Do You Understand?

An Ethical Assessment of Researchers' Description of the Consenting Process

Sandra L. Titus and Moira A. Keane

Research Question

How do researchers describe their own interactions with possible subjects when they obtain informed consent from them? We will study this question by examining what they say to subjects about the research, how they assess the level of a subject's understanding, who is delegated the role of obtaining consent, and when the written consent is gained.

Methods

THE INSTRUMENT

The following four questions were part of the IRB application process. Prior to the four questions, the following statement introduced the expecation that the consenting process was more than just a paper-and-pen process:

> Simply giving a consent form to subjects does not constitute informed consent. The following questions pertain to the consenting process:
>
> 1. Please describe what you will say to subjects to explain the research. Write your explanation as if you were speaking to the subject. (Do not copy the written consent form into this area.)
> 2. What questions will you routinely ask to assess subjects' understanding?
> 3. In relation to actual data gathering, please describe how much time you will typically allow the subject to think about the study before expecting them to sign. (Be explicit—3 days before, 10 minutes before surgery, 2 hours before, etc., and describe your constraints which influence the time choice.)
> 4. Name *all* individuals who may obtain informed consent. (All responsible parties who are going to obtain consent must be listed here.)

The Sample

The subjects in this study were a convenience sample of researchers who applied to one of four Midwestern institutional review boards for approval over a six-month period. Three of the institutional review boards (IRBs) were part of a

Excerpt from Sandra A. Titus and Moira A. Keane, "Do You Understand? An Ethical Assessment of Researchers' Description of the Consenting Process," *The Journal of Clinical Ethics*, 7, no. 1, Spring 1996, 60–68. (Original footnote numbering retained.)

university system and the fourth was an IRB in a free-standing medical center. All types of research studies were submitted, including clinical trials, drug and device studies, surveys, and interviews.

Since we examined existing IRB forms (minus identifiers), we had received an exemption from IRB review. The researcher-subjects were unaware that they were being studied and thus, the data can be considered unobtrusive. The value of obtaining data from those who are unaware that they are being studied is that the subjects are unable to alter their behaviors. Thus, these data are generally thought to be more likely to represent reality and less likely to merely reflect what the subjects considered to be socially desirable.

Findings

We studied 167 independent principal investigators from varied educational backgrounds: physician-researchers, 45 percent; PhDs, 27 percent; graduate students, 18 percent; and social or medical scientists, 10 percent.

How is the Research Described?

One-third of the researchers in the sample gave no indication that they knew how to speak about their research projects at all. Although they were cautioned against doing so in the application, many researchers did transcribe sections of their written consent forms. We determined whether a researcher had "oral skills" by comparing the written consent form with the response. We coded answers that elaborated or were written in a manner that was clearly different from the written consent form as demonstrating "oral" skills. The responses of those that provided statements sounding like oral descriptions (66 percent) were further analyzed and coded for their descriptions of the purpose, procedures, risks, benefits, alternatives, costs, confidentiality of the research; option to withdraw or refuse; and offer to answer questions. These categories parallel the expectations described in the regulations.[5]

We found that about 50 percent of the researchers focused on describing the study's purpose or its procedures (see table 1). Researchers indicated only infrequently that they discussed benefits, risks, alternatives, costs, confidentiality, nonparticipation, or withdrawal, or that they gave subjects time to ask questions or think about the project.

We also judged whether the researchers' statements were "meaningful" or not (see table 1). A "meaningful" statement was one that we perceived to be complete and useful, as opposed to casual and not particularly developed. In short, we took the point of view of participants, and if we found that we knew more after reviewing the responses, we considered the researcher's statement to be meaningful. About one third of the investigators gave a detailed description of the purpose of the research and what they wanted subjects to do in their studies. A meaningful discussion on all other areas was virtually nonexistent.

WHAT QUESTIONS ARE ASKED TO ASSESS THE UNDERSTANDING
OF SUBJECTS?

Once the researchers presented the study's content to a subject, the researcher is responsible for assessing whether or not the person understands the study, including the risks of the research. The researcher has to take responsibility for assessing, not assuming, the subject's understanding.[5]

CLOSED-ENDED VERSUS OPEN-ENDED QUESTIONS

We coded the answers for the types of questions the researchers used to assess understanding. Closed-ended questions asked for bipolar answers (typically "yes" or "no"). This narrow response range is better suited to gathering quantitative data, in which the proportion of responses in each category is counted. To assess qualitatively whether a subject understands, an open-ended question that does not direct the respondent is preferred.[6]

Closed-ended questions. Out of all the researchers, 80 percent demonstrated using closed-ended questions, the two most typical being, "Do you understand?" and "Do you have any questions?"

Open-ended questions. Of the researchers, 20 percent demonstrated using one or more open-ended questions to assess what a potential subject understood about the research. Open-ended questions gave the respondent an opportunity to fully describe perceptions, understanding, and what he or she heard. Open-ended questions were typically formed by using words and phrases such as "what," "where," "how often," "when," "please describe," and "please review what you heard me say":

- "Just so that I'm sure you understand what is expected of you here, would you please explain to me what you think we are going to ask you to do?"
- "Please tell me again."
- "Describe in your own words the purpose of study."
- "What more would you like to know?"
- "What is the possible benefit to you of taking the new experimental drug? What are the possible risks to you of taking this new drug?"

ASSESSING HOW INFORMED A SUBJECT IS ABOUT HIS/HER
MEDICAL CONDITION

A few investigators with very complex medical-research protocols assessed their subjects' general medical understanding prior to discussing the technical aspects of the consent forms. The following types of open-ended questions helped the researchers examine understanding:

- "Generally, I'd start out with, 'What do you know about your disease? What is a platelet? What are antibodies?' and questions of that sort."
- "What does it mean to have a defective gene?"
- "Tell me what phlebitis means."

TABLE 1
Consenting Process: Content Areas Researchers Discuss
with Respondents (n = 167)

Content Areas	Oral Skills		Meaningful	
	n	%	n	%
Says this is a study/research	57	34.0	22	13.0
Invites person to consider participating	0	0.0	0	0.0
Gives purpose of study	87	52.0	54	32.0
Discusses procedure of study	79	47.0	50	30.0
Discloses research risks	15	9.0	10	6.0
Discusses direct benefits	8	5.0	6	4.0
Discusses indirect benefits	5	3.0	4	2.0
Gives alternatives to study	0	0.0	0	0.0
Discusses confidentiality	11	7.0	7	4.0
Tells person he/she can withdraw	7	4.0	6	4.0
Tells person he/she can choose not to participate	10	6.0	5	3.0
Discusses meaning of signature	0	0.0	0	0.0
Tells person he/she can have time to think about participating	1	0.5	1	0.5
Discusses costs of being in the study	0	0.0	0	0.0
Tells person it is ok to ask questions	3	2.0	3	2.0

TIMING OF THE CONSENTING PROCESS IN RESEARCH

The researchers were asked to indicate when they obtained the written consent and to describe the time frame explicitly. Of the researchers, 45 percent (n = 75) appeared to have documented obtaining written consent just prior to beginning the study, while 30 percent (n = 49) demonstrated that they gave the subject some time to consider participating. In addition, 25 percent gave ambiguous answers that could not be evaluated.

Only one investigator in this study indicated that he had considered how to be less coercive. He stated, "After I talk about the study, I leave the subject alone to read and sign consent."

Next, we evaluated the time period to assess whether the researcher might have had enough lead time to allow the subject more of an opportunity to think about participating. We determined that in nonacute or nonemergency situations, subjects should have been given additional time to consider participating. We evaluated and judged that one-third of the 124 researchers who answered this question were initiating studies in which more time could have been allowed for the subjects to consider the request.

GAINING MULTIPLE CONSENTS FOR CONTINUING A STUDY

In one unique study, the researcher described a plan to obtain multiple consents in order for the subjects to remain in the study. We think this kind of staging needs to become more commonplace and that researchers need to be encouraged to consider this option. This research group, in fact, informed the IRB that reconsenting increased cooperation:

> The first consent form is the cover letter that will be sent to subjects. It will not be signed, but rather the questionnaire, itself, will be completed only by those who do, in effect, consent to do so. Prior to the Preliminary Run-in Trial, a second consent form will be signed, and then, prior to the Clinical Trial, a third consent form will be signed. The purpose of repeating this process is that it not only renews awareness on the part of the subject, but it also has been shown to increase compliance to the experimental protocol.

WHO EXPLAINS THE STUDY AND CONSENT PROCESS?

The fourth area we investigated was who actually obtained the signed consent. In 136 cases, we were able to calculate the number of names or professional categories of those who might have been delegated to obtain the written consent. The mean number of investigators obtaining written consent for each of these projects was 2.9 (S.D. = 2.7). In 63 percent of these studies, investigators indicated that they were the only ones who obtained the signed consent. In 37 percent of the proposed studies, more than one individual obtained the consent; of these 60, however, only 45 percent identified the names and credentials of those others, while 55 percent ignored the question.

THE PHYSICIAN-RESEARCHER

Our findings on physician-researchers, who comprised almost half of the researchers studied, were no different from our findings for other researchers in terms of what they reported saying to possible participants. When they described their verbal consenting process, 50 percent of the physicians ($n = 37$) incorporated the words "study" or "research." The physician-researcher, as with other researchers, focused on procedures and purpose of the study, while omitting other essential components from the discussion. Physicians asked open-ended questions in 15 cases (20 percent), and their level of ambiguity in describing when they obtained consent was no different from that of the overall sample. However, the physician teams were larger and more likely to indicate categories of people (rather than the names of individuals) who might be involved in obtaining consent.

Discussion

We focused our research effort on examining the written answers that researchers gave about their verbal consenting processes. One of the limitations of our research is that investigators might have minimized their answers because they perceived the form to be merely a bureaucratic procedure. Another possible limitation in interpreting the findings is that people may not be able to describe their behavior. To be aware of what one does and to record it may require a sophistication and an understanding that few people possess.

However, we believe that the responses do measure some degree of reality. While the researchers' descriptions of their behavior do not necessarily reflect what actually happened when they met with subjects, they do show that on a "dress rehearsal" level, the researchers did little to demonstrate knowledge of, or proficiency at, conversing with subjects about informed consent. This finding leads us to speculate that researchers generally do not go beyond the self-reported description. Either researchers did not feel that they had to demonstrate their "best (informed-consent) behavior" to IRBs, or they felt that they *were* demonstrating their best behavior. In either case, it seems safe to assume, then, that these researchers did not know what the IRB was trying to encourage with its questions, and/or how to go about implementing a verbal consenting process. Thus, the researchers' behavior in orchestrating the informed-consent process seems to make it unlikely that their subjects would be able to make autonomous decisions, as Faden and Beauchamp envisioned.[7]

We will review and highlight specific deficits in the self-descriptions of researchers behaviors. These deficits can be viewed as coercive strategies used to ensure that sample sizes were adequate and to dominate subjects or to force compliance with the researchers' wishes.

The researchers did not appear to extend an invitation to participate to their potential subjects, as if researchers thought that the subjects would already know that the researcher was extending an invitation. Yet, to subjects, the professional was likely to appear commanding and demanding of participation.

The researchers did not fully discuss their reasons for wanting to conduct the research with the subjects. Full disclosure about the purpose of the research would naturally have led researchers to more completely describe what information was known and what was unknown. Subjects then would be better equipped to make decisions and engage in dialogue with the researchers.

We also found that researchers talked to subjects primarily about what they wanted the subjects to do. Half of the researchers described discussing procedures. The researchers appeared to place a great deal of value on this component of the process. While, at first sight, this seems to be positive, we believe that it may also represent the coercive nature of the consenting process. Applying Nusbaum's theoretical model to the consenting process, we suggest that researchers spend a lot of time describing the procedures in order to "entice" subjects to participate and to minimize real discussion.[8] At the same time, most researchers failed to discuss risks, benefits, and alternatives with subjects, further minimizing the ability of a subject to make an informed decision.

MINIMIZING CONVERSATION VIA THE "NONQUESTION"

Once the researcher described the research and extended an invitation to the study, the researcher must then assess how informed the potential subject is and whether his or her grasp of the information was accurate and complete enough to allow for a truly informed decision. From our study we conclude that few researchers have any appreciation of the need to assess a potential subject's understanding. Of the researchers, 80 percent demonstrated to us that they relied exclusively on asking closed-ended questions, questions that are likely to preclude conversation.

The classic and overused closed-ended question, "Do you understand?" is, in reality, a non-question. It does not truly invite conversation. Interrogators ask it to gain the self-gratifying answer, "Yes." Closed questions are of little value in evaluating whether another person understands a complex issue. An absurd analogy—imagine that high school tests were designed around the question, "Pupil, do you understand?"—highlights how empty and inadequate the question "Do you understand?" is. The failure of researchers to appreciate the need to assess a possible participant's understanding is extremely troublesome, because it indicates to us how highly coercive the process remains, even with all of the attempts dictated by regulation. By bypassing or sidestepping assessment, the researcher speeds up the process and minimizes any dialogue that could occur. This observation is similar to Katz's argument that a physician communicates mainly in monologue, not dialogue.[9] Katz calls such conversation a monologue because it is one-sided and does not allow patients the opportunity to be partners in their own care or in research. If we apply Nusbaum's model, the avoidance of open-ended questions would be defined as a minimizing strategy that is used to reduce the importance of the interview and maximize the stature of the researcher.[10]

One researcher had a discussion with one of the authors and asked quite frankly what the question on assessing informed consent meant. The author dissected the question and answered explicitly that closed-ended questions did not really promote dialogue, while open-ended questions invited further discussion. The researcher indicated that this still made no sense. So the author gave a specific example and encouraged the researcher to think of other ways to ask the participant questions that would promote dialogue. On the application, the researcher was able to write one open-ended question: "What are the side effects for each of the possible drugs?" Clearly, one-on-one coaching will be needed before any long-term changes in behavior are to be expected.

TIMING CAN BE COERCIVE

An investigator's selection of when to talk to participants about the research and when to obtain written consent can be very coercive. Researchers may find it easier to obtain consent just prior to procedures. However, they need to become more cognizant that the informed-consent process requires allowing subjects a period of time to think and to formulate questions. Mackillop and Johnston pointed out the inherent danger of pressing patients for consent, implying a parallel with conscription.[11] Researchers who demand that subjects sign the consent form immediately are invalidating the process of gaining "informed consent."

DIFFUSION OF RESPONSIBILITY IN OBTAINING CONSENT

We were surprised by the large teams of researchers designated to obtain the written consents. Often, the researchers were not responsible for discussing their studies and obtaining the written consent. The researchers' careless responses, which described categories of people rather than names of individuals, indicate to us that they were unaware that an IRB would not approve a study without assurance that capable staff was involved in the consenting process.

PHYSICIAN'S CONFLICT WHEN WEARING TWO HATS

A highly coercive situation occurs when the researcher is also a person's physician.[12] The subject then undoubtedly would feel obligated to participate and probably would also be concerned that declining to participate could alienate the physician. Indeed, we wondered if this potential conflict of interest between patients and physician/researchers could be improved only if the profession barred physicians from enrolling their own patients into studies. Physician/researchers must become more responsive to the conflict of interest that occurs when they combine the roles of therapist and researcher. Admitting that the conflict in roles exists heightens awareness, but does not necessarily correct injustice. A patient/subject can say no to someone when he or she does not expect to interact with the person in the future, but how can he or she say no when he or she relies on that person for medical care?

Overall, we conclude from the self-reported data that researchers failed to demonstrate that they knew how to educate subjects on the pros and cons of participation. For a potential subject to actually make an informed choice, a researcher must be willing to converse at length to foster the subject's complete understanding. The researcher must be willing to discuss all mandated elements in the written consent form. The researcher must also be willing to assess the subject's understanding, always sensitive to the possibility that he or she was being coercive. Although informed consent relies heavily on effective communication for increasing understanding,[13] we have found, in reality, that any communication is likely to be as truncated and abbreviated as possible. Furthermore, we suggest that the consenting process is rife with behavior that is coercive and that does not promote the subject's autonomous decision making. While it is true that a person may benefit from being in a cutting-edge study, emphasizing the patient's benefits may obscure the predominance of the researcher's benefits.

An Ethical Imperative: How to Effect Change

How can true informed consent be assured? Katz has written eloquently that physician-researchers must strive to increase dialogue with patients.[14] His writings continually emphasize that medical schools must strive to convince doctors that talking with patients is as important as diagnosing them. He has argued that medical education needs to focus on teaching doctors to talk in nonmedical terms and to let patients participate in their own care or research. Katz also believes that physicians need to indicate openly the ambiguities in treatment. A natural extension of his thesis leads us to state that researchers also need to be able to address ambiguity in research by explaining that the reason for research is to reduce a specific area of ambiguity. All researchers, not only physicians, must converse rather than command. Since the authors alone cannot alter medical-school or other professional curricula, we instead propose alternatives that may change the behavior of investigators. We believe that IRBs could and should play a more active and/or proactive role to help researchers learn how to gain a truly informed consent.

First, IRBs' applications and continuing review forms should include questions regarding what researchers say to subjects during discussions of their studies. Careful wording would sensitize researchers to recognize that conversation is an essential, necessary part of the informed-consent process for research.

Secondly, IRBs need to concern themselves more with the potential for coercion inherent in the timing of the consent process. Timing has received little attention from researchers or regulators. IRBs must ask specific questions to determine how to protect potential subjects so that they have the opportunity to think and reflect on the request to participate without being forced to decide immediately. IRBs might generate standard timelines for both acute and nonacute situations, thus directing researchers toward instituting a post-discussion waiting period prior to the subject's signing or declining consent. Along with codifying the consent-process time line, IRBs might direct the use of patients' advocates. Patients' advocates, with no vested interest in the outcome of research, would encourage potential subjects to discuss the pros and cons of enrolling in the studies.

IRBs also should concern themselves about the proliferation of players who are responsible for obtaining written consents. This means that IRBs must understand the situation clearly for their constituents and create training programs for those involved in the consenting process. Perhaps all research team members who are involved with obtaining consent need to obtain research "licenses" for which they have demonstrated at least minimal knowledge.

One of the components of a "research license" might be to have the investigator demonstrate his or her mastery of evaluating a potential subject's level of understanding. Most researchers can readily hear the contrast between open and closed questions. With some effort, they can learn to revise a poor closed-ended question to an open-ended question, thus increasing the likelihood of creating a dialogue. Instead of a typical closed-ended question such as, "Do you understand that neither you nor your doctor will know until the end of the study whether you have been taking the drug or the placebo?" they could learn to ask an open-ended question: "Some people get confused about what it means to be in a study in which some people get the drug and some people only get a fake drug that we call a placebo. Can you tell me what you have heard me say about the placebo? How is it determined who will get the placebo or fake drug and who will get the real drug?"

Another component of the "research license" might be to require that researchers videotape or audiotape themselves during the process of gaining a first or second consent. A knowledgeable communication consultant would then review each tape with the appropriate researcher, examining the content and style of disclosure. If a researcher demonstrated skills in enhancing subjects' autonomy and decision making, she or he could then proceed to enroll subjects into the study. If a researcher asked closed questions, minimized information, and forestalled conversation, then she or he would work on altering his or her discourse. In this scenario, researchers might then produce additional tapes for evaluation. Benson, Roth, and Winslade have also recommended, and successfully used, a feedback strategy in their studies to change the behavior of physician-researchers.[15] While IRBs (and researchers) may initially feel that this is an impossible goal, we think that IRB committee members may also agree that finding new ways to protect human subjects is the *sine qua non*. IRB members and administrators must now implement their roles creatively, protecting subjects even more than our current regulation-driven standards encourage. Indeed, Katz has pointed out that the drafters of the regulations

> should have explicitly warned investigators that taking informed consent seriously in research negotiations requires them to spend considerable time with prospective patient-subjects. They should have provided explicit instructions on the length to which investigators must go in explaining themselves and their intentions so that the patient-subjects will know what is being asked of them. Respect for subjects' human rights dictates that they appreciate that the decision to participate in research entails making a gift for the sake of others.[16]

A third focus of the "research license" class might be a discussion about the relationship between coercion and low rates of refusals by those who are asked to participate in the research. Shimm urges us to collect data on the number of eligible potential subjects versus those who actually do give informed consent to participate.[17] He theorizes that if we had a national data base on refusals to participate in research, we would be able to determine which researchers were enrolling as many subjects into a study as quickly as possible and rendering the informed-consent process suspect. Without such a national data base, we can still scrutinize the rates of refusals, as part of IRBs' continuing the review process. This would be another mechanism that may sensitize researchers to the fact that 100 percent enrollment can mean that the subjects were likely to be under duress to participate. We could also expect that this focus would help study coordinators feel that they did not have to "sell" the study to participants in order to look good to the principal investigator, or "boss."

In addition to altering the behavior of researchers, IRBs can also play a greater role in educating possible participants. First IRBs need to actively study how informed participants appear to be after they have discussed a study with a researcher. This would be the quintessential research question that IRBs must ask. Once IRBs have more information about what subjects understand about research, IRBs can begin to try different means to educate subjects about the research process. Subjects could be informed about their rights, the information needed to make choices, what it means to sign the consent form, and how to participate actively in the decision making. To describe the decision-making process, educators could develop a videotape that would emphasize and encourage asking questions, address the validity of doubts about participation, and suggest that discussion with certain other people is a typical and useful way to make such a complex decision. Others have suggested that IRBs could employ neutral third parties to talk with subjects and foster more active thinking by participants. We think that evaluating the needs of consumers—along with educating them—is a vital outreach activity that IRBs need to establish.

In conclusion, we think that in the past 20 years the groundwork for informed consent has been firmly established. While medical and professional education have a role in continuing to improve the research-consenting process, we firmly believe that the IRB is also in a powerful position to both educate and expect researchers to demonstrate their informed-consent process. IRBs need to develop training programs and to give feedback to individual researchers. IRBs need to do observational studies on researchers and subjects during the consent process to identify specific deficits, because the process is not uniform across the field. High-stress situations may require alternative standards: perhaps in such acute situations IRB-mandated advocates might be required to talk with both subjects and researchers. The role of the human subjects' review process needs to be actively expanded. IRBs must go beyond relying on the rhetoric of protecting study subjects via the consent document. If IRBs can expand their role from merely being administrative gatekeepers to being educators, the consent ritual can become a respectful discussion about the possibility of participating in a research study.

Acknowledgements

We thank Jay Katz, MD, Colleen Cashdollar, Johannah Bomster, MFA, and two unidentified reviewers for their thoughtful critiques of prior versions of this manuscript.

Notes

[5] The primary regulations which protect human subjects are the following: *Department of Health and Human Services Rules and Regulations,* Title 45; *Code of Federal Regulations:* Part 46: Revised 8 March 1983 and amended 18 June 1991. *Food and Drug Administration Rules*

and Regulations. Title 21; *Code of Federal Regulations;* Part 50 and 56; from the *Federal Register,* vol. 46, No. 17, Tuesday, 27 January 1981 and amended 18 June 1991.

[6] Nusbaum and Chenitz, "Grounded Theory;" R. R. Faden and T. L. Beauchamp, *History and Theory of Informed Consent* (Oxford, U.K.: Oxford University Press, 1986); C. L. Briggs, *Learning How to Ask: A Sociolinguistic Appraisal of the Role of the Interview in Social Science Research* (Cambridge: Cambridge University Press, 1986); E. F. Cassell, *Talking with Patients: Volume 1: The Theory of Doctor-Patient Communication & Volume 2: Clinical Technique* (Cambridge, Mass: MIT Press, 1985); L. R. Frey et al., *Investigational Communication: An Introduction to Research Methods* (Englewood Cliffs, N.J.: Prentice-Hall, 1986); S. W. Littlejohn, *Theories of Human Communication* (Belmont, Calif.: Wadsworth, 1989); D. Pendleton and J. Hasler, eds., *Doctor-Patient Communication* (London: Academic Press, 1983); C. Selltiz et al., *Research Methods in Social Relations* (New York, N.Y.: Holt Rinehart and Winston, 1984); C. West, *Routine Complications: Troubles with Talk between Doctors and Patients* (Bloomington, Ind.: Indiana University Press, 1984); J. Katz, *The Silent World of Doctor and Patient* (New York: Free Press, 1984); and J. Katz, " 'Ethics and Clinical Research' Revisited: A Tribute to Henry Beecher," *Hastings Center Report* 23 (1993): 32–39. All of the above explore communication concerns.

[7] Faden and Beauchamp, *History and Theory.*

[8] Nusbaum and Chenitz, "Grounded Theory."

[9] Katz, *Silent World.*

[10] Nusbaum and Chenitz, "Grounded Theory."

[11] W. J. MacKillop and P. A. Johnston, "Ethical Problems in Clinical Research: The Need for Empirical Studies of the Clinical Trial Process," *Journal of Chronic Diseases* 39 (1986): 177–88.

[12] Katz, *Silent World.*

[13] Faden and Beauchamp, *History and Theory;* Katz, *Silent World.*

[14] Katz, *Silent World.*

[15] Benson, Roth and Winslade, "Informed Consent in Psychiatric Research: Preliminary Findings from an Ongoing Investigation," *Social Science and Medicine* 20 (1985): 1331–41.

[16] Katz, "'Ethics and Clinical Research' Revisited."

[17] D. S. Shimm and R. G. Spece, Jr., "Rate of Refusal to Participate in Clinical Trials," *IRB* (March–April 1992): 7–9.

Chapter 5
Treatment of Vulnerable Subject Populations

5.1 INTRODUCTION

The preceding chapter presented some of the issues surrounding human subject protections. Human subjects should be used in research only if the risk/expected-benefit ratio is favorable and if provisions are made to reduce all possible risks to human subjects during their participation in the research. Human subjects should be recruited without coercion. Coercion can occur in a number of ways, such as when potentially intimidating authority figures solicit subject participation or offer inducements that undermine the ability of the subjects to decline participation. Informed consent statements, either oral or written, should include a description of the possible risks and benefits of subjects' participation, the data-collection process, and a clear explanation that the subjects have the freedom to leave the experimental situation at any time without loss of benefit. An understanding of these facts, and consent to participation in light of this understanding, is the groundwork for informed, voluntary participation. Finally, privacy and confidentiality of experimental data should be guaranteed to all subjects, within the limits of the law.

All of the above provisions assume a great deal of autonomy on the part of the prospective research subjects. The presumption is that the research subjects are in a position to make autonomous decisions regarding participation based upon an understanding of a consent document. However, this ideal of autonomy is not always applicable, even in the best of circumstances. Vulnerable subject populations often start out as less-than-autonomous individuals, and thus are not able to act with full autonomy in choosing to become research subjects. In such cases, conventional methods by which researchers protect the interests of research subjects may be insufficient. For example, mentally disabled individuals may not be able to fully understand the risks and expected benefits of participation in research. Children may not be able to make informed choices based upon the typically complex claims in informed consent documents. Institutionalized individuals, such as prisoners, may not be in a position to consent voluntarily to participation in research. As they are not always able to protect their own interests, subject populations such as these create a special set of problems for researchers.

In some cases the problems mentioned above may be solved by choosing a different population of research subjects. There may be no reason to single out research subjects from a particularly vulnerable population when those from an autonomous population are available for study. Researchers should first ask whether their subject population is a convenience population that has been chosen in part because they are more vulnerable, or less likely to refuse participation. Captive populations of students, prisoners, interns, and residents make the job of subject selection easier for researchers, but the ethics of using such populations are questionable if the subjects are unable to make a voluntary decision to participate. Using a less vulnerable population can allay some of the ethical concerns; however, this strategy is not always effective.

There are two common reasons for choosing a vulnerable population as the subject population in research. First, justice may demand that a vulnerable subject population be studied. For example, it is possible that clinical trials have already taken place establishing that a particular drug or therapy is efficacious for a population that is able to consent autonomously. The results of these trials may not be applicable to some vulnerable populations, such as children or pregnant women. Justice requires that the benefits of medical science not be arbitrarily withheld from any one group. Yet, without testing drugs or new therapies on vulnerable populations, scientists may not be able to prove the efficacy of these experimental treatments or determine safe dosage levels across different subject populations.

A second reason that a vulnerable population would be called upon to serve as research subjects is that some generalizable knowledge can be obtained only after studying such a population. It would be impossible to learn, for example, of the success of a new treatment for schizophrenia, without actually testing the treatment on people who have this disorder. It would be impossible to learn about successful methods for counseling prisoners without actually performing research on prisoners.

In this chapter, several but not all classes of vulnerable populations are examined. Responsible researchers should first consider the circumstances of their subject populations to determine if the populations are vulnerable. Are the subjects in a population with inherent problems in comprehending information, a population that is inherently unable to make voluntary decisions, or a population that has historically been unable to exercise autonomy? The factors that make a population vulnerable tell a researcher a great deal about the steps that must be taken to protect the interests of the subjects. It is also notable that the classes of vulnerable populations discussed in this chapter should not be perceived as homogeneous populations. Research subjects are individuals, with individual strengths, weaknesses, concerns, and questions. Therefore, responsible researchers should not overgeneralize about their subject populations. The discussion of this chapter focuses on what makes each population vulnerable, and some of the ethical challenges in performing research on each population. Some practical solutions are offered, both in performing research on these populations and in locating additional ethical issues relevant to each vulnerable subject group. The reader will observe that methods of protection for some vulnerable population groups may be similarly effective for other vulnerable populations.

A final word on the vulnerable subject populations discussed in this chapter: As mentioned above, vulnerable subject populations may be vulnerable for any number of reasons, such as their inability to comprehend information or make voluntary choices or a group history that has prevented them from exercising autonomy. Women and members of some minority populations fall into the last category. The Tuskegee Syphilis Study, discussed in section 1.2, is only part of the shameful historical record of oppression of minority populations as research subjects in the United States. Because of the historical oppression of women and minority populations, researchers should be cautious when soliciting the participation of research subjects from these populations. At the same time, we contend that there is *nothing* about being a woman or a member of a minority group that inherently compromises one's autonomy in the way that being a young child or a person with a mental disorder compromises autonomy. Since the focus of this chapter is subjects whose autonomy is inherently compromised, we have not focused on the special circumstances of women or minority populations here. Readers are directed to one of the essays accompanying the text, Lisa A. Eckenwiler's "Attention to Difference and Women's Consent to Research" for a discussion of those issues.

5.2   YOUNG CHILDREN

Researchers may wish to circumvent the ethical problems associated with using children as research subjects by simply not using them and dealing only with autonomous adults in their research. However, in recent years there has been a greater emphasis on involving children in research projects. Considerations of justice demand that more children be used as research subjects, so that they are able to benefit from scientific advances to the same extent as adults. The National Institutes of Health (NIH) has responded to this newfound interest in the use of children as research subjects by placing the onus on researchers to defend the lack of child research subjects in NIH-sponsored research, when the researcher intentionally restricts subject pools to adults.

'Minor' is a legal term, meaning an individual who has not yet reached the age of majority. Minor children then are individuals who cannot legally consent to participate in research. However, minors can be in very different circumstances. In this section we will consider the use of younger minors as research subjects. In the following section we will examine the ethical considerations of using older minors, adolescents, as research subjects.

Children are a vulnerable subject group for a number of reasons. First, very young children may not be able to understand the risk/expected-benefit ratio, the procedures that they will be subjected to as part of research, or the entirely voluntary nature of their participation. Because they may be unable to understand these facts, any consent that they give to participate in research may not be *informed* consent. Insofar as some children are able to nod and agree superficially to participate in research, without fully comprehending their role as research subjects or making a decision on the basis of their understanding, what appears to be consent on their part may not be informed. However, it seems inaccurate to say that these children have no role in the consent process. Young children, while unable to offer informed consent, are nonetheless able to offer **assent** to participation in research. Assent is mere agreement to participate. Researchers should get assent from children who will be participating in research in most cases, especially when the potential subjects may not directly benefit from participation and are able to understand some portion of the risk/expected-benefit calculation. Research on children, such as infants or toddlers, who are so young that they are unable to offer assent does not require it. However, as discussed below, this type of research should also incorporate other considerations, such as those that involve the waiving of assent or informed consent.

Legal guardians should be solicited for informed consent on behalf of children. Both parents should offer consent, unless one is not reasonably available, for example, unknown, or incompetent. However, this is not to say that children have no say in the decision to participate as research subjects. If a child is asked to serve as a research subject and says no, then in most cases it is inappropriate to use that child in research. Failure to say "no" should not be construed as assent—assent is a positive, active agreement to participate. The Nuremberg Code makes it clear that the responsibility to obtain informed consent rests with the researcher. Therefore, "passive assent," in which children are expected to be willing participants unless they explicitly decline participation, puts too great a burden on children.

Just as informed consent documents should be written in language that the readers can understand, children's assent should be similarly obtained using language that is appropriate to the age group that is being solicited for participation in research. Researchers may wish to double-check any assent script, replacing words like 'participate' and 'observe' with words like 'join in' and 'look at', to cite just two examples. Some words may be coercive, however, and should be avoided. Children who are asked to 'help out the adults' may feel pressure to assent. Thus, researchers should be careful to check their assent scripts not only for comprehensibility, but also for subtle forms of coercion.

Questions of assent should be put to children orally when children who are not old enough to read are asked to participate in research. As with adults who are asked for informed consent, the assent should be solicited by individuals who are not authority figures, so that the children will not feel pressure to participate. Parents, teachers, physicians, and the like are all authority figures to whom children may be reluctant to say "no." However, avoiding these conflicts may be difficult in some circumstances, for some children look upon all adults as authority figures.

There are some cases in which it is permissible to waive children's assent to participate in research. In cases in which the children will benefit directly from participation, and cannot receive these benefits except via the participation in the research, assent may not be necessary. For example, Phase II and III clinical trials, which hold out the possibility of direct benefit to the subjects, and for which these benefits are not believed to be available using non-experimental methods, may not require child assent for child participation. Additionally, it may be permissible to override children's dissent if they will receive these benefits only by virtue of participating as research subjects.

The requirement for parental informed consent may be waived only if the research in question meets the following three criteria. First, the research must involve no more than minimal risk. Second, a waiver of parental consent is permissible if the waiver would not adversely affect the rights and welfare of the subjects. Children have the same rights as adults when they are used as research subjects. They have the right to an assessment of the risk/expected-benefit ratio, to voluntary participation, and to understand the procedures to which they will be exposed during the research process. However, as noted during the discussion of deception research in section 4.3, these rights can be waived if it appears that there would be greater benefit to the subjects in waiving the rights than in maintaining the rights. In the case of deception research, the right to informed consent before the research occurs is waived, because the benefits of the research are presumed to outweigh the harms of not obtaining informed consent before the research takes place. A third, more complex requirement for waiving informed consent is that the research could not practicably be carried out without the waiver. This is not to allow an exception whenever obtaining informed consent from the parents is difficult or time-consuming or when the researcher is under a publication deadline that makes it inconvenient to spend the time required to obtain both assent and informed consent. Rather, the exceptional case is one in which the parents are somehow not available at all for informed consent. One example would be research on children who have run away from home. The parents of these subjects are not usually available to give informed consent. It would be prohibitive to expect a researcher to obtain informed consent from the parents of children who have run away from home. However, there may be benefits, both to the subjects directly as well as a contribution to generalizable knowledge that could help future runaways, if this research takes place. Thus, a waiver of parental informed consent may be appropriate in this case. There is a fourth criterion for waiving informed consent, which applies in some, but not all, cases. Waivers of informed consent are permissible only if, when appropriate, the subject will be provided with additional pertinent information after participating in the research. Again, cases of deception research, discussed in section 4.3, prove a helpful guide in this case. After deception research takes place, researchers debrief their subjects by telling them the nature of their participation, and allow the subjects to make an informed choice, albeit *post hoc*, about the use of data obtained during their participation. In cases in which informed consent is waived, it may be appropriate to give additional information after data collection has taken place, which will further protect the rights of the subjects.

Researchers should be aware of both the psychological and the physiological differences between children and adults when undertaking research. This recommendation is an elaboration of a previous recommendation: researchers should be familiar with their area of study before undertaking projects that involve human research subjects. A lack of familiarity with the area of study could result in research subjects being placed in greater harm than they otherwise would if the researcher were entirely conversant with the area of study. The physiological differences between children and adults should be quite apparent to researchers. For example, when considering the possible side effects of a drug, it is fairly elementary to recognize that children are smaller than adults, and as such may have a stronger reaction to some drugs than an adult might.

The psychological differences between children and adults are not as obvious in some cases. The level of psychological maturity, degree of trust, self-concept, and respect for authority may be very different when dealing with young children as opposed to adults. These and other differences may have tremendous impact on the ethical treatment of child research subjects. One example may be the psychological differences that would affect a debriefing when engaging in deception research on children. It is important to debrief subjects as soon as possible after a deception study, because the nonvoluntary nature of deception studies demands that subjects be offered full disclosure as soon as possible. However, the researcher who is focusing on children in a deception study may wish to re-examine the rule that says that subjects should always be debriefed after deception studies. Is the debriefing ultimately going to benefit the subject, or might it do the subject more harm than good? Some young children may be harmed by a debriefing, especially when they are told by adults, whom they trust, that in fact the adults lied to them during the course of the research process. Might children be better served by not being debriefed in some research studies? Awareness of the differences between children and adults, both physiologically and psychologically, is a requirement of all responsible research.

As mentioned in the previous chapter, what counts as a harm may be subjective. Implicitly, what counts as a benefit may also be subjective. When soliciting the participation of children, it should be clear that *what counts as coercion is subjective;* a seemingly noncoercive incitement for participation may be quite coercive to a child. Researchers should be careful not to offer inducements for participation which are coercive for younger individuals. Candy, free movie tickets, or stuffed animals don't mean that much to adults, but can be extremely powerful incentives for children. Incentives may be appropriate, but an unduly attractive incentive may compromise an already vulnerable subject. The unique social situations of children should also be taken into account by researchers when performing research on children. Research on children may directly or indirectly be research on the other members of that child's family, and as such the researcher may need to obtain informed consent from other family members in addition to the child. An example of such a project was discussed in section 1.4. The project described involved giving cameras to children, allowing them to explore the creative process. However, giving young children cameras may yield images of the children's families which the family may wish to remain private. In light of this type of episode, researchers may wish to obtain informed consent from the entire family for some research involving children.

5.3   ADOLESCENTS

A different set of ethical concerns arises with respect to adolescents. First, adolescents have emerging cognitive, psychological, and social abilities that may allow them to provide genuine consent, and not merely assent, on their own behalf. However, legally adolescents are minors and as such cannot offer informed consent to participate in research except when they have become emancipated through special circumstances. Those who are already married or have obtained legally autonomous status by virtue of performing activities that demonstrate adult responsibilities (such as being financially self-supporting or raising children) may legally offer informed consent to research. Additionally, some adolescents may petition for "mature minor" status. Mature minor status designates the minor as one who is psychologically capable of making important decisions, such as health care decisions. With mature minor status adolescents may give informed consent to participate as research subjects.

Adolescents who are legally emancipated or who have mature minor status are the exception, not the rule. For this reason, researchers should be aware that even if adolescents are psychologically able to offer informed consent the researcher may still have the responsibility of obtaining informed consent from the parents or guardians of the adolescents while obtaining assent from the adolescent subjects. The researcher is well advised to learn the applicable laws in the states in which the research is taking place before performing research on adolescents who may or may not have the legal status to consent to certain types of procedures.

An important consideration for adolescent research subjects is privacy and confidentiality. On one hand, since parents are the legal representatives who are offering informed consent, they may be entitled to data gathered during the research process. On the other hand, adolescents may not wish for their parents to be informed of the data generated during a research study. Many adolescents guard their privacy carefully and would not be comfortable disclosing to their parents even seemingly innocuous data, such as food, music, or clothing preferences. Furthermore, in some cases release of data about adolescents may increase the risk to those adolescents, thereby violating the spirit of beneficence that guides the need for informed consent and data disclosure. For example, adolescents who answer questions about illegal drug use, sexual activity, or their relationships with their parents may not wish for their parents to be informed of their answers. Some answers may put the adolescents at risk of harm, because parents may react negatively when they receive the data about their children. Researchers who are unable to guarantee privacy to their research subjects may collect tainted data, as sophisticated adolescents attempt to alter their answers in light of the perceived lack of privacy. Tainted data will not yield generalizable knowledge, and one of the definitive aims of performing the research may be thwarted. One solution is that researchers should make clear in the informed consent documents, which parents are signing, what privacy and confidentiality protections the researchers are guaranteeing the adolescent subjects. The adolescents' assent documents should reflect the same information. This will allow the parents to make a choice about their children's participation knowing that some of the data may be withheld from them, and it will encourage the adolescents to give honest responses in light of this assurance of confidentiality. Another solution is to collect all data that deals with sensitive subject matter anonymously, so that confidentiality can be maintained for all adolescent subjects. Reporting anonymous data in the aggregate may provide some of the protections of confidentiality that the adolescent subjects desire. This strategy may work in some large-scale studies, but studies that use smaller samples or demographic identifiers that may link subjects to data may not appropriately utilize this methodology.

A changing sense of self, issues of privacy, and emerging doubts about authority figures may cause adolescents, in particular, to be suspicious of researchers, and assent documents may be written accordingly. These evolving psychological factors may also make adolescents more sensitive to peer pressure, which can manifest itself in subtle coercion to participate (or not participate) in a research project. Researchers should be careful to ensure that the participation of their adolescent research subjects is entirely voluntary. Insofar as it is possible, researchers should allow research subjects to participate in research projects anonymously, so that any stigma associated with participation is diminished. One recommendation is to allow members of the adolescent population to review and offer suggestions about the informed consent document before it is actually used.

Finally, many of the recommendations and protections in section 5.2, on children, may also be applicable to adolescents. Waivers of informed consent may be appropriate if obtaining assent alone can protect the rights and welfare of the adolescent subjects. Assent scripts should be written in language that adolescents can understand. Debriefings after deception research may do more harm than good. These and similar considerations, though not applicable to every adolescent population, are matters that researchers should take into account before using an adolescent population. Once again, the best advice is to know the subject population before data collection begins. Some 13-year-olds are surprisingly sophisticated, others are less so. It is the responsibility of the researcher to know his or her subject population and to take the appropriate measures so as to ensure that the subjects are as well-protected as possible.

5.4   THE ELDERLY

The elderly, like adolescents, are not a homogeneous group. Some elderly are entirely competent to assess risk/expected-benefit ratios of participation, are able to autonomously volunteer to participate in research, and are no more likely to be harmed by participation in research than their younger counterparts. Other elderly participants may not have full mental or physical capacities or are more likely to be harmed by their participation in some study designs, and as such they will require special consideration as research subjects.

Perhaps the most important step that the responsible researcher can take when soliciting the participation of elderly research subjects is to recognize that informed consent is an on-going process. Informed consent should be understood as much more than a document that is signed once and then stuffed in a file cabinet so that the data-collection process can begin. Responsible researchers should continue the informed-consent process during the data-collection phase; each personal contact with the research subjects can be an opportunity to review the data-collection procedures, the risk/expected-benefit ratio, and the voluntary nature of the subjects' participation. This on-going conversation will allow the researcher to correct for any problems that may arise because of forgetfulness on the part of the subjects, or former misunderstandings about the research project. Additional considerations in obtaining informed consent, such as documents with large type size, may also be appropriate for some elderly subjects.

Just as adolescents are, by and large, a subject population that views authority figures with mistrust and suspicion, some members of elderly populations may view authority figures with a surprising amount of trust and respect. This may be due to generational differences: Previous generations have granted authority figures more respect than younger generations do, perhaps because many elderly are themselves authority figures, and as such believe that authority figures are not as bad as some people think. The responsible researcher will be cautious, because subject populations that are more likely to follow the advice of physicians, psychologists, or research professors may not be participating in research voluntarily or may be doing so based upon mistaken impressions. One example is the elderly patient who is invited to participate in a research study by her physician. She may ask her physician questions about the study, the nature of the study, and whether she should participate. Even the most conscientious physician, careful not to say anything coercive to his patients, may end up saying something confusing to his patients. Consider the following exchange:

> **Physician:** So, do you understand what would be expected of you if you participate in this study?
> **Patient:** Yes, I think I do. I just cannot decide if I should participate or not.
> **Physician:** I understand. It is a difficult decision.
> **Patient:** Oh, doctor, I just don't know! What would you do if you were me?
> **Physician:** Well, if I were you, I think I'd participate.

This exchange may be seen as an endorsement to participate, bordering on co-ercion, by a person who is respectful of authority figures. This may also be an ex-ample of the "two hats" problem, discussed in sections 4.3 and 4.4, as well as in case 3.1. Subject populations who are more likely to defer to authority figures, or blur the line between authorities in one arena and authorities in another, fur-ther exacerbate the two hats problem.

5.5   PREGNANT WOMEN

As mentioned in section 5.1, some individuals may not be inherently nonau-tonomous, but nonetheless may be members of populations which require spe-cial treatment. Women and members of minority populations may fall under the category. Pregnant women may also fall under the category.

If women are excluded from research studies because they are, or might be, pregnant, then an unjust state of affairs may result. Women who are or may be pregnant will then not reap the benefits of advances in generalizable knowledge. As a result, it is important that women who are or may be pregnant serve as re-search subjects. However, when including women who are or may be pregnant, researchers must make special considerations based on three factors. The first is that the risk/expected-benefit ratio of a study may be different for pregnant women than for other subjects. The second is that the fetuses are not voluntary participants in any research, and precautions must be taken to ensure that the fetuses are subject to minimal risk. The third is that both the mothers and the fa-thers may have a role in providing informed consent for the mothers' participa-tion in research.

The researcher is responsible for assessing the potential risks of allowing pregnant women to participate as research subjects. Some research studies do not pose greater risk to pregnant women than to women who are not preg-nant. For example, psychological studies that are expected to induce moderate stress or include moderate exercise should not pose a greater risk to pregnant women than to anyone else. Other studies, such as some drug studies or max-imal exercise, could have more harmful effects on pregnant women than on other subjects. Thus, the researcher's first responsibility is to assess the risk/expected-benefit ratio from the perspective of pregnant women. If the ratio changes by virtue of the fact that the research subjects are pregnant, then this fact should be incorporated into the informed consent for the study. The informed consent documents for projects that involve women of childbearing age should adequately address the possibility of harm to both the study subjects and the fetuses.

Since the fetuses cannot give informed consent, it is important that their risk be minimized in all cases. As discussed in section 4.3, *nonvoluntary* participation is that to which subjects did not explicitly consent, but can be reasonably ex-pected to consent to in the future. Participation in most deception research is presumed to be non-voluntary. Strictly speaking, the participation of fetuses is not non-voluntary either, because no one believes that fetuses will later be debriefed and offer *post hoc* consent. Because fetuses are participants, albeit neither voluntary nor non-voluntary, their risks should be minimized. A notable exception may be those cases in which the research is undertaken for the health benefits of the women.

In addition to posing minimal risk for a fetuses, the informed consent for participation in research must be administered both to the mothers and the fathers for the participation of pregnant women. There are some exceptions to this rule. For example, if the research is undertaken for the health benefit of the mothers, or the fathers are not reasonably available, then this requirement can be waived. The ethical justification for such exceptions should be clear: If research is of greater minimal risk but may be of direct benefit to the research subjects (the mothers) then the mothers should be able to approve their own participation, as long as there are no greater than minimal risks for the fetuses.

5.6   INDIVIDUALS WITH MENTAL DISABILITIES

Different cognitive disabilities have different symptoms, and consequently the protections that should be afforded to persons with mental disabilities vary. For example, a mental disorder such as depression would raise different concerns than Alzheimer's Disease would. As with any research subjects, the first and best option is for them to personally offer informed consent to participation. However, if the subjects are unable to offer consent due to a mental disorder that affects autonomous decisionmaking, a few guidelines may be helpful in soliciting participation.

The researcher should first assess the cognitive abilities of the prospective research subjects. Some mental disorders may result in a complete inability to render an informed decision to participate. Other subjects may have a fluctuating capacity to make such decisions—better one day, and not as strong the next. The researcher, or another trained professional, should examine any potential subjects with mental disorders to assess their decision-making capacity. It may be the case that subjects can make a decision to participate, but that this capacity is not static and needs to be assessed on a continuing basis. The decision-making capacity of the subjects should be under continuing review by the researcher, by a trained professional who can monitor the subjects' capacity, and by an Institutional Review Board (IRB) that can oversee the experimental procedures and informed consent process. The requirement that the subjects be able to withdraw from the study at any time is complicated in some cases for persons of declining mental capacity. What should the researcher do when the subjects have the capacity to make an informed decision at the beginning of a research protocol, but as the protocol progresses, the subjects' ability to understand deteriorates? Is the inability to make a voluntary decision throughout the experimental procedure sufficient to withdraw the subjects from the study? What if the subjects have made clear to the researcher the desire to remain in the study, despite the fact that they anticipate the loss of their capacity to reflect on this decision? In such cases, the researcher has a responsibility to understand not only the current, but future, decision-making capacities of the subjects.

As suggested in section 5.2, members of the target population may be helpful in assessing any informed consent statement for readability and comprehensiveness. When assessing the capacity of potential subjects to make an informed decision, the researcher should recognize that the ability to make an autonomous decision is relative to the decision that is being made. For example, some individuals are entirely autonomous when choosing the clothing that they wish to wear, or the food that they will eat, but are not autonomous when making more significant decisions, such as how to spend a large inheritance. Similarly, some individuals may be autonomous with regard to their decision to participate in minimal risk research, but their decision-making capacity is questionable when they are asked to consider their participation in placebo-controlled cross-over studies that do not hold out the possibility of direct benefit and pose greater than minimal risk. Thus, assessing the decision-making capacity of subjects should take into consideration their abilities and the decision under consideration.

There may be several barriers to informed decisionmaking for persons with mental disorders. First, the subjects may be unable to comprehend fully the risk/expected-benefit ratio or its implications for their participation. Some seemingly minimal risks may appear far more daunting to individuals with some mental disorders. Audiotaping, videotaping, or taking a small amount of blood may seem innocuous to some persons, but to others these experimental procedures may be prohibitive. Again, the best recommendation for researchers is to know their subjects well before they attempt to solicit participation in research projects. The assessment of the risk/expected-benefit ratio is further complicated in the case of persons with some types of mental disorders, in that they may be able to understand the information regarding the risks of the experimental procedures but demonstrate a lack of interest or attention to these risks. For example, a person with clinical depression may recognize that an experimental design involves greater than minimal risk but may simply not care about these risks. This attitude may demonstrate a lack of decision-making capacity, inasmuch as fully autonomous individuals typically do demonstrate concern about possible risks.

A second consideration is that the subjects may be institutionalized and as a result may have severe constraints on voluntary decisionmaking. As mentioned earlier, researchers should avoid any type of coercion when recruiting subjects. Additional considerations may also be in order to avoid the "two hats" problem. Finally, given the negative stigma associated with mental illness, the researcher may be required to undertake special procedures to ensure the privacy and confidentiality of the data and subject identifiers. Audiotapes and videotapes that do not mask the identity of the research subjects should be disposed of if the researcher promises confidentiality.

In the event that the subjects are unable to offer informed consent, the researcher may rely on a surrogate to make the decision to participate on behalf of the subjects. A surrogate is a stand-in decision maker, typically the legal guardian of an individual who has been determined to lack significant decision-making capacity. Surrogates are often chosen because they have a special relationship to the person whose interests they are representing. As such, they are able to articulate what the individual would have wanted, if he or she were able to offer consent. As not all legally authorized representatives stand in this special relationship to the subjects, lack of knowledge about subjects' beliefs and preferences could render representatives morally unqualified to make surrogate decisions.

Even in cases in which the surrogates intimately know the preferences of the subjects, the surrogates' consent alone may not be sufficient to allow the participation of some individuals with mental disabilities. If the subjects did not make advance declarations that authorized participation in research, it may be inappropriate to use them, especially in research that poses greater than minimal risk, or does not hold out the prospect of direct benefit to the subjects. Also, advance declarations may lack specificity regarding the type or scope of research that the subjects would have agreed to, and consequently, advanced directives for participation as research subjects are not always illuminating. Finally, even with a surrogate's consent, it is appropriate to obtain assent directly from the subjects, as long as they are able to offer it.

5.7   INSTITUTIONALIZED INDIVIDUALS

The use of prisoners as research subjects is problematic. Serving as imprisoned research subjects may be construed as punishment beyond that which prisoners are expected to serve or as a reward to which not all prisoners are entitled. Researchers should carefully consider the risk/expected-benefit ratio when using prisoners as research subjects, as it may not be the same ratio the research would generate for non-prisoners.

Additionally, prisoners are often beholden to others. Many everyday activities that non-prisoners autonomously choose to engage in are determined for prisoners by others. As a result, prisoners may feel coerced into participating as research subjects. For example, in ordinary circumstances when a physician asks a patient to participate in a research project, the patient may feel undue coercion from the physician. However, even when a physician exerts undue authority, directly or indirectly, it would be an extreme reaction for the patient to fear that if he did not agree to participate as a research subject all medical care would be withheld. In a prison setting, in which there is only one physician, a prisoner may feel additional coercion when asked by the prison physician to participate in a research project. The prisoner may feel that if he declines to participate, then there will be some type of retaliation. For this reason, researchers should take special care to ensure that participation of prisoners truly is voluntary.

Finally, coercion in prison settings may result from unduly enticing rewards offered to prisoners for their participation. As discussed in section 5.2, what counts as great enticement for children may seem fairly innocuous to an adult. For prisoners, a similar problem arises, by virtue of the fact that prisoners live in a highly controlled environment. Thus, even seemingly mundane rewards for participation, such as novel food or clothing items, could be coercive for prisoners. Researchers are well-advised to consult with the prison authorities who are in charge of the potential subject population, to make sure that the researchers are not unjustly enticing involvement in the research study. As always, the best advice is to be well-acquainted with the concerns of the population of study before embarking on the research.

5.8   SUMMARY

In many cases, research subjects who are not able to make autonomous decisions about participation should not be used as research subjects. However, this view does not take into account the fact that justice often demands that nonautonomous individuals be used as research subjects. When using research subjects of compromised autonomy, responsible researchers will take precautions so that the rights and welfare of their subjects are protected.

Minor children should offer assent, when they can, to participation in research, and their legal guardians should offer informed consent for the children. Denial of assent should preclude the use of children; however, mere failure to deny assent should not be construed as assent. Assent should be obtained in a way that is appropriate to the age and cognitive abilities of the children. Assent may be waived in special circumstances, such as for research that holds out the possibility of direct benefit to the subjects. Additionally, informed consent may be waived from the parents if the research could not practicably be carried out without the waiver, provided that the research involves no more than minimal risk, the waiver does not adversely affect the children's rights or welfare, and, when appropriate, additional information will be provided after the research has been performed. These, and other special provisions, should appropriately incorporate the researcher's knowledge about the physically, psychologically, and socially unique aspects of children as research subjects.

Adolescents have greater self-concept, greater abilities to make decisions, and may have more complex social networks than younger children, all of which may affect their roles as research subjects. However, most adolescents are legally unable to choose to participate as research subjects. Privacy and confidentiality, even from the parents or guardians who are offering informed consent, are important to adolescents. The best advice to researchers is to know the subject population well, so that the concerns of the population can be appropriately addressed.

Researchers may also need to take special care with populations of elderly individuals who serve as research subjects, due to the possibility of forgetfulness or mere misunderstanding. Voluntariness may also be an issue that merits additional consideration. Researchers should be especially mindful of coercive practices, as well as the two hats problem in such cases.

Pregnant women are not usually a non-autonomous class; however, they may merit special consideration. The possibility that otherwise innocuous experiments would result in greater harms, the fact that the fetuses cannot voluntarily consent to participation in research, and the interests of the fathers all play an important role in the selection of pregnant women as research subjects.

When using individuals with mental disabilities as research subjects, researchers should first assess whether the subjects are able to offer informed consent on their own, keeping in mind that this capacity may fluctuate. Surrogate decision makers may be called upon to offer informed consent, but they should be asked to do so only with caution and in general only when the experiment involves minimal risk or direct benefit to the subjects.

Finally, prisoners may also be used as research subjects, but only after special considerations are made. Coercion is a significant barrier to autonomous decision making prisoners, and as a result, their voluntary participation should be absolutely assured.

5.9 CASE STUDIES

Case 5.1: Casey wishes to run a series of experiments that will calibrate the degree of mental functioning in patients with Alzheimer's Disease. Her study will take two years, during which time she will administer the same educational test at four-month intervals to patients with Alzheimer's. During the first session, Mrs. H. is surprisingly lucid. Mrs. H. chats with Casey, and it is clear that Mrs. H understands the informed consent document that she has signed. At the second session, four months later, Mrs. H. does not remember Casey, but she does remember the experiment and is happy to perform the tasks involved. But at the third session, Mrs. H keeps asking Casey why Casey "is making her do this" and wants to know when she can finally stop. Mrs. H. is entirely able to perform the tasks, she just doesn't seem to want to do them any more. Casey knows that when Mrs. H. was lucid she was happy to accommodate. Casey also knows from Mrs. H.'s nurses that Mrs. H. "just isn't who she used to be." Should the prior consent that Casey received from Mrs. H. still stand? Should Casey withdraw Mrs. H. from the study? What if Mrs. H.'s spouse, her legally authorized surrogate, insists that Mrs. H. stay in the study, because "that is what she would have wanted—she was a great believer in education"?

Case 5.2: Both adolescents and their parents are invited to take part in an experiment on communication styles and conflict resolution. In the first part of the study, a parent and an adolescent each write a one-page description of a conflict they have had in the past. The researcher reads the papers and then chooses one of the issues as a starting-point for a discussion. The parent-adolescent pairs are then brought together and videotaped with a moderator who asks about the conflict. The moderator attempts to provoke an argument, so that the videotape can record the method of communication between the parent and adolescent, and the means by which they resolve the conflict. In exchange for participation, the parent and the adolescent each receive $40.00. Keeping in mind that the researcher wants the arguments to be as authentic as possible, what should the pairs be told about the experiment before they agree to participate? What are the issues surrounding the voluntary participation of the adolescents?

REFERENCES AND FURTHER READING

Paul S. Appelbaum, "Drug-Free Research in Schizophrenia: An Overview of the Controversy," *IRB: Human Subjects Research,* volume 18, no. 1, January-February 1996, pp. 1–5.

Stephan Haimowitz, Susan J. Delano, and John M. Oldham, "Uninformed Decisionmaking: The Case of Surrogate Research Consent," *Hastings Center Report,* volume 27, no. 6, 1997, pp. 9–16.

Allen M. Hornblum, *Acres of Skin: Human Experiments at Holmesburg Prison: A Story of Abuse and Exploitation in the Name of Medical Science,* New York: Routledge, 1998.

Kathleen Mammel and David W. Kaplan, "Research Consent by Adolescent Minors and Institutional Review Boards," *Journal of Adolescent Health,* volume 17, 1995, pp. 323–30.

Office for Protection from Research Risks, *Protecting Human Subjects: Institutional Review Board Guidebook,* Washington, DC: Government Printing Office, 1993.

B. Stanley and J. E. Sieber, *The Ethics of Research on Children and Adolescents,* Newbury Park, CA: Sage Publications, 1991.

A Relational Perspective on Ethics-in-Science Decisionmaking for Research with Vulnerable Populations

Celia B. Fisher

In the wake of recent revelations concerning the government radiation studies[1] and concerns that diminished public trust in human subjects research may jeopardize the willingness of our most vulnerable citizens to become research participants, the President has appointed a National Bioethics Advisory Commission to review the adequacy of current federal guidelines for the protection of human

Celia B. Fisher, "A Relational Perspective on Ethics-in-Science Decisionmaking for Research with Vulnerable Populations," *IRB: A Review of Human Subjects Research,* 19, no. 5, September–October 1997, 1–4.

subjects. This article advances the argument that to insure that such protections are indeed adequate, revised research regulations will need to reflect the perspectives of those who design, implement, and participate in research. In the everyday practice of science, investigators often find that guidelines designed to protect vulnerable children and adults inadvertently create institutional obstacles that limit participants' autonomy and access to research protocols that may advance scientific understanding and treatment of their disorders. Moreover, healthy adults, adults with physical or mental disabilities, children and adolescents, and individuals from diverse economic and cultural backgrounds react differently to controlled procedures, and their perspectives can differ from those of well-meaning decisionmakers. Creating federal regulations without considering the expectations of and special relationship between investigator and participant thus risks decreasing the adequacy of ethical procedures. Constructing national guidelines that emerge from careful consideration of investigator and participant perspectives will facilitate collaborations between scientist and subject that enable the construction of the best ethical procedures possible within each unique research context.

Limitations of Traditional Moral Ideologies Applied to Ethics-in-Science Decisionmaking

Researchers applying the scientific method to describe, explain, and enhance the status of individuals with physical, psychological, and social vulnerabilities are encountering ethical dilemmas to which current federal regulations offer incomplete answers. In such work scientific and ethical duties often appear to have mutually exclusive goals. Whereas scientific responsibility involves a search for truth through experimental controls, ethical duties are directed toward protecting participant welfare through means that often appear to jeopardize such controls.[2] When the goals of science and ethics appear to conflict, investigators studying vulnerable populations draw upon their own moral compass, the advice of colleagues, and recommendations of institutional review boards (IRBs) to make decisions about ethical procedures that will have immediate and possibly long-term impact on individual subjects, their families, and the communities they represent.

Historically, these decisions have been grounded in two metaethical traditions.[3] According to the first tradition, utilitarianism or consequentionalism, the morally right action is the one that produces the most pleasing consequences.[4] Utilitarianism can thus promote a value structure in which potential benefits of science to society take on higher priority than concrete and measurable risks to research participants. In the second tradition, deontology, the moral rightness of an action is evaluated without regard to the consequences.[5] Although the Kantian tradition has been interpreted by some as promoting an inherent respect for the dignity of persons and thus would appear to encourage scientists to seek to incorporate the perspective of participants into their ethical decisionmaking, in practice its focus on the universality of moral principles often leads investigators and IRBs to believe they can determine which research procedures are ethical without consulting members of the population that will be studied. Thus, even though both utilitarianism and deontology are important theoretical resources for ethics-in-science decisions, applied in isolation from subjects' own understanding of the research context these moral frameworks have the potential to minimize a scientist's special relationship and subsequent moral obligations to individual research participants, fostering a psychological distance between scientist and subject.[6]

In the absence of knowledge concerning what research subjects think about ethical alternatives, investigators have incomplete moral guidance when confronting such questions as:

- Does prevention research requiring public identification of risk factors in persons with cognitive, physical, or psychological disorders violate their privacy or lead to social stigmatization?
- Is requiring guardian consent always in the best interest of minors or individuals with cognitive impairments?
- Under what conditions is it ethically responsible to use placebos, control groups, and randomized assignment to evaluate the efficacy of a treatment for persons identified with physical or mental disabilities?
- When is payment for research participation coercive for the cognitively impaired or those from impoverished backgrounds; and when is withholding of such payment inequitable?

The Justice-Care Perspective

Moral arguments for the duty to consider participant perspectives in ethics-in-science decisionmaking derive from a synthesis of principle-based justice ethics and relation-based care ethics. The justice perspective emphasizes moral agency based upon principles of mutual respect, beneficence, and fairness.[7] It stresses impartiality and distance from both the scientist's own interests and her or his connectedness to participants. The ethics of care emphasizes the duty to interact with research participants on their own terms and to respond to their needs as they extend over time.[8]

In recent years there has been growing recognition in philosophical and scientific circles that a morality based on justice can and does coexist with a morality based on interpersonal obligations.[9–12] A justice-care framework recognizes that ethical principles can mediate our understanding of participant perspectives without placing a priority on the investigator's interpretation of these principles over the moral frameworks of others, and that respecting research participants involves responding to them on the basis of their own self-conceptions.

Participant Perspectives. The justice-care perspective, by integrating the perspectives of both justice-based and interpersonal-based ethical frameworks,[13–16] supports several moral arguments for including the views of prospective research participants and their families in federal regulations and ethics-in-science decisionmaking. First, formulating regulations and ethical judgments solely on the bases of opinions expressed by experts in the scholarly community and IRB members risks treating subjects as "research material" rather than as moral agents with the right to judge the ethicality of investigative procedures in which they are asked to participate. Second, failure to consider prospective participants' points of view leads to a reliance on scientific inference or professional logic. This in turn can lead to the acceptance of research procedures causing significant participant distress or to the rejection of potentially worthwhile scientific procedures that subjects and their families would perceive as benign and/or worthwhile. Third, consistent with the community consultation model advanced by ethicists and investigators concerned with ethical practices and policies for clinical research on HIV/AIDS, engaging prospective participants in partnership in the design and implementation of research: (1) assures that adequate consideration is given to the ethical values of beneficence, respect, and justice; and (2) increases the probability of community support and cooperation.[17,18] Finally, understanding the point of view, needs, and expectations of others can enhance an investigator's own moral development through a better understanding of the reciprocal relationship between the participant's expectations and the scientist's obligations.

Investigator Experiences. Another aspect of this relational perspective is the importance of grounding ethics-in-science principles and federal guidelines in the practical, day-to-day experiences of researchers. As my colleagues and I found in a recent NIMH survey, investigators striving to meet the dual obligations of protecting participants and producing valid scientific knowledge have developed innovative ways of identifying and minimizing research risks without forfeiting the integrity of their studies.[19] Researchers studying vulnerable populations can provide ethicists, policymakers, members of IRBs, and citizens an enhanced understanding of the ethical challenges that arise during the actual design and implementation of human subjects research, the barriers that current ethical guidelines sometimes place on good scientific and ethical practice, and the practical and innovative steps that have been taken to meet these challenges. *The practice of science without guidance from ethical principles is morally blind, but the establishment of federal guidelines without relevance to real world application will be empty.*

Understanding Participant Perspectives: A Co-Learning Model

If one believes that knowledge concerning participant perspectives is essential to good ethical decisionmaking, how does one go about generating this knowledge? To engage individuals in a morally ambiguous study for the purpose of eliciting their reactions is ethically problematic, since it exposes persons to what the investigator believes may be procedures that potentially violate their autonomy and welfare. To give prospective participants open-ended questions concerning research ethics is equally problematic, since it asks individuals to provide spontaneous and decontextualized responses to moral questions which require informed deliberation.

Over the years my colleagues and I have developed empirical methods based upon a co-learning model of scientist-participant relationships. Individuals in our studies learn about how the scientific method is applied to examine questions of societal import and are introduced to areas of current ethical concern. We, in turn, learn what prospective participants think about specific ethically relevant issues, their views on whether certain types of studies should be conducted, and the moral frameworks applied to their decisions. We have established dialogues about guardian consent procedures with Latin-American mothers, about confidentiality in research with urban adolescents, and about randomized clinical trials and deception research with young adults.

Adolescent Perspectives on Confidentiality: A Case Example. Our endeavors have challenged stereotypes about how participants view ethical procedures. For example, in one study we found that urban high school students do not endorse maintaining confidentiality when during the course of research an investigator discovers a teenage subject is a victim or engaged in behaviors adolescents themselves perceive as serious problems.[20] Teenagers often indicated that upon such a discovery a researcher should tell a concerned parent or adult. Students' responses thus indicated that *they saw the investigator as having a moral role in relationship to their problems.* Their views raised heretofore unasked ethical questions concerning the consequences if scientists fail to fulfill this role. For example, an investigator's failure to help may unintentionally communicate to a troubled high school research participant that his or her problem is unimportant, that no services are available, or that knowledgeable adults cannot be depended upon to help children in need.

Additional Areas of Ethical Inquiry. A relational ethic of scientific responsibility and care that considers the interpersonal dimensions of the scientist-participant relationship can lead to the examination of other underexplored areas of ethical inquiry.[21-24] An ethical attitude that seeks information on prospective participant perspectives can lead to moral discourse on the following questions:

1. Is the current emphasis on harm avoidance sufficient ethical justification for conducting research on mentally infirm or marginalized populations if it places the ethical burden on participants or their guardians to demonstrate that they have been harmed, and away from the investigators who need not demonstrate that their research will result in any good?

2. If research findings can have direct impact on public attitudes and policies directed toward individual research participants, their families, and communities, to what extent should group stigmatization be considered in determining research risks, and should the nature of such risks be described during informed consent?

3. Who should represent participant and community interests on IRBs, and do community leaders always represent the views of their individual constituents?

4. When do tests of competency for consent to research decisions place an unjust burden on those with identified mental deficiencies?

5. How can risk be better defined across diverse populations so that norms based upon healthy or advantaged persons do not overinclude or exclude vulnerable populations from research?

6. What role should the altruistic benefits of research participation play in the cost-benefit calculus for research presenting greater than minimal risk?

7. Given the scandals surrounding the Tuskegee and Willowbrook studies, the government radiation and UCLA schizophrenia experiments, and the recent controversial adolescent violence research initiative,[1,25–28] how can scientists win the confidence of vulnerable persons and their appreciation of the potential positive value of research?

Ethical Challenges of the Relational Perspective

Including participant perspectives and the practical concerns of scientists conducting research with vulnerable populations in the establishment of federal guidelines raises its own ethical challenges.[29] For example, when including participant perspectives in the ethical evaluation of federal regulations, bioethicists need to address issues raised by the potential *tyranny of the majority.* Principles of respect, beneficence, and justice, informed by participant and investigator perspectives, can guide policymakers in their struggle with the question whether a particular procedure can be justified if a substantial or even small *minority* of prospective participants believe the costs of participation outweigh potential benefits or that procedures selected are in conflict with individual moral frameworks.

Consideration of participant or investigator opinion also runs *the risk of accepting descriptions of ethical decisionmaking as prescriptions for ethical decisions.* The fiduciary nature of the scientist-participant relationship obliges the investigator to take ultimate responsibility for the welfare of research subjects. A relational perspective based upon the ethics of both justice and care proposes that an understanding of participant views can assist, but not substitute for the ethical decisionmaking obligation of individual scientists and policymakers as moral agents. Thus the opinions of those from the scientific and participant communities need to inform, but not dictate federal guidelines and ethics approval or disapproval of research practices.

Conclusions

Attention to the interpersonal nature and obligations inherent in the scientist-participant relationship expands ethics-in-science decisionmaking to include the importance of intersubjectivity, particularity, and context, and moves scientists toward a reinterpretation of their own moral agency.[30] The relational perspective enhances the ability to engage scientists and research participants as partners in creating federal guidelines reflecting both scientific and interpersonal integrity. Scientific ethics is a process that draws upon our human responsiveness to those who participate in research and our awareness of our own boundaries, competencies, and obligations. If becoming a moral subject is the critical moral task for all persons,[31] then recognizing that morality is embedded in the investigator-participant connection is the essential moral activity of human subjects research.

References

[1] Advisory Committee on Human Radiation: *The Human Radiation Experiments: Final Report of the President's Advisory Committee.* New York: Oxford University Press, 1996.

[2] Fisher CB: Integrating science and ethics in research with high-risk children and youth. *SRCD Social Policy Report* 1993; 7:1–27.

[3] Beauchamp TL, Childress JF: *Principles of Biomedical Ethics,* 3rd ed. Oxford: Oxford University Press, 1989.

[4] Mill JS: *Utilitarianism.* New York: Bobbs-Merrill, 1957 [1861].

[5] Kant I: *Foundations of the Metaphysics of Morals.* Indianapolis: Bobbs-Merrill, 1959 [1785].

[6] Fisher CB: Reporting and referring research participants: ethical challenges for investigators studying children and youth. *Ethics & Behavior* 1994; 4:87–95.

[7] Kohlberg L: *Essays on Moral Development: Vol. V. The Psychology of Moral Development.* San Francisco: Harper & Row, 1984.

[8] Gilligan C: *In a Different Voice.* Cambridge, Mass.: Harvard University Press, 1982.

[9] Dillon R: Care and respect. In *Explorations in Feminist Ethics,* ed. Cole EB, Coultrap-McQuin S. Bloomington, Ind.: Indiana University Press, 1992: 69–81.

[10] Higgins A: The just community educational program: the development of moral role-taking as the expression of justice and care. In *Who Cares? Theory, Research, and Educational Implications of the Ethic of Care,* ed. Brabeck MM. New York: Praeger, 1989: 197–215.

[11] Killen M: Justice and care: dichotomies or coexistence? *Journal for a Just and Caring Education* 1996; 2: 42–58.

[12] Waithe ME: Twenty-three hundred years of women philosophers: toward a gender undifferentiated moral theory. In *Who Cares? Theory, Research, and Educational Implications of the Ethic of Care,* ed. Brabeck MM. New York: Praeger, 1989: 3–18.

[13] Farr JL, Seaver WB: Stress and discomfort in psychological research: subject perceptions of experimental procedures. *American Psychologist* 1975;30: 770–3.

[14] Sullivan DS, Deiker TE: Subject-experimenter perceptions of ethical issues in human research. *American Psychologist* 1976; 28: 587–91.

[15] Veatch RM: *The Patient as Partner.* Bloomington, Ind.: Indiana University Press, 1987.

[16] Wilson DW, Donnerstein W: Legal and ethical aspects of non-reactive social psychological research: an excursion into the public mind. *American Psychologist* 1976; 31: 765–73.

[17] Levine C, Dubler NN, Levine RJ: Building a new consensus: ethical principles and policies for clinical research on HIV/AIDS. *IRB* 1991; 13(1–2): 1–17.

[18] Melton GB, Levine RJ, Koocher GP, Rosenthal R, Thompson WC: Community consultation in socially sensitive research: lessons from clinical trials of treatments for AIDS. *American Psychologist* 1988; 43: 573–81.

[19] Fisher CB, Hoagwood K, Jensen PS: Casebook on ethical issues in research with children and adolescents with mental disorders. In *Ethical Issues in Mental Health Research with Children and Adolescents,* ed. Hoagwood K, Jensen PS, Fisher CB. Mahwah, N.J.: Lawrence Erlbaum Associates, 1996: 135–238.

[20] Fisher CB, Higgins-D'Allesandro A, Rau MB, Kuther T, Belanger S: Referring and reporting research participants at-risk: views from urban adolescents. *Child Development* 1996; 67: 2086–2100.

[21] Casas JM, San Miguel S: Beyond questions and discussions, there is a need for action: a response to Mio and Iwamasa. *The Counseling Psychologist* 1996; 21(2): 233–9.

[22] Fisher CB, Jackson JF, Villarruel F: The study of African American and Latin-American children and youth. In *Handbook of Child Psychology: Vol. 1. Theoretical Models of Human Development*, 5th ed., ed. Lerner RM, Damon W. New York: Wiley, 1997: 1145–1207.

[23] Sarason SB: If it can be studied or developed, should it? *American Psychologist* 1984; 39: 477–85.

[24] Scott-Jones D: Ethical issues in reporting and referring in research with low-income minority children. *Ethics & Behavior* 1994; 4: 97–198.

[25] Jones, JH: *Bad Blood: The Tuskegee Syphilis Experiment* rev. ed. New York: Free Press, 1993.

[26] Katz J: *Experimentation with Human Beings.* New York: Russell Sage Foundation. 1972.

[27] Appelbaum PS: Drug-free research in schizophrenia: an overview of the controversy. *IRB* 1996; 18(1): 1–5.

[28] Wheeler DL: Ambitious federal plan for violence research runs up against fear of its misuses. *The Chronicle of Higher Education*, 4 November 1992.

[29] Fisher CB, Fyrberg D: Participant partners: college students weigh the costs and benefits of deceptive research. *American Psychologist* 1994; 49: 417–27.

[30] Walker MW: Moral understandings: alternative "epistemology" for a feminist ethics. In *Explorations in Feminist Ethics*, ed. Cole EB, Coutrap-McQuin S. Bloomington, Ind.: Indiana University Press, 1992: 165–75.

[31] Smith RL: Feminism and the moral subject. In *Women's Consciousness, Women's Conscience*, ed. Andolsen BH, Gudorf CE, Pellauer MD. Minneapolis: Winston Press, 1985: 235–50.

Attention to Difference and Women's Consent to Research

Lisa A. Eckenwiler

There is, in research ethics, a history of acknowledging the moral relevance of differences among potential participants. The need for special provisions in research involving children, prisoners, the institutionalized mentally disabled and others who are cognitively impaired, the emergently ill, and cultural minorities, has

Lisa A. Eckenwiler, "Attention to Difference and Women's Consent to Research," *IRB: A Review of Human Subjects Research*, 20, no. 6, November–December 1998, 6–11.

been established by thoughtful contributors to discussions concerning research ethics.[1] My aim here is to support the line of argument that suggests we must consider difference and group membership as it relates to constraints on members of a group to exercise self-determination in consenting to research participation. Rather than drawing attention to physiologically based limitations, physical confinement, age, and cultural pluralism, I seek to shine the moral light on constraints on moral agency that stem from social and institutional structures, relations, and processes embedded in and related to research. Such restrictions, attributable to certain norms, unquestioned assumptions, stereotypes, and economic structure, undermine persons' opportunities to lead healthy lives and inhibit their capacities to make choices concerning the conditions of their lives. These social and institutional constraints have special pertinence for women. While the case for women's inclusion has been made and initiatives aimed at promoting it launched, more needs to be said about certain lingering hindrances to the realization of social equality and women's self-determination in research.

Here I shall discuss how features of social and institutional context support an inattention to difference in research and why this compromises social equality and self-determination for women; show that even when difference is recognized, where women are concerned these ideals can be undermined; and explain how, in research involving women, and specifically, in the consent process, we can attend to differences in a way that promotes equality and enhances rather than undermines self-determination.

Undermining Social Equality and Self-Determination for Women

The particularities of women's bodies have been both identified and neglected in clinical research. Researchers have often argued that in a clinical trial, valid interpretation requires that subjects be as homogeneous as possible. By using uniform subjects they believe they can better determine which effects are attributable to a drug or other intervention as opposed to some other variable. Rather than taking such differences as the cyclical variation of women's hormones, their body size and composition, and the use among many of steroidal contraceptives as reasons to study women, they have been seen as confounding factors or methodological problems, and thus used as rationales for exclusion.[2] Older women have been regarded as especially problematic because they may have multiple health conditions and take concomitant medication.[3]

Where women have been included in research, there has been a general failure to examine gender-specific differences. A revealing example comes from clinical research on HIV and AIDS. In the summer of 1992 at the VIII International Conference on AIDS, members of a panel suggested that the symptoms of HIV were the same for men and women. Advocates for women's health, however, questioned the results of the research presented as evidence for the claim because gynecological data were not collected, nor were hormone levels, reproductive impacts, or changes in menstruation. Instead:

the scientists categorized women as men and studied them only in accordance with their biological similarities to men. . . [T]he disease was studied as a male disease in female bodies that were in fact treated throughout the research as male bodies.[4]

Further, research has been found to be deficient with respect to gender-specific analyses in the pharmacokinetics and pharmacodynamics of drugs despite good reasons to believe that gender differences exist in absorption, distribution, and metabolism of drugs, and that taking oral contraceptives may affect drug interactions.[5] In sum, epistemological assumptions—specifically, views about how reliable knowledge is produced—have encouraged inattentiveness to difference in research and played a crucial role in generating results that are not clearly applicable to women.

To the extent that women are excluded or underincluded in research, or gender-specific analyses are not performed, health care providers have insufficient information on the etiology, symptoms, and progression of particular diseases, disorders, and conditions in women, and on preventive strategies and diagnostic testing.[6] When women are excluded or underrepresented as participants in investigations of drugs and other medical interventions, or when gender-specific differences fail to be assessed, health care providers do not have accurate and complete information on their safety and efficacy. With respect to drugs, they lack information on such specifics as appropriate dosages, timing of administration, and indications for use. When such information is absent or otherwise insufficient, health care providers may be reluctant to prescribe drugs for women, a consequence described as "residual exclusion."[7] In the event that medications not analyzed in women *are* prescribed for their use, potential risks are shifted outside of the research context. After marketing, women use many of the same drugs that men use, and may even be the primary users of these drugs.[8] But there is no basis for predicting the effects of such drugs in women. Not only will side effects inevitably occur in a certain percentage of women who take drugs, these side effects involve many more women, because the exposed population is much larger during marketing than during phase I, II, and III clinical trials.[9] When other interventions are not adequately studied in women they may not receive them; when they do, they may present unknown risks and contribute to adverse prognoses.[10]

Such research deficiencies extend even further in inhibiting women's prospects for leading healthy lives. For example, the failure to study the incidence and unique progression of AIDS in women ultimately skewed statistics used to determine funding levels for services and other resources, and led to the denial of social security benefits for them.[11]

Recent legislative and policy initiatives have taken important steps toward promoting the inclusion of women.[12] Nevertheless, women's capacities to authorize their own participation in research continue to be constrained. National Institutes of Health guidelines, for instance, allow for women's exclusion when it is deemed appropriate by research sponsors, investigators, and others with decision-making authority in the institutional structures of research. The requirement to include women, in other words, shall not apply when this is considered "inappropriate with respect to the health of the subjects; . . . the purposes of research; or . . . under such circumstances as the Director of the NIH may designate."[13] It is not hard to imagine researchers citing homogeneity as important to research purposes, or concern for women's reproductive health (a matter to be addressed below), and arguing for their exclusion.

If we shift to consider attention to difference in another area of research, the consent process, we can look to the standard that governs the conveyance of information to potential research participants, the "reasonable volunteer" standard.[14] Like its cousin the "reasonable person," this standard has its origin in tort negligence law and reflects an effort to establish—granting certain exceptions—a *universally applicable* measure for researchers' conduct in disclosing information about a trial's purposes and procedures, benefits and risks, available treatment alternatives, the voluntariness of participation, the privilege of withdrawal, costs and payments, and so on. Coupled with this is the expectation that researchers eliminate bias in their treatment of subjects. With the aim of achieving "valid" results, researchers may subject themselves to epistemic constraints. In other words, they may ignore or seek to suppress knowledge about participants except for that which is related to inclusion and exclusion criteria. This model for organizing the consent process—grounded in the view that all persons are of equal worth and have the same rights to bodily integrity and self-determination—aims at promoting social equality by treating all according to the same moral rules. Notwithstanding those groups noted earlier, however, the reasonable volunteer standard has not been extended to all persons.

In society generally as well as in clinical settings, women have often been denied respect as capable thinkers and decisionmakers. Evidence suggests that some physicians treat female patients differently, as intellectually inferior, and dominate the structure and content of exchanges.[15] It is not unreasonable to assume that this also describes the behavior of some researchers. The pervasive assumptions that persons not trained in science cannot understand the complexity of the research process or the details of an idea under investigation, and that women *in particular* are lacking in rationality, undermines their decision-making in research.[16]

Evidence reveals especially strong biases against particular groups of women. The first group includes women of color.[17] In one study, for example, Mexican-American women believed they were receiving effective birth control, but some were given placebos. When questioned about this, the chief investigator responded, "If you think you can explain a placebo test to women like these, you never met Ms. Gomez from the West Side."[18]

In addition, pregnant women continue to be excluded from the company of the "reasonable." The view that they cannot be trusted to make a "good" decision— whether because someone is pressuring them into enrolling in research for their benefit or that of the fetus,[19] because any decision about research participation would be made without full or adequate appreciation of the possible consequences; and/or because the responsibility for these consequences might fall to those who sponsor, carry out, and/or review research—endures in settings where research is planned and discussed. Fears among those with financial interests in research—pharmaceutical companies, manufacturers of medical devices, researchers, and institutions that carry out protocols—of causing harm to fetuses and the financial losses that might follow liability claims serve to deny pregnant women the opportunity to consent to research participation.[20]

Prevailing interpretations of scientific norms and ethical ideals, gender and cultural stereotypes, the relationship between the economic growth imperative and scientific endeavors, and hierarchical decisionmaking processes—a confluence of social and institutional relations, processes, and structures embedded in and related to research—have resulted in inattention to relevant differences as well as in practices that transform real or perceived differences into disadvantage for women. Denying the uniqueness of persons and/or allowing the views and experiences of dominant groups[21] to prevail undermine women's potential to live under health policies and standards of care formulated from research involving women, and to pursue the benefits of participation in research. These features of social and institutional context have ultimately served to tarnish the ideal that basic equalities among persons are fundamental to a just society. Moreover, they have functioned to deny women respect as persons capable of making sound decisions, including decisions that may affect their health. In essence, they have served to constrain women's healthy development and the exercise of their self-determination.

Women, Difference, and Informed Consent

Recognizing how social and institutional structures, relations, and processes in research compromise social equality and constrain women's moral agency, we are compelled to develop mechanisms that treat women and differences among them in a way that enhances rather than undermines their potential to develop and exercise their capacities and realize their choices. The informed consent process is a critical place for incorporating attention to particularity and promoting social equality and self-determination for women in research. While respect for human dignity—the corner-stone of ethical research involving humans—must be universal, if the primary goal of informed consent is to enhance the self-determination of participants, the process of disclosing information and assessing comprehension and voluntariness can and should incorporate certain variations. Specifically, we ought to invoke a standard that attends to constraints upon women as a social group and to the situations of particular women considering research participation.

In confronting hindrances to the realization of social equality and women's self-determination, researchers must first reckon with stereotypes that portray them—especially those who are members of cultural minority groups[22]—as incapable, less capable, or untrustworthy decisionmakers. The consent process, as well, should incorporate attention to gender norms that encourage women's subordination. Some women may defer to physician authority and be concerned about politeness, for instance, leading researchers to question their intelligence and in turn, their capacities to make decisions.[23] These norms have particular force for some women: older women may be especially reluctant to ask questions, state their concerns, or assert themselves. Moreover, immigrant and refugee women may lack knowledge about their basic human rights in the United States and come from countries that restrict freedom of expression.[24] IRBs can help to educate researchers on these points.

Additionally, in carrying out research that involves women it is crucial to acknowledge the disproportionate representation of women among the poor. The "feminization of poverty" has contributed to the economic inaccessibility of health care for women.[25] Participation in research may be especially compelling when services including health education, monitoring, referral, and follow-up are provided to those otherwise unable to secure them.[26] When those who lack access to health care services consider their best chance for obtaining services to be through research, the ideal of voluntary participation cannot be realized. Poor women therefore merit mechanisms that will enable them to make sound decisions in circumstances that can undermine self-determination. At minimum researchers and IRBs are morally required to ensure that advertisements which offer free medical services to subjects note that the purpose of research is to develop generalizable knowledge, not to benefit individuals, although this is possible; that it poses *risks;* and to help poor women who seek to enroll understand that they may not be among the beneficiaries of the knowledge that emerges from a study due to their diminished access to health care.[27] While promoting the health of all members of the public requires the increased participation of women, the economic structure of health care in the United States makes research a likely venue for exploitation, where the disenfranchised are subject to the risks of research, transferring their labors for the benefit of others who can avail themselves of the best science and medicine have to offer. A strengthened consent process can enable poor women to exercise reasonable choices even under conditions that compromise free moral agency and tarnish social equality.

Women who plan to bear children warrant differential treatment of the sort that helps them develop and exercise their capacities and participate in determining their actions and the conditions within which they act. Social equality requires that women of childbearing potential be participants in research. Researchers can support their self-determination through the consent process. IRBs can help investigators tailor consent in ways that highlight risks to reproductive health, and encourage them to provide participants with information on known and anticipated risks of the experimental intervention and the unknown potential for harm, along with the nonexperimental alternatives available, if any. At minimum, federal regulations and state tort law should be upheld, but the stronger the standard for disclosure, the greater the prospects for promoting women's self-determination through informed consent.

Restrictions on pregnant women's inclusion undermine their self-determination and, ultimately, the ideal of social equality. Although recent years have brought progress in seeking to address other women's health needs through research, health care providers continue to care for pregnant patients without adequate information regarding conditions they may have during pregnancy or the safety and efficacy of interventions.[28] Moreover, in some cases experimental interventions may carry the prospect of direct benefit to pregnant women with debilitating or life-threatening diseases.[29] Constraints on the exercise of choice, then, can deny these women potential health benefits.

Research on conditions that are unique to or especially prevalent or serious among pregnant women, as well as on the safety and effectiveness of interventions, is necessary if women are to experience healthy pregnancies. Moreover, where an experimental intervention holds out the prospect of direct benefit to a pregnant woman, even when there is a risk to the fetus, decisionmaking authority regarding participation should rest with her. This position is supported not only by appeals to social equality and the self-determination of women and by stronger personhood claims, but also, in cases where the prospect for benefit to the woman is substantial and the risk of harm to the fetus minimal, by utilitarian arguments.[30] Several legal precedents also support the view that restrictions on pregnant women in research are wrong.[31] Most recently, the Supreme Court's argument in *Johnson Controls* upholds women's decisionmaking authority: ". . . decisions about the welfare of future children [should be] left to the parents who conceive, bear, support, and raise them."[32] The consent process can enable pregnant women to make informed, voluntary decisions, and thereby support the ideals of self-determination and social equality in the research context.[33]

Industries driven by goals of production and capital accumulation have thwarted research for women. Concern for legal liability has permeated the research process for at least three decades. Close inspection of legal doctrines, however, reveals that undue attention is focused here. The doctrine of parental immunity, which protects parents from suits by future children for alleged fetal damage, may serve to shield women from tort claims tied to previous research participation through the principle of respect for the exercise of ordinary discretion regarding medical care. When a case concerns conduct prior to conception and the person harmed did not exist—for example, when a woman is *not pregnant* at the time of the research—the difficulty of establishing causal links makes the success of liability claims unlikely. Such causal links, significantly, may be broken by the consent process. As well, in the more controversial case in which a woman is pregnant and research participation affords an intervention that can conceivably benefit her directly, or provides an opportunity to yield generalizable knowledge about conditions affecting pregnant women, adherence to high standards for informed consent can insulate her, researchers, institutions, and manufacturers from liability. The consent process, again, may highlight risks that are known or suspected, and incorporate a discussion about unknown harms to fetal health. Adherence to high standards for consent should not only promote women's health and self-determination, it should also make conditions less favorable for liability claims.[34]

Conclusion

Attending to difference is a vital component of ethical research. Although protective provisions for specific groups and recent measures to encourage the inclusion of women and assess physiological differences represent significant strides in promoting social equality and self-determination, more work is needed if we are to see these ideals realized in the research context. The process of informed consent can figure prominently here by attending to constraints on women as a social group and on those affecting particular groups of women who might contemplate research participation. The crucial insight is that this is not just a matter of improving the efforts of individual researchers and IRBs. We must also look at the social and institutional context in which research is conducted and reviewed and, in particular, consider how gender and cultural stereotypes, the sexual division of labor, economic structures, and particular conceptions of scientific and moral ideas can hinder women's self-determination and undermine social equality.

A lingering question concerns whether informed consent has been overemphasized as a mechanism for upholding participants' rights in research. There are indeed serious limitations to what informed consent can do to promote equality and self-determination. Other changes in the research process should be pursued.[35] Yet part of giving informed consent its due is acknowledging the sea change it has brought about in research ethics, and that its potential to accommodate and even to further reform is far from exhausted. While it must be regarded modestly, as a small part of a much larger transformation required in research, informed consent can play a salutary role in promoting social equality and self-determination in this context.

Acknowledgments

The author wishes to thank James Lindemann Nelson and Françoise Baylis for their comments on earlier versions of this manuscript.

References

[1] The provisions for children and prisoners are discussed in 45 CFR 46.401–409 and 45 CFR 46.301–306. Although never finalized, guidelines for research on the institutionalized mentally disabled were proposed. See Department of Health, Education, and Welfare. Proposed regulations on research involving those institutionalized as mentally disabled. *Federal Register* 1978; 17(43):53950–6. The National Bioethics Advisory Commission is presently developing guidelines for research on the cognitively impaired. Commentaries

include: Dresser R. Mentally disabled research subjects: the enduring policy issues. *JAMA* 1996; 276(1):67–72; Karlawish JHT, Sachs GA. Research on the cognitively impaired: lessons and warnings from the emergency research debate. *Journal of the American Geriatrics Society* 1997; 45(4):474–81; Marwick C. Bioethics commission examines informed consent from subjects who are decisionally incapable. *JAMA* 1997; 278(8):618–9.

For final rules on emergency research see: Informed consent and waiver of informed consent requirements in certain emergency research. *Federal Register* 1996; 61(192): 51497–533. For a discussion of cultural pluralism and informed consent, see Gostin LO. Informed consent, cultural sensitivity, and respect for persons. *JAMA* 1995; 274(10):844–5.

[2] See Hamilton JA. Women and health policy: on the inclusion of females in clinical trials. In Sargent CF, Bretell CB, eds. *Gender and Health: An International Perspective.* Englewood Cliffs, N.J.: Prentice Hall, 1996:298–9; Merkatz, RB, Temple R, Solomon S, et al. Women in clinical trials of new drugs: a change in Food and Drug Administration policy. *NEJM* 1993; 329(4):292–6.

[3] Gurwitz JH, Col NF, Avorn J. The exclusion of the elderly and women from clinical trials in acute myocardial infarction. *JAMA* 1992; 268(11): 1417–22; Wenger NK. Exclusion of the elderly and women from coronary trials: is their quality of care compromised? *JAMA* 1992; 268(11): 1460–1.

[4] Caschetta MB. The identity politics of biomedical research: clinical trials, medical knowledge, and the female body. *SIECUS Report* 1993; 22(1):3.

[5] Hamilton JA, Parry B. Sex-related difference in clinical drug response: implications for women's health. *Journal of the American Medical Women's Association* 1983; 38(5): 126–32; see also Note 2, Merkatz et al. 1993.

[6] For example, see Bell NK. Women and AIDS: too little, too late? In Holmes HB, Purdy LM, eds. *Feminist Perspectives in Medical Ethics.* Bloomington: Indiana University Press, 1992:46–62; Wenger NK, Speroff L, Packard B. Cardiovascular health and disease in women. *NEJM* 1993; 329(4):247–56.

[7] Minkoff H, Moreno J, Powderly K. Fetal protection and women's access to clinical trials. *Journal of Women's Health* 1992; 1(2):137.

[8] See note 3, Gurwitz et al. 1992; Raskin R. Age-sex differences in response to antidepressant drugs. *Journal of Nervous and Mental Disease* 1974; 159(2):120–30; Yonkers KA, Harrison W. The inclusion of women in psychopharmacologic trials. *Journal of Clinical Psychopharmacology* 1993; 13(6): 380–2.

[9] See Kinney EL, Trautman J, Gold JA, et al. Underrepresentation of women in new drug trials: ramifications and remedies. *Annals of Internal Medicine* 1981; 95(4):495–9.

[10] Ayanian JZ, Epstein AM. Differences in the use of procedures between men and women hospitalized for coronary heart disease. *NEJM* 1991; 325(4):221–5; Tobin JN, Wassertheil-Smoller S, Wexler JP, et al. Sex bias in considering coronary bypass surgery. *Annals of Internal Medicine* 1987; 107(1):19–25; Wenger NK. Gender, coronary artery disease, and coronary bypass surgery. *Annals of Internal Medicine* 1990; 112(8):557–8.

[11] Merton V. The exclusion of pregnant, pregnable, and once pregnable people (a.k.a. women) from biomedical research. *American Journal of Law & Medicine* 1993; 19(4):384.

[12] National Institutes of Health. NIH guidelines on the inclusion of women and minorities as subjects in clinical research. *Federal Register* 1994; 59(59):14507–13; Food and Drug Administration. Guidelines for the study and evaluation of gender differences in the clinical evaluation of drugs. *Federal Register* 1993; 58(139):39405–16; Food and Drug Administration. Investigational new drug applications: proposed amendment to clinical hold regulations for products intended for life-threatening disease. *Federal Register* 1997; 62(185):49946–54.

[13] See note 12, National Institutes of Health 1994:14509.

[14] National Commission for the Protection of Human Subjects of Biomedical and Behavioral Research. *The Belmont Report: Ethical Principles and Guidelines for the Protection of Human Subjects of Research.* Washington, D.C.: U.S. Government Printing Office, 1979: 5–6.

[15] Secker B. Destroying the right/power to decide: the gender politics of incompetence labeling. Presented at International Social Philosophy Conference, De Pere, Wisconsin, 16 August 1996; Council on Ethical and Judicial Affairs, American Medical Association. Gender disparities in clinical decision making. *JAMA* 1991; 266(4): 559–62; Fisher SM. *In the Patient's Best Interest: Women and the Politics of Medical Decisions.* New Brunswick, N.J.: Rutgers University Press, 1988.

[16] See Harding S. Rethinking standpoint epistemology: what is 'strong objectivity'? In Alcoff L, Potter E, eds. *Feminist Epistemologies,* New York: Routledge, 1993:49–82; Lloyd G. *The Man of Reason: 'Male' and 'Female' in Western Philosophy.* Minneapolis: University of Minnesota Press, 1984.

[17] Gamble VN. Under the shadow of Tuskegee: African-Americans and health care. *American Journal of Public Health* 1997; 87(11):1773–8. Sherwin S. Gender, race, and class in the delivery of health care. In Sherwin S. *No Longer Patient: Feminist Ethics and Health Care.* Philadelphia: Temple University Press, 1992:222–40.

[18.] Seaman B. *Free and Female.* New York: Fawcett, 1972:180–1. As well, see Mouton CP, Harris S, Rovi S. Barriers to Black women's participation in cancer clinical trials. *Journal of National Medical Association* 1997:89:721–7; Allen M. The dilemma for women of color in clinical trials. *Journal of American Medical Women's Association* 1994; 49(4):105–9.

[19] Department of Health and Human Services. Protection of human research subjects: proposed rule. *Federal Register* 1998; 63:27793–804, p. 27800.

[20] Oberman M. Real and perceived legal barriers to the inclusion of women in clinical trials. In Dan AJ, ed. *Reframing Women's Health: Multidisciplinary Research and Practice.* Thousand Oaks, Calif.: Sage, 1994:266–76; see note 11, Merton 1993:400–2.

[21] Groups whose experience and culture find expression and, moreover, define social norms.

[22] Those whose experience and culture do not find expression in the dominant society.

[23] Tannen D. *You Just Don't Understand: Women and Men in Conversation.* New York: William Morrow and Co., 1990.

[24] Yu ESH. Ethical and legal issues relating to the inclusion of Asian/Pacific Islanders in clinical studies. In Mastroianni AC, Faden R, Federman D, eds. *Women and Health Research: Ethical and Legal Issues of Including Women in Clinical Studies,* vol. 2. Washington, D.C.: National Academy Press, 1994:216–31.

[25] Mahowald MB. The feminization of poverty: its impact on women's and children's health. In Mahowald MB. *Women and Children in Health Care: An Unequal Majority.* New York: Oxford University Press, 1993:217–35.

[26] Goldberg C. Cutting a lifeline to AIDS study. *New York Times,* 30 January 1996; Murphy TF. Women and drug users: the changing face of HIV clinical trials. *QRB* 1991; 17:26–32.

[27] This notion, indeed, is reminiscent of a standard expressed in the CIOMS *International Ethical Guidelines for Biomedical Research Involving Human Subjects.* More specifically, when research is carried out in a "developing country" by sponsors and investigators from a "developed country," and this research is designed to develop a diagnostic, preventive, or therapeutic product, the stand set forth in the *Guidelines* is that there must be assurance that the product, once developed, will be made reasonably available to the inhabitants of the country in which the research is carried out. I am thankful to Robert J. Levine for drawing this important connection to my attention. To return to my specific point, however, the stronger position, whose defense is beyond the scope of this paper, is that given the potential for exploitation, poor women should not be recruited for research that presents more than minimal risk, except where the investigational intervention holds

some prospect for direct health benefit to them, or where the research is likely to yield generalizable knowledge about a condition that disproportionately affects the poor.

[28] Frederiksen MC. Clinical trials in pregnancy. *Food and Drug Law Journal* 1993; 48(2): 195–6; Charo A. Protecting us to death: women, pregnancy, and clinical research trials. *Saint Louis Law Journal* 1993; 38(1):135–88.

[29] Kass NE, Taylor HA, King PA. Harms of excluding pregnant women from clinical research: the case of HIV-infected pregnant women. *Journal of Law, Medicine & Ethics* 1996; 24(1):36–46.

[30] Baylis F. Women and health research: working for change. *Journal of Clinical Ethics* 1996; 7(3):229–42.

[31] The Pregnancy Discrimination Act of 1978, and the following Supreme Court cases also support this view: *Cruzan v. Director, Missouri Department of Health,* 497 U.S. 261 (1990); *Griswold v. Connecticut,* 381 U.S. 479 (1965); *Roe v. Wade,* 410 U.S. 113 (1973); and *International Union, United Automobile, Aerospace, and Agricultural Implement Workers v. Johnson Controls Inc.,* 499 U.S. 187(1991).

[32] See note 31, *Johnson Controls* 1991.

[33] As of this writing, proposed changes to Subpart B of 45 CFR 46 embrace a strengthened role for the consent process in research with pregnant women. Save for one notable suggested revision—that the consent of the woman alone is adequate—the proposed regulations are no less restrictive with respect to their inclusion than those in place. See note 19, Department of Health and Human Services 1998.

[34] It is important to add that these suggestions should not be interpreted as an argument for asking a research subject to waive her entitlement to litigate. These issues are discussed in great detail by legal commentators. See: Gorenberg H, White A. Off the pedestal and into the arena: toward including women in experimental protocols. *N.Y.U. Review of Law and Social Change* 1991–1992;19:223–8; see note 11, Merton. 1993:402–14; Rothenberg KH. Gender matters: implications for clinical research and women's health care. *Houston Law Review* 1996; 32:1259–63. Also instructive is the work of Lucinda Finley. See Finley L. Female trouble: the implications of tort reform for women. *Tennessee Law Review* 1997; 64:847–79.

[35] Department of Health and Human Services, Office of the Inspector General. *Institutional Review Boards: A Time for Reform.* Washington, D.C.: Office of Inspector General, 1998; Eckenwiler LA. Women and the Ethics of Clinical Research: Broadening Conceptions of Justice. Doctoral Dissertation. University of Tennessee, Knoxville, Tennessee, 1997.

Moving Ahead in Research Involving Persons with Mental Disorders: Summary and Recommendations

This report stands in a long line of statements, reports, and recommendations by governmental advisory groups and professional organizations on the ethical requirements of research involving human subjects. Each of these has left an important legacy. For example, in 1947 the Nuremberg Code established the importance of voluntary consent to research participation. The Declaration of Helsinki in 1964 distinguished between research intended partly to benefit the subject and research intended solely for others' benefit. The Guidelines developed by the Council of International Organizations of Medical Sciences allow legal guardians to consent to low-risk research that is potentially beneficial to the human subject involved. In addition to proposing ethical principles that should govern all human subjects research and developing guidelines for research with special populations, the National Commission in 1978 proposed additional protections for those institutionalized as "mentally infirm." Even though these protections resembled those proposed by the National Commission for research with children (which were adopted), the proposed protections for those institutionalized as mentally infirm were never adopted in federal regulations.

Much has changed since the National Commission's work 20 years ago. There is a greater sensitivity on the part of many to the variety of mental disorders and an improved understanding of the ways that these disorders can be recognized and ameliorated. Diagnostic procedures and treatments have progressed, sometimes in breathtaking ways, with the promise of still greater breakthroughs on the horizon. More research is being conducted than ever before, and the research environment has become far more complex, involving both a larger societal investment and a greater role for the private sector. While by no means vanquished, the stigmatization of those who suffer from mental illnesses shows signs of abating due to greater understanding of these disorders and, in some cases, the underlying biological and genetic etiology of these disorders.

NBAC [the National Bioethics Advisory Commission] hopes that the legacy of this report will be to bring persons with mental disorders more fully and specifically under appropriate additional research protections, such as those that have been extended to other potentially vulnerable persons. It recommends these new protections with the deepest respect for those involved in research on these disorders: the person with a disorder that may affect decisionmaking capacity, whose

Reprinted from *Research Involving Persons with Mental Disorders That May Affect Decisionmaking Capacity,* a report of the National Bioethics Advisory Commission. (Original footnote numbering retained and references to the appendix omitted.)

autonomy must be protected and, when possible, enhanced; the clinical investigators who are dedicated to the alleviation of these terrible afflictions; and informal caregivers, whose own lives are often absorbed by the tragedy that has befallen their loved ones. In view of the ethical uncertainties noted by those involved in such research—as investigators, subjects, or family members—NBAC believes that enhanced protections will promote broad-based support for further research by engendering greater public trust and confidence that subjects' rights and interests are fully respected. This concluding chapter presents NBAC's recommendations and identifies, where possible, those who should be responsible for their implementation.[243]

Concerns have been expressed that requiring new protections in research involving persons with mental disorders might limit such research and thereby impede the development of new methods of diagnosis or treatment.[244] It is difficult to evaluate such claims because there is, to date, insufficient evidence to support or reject them. NBAC does not believe, however, that the additional protections recommended in this report will excessively burden research or hamper the development of effective new treatments. Moreover, it is useful to note that many share the responsibility to protect the interests of those without whom this research could not be done—especially those who may be unable to give full informed consent and who may not themselves directly benefit from the research. All research involving human beings must satisfy appropriate ethical standards. That is, both the means and ends of individual studies must be morally acceptable. This moral imperative is especially acute for potentially vulnerable populations such as children, pregnant women, prisoners, or, NBAC believes, individuals with mental disorders that may affect decisionmaking capacity.

A cogent case can be made for requiring additional special protections in research involving as subjects persons with impaired decisionmaking capacity. Indeed, most of the additional protections NBAC recommends could also be considered for research in that larger population. However, NBAC has chosen to focus this report on persons with mental disorders, in part because of this population's difficult history of involvement in medical research. NBAC believes that in addition to the regulations that are already applicable, IRB deliberations about research involving subjects with mental disorders that may affect decisionmaking capacity should be governed by other specific regulations.

Recommendations for New Regulations

In the United States, regulations have provided perhaps the most important means of protecting the rights and welfare of human subjects. But they have not been the only means. Clearly, for example, widely accepted and enduring professional norms have also played a role. The desirability of additional governmental regulation depends not only on the nature and importance of the problems the proposed new rules aim to address, but also on the regulation's ultimate efficacy. Presumably, the least complex measures taken by governmental entities are the preferred ones, as long as those measures can achieve the important societal goals that have been identified. Many who are familiar with the federal regulations currently governing human subjects research complain that they are already too complex and bureaucratic. Some of those engaged in research on conditions related to mental disorders fear that further regulation will unnecessarily slow scientific progress and inappropriately stigmatize individuals who may be suitable and appropriate research subjects.

Whatever one's view of the current regulations, the period since their adoption has been, in the judgment of some, largely free of the sorts of large-scale problems and abuses that led to their initial promulgation. Others, however, stress that the issues discussed in this report illustrate some of the shortcomings of the Common Rule. In this context, NBAC was obliged to determine whether the outstanding issues and problems in research involving persons with mental disorders warrant new regulations and/or whether some or all of the required reforms could be advanced through other mechanisms. These might include statements of principle; the adoption of guidelines by those individuals or professional groups involved in reviewing, regulating, and carrying out these projects; and the development of educational materials for all relevant parties.

Although NBAC proposes a number of recommendations that would require changes in the language of the Common Rule, it is mindful that the time frame for such reforms might be long and the process labor intensive. Many of the regulatory proposals made by NBAC could, however, also be accomplished by the creation of a new subpart in 45 CFR 46. Adoption of a subpart has the advantage of permitting affected federal agencies to act as expeditiously as they choose to change the regulatory requirements for their own intramural and extramural research. *Regardless of which regulatory route is taken, NBAC encourages researchers and institutions to adopt the spirit and substance of these recommendations immediately.*

NBAC proposes 21 recommendations. A number propose the development of new federal regulations for the protection of human subjects; others are directed to investigators and IRBs, state legislatures, NIH, DHHS, health professionals, federal agencies subject to the Common Rule, and others responsible for human subjects' protection. These recommendations provide both a set of requirements that NBAC believes must be satisfied in all research protocols involving persons with mental disorders, and several additional or optional protections that may be appropriate in particular circumstances. Taken together, these recommendations would both enhance existing protections and facilitate broad public support for continued research on mental disorders.

The several recommendations for changes in federal regulations and for other governmental, institutional, and organizational actions are interconnected. Even though only a few recommendations are explicitly cross-referenced, it is important to view each recommendation in the context of the others. Only then is it possible to see exactly how NBAC proposes to protect human subjects with mental disorders that may affect decisionmaking capacity and also allow important research to proceed. Finally, in some cases, only brief justifications, explanations, and interpretations follow each recommendation in this chapter; additional support and explication appear in the preceding four chapters. The following recommendations are clustered into six sections relating to: review bodies; research design; informed consent and capacity; categories of research; surrogate decision making; and education, research, and support.

I. Recommendations Regarding Review Bodies

INSTITUTIONAL REVIEW BOARD (IRB) MEMBERSHIP

> *Recommendation 1.* All IRBs that regularly consider proposals involving persons with mental disorders should include at least two members who are familiar with the nature of these disorders and with the concerns of the population being studied. At least one of these IRB members should be a member of the population being studied, a family member of such a person, or a representative of an advocacy organization for this population. These IRB members should be present and voting when such protocols are discussed. IRBs that only occasionally consider such protocols should involve in their discussion two ad hoc consultants who are familiar with the nature of these disorders and with the concerns of the population being studied; at least one of these consultants should be a member of the population being studied, a family member of such a person, or a representative of an advocacy organization for this population.

The issues considered in this report are as complex and as multifaceted as the research protocols designed to advance medical knowledge about mental disorders. Some of these issues are likely to arise routinely in protocols involving research subjects with such disorders. By increasing the representation of the subject population on IRBs and involving them in planning clinical research relevant to their disorders, investigators and their research institutions increase the likelihood that protocols will be both better designed and more responsive to the interests of the affected groups.[245] It is for these reasons that the Common Rule directs IRBs that regularly review research involving a vulnerable subject group to consider including as reviewers persons "knowledgeable about and experienced in working with these subjects."[246] This provision is advisory only. Another provision permits an IRB to seek assistance in the "review of issues which require expertise beyond or in addition to that available on the IRB," but disallows these individuals of special competence from voting with the IRB.[247] Thus, some agencies and research institutions have already required the inclusion of such individuals on IRBs. For example, the Department of Education's National Institute for Disability and Rehabilitative Research (NIDRR) must comply with a regulation that, "[w]hen an IRB reviews research that purposefully requires inclusion of children with disabilities or individuals with mental disabilities as research subjects, the IRB must have at least one person primarily concerned with the welfare of these research subjects."[248]

After evaluating schizophrenia studies at UCLA, OPRR took the stronger measure of directing the UCLA School of Medicine's IRB to "engage one or more subject representatives as IRB members who will assist the IRB in the review of issues related to the rights and welfare of subjects with severe psychiatric disorders."[249]

OPRR issued this directive even though the IRB already had a psychiatrist and a psychologist as members.[250]

NBAC's recommendation aims to ensure that the special concerns and knowledge of this population are represented in IRB deliberations and conveyed, as appropriate, to investigators. Persons who have suffered from mental disorders, or those who are familiar with the problems caused by these disorders, are often uniquely helpful for evaluating the potential problems posed by a specific research protocol.

CREATION OF A SPECIAL STANDING PANEL (SSP)

Recommendation 2. The Secretary of the Department of Health and Human Services should convene a Special Standing Panel (SSP) on research involving persons with mental disorders that may affect decisionmaking capacity. The panel's tasks should include:

1. reviewing individual protocols that cannot otherwise be approved under the recommendations described in this report, that have been forwarded by IRBs to the SSP for its consideration. If the SSP finds that a protocol offers the possibility of substantial benefit to the population under study, that its risks to subjects are reasonable in relation to this possible benefit, and that it could not be conducted without the proposed population, then the SSP may approve the protocol if it is satisfied that all appropriate safeguards are incorporated. Under no circumstance, however, should the SSP approve a protocol that reasonable, competent persons would decline to enter;

2. promulgating guidelines that would permit local IRBs to approve protocols that cannot otherwise be approved under the recommendations described in this report. Such guidelines could suggest that a particular class or category of research, using specified research interventions with certain identified populations, could be considered by local IRBs without the need to resort to the SSP for further approval. Under no circumstances, however, should the SSP promulgate guidelines permitting IRBs to approve research that would enroll subjects who lack decisionmaking capacity in protocols that reasonable, competent persons would decline to enter.

The SSP should have members who can represent the diverse interests of potential research subjects, the research community, and the public. The panel's protocol approvals and guidelines should all be published in an appropriate form that ensures reasonable notice to interested members of the public.

Those federal agencies that are signatories of the Common Rule should agree to use the SSP, and the SSP's effectiveness should be reviewed no later than five years after inception.

In the case of research involving greater than minimal risk that does not hold out the prospect of direct medical benefit to subjects, there may be protocols that, while not meeting the requirements of Recommendation 12 below, nevertheless may present a compelling balance of risks and benefits, and thus warrant further review. IRBs could refer such protocols to the SSP, which would review them on a case-by-case basis. Over time, the SSP could also set guidelines for entire categories of research. Once these guidelines were promulgated, protocols consistent with these guidelines could be reviewed and approved by the local IRB. In reviewing individual protocols and considering particular categories of research, the SSP should determine whether the protocol is of substantial importance, its risks are reasonable in relation to the potential benefits, and it could not be conducted without involving subjects with mental disorders. In addition, the SSP should specify (1) any special procedures or protections needed to ensure that the risks to subjects are minimized; (2) the means to maximize the informed and voluntary nature of participation, including the permission obtained from subjects' LARs [legally authorized representatives]; and (3) the IRB's special obligations to monitor the progress of the research and the ongoing adequacy of the protection afforded subjects. The SSP should include members from among the following groups: persons with mental disorders, members of their families, advocates for the rights and welfare of this population of persons, experts in the law and ethics of experimentation, researchers, and clinicians with expertise in the area of research.

This recommendation is intended to provide some genuine flexibility for the system to respond to new knowledge and to create a greater uniformity of understanding in what is a controversial area. As stressed throughout this report, there remain certain concerns about the adequacy of protections for persons with mental disorders in research. NBAC believes, however, that with advances being made in research, and the increased sensitivity of investigators and IRBs to ethical issues arising in research involving persons with mental disorders, there will be more examples of research that promises either significant scientific benefits for persons with mental disorders or significant increases in understanding their conditions. By assessing these examples on a case-by-case basis through an open consensus process, the Secretary would have access to a gradually evolving list of research examples (including the procedures used and any special protections required). Such a process might eventually result in an informed delegation to IRBs of the authority to approve a particular class of research protocols.

NBAC believes that the SSP could provide careful and timely evaluation of controversial research protocols that could not otherwise be approved under the other recommendations in this report. As already noted, the Secretary's authority within the regulations pertaining to research with children includes a provision for a special review process, which has been rarely used. The intent of NBAC's recommendation is to provide the Secretary with a more viable and flexible mechanism to address important concerns of researchers and the public: How, if at all, can potentially important research that involves greater than minimal risk and does not hold out the prospect of direct benefit to subjects be conducted on persons with mental disorders who lack decisionmaking capacity, when the very ability of the individual subjects to assess the risks of such research may be lacking? How can potential subjects and their families be assured that their rights and welfare are protected? This mechanism may provide a way forward for some protocols in this area.

II. Recommendations Regarding Research Design

APPROPRIATE SUBJECT SELECTION

> *Recommendation 3.* An IRB should not approve research protocols targeting persons
> with mental disorders as subjects when such research can be done with other subjects.

One important justification for research involving those with mental disorders
is the need for progress in the treatment of these very conditions. However, because of this population's potential vulnerability, we should prohibit research
targeting them if that research can be conducted equally well with other subjects.
At least two reasons support this prohibition. First, it is important, on grounds
of justice and fairness, to discourage any tendency to engage these persons in research simply because they are in some sense more available than others. Second,
this prohibition would further reinforce the importance of informed consent in
human subjects research. The principles of justice and respect for persons jointly
imply that IRBs should not approve research protocols targeting persons with decisional impairments due to mental disorders when the research does not, by
design, require such subjects.

There are circumstances, however, under which the use of subjects without
these disorders may not be scientifically valid or appropriate. For example,
if the research bears directly on a disorder that underlies the subject's decisional impairment, and the disorder is commonly associated with such an impairment, then it may not be possible to learn how to improve diagnosis and
treatment for that disorder without, at some stage, involving subjects who are
so affected. But if the research involves new ways to protect against diseases that
are also common among those who do not have mental disorders that affect
their decisionmaking capacity, then individuals with impaired decisionmaking capacity should not be targeted for recruitment. To do so would be a form
of exploitation.[251]

NBAC is not suggesting that individuals with mental disorders should be
precluded from participating in research unrelated to their mental disorder. These
same individuals, if they are able to consent, would be permitted, as any person
would, to choose to enter a study unrelated to their condition. This recommendation is in line with current regulations, which provide additional protections
to certain potentially vulnerable populations to ensure that they are not unfairly
burdened with involvement in research simply because, for example, they may
be more easily available.

JUSTIFYING RESEARCH DESIGN AND MINIMIZING RISKS

> *Recommendation 4.* Investigators should provide IRBs with a thorough justification
> of the research design they will use, including a description of procedures designed
> to minimize risks to subjects. In studies that are designed to provoke symptoms,
> to withdraw subjects rapidly from therapies, to use placebo controls, or otherwise
> to expose subjects to risks that may be inappropriate, IRBs should exercise height-
> ened scrutiny.

The protection of human subjects begins with an ethical study design that not only ensures the scientific validity and importance of the proposed protocol (ensuring the moral acceptability of its objective) but that also minimizes risks to subjects while still allowing the study objectives to be met. This process is accomplished by a variety of approaches, including the use of prior scientific evaluation by established peer review groups and review by an IRB. In many institutions, separate scientific review precedes an IRB's assessment of a protocol. In some institutions, IRBs also ensure the scientific merit of a protocol through using their own members or outside consultants. Whatever procedure is used, investigators and IRBs must consider ways to assess how the particular proposed research protocol would affect subjects in order to determine that a protocol will incorporate appropriate protections.

Because several specific designs used in research on mental disorders have raised concerns about increased risks to subjects, whenever an ethically controversial research design is proposed, the investigators are obligated to make every effort to minimize its associated risks. In particular, IRBs should require a clear justification for studies that include symptom provocation, placebo controls, or washout periods (particularly those involving rapid medication withdrawal), and should review carefully the criteria for including or excluding individuals from a study as well as the likely reasons for subject withdrawal, and the availability of follow-up care. In such research, the researcher and the IRB have a special obligation to ensure that the subjects or their legally authorized representatives are fully cognizant of the nature of the research design and its possible consequences.

Because many decisional impairments are associated with mental disorders that can be managed symptomatically with anti-psychotic medication, it can be argued that it is unethical to include a placebo arm in the study when a known risk is the return of symptoms. Thus, some contend that new drug investigations should always use standard therapy as a control, in spite of the additional methodological difficulties of such designs.[252] Relevant grounds for excluding placebo arms in particular studies include the following: (1) an individualized assessment reveals that certain patients would be at high risk for relapse if a current or prospective therapeutic regimen were discontinued; (2) a washout period would not be contemplated for these patients if they were not enrolling in a study; or (3) standard therapy has previously proven to be effective.

When drug-free research is considered necessary, it is important to control risks and to follow subjects who are at risk for relapse. IRBs currently have the authority to follow-up studies that they approve. In studies in which patients are at risk of relapse, IRBs should give particular attention to exercising this authority.

EVALUATING RISKS AND BENEFITS

Recommendation 5. Investigators should provide IRBs with a thorough evaluation of the risks and potential benefits to the human subjects involved in the proposed protocol. The evaluation of risks includes the nature, probability, and magnitude of any harms or discomforts to the subjects. The evaluation of benefits should distinguish possible direct medical benefits to the subject from other types of benefits.

This recommendation reaffirms what is already in the federal regulations, with a particular emphasis on tailoring the risk assessment to the population under study. The assessment should include consideration of the particular procedures proposed and their relationship to the specific conditions of the individuals who may be involved as study subjects. IRBs should be alert to the possibility that researchers and subjects may not evaluate the risks and benefits of a particular study in the same way.

Because there has been some confusion about what the current federal regulations say about levels of risk, it must be emphasized that only the regulations relating to children, found at Subpart D of the DHHS regulations (and the comparable set of regulations in the Department of Education), refer to three levels of risk. These regulations are not part of the Common Rule (which is limited only to Subpart A), and hence are not applicable to all agencies that are signatories to the Common Rule. Under current regulations agencies, investigators, and IRBs may voluntarily choose to adopt a three-tiered approach to risk assessment, should they find it to be useful. In NBAC's view, no change is needed in this component of the Common Rule, but greater attention should be given to the assessment of the nature and levels of risk by IRBs and investigators so that judgments of risk in relation to potential benefit and the level of protection provided to subjects can be more appropriately related to the risks inherent in the protocols themselves. In particular, this will be important for research in which disagreement exists about whether the risk is minimal. Although the regulations contain language that defines minimal risk, care is needed when determining whether (or how) the definitional category applies to research involving persons with mental disorders.

The risk categories in the current regulations do not automatically apply to particular procedures, but must be applied contextually in light of specific study conditions. Recently, OPRR published a revised list of the categories that may be reviewed by IRBs using an expedited review procedure.[253] The need for sensitivity in the application of risk categories is especially great when persons with mental disorders are among the potential subjects of a study. For some persons with mental disorders, their limited ability to understand the rationale for a specific intervention could cause them more distress than it would someone who fully understood the reason for the intervention. For example, repeated venipunctures (blood draws), which might be innocuous to many people, could be quite disturbing to persons with limited understanding. Thus, a procedure that *per se* presents minimal risk could nonetheless be highly threatening to those who are unable to appreciate the procedure's context or the nature of their current situation.

In particular, those who lack the practical ability to function autonomously, as in the case of institutionalized persons, may have distorted perceptions of otherwise minor interventions. Those whose treating doctor is also the researcher may feel unable to withdraw from a study and may feel more threatened by the risks of a procedure than is objectively the case. Thus, *a priori* assessments of risk levels to the subject population as a whole may need to be adjusted according to the circumstances of individual subjects. Even within a given protocol, the same intervention may entail different risk levels for different individuals depending on their particular condition. When the level of risk may be perceived to be higher for some subjects than for others, the determination of risk for the entire subject group should be made conservatively. Moreover, the range of special protections should increase as the level of risk increases. Both investigators and IRBs should be sensitive to different levels of risk and adjust the required set of protections accordingly. As a consequence, investigators who propose to involve persons with mental disorders as subjects in research must carefully articulate to IRBs the nature of their risk evaluation procedures for potential subjects.

III.   Recommendations Regarding Informed Consent and Capacity

INFORMED CONSENT TO RESEARCH

> *Recommendation 6.* No person who has the capacity for consent may be enrolled in a study without his or her informed consent. When potential subjects are capable of making informed decisions about participation, they may accept or decline participation without involvement of any third parties.

Regardless of a diagnosis of a mental disorder, persons capable of making informed decisions cannot be enrolled in a study without their informed consent unless, of course, consent is waived under existing regulations. Indeed, nothing in this report is intended to supplant federal rules governing consent waivers, which may be granted for minimal risk research that meets certain criteria. This merely reaffirms what is already in the federal regulations. A third party, such as a relative or friend, may not override the informed decisions of capable people. This is an implication of respect for persons, including their autonomous choices. Special moral and practical difficulties may arise, however, when a person's capacity can be expected to decline, either temporarily or permanently, or to fluctuate during the period of the protocol. In such cases, IRBs should ensure that the potential subject will be offered the opportunity to appoint a legally authorized representative (LAR) to make decisions, consistent with Recommendation 14 below, if the subject's decisionmaking capacity becomes impaired or is lost. As part of an informed consent process, such potential subjects must be able to understand all the usual information about the nature and purpose of the research, the procedures involved, the reasonably foreseeable risks or discomforts, potential benefits, and other relevant items.

In addition, they should also understand that consent to participate in a research protocol constitutes an agreement to take part in a project that will occur over a specified and perhaps extended period of time, during which their autonomous decisionmaking capacity may become impaired, either temporarily or permanently. Finally, investigators should be aware—and IRBs should remind them—of their responsibility to provide reasonable accommodations so that persons with impairments can, if possible, make their own decisions about research participation.

It is often possible for investigators and others to enable persons with some decisional impairments to make voluntary and informed decisions to consent or refuse participation in research. Creative measures include repetitive teaching, group sessions, videotapes, computer programs, and involvement of family members, among other approaches. Of course, some potential subjects simply cannot be enabled to make their own decisions, whatever approach is used. But creative approaches should be tried because, as Paul Appelbaum stresses, "one way of protecting people's rights and interests is to help them make decisions for themselves."[254] (See also the discussion of Recommendation 8 below.)

OBJECTION TO PARTICIPATION IN RESEARCH

Recommendation 7. Any potential or actual subject's objection to enrollment or to continued participation in a research protocol must be heeded in all circumstances. An investigator, acting with a level of care and sensitivity that will avoid the possibility or the appearance of coercion, may approach people who previously objected to ascertain whether they have changed their minds.

Even when decisionmaking capacity appears to be severely impaired, respect for persons must prevail over any asserted duty to serve the public good as a research subject. Hence, a potential or actual subject's objection must be heeded, regardless of the level of risk or potential benefit, just as it would in the case of an individual who clearly retains decisional capacity. Respect for persons requires that we avoid forcing an individual to serve as a research subject, even when the research offers the possibility of direct medical benefit to the individual, when his or her decisional capacity is in doubt, or when the research poses no more than minimal risk. While objection must always be respected, situations may arise in which the investigator could legitimately return to the subject at a later point to ascertain whether the previous objection still stands.

ASSESSING POTENTIAL SUBJECTS' CAPACITY TO DECIDE ABOUT PARTICIPATING IN A RESEARCH PROTOCOL

Recommendation 8. For research protocols that present greater than minimal risk, an IRB should require that an independent, qualified professional assess the potential subject's capacity to consent. The protocol should describe who will conduct the assessment and the nature of the assessment. An IRB should permit investigators to use less formal procedures to assess potential subjects' capacity if there are good reasons for doing so.

All potential human subjects are presumed to be capable of making decisions for themselves unless there is a particular reason to suspect that a capacity assessment will be necessary. Because of this presumption, capacity assessments are usually undertaken only when there are reasons to believe that potential subjects may not be capable of making voluntary and informed decisions about research participation. IRBs should be aware, however, that decisional impairment and incapacity may be more frequent among some people with certain mental disorders than in the general population. It is thus appropriate for IRBs to assume that capacity assessments may be needed more often in certain populations and to require investigators to explain why such assessments would be unnecessary for a particular group, especially if the research protocol poses greater than minimal risk.

Therefore, for research protocols that involve as subjects persons with mental disorders that may affect decisionmaking capacity and that also pose greater than minimal risk, NBAC believes that IRBs should generally require investigators to use independent and qualified professionals to assess whether potential subjects have the capacity to give voluntary, informed consent. As a result, investigators should provide in their research protocols a description of who will perform the assessment and what instruments they will use in doing so.

NBAC recognizes that a range of professionals may be qualified to assess capacity, and thus does not indicate which professionals should perform the assessment. NBAC also does not recommend any particular method of capacity assessment, since there is vigorous debate about methods, in part because of their different presuppositions. Instead, it recommends that investigators include in their research protocols a description of the nature of the capacity assessment that will be used as well as an indication of who will perform it. The IRB should consider, in particular, not only whether the proposed professional is qualified to perform the assessment but also whether he or she is sufficiently independent of the research team and institution. This requirement of independence is based on NBAC's conviction that conflicts of interest can, in some cases, distort professional judgment, and that they should be eliminated whenever possible.

IRBs would have the discretion to permit investigators to use less formal procedures for capacity assessment when there are good reasons for doing so. Such good reasons might include considerations of feasibility; for example, no independent, qualified professionals are available in a particular area. Less formal procedures could include the ways professionals often make judgments about capacity in routine interactions.

Requiring a formal procedure for capacity assessment, administered by an independent professional, for all potential research subjects with mental disorders does not appear to be necessary. It would perpetuate an incorrect assumption about individuals with mental disorders, namely that they are incapable unless assessed as capable. In a practical sense, requiring that IRBs approve research protocols (irrespective of their risk level), only when a formal capacity assessment will be undertaken, would impose additional and unnecessary burdens on researchers. Of course, if potential subjects appear to lack capacity, their capacity should be assessed before recruiting them for participation in research protocols.

NBAC notes that for research involving only minimal risk, IRBs would, of course, have the authority to require that a particular study include a capacity assessment if there are reasons to believe that potential subjects' capacity may be impaired. The value of such a capacity assessment prior to enrollment of a subject in a minimal risk study is clear: by finding a potential subject incapable of deciding about participation in such a study, investigators would then be obligated, unless there is a consent waiver, to ensure that such a person is enrolled only when permission has been obtained from an LAR in light of what that person would have chosen if he or she had been capable of making a decision.

NOTIFYING SUBJECTS OF INCAPACITY DETERMINATIONS AND RESEARCH ENROLLMENT

> *Recommendation 9.* A person who has been determined to lack capacity to consent to participate in a research study must be notified of that determination before permission may be sought from his or her LAR to enroll that person in the study. If permission is given to enroll such a person in the study, the potential subject must then be notified. Should the person object to participating, this objection should be heeded.

To be found decisionally incapable and then enrolled as a subject in a research protocol on the basis of alternative decisionmaking arrangements is to have certain rights curtailed, however justifiable the curtailment may be. Thus, whenever potential research subjects are found to be decisionally incapable, investigators should notify them of this determination prior to approaching their LAR for permission to enroll them as subjects in research (in accord with the relevant recommendations below).[255] Such a notification process might seem, at times, to be an empty ritual that could undermine researchers' respect for the regulatory system. Nevertheless, ethical treatment of human subjects demands that this process be observed; failure to do so may deprive the subject of the right to seek review of the decision and to pursue possible judicial intervention. People deserve to know that they have been found to lack the capacity to make a decision for themselves. At a minimum, this is a gesture of respect. Furthermore, it will allow them to assent or object to participation in research. Thus, only with unconscious persons is this interaction no more than an empty ritual.

IV. Recommendations Regarding Categories of Research

RESEARCH PROTOCOLS INVOLVING MINIMAL RISK

> *Recommendation 10.* An IRB may approve a protocol that presents only minimal risk, provided that:
>
> A. consent has been waived by an IRB, pursuant to federal regulations; or
>
> B. the potential subject gives informed consent; or
>
> C. the potential subject has given Prospective Authorization, consistent with Recommendation 13, and the potential subject's LAR gives permission, consistent with Recommendation 14; or
>
> D. the potential subject's LAR gives permission, consistent with Recommendation 14.

Persons who are capable of giving informed consent may choose to participate in research protocols that present minimal risk, whatever the prospect of direct benefit. The types of risk falling into this category of minimal risk are defined by federal regulation: "the probability and magnitude of harm or discomfort anticipated in the research are not greater in or of themselves than those ordinarily encountered in daily life or during the performance of routine physical or psychological examinations or tests."[256] This report has previously examined some of the difficulties in determining minimal risk. Additional guidance can be gleaned from the recent revision to the categories of research that may qualify for expedited IRB review. For instance, it might be argued that studies involving magnetic resonance imaging now fall within the category of minimal risk because federal regulations consider it a type of research that is approvable through expedited IRB review. But NBAC stresses, as do the federal regulations themselves, that the procedures qualifying for expedited review are not to be considered minimal risk solely because they appear on this list.[257] In the end, the determination that a procedure is less than, equal to, or greater than minimal risk rests with the local IRB, and it must take into account the specific conditions and vulnerabilities of the particular subject population.

RESEARCH PROTOCOLS INVOLVING GREATER THAN MINIMAL RISK
THAT OFFER THE PROSPECT OF DIRECT MEDICAL BENEFIT TO SUBJECTS

> *Recommendation 11.* An IRB may approve a protocol that presents greater than minimal risk but offers the prospect of direct medical benefit to the subject, provided that:
>
> A. the potential subject gives informed consent; or
> B . the potential subject has given Prospective Authorization, consistent with Recommendation 13, and the potential subject's LAR gives permission, consistent with Recommendation 14; or
> C . the potential subject's LAR gives permission, consistent with Recommendation 14. The research must also comply with Recommendations 7, 8, and 9.

Some important research cannot be done without the involvement of persons with mental disorders and some of that research may offer the prospect of direct medical benefit to those who participate. An example is the study of dopamine receptor function and schizophrenia, for which there are currently no suitable alternative models, and which could aid the treatment of individuals participating in the study.[258]

No one is obligated to participate in a study, even if it may be of direct medical benefit to him or her. Therefore, in order for research in this category to go forward, (1) the potential subject's informed consent must be obtained, or (2) the potential subject must have given Prospective Authorization to participate and his or her LAR must give permission, or (3) the potential subject's LAR must give permission in accord with what that person would have chosen if he or she had been capable of deciding. Recommendations that follow, particularly 13 and

14, indicate the circumstances under which prospective authorization and LAR permission can be given. Persons have the right to object to research participation before or during the research, and their objection must be heeded, even if they gave prior consent or Prospective Authorization, the LAR gives permission, and the research offers the prospect of direct medical benefit.

RESEARCH PROTOCOLS INVOLVING GREATER THAN MINIMAL RISK RESEARCH THAT DO NOT OFFER THE PROSPECT OF DIRECT MEDICAL BENEFIT TO SUBJECTS

Recommendation 12. An IRB may approve a protocol that presents greater than minimal risk but does not offer the prospect of direct medical benefit to the subject, provided that:

A. the potential subject gives informed consent; or

B . the potential subject has given Prospective Authorization, consistent with Recommendation 13, and the potential subject's LAR gives permission, consistent with Recommendation 14; or

C . the protocol is approved on the condition of its approval by the panel described in Recommendation 2, or falls within the guidelines developed by the panel, and the potential subject's LAR gives permission, consistent with Recommendation 14. The research must also comply with Recommendations 7, 8, and 9.

As the most controversial category of research involving subjects with mental disorders, research protocols that present greater than minimal risk but do not offer the prospect of direct medical benefit require special attention. Such research should be conducted only under the conditions outlined in this recommendation.

First, potential subjects who have the capacity to decide whether they want to participate in such a study cannot be enrolled without their informed consent. This condition expresses what is implied by the principle of respect for persons, including their autonomous choices.

Second, potential subjects who now lack the capacity to give informed consent may be enrolled in such research if, while capable, they gave Prospective Authorization for participation in a particular class of research and their LAR now gives permission in accord with that authorization. The requirements for Prospective Authorization and LAR permission are spelled out in subsequent recommendations, especially Recommendations 13 and 14.

The third possibility (C) is for the research protocol to pass the scrutiny of the SSP proposed in Recommendation 2—or to fall within the guidelines developed by that panel—and for the potential subject's LAR to give permission in accord with the conditions specified in Recommendation 14.

For (B) and (C) above, the subject must be notified of the results of a formal capacity determination and of the LAR's decision to enroll him or her in research. The subject's objection to participation in the research protocol at the outset or during the research must be heeded.

V.   Recommendations Regarding Surrogate Decision Making

PROSPECTIVE AUTHORIZATION

> *Recommendation 13.* A person who has the capacity to make decisions about participation in research may give Prospective Authorization to a particular class of research if its risks, potential direct and indirect benefits, and other pertinent conditions have been explained. Based on the Prospective Authorization, an LAR may enroll the subject after the subject has lost the capacity to make decisions, provided the LAR is available to monitor the subject's recruitment, participation, and withdrawal. The greater the risks posed by the research protocol under consideration, the more specific the subject's Prospective Authorization should be to entitle the LAR to permit enrollment.

The principle of respect for persons, including respect for their autonomous choices, extends to their choices made while capable to cover future periods of mental impairment or incapacity. NBAC believes that one of the ways in which individuals can be respected in their choices is to provide them opportunity to express their preferences (where they have them) regarding future research participation, within certain limits.

This Prospective Authorization cannot be a "blank check" for research participation. Hence, NBAC limits valid Prospective Authorization to "a particular class of research" and then only if the potential subject, while capable, understood the "risks, potential direct and indirect benefits, and other pertinent conditions" of this particular class of research. Furthermore, the degree of specificity of the Prospective Authorization should correlate with the level of risk of the research protocol for which the person is a potential subject: as the research protocol's level of risk rises, so must the degree of specificity of the prospective authorization before the LAR may legitimately grant permission for research participation.

Finally, the prospective authorization is not by itself valid for enrollment in research. It must be accompanied by the LAR's permission and availability for monitoring. The conditions for the LAR's permission are further specified in Recommendation 14.

LEGALLY AUTHORIZED REPRESENTATIVES (LARS)

> *Recommendation 14.* An LAR may give permission (within the limits set by the other recommendations) to enroll in a research protocol a person who lacks the capacity to decide whether to participate, provided that:
>
> A. the LAR bases decisions about participation upon a best estimation of what the subject would have chosen if capable of making a decision; and
>
> B . the LAR is available to monitor the subject's recruitment, participation, and withdrawal from the study; and
>
> C . the LAR is a person chosen by the subject, or is a relative or friend of the subject.

Currently, an LAR is an individual authorized by law (statutory or judicial) or previously published institutional rules to make medical decisions on behalf of another individual. Sometimes it is appropriate for the LAR to give permission for a currently incapable person to be enrolled in a research protocol. This recommendation sets forth the basis on which the LAR should grant or withhold such permission; the requirement that the LAR be available to serve as monitor during the research; and some limits on who may serve as an LAR.

The standard for LAR decisions should be what the potential subject would have chosen if they had been capable of making a decision. Often called "substituted judgment," this standard requires that the surrogate decision maker, the LAR, make a decision according to his or her "best estimation" of what the subject would have chosen. Where the potential subject made a Prospective Authorization, the LAR can be more confident about conveying what he or she would have chosen. And, in accord with Recommendation 13, as the level of research risk increases, it is important that the Prospective Authorization be more specific. In the absence of a Prospective Authorization, the LAR must rely on other sources of information about the potential subject's values and preferences. Where the LAR lacks any evidence about the person's values and preferences, the LAR may not grant permission to investigators to enroll him or her in research unless judgments about that person's "best interests" could warrant such permission. Great caution is needed, however, because LARs also may succumb to the therapeutic misconception, and, in the absence of information about the subject's values or choices, make inappropriate judgments about the subject's best interests.

Another necessary condition (B) is the LAR's availability for appropriate involvement with the research subject through the process of recruitment for participation in and withdrawal from the research protocol. If the LAR is not available for such a role, then his or her permission to enroll the potential subject in research should not be accepted.

Finally, the LAR should be someone selected for this role by the potential subject or "a relative or friend" of the potential subject, as authorized by state law or institutional rules. Ideally, the LAR should be chosen by the potential subject. Potential subjects are often able to select their LARs even when they lack the capacity to make a voluntary, informed decision about research participation or a Prospective Authorization for research participation. If the LAR is assigned by state law or institutional rules, rather than selected by the potential subject, investigators should rely on that LAR's permission only if he or she is a relative or a friend of the potential subject. Such a relationship may increase the likelihood that the available LAR will in fact conscientiously "monitor the subject's recruitment, participation, and withdrawal from the study" as well as being "available" to do so.

EXPANSION OF THE CATEGORY OF LEGALLY AUTHORIZED REPRESENTATIVES
AND OF THE POWERS GRANTED UNDER STATUTES FOR DURABLE POWERS
OF ATTORNEY (DPA) FOR HEALTH CARE

Recommendation 15. In order to expand the category of LARs:

A. an investigator should accept as an LAR, subject to the requirements in Recommendation 14, a relative or friend of the potential subject who is recognized as an

LAR for purposes of clinical decision making under the law of the state where the research takes place.

B . states should confirm, by statute or court decision, that:

1. an LAR for purposes of clinical decision making may serve as an LAR for research; and

2. friends as well as relatives may serve as both clinical and research LARs if they are actively involved in the care of a person who lacks decisionmaking capacity.

Recommendation 16. States should enact legislation, if necessary, to ensure that persons who choose to plan for future research participation are entitled to choose their LAR.

Although their scope varies considerably, statutes in 36 states and the District of Columbia authorize surrogates (without need of judicial appointment) to make health care decisions when a person lacks decisionmaking capacity. In the other states, custom recognizes family members as surrogates. Most statutes relating to substitute decision making do not explicitly refer to research, although they may be construed as implicitly authorizing surrogate consent for participation in research that holds out the prospect of direct medical benefit. NBAC is not aware of any state statutes that authorize a third party to enroll an incapable person in research that does not offer the prospect of direct medical benefit, even if the risk is minimal. In addition, every state recognizes the DPA for health care or an equivalent proxy designation mechanism. As is true of laws relating to substitute decision making, no state statutes authorize a proxy designated under a clinical DPA to consent to the patient-subject's participation in research that does not hold out the prospect of direct benefit to the subjects.

Although NBAC does not endorse the idea of authorizing third parties to enroll incapable subjects in research involving greater than minimal risk without the prospect of direct medical benefit, it is undoubtedly true that matters related to proxy decision making are ordinarily the province of state law, and principles of federalism suggest that deference be given to these state policy judgments. Here, however, each state has already decided to give clinical decisionmaking authority to these proxies. It would do no violence to state prerogatives if, for the reasons stated in this report, the federal government were to extend the authority of these proxies so that they could grant permission for participation in certain federally conducted or funded research. This could be accomplished by an amendment to the Common Rule that would define the term "legally authorized representative" to include those who, under the law of the state where the research is conducted, may serve as proxy decision makers for clinical care. Without Prospective Authorization, the authority of the LAR to enroll subjects would, however, extend only to minimal risk research or research involving greater than minimal risk where there is a prospect of direct medical benefit. Where research involves greater than minimal risk and does not hold out the prospect of direct medical benefit, and where the protocol has not been approved by the panel described in Recommendation 2, the authority of the LAR would extend only to permitting continued enrollment, withdrawing the subject, or enrolling the subject pursuant to the subject's Prospective Authorization.

INVOLVING SUBJECTS' FAMILY AND FRIENDS

> *Recommendation 17.* For research protocols involving subjects who have fluctuating or limited decisionmaking capacity or prospective incapacity, IRBs should ensure that investigators establish and maintain ongoing communication with involved caregivers, consistent with the subjects' autonomy and with medical confidentiality.

This report has stressed several times the important role of "involved caregivers," especially family members. Communication between these caregivers and the research team may be important in the relationships between both parties and the research subject. It may, for example, enable involved caregivers to respond more appropriately to the subject's particular needs, some of which may be affected by participation in the research protocol, and it may provide researchers with helpful information about the subject's responses during the research. Such communication should, of course, be limited by the ethical and legal requirements of respect for personal autonomy and medical confidentiality. Concerned parties, including professional and patient/family organizations, should begin discussions about ways to improve communication while, at the same time, respecting subjects' choices about confidential information.

VI.   Recommendations Regarding Education, Research, and Support

REVIEWING AND DEVELOPING EDUCATIONAL MATERIALS REGARDING RESEARCH

> *Recommendation 18.* Professional associations and organizations should develop (or review their existing) educational materials pertaining to research involving persons with mental disorders to ensure that they are adequate to inform the health care community and the public of ethical issues related to the involvement of such persons as research subjects, and to convey the importance of measures to ensure that their rights and welfare are adequately protected.

A serious commitment to ethical research must be maintained at all levels of the research endeavor. Educational outreach through public and private organizations can serve as a valuable tool for ensuring the continuation of this commitment in the field. Agencies should develop educational materials on research ethics for IRB members and investigators involved in research with persons who have mental disorders. These materials should emphasize that many persons with mental disorders have the capacity to make decisions for themselves. NBAC further supports the development of educational materials to assist the general public (specifically populations of persons—and their families—who may encounter difficulties with decisionmaking capacity) in deciding about research participation. These materials should include information about risks and potential benefits of participation, and should offer guidelines for making informed choices about research participation (e.g., how to protect oneself as a research subject, what questions to ask, who to ask). NBAC recommends that all materials be circulated widely in order to encourage a more general public dialogue regarding the social and scientific issues engendered by research in this field.

EXPANDING KNOWLEDGE ABOUT CAPACITY ASSESSMENT AND INFORMED CONSENT

> *Recommendation 19.* The National Institutes of Health (NIH) should sponsor research to expand understanding about decisionmaking capacity, the best means for assessing decisionmaking capacity, techniques for enhancing the process of informed consent, and the possible roles of surrogate decision makers in research. It should sponsor research to evaluate the risks of various research interventions, and the attitudes of potential subjects toward the prospect of participating in research. Particular attention should be paid to attitudes toward participating in research of greater than minimal risk that does not offer the prospect of direct medical benefit to subjects. These data may be of particular value to the panel described in Recommendation 2.

The NIH should ensure that proposals for training grants and center grants include appropriate provisions for training and technical assistance in the issues discussed in this report. Where appropriate, NIH and OPRR should consider using consensus development conferences or workshops to advance discussion of these issues.

NIH has been active in sponsoring research on informed consent,[259] in supporting training opportunities and grants for courses in research ethics, and in sponsoring a helpful meeting on the subject of research involving persons of questionable capacity, which has been extensively referenced in this report. In NBAC's view, NIH is ideally positioned to support further intensive research on many of the issues identified in our report.

INSTITUTE OF MEDICINE REVIEW OF RESEARCH STUDIES

> *Recommendation 20.* The Department of Health and Human Services should contract with the Institute of Medicine (IOM) to conduct a comprehensive review and evaluation of the nature and extent of challenge, washout, and placebo controlled studies with subjects with mental disorders that may affect decision making.

Recommendation 4 requires investigators to submit a "thorough justification" of their research design and IRBs to exercise "heightened scrutiny" when examining research protocols that involve drug challenges, drug washout, and placebo controls. It would be helpful to investigators, IRBs, and the SSP to have comprehensive data available about the extent of research involving these designs, the actual and potential contributions of research using these designs, the medical conditions of the persons who are commonly recruited, and the process of obtaining informed consent or permission (including the use of consent forms). Data about symptom provocation and washout studies are needed, because these are controversial designs for which few data are currently available. Moreover, NBAC heard the greatest expression of concern from the public about these designs. Since NBAC does not have the resources or authority to conduct a comprehensive study, a focused effort by the IOM would be very valuable. The proposed review and evaluation should also include placebo-controlled research, about which there is also considerable controversy, especially when effective treatments are available for some disorders.

INCREASED FUNDING TO SUPPORT NECESSARY PROTECTIONS OF HUMAN SUBJECTS

> *Recommendation 21.* Compliance with the recommendations set forth in this report will require additional resources. All research sponsors (government, private sector enterprises, and academic institutions) should work together to make these resources available.

Several recommendations, for example, the requirement for independent capacity assessment and the establishment and use of additional review procedures, may require funds over and above the direct and indirect costs usually provided through federal grants. In NBAC's view, these additional protections are necessary, and important research should not be thwarted because the resources are not available to provide the necessary protections.

Additional Guidance for IRBs

It will take time for the regulatory recommendations listed above to be considered, further evaluated, and perhaps implemented in whole or in part. Meanwhile, NBAC hopes that individual IRBs will adopt, on a voluntary basis, the spirit and substance of many of the additional protections described above. Those IRBs that choose not to adopt such policies should consider publicly disclosing their reasons and the resulting differences in their policies.[260]

THE RESEARCH CONTEXT

IRBs should further consider whether the particular context of a proposed research protocol would tend to undermine the capacity of persons with mental disorders to provide informed consent due to their psychosocial vulnerability or to their misconception of therapeutic efficacy. IRBs should be alert to potential conflicts arising from the dependence that in-patient or continuing-care subjects may have on their institutions, or from the dual role played by the potential subject's physician as a member of the research team (e.g., as a recruiter or as a source of names of potential subjects).

CONSIDERATIONS IN RESEARCH DESIGN

Subjects with serious illnesses are often more vulnerable than others to exploitation when they are involved in randomized clinical trials. Although the study itself must satisfy the condition of clinical equipoise, and may offer the prospect of direct medical benefit, there will be instances in which the experimental arm of a study turns out to be more beneficial to subjects than the placebo arm (or standard care). One way to ameliorate this problem is to incorporate into the study design a non-research or "wraparound phase" which, following the conclusion of the research period, could provide the subject with some beneficial intervention independent of the study itself. Using such a wraparound phase can be problematic, however, because it may shift the balance of protection in the opposite and equally problematic direction by providing an inappropriate incentive to participate in studies, that is, to derive perceived benefits without having to pay for the treatment. Nevertheless, wraparound phases are suitable follow-ups to certain kinds of research, including those that provoke symptoms. In appropriate circumstances, IRBs could require a wraparound phase as part of the overall study design.

Subjects who are included in study arms in which they receive an experimental drug are also vulnerable to unfair treatment if the research results indicate that the drug is effective, but the subjects do not receive it after the study concludes. In such circumstances, IRBs could condition study approval on the manufacturer's commitment to continue to supply the medication to research participants (including any subjects, such as placebo or standard therapy controls, who did not receive it during the study). Here again, such a condition would have to be considered carefully in view of its potential for inappropriate inducement.

POSSIBLE ADDITIONAL PROTECTIONS FOR THE CONSENT PROCESS

The use of a consent auditor has been suggested as an additional procedural protection in the recruitment of research subjects who may be decisionally impaired. A consent auditor, who cannot be a member of the study team but may be, for example, a member of the IRB or an institutional ethicist, witnesses the consent process and then either certifies it as valid or informs the principal investigator that, due to the inadequacy of the process, an individual is not able to give valid consent. IRBs could require consent auditors for potential subjects who have conditions often associated with a decisional impairment. A system of audited consent would involve a substantial investment by research institutions, but the requirement could be limited to studies that have certain characteristics, such as those that involve greater than minimal risk and/or those that do not offer the prospect of direct medical benefit to the subject.

In addition, studies with subjects who are decisionally impaired may take place over extended periods. One of the essential conditions of ethical research is the subject's continued voluntary participation, but those who are deeply involved with and dependent on the health care system may feel unable to withdraw from a study. A requirement for periodic re-consenting would help ensure that a patient's continued involvement is truly voluntary, would provide the occasion to reassess decisionmaking capacity and, if necessary, would trigger an advance directive or surrogate arrangement. Re-consent arrangements conform with the spirit of informed consent as a process rather than a single event, and with the view that human research participants are partners in the study process rather than passive subjects.[261]

Although re-consenting is another potentially labor-intensive measure that might add to the cost and complexity of the human research system, some long-term studies supported by the National Institute on Aging already include such a procedure.[262] IRBs should consider attaching a re-consent requirement to certain studies based on their length, on their risks and benefits, and on the potential decisional impairment of persons participating as subjects, such as those with progressive neurological disorders or fluctuating capacity.

FURTHER CONSIDERATIONS ABOUT LARS

In NBAC's view, an LAR ideally should be appointed by the potential subject. As the above recommendations reflect, the twin goals of appropriate protection of subjects and the conduct of high-quality research can often be accomplished by utilizing a carefully described advance planning process. Anticipatory planning for research participation is not a "research advance directive" but a version of the standard informed consent process. A critical difference between the planning and informed consent process is that the planning process should include the prospect of a loss of decisionmaking capacity during the study period, a consideration that is not routinely part of an informed consent process. Planning for research participation should involve the following elements: (a) the identification of an LAR; and (b) the completion of a DPA document, which identifies the person designated as an LAR, and provides any specific and relevant information that would assist the LAR in making research decisions on behalf of the subjects should they later become incapable of deciding about research participation on their own.

For persons with fluctuating capacity and those who are at risk for loss of capacity during a study, NBAC's view is that comprehensive anticipatory planning for research participation should involve identifying an LAR who can function as a surrogate decision maker. There is always the possibility that unanticipated incidents will occur in a research study, incidents that a surrogate may find relevant to the subject's continued welfare and his or her participation in research. The surrogate could be an informal caregiver—for example, a family member or close friend—but not a member of the study team. Because of its concern that LARs could, at times, have some significant self-interest in enrolling a now incapable person into a study, NBAC recommends that IRBs request documentation of the designation of the LAR.

In such anticipatory planning, the potential subject must understand that he or she has appointed an LAR as a surrogate to make decisions concerning continuing research participation in a particular class of research protocols should the subject become unable to make these decisions. The subject must further understand that the LAR may never overrule the subject's wish not to participate in the research protocol or in any part of it, but may overrule the subject's instructions to continue participation, under certain conditions. Potential subjects must be aware that they have given the researchers permission to provide their LAR and their health care provider with information about treatment. They should also appreciate that, should their preferences change, they may alter their instructions at any time they have the capacity to do so, and that they may withdraw from the study at any time, whatever their level of decision-making capacity.

In turn, the researchers should agree to discuss information about the research site and the subject's treatment in the study (e.g., possibilities of decompensation, description of likely symptoms, data about medications and potential side effects, and possible danger to self or others) with the LAR. The research team should also make adequate provision for a thorough diagnostic assessment of the subject's current clinical status and develop an appropriate continuing treatment plan should the subject decompensate, become unable to cooperate, and drop out of the study.

During the course of the study, it is highly desirable for the subject's LAR to work closely with the subject's independent health care professional to ensure the subject's welfare. This health care professional should have no relationship with the research and, therefore, should be concerned only with subject's well-being and interests, should follow the subject's treatment, and should be in communication with the surrogate.

INDEPENDENT HEALTH CARE PROFESSIONAL ADVISORS

For greater than minimal risk research, whether or not direct medical benefit is possible, IRBs should consider whether to require that an independent health care professional be identified in advance of the research to serve as a consultant to the subject or their representative. Subjects or their LARs may or may not choose to utilize the independent health care professional. Investigators should consider making available or accessible (to the subject or the LAR) any information the independent health care professional requests in relationship to the protocol.

VOLUNTARY SELF-EVALUATION

IRBs may consider, alone, with other IRBs, or in collaboration with professional organizations, voluntarily adopting NBAC's recommendations and then, after a suitable period of time, assessing their effect on the quality of the IRB review process. For example, since there has been considerable discussion in this report about the appropriateness of using two levels of risk in IRB review, it might be worthwhile to review protocols using this strategy, as compared with a strategy in which three (or more) risk levels are explicitly used. Where this evaluation is conducted in a more formal manner, the results could be published and shared with the IRB and research communities.

Guidance for Institutions

While investigators and IRBs bear a considerable responsibility for ensuring the ethical conduct of research involving human subjects, the institutions in which research occurs share some of this responsibility. In particular, since federal grants are awarded to institutions, not individual investigators, and since an Assurance of Compliance is negotiated between an institution and OPRR, the behavior of institutions may be thought of as the foundation upon which ethical practice is built.

AUDIT AND DISCLOSURE

The policies of IRBs and the institutions they serve play a central role in protecting human subjects, particularly vulnerable populations. Thus, IRBs should consider voluntarily undertaking a series of measures to open their activities to greater public view and accountability. In this regard, NBAC makes the following general recommendations.

1. Each IRB should make publicly available brief descriptions of the policies and procedures that characterize the key aspects of its ongoing work.
2. Each IRB should provide, on an annual basis, appropriate summary statistics regarding the overall nature and scope of the activities it has approved.
3. Each institution incorporating an IRB should adopt appropriate internal audit procedures to assure itself that its IRBs are following all appropriate rules and regulations.

It is NBAC's view that IRBs can effectively use the mechanisms of audit (both internal and external) and disclosure to improve accountability and inspire public confidence in their oversight activities. Indeed, these oversight tools can be an excellent substitute for a wide variety of excessively detailed rules and regulations. Furthermore, such mechanisms can be used by all institutions, for all research involving human subjects.

Notes

[243] The conclusions and recommendations directly address research that involves adult patients or subjects in research. They do not supplant the regulations governing research involving children.

[244] Expert Panel Report to the National Institutes of Health, *Research Involving Individuals with Questionable Capacity to Consent*, 1.

[245] Expert Panel Report to the National Institutes of Health, *Research Involving Individuals with Questionable Capacity to Consent*, 3.

[246] 45 CFR 46.107(a) (1998).

[247] 45 CFR 46.107(f) (1998).

[248] 34 CFR 356.3(c)(2) (1998).

[249] Office for Protection from Research Risks, supra, 21–22.

[250] Id.

[251] An individual with impaired decisionmaking ability who, for any reason, is not otherwise an appropriate subject for a particular protocol may have a life-threatening condition for which there is no satisfactory treatment. Under these circumstances, when the protocol is designed to ameliorate or potentially cure the life-threatening condition, current regulations permit these individuals, on compassionate grounds, to obtain the investigational treatment. Therefore, as a matter of justice, all persons, regardless of their decisionmaking capacity, whose best therapeutic alternative may be an innovative treatment, should

have access to that treatment. The specific term used in the regulations is "treatment use." Criteria for "permitting an investigational drug to be used for treatment use under a treatment protocol or treatment IND" are: "(1) FDA shall permit an investigational drug to be used for a treatment use under a treatment protocol or treatment IND if: (i) The drug is intended to treat a serious or immediately life-threatening disease; (ii) There is no comparable or satisfactory alternative drug or other therapy available to treat that stage of the disease in the intended patient population; (iii) The drug is under investigation in a controlled clinical trial under an IND in effect for the trial, or all clinical trials have been completed; and (iv) The sponsor of the controlled clinical trial is actively pursuing marketing approval of the investigational drug with due diligence." 21 CFR §312.34(b) (1998).

[252] Donald Addington, "The Use of Placebos in Clinical Trials for Acute Schizophrenia," *Canadian Journal of Psychiatry* 40 (1995): 171–76; Kenneth J. Rothman and Karin B. Michels, "The Continued Unethical Use of Placebo Controls," *New England Journal of Medicine* 331 (1994): 394–98.

[253] See, Categories of Research That May Be Reviewed by the Institutional Review Board (IRB) Through An Expedited Review Procedure, 63 Fed. Reg. 60,364 (1998) (to be codified at 45 CFR 46).

[254] Paul S. Appelbaum, "Missing the Boat: Competence and Consent in Psychiatric Research," *American Journal of Psychiatry* 155 (1998): 1486–88, 1488.

[255] Another way to express this issue is whether the assent of incapable subjects should be required. Rebecca Dresser, *Research Involving Persons With Mental Disabilities: A Review of Policy Issues and Proposals* (contract paper for the National Bioethics Advisory Commission, September 1997). See volume II of this report.

[256] 45 CFR 46.102(i) (1998).

[257] 45 CFR 46.110(b)(1) (1998).

[258] See, for example, Anthony F. Lehman et al., "Translating research into practice: the Schizophrenia Patient Outcomes Research Team (PORT) treatment recommendations," *Schizophrenia Bulletin* 24 (1998): 1–10.

[259] See for example: Informed Consent in Research Involving Human Subjects, *NIH Guide to Grants and Contracts*, RFA-OD-97-001, vol 25, no. 32. (September 27, 1997).

[260] NBAC is currently reviewing the federal system for overseeing human subjects protection, including the IRB system, and will issue a separate report on this subject. For this reason, this report offers only a few additional areas of guidance for IRBs; other, more comprehensive, recommendations for IRBs will appear in this later report.

[261] An expert panel convened by NIH also notes that "repeated exposure to information in 'small doses' over time may greatly improve comprehension." Expert Panel Report to the National Institutes of Health, *Research Involving Individuals with Questionable Capacity to Consent*, 14.

[262] One such example is the Baltimore Longitudinal Study of Aging (BLSA). The protocol for reconsenting participants was described to NBAC as follows: "At this time, competency evaluations are done by a working group in the Laboratory of Personality and Cognition composed of Susan Resnick (NIA neuropsychologist), Claudia Kawas (a collaborating neurologist from JHMI), Jeff Metter (physician), and if necessary Chester Schmidt (Chief of Psychiatry at JHBMC). Each BLSA participant has a baseline cognitive assessment done upon entry to the study. Cognition is not formally assessed by serial determinations until participants are 55 years of age when most patients undergo the cognitive battery administered by the Cognition Section of LPC. Once patients enter this phase of the study, their test results are reviewed and if substantial loss of cognitive function is suspected the participant and his/her records (medical

and psychometric) are reviewed by Drs. Resnick, Kawas, and Metter. At this time, Dr. Kawas performs a formal neurological evaluation to determine a medical cause of the cognition decline. In the case in which affective disorders are suspected, Dr. Schmidt will be consulted. Family members are immediately involved in the status of the evaluation and if competency is judged to be impaired, family members are asked to provide consent for further participation if the patient is agreeable and the family members believe that participation is in the interest of the patient. Since the BLSA is an observational study, not an interventional clinical one, issues of study-related risks (morbidity and mortality) have not been raised in terms of greater than minimal risk. Personal communication, Dr. Terrie Wetle, Deputy Director, National Institute on Aging, July 2, 1998.

Chapter 6
The Use of Animals and Other Resources in Research

6.1 INTRODUCTION

The use of animals in research remains a controversial topic. Like some of the vulnerable human populations discussed in the previous chapter, animals are not able to consent to their participation as research subjects. Unlike members of some of these vulnerable human populations, animals are not able to assent to participate in research either. Furthermore, the justifications for using some vulnerable human populations in research do not always work for animals. One justification that is occasionally offered for using humans who are unable to offer consent is that they would consent to participation as research subjects if they were able. However, the same is not often said of animals, for two reasons. First, we do not know what animals would consent to, if they were able to consent. Some people even think that it is a mistake to say of certain animals that they are having the kind of thoughts that would allow one to assess whether they would wish to serve as subjects of scientific research. Perhaps some animals can make these assessments, but many certainly cannot. Perhaps, then, some animals can be used as research subjects, and some cannot. Second, many people who are confident that animals would be able to assess what they would want under these circumstances claim that animals would not consent to be the subjects of research experiments. Unlike some vulnerable human populations, for whom surrogates or legal guardians can truly say "this individual would want to participate in research, but simply is unable to consent," we are less likely to attribute thoughts about consent to research participation to animals.

The decreased likelihood that animals would, if they were able to, consent to be subjects in research, is caused by the kinds of experiments that are often performed on animals. Some experiments on animals involve the first stages of testing a scientific hypothesis. When Phase I, II, or III clinical trials are performed, there is already some evidence that the drug or therapy being tested may be of use. In the case of Phase II and III clinical trials, testing for toxicity and dosage levels on other human subjects has already taken place. In the case of Phase I clinical trials, animal testing has already taken place. But what testing takes place before the animal testing? Animal experiments are often the beginning of research, and as a result the likelihood of a favorable risk/expected-benefit ratio, for benefit that accrues directly to the animal or to science as a whole, may be small.

A second reason for believing that animals would be unlikely to consent to their own participation in research is that in some cases, the end-point of animal experimentation is death or a similarly undesirable end. The Nuremberg Code, included in the Chapter 2 readings, prohibits experiments in which the expected outcome is that human subjects will die due to the experimental procedure. However, some animal experiments are designed with the expectation that the animals will die in the course of the experiment. For example, in testing a drug that may be efficacious in fighting AIDS, it is best to first give animals AIDS and then give the drug in order to see whether the drug has any effect. Forcing an animal to contract AIDS may guarantee the animal's death. It is unlikely that any animal would consent to be part of such an experiment. Other experiments that test, for example, for the carcinogenic nature of household products or pharmaceuticals presuppose that some of the animals involved will become ill during the scientific process. Even if the animals are not killed, if the experimental process leaves them in an undesirable condition, it may be appropriate to kill them after the experiment is over. It is unlikely that the animals would, if they were able to, consent to these procedures. Hence, judgments by human beings that animals would consent to participate as research subjects are probably unfounded.

Despite how unlikely it is that animals would consent to being the subjects of research studies, there nonetheless may be justifications for the use of animals in research. In this chapter we will first look at some of the arguments against the use of animals in research. The animal rights movement remains a powerful force in the United States. There continue to be legal challenges to the use of animals in research, despite the fact that it is a common practice.

After an examination of the arguments against, we will turn to some of the arguments in favor of using animals in research. Scientists have defended animal experimentation for years, primarily based on claims about the benefits of using animals as research subjects. Currently, there are regulations governing the use of some species of animals in research in the United States, and we will examine some of these regulations. Finally, we will examine the use of the environment and other resources in scientific experimentation. Scientists have a moral obligation to use limited resources responsibly, based upon their obligations to other scientists, to the public at large, and possibly to the environment itself.

6.2   ARGUMENTS OBJECTING TO ANIMAL RESEARCH

The most extreme objections to the use of animals as research subjects conclude that any use of animals in experimentation is always wrong. There are several arguments to support this claim. One argument says that it is wrong to use anyone, human or animal, for experimentation unless the individual is able to consent. Thus, since animals are unable to consent, it is wrong to use them as subjects in experimentation. Some might argue from a Kantian perspective that using anyone is always morally wrong. However, opponents of this argument observe that Kant said that using rational beings merely as a means is morally wrong, and that animals are not rational beings. Some people try to widen the Kantian sphere by saying that at least some animals are sufficiently rational and that those animals should never be used for experimentation. Some primates may be sufficiently rational, whereas other mammals, such as mice, are not. This response still allows for using some animals, namely those that are determined to be insufficiently rational, as the subjects of research.

Another argument for the claim that it is wrong to use animals in research is that animals should not be used for experiments that will ultimately benefit humans and not animals, and most of the experiments involving animals do ultimately benefit humans more than animals. The strength of this argument becomes apparent when a comparison is made between human populations and animal populations. Experiments that will benefit one human population, but force a different human population to assume all of the risks and harms of the research, are considered unjust. Many people observe that the use of animals in research involves the same type of injustice. For example, mouse populations may be injected with cancer cells and then given drugs to test their efficacy. The drugs may prevent the spread of the cancer, or even to kill cancer cells in some cases, but these drugs are being developed ultimately for human populations. However, animals have reaped the benefits of some animal experimentation, such as vaccines for rabies and tetanus. Thus, to say that animal experimentation solely benefits humans is mistaken. It remains the case, however, that human populations have benefited much more, and will continue to benefit much more, from animal experimentation than do animal populations.

Some advocates for the claim against animal research have argued that at one time animal experimentation was morally permissible but that it no longer is. Early animal experimentation was justified because science was less sophisticated than it is now. Basic physiology was best understood initially by performing experiments on animals. Early drugs were best tested initially on animals. However, the progress of science has rendered animal tests unnecessary, the proponents of this argument claim. The gains in knowledge no longer outweigh the harms that the animals suffer in these experiments. Furthermore, alternative methods, such as computer modeling, make many animal tests obsolete. Detractors question the likelihood that science has exhausted itself and that no beneficial discoveries requiring animal testing are possible. A second objection to this argument questions the viability of alternatives to animal testing, such as computer models. Although computer models may be appropriate in some cases, it is not clear that computer modeling, or other technological advances, can match the effectiveness of animal testing, at least at this time.

Finally, some people object to animal experimentation by observing that much of what plagues human beings, such as world hunger, cannot be cured by using animal experimentation. Although this point is true, it does not seem to address the question of animal experimentation. No one will dispute that much of what ails humanity cannot be cured by animal experimentation. However, there is a great deal that can be helped, at least in part, by medical and psychological experiments, and some of these experiments may involve animals. Many diseases remain to be cured, or their symptoms alleviated, by scientific advancement. Hence, it seems reasonable to allow some animal experimentation.

6.3   ARGUMENTS DEFENDING ANIMAL RESEARCH

One argument for the use of animals in research stems from a belief that animals do not feel pain in the way that we do, and perhaps do not feel pain at all, and that any animal research is morally permissible. This view was held most prominently by the philosopher René Descartes, who claimed that animals are akin to machines in their inability to feel pain. This view is widely discredited today. Those who hold that animal research is morally permissible now draw the line at experiments that gratuitously inflict pain or that place animals in unacceptable conditions.

A second argument for the permissibility of animal experimentation acknowledges that animals feel pain but asserts that animal lives are simply less valuable than humans lives. For this reason, we can do to animals anything we wish, as long as it protects or promotes human lives. To understand this argument best, we must inquire about what makes human lives so valuable. The answer to this question is too involved to treat completely here. However, it is possible that on reflection we will find that some of the properties or experiences that make human lives valuable are not unique to humans. Consciousness, happiness, family, friendships, accomplishments, or the experience of beauty might be on some people's short list of what makes life valuable. If these are not unique to humans, and yet they are part of what make human lives so valuable, then it stands to reason that some animals may have lives that are comparably valuable to human lives.

A second problem with this argument is that it denies the possibility of degrees in the "human" life qualities found in animal lives. Some animals experience those emotions and activities that make human lives so valuable to a lesser degree, and some experience them to a greater degree. Some humans are comfortable with the claim that a human life is more valuable than the life of a grasshopper. However, the claim that a human life is more valuable than the life of a mammal, especially one of the mammals that appear to share many "human" qualities, is one that fewer humans are comfortable asserting. The implication here is that we may be safe using grasshoppers in scientific experiments, because they have less of what makes lives valuable. Dogs or primates, on the other hand, should not be used as subjects in medical experiments, because they share many of the emotions and activities that make human lives valuable. This conclusion tempers the argument in favor of using animal subjects for research.

The argument that human lives are more valuable than animal lives is one that underlies some of the more complex experimental procedures performed today. Xenotransplantation, for example, is the procedure of taking an organ or other part of an animal, such as the pancreas of a pig, and transplanting it into a human being whose organ is no longer functioning. Xenotransplantation assumes that the life of the pig, in this example, is not as valuable as the life of the human who is being saved by the organ donation. Many opponents of the use of animals in research will agree that saving a human's life at the expense of an animal's life is morally permissible.

A variation of this argument does not claim that humans are more valuable than animals, but rather claims that animals are on earth in part to serve humans. Since animals are here to serve humans, animal experimentation is morally permissible. The claim that animals are on earth to serve humans is controversial. Some people have tried to support it with religious teachings that claim that humans are the stewards of the earth. As the stewards of the earth, humans have a moral responsibility to deal with animals fairly, but at the same time humans are ultimately at the "top of the pyramid," and if animals must be sacrificed for the good of humans, then this is morally acceptable.

The strongest arguments for the use of animals in research are those that focus on the benefits of using animals in research. These arguments are utilitarian in nature, citing the fact that if the benefits outweigh the harms of the research, then the moral concerns about the use of animals have been alleviated. Scientists point out the remarkable advances that have been made due to animal experimentation. Many drugs, medical procedures, and treatments have come about due to animal experimentation. It is difficult to dispute the value of vaccinations against small pox, polio, and measles, to name a few, all of which were made possible by animal experimentation. Many antibiotics were first tested on animals. Many of the more promising cancer treatments originated in animal research. Furthermore, as mentioned earlier, animals have benefited from these experiments, with the invention of vaccines for diseases that are found in animal populations, such as rabies and tetanus. The benefits of animal research touch every one of us, every day, and these benefits have come at a great price to many animals. Proponents of this argument state that the benefits outweigh the harms.

Objectors claim that the advances in science as a result of animal research have been wildly exaggerated. A comprehensive account of either the benefits of scientific research or the claim that these benefits have been exaggerated is beyond the purview of this chapter. So, we set this objection aside and consider an even stronger objection.

Most problematic for the defender of using animals in research are the already-mentioned questions surrounding the similarities between humans and animals. On one hand, if the defender of using animals in scientific experiments claims that the similarities between humans and animals are not that great, thereby paving the way for a moral justification for using animals, then the question arises, "Why use animals in research to benefit humans if the animal models are not sufficiently like humans so as to draw any reliable conclusions?" When using animal subjects the responsible scientist must give a justification for methodology that raises this concern. On the other hand, if the defender of using animals in scientific experiments claims that the similarities between humans and animals are sufficient to draw valid conclusions about humans from animal studies, then the question arises, "Why, if animals are so like humans, is it permissible to use them without their consent?" The more like humans animals seem to be, the more appropriate it appears to give animals moral standing similar to that of human beings. After all, irrespective of any "benefits" of coercing humans into participating as research subjects, as was done in the Tuskegee Syphilis Study or the Nazi experiments that prompted the Nuremberg Code, these experiments remain morally impermissible. These experiments were morally wrong because humans were used without their consent and horribly hurt or killed by the experimental procedures. These harms outweigh any gains in knowledge from these experiments. The benefits argument then must be supplemented by one of the earlier arguments, which attempt to draw disanalogies between animal and human subjects.

Although these arguments appear inconclusive, research on animals continues in the United States. Research on some animals is regulated. We turn now to some of the regulations that have been enacted to protect the interests of experimental animal populations.

6.4   LEGAL PROTECTIONS FOR ANIMALS IN RESEARCH

The federal Animal Welfare Act (AWA), enacted in 1966 and revised several times, most recently in 1990, governs the proper use of animals such as dogs, cats, and primates in the United States. The AWA does not cover the use of mice, rats, or birds. The National Association for Biomedical Research estimates that 23 million mammals are used for research in the United States annually. Of these, about 95 percent are mice and rats.

Institutional Animal Care and Use Committees (IACUCs) are the animal equivalent of Institutional Review Boards (IRBs), which oversee the ethical use of human research subjects. IACUCs are charged by the federal government to oversee and approve procedures for the ethical care and use of experimental animals. Just as with IRBs, local IACUCs may have special regulations, and it is the responsibility of each researcher to be familiar with the local, as well as federal, requirements. Just as with human subject research, which must be IRB-approved before federal money can be used to fund that research, federal funding agencies such as the NIH require IACUC approval before federal money can be used for research projects involving animals. Unlike IRBs, which grapple with appropriate informed consent and assent procedures, IACUCs of course do not consider informed consent. Instead, one of the more significant issues that IACUCs deal with is the methodological justification of the proposed research. For example, researchers may be called upon to defend the use of animals in an experiment, to demonstrate that the experiment does not duplicate research that has already been done, and to show the methodological soundness of the experiment being considered. The reason for such careful scrutiny of the methodology and contribution of the experiment is that it is always preferable not to use animals. An explanation of the alternative methods that would not require the use of animals, and why those methods have been eschewed in favor of methods which will put animals at risk, may be required. An additional consideration of IACUCs is the number of animals that will be used in the study. In an attempt to reduce the possible harms to animals, researchers are unlikely to use too many animals in an experiment. However, it is important that researchers avoid using so few animals that the data set is inconclusive. In such circumstances, the data from the animals that were used as subjects would not be useful and the researcher would have needlessly compromised the lives or safety of the animals used in the experiment.

There are several guiding principles, developed by the Interagency Research Animal Committee and adopted in 1985 by the White House Office of Science and Technology Policy, which help to foster the ethical use of animals in research in the United States. For example, all animal research should be in compliance with the AWA. Animal experiments should not be gratuitously performed, but instead should be performed only in cases that benefit humans, animals, or in cases that are expected to contribute to the generalizable knowledge. A guiding recommendation is similar to a recommendation made earlier when using human research subjects: The first responsibility of any researcher before exposing research subjects to potential harm is to have an adequate scientific background in the relevant field of inquiry. Following this recommendation is a step toward ensuring a favorable risk/expected-benefit ratio in the experiment, because the presumption is that benefits can accrue from an experiment only if the researcher is familiar with the field of inquiry. Researchers who begin an experiment without the proper training in their field cannot be reasonably expected to yield valuable data that may contribute to the generalizable knowledge.

Animals have a right to be housed in appropriate conditions and to be cared for by appropriately trained individuals. For example, a veterinarian may be required to be on hand to look after the animals being used. Some objectors to the use of animal research subjects have observed that the procedures to which animals are subjected are not as great a harm to the animals as the living conditions that some animals endure while being housed as potential research subjects. One recent law, for example, states that healthy dogs should not be tethered outdoors while being used as research subjects. Tethering reduces the quality of life for dogs. Questions of quality of life, such as the kind of enclosures that house dogs and cats, are important ones that affect the animals and are rightly under the purview of IACUCs.

Researchers should also consider the direct harm to the animal subjects. What is seen to cause harm or distress in humans can be reasonably expected to cause harm or distress in animals in many cases. Researchers have a responsibility to reduce harms to animals as much as possible. The appropriate procedures to reduce pain, such as the use of anesthesia, may be called for in some cases. Some cases may require researchers to kill animal subjects after an experimental procedure, rather than to allow the animals to continue living in pain.

6.5   ENVIRONMENTAL AND OTHER RESOURCE CONSIDERATIONS

Scientists must use resources in their attempt to further scientific progress. Some of these resources are natural resources, such as plant life, water, or fossils. These environmental resources are limited. Other resources are man made, but are similarly limited, such as expensive data-gathering equipment, laboratory space, or computers. Ethical scientific practice demands that scientists use these resources responsibly. The first step toward the ethical use of resources is the recognition that these resources are limited, which leads to inevitable questions: To whom are these resources valuable? To whom is the responsible researcher obligated when undertaking a project that uses valuable resources? There are three parties whose interest in these resources contribute to an ethical assessment of their use: other scientists, the general public, and perhaps the resources themselves.

Scientists have a responsibility to other scientists to allow a continued quest for generalizable knowledge. Squandering resources irresponsibly prevents other scientists from using them in the future. For example, overcollecting specimens may leave other scientists without the opportunity to collect data. Collecting specimens in an irresponsible fashion, leaving destruction in one's wake, is also irresponsible. Using valuable equipment without giving other researchers an opportunity to use this equipment may also be unethical. The ethics of responsible sharing of resources and equipment often boils down to the intentions of the researcher. If the intention in monopolizing an expensive piece of equipment is to collect a large data set, and if the only way to correctly process or collect the data requires the researcher to monopolize the equipment, then this may be permissible. If the researcher's actions, however, are tainted by the motive to monopolize the equipment so that competing researchers are thereby unable to collect their own data, then this is an unethical use of a limited resource. The intention behind the researcher's actions is significant in this case. A similar lesson is found in section 7.1; the line between permissible statistical manipulation and fabrication or falsification may lie in the intentions of the researcher. Scientists should also recognize that they are part of a community of scientists, many of whom have similar goals. Sometimes these goals appear a bit too similar, and scientists find themselves competing for limited data sets, limited funds, or limited opportunities. The responsible researcher shows restraint, being careful not to allow conflicting roles to compromise the goal of generalizable knowledge. A cooperative effort may be required so that the goals of science can be accomplished with limited resources.

Researchers should also recognize that many of the resources they use are sought after not merely by other researchers, but by the community at large. The public often cherishes the environment and may look unfavorably on scientists who seem recklessly to be using the environment for their own purposes. Scientists have a two-fold responsibility in light of public interest in limited resources. First, researchers have an ethical obligation to use resources responsibly, so that the public also has an opportunity to enjoy these resources. Sharing limited resources is usually the best solution, because it is an attempt to maximize both the contribution to generalizable knowledge and the public's direct experience with wildlife and other natural resources. However, sharing resources requires scientists to first make their case for their own use of these limited resources; this is the basis of researchers' second responsibility in light of these limited resources.

Researchers have a responsibility to educate the public about their work, so that the public can better understand researchers' interest in these limited resources. If the general public is ignorant about the value of research, then it is harder for researchers to make their case for their own interest in limited resources. The responsible scientist will make clear to the public the contributions to generalizable knowledge that may be gained by using limited resources for research in order that the public can better understand the value of scientific inquiry. Issues surrounding the responsibilities of researchers to the community at large are discussed in greater detail in section 9.4.

Finally, it is possible that researchers have a responsibility to the environment itself. For example, scientists who do research on the Amazonian rain forest may have a responsibility to the rain forest—to protect and preserve it. In this case, researchers recognize that the rain forest is not a means to an end, preserved for other researchers' or the public's use, but that the rain forest is an end in itself and should be preserved for its own sake. The arguments for the environment as an end in itself, having its own interests that should be protected in the same ways as animals' or humans' interests, are many and controversial. Perhaps it is sufficient for our purposes to observe that the scientists who work most closely with the Amazonian rain forest, for example, likely do not need persuading that the forest is valuable as an end in itself, valuable not merely because it harbors rich research opportunities.

6.6   SUMMARY

It is unlikely that research on animals will cease at any time in the near future. However, given the controversial nature of animal experimentation, a review of the arguments for and against the use of animal research subjects merits some attention.

In this chapter we first discussed the arguments against the use of animal research subjects. The first of these arguments claims that using any subject in experimentation, human or animal, is always wrong, unless the individual can give consent. A less extreme version of this argument states that using rational beings as subjects in experimentation is always wrong, and that at least some animals are sufficiently rational such that their use in experiments is wrong. A second argument against the use of animals as research subjects is one that states that it is unjust to use animals in experiments that are designed to ultimately benefit humans. A third argument proceeds from the claim that at one time animal experiments were morally permissible, but they have since become obsolete. A final argument questions the value of animal experimentation, when there are other means of benefiting human lives that do not require the taking of animal lives.

There are many arguments in support of the use of animals as research subjects. The first of these arguments states that any animal experimentation is permissible, because animals do not feel pain in the way that humans do. A second argument proceeds from the claim that though animals may feel pain, their lives are less valuable than human lives, and as a result, animals may be used as experimental subjects. A similar argument claims that animals are supposed to serve humans; thus, humans are permitted to use animals in ways that will ultimately benefit humans. Finally, the moral permissibility of animal experimentation may be justified by an argument from the benefits of animal experimentation. Objections exist to every one of these arguments, both those against and those for the use of animal research subjects. Questions about the moral permissibility of the use of animal research subjects remain.

Just as there are guidelines mandated by the federal government to protect human research subjects in many research settings, there are also laws that are designed to protect some animal research subjects. Institutional Animal Care and Use Committees (IACUCs) oversee the use of animals in research. Methodological considerations are at the forefront of any IACUC's judgment about the use of animal subjects. Appropriate care of animals by trained professionals is important in any research setting that uses animals. Finally, harms such as physical pain should be minimized for animal research subjects.

Just as animal research subjects may be looked upon as valuable resources that should be handled with due respect and consideration, other resources, such as environmental or man-made resources, should be used responsibly. The responsible use of these resources requires researchers to first recognize others who have an interest in protecting these limited resources. Other researchers, the public, and the environment itself may be among those with interests in protecting these resources. Thus, researchers should look to these parties, determine their interests in limited resources, and make responsible choices accordingly.

6.7   CASE STUDIES

Case 6.1: Professor Davis is interested in testing a chemical compound found in paint. Previous studies have suggested that this compound may cause headaches and, in some cases, sterility. If it turns out that this compound causes headaches or sterility, Professor Davis will publish the data and recommend that safer products be tested for the market. In the first phase of his experiment, Professor Davis plans on exposing mice to the paint, by painting the inside of their cages, and see if they demonstrate evidence of headaches. He will do this by measuring brain-wave activity, to see if the activity is in any way indicative of pain on the part of the mice. He will do further tests, after long-term exposure, to see if the paint causes sterility. His colleague, Professor Chatterjee, argues that it would be best if Professor Davis used analgesics for the mice who will have long-term exposure to the paint, so that they will not be forced to experience more pain than need be. Professor Davis argues both that the painkillers may alter the data set and that the use of the painkillers may require him to use even more mice than he would if he could combine the headache and sterility populations. What should Professor Davis do at this point? If the animals in the experiment were cats or primates, instead of mice, would this change the ethics of the experimental design?

Case 6.2: A group of anthropologists has located preliminary evidence that an ancient people lived in a desert that is currently the habitat of a rare lizard. A group of animal behaviorists wishes to observe the lizards, so steps may be taken to increase the population of this species. Though not on the endangered species list, the lizard population is dwindling rapidly. Since the lizard is not an endangered species, its habitat is not under federal protection, and researchers are permitted to collect data at the site. The animal behaviorists fear that allowing the anthropologists into the desert to collect data about the ancient people will disrupt the habitat of the lizard, speeding the decline in the lizard population and making the lizards nearly impossible to study in the future. The anthropologists fear that allowing the animal behaviorists into the desert will result in unintentional destruction of rare artifacts of this ancient culture. Which of the scientists has a greater claim to the valuable resources located in the desert? How should such a disagreement be settled?

REFERENCES AND FURTHER READINGS

C. Cohen, "The Case for the Use of Animals in Biomedical Research," *New England Journal of Medicine*, volume 315, pp. 865–69, 1986.

Mary Midgley, *Animals and Why They Matter.* Athens, GA: University of Georgia Press, 1983.

Barbara F. Orlans, Tom L. Beauchamp, Rebecca Dresser, David B. Morton, and John P. Gluck, *The Human Use of Animals: Case Studies in Ethical Choice*, New York: Oxford University Press, 1998.

James Rachels, *Created from Animals: The Moral Implications of Darwinism*, New York: Oxford University Press, 1990.

Tom Regan, *The Case for Animal Rights*, Berkeley: University of California Press, 1983.

Peter Singer, *Animal Liberation*, second edition. New York: New York Review of Books, 1990.

The Ethics of Animal Research: What Are the Prospects for Agreement?

David DeGrazia

Few human uses of nonhuman animals (hereafter simply "animals") have incited as much controversy as the use of animals in biomedical research. The political exchanges over this issue tend to produce much more heat than light, as representatives of both biomedicine and the animal protection community accuse opponents of being "Nazis," "terrorists," and the like. However, a healthy number of individuals within these two communities offer the possibility of a more illuminating discussion of the ethics of animal research.

One such individual is Henry Spira. Spira almost single-handedly convinced Avon, Revlon, and other major cosmetics companies to invest in the search for alternatives to animal testing. Largely due to his tactful but persistent engagement with these companies—and to their willingness to change—many consumers today look for such labels as "not tested on animals" and "cruelty free" on cosmetics they would like to buy.

Inspired by Spira, this paper seeks common ground between the positions of biomedicine and animal advocates. (The term "biomedicine" here refers to everyone who works in medicine or the life sciences, not just those conducting animal research. "Animal advocates" and "animal protection community" refer to those individuals who take a major interest in protecting the interests of animals and who believe that much current usage of animals is morally unjustified. The terms are not restricted to animal activists, because some individuals meet this definition without being politically active in seeking changes.) The paper begins with some background on the political and ethical debate over animal research. It then identifies important points of potential agreement between biomedicine and animal advocates; much of this common ground can be missed due to distraction by the fireworks of the current political exchange. Next, the paper enumerates issues on which continuing disagreement is likely. Finally, it concludes with concrete suggestions for building positively on the common ground.

Background on the Debate over Animal Research

What is the current state of the debate over the ethics of animal research? Let us begin with the viewpoint of biomedicine. It seems fair to say that biomedicine has a "party line" on the ethics of animal research, conformity to which may feel

David DeGrazia, "The Ethics of Animal Research: What Are the Prospects for Agreement?" *Cambridge Quarterly of Healthcare Ethics* 8, (7), 1999, pp. 23–34.
Acknowledgment—My thanks to Arlene Klotzko and Peter Singer for their suggestions regarding this paper. Author.

like a political litmus test for full acceptability within the professional community. According to this party line, animal research is clearly justified because it is
necessary for medical progress and therefore human health—and those who disagree are irrational, antiscience, misanthropic "extremists" whose views do not
deserve serious attention. (Needless to say, despite considerable conformity,
not everyone in biomedicine accepts this position.)

In at least some countries, biomedicine's leadership apparently values conformity to this party line more than freedom of thought and expression on the
animal research issue. (In this paragraph, I will refer to the American situation
to illustrate the point.) Hence the unwillingness of major medical journals, such
as *JAMA* and *The New England Journal of Medicine*, to publish articles that are
highly critical of animal research. Hence also the extraordinary similarity I have
noticed in pro-research lectures by representatives of biomedicine. I used to be
puzzled about why these lectures sounded so similar and why, for example, they
consistently made some of the same philosophical and conceptual errors (such
as dichotomizing animal welfare and animal rights, and taking the latter concept
to imply identical rights for humans and animals). But that was before I learned
of the "AMA [American Medical Association] Animal Research Action Plan"
and the AMA's "White Paper." Promoting an aggressive pro-research campaign,
these documents encourage AMA members to say and do certain things for public relations purposes, including the following: "Identify animal rights activists
as anti-science and against medical progress"; "Combat emotion with emotion
(eg [sic], 'fuzzy' animals contrasted with 'healing' children)"; and "Position
the biomedical community as moderate—centrist—in the controversy, not as a
polar opposite."[1]

It is a reasonable conjecture that biomedicine's party line was developed
largely in reaction to fear—both of the most intimidating actions of some especially zealous animal advocates, such as telephoned threats and destruction of
property, and of growing societal concern about animals. Unfortunately, biomedicine's reaction has created a political culture in which many or most animal
researchers and their supporters do not engage in sustained, critical thinking
about the moral status of animals and the basic justification (or lack thereof) for
animal research. Few seem to recognize that there is significant merit to the opposing position, fewer have had any rigorous training in ethical reasoning, and
hardly any have read much of the leading literature on animal ethics. The stul-
tifying effect of this cultural phenomenon hit home with me at a small meeting
of representatives of biomedicine, in which I had been invited to explain "the
animal rights philosophy" (the invitation itself being exceptional and encouraging). After the talk, in which I presented ideas familiar to all who really know
the literature and issues of animal ethics, several attendees pumped my hand
and said something to this effect: "This is the first time I have heard such rational and lucid arguments for the other side. I didn't know there were any."

As for the animal protection community, there does not seem to be a shared
viewpoint except at a very general level: significant interest in animal welfare and

the belief that much current animal usage is unjustified. Beyond that, differences abound. For example, the Humane Society of the United States opposes factory farming but not humane forms of animal husbandry, rejects current levels of animal use in research but not animal research itself, and condemns most zoo exhibits but not those that adequately meet animals' needs and approximate their natural habitats.[2] Meanwhile, the Animal Liberation Front, a clandestine British organization, apparently opposes all animal husbandry, animal research, and the keeping of zoo animals.[3] Although there are extensive differences within the animal protection community, as far as our paper topic goes, it seems fair to say that almost everyone in this group opposes current levels of animal research.

That's a brief sketch of the perspectives of biomedicine and animal advocates on the issue of animal research. What about the state of animal ethics itself? The leading book-length works in this field exhibit a near consensus that the status quo of animal usage is ethically indefensible and that at least significant reductions in animal research are justified. Let me elaborate.

Defending strong animal rights positions in different ways, Tom Regan and Evelyn Pluhar advocate abolition of all research that involves harming animals.[4] Ray Frey and Peter Singer, by contrast, hold the use of animals to the very stringent utilitarian standard—accepting only those experiments whose benefits (factoring in the likelihood of achieving them) are expected to outweigh the harms and costs involved—where the interests of animal subjects (e.g., to avoid suffering) are given the same moral weight that we give comparable human interests.[5]

Without commiting either to a strong animal rights view or to utilitarianism, my own view shares with these theories the framework of equal consideration for animals: the principle that we must give equal moral weight to comparable interests, no matter who has those interests.[6] But unlike the aforementioned philosophers, I believe that the arguments for and against equal consideration are nearly equal in strength. I therefore have respect for progressive views that attribute moral standing to animals without giving them fully equal consideration. The unequal consideration view that I find most plausible gives moral weight to animals' comparable interests in accordance with the animals' cognitive, affective, and social complexity—a progressive, "sliding scale" view. Since I acknowledge that I might be mistaken about equal consideration, my approach tracks the practical implications both of equal consideration and of the alternative just described.

Arguing from pluralistic frameworks, which are developed in different ways, Steve Sapontzis, Rosemary Rodd, and Bernard Rollin support relatively little animal research in comparison with current levels.[7] Drawing significantly from feminist insights, Mary Midgley presents a view whose implications seem somewhat more accepting of the status quo of animal research but still fairly progressive.[8] Of the leading contributors to animal ethics, the only one who embraces the status quo of animal research and does not attribute significant moral status to animals is Peter Carruthers.[9] (It is ironic that while biomedicine characterizes those who are critical of animal research as irrational "extremists," nearly all of the most in-depth, scholarly, and respected work in animal ethics supports such a critical standpoint at a general level.)

In discussing the prospects for agreement between biomedicine and animal advocates, I will ignore political posturing and consider only serious ethical reflection. In considering the two sides of this debate, I will assume that the discussants are morally serious, intellectually honest, reflective, and well informed both about the facts of animal research and about the range of arguments that come into play in animal ethics. I will not have in mind, then, the researcher who urges audiences to dismiss "the animal rights view" or the animal activist who tolerates no dissent from an abolitionist position. The two representative interlocutors I will imagine differ on the issue of animal research, but their views result from honest, disciplined, well-informed ethical reflection. Clearly, their voices are worth hearing.

Points on Which the Biomedical and Animal Protection Communities Can Agree

The optimistic thesis of this paper is that the biomedical and animal protection communities can agree on a fair number of important points, and that much can be done to build upon this common ground, I will number and highlight (in bold) each potential point of agreement and then justify its inclusion by explaining how both sides can agree to it, without abandoning their basic positions, and why they should.

1. The use of animals in biomedical research raises ethical issues. Today very few people would disagree with this modest claim, and any who would are clearly in the wrong.[10] Most animal research involves harming animal subjects, provoking ethical concerns, and the leading goal of animal research, promotion of human health, is itself ethically important; even the expenditure of taxpayers' money on government-funded animal research raises ethical issues about the best use of such money. Although a very modest assertion, this point of agreement is important because it legitimates a process that is sometimes resisted: *discussing* the ethics of animal research.

It is worth noting a less obvious claim that probably enjoys strong majority support but not consensus: that animals (at least sentient ones, as defined below) have moral status. To say animals have moral status is to say that their interests have moral importance independently of effects on human interests. ('Interests' may be thought of as components of well-being. For example, sentient animals have an interest in avoiding pain, distress, and suffering.) If animals have moral status, then to brutalize a horse is wrong because of the harm inflicted on the horse, not simply because the horse is someone's property (if that is so) or because animal lovers' feelings may be hurt (if any animal lovers find out about the abuse). The idea is that gratuitously harming the horse *wrongs the horse.* Although nearly every leader in animal ethics holds that animals have moral status—and though most people, on reflection, are likely to find this idea commonsensical—Carruthers argues that it is mistaken.[11]

2. Sentient animals, a class that probably includes at least the vertebrates, deserve moral protection. Whether because they have moral status or because needlessly harming them strongly offends many people's sensibilities, sentient animals deserve some measure of moral protection. By way of definition, sentient animals are animals endowed with any sorts of feelings: (conscious) sensations such as pain or emotional states such as fear or suffering. But which animals are sentient? Addressing this complex issue implicates both the natural sciences and the philosophy of mind. Lately, strong support has emerged for the proposition that at least vertebrate animals are very likely sentient.[12] This proposition is implicitly endorsed by major statements of principles regarding the humane use of research animals, which often mention that they apply to vertebrates.[13] (Hereafter, the unqualified term "animals" will refer to sentient animals in particular.)

3. Many animals (at the very least, mammals) are capable of having a wide variety of aversive mental states, including pain, distress (whose forms include discomfort, boredom, and fear), and suffering. In biomedical circles, there has been some resistance to attributing suffering to animals, so government documents concerned with humane use of animals have often mentioned only pain, distress, and discomfort.[14] Because "suffering" refers to a *highly* unpleasant mental state (whereas pain, distress, and discomfort can be mild and transient), the attribution of suffering to animals is morally significant. An indication that resistance may be weakening is the attribution of suffering to sentient animals in the National Aeronautics and Space Administration's "Principles for the Ethical Care and Use of Animals."[15] Whatever government documents may say, the combined empirical and philosophical case for attributing suffering to a wide range of animals is very strong.[16]

4. Animals' experiential well-being (quality of life) deserves protection. If the use of animals raises ethical issues, meaning that their interests matter morally, we confront the question of what interests animals have. This question raises controversial issues. For example, do animals have an interest in remaining alive (life interests)? That is, does death itself—as opposed to any unpleasantness experienced in dying—harm an animal? A test case would be a scenario in which a contented dog in good health is painlessly and unwittingly killed in her sleep: Is she harmed?

Another difficult issue is whether animal well-being can be understood *entirely* in terms of experiential well-being—quality of life in the familiar sense in which (other things equal) pleasure is better than pain, enjoyment better than suffering, satisfaction better than frustration. Or does the exercise of an animal's natural capacities count positively toward well-being, even if quality of life is not enhanced? A test case would be a scenario in which conditioning, a drug, or brain surgery removes a bird's instinct and desire to fly without lowering quality of life: Does the bird's transformation to a new, nonflying existence represent a harm?

Whatever the answers to these and other issues connected with animal well-being, what is not controversial is that animals have an interest in experiential well-being, a good quality of life. That is why animal researchers are normally expected to use anesthesia or analgesia where these agents can reduce or eliminate animal subjects' pain, distress, or suffering.

   5. **Humane care of highly social animals requires extensive access to conspecifics.** It is increasingly appreciated that animals have different needs based on what sorts of creatures they are. Highly social animals, such as apes, monkeys, and wolves, need social interactions with conspecifics (members of their own species). Under normal circumstances, they will develop social structures, such as hierarchies and alliances, and maintain long-term relationships with conspecifics. Because they have a strong instinct to seek such interactions and relationships, depriving them of the opportunity to gratify this instinct harms these animals. For example, in some species, lack of appropriate social interactions impedes normal development. Moreover, social companions can buffer the effects of stressful situations, reduce behavioral abnormalities, provide opportunities for exercise, and increase cognitive stimulation.[17] Thus in the case of any highly social animals used in research, providing them extensive access to conspecifics is an extremely high moral priority.

   6. **Some animals deserve very strong protections (as, for example, chimpanzees deserve not to be killed for the purpose of population control).** Biomedicine and animal advocates are likely to disagree on many details of ethically justified uses of animals in research, as we will see in the next section. Still, discussants can agree that there is an obligation to protect not just the experiential well-being, but also the lives, of at least some animals. This claim might be supported by the (controversial) thesis that such animals have life interests. On the other hand, it might be supported by the goal of species preservation (in the case of an endangered species), or by the recognition that routine killing of such animals when they are no longer useful for research would seriously disturb many people.[18]

   Without agreeing on all the specific justifications, members of the National Research Council's Committee on Long-Term Care of Chimpanzees were able to agree (with one dissent) that chimps should not be killed for the purpose of population control, although they could be killed if suffering greatly with no alternative means of relief.[19] This recommended protection of chimps' lives is exceptional, because animal research policies generally state no presumption against killing animal subjects, requiring only that killings be as painless as possible.[20] Since this committee represents expert opinion in biomedicine, it seems correct to infer that biomedicine and the animal protection community can agree that at least chimpanzees should receive some very strong protections—of their lives and of certain other components of their well-being, such as their needs for social interaction, reasonable freedom of movement, and stimulating environments.[21]

   7. **Alternatives should now be used whenever possible and research on alternatives should expand.** Those who are most strongly opposed to animal research hold that alternatives such as mathematical models, computer simulations, and in vitro biological systems should replace nearly all use of animals in research.

(I say "nearly all" because, as discussed below, few would condemn animal research that does not harm its subjects.) Even for those who see the animal research enterprise more favorably, there are good reasons to take an active interest in alternatives. Sometimes an alternative method is the most valid way to approach a particular scientific question; often alternatives are cheaper.[22] Their potential for reducing animal pain, distress, and suffering is, of course, another good reason. Finally, biomedicine may enjoy stronger public support if it responds to growing social concern about animal welfare with a very serious investment in non-animal methods. This means not just using alternatives wherever they are currently feasible, but also aggressively researching the possibilities for expanding the use of such methods.

8. **Promoting human health is an extremely important biomedical goal.** No morally serious person would deny the great importance of human health, so its status as a worthy goal seems beyond question. What is sometimes forgotten, however, is that a worthy goal does not automatically justify all the means thereto. Surely it would be unethical to force large numbers of humans to serve as subjects in highly painful, eventually lethal research, even if its goal were to promote human health. The controversy over animal research focuses not on the worthiness of its principal goal—promoting human health—but rather on the means, involving animal subjects, taken in pursuit of that goal.

9. **There are some morally significant differences between humans and other animals.** Many people in biomedicine are not aware that the views of animal advocates are consistent with this judgment. Indeed, some animal advocates might not realize that their views are consistent with this judgment! So let me identify a couple of ideas, to which all should agree, that support it.

First, the principle of respect for autonomy applies to competent adult human beings, but to very few if any animals. This principle respects the self-regarding decisions of individuals who are capable of autonomous decisionmaking and action. Conversely, it opposes paternalism toward such individuals, who have the capacity to decide for themselves what is in their interests. Now, many sentient beings, including human children and at least most nonhuman animals, are not autonomous in the relevant sense and so are not covered by this principle.[23] Thus it is often appropriate to limit their liberty in ways that promote their best interests, say, preventing the human child from drinking alcohol, or forcing a pet dog to undergo a vaccination. We might say that where there is no autonomy to respect, the principles of beneficence (promoting best interests) and respect for autonomy cannot conflict; where there is autonomy to respect, paternalism becomes morally problematic.

Second, even if sentient animals have an interest, others things equal, in staying alive (as I believe), the moral presumption against taking human life is stronger than the presumption against killing at least some animals. Consider fish, who are apparently sentient yet cognitively extremely primitive in comparison with humans. I have a hard time imagining even very committed animal advocates maintaining that killing a fish is as serious a matter as killing a human being. Leaders in animal ethics consistently support—though in interestingly different ways—the idea that, ordinarily, killing humans is worse than killing at least some animals who have moral status. (It is almost too obvious to mention that it's worse to kill humans than to kill animals, such as amoebas, that *lack* moral status.[24])

The only notable exception seems to be Sapontzis, who tries to undermine the major arguments proffered to support such comparative claims. But the comparisons he opposes always involve humans and other mammals or birds.[25] The farther one goes down the phylogenetic scale, the more incredible it becomes to hold that it is equally prima facie wrong to kill humans and to kill other animals. At the very least, someone like Sapontzis will have to admit that killing humans tends to be worse than killing fish in that (1) humans tend to live much longer, so that untimely death generally robs them of more good years, and (2) untimely human death causes deep social sorrow and anguish to others in a way that is not paralleled in the fish world. So I believe that the comparative judgment I have made is well justified and embraceable by all parties to the present debate. There may be other morally interesting differences to which all should agree,[26] but these examples will suffice for present purposes.

10. Some animal research is justified. Many animal advocates would say that they disagree with this statement. But I'm not sure they do. Or, if they really do, they shouldn't. Let me explain by responding to the three likeliest reasons some animal advocates might take exception to the claim.

First, one might oppose all uses of animals that involve *harming them for the benefit of others* (even other animals)—as a matter of absolute principle—and overlook the fact that some animal research does not harm animal subjects at all. Although such nonharmful research represents a tiny sliver of the animal research enterprise, it exists. Examples are certain observational studies of animals in their natural habitats, some ape language studies, and possibly certain behavioral studies of other species that take place in laboratories but do not cause pain, distress, or suffering to the subjects. And if nonsentient animals cannot be harmed (in any morally relevant sense), as I would argue, then any research involving such animals falls under the penumbra of nonharming research.

Moreover, there is arguably no good reason to oppose research that imposes only *minimal* risk or harm on its animal subjects. After all, minimal risk research on certain human subjects who, like animals, cannot consent (namely, children) is permitted in many countries; in my view, this policy is justified. Such research might involve a minuscule likelihood of significant harm or the certainty of a slight, transient harm, such as the discomfort of having a blood sample taken.

Second, one might oppose all animal research because one believes that none of it actually benefits human beings. Due to physical differences between species, the argument goes, what happens to animal subjects when they undergo some biomedical intervention does not justify inferences about what will happen to humans who undergo that intervention. Furthermore, new drugs, therapies, and techniques must always be tried on human subjects before they can be accepted for clinical practice. Rather than tormenting animals in research, the argument continues, we should drop the useless animal models and proceed straight to human trials (with appropriate protections for human subjects, including requirements for informed or proxy consent).

Although I believe a considerable amount of current animal research has almost no chance of benefitting humans,[27] I find it very hard to believe that no animal research does. While it is true that human subjects must eventually be experimented on, evidence suggests that animal models sometimes furnish data relevant to human health.[28] If so, then the use of animal subjects can often decrease the risk to human subjects who are eventually involved in experiments that advance biomedicine, by helping to weed out harmful interventions. This by itself does not justify animal research, only the claim that it sometimes benefits humans (at the very least human subjects themselves and arguably the beneficiaries of biomedical advances as well).

Note that even if animal research never benefited humans, it would presumably sometimes benefit conspecifics of the animals tested, in sound veterinary research.[29] It can't be seriously argued that animal models provide no useful information about animals! Moreover, in successful *therapeutic* research (which aims to benefit the subjects themselves), certain animals benefit directly from research and are not simply used to benefit other animals. For that reason, blanket opposition to animal research, including the most promising therapeutic research in veterinary medicine, strikes me as almost unintelligible.

Almost unintelligible, but not quite, bringing us to the third possible reason for opposing all animal research. It might be argued that, whether or not it harms its subjects, all animal research involves *using animals (without their consent) for others' benefit,* since—qua research—it seeks *generalizable knowledge.* But to use animals in this way reduces them to *tools* (objects to be used), thereby *disrespecting* the animals.

Now the idea that we may never use nonconsenting individuals, even in benign ways, solely for the benefit of others strikes me as an implausibly strict ethical principle. But never mind. The fact that some veterinary research is intended to benefit the subjects themselves (as well as other animals or humans down the road) where no other way to help them is known shows that such research, on any reasonable view, is *not* disrespectful toward its subjects. Indeed, in such cases, the animals *would* consent to taking part, if they could, because taking part is in their interests. I fully grant that therapeutic veterinary research represents a minuscule portion of the animal research conducted today. But my arguments are put forward in the service of a goal that I think I have now achieved: demonstrating, beyond a shadow of a doubt, that some animal research is justified.

If animal advocates and representatives of biomedicine were aware of these ten points of potential agreement, they might perceive their opponents' views as less alien than they had previously taken them to be. This change in perception might, in turn, convince all parties that honest, open discussion of outstanding issues has a decent chance of repaying the effort.

Points on Which Agreement between the Two Sides Is Unlikely

Even if biomedicine and the animal protection community approach the animal research issue in good faith, become properly informed about animal ethics and the facts of research, and so forth, they are still likely to disagree on certain important issues. After all, their basic views differ. It may be worthwhile to enumerate several likely points of difference.

First, disagreement is likely on the issue of *the moral status of animals in comparison with humans*. While representatives of biomedicine may attribute moral status to animals, they hold that animals may justifiably be used in many experiments (most of which are nontherapeutic and harm the subjects) whose primary goal is to promote human health. But for animal advocates, it is not at all obvious that much animal research is justified. This suggests that animal advocates ascribe higher moral status to animals than biomedicine does.[30]

Second, disagreement is likely to continue on the issue of *the specific circumstances in which the worthy goal of promoting human health justifies harming animals*. Biomedicine generally tries to protect the status quo of animal research. Animal advocates generally treat not using animals in research as a presumption, any departures from which would require careful justification. Clearly, animal advocates will have many disagreements with biomedicine over when it is appropriate to conduct animal research.

Third, in a similar vein, continuing disagreement is likely on the issue of *whether current protections for research animals are more or less adequate*. Biomedicine would probably answer affirmatively, with relatively minor internal disagreements over specific issues (e.g., whether apes should ever be exposed to diseases in order to test vaccines). Animal advocates will tend to be much more critical of current protections for research animals. They will argue, for example, that animals are far too often made to suffer in pursuit of less than compelling objectives, such as learning about behavioral responses to stress or trauma.

In the United States, critics will argue that the basic principles that are supposed to guide the care and use of animals in federally funded research ultimately provide very weak protection for research animals. That is because the tenth and final principle begins with implicit permission to make exceptions to the previous nine: "Where exceptions are required in relation to the provisions of these Principles, ..."[31] Since no limits are placed on permissible exceptions, this final principle precludes any absolute restraints on the harm that may be inflicted on research animals—an indefensible lack of safeguards from the perspective of animal advocates. (Although similar in several ways to these American principles, including some ways animal advocates would criticize, the *International Guiding Principles for Biomedical Research Involving Animals* avoids this pitfall of a global loophole. One of its relatively strong protections is Principle V: "Investigators and other personnel should never fail to treat animals as sentient, and should regard their proper care and use and the avoidance or minimization of discomfort, distress, or pain as ethical imperatives."[32])

Although protections of research animals are commonly thought of in terms of preventing unnecessary pain, distress, and suffering, they may also be thought of in terms of protecting animal life. A fourth likely area of disagreement concerns *whether animal life is morally protectable.* Return to a question raised earlier: whether a contented animal in good health is harmed by being painlessly killed in her sleep. Since government documents for the care and use of research animals generally require justification for causing pain or distress to animal subjects, but no justification for painless killing, it seems fair to infer that biomedicine generally does not attribute life interests to animals. Although I lack concrete evidence, I would guess that most animal advocates would see the matter quite differently, and would regard the killing of animals as a serious moral matter even if it is justified in some circumstances.

The four issues identified here as probable continuing points of difference are not intended to comprise an exhaustive list. But they show that despite the fact that the biomedical and animal protection communities can agree on an impressive range of major points, given their basic orientations they cannot be expected to agree on every fundamental question. Few will find this assertion surprising. But I also suggest, less obviously, that even if both sides cannot be entirely right in their positions, differences that remain after positions are refined through honest, open-minded, fully educated inquiry can be reasonable differences.

What Can Be Done Now to Build upon the Points of Agreement

Let me close with a series of suggestions offered in the constructive yet critical-minded spirit of Henry Spira's work for how to build on the points of agreement identified above. For reasons of space, these suggestions will be stated somewhat tersely and without elaboration.

First, biomedical organizations and leaders in the profession can do the following: openly acknowledge that ethical issues involving animals are complex and important; educate themselves or acquire education about the ethical issues; tolerate views departing from the current party line; open up journals to more than one basic viewpoint; and stop disseminating one-sided propoganda.

Second, the more "militant" animal advocates can acknowledge that there can be reasonable disagreement on some of the relevant issues and stop intimidating people with whom they disagree.

Third, biomedicine can openly acknowledge, as NASA recently did in its principles, that animals can suffer and invite more serious consideration of animal suffering.

Fourth, the animal protection community can give credit to biomedicine where credit is due—for example, for efforts to minimize pain and distress, to improve housing conditions, and to refrain from killing old chimpanzees who are no longer useful for research but are expensive to maintain.

Fifth, animal researchers and members of animal protection organizations can be required by their organizations to take courses in ethical theory or animal ethics to promote knowledgeable, skilled, broad-minded discussion and reflection.

Sixth, the animal protection community can openly acknowledge that some animal research is justified (perhaps giving examples to reduce the potential for misunderstanding).

Seventh, more animal research ethics committees can bring aboard at least one dedicated animal advocate who (unlike mainstream American veterinarians) seriously questions the value of most animal research.

Eighth, conditions of housing for research animals can be improved—for example, with greater enrichment and, for social animals, more access to conspecifics.

Ninth, all parties can endorse and support the goal of finding ways to *eliminate* animal subjects' pain, distress, and suffering.[33]

Tenth, and finally, governments can invest much more than they have to date in the development and use of alternatives to animal research, and all parties can give strong public support to the pursuit of alternatives.

Notes

[1] American Medical Association. Animal Research Action Plan. (June 1989), p. 6. See also American Medical Association. White Paper (1988).

[2] See the Humane Society of the United States (HSUS). *Farm Animals and Intensive Confinement*. Washington, D.C.: HSUS, 1994; *Animals in Biomedical Research*. Washington, D.C.: HSUS, revised 1989; and *Zoos: Information Packet*. Washington, D.C.: HSUS, 1995.

[3] Animal Liberation Front. Animal Liberation Frontline Information Service: the A.L.F. Primer. (website)

[4] Regan T. *The Case for Animal Rights*. Berkeley: University of California Press, 1983; Pluhar E. *Beyond Prejudice*. Durham, North Carolina: Duke University Press, 1995.

[5] Frey RG. *Interests and Rights*. Oxford: Clarendon, 1980; Singer P. *Animal Liberation*, 2d ed. New York: New York Review of Books, 1990.

[6] DeGrazia D. *Taking Animals Seriously*. Cambridge: Cambridge University Press, 1996.

[7] Sapontzia SF. *Morals, Reason, and Animals*. Philadelphia: Temple University Press, 1987; Rodd R. *Biology, Ethics, and Animals*. Oxford: Clarendon, 1990; and Rollin BE. *Animal Rights and Human Morality*, 2d ed. Buffalo, New York: Prometheus, 1992.

[8] Midgley M. *Animals and Why They Matter*. Athens, Georgia: University of Georgia Press, 1983.

[9] Carruthers P. *The Animals Issue*. Cambridge: Cambridge University Press, 1992.

[10] In a letter to the editor, Robert White, a neurosurgeon well known for transplanting monkeys' heads, asserted that "[a]nimal usage is not a moral or ethical issue . . ." (White R. Animal ethics? [letter]. *Hastings Center Report* 1990;20(6):43). For a rebuttal to White, see my letter, *Hastings Center Report* 1991;21(5):45.

[11] See note 9, Carruthers 1992. For an attempt in undermine Carruthers' arguments, see note 6, DeGrazia 1996:53–6.

[12] See Rose M, Adams D. Evidence for pain and suffering in other animals. In: Langley G. ed. *Animal Experimentation*. New York: Chapman and Hall, 1989:42–71; Smith JA, Boyd KM. *Lives in the Balance*. Oxford: Oxford University Press, 1991:ch. 4. See also note 7 Rodd 1990: ch. 3; and DeGrazia D, Rowan A. Pain, suffering, and anxiety in animals and humans. *Theoretical Medicine* 1991;12:193–221.

[13] See, e.g., U.S. Government Principles for the Utilization and Care of Vertebrate Animals Used in Testing, Research, and Training. In: National Research Council. *Guide for the Care and Use of Laboratory Animals.* Washington, D.C.: National Academy Press, 1996:117–8; National Aeronautics and Space Administration. *Principles for the Ethical Care and Use of Animals.* NASA Policy Directive 8910.1, effective 23 March 1998; and Council for International Organizations of Medical Sciences. *International Guiding Principles for Biomedical Research Involving Animals.* Geneva: CIOMS, 1985:18.

[14] See note 13, National Research Council 1996; CIOMS 1985.

[15] See note 13, NASA 1998.

[16] See note 12, Rose, Adams 1989; DeGrazia, Rowan 1991. And see note 7, Rodd 1990: ch. 3. There is also much evidence that at least mammals can experience anxiety. (See note 12, DeGrazia, Rowan 1991; note 12, Smith, Boyd 1991:ch. 4.)

[17] See note 13, National Research Council 1996:37.

[18] Note that the term "euthanasia," which means a death that is good for the one who dies, is inappropriate when animals are killed because they are costly to maintain or for similarly human-regarding reasons.

[19] National Research Council Committee on Long-Term Care of Chimpanzees. *Chimpanzees in Research.* Washington, D.C.: National Academy Press, 1997:38.

[20] Such policies typically state that animals who would otherwise experience severe or chronic pain or distress should be painlessly killed. See, e.g., note 13, National Research Council 1996:117; CIOMS 1985:19; and [British] Home Office. *Home Office Guidance on the Operation of the Animals (Scientific Procedures) Act 1986.* London: Home Office, 1986. Although this directive addresses what to do with animals who could survive only in agony, it does not state any presumption against killing animals who could live well following research.

[21] The committee addresses these chimpanzee interests in note 19, National Research Council 1997:ch. 3.

[22] See note 12, Smith, Boyd 1991:334.

[23] See note 6, DeGrazia 1996:204–10.

[24] Admittedly, some unusual individuals would claim that amoebas have moral status, either because they think amoebas are sentient or because they think that sentience is unnecessary for moral status. I know of no one, however, who would claim that killing amoebas is as serious a matter as killing humans.

[25] See note 7, Sapontzia 1987:216–22.

[26] For example, if I am right, just as the moral presumption against taking life can differ in strength across species, so can the presumption against confining members of different species (the interest at stake being freedom). See note 6, DeGrazia 1996:254–6.

[27] That is, except those humans who benefit directly from the conduct of research, such as researchers and people who sell animals and laboratory equipment.

[28] See, e.g., note 12, Smith, Boyd 1991:ch. 3.

[29] Peter Singer reminded me of this important point.

[30] The idea of differences of moral status can be left intuitive here. Any effort to make it more precise will invite controversy. (See note 6, DeGrazia 1996:256–7.)

[31] See note 13, National Research Council 1996:118.

[32] See note 13, CIOMS 1985:18.

[33] This is the stated goal of a new initiative of the Humane Society of the United States, which expects the initiative to expand to Humane Society International.

Animal Experimentation and the Argument from Limited Resources

Charles K. Fink

Animal rights activists are often accused of showing more concern for animals than for human beings. How, it is asked, can activists condemn the use of animals in research that might eventually provide a cure for cancer, AIDS, muscular dystrophy, or diabetes? C. R. Gallistel speaks for many critics of the animal liberation movement when he writes:

> It is an affront to my own ethical sensibility to hear arguments that the suffering of animals is of greater moral weight than the advancement of human understanding and the consequent alleviation of human suffering (214).

Gallistel's appeal to the humanity of the scientific enterprise is not uncommon among apologists for vivisection. The argument is that animal research is an indispensable tool in the treatment of disease and, consequently, to condemn such research, as activists do, is to condemn indefinitely many people to misery and death. One should accept restrictions on animal research, Gallistel insists, "only if one believes that the moral value of . . . scientific knowledge and of the many human and humane benefits that flow from it cannot outweigh the suffering of a rat" (214).

Some activists have questioned the sincerity of this humanitarian appeal. In his classic study on vivisection, *Victims of Science,* Richard Ryder observes:

> Those with genuinely humane motives are most likely to prolong life or alleviate suffering by bringing existing medical knowledge to bear in those parts of the world where men and women are suffering and dying because they cannot afford any treatment. Yet many scientists prefer to spend their lives in laboratories causing untold suffering to animals in questionable medical research with a strong commercial motive; these researchers are not convincing when they plead that humanity is their overriding concern (22).

Ryder's point is that health care professionals have a choice between applying their knowledge and skills in laboratory research or devoting themselves instead to providing basic medical care to the poor. The first choice involves inflicting

Charles K. Fink, "Animal Experimentation and the Argument from Limited Resources," *Between the Species*, 1991, pp. 90–96.

untold suffering and death upon any number of animals in research which may never yield beneficial medical results. The second choice involves helping people directly without any harm coming to animals. It is this second choice, Ryder urges, that is the truly humane one.[1]

In a more recent study, Rosemary Rodd alludes to Ryder's argument:

> No-one (I think) would attempt to argue that the lives of Third World children are less valuable than those of children in the developed countries, so there seems to be some merit in the argument of Richard Ryder that resources ought preferentially to be used to save human lives by means which do not involve contingent suffering for research animals. It certainly appears that there is no reason why an individual should not make a principled decision to support famine relief rather than, say, heart research (59).

The choice between supporting animal research or supporting other forms of humanitarian work is not one which only health care professionals must make, it is one faced by virtually all members of an affluent society. For example, the Muscular Dystrophy Association collects many millions of dollars each year from individual contributors. While not all of this money is used in animal research, a considerable portion of it is. Now, this charitable organization is only one among numerous others which compete with one another for our support. And while muscular dystrophy is a horrible and debilitating disease, so are many of the diseases, including chronic hunger, which afflict so many in the Third World. Further, diseases of poverty, unlike muscular dystrophy, are often preventable and curable. All things considered, therefore, would it not be better for contributors to support organizations—such as Food First, Grassroots International, and Co-op America—devoted to improving the circumstances of people in the Third World than to support the Muscular Dystrophy Association?

This, I believe, amounts to a very powerful argument against animal experimentation, though it is only implicit in the writings mentioned above. The thrust of the argument is that whatever resources are currently being used to support animal research might alternatively be used for other humanitarian purposes, so that, all things considered, we might serve humanity as well or even better by altogether abandoning animal experimentation. Fully stated, the argument proceeds as follows. First:

> Those individuals and organizations involved in animal research (whether directly as health care professionals or indirectly as supporters) might alternatively devote their energies and resources to other humanitarian causes.

Thus, physicians and health care organizations now engaged in animal research might instead devote their time and resources to providing medical care directly to those in need; and contributors to charitable organizations (which would include not only individuals, but private foundations and governmental agencies) might choose to donate whatever money they would otherwise contribute to animal research organizations to other public or charitable organizations. (For example, rather than contributing ten dollars to the

Muscular Dystrophy Association, one might donate this money to a famine relief fund.) Second:

> There is humanitarian work that is at least as beneficial to humanity as medical research, and moreover, does not involve harming laboratory animals.

For example it is estimated that between 700 million and 1 billion people in the Third World are chronically malnourished.[2] Over 2 billion do not have access to clean drinking water.[3] Some 14,000 children go blind each year in India alone from insufficient protein.[4] And worldwide between 18 and 20 million die from malnutrition and preventable diseases.[5] Experts say that most of these deaths could be prevented by access to clean water, vaccines, oral hydration salts, and vitamins.[6] In fact, over 60,000 children die each week from dehydration caused by diarrhea.[7] Yet affluent nations continue to invest billions of dollars to research diseases that afflict comparatively few people.[8] If the resources currently used to research diseases of affluence[9] were instead devoted to providing food and basic medical care to the poor, the benefit to humanity would be far greater (and the cost to animals far less) than whatever benefits flow from animal research. Therefore:

> Even if there are serious diseases that are treatable only by conducting animal research, we would still be justified in not conducting this research, but in devoting our limited resources to other forms of humanitarian aid.

In fact, the two premises seem to support an even stronger conclusion:

> Even if animal experimentation might eventually provide cures for many serious diseases, given the present state of the world, we are definitely *not* justified supporting this research; rather we ought to devote our limited resources to other forms of humanitarian assistance.

I shall refer to this argument, with either the stronger or the weaker conclusion, as the Argument from Limited Resources.

This argument, I believe, has an important place in the debate over animal experimentation. Much of this debate revolves around the following three points. First, most experiments on animals are performed not for valid scientific or medical reasons, but for commercial purposes.[10] Second, because of well-known difficulties of extrapolating from one species to another, the results of animal experimentation are often unreliable.[11] And third, in many cases, there exist alternatives to animal models in medical research, so that even when animal experimentation does yield important and reliable medical information, the use of animals may have been unnecessary.[12] Still there remains a considerable amount of animal research (just how considerable it is is the subject of much controversy) which does provide important medical insights and, furthermore, cannot be replaced by other known research methods. One important strength of the Argument from Limited Resources is that it concedes this point, yet still provides a compelling reason to abandon animal experimentation. Even if cancer, for instance, might only be cured through extensive animal research, we would not be justified in conducting this research, because there are other even more serious social problems that have priority. Today some 14,000 Americans will die from cancer.[13] In combating this disease, the National Cancer Institute will spend $3 million, and the American Cancer Institute another $1 million.[14] Yet 40,000 children in the Third World will die from malnutrition and treatable diseases.[15] According to World Vision, just 50 cents could feed a hungry child for two days. As Rosemary Rodd points out, no one can reasonably argue that the interests of Americans count for more than those of children in developing nations. Yet this is precisely the implication of a social policy that favors the welfare of American cancer patients over that of malnourished children in the Third World.

Another important feature of the Argument from Limited Resources is that it does not take a controversial stand concerning the moral status of nonhumans. Richard Ryder, Peter Singer, Tom Regan, and many others have argued against animal experimentation on the basis of the moral considerability of animals. Since animals have moral rights or are otherwise deserving of moral consideration, and since animal experimentation fails to show animals the moral respect they deserve, it follows that such experiments are immoral. While I believe that this argument, fully developed, is sound, defenders of animal experimentation have been very critical of the view that nonhuman animals are morally comparable to human beings. If animals are not, this would undermine the moral arguments of many philosophers, but it would not vitiate the Argument from Limited Resources. The point of this argument is not that animal research is wrong because of how it affects animals, but that it is wrong because of how it affects human beings. By investing whatever funds would otherwise be used in, say, cancer research in famine relief, the benefit to the human community would be far greater.

Finally, the Argument from Limited Resources provides a response to the complaint, noted earlier, that animal rights activists show more compassion for animals than for human beings. For now it can be argued that it is the activist and not the vivisectionist who shows true compassion for humanity. Every day millions of dollars are spent in animal research which provides no alleviation of human suffering, and may never do so. According to the animal rights activist, this money, if properly spent, could do far more for mankind than animal research has ever done.

This summarizes the important strengths of the Argument from Limited Resources. Let us now consider some possible objections to the argument.

One objection which might be raised is that the moral reasoning involved in the argument cannot be generalized without unacceptable consequences. If it is true, the objection goes, that we should not spend money on cancer research so long as there are starving children in the world, then it must also be true that we should not spend money on space exploration, transportation systems, industrial development, or the Strategic Defense Initiative, since the money expended on these endeavors could also be used to assist the poor. Yet these consequences are surely unacceptable. While there is, perhaps, much more that could be done to help the poor, doing so need not preclude other important and worthwhile endeavors; it need not, in particular, preclude animal research.

I agree with this objection up to a point. It is true that animal research is only one among many other immensely costly endeavors, and that there is no special reason why animal research, in consideration only of its neglect for humanity, should be singled out for criticism. While I concede this point, I think the proper conclusion to draw is not that animal research is excusable because space exploration is, but that neither one is excusable. In a much better world than our own, no one would seriously consider spending millions of dollars in space exploration when thousands of children die each day from starvation; and no one would consider spending millions on animal research when every day thousands of people die from treatable diseases.

Still, it may be argued, by redirecting funds from other sources it might very well be possible to combat poverty without abandoning animal research. If there is, in other words, no special reason why animal research should be singled out for condemnation, then there is no special reason why animal research rather than certain other costly practices should be abolished. If not all have to be abolished, then no one in particular does.

But this objection completely misses the point. It may well be true that not all people in affluent nations need to make sacrifices to improve the standard of living of people in developing nations, but this would hardly excuse any particular person from making no effort to improve things. Similarly, it may be true that by redirecting other resources significant improvements could be made in the health care of the poor without abandoning animal experimentation. But this does not excuse health care professionals for engaging in animal research rather than bringing their knowledge and skills to those people who need them most; nor does it undermine the point that contributors to charitable organizations (as well as all taxpayers) should think twice about donating their money to those organizations involved in animal research, and choose instead to donate their money to other worthy organizations. Since the objection does not undermine these two points, it does not vitiate the Argument from Limited Resources (certainly not the weaker version of this argument).

Another objection which might be raised is that the Argument from Limited Resources involves a certain inconsistency. The inconsistency consists in arguing that animal research should be abolished and our resources devoted to providing, among other things, basic medical care when, in fact, what we now recognize as basic medical care was made possible largely through the use of animal experimentation. The anti-vivisectionist, so it seems, wants to have the benefits of animal research without paying the price.

This objection has great rhetorical force, but little more. One response is to challenge the alleged importance of animal experimentation in the advancement of medical science. This is a highly controversial subject, but some critics of the medical establishment maintain that animal research, far from contributing significantly to the growth of medical knowledge, has actually *hindered* the advancement of medicine.[16]

Another possible response is to indicate that there are many forms of humanitarian assistance other than medical care. Each year many millions of people die from starvation or from diseases caused by various factors—such as inadequate sanitation—endemic to poverty. Even if these people received no direct medical care, it would still be possible to save millions of lives by supplying them with food and other forms of aid. (It has been argued, for instance, that the decline in mortality rates associated with infectious diseases is due less to medical discoveries based on animal research than it is to improved hygiene and sanitation.[17]) A proponent of the Argument from Limited Resources need not maintain that medical care should be provided to the poor but only that there are other forms of humanitarian work of greater potential value to mankind than animal research.

Yet, having said this, why shouldn't anti-vivisectionists accept the use of medical technology developed through animal research *provided that* this would not encourage further animal research? If this technology already exists, and if it would be possible to save lives or otherwise improve human health by making use of it, then, other things, being equal, we should. The position of anti-vivisectionists, as I understand it, is that we should not *continue* the practice of animal experimentation (which is not to suggest that we ever were justified in this practice), and that we should not make use of whatever products or drugs have been tested on animals because doing so only encourages further animal testing and supports those institutions that conduct it. It is not, or need not be, the position of anti-vivisectionists that even if animal experimentation is abolished, we should still not make use of any products or drugs that were developed through animal research.

Another possible objection to the Argument from Limited Resources is that while it may be true that most animal experiments do not yield valuable medical results, some experiments certainly do. For example, it has been estimated that as many as 130 million lives have been saved by the discovery of insulin for the treatment of diabetes. The research upon which this discovery was based was made in 1921 by Frederick Banting and Charles Best working with several dogs who had been surgically rendered diabetic.[18] Now, whatever objection there might be to this research, it cannot reasonably be argued that Banting and Best might have made a more significant contribution to humanity by devoting themselves to some other form of humanitarian service, such as providing basic medical care to the poor. Therefore, even if the Argument from Limited Resources does apply in some cases, it does not apply in all.[19]

I am willing to concede this point, but I do not believe it is a very forceful one. The objection admittedly applies only in those cases in which the resources (human or monetary) invested in animal research could not have been put to some more beneficial use. These cases may well be rare. But even if they are not, there is still some merit to the argument I advance. First of all, scientific research rarely proceeds in a vacuum. The work of one research team builds upon and complements the work of others, so that when success is achieved this is largely the result of a collaborative effort. Because of this, it is difficult to isolate individual experiments and defend them along the lines considered here. The true cost of success is often much greater than it appears. (There certainly were, for example, many scientists other than Banting and Best researching diabetes prior to the discovery of insulin.) Second, when animal experiments truly are medically necessary (that is, necessary in order to achieve certain medical results) it is never known beforehand what the results might be; otherwise these experiments were not truly necessary. C. R. Gallistel, in defending unrestricted animal research, argues that "There is no way of discriminating in advance the waste-of-time experiments from the illuminating ones with anything approaching certainty"(211). If this is true, then one can never know *beforehand* whether some animal research project will truly benefit mankind. This, coupled with the fact that one *can* know beforehand what the results of various forms of humanitarian aid will be (not to mention the certainty of the suffering and deaths of laboratory animals), seems to undermine the argument that animal research is justified because of the important medical results it sometimes yields.

Both points suggest that animal experimentation cannot be considered piecemeal, but only as a whole institution. Individual research projects may prove to be of immense importance to mankind. But because of the difficulty of isolating individual projects and predicting their results, we must ask whether the institution *as a whole* is morally defensible. The thrust of the Argument from Limited Resources is that the many billions of dollars invested each year in the animal research establishment might be put to better humanitarian use.

These, I believe, are the main objections to the Argument from Limited Resources. Throughout I have defended the argument on humanitarian or even humanist[20] grounds. If my defense is satisfactory, then even those with no sympathy whatever for animals should still be critical of animal experimentation. For, as I have argued, to support this institution is to support a social policy which neglects the vital interests of the vast majority of humankind.

There remains one final point to consider. And this is that my argument has social application only so long as there exist more serious social problems than those which might be solved through animal research. I acknowledge this limitation, but sadly it is one that need not concern us for the foreseeable future.

Notes

[1] In a similar vein, Peter Singer remarks: "Those who are genuinely concerned about improving health care would probably make a more effective contribution to human health if they left the laboratories and saw to it that our existing stock of medical knowledge reached those who need it most" (92).

[2] See *World Hunger:* 2 and *Roots of Failure:* 195.

³ *Roots of Failure:* 195.

⁴ *Applying Ethics:* 324

⁵ *World Hunger:* 3.

⁶ *Christian Science Monitor,* 20 September 1990: 10.

⁷ "The Cost of AIDS," *New Scientist,* 17 March 1988: 22 (as reported in *Animal Liberation:* 92).

⁸ Furthermore, many of these diseases are preventable. For example, studies indicate that a vegetarian diet can prevent 97% of all coronary occlusions, and up to 80% of all cancers may be due to diet and tobacco products. (Information from *Diet for a New America:* 247, and from a pamphlet provided by Physicians Committee for Responsible Medicine.) The position of animal rights activists is that the medical establishment could be far more effective in improving the health of the general population by concentrating upon the *prevention* rather than the *treatment* of disease. If it is true, for instance, that 80% of all cancers are caused by environmental factors, then the control of these factors would be far more effective in the war on cancer than any "magic bullet" developed through extensive animal research might possibly be.

⁹ These are diseases—such as cancer, heart disease, osteoporosis, and diabetes—that are endemic to affluent societies. For more information on this topic, see Robbins' *Diet for a New America.*

¹⁰ Ryder, for instance, reported back in 1975 that only one-third of the British research on animals fell into categories recognized as "medically necessary" (36).

¹¹ One notorious example is the thalidomide tragedy. Thalidomide was a drug widely used by pregnant women resulting in thousands of birth defects. Yet this drug was thoroughly tested on animals and thought to be perfectly safe. See *Victims of Science:* 42–43 and *Animal Liberation:* 50–51.

¹² Critics of animal experimentation have argued that computer models, insentient organisms, tissue cultures, and human subjects, among other alternatives, may replace the use of animals in some medical research. For a complete discussion, see Gendin's "The Use of Animals in Science."

¹³ *Diet for a New America:* 251.

¹⁴ *Diet for a New America:* 248.

¹⁵ *Christian Science Monitor:* 10.

¹⁶ See Sharpe's *The Cruel Deception.*

¹⁷ Fuchs makes this argument in *Who Shall Live?* (as noted by Nelson in "Animal Models in 'Exemplary' Medical Research").

¹⁸ My discussion of the discovery of insulin is based upon Nelson's account in "Animal Models in 'Exemplary' Medical Research."

¹⁹ The American Anti-Vivisection Society has produced a pamphlet, written by Brandon Reines, which is very critical of the actual role of animal experimentation in the discovery of insulin.

²⁰ The humanist, as I understand it here, is someone who maintains that only human beings are morally considerable.

References

Fuchs, Victor. *Who Shall Live?* (New York: Basic Books, 1975).

Gallistel, C. R. "The Case for Unrestricted Research Using Animals." *Animal Rights and Human Obligations:* 209–215.

Gendin, Sidney. "The Use of Animals in Science." *Animal Rights and Human Obligations:* 197–208.

Gurtov, Melvin and Maghroori, Ray. *Roots of Failure* (Connecticut: Greenwood Press, 1984).

Lappé, Frances Moore and Collins, John. *World Hunger* (New York: Grove Press, 1986).

Nelson, James Lindermann. "Animal Models in 'Exemplary' Medical Research." *Between the Species* 5(1989) 195–204.

Olen, Jeffery and Barry, Vincent (eds.) *Applying Ethics* (California: Wadsworth, 1989).

Regan, Tom. *The Case for Animal Rights* (California: University of California Press, 1983).

Regan, Tom and Singer, Peter (eds.). *Animal Rights and Human Obligations* (New Jersey: Prentice Hall, 1989).

Robbins, John. *Diet for a New America* (New Hampshire: Stillpoint, 1987).

Rodd, Rosemary. "Pacifism and Absolute Rights for Animals: a comparison of difficulties." *Journal of Applied Philosophy* 2 (1985): 53–61.

Ryder, Richard. *Victims of Science* (London: Davis-Poynter, 1975).

Sharpe, Robert. *The Cruel Deception* (Wellingborough, Northants: Thorsons, 1988).

Singer, Peter. *Animal Liberation* (New York: The New York Review of Books, 1990).

Chapter 7
Misconduct in Research

7.1   INTRODUCTION

The very idea of *misconduct* in research suggests a certain picture. Research, as we saw in Chapter 1, is a systematic investigation (i.e., the gathering and analysis of information) intended to develop or contribute to the generalizable knowledge. To say that misconduct in research exists, we must assume that research activities may be done *well* or *poorly*. In Part II, we explored the standards to which researchers hold themselves when they use human subjects—vulnerable or otherwise—or animals in the course of gathering data for their research. We also learned about the oversight committees that researchers have instituted to ensure compliance with those standards, as well as the ethical justifications for both standards and oversight in these matters. In Part III, we will look into the standards used to distinguish the proper conduct of research from misconduct. These standards are essential to ethical research and are a part of every step in the research process, from the initial conception of a research project, through the data-collection process, to the dissemination of the conclusions once the data have been gathered.

Imagine that in a particular set of experiments the rights and interests of research subjects have been guarded and the subjects have been treated well and used fairly for important and valuable scientific research. Can we conclude that the research has been conducted ethically? Not yet. A central element of research is *teaching* or *communicating* to others what we have learned about the world. What researchers do after the data have been gathered still counts toward the ethical assessment of their research. Some of these concerns have already been raised, in order to emphasize that subjects can be affected by research even after—sometimes long after—the experiments involving them are complete.

We now must examine the standards applied to the use and dissemination of data as well as the results of research. The present chapter will explore what happens to data and results between the time they are gathered and the time they are reported. The standards and principles we find—prohibiting plagiarism and interference with research, for example—are widely applicable, even beyond the sciences. In addition to exploring the reasons that various forms of misconduct are wrong, we will attempt to clarify two issues related to the principles prohibiting misconduct: First, it is not always clear whether a particular case counts as an instance of, say, falsification, or whether it is rather good science. The solution is not one that any ethics book can provide; the application of rules requires good judgment, experience, and dedication to the goals of science. Second, there are several factors that might motivate someone to engage in misconduct. We believe that an exploration of those factors might help people better understand what is at stake in such violations. Frequently more is at stake than simply "wrongdoing."

7.2   MISREPRESENTATION OF DATA

Rita is a psychology graduate student who is involved in a research project on auditory perception. She has spent months painstakingly gathering data designed to elicit a correlation between harmonics and perceived pitch. The experiments consume a great deal of time: The briefing of subjects is elaborate, and the experiment itself takes several hours to run. Since Rita is a member of a small department, she has had to work with little assistance or supervision. After several months of gathering data, she is ready to analyze her results.

When Rita begins to plot the data, her disappointment mounts. The data points do not seem to demonstrate any discernible correlation. She is concerned that her months of hard work might amount to little. Rita has conducted only 20 trials, and 4 of them had to be discarded due to the fact that her research subjects withdrew from the experiment. She does not have time to set up the experiment, locate subjects, and run the tests again in order to gather more data. As she completes her plotting, her fears are confirmed: No statistically significant correlation appears in this data set.

Although the absence of a correlation can be a useful scientific result, it conflicts with some related work by her director. Rita is therefore not inclined to report these results. She looks again at her data points scattered on the graph, and she notices that the addition of two more points would dramatically change the nature of her results. She could fit a curve much more plausibly, and a significant correlation might emerge. Just out of curiosity, she drops the points in and checks for a correlation. In fact, the correlation turns out to be not only statistically significant, but almost exactly what she had initially predicted when she proposed the research! She is delighted that her experimental results were so close after all. Perhaps, Rita thinks, some of the discarded trials would have put data points just where these two additional points occurred. Again, just out of curiosity, she checks. Of her four discarded runs, one yields a point not far from the ones she has added. In light of this outcome, and given her pressures and her situation, she considers leaving the two additional data points in, recognizing that she would have to add the documentation necessary to prove that these data were gathered in an actual experimental trial.

If she goes through with it, Rita will have fabricated data. **Fabrication is the creation of data or results that are not supported by one's own experimental results.** The creation of data, in whole or in part, that do not reflect genuine results is a form of deliberate deception. Rita proposes to deceive her director, her committee, and perhaps the scientific community into thinking that her results are other than they in fact were. Fabrication is a kind of lying, a form of dishonesty. Since it is part of a scientist's obligation to the scientific community to report the truth about experiments, fabrication fails to give others what they are due. Hence fabrication is also a form of injustice. Finally, Rita's conclusions are based upon fabricated data and may not be reproducible. She may not have contributed to generalizable knowledge at all, which is a cornerstone of research. Thus, fabrication is unethical for three separate reasons: It is a form of lying; it is a form of injustice; it does not yield genuine research.

Rita might decide not to fabricate data. It could be that the supporting documentation is too elaborate for this particular experiment, and so fabrication would be too easy to detect, or she might think that fabrication is too gross a violation. She might consider it a less significant violation if she were to alter slightly some of her data points so that they produce the desired correlation. After tinkering with the numbers a bit, she might find that slight changes are necessary to only three data points.

Rita is now considering falsifying her data. **Falsification is the deliberate misreporting of data, saying that an experiment or result turned out one way when in fact it turned out differently.** Falsification is distinct from fabrication in that falsified data reflect the misreported results of an actual experimental trial, whereas fabricated data are invented without having performed any trial. We generally regard falsification as wrong for the same reasons that fabrication is: it is a kind of deception, a kind of lying. It, too, violates the scientist's responsibility to report the truth about the world as experiments disclose that truth. Because falsified data is unlikely to be reproducible or to contribute to generalizable knowledge, it plays no part in genuine research. Finally, this illegitimate research costs money: whatever funding supports falsified or fabricated data is wasted, since these data contribute nothing to science.

Another topic that deserves mention here is statistical analysis. Some form of statistical analysis is a part of virtually every kind of scientific research. As a result, opportunities for manipulating the analysis in favor of a preferred result may present themselves, depending on the complexity of statistical analyses in a given piece of research. One means of manipulating an experiment in order to generate a preferred result is by **cooking** the data. Cooking the data is running an experiment knowing that one will get a particular result. This is unethical because it is a scientific "set-up"—the experiment is a sham, orchestrated in an attempt to get a particular set of data. As with falsification, in which it may be difficult to judge when a researcher has crossed the line from responsible statistical practices to scientific misconduct, it is difficult to judge when cooking has actually occurred. There is a sense in which the forming of a hypothesis and the testing of that hypothesis is a kind of cooking of data, because the experiment is designed to locate a particular result. If Rita is responsible and familiar with the accepted methodology in her field, she should be able to discern the difference between a genuine scientific experiment and one that is orchestrated to get a preconceived set of results.

One of the most common forms of misrepresentation is the omission of "statistical outliers," or data points that tend to weaken a correlation. This practice is also called **trimming**—failing to report results so that the data look better than they really are. A famous example is Millikan's experiments to calculate the charge of an electron. Millikan atomized droplets of oil and examined their rate of descent between two charged plates. The electrical charge on the droplets tended to slow the oil droplets' rate of fall, thereby allowing Millikan to measure the electrical charge of each droplet by measuring the rate of fall. Millikan performed 140 runs of this experiment, which he evaluated on a scale between "best" and "fair." In his notebooks, he recorded all trials of the experiment and explained his evaluations; but in the published paper that eventually helped to earn him the Nobel Prize, Millikan omitted 49 of the trials that he had judged only "fair," and he included none of the evaluative information of the notebooks. Consequently, his results were more elegant, and he was able to report exact multiples of charges rather than fractional charges, as earlier experiments had reported. Millikan's omission laid part of the groundwork for quantum mechanics, suggesting as it did that only certain "levels" or "quanta" of electrical charge were possible and that all electrical charges were exact multiples of some basic quantum charge.

This case is useful in illustrating the point that it is often difficult to distinguish between good and bad science. Millikan might have been right to report only part of his data; researchers sometimes botch experimental trials. To avoid ethical concerns, however, Millikan might have provided a complete report of the data together with his account of which data he selected as significant and why. We have no general principle governing statistical analysis. The tools of different disciplines are too diverse, and assumptions and practices are not shared across the various branches of scientific research. Just as it is a requirement of human subjects research to be familiar with the literature before performing an experiment involving human subjects, so that subjects are not exposed to harms without a genuine contribution to generalizable knowledge as a benefit, it is a requirement of all researchers to be familiar with the statistical methods used in their disciplines before they begin to analyze their data.

Although the scientific practices and goals embodied in the use of statistical analysis are too diverse to yield to a few governing general principles, this diversity of practices does not imply that no standards exist for their proper implementation in each discipline. It would be a mistake to assume that just because it is difficult to articulate the standards for the proper use of statistics, or just because different standards may exist in different disciplines, that there is no right or wrong way to use statistics in research. It is the responsibility of the scientist to be familiar with these techniques and to use them toward the goal of scientific progress. The best indication of responsible handling of statistics is to look at the intention behind the statistical manipulation. What was the intention behind the trimming of statistical outliers? Was it an attempt to make the data look better than they really are? Was it part of acceptable scientific practice? The researcher who trims outliers in an attempt to mislead others about the quality of the experimental results has committed scientific fraud. The researcher who trims outliers in an attempt to discount data which do not reflect the truth behind the observed phenomena is practicing good science. Understanding the hallmarks of good science is difficult, but a researcher's understanding of the intentions behind statistical manipulation should be apparent to the researcher.

Rita might cause herself trouble if she fabricates or falsifies data. Fabrication and falsification are widely prohibited, either explicitly or implicitly. Trimming and cooking data may also be discouraged and, if sufficiently extreme, punished. If her misconduct is discovered, then Rita could be suspended or expelled from her program and her work will be unpublishable. Does this give Rita a reason *not* to misreport data? It might, if she thinks it likely that she would be caught. It might instead give her a reason to be as crafty and deceptive as possible, to make her lie as convincing as she can.

These considerations raise the question of what Rita thinks she is doing. What goal or goals does she hope to achieve with this experiment? She is nearly finished with her doctorate, and she wishes to graduate and go on to a fellowship or faculty position, or perhaps a research career in the private sector. She may aim to support herself and her family and to cultivate friendships with her colleagues. She probably hopes to establish a favorable reputation for herself and her research. These are all worthy goals, and many of us would like to accomplish these.

Notice that if these are the *only* reasons for Rita to engage in scientific research, then perhaps she should misreport the data. She might best accomplish these goals by graduating quickly and receiving positive recommendations from her director. Assuming that she can fabricate or falsify the data effectively and without detection, doing that may provide her the best chance of achieving a good career, a steady income, and a sound reputation.

This analysis might seem shocking in an ethics textbook, but it allows us to bring into focus the question of what Rita thinks she is doing in performing her research. The goals just mentioned—career, money, reputation—are **external to research.** One can achieve these goals by doing many sorts of activity. The law, medicine, and finance can all provide stable career opportunities, secure income, and a favorable reputation. Therefore, these goals give Rita no real reason to report her data responsibly. They give her at most a reason to *give the appearance* of responsibly reporting her data, in order to avoid detection.

It is just as important to notice, however, what Rita *cannot* achieve by her contemplated misconduct. She cannot become a *good scientist*. A good scientist must be more than one who earns a good income and has a good reputation.

A good scientist is committed to the scientific method and other practices and procedures that scientists have devised for discovering the truth about the natural and social worlds. Only by engaging in the responsible reporting of data can Rita *deserve* a good reputation. These goals are **internal** to research: They can be achieved only by meeting the standards of excellence set by researchers for the reporting of data and other activities of scientific research. Therefore, if Rita hopes to attain *these* goals, she has every reason not to fabricate or falsify her data.

Goals External to Research	Goals Internal to Research
• Career	• Being a good researcher
• Income	• Scientific discovery and pursuit of the truth
• Reputation	• Deserving good reputation

Do researchers always enter their respective fields hoping to achieve goals that are internal to research? Perhaps not, but the goals external to research can be achieved in other, less demanding lines of work. Most researchers, we believe, aim primarily to achieve the goals internal to research, and they would frustrate their own goals and those of the scientific community by misreporting their data. Sometimes, under the pressure of deadlines and other demands—demands which themselves are usually external to scientific research—it is possible to lose sight of the difference between these two kinds of goals, and that is when many instances of misconduct occur.

Can we imagine any circumstances where fabrication or falsification of data would be ethical? Perhaps: If some corrupt government were to kidnap Rita's family and threaten to kill them if she did not contribute to their weapons research, it might be right to participate yet misreport the data in order to prevent the advancement of their projects. Utilitarian and virtue-centered moral theories would likely agree about this conclusion, as would some versions of deontological theory that allow exceptions in such unusual cases.

We should, however, recognize two points about this case. First, Rita's actual case is not like this extreme one, since no one has threatened her and no corrupt government intends to abuse her results. Although Rita may have concerns about finishing her program on time or contradicting her advisor, these worries are not the dire concerns about protecting others' lives that might motivate and justify fabrication or falsification. The benefits and harms of Rita's contemplated misconduct are quite different, as are her obligations under justice—both to other scientists and to the wider community. So Rita cannot appeal to the same kinds of consideration that might justify fabrication or falsification in the extreme case.

Second, we might argue that in the extreme case the corrupt government had removed Rita from the practices of scientific research altogether by forcing her to provide them with more effective means of domination and control. Her misreporting of data could in that case be better understood as political resistance than as scientific misconduct. Not every instance of working in a lab counts as science: One could perform the same actions on stage for a play, and that would not be genuine research. By directing Rita's experimental results to their own ends rather than those of scientific research, the corrupt officials have effectively prevented her from doing genuine research as we have defined it. In this case the goals internal to research have been undermined by other goals, so the virtues of honest reporting of data are no longer applicable. The important point for our purposes is that it can be ethically correct to fabricate or falsify data in extreme situations when the goals internal to research are not at stake or are suspended temporarily.

This example should remind us that moral rules hold generally, or most of the time. Extreme cases may require that we make an exception, but we may nonetheless be called upon to justify our decision to others. An example of a reasonable exception was discussed in section 5.2, in which we discussed deception research on children. It is generally recognized that if a researcher is going to deceive subjects, the researcher has the obligation to later disclose this deception to the subjects. However, disclosure of deception may do more harm than good to young children, who may not understand why adults lied to them. This fact might provide an appropriate justification for the failure to debrief subjects in such a case. In the case of the falsification or fabrication of data, a justification will have to explain why in particular circumstances it was best to pursue goals other than those internal to science. In the ordinary course of most natural and social scientific research, it will not be possible to give such a justification, since research nearly always aims to achieve those goals.

7.3 PLAGIARISM

Just as fabrication and falsification are forms of deception or lying, plagiarism is a form of stealing. **Plagiarism** is the misrepresentation of the words, ideas, or data of another person as one's own. Plagiarism, like fabrication and falsification, involves deception, but it is also stealing. It corrupts the scientific record by misrecording the origin of research. Plagiarism represents a distinct kind of violation within the scientific community and hence another form of injustice.

Plagiarism does not always involve copying the published words of another. Paraphrasing published works without proper citation, claiming the spoken words of another person, misrepresenting another's ideas as one's own, and even summarizing another's work without citation are all instances of plagiarism. This is not the place to identify every kind of writing that constitutes plagiarism; writing handbooks and style guides are useful for those who are uncertain whether using a particular passage of a work constitutes plagiarism. These examples suggest, however, that the definition of plagiarism is broader than many people realize.

Committing plagiarism, like committing fabrication or falsification, precludes a researcher from achieving goals internal to science. Presenting the ideas of another as one's own obviously cannot lead to authentic scientific discovery or original work. One who uses another's ideas without citation is a poor researcher, by the standards of the scientific community. It should be equally clear that the plagiarist does not deserve a good reputation.

The distinctive form of injustice constituted by plagiarism is condemned by all major moral theories. Utilitarians can justify the prohibition of plagiarism on the grounds that people in general—and often researchers themselves—can be expected to benefit more from an uncorrupted scientific record. Scientists are more likely to share what they know and continue to contribute if they are confident that they are going to be appropriately recognized for their contribution. The utilitarian argument for prohibiting plagiarism is that giving credit where credit is due will result in more open, and more productive, science.

Deontologists recognize a duty to cite the work of others as a central responsibility of researchers, and they justify the prohibition of plagiarism to prevent the violation of this duty. Kant's claim that we should not use other persons merely as a means is the basis for the deontological prohibition of plagiarism. Failure to give credit to others for their work, and instead representing that work as one's own, is an instance of using another person "merely as a means."

Libertarians maintain that one's research is one's intellectual property, and that plagiarism may be prohibited on the same grounds as other forms of theft. We have acknowledged that in some extreme cases, actions that would ordinarily constitute research misconduct may be morally justifiable. Once again, we should emphasize that the rare exception does nothing to undermine the applicability of such widely acknowledged rules as those prohibiting plagiarism.

The best way to avoid plagiarizing is through the diligent use of proper citation techniques. Any words, ideas, or data, spoken or written, can be cited in your work. The format to use for such citation will depend on the ultimate purpose of your work. A research paper for a graduate or undergraduate course should conform to the requirements established by the instructor. Students who are writing dissertations should consult their university's style document, which indicates the format for proper citation. Researchers who intend to publish their research in an academic journal or in a book may contact the publisher to learn the requirements for proper citation. When all else fails, consult a commercially available style guide, such as the *Chicago Manual of Style,* Turabian's *Manual for Writers of Term Papers, Theses, and Dissertations,* or a style guide specific to a particular discipline such as the *APA Style Guide.*

Citation of sources is *always* the researcher's responsibility. Do not assume that a publisher, advisor, editor, journal referee, proofreader, or anyone else will take care of citations. When collaborating, each collaborator must ensure that proper citations are included for any sources used. If one collaborator will be responsible for all citations, this arrangement must be clarified in advance.

Authors may always use common or general knowledge without citing any particular source, even if the information came from a particular source. Common knowledge is any piece of information that can be found in multiple sources without citation. Most information in encyclopedias, dictionaries, and other reference works, for example, constitutes common knowledge. It is important to realize, however, that the distinctive phrases and presentation of information in any given encyclopedia are copyrighted and may not be used without citation. Copying from the encyclopedia or dictionary is, of course, plagiarism. Authors may look up the atomic number of gold (79), the number of Roman Catholics in the world (1 billion), or the area of Sierra Leone (27,699 square miles) and use that information without citation (as we just did). If any doubt remains as to whether a particular piece of information is common knowledge, it generally does no harm to cite the source.

Plagiarism can happen "by accident." Researchers read a lot, and it is easy to pick up information and ideas without recalling the source. Should such a researcher use the idea or information without proper citation, however, he would be guilty of plagiarism. Why, if the omission was accidental, is this a case of plagiarism? The penalties for plagiarism are usually severe; why should an accident of this kind deserve a harsh sanction?

The reason is twofold. First, the scientific community values knowing whose work is whose. In part, knowing who thought of an idea first is important in order to properly reward achievement, whether that reward takes the form of graduation, publication, promotion, a new job, recognition, or money. Furthermore, knowing the origin of ideas is also important to a complete understanding of the history of science and knowledge and the development of our various theories of the world. It can be crucial to the evaluation of a particular theory that it was thought of by one person rather than another. The first reason that plagiarism—even if inadvertent—is punished severely is to impress upon researchers the importance of respecting authorship and maintaining the scientific record.

Second, a serious penalty for plagiarism indicates that omitting citation is a kind of *blameworthy negligence.* Sometimes, our accidents are not blameworthy or wrong. If the tire of my car has a blowout, I lose control, and subsequently sideswipe another car, my action need not be blameworthy. In this sort of case, we say it was just an accident. On the other hand, perhaps my mechanic has been telling me for a year that my tires are bad and need to be replaced as soon as possible. Now the case is different: By neglecting to buy new tires, I have made an accident more likely. My negligence in this case directly contributed to the accident, and I am somewhat at fault.

In the case of the researcher who neglects to cite a source—and the *reason* he neglected to do so is rarely important—the scientific community almost always regards such neglect as blameworthy and assesses the relevant penalty for plagiarism. Researchers expect their original ideas to be acknowledged by others, and so they agree to acknowledge others' ideas. Consequently, researchers have an obligation or duty to seek out sources that might have influenced their work. Part of responsibly conducted research is familiarity with the relevant literature on a particular topic, and this familiarity should preclude negligent failure to cite sources.

7.4   MISAPPROPRIATION

Like plagiarism, misappropriation is a kind of theft. **Misappropriation** is the intentional or negligent misrepresentation of the work, including data, analysis, interpretations, or conclusions, of one's colleague as one's own work. It is therefore, like plagiarism, a form of lying as well as stealing. In fact, as we define it, misappropriation is a form of plagiarism, plagiarizing the work of a colleague.

Misappropriation can take a variety of forms. It occasionally occurs when a supervisor misrepresents a student's work as his or her own. At one university, for instance, a member of the biochemistry faculty wrote a paper for publication in a journal. Her team included a colleague and two graduate students. The graduate students did much of the actual laboratory work, including running the trials, collecting the data, and preparing the analysis. The graduate students wrote up the results and submitted them to the faculty members, who revised the paper and submitted it to the journal. All four members of the team were listed as authors of the paper.

The paper was rejected by the journal, which encouraged the authors to revise it and resubmit it. The editors objected to an important part of the analysis of the data, and they suggested revisions to this part of the paper. Between the time of submission and the time the paper was returned, a personal conflict developed between the principal investigator and one of the graduate students. As a consequence of this conflict, the graduate student left the project. As it turned out, this same graduate student was responsible for the part of the analysis to which the editors had objected. So when the paper was returned, the principal investigator revised the paper herself, without consulting the graduate student. She subsequently removed his name from the list of authors and resubmitted the paper.

The faculty member's behavior in this case probably constitutes misappropriation because by failing to mention the student as an author, she misrepresented his contribution as her own. Although she reasoned that she had revised the analysis—perhaps even thoroughly reworked it from beginning to end—and so could claim that his contribution had been eliminated from the final version, the fact is that her changes were based on the work of a colleague or co-worker.

Misappropriation also occurs when a person who contributed nothing to a research project is nonetheless given credit for the project. On the face of it, it seems unusual for someone to voluntarily give credit to a person who did not make a contribution to the research effort. However, there are several circumstances under which misappropriation of this kind might occur. For example, in an attempt to get a paper published in a prestigious journal, a "big name" may be given gift authorship. In another case, a grant application may be strengthened by listing a colleague as a co-Principal Investigator, when in fact that person's contributions do not merit standing as a co-PI.

To offer or take such a gift is misappropriation because it confers authorship or other types of responsibility on someone who does not deserve credit. Like other forms of misconduct, this kind of misappropriation corrupts the scientific record by falsely indicating the origin of a particular piece of research. Furthermore, this type of misappropriation is also a form of injustice, because it frustrates the ability of other researchers to get what they deserve. Articles that falsely attribute authorship to "big names," or grant applications that falsely attribute substantial contributions to "big names," may undermine the opportunities for other researchers to publish or fund their work. Grant applications that list a prominent scholar as a co-PI, despite the fact that that scholar's actual contributions on the project are expected to be minimal, may be chosen over more-deserving applications because the grant reviewers trust the integrity of the application. For this reason, as well as other reasons discussed above, misappropriation is wrong and should be avoided by researchers whose goals are the advancement of scientific knowledge.

The straightforward solution to some of the dangers of misappropriation are to practice responsible co-authoring. Co-authoring, or the collaboration of two or more people in writing and publishing research, is common in many scientific disciplines, especially in the natural sciences. It is a useful and helpful practice that serves to initiate students into the rigors of publishing scientific research, to distribute credit for complicated experiments performed collaboratively, and to indicate the shared responsibility for the research. Co-authoring can raise some ethical difficulties, including some of the problems we have discussed in this chapter.

The best way to avoid the problems that arise in co-authoring is to agree upon the rules for authorship even before the research project has begun. Just as a team of researchers set up a schedule for who will run the lab, who will run each phase of the experimental procedure, and who will do the statistical analysis, the team should begin the project with an understanding of who will receive authorship credit and what kind of credit each person should receive. Seeming subtleties such as the order of the names on a manuscript can make a tremendous difference, especially when multiple authors may be relegated to "et al." status. The problems that arose in the case discussed earlier, in which a graduate student lost authorship, may have been avoided if the authorship protocol for the project had been clear in the beginning.

7.5 INTERFERENCE

Interference is the manipulation of the experimental apparatus, data, analysis, results, or report of another, at any stage of scientific inquiry, with the aim of impeding or preventing the successful execution and recording of a scientific project.

Interference may also take place beyond the lab, when, for instance, a journal referee recommends rejecting an article so that his own, previously written article on the same topic, might be published first.   ✓ ₐₗₗ.

Interference certainly contributes nothing to generalizable knowledge; indeed, it hinders others' efforts to contribute. Obviously, interference is a grave ethical violation, constituting in some instances vandalism or even assault. It is, moreover, an infringement of autonomy inasmuch as interfering with researchers' work fails to respect their choices. Finally, interference is always unjust, since it represents a failure to fulfill one's obligations to other researchers, to the scientific community, and to the public.

One interesting issue that sometimes arises is the question of whether the denial of funding constitutes interference. If a researcher applies to a funding agency for a grant, and the application is denied, then the researcher may not be able to continue the research. The same may be said when continuing funding is interrupted: By cutting support for a research project, the funding agency can effectively kill the project. Does the denial of funding constitute interference?

The answer to this question will depend on the reasons for the denial of funding. If a grant application is reviewed by competent, knowledgeable referees, and if those referees decide on adequately scientific grounds that a project does not merit funding, then such a decision should not be considered interference. The reason that such an evaluative process is not interference is that the aim of the funding agency, as embodied in the decision of the referees and reviewers, is to spend the agency's money on the best research project possible. The criteria for "best" will vary from agency to agency, but generally considerations of scientific promise—both for the particular project and for the particular individuals proposing to conduct the research—will or should guide the referees' decisions about which projects to fund. To the extent that evaluators and reviewers succeed in applying a funding agency's legitimate criteria, denial of funding should not count as interference.

Funding agency referees can, however, undermine the integrity of the review process at many points, and sometimes such failures will constitute interference. Referees are often drawn from the ranks of scientific researchers themselves, and rightly so: Funding agencies want knowledgeable experts to evaluate the scientific potential of their grant applications and applicants. If a referee is planning to submit a grant proposal in a particular area and is asked to review a proposal submitted by another investigator in the same area, then he might find himself in a conflict of interest. Chapter 8 considers further questions of conflict of interest. On the one hand, a referee's role as referee requires him to represent the funding agency's interests; on the other hand, he also has an interest in securing funding for his own research. Such a conflict might lead a referee to recommend rejecting a grant proposal that would otherwise have received funding. That sort of case might indeed constitute interference, as the referee's aim is to prevent the successful performance of the proposed research. Here again, a forthright application of the funding agency's criteria is the best way to prevent this kind of interference. Fortunately, most funding agencies rely on several reviewers, partly to avoid conflicts of this kind.

7.6   WHISTLEBLOWERS

The issue of whistleblowers is one of the most difficult in the ethics of scientific research. A **whistleblower** is a person who exposes an instance of misconduct, especially in a scientific, corporate, governmental, or other public setting. One difficulty lies in motivating people to become whistleblowers. Why would anyone call attention to misconduct, especially given the risks of doing so? A second difficulty concerns what protections we owe whistleblowers after they have come forward.

An institution may have a rich and supportive environment for conducting research. It may have superior personnel at every level. Yet research misconduct *does* occur, and presumably it may occur at any institution. No matter how well-written a professional code of ethics may be, no matter how fair and confidential an institution's grievance procedures may be, no matter how carefully monitored research might be, misconduct generally would go undetected were it not for whistleblowers. They play a crucial role in the detection and exposure of research misconduct. Whistleblowers uncover policies or practices that harm either the public or the cause of science, and they act in order to protect the interests of the public or of science. The fact of the matter is that no one is better placed to detect misconduct than a person actually involved in the research. Whistleblowers are typically laboratory assistants, graduate students, or other employees of a researcher, and it is this relationship that causes the problem.

Whistleblowers are almost always subordinates. They accuse their superiors of wrongdoing, and their subordinate position makes their accusations dangerous. Superiors, being in a position of greater power, may choose to exercise their power against whistleblowers. They may accuse whistleblowers of harboring a grudge. Whistleblowers may be subjected to retaliation; they may be fired, harassed, threatened, or otherwise harmed. They may be blackballed and prevented from working in research or have their careers ended. They often receive little institutional support, despite providing a crucial service. Whistleblowers have been diagnosed with post-traumatic stress disorder after losing their careers, families, and health. In light of these consequences, we should perhaps expect few people to come forward with evidence of misconduct. As pointed out already, without whistleblowers, enforcement provisions of ethics codes are virtually useless: One cannot punish misconduct if it is never reported. However, if we do not protect whistleblowers, then the enforcement of rules prohibiting misconduct may suffer.

Fortunately, many institutions have recognized the important role whistleblowers play and have begun, here and there, to take steps to protect them. The first such steps include defining a code of ethical conduct, both at the institutional level and at the federal level. Once a code of conduct is in place to oversee research projects, whistleblowers who expose research misconduct will be better protected. Having a code of ethics and a set of rules that must be followed in the event of a charge of misconduct may itself be a deterrent for researchers who are considering misconduct. In fact, everyone needs protection, both accuser and accused. A researcher's credibility can be ruined by an accusation of misconduct, even a false and malicious one; conversely, a high-powered researcher often has sufficient resources and power to retaliate and ruin the lives of subordinates, even if their accusations are true. In order to protect both parties, accusations of misconduct must be investigated thoroughly, while protecting the confidentiality of the parties. Should the accusations turn out to be true, the institution has opportunities later to publicize the misconduct and punish the offender. Should the accusations be false—either merely mistaken or motivated by envy, spite, or malice—the whistleblower need not be subjected to retaliation (though some disciplinary action may be appropriate if the accusations are malicious or negligent). Many research institutions have already taken steps in the direction of protecting all parties when alleged cases of misconduct arise.

The Office for Research Integrity, which is part of the Department of Health and Human Services (DHHS), has crafted a Whistleblower's Bill of Rights. All research that is funded through the DHHS carries the protections stated in this bill. Some of them include protection from retaliation, the guarantee of fair procedures following an allegation of research misconduct, and the guarantee that the allegation will be dealt with in a timely fashion. The Whistleblower's Bill of Rights is an important step in protecting the rights of whistleblowers.

A less obvious area for improvement addresses the disparity in power between researcher and assistant. Part of the disincentive for potential whistleblowers to come forward with their accusations lies in the immense power wielded by their superiors. The idea of "betraying" one's teacher, mentor, friend, superior, and so forth, carries great emotional force. As we have mentioned, the consequences for the subordinate can be disastrous should the superior decide to retaliate. Protections for both parties help with this problem to a great degree, but it might also help if institutions could somehow reduce the disparity in power. One possibility is to make clear to all parties that "no one is above the law." That is, codes of conduct, expectations of professional responsibility, and the explicit and implicit standards of ethical research must apply equally to all, regardless of how much power within the institution is held by a particular individual. If an institution's culture embodies this principle, supported by sound judgment, fair application, and concern for the well-being of all parties, then the task of a whistleblower becomes more tolerable. Institutional codes that both elaborate what constitutes misconduct and set out guidelines for investigation into misconduct allegations are an excellent step towards a culture of responsible research.

7.7 SUMMARY

In this chapter we have explored the varieties of misconduct in research. Many of these are forms of fraud or deception. Fabrication is the creation of data that are not supported by experimental trial. Falsification relies on actual experiments but misreports the data in order to present a false result that better supports the researcher's hypothesis. These fraudulent activities, we have suggested, are ethically wrong for three reasons. First, they amount to lying, since researchers assert what they know to be false in order to deceive those who deserve the truth. Second, these forms of misconduct are forms of injustice inasmuch as researchers who engage in these activities fail to fulfill their responsibilities to discover and disseminate the truth about the world. Third, these activities are a sham and not genuine research at all. Fraudulent research does not contribute to generalizable knowledge because it is not true. And even if a researcher's theory is ultimately accepted as true, the money and resources spent proving that theory are wasted if the researcher falsified or fabricated the data supporting it.

Plagiarism and misappropriation are forms of theft. They involve taking the property—in this case, intellectual property, which we discuss in Chapter 8—of others. Plagiarism and misappropriation are wrong for three reasons. First, they are forms of theft, and so they fall under the general prohibition of taking what belongs to others. Even cases of negligent plagiarism are blameworthy, since researchers need to be especially vigilant about respecting the rights of others. Second, these forms of misconduct are forms of injustice, since researchers who plagiarize fail to fulfill their responsibilities to themselves, their institutions, and the scientific community. Misappropriation is a form of injustice because it may prevent other researchers, who do not engage in this deceptive practice, from receiving what they deserve. Third, plagiarism is not research because it contributes nothing to the generalizable knowledge. Even if what the plagiarist reports is true or accurate, it is not original and so represents no distinct contribution to our knowledge. Finally, interference is the unjust hindrance of research.

We learn about instances of misconduct, when we do, because someone has called our attention to them. Often misconduct surfaces when someone in the researcher's lab or institution reports it. These whistleblowers are subjected to tremendous scrutiny, and they need protections; those accused of misconduct also need protection from malicious accusations. Therefore, all institutions that sponsor research need clear and confidential policies for the handling of accusations of misconduct. These policies must strive to take the best interests of all parties into account. Whistleblowers must not be attacked or punished for reporting what they take to be genuine ethical violations; on the other hand, we should not naïvely take at face value every accusation of misconduct. Reports of violations must be investigated thoroughly, impartially, and quickly. Malicious, incorrect accusations, as well as correct ones can then be addressed, regardless of the status of the affected parties.

7.8   CASE STUDIES

Case 7.1: Review the case of Rita, first introduced in section 7.2. At each stage where Rita must make a decision, explore how she might think about her choices in ways that would make various kinds of misconduct less tempting.

Case 7.2: Guy is a post-doctoral fellow in a respected molecular biology department. He believes that his research assistant has engaged in research misconduct, but he has only hunches and intuition to support his suspicions. He considers asking the assistant about the data, but he worries that this may accomplish no more than alienating the assistant. He is also reluctant to do much investigative work, since that would be time-consuming and, if discovered, undermine the trust of the lab. He believes he should do something to determine how accurate the data are, since the project is important for his career. What are Guy's options, and how should he proceed? If he discovers misconduct, what steps should he take? How would the situation change if the research assistant harbored suspicions about the post-doctoral fellow?

REFERENCES AND FURTHER READING

American Association for the Advancement of Science(AAAS), *Misconduct in Science, Executive Summary of Conference,* Washington, DC: AAAS, 1991.

Sisela Bok, *Lying,* New York: Pantheon Books, 1978.

William Broad and Nicholas Wade, *Betrayers of the Truth,* New York: Simon & Schuster, 1993.

R. Chalk and F. van Hippel, "Due Process for Dissenting Whistle Blowers," *Technological Reviews* 8(1979):48.

Gordon Harvey, *Writing With Sources,* Indianapolis: Hackett, 1998.

Darrell Huff, *How To Lie With Statistics,* New York: Norton, 1954.

E. Huth, "Irresponsible Authorship and Wasteful Publication," *Annals of Internal Medicine,* 104(1986):257–59.

Daniel J. Kevles, *The Baltimore Case,* New York: Norton, 1998.

U. Segerstrale, "The Murky Borderland Between Scientific Intuition and Fraud," *International Journal of Applied Ethics,* 5(1990):11–20.

J. Woodward and D. Goodstein, "Conduct, Misconduct, and the Structure of Science," *American Scientist* (September/October, 1996):479–90.

Inappropriate Authorship
in Collaborative Science Research

Robert T. Pennock

A recent statement from the National Academy of Sciences, the Institute of Medicine and the National Academy of Engineering decried the lack of progress in instituting ethical standards for scientific research, and among the sorts of misconduct they mentioned was "inappropriately assigning authorship to research papers" (Hilts 1994).

Kristin Shrader-Frechette terms this unethical practice "loose authorship" in her *Ethics of Scientific Research* and defines it as "inserting or removing names of persons who may or may not have helped with the work," but she does not discuss it beyond noting that it is a "controversial" form of deception or fraud (Shrader-Frechette 1994, p. 52). In this paper I take up this issue of inappropriate authorship in collaborative scientific research and examine it in detail. The first section presents the current situation in which this sort of misconduct has become problematic and analyzes specific forms that it can take. The second section discusses three major ethical principles—truthfulness, responsibility and justice—that are violated in inappropriate authorship and lays out what they demand for proper attribution. Next, I review current attribution conventions and show how they make it difficult for even well-intentioned researchers to satisfy the ethical principles. I propose two alternative attribution strategies that may help avoid some of these problems, and defend them against possible objections. In the final section I summarize the conclusions and make some additional recommendations that could facilitate change. My central contention in the paper is that the authorship model itself, with its vague and conflicting tacit conventions, is to blame for many of the ethical difficulties and that many of these difficulties could be avoided if scientific associations endorsed and scientific journals adopted an explicit and more carefully differentiated set of attribution conventions.

*   *   *

To illustrate the current situation in science in which the problem of inappropriate authorship has come to the fore, let us review a few telling statistics. The Institute for Scientific Information noted in 1994 there were 37 papers in the life-sciences published with over 100 authors, compared to almost none in the 1980's. In physics, papers with over 100 authors totaled almost 140. For the last few

Robert T. Pennock, "Inappropriate Authorship in Collaborative Scientific Research," *Public Affairs Quarterly* (1996), vol. 10, 379–391. Reprinted with permission of the publisher.

years a dozen or so papers have had over 500 authors! These represent the extreme, but in 1994 there were almost 400 papers published with over 50 authors (Regalado 1995). Even for papers with a dozen or so names, one wonders whether all these people deserve authorship credit.

Of course, most cases are ethically unproblematic. Scientific research has increased in complexity, leading to a greater need for collaboration, and this has naturally resulted in an increase in multi-authored papers. Indeed, most of the heavyweight papers come from high-energy physics and multi-center medical clinical trials, which require dozens or hundreds of researchers for the implementation, if not the design, of an experiment. So, probably in most cases most of those listed do deserve some credit. Unfortunately, in many cases we know that authorship is given improperly. A 1993 survey of faculty in chemistry, civil engineering, microbiology and sociology revealed that almost one-third of faculty members knew of inappropriate assignment of authorship credit of research papers by their peers (Swazey and others 1993). No doubt some of these were referring to the same incidents, but, even so, the statistic indicates that the problem is not insignificant.

What sorts of behavior fall under the heading "inappropriate authorship credit" and why are they thought to be unethical? Of course, merely including a large number of names is not unethical if a large number of people in fact made significant contributions. Ethical problems arise in three ways: when people who contributed in a significant manner are not properly recognized, when those whose contribution was minimal or nil are included as co-authors, and, the general case, when researchers are not properly recognized for their actual contributions.

The first sort of case may appear as plagiarism, but there are other ways to fail to give proper credit. What probably occurs most commonly is that a person in authority takes credit as the main author while an underling who played the more significant role, perhaps in the conception and execution of the experiment, merely appears as one of the subsidiary authors. Completely omitting mention of someone who played a significant role is the most flagrant sort of violation, but occurs rarely.

These days the trend seems to be to include too many people, and this second sort of case is what is most typically thought of under the heading of inappropriate authorship credit. Again, it may occur in a variety of ways. For example, a researcher may include a colleague as an author either to curry favor or with the tacit understanding of being listed in return in the colleague's articles. Or researchers may use the briefest of conversations to rationalize inclusion of a "big name" scientist among the authors to heighten the prestige of a paper and the chance that readers will take it seriously; at the very least this increases the likelihood that the article will be found and read when someone does a literature search. In other cases the impetus may come from the other side: someone may agree to provide a bit of information or a sample to a researcher only on condition of receiving authorship credit.

Sometimes the motivation is less self-serving, but practices that give recognition out of proportion to input or fail to properly recognize actual contributions are still ethically problematic. The job market is tight even for researchers with a Ph.D. and one or more post-doctorate degrees, and professors may feel a need to help their graduate students by including all their lab members as authors on papers when only a subset actively collaborated in the particular project. Students who benefit from this practice may not complain, but it is clearly unfair to other students on the job market who earned their credits by their own labors. Also, conferring authorship is sometimes the only way that a project leader can publicly recognize those who were helpful in some way. According to Curt Furberg, chair of the publication committee for the Women's Health Initiative at N.I.H., "If you give credit, you give it to everyone" (Regalado 1995). The point seems to be that anyone who contributed at all gets to be an author, even if their only contribution was to solicit a few patients for the study. Although one can sympathize with the difficulties that researchers face that would lend them to adopt this sort of maxim, it is hardly an equitable solution. For one thing, it is false—how often are the names of lab technicians, nurses, and other supporting staff included, even though they were essential to the execution of a study? Second, it is unfair in that those included as "authors" for some minor consultation or service receive equal credit to those who contributed in a substantial manner. To confer "honorary authorship" in these ways is to abdicate one's responsibility to make fair and honest judgments, rather like a teacher who gives any student a grade of 'A' who was a personal favorite or who turned in at least one assignment.

* * *

If one were to adopt the model that ideas and other sorts of intellectual input are kinds of property, then one could argue that the various forms of inappropriate authorship mentioned are all forms of theft. When someone who contributed is not included as author or when someone's ideas are used without attribution, then these clearly would be cases of stealing. One could argue that theft occurs in the other sorts of case as well; for example, by including as authors people who made little or no contribution one indirectly takes something of value—the exclusivity of property—from those who did contribute. However, the notion of intellectual property is controversial and I do not believe that it should be endorsed generally in scientific research, so I will not use it as part of the ethical argument here, and will instead appeal to a few more basic ethical principles. In particular, I want to argue that there are three major ethical principles that are violated in cases of inappropriate authorship: truthfulness, responsibility and justice. Let us consider them in turn.

The first ethical principle that applies to the question of appropriate authorship is that of simple truthfulness or honesty. A commitment to truth is an especially important virtue in science, given that a central goal of research is to search for empirical knowledge, which necessarily requires truth. We should naturally expect the virtue of truthfulness to hold generally and not to stop with the reporting of experimental results but also include honest attributions of contribution.

One might object that reporting authorship is not comparable to reporting experimental data, because the latter is evidentially significant to the investigation whereas the former is not. Even if we were to accept the purported difference this would not justify a departure from the principle of truthfulness, but in any case we should not grant the premise for it ignores the possibility of an indirect form of evidential relevance of authorship. For instance, if a researcher has been found to be negligent or to commit fraud in a particular instance, that information would cast doubt upon that person's other work as well, and in this way turn out to make a difference to one's evidential assessment. On the positive side, it may also make an evidential difference to know that someone who is particularly skilled or trustworthy was in charge of a particular aspect of a research project. Clearly, who did what can be evidentially relevant, so it is not merely that ethics demands honesty in general that supports accurate, objective reporting of researcher input.

A second general ethical principle that stands behind proper authorship attribution is that of responsibility—we attach the names of researchers to a report to indicate that they were responsible for the work. The idea of *bearing responsibility* is a basic concept in any framework of moral action. Moral agents are accountable for their actions and consequences thereof, and failure to take responsibility and recognize responsibility is a serious omission.

Critics should not minimize the idea of responsible action as merely an abstract philosophical notion, nor think that proper attribution is simply a matter of etiquette, because with responsibility may come reward. In the case at hand there are tangible benefits that can accrue from authorship. Authorship determines not only reputation in the field, but also salaries, tenure, promotion, bonuses and grant funding. Other things being equal, researchers who author no or only a few papers typically find themselves receiving fewer of these benefits than those who publish more because administrators who divvy up the rewards do so largely on the basis of numbers of publications. As a sign of responsibility, authorship lets us know who is deserving and so whom we ought to reward.

The other side of the coin of responsibility is responsibility for wrong-doing or error. In legal terms we might think of this as liability; we need to know who to blame when there is negligence or fraud. On the current system of co-authorship, it would follow that all the named researchers would be liable for wrong-doing in the same way that they are all claiming and would receive credit if that is due. But how many scientists are willing to accept responsibility for "someone else's" negligence or fraud? One sometimes sees a subset of authors of a report publishing a retraction and distancing themselves from their co-authors when there has been a charge of data-fabrication or some other wrong-doing. If someone is willing to accept credit as an author, it is reasonable to expect them to accept blame as well.

On the other hand, it is also important that we not hold responsible for some outcome someone who had no control over it. For persons to have moral responsibility requires that they have a role that gives them the ability to choose and to take one course of action rather than another, and thus potentially to make a difference to the outcome. Those who could take no action (or no significant action) in a situation bear no responsibility and so cannot properly share either the blame or the credit. Therefore, what we should expect to see in ethically grounded attribution is a report of those researchers who were in a position to act and make a difference and who take responsibility for the same.

A third ethical principle that applies to authorship is that of justice. We mostly speak of justice in contexts of political or social rights, but the ethical notion properly has a much broader scope. Aristotle's formal principle of justice tells us we should treat equals equally and unequals unequally. (This is a "formal" principle in the sense that it describes the logical structure for just judgment and action, but does not provide the content.) Justice demands "discrimination" in the positive sense that those who deserve greater reward should receive greater reward and those who deserve less should receive less. In the case at hand, justice requires that recognition be given to whom it is due by virtue of their contributions to the research and not to others who do not deserve it (and similarly for blame).

To try to counter the justice argument, one might appeal to a sports model and argue that differentiation is inappropriate in science because successful collaborative research is necessarily a team effort. Scientists undertake joint research in part because there are problems that cannot be tackled by an individual. So, given that a project could not have succeeded without everyone's contribution, everyone deserves equal credit. However, there are two problems to note about this argument. In cases in which every participant's contribution was necessary it is certainly true that they all deserve credit, but that does not imply that they all deserve equal, undifferentiated credit. That is, keeping with the sports analogy, the fact that the team as a whole was responsible for the win does not mean that we should ignore the members' individual roles—kicker, receivers, quarterback and so on. A second problem is that one of the main issues at hand is that in extreme cases individuals are being included as authors even when they were not "on the team." Here the injustice is clear: people whose contribution was minimal or nonexistent are included as "equals" with those whose contribution was essential and significant.

To summarize, we can say that inappropriate authorship is attribution that does not honestly report the researchers' true roles, give proper assignment of responsibility, or justly apportion differential contributions, and that ethically proper attribution should do these things. Of course, there is little that the scientific community can do to prevent willful misconduct beyond setting up policies that make it difficult and costly, and then being diligent about oversight and enforcement. However, I suspect that egregious cases of willful misconduct are rare, and I want to suggest that many of the ethical problems involving inappropriate authorship arise inadvertently, because of the authorship model itself and the simplistic modes of attribution that are available. If we examine the authorship conventions now used we will see that they make it difficult to adequately follow these ethical principles even when one tries. Indeed, it is remarkable that the scientific enterprise, which is based upon precision and clarity, should allow such a vague and internally-conflicting "system" of credit attribution as we now find.

*   *   *

When a research report lists a single person as author, the reader knows that this person is to get full credit, but otherwise the division of responsibility is unclear. If two or more names appear it is difficult to know whether they are to share credit equally or whether some differentiation is intended because there are some tacit ranking conventions—ordinal position, alphabetization, and correspondence priority—that may (or may not) come into play and that lead to ambiguous or conflicting rankings.

The most common tacit convention in scientific research reports that may differentiate responsibility is that major credit supposedly goes to the person who is "first author," that is, whose name comes first in the list. Sometimes this pride of place gets emphasized when the subsequent names stand alone in alphabetical order, as in (Yellin and others 1995). In more complex cases one finds the first two or three names listed in some order, followed by the rest alphabetized, as in (Boujrad and others 1995). In such cases, if the initial names are also alphabetized one might conclude that these are meant to be of equal "first author" status, and if not that some ranking of importance is implied. Of course, none of this will work if the primary investigator happens to have a surname that comes first in alphabetical order. Indeed, if all the names are in alphabetical order, then one may not give any special credit to the first author, on the assumption that the order was not meant to be indicative of credit. In other cases one finds a list without any alphabetization, as in (Endrizzi and others 1995). Such cases are especially unclear. One probably would tend to credit the first author, but was the intention to indicate descending order of credit or were the names arranged at random to de-emphasize this?

A second main strategy—the "starred author"—gets around some of these problems. In this approach, an asterisk by a name refers the reader to a footnote that usually indicates that this is the author "to whom correspondence should be addressed." The unspoken convention here seems to be that the person from whom one would request reprints or direct inquiries would be the key figure. However, sometimes one finds more than one starred author to whom correspondence should be addressed, occasionally with the names at different places in a list that may or may not be alphabetized. (For example: "T. C. Shen,* C. Wang, G. C. Abeln, J. R. Tucker, J. W. Lyding, Ph. Avouris,* R. E. Walkup" (Shen and others 1995)) Is this a sign of equal contribution or is some ranking implied? Some researchers are explicit that stars indicate credit—in a few cases multiple identical asterisks lead to a footnote that says specifically that those authors contributed equally to the work, as in (Karlovich and others 1995). More and more often one finds papers with several sorts of footnote marks by names—stars, daggers, crosses, etc.—some indicating correspondence precedence, others shared credit, and others alternative addresses, as in (Mougneau and others 1995). How are these and other such mixed signals to be interpreted?

Things get especially confusing when the two conventions clash. For example, often the starred author is not the same as the first author, as in (Hsieh and Hayward 1995). In such cases one might judge that the starred author runs the lab or was project leader and that the first author played the main role for this particular result, but it is doubtful that this is a general rule. Except in the cases in which footnotes explicitly mention contribution, the reader mostly must guess how to assign credit and responsibility, because the various signs of differentiation are inconsistent.

I will not multiply examples. This brief review is enough to show that although current attribution strategies make some attempt to address the need for differential attribution as required by the ethical principles, they are structurally inadequate to the task. They make it difficult to honestly report the researchers' true roles, they do not allow proper assignment of responsibility, and they do not justly apportion differential contributions.

*   *   *

Despite the national calls for attention to inappropriate authorship and the studies that show that it is a real problem, I do not think it common that scientists are intentionally flouting the demands of truth, responsibility and justice when they assign authorship credit. While there are certainly instances of misconduct of this sort, I believe that most violations are unintentional—the inadvertent result of accepting without question a standard, but archaic and flawed, model of attribution. Indeed, it is of little help that a scientific report writer understands and conscientiously attempts to follow what ethics demands for appropriate standards of authorship, if there is no adequate mechanism for implementing them.

To be adequate, a set of attribution conventions must make it possible to fulfill the ethical principles we have noted. Primarily, they must allow honest and just differential attribution of credit and responsibility. They should recognize essential, though perhaps minor, contributions while discouraging unearned authorship. They should reflect the ethical ideal while still being grounded in the practical realities of the work structure within the laboratory and the social reward (and punishment) structure without. Let me now propose a couple of possible attribution models that science could adopt to accomplish these goals.

One approach would be to keep an authorship model, but to abandon the ambiguous "first author" convention in favor of an extended method of explicit "starred" crediting. Rather than vague mention of correspondence priority, footnotes could note researchers' actual contributions and especially should indicate those who had primary responsibility. Those who had only consulting or supporting roles should not be included in the author list at all. For example, someone who merely provided samples or subjects should be credited in a different manner, perhaps by a citation within the report in the same way that information from another published work is referenced. Similarly, someone who provided expert advice on a particular point deserves recognition for that but not as co-author, and instead could be acknowledged in a footnote. We already have a precedent for this sort of credit attribution in the long-standing method of bibliographic referencing, which gives targeted credit for background information in published or unpublished forms. This approach has the advantage of resolving some of the ambiguities of credit without making a radical change; it simply extends a current trend in attribution. However, it may be that we need to break with the current model in a more significant way.

A second approach is for science to do away with the very notion of authorship, which is, after all, a completely inappropriate category to use to describe the scientist's work. Scientists are researchers, experimentalists, theoreticians and investigators first, and authors only incidentally. Scientists should take their actual roles and responsibilities seriously and attribution conventions should reflect this. I therefore propose that science journals institute a section in research reports devoted to delineation of contributions, following the model of "the credits" in a film. Rather than a generic or vaguely differentiated list of "authors" the credits should name the participants together with their scientific responsibilities in the research project. I will not here offer a specific list of such responsibilities because most categories will depend upon the field of research. We might expect to see roles such as Statistician, Laser Spectrographer or Subject Interviewer, or categories that list responsibilities such as instrument design, equipment engineering, computer simulation programming, and so on. Perhaps there ought to be a spot for an ethicist! Of course, individuals may have more than one role, and the level of detail that is appropriate will vary depending upon the actual division of responsibilities in any given project, so these examples should be taken merely as possibilities. The significant point is that by signing off on a role a scientist accepts credit for that function and possible blame in the case of negligence or fraud.

I do propose one cross-disciplinary category, that of "Principal Investigator," a title that is already generally recognized, though not in published reports. This key role is to be reserved for those who conceived and oversaw execution of the research and who thus bear overall responsibility. These are the scientists who had the theoretical insight, formed the hypothesis, designed and implemented the protocol, analyzed the data. We should expect relatively few people to be listed as principal investigators for any given research report. Even the mammoth projects with over 500 authors that we saw in physics and medicine would probably have fewer than a dozen principal investigators, and the vast majority of projects would have only one, two or three. The title should identify just those scientists who had the primary positions of design and general oversight of the research being reported and who will sign off on all the steps of the process and take responsibility for the accuracy of its results. The principal investigators should receive primary overall credit and if error or fraud is discovered they will be the ones to hold accountable. Listing just a few scientists as principals is not meant to deny credit to those who played other roles—such people deserve specific credit for their specific roles (and specific blame if they violate their responsibilities). Again, the point is to reflect the actual contribution of the participants, and typically there are only a few scientists in any given project who really exercise overall design and control.

Finally, I suggest that there be a second generally recognized role—perhaps "Consulting Scientist" would serve—that would allow a way to credit those auxiliary contributors who provided some expert advice or professional service, for example, but who were not actively involved as researchers on the project. This provides a way for the Primary Investigator to recognize important professional help from other scientists without having to inappropriately elevate such contributors to the status of an "author."

The general strategy behind these proposals is to make attributions of differential responsibility explicit. Besides permitting researchers to be given credit for their true contributions as scientific investigators (rather than as "authors"), an explicit system of attribution will also make it harder to inappropriately tuck in "honorary" researchers as is now so easily done in the generic author list.

*   *   *

Let us now consider possible arguments against these proposals and try to rebut them in turn.

First, we may dismiss some rather self-serving reasons one might offer in favor of the status quo. The undifferentiated author list might make it easier to evade responsibility and duck blame if there are accusations of fraud or negligence. The current system also makes it easier to claim credit if the project turns out to be a major success. Moreover, if the paper simply sinks into the morass of uncited papers, the authorship credit still helps increase the length of one's publication list. The ethical cynicism here should be obvious, but even the supposed benefits are not unadulterated. Innocent researchers may be tarred in a case of research fraud by having appeared as an equal author when they had no knowledge or control over the fraudulent aspect of the research. Also, multiple authorship will eventually dilute the benefits of authorship in the same way that grade inflation has decreased the value of B's and A's. The impression one has now upon seeing reports of the "most published" researchers, often with hundreds of articles, is not of their quality in scholarship. Instead, one suspects that it is mostly a sign of their ability to network politically. Nevertheless, we must admit that these "reasons" will continue to have some unfortunate practical force unless institutional and administrative attitudes change. When universities emphasize number of publications over content and quality when making judgments about tenure or promotion it is not surprising that people will be tempted to find ways to increase their "output" quantity. Concomitant with the proposed change in attribution policy, we should expect administrators to become more sophisticated in their judgments and more careful and consistent in dividing rewards based upon a scientist's record of work.

Second, one might offer some practical arguments against the proposals. For example, one may argue that it is difficult or impossible to categorize the various contributions individual scientists make to a research project. Credits in films are possible because responsibilities are mostly pre-defined by unions, but someone could argue that no such categories are available in scientific research. It is true that research roles are not contractually defined as they are in films, but it is not correct to say that divisions of responsibilities do not exist. In some cases roles may indeed be quite clearly laid out in job descriptions or grant applications, and in other cases differential responsibilities are understood informally within a lab or research group, with the participants well aware of who conceived and/or oversaw implementation of a given experiment or provided the key elements of a theoretical analysis, and who served the various supporting roles. Except for the role of Principal Investigator, I do not propose that there be a pre-set classification either between or within disciplines, but simply one that accurately reflects the divisions of responsibilities as they occurred in the particular research project that is being reported.

Another pragmatic argument against these attribution proposals is that they will unduly focus attention upon the participants' places in the research hierarchy. Instead of regarding all the participants as co-operative seekers of knowledge we now will be concerned about whose name goes where on the marquee. This point has some merit. Unlike the case of creative works of art in which our interest is often as much in the artist as in the work, in science the content of an article is what is important—what knowledge has been gained—and the identity of the researchers is of little importance and so should not be emphasized in this way. On the other hand, we have already mentioned a way in which researcher identity may be indirectly evidentially relevant. Furthermore, although we might find the notion of the "abstract researcher" who is interested only in advancing knowledge to be an appealing ideal, the argument is somewhat disingenuous given that we already do pay attention to the place of the researchers' names on the author billboard as we have earlier seen. Given limited funds for research support and the competitive nature of the scientific career, individual achievement must be recognized and documented, and it is not right to expect researchers to give up the possibility of distinguishing themselves. The attribution methods that I propose have the advantage of making recognition and documentation explicit and "above board."

There is one more serious practical consequence that could result from changes to the present system, namely, they could have a chilling effect upon collaboration in general. Anecdotal evidence from research departments in which authorship is shared as a matter of policy shows greater interaction and sharing of information, high productivity, and better morale. If we remove the incentive of co-authorship, researchers may be less willing to co-operate with other scientists, especially in supportive roles. Such a result would be detrimental to the advancement of science, so the change is ill-advised. If such a chilling effect would indeed occur as the result of the proposed changes, then this would be a good argument. Of course it would take an empirical study to check the claim, but given general knowledge of human psychology it does not seem unreasonable to think that removing the co-authorship incentive to co-operation would have that effect. At this point one might argue that thorough-going competition is more productive than co-operation, and dismiss the argument by granting the second premise while rejecting the first. For example, Philip Kitcher, in a different context, has argued that competition among scientists is an important impetus to science's continued success and advancement (Kitcher 1993). However, although a certain level of competition is healthy, substantial co-operation is also required, so we should encourage or at least not discourage it. Nevertheless, I would claim that there is little danger that collaborative research will be unduly discouraged for the simple reason that, as was mentioned, most scientific research today is sufficiently complex that it simply cannot be done alone. Furthermore, the proposed attribution schemes will continue to reward collaboration by making scientists' contributions explicit. Some self-serving co-operation will no doubt be lost, but that may be the price to be paid for ethical attribution.

Finally, we must consider an ethical argument that is the most persuasive reason for not adopting the proposals, namely, that in the established research culture authorship is the accepted coin of the realm. Although the final goods may be research funds or promotions, the immediate unit of payment for the researcher is authorship, and from this is derived recognition, reputation and reward. In such a culture the proper way to recognize someone's contribution to a research project is to confer authorship. One can argue this point from a Contractarian theory of ethics, reasoning that the present system of co-authorship is moral because it is what professional scientists have agreed to or would agree to under some fair decision-making procedure. This viewpoint also would explain why lab technicians and other support staff are not typically included as authors. Hired technicians have chosen a career in which they hone their ability to carry out assigned technical tasks without needing to understand the conceptual protocol in which those procedures are embedded, and their primary, accepted remuneration for this limited but essential role is the wage they receive. For the professional, on the other hand, who has devoted years of effort and resources to reach a high level of both practical knowledge and theoretical understanding, "payment" for contributions to a research project is not wage but recognition, and in the present system this can only come from being listed as an author.

We may admit that it is certainly proper that professionals receive credit for their contributions by providing them with recognition, given that this is the accepted form of "payment." Nevertheless, it does not follow that everyone should receive equal recognition, which calling everyone an "author" does. To stay with the currency analogy, it would be as if the only monetary denomination were the hundred dollar bill so one could not be paid less than that no matter how large or small one's contribution. The situation is in fact a bit worse than this, because neither can one be paid any more than this. The current attribution strategies attempt to refine things a little in that the "first" or "starred" authors could be thought to be more equal than the other authors, but, as we saw, these tacit conventions are vague and inconsistent. The arguments from truthfulness, responsibility and justice show that more fine-grained acknowledgment is required. My proposed attribution methods that depart from the simple authorship model are possible solutions in that they keep the special sort of credit that research professionals expect, but also allow us to respect the ethical need to differentiate levels and varieties of contributions.

*   *   *

We may now summarize our conclusions. Inappropriate authorship in scientific research occurs when one or more of the principles of truthfulness, responsibility and justice are not respected when reporting researcher contribution in a published report of a scientific investigation. Some cases of loose authorship are the result of willful misconduct, but often problems arise because of the authorship model itself and the vague and conflicting conventions that are available to differentiate responsibility among "authors." Alternative attribution conventions that can more accurately reflect the actual roles and contributions of scientists are ethically preferable and should be pursued.

Two further recommendations may facilitate the proposed change to a more ethically sound system of attribution. First, professional journals (or perhaps scientific societies) should adopt a convention of explicit responsibility attribution such as I have defended in the same way that they adopt stylistic conventions, thus providing a consistent model that researchers can follow and readers can use to make judgments. Second, administrators should review their institutional policy for judging and rewarding researchers; as long as administrators continue to emphasize quantity and simply count numbers of "authored papers" to determine reward, scientists will have little practical incentive to change the present system.

Of course, even if the proposed attribution procedures are adopted, they do not by themselves solve the problem of intentionally unethical actions; they cannot prevent researchers from engaging in outright fraud. What they will do is mitigate many of the ethical problems of credit attribution that the current authorship model exacerbates. They provide a way to honestly report and justly differentiate the particular contributions that individuals actually made. They allow a way to indicate who bears responsibility for what. And they provide a structure in which consultants and others who provide important auxiliary support may be given credit for their contributions without improperly exaggerating their role to that of co-author. In the end, however, it will still be up to researchers to choose to do the right thing.

Bibliography

Boujrad, Noureddine, Stephen O. Ogwuegbu, Marine Garnier, Choong-Hyu Lee, Brian M. Martin, and Vassilios Papadopoulos. "Identification of a Stimulator of Steroid Hormone Synthesis Isolated from Testis." *Science* 268 (16 June 1995): 1609–12.

Endrizzi, James A., Jeff D. Cronk, Weidong Wang, Gerald R. Crabtree, and Tom Alber. "Crystal Structure of DCoH, a Bifunctional, Protein-Binding Transcriptional Coactivator." *Science* 268 (28 April 1995): 556–59.

Hilts, Philip J. "Scientists Lament Lack of Action on Misconduct." *The New York Times*, Feb. 6 1994, 13.

Hsieh, James J.-D and S. Diane Hayward. "Masking of the CBF1/RBPJk Transcriptional Repression Domain by Epstein-Barr Virus EBNA2." *Science* 268 (28 April 1995): 560–63.

Karlovich, Chris A., Laura Bonfini, Linda McCollam, Ronald D. Rogge, Andrea Daga, Michael P. Czech, and Utpal Banerjee. "In Vivo Functional Analysis of the Ras Exchange Factor Son of Sevenless." *Science* 268 (28 April 1995): 576–79.

Kitcher, Philip. *The Advancement of Science: Science without Legend, Objectivity Without Illusions.* New York: Oxford Univ. Press, 1993.

Mougneau, Evelyne, Frédéric Altare, Adil E. Wakil, Shichun Zheny, Thierry Coppola, Zhi-En Want, Rainer Waldmann, Richard M. Locksley, and Nicolas Glaichenhaus. "Expression Cloning of a Protective *Leishmania* Antigen." *Science* 268 (28 April 1995): 563–66.

Regalado, Antonio, "Multiauthor Papers on the Rise." *Science* 268 (7 April 1995 1995): 25.

Shen, T. C., C. Wang, G. C. Abeln, J. R. Tucker, J. W. Lyding, Ph. Avouris, and R. E. Walkup. "Atomic-Scale Desorption Through Electronic and Vibrational Excitation Mechanisms." *Science* 268 (16 June 1995): 1590–92.

Shrader-Frechette, Kristin. *Ethics of Scientific Research.* Issues in Academic Ethics, ed. Steven M. Cahn. U.S.A.: Rowman & Littlefield Publishers, Inc., 1994.

Swazey, Judith P., Melissa S. Anderson, and Karen Seashore Lewis. "Ethical Problems in Academic Research." *American Scientist* 81 (6 1993): 542–53.

Yellen, John E., Alison S. Brooks, Els Cornelissen, Michael Mehlman, and Kathlyn Stewart. "A Middle Stone Age Worked Bone Industry from Katanda, Upper Semliki Valley, Zaire." *Science* 268 (28 April 1995): 553–56.

The Voice of Experience

Robert L. Sprague

Introduction

The title of this paper, "The Voice of Experience," was selected because it implies that personal experience in whistleblowing adds a dimension to the understanding of scientific misconduct.[1] Those purely scholarly accounts of whistleblowing by authors who have not experienced the often traumatic events associated with whistleblowing lack an important aspect of the activity, i.e.[2-3] This will be the main point of this paper.

Perhaps the best way of explaining the value of experience in understanding whistleblowing in science can be derived from analogies. In preparing this paper, I talked with several well-known whistleblowers, mainly from areas of science. From time to time I will refer to their comments and reactions because most of them have experienced far more dramatic events and emotional trauma than I have experienced.[4,5] Heidi Weissmann[6] suggested to me that the whistleblowing experience is very similar to that of people who have encountered disasters, such as hurricanes, fires, flooding, or displacement due to riot or war. The disaster experience is certainly bad enough in itself, but after it passes, the individual has to put her/his life back together. Reorganizing one's life is probably the most important similarity between surviving a disaster and whistleblowing. Thus, the trauma is prolonged as readjustment to life occurs, sometimes taking years. The severity of the analogy to a disaster is not accidental but deliberate. Many whistleblowers never recover from the experience, especially if their family ties are not strong[7] as pointed out to me recently by Roger Boisjoly. As is widely known, Boisjoly tried to stop the launch of the Challenger space shuttle because of concern about faulty O-rings, but his consultation was ignored.[8-10] Also, see Boisjoly's comments in this issue of the Journal.[11]

The initial shock of the scientific community in response to whistleblowing, particularly to the revelations that some scientists fabricate, lie, and in one instance murder[12], has passed. The scientific community moved to accepting, and in some cases, honoring the whistleblower.[13-14] Now I believe the scientific community is moving toward suspicion of the whistleblower as being personally motivated for the wrong reasons, for example, greedily seeking a large financial settlement from a lawsuit.[15-16] While I do not deny that a few whistleblowers may be motivated by the lure of large financial settlements, I vigorously deny that is the primary motivation of the majority of people who bring cases of scientific misconduct to light.[7]

Robert Sprague, "The Voice of Experience," *Science and Engineering Ethics*, (1998), vol. 3, 34–44.

Thus, my main point is that in studying integrity in science, (or sometimes the reverse side of the coin, scientific misconduct), the personal experiences of scientific whistleblowers provide considerable information useful to understanding and, hopefully, improving integrity in science. Many of the whistleblowers have used their personal experiences to develop new activities which contribute to science as a whole. In fact, I will postulate that one of the most effective ways of overcoming the often very traumatic experience of whistleblowing is to attempt to use the experience to move on to a new phase of life in which a new activity can contribute to science, in particular, and society, in general.

The Subjective Experience of Whistleblowing: Quality of Life Issues

Well-being is very important in everybody's life, and it is crucially important when disasters of life strike. In the many psychological studies that have been done in this area, subjective well-being is measured with checklists and rating scales generally called "quality of life." The quality of life is a very important factor in medicine, and it influences crucial measures such as morbidity and mortality. For example, recovery from cardiac trauma[17] is often heavily influenced by the patient's quality of life perspective. This important factor was pointed out by Engel[18] who developed the biopsychosocial model for explaining individual differences in response to medical treatment.* Sometimes quality of life measures are more important in predicting the patient's outcome than more scientifically rigorous biological or physiological measures. Quality of life is an enduring factor in the human condition that is highly related to "happiness," a concept which all of us understand and seek. Measurements of quality of life have been replicated in several studies over many cultures.[19] Quality of life measures can only be obtained from people directly involved with the environment or event of interest. There is no substitute for this measure that can be obtained from others. Thus, the point is that whistleblowers themselves are the only source of information if one wants to obtain data about their quality of life.†

Breuning Case

It is obvious that I know more about the case of scientific misconduct in which I blew the whistle than any other case. In fact, I am the only source of information about subjective feelings of the whistleblower in the Breuning case.** [4-5] The case of Stephen E. Breuning, University of Pittsburgh, officially began when I wrote an eight-page letter with 44 pages of appendices—I rarely write such detailed letters—to the National Institutes of Mental Health (NIMH) in December 1983.[5]

This lengthy letter contained detailed information about data fabrication in a very sensitive area of research, namely the use of psychotropic medication with mentally retarded people who are very vulnerable. Because mentally retarded people in institutions typically do not have the verbal ability to inform their physician about their complaints, pains, and reactions to treatment, they need special care and protection. At the time of the Breuning case, psychotropic medication was used extensively in institutional facilities[20] for the mentally retarded and also in community settings.[21] In fact, psychopharmacological treatment of mentally retarded people is still an area of considerable interest and controversy.[22]

The evidence presented in my letter was detailed and supported by extensive documentation.[5] The essential points in the letter were confirmed by Breuning's confession of fabrication only 3 months after my letter was sent. Yet in spite of that smoking gun confession, 5.5 more long years (December 1983 to July 1989) of emotional upheaval continued before an NIMH report was issued and other aspects of the case were settled. It seems that pressure from media exposure speeded up events in this glacier-like pace of NIMH. In chronological order some of these reports appeared in: *Science*,[23] *Time*,[24] *U. S. News & World Report*,[25] and *60 Minutes*.[26]

SCHRIVER'S INVESTIGATION

About 3 months after my initial letter, Breuning confessed[5] to a University of Pittsburgh committee about his fabrication of data. University of Pittsburgh committees investigated Breuning during the next 6 months. Following these investigations, the Dean of the School of Medicine wrote to Lorraine Torres at NIMH, who was in charge of the federal investigation, that he could "find no serious fault with Dr. Breuning's activities here at Pittsburgh" (p. 115)[5] in spite of Breuning's confession to part of the scientific misconduct.

Given this discrepancy between the University of Pittsburgh's report and the facts known about the case, NIMH appointed an investigator, James W. Schriver, to "conduct a comprehensive investigation of . . . [Sprague's] allegations against Dr. Breuning." (p. 41)[4]

Much to my surprise and anger, Schriver started his investigation by interrogating me and examining my files apparently because I made the allegations. This seems to me most unusual because in most investigations of illegal activity with which I am aware, the police or investigating agents begin with the accused and the scene of the misdeeds, not the person who called the police; certainly not investigating the laboratory of the person who reported the incident, which was far from the location of the alleged misdeeds.

It is difficult to convey in words the emotional reaction of being officially investigated for responsibly alleging scientific misconduct (recall the initial eight page letter with 44 pages of appendices) in an area where great potential public health harm is possible. Most ethical codes indicate that it is the responsibility of a person, particularly a professional, to report to authorities suspected improper activities when those activities have the potential for producing great harm. But in this situation, the person doing the reporting was investigated first—a dramatic departure from customary practice.

Wife's Terminal Illness

As indicated in a previous publication,[27] Joyce, my wife, was terminally ill during almost the entire duration of the Breuning case and died in the same month (April 1986) the NIMH report was finally issued. The terminal illness and death of a spouse is one of the most trying and emotional experiences anybody can encounter without the added burden of defending one's self from whispered insinuations about conspiracy in a scientific misconduct case.

Because Joyce's kidneys failed following about 28 years as a diabetic, she was started on 3 times a week hemodialysis in a local hospital. She was unable to drive herself home from the hospital after the hemodialysis; thus, I always took her to the hospital and returned for her about 3 hours later after the treatment was finished. The University of Illinois was gracious enough during the 2.5 years of these treatments to allow me to be absent from my position for extended periods of time at least 3 afternoons a week. Ironically, her hemodialysis treatments started the same month (September 1984) that Schriver first contacted me. Additionally, there were other trips to the hospital for medical tests. Often Joyce would awaken me during the nights, and my sleeping pattern during this time was often interrupted. Needless to say, the time demands, interrupted sleep, and emotional strain of the treatments were quite stressful. Nevertheless, I was required during the last few years of her life to meet with Schriver, obtain documentation for him, correspond and obtain data for NIMH, prepare and meet with the NIMH panel, and carry on my regular duties at the University of Illinois as well as I could. As I look back on the situation, I sometimes wonder how I made it through those times with all the demands being placed on me.

End of the Breuning Case

In fact, the final resolution of the Breuning case did not come until the summer of 1989, more than 5.5 years after the start of the case. The case ended when the President of the University of Pittsburgh wrote a letter of apology to me. In June 1989, I testified before a United States House of Representatives Committee about scientific misconduct.[28] In that testimony I stated I thought there was a cover up in the case because the confession of Breuning was ignored. Moreover, the University of Pittsburgh did not investigate Breuning's work at Pittsburgh until very late in the process although Torres had sent two letters ordering such an investigation.[5,28] About 2 weeks after the testimony, I received a letter from an attorney from the University of Pittsburgh threatening me for a libel lawsuit because of my Congressional testimony.[5]

As I understand the law particularly after this episode, Congressional testimony is protected because it would be impossible for the committees of Congress to obtain necessary information from witnesses if those witnesses could be intimidated into silence by the threats of libel lawsuits by wealthy corporations. This final threat really upset me because I knew the legal budget of the University of Pittsburgh was many times larger than my ability to retain attorneys to defend myself even against a frivolous lawsuit. However, Representative John Dingell (D-Mich) had told me in my previous testimony before his Committee that he and his staff wanted to know if I was ever intimidated because of my Congressional testimony.[29] Congressman Dingell wrote a strongly worded letter[5] to the President of the University of Pittsburgh, who subsequently sent me a letter of apology. However, if I had not had the good fortune of testifying before Congressman Dingell's Subcommittee, I might have been in legal and subsequent financial difficulties.

Finally, it should be noted that a number of other people were harmed in the Breuning case in addition to the mentally retarded people who were treated according to the findings of his bogus experiments. The capable young psychologists and other researchers who were enticed to be his coauthors found their careers jeopardized or, at the very least, were forced to explain their coauthorship with him.[30-31]

Experiences of Other Whistleblowers

Roger Boisjoly

Roger Boisjoly, an engineer working on the shuttle spacecraft, tried to persuade NASA not to launch the Challenger in April 1986 because he and some of his colleagues believed that unusually cold weather at the launch pad in Florida would cause malfunctioning of the O-rings that were essential to a safe flight. However, his engineering expertise was silenced, the Challenger was launched, and within a few minutes of launching, it exploded in a ball of fire when the O-rings failed, allowing hot gases to ignite the propellant. As a result, the astronauts all died including the civilian teacher who had been selected to go on the mission. If Boisjoly's warnings had been heeded, the astronauts' lives would have been spared. Boisjoly, although a national hero, was subjected to considerable harassment and eventually left the company and formed his own engineering consulting firm. The Boisjoly consulting firm specialized in engineering cases in which defective equipment had been sold to the public and subsequently caused injury and damage. Thus, one of the factors in his lengthy recovery from a devastating whistleblowing experience[8] was developing a new activity that built upon his traumatic experiences. Boisjoly is now spending a considerable amount of his time lecturing and speaking about engineering and professional ethics and integrity.

Heidi S. Weissmann

Heidi S. Weissmann, formerly of the Einstein School of Medicine, spent years in federal courts trying to protect her writings from plagiarism using the copyright laws of the United States.[6] Although Weissmann's entire article was plagiarized, except the title and her name,[6] she spent many long difficult years in investigations by the university and court proceedings filled with many adverse and strange events. Leonard Freeman who copied her article was promoted, and Weissmann lost her job.[32-33] She was subsequently charged with misconduct at the university,[34] and observed incredulously as Freeman was honored by a medical honor society.[35] However, there was some levity along the way when the university issued a policy with a flawed title, "Policy to Protect Misconduct in Research."[36] The resistance to settle her case persisted for years,[37] and it included an attempt to entice her to alter her Congressional testimony.[38]

In a 1991 meeting in New York City sponsored by the American Chemical Society, Weissmann discussed her case and acknowledged to the audience that the trauma of the situation had resulted in her developing post traumatic stress disorder (PTSD).

Weissmann finally won a decisive federal appellate court ruling that strengthens the copyright protection of all of us who engage in writing and publishing of scholarly and research papers.[39] She also recovered a significant financial judgment although not enough to cover her legal expenses and recoup the years of lost salaries.[40] As part of her recovery from the PTSD that resulted from her experience, she has formed the Center for Women in Medicine and Health Care to aid victims of abuse in the health care system.

CAROLYN PHINNEY

Carolyn Phinney, formerly of the University of Michigan, turned to the local county court after the University system failed to rectify plagiarism of her ideas and writings in a grant application. As in other cases, after several years of battling in court, she won a $1,000,000 damage award from the University of Michigan and the faculty members involved in preventing a fair hearing of her case at the university level.[41] During this stressful time, she also developed PTSD.[42]

The University of Michigan appealed the decision of the jury award from the county court, and a decision was reached by the Michigan appellate court on her case in August 1997.[43] The three judge court unanimously upheld the jury's damage award. The award is now worth about $1,600,000 considering the interest earned on the award from the time of the original decision in 1993.

During the several years Phinney has been seeking a decision in her case, she has been busy working on local political campaigns, and she raised a significant amount of funds for the Congressional candidate from her Michigan district.

Phinney has spent many hours on the phone talking to other individuals who have blown the whistle on various kinds of scientific misconduct. She is probably contacted by various other people because her case is the only case, to the best of my knowledge, in which a person has won a substantial damage award by going into the local courts and deliberately avoiding the federal procedures for adjudicating scientific misconduct in cases involving federal grant funds.[44-45] The federal procedure involves the Office of Research Integrity (ORI) which represents another potentially cumbersome bureaucratic layer that might delay a case for several more years often while the whistleblower may suffer a variety of indignities. It appears that the ORI has so defined its mission to exclude authorship disputes of the kind reviewed above from its purview.[46] Thus, the ORI has ruled out of its purview many of the difficult issues which plague university communities where disputes may arise between investigators over coauthorship of papers derived from federally funded research projects.

THOMAS CONDIE

Another legal procedure open to individuals in situations where federal research funds have been misused is the federal False Claims Act. There has been one case in which Thomas Condie at the University of Utah filed a lawsuit under this act and, after years of waiting, won a substantial award for reporting scientific misconduct.[47] There has been a substantial increase in such lawsuits in recent years, and it remains to be seen whether this might be an effective avenue for seeking justice for those who have been ignored when misconduct has been reported. Of course, critics may ignore the larger contest of the situation and imply that the primary reason for whistleblowing in such cases was the lure of large monetary rewards, a type of criticism noted above.[15-16]

What Can Be Learned From These Experiences

There are lessons that may be learned from these few whistleblowing episodes described above. As has already been indicated, the person who plans to make a public complaint about suspected misconduct in science should be prepared to face a very difficult time as has been adequately documented in a study of whistleblowers in general.[7] Probably the harsh treatment of whistleblowers should have been suspected from the beginning because one only has to consider the English words used to describe whistleblowing to obtain an appreciation of how society views this activity. Consider these words: tattletale, rat fink, squealer, etc. Because of these negative connotations, a few writers have attempted to coin more neutral words to describe the activity, none of which seems to have been widely accepted: allegator and ethical resistor.

What I Learned

At the beginning of the Breuning case, I was incredibly naïve about how universities and governmental agencies might respond to allegations of scientific misconduct. I thought all I had to do was to point out the misconduct, thoroughly document my allegations, and then sit back and wait for the agencies to accomplish what clearly is their moral obligation and, in some instances, their legal responsibility. I am disappointed to write that I was never more wrong in my life. However, I learned a great deal from this experience. Unfortunately, all too often one must apply pressure to organizations to encourage them to do the right thing. I quickly learned that pressure can be applied through the media and that the whistleblower may need to contact actively a number of journalists until one finds an interested and motivated reporter. Communication with members of Congress is important, I believe, in situations where federal funds are involved or the public health is at stake. Reports in the media and Congressional interest go hand in hand, that is, media reports attract the interest of Congressmen who may arrange hearings on the topic. Such hearings attract the interest of more media people. Finally, persistence is vital to blowing the whistle successfully. If one is not able or willing to pay the price of time, money, and possibly intense criticism, successful whistleblowing is not possible. Hopefully, this situation will change in the future.

What Should a Whistleblower Do?

There are several actions which a prospective whistleblower should take: 1) One should expect that subsequent to making a public complaint about scientific misconduct, one's life will become far more difficult. One will need the support of family. 2) One should keep thorough and voluminous records particularly of important discussions and telephone calls. 3) One should talk often to close colleagues about the situation to have them reflect your feelings, attitudes, and, especially, your plans for the case. 4) One should attempt to network with other successful whistleblowers. Plans are underway to establish a foundation, WISE (Whistleblowers for Integrity in Science and Education), to provide networking and information to prospective whistleblowers.‡ 5) It is often valuable to contact a lawyer to obtain information about the legal implications of the situation. One should seek a lawyer with experience in the area, and it may be difficult to find such a lawyer.*** Finally, 6) if federal funds are involved, one should write to his/her representative in Congress.

Recommendations

A panel of the National Academy of Sciences issued a report with 10 recommendations in the area of scientific integrity.[48] Two especially relevant recommendations are: "Recommendation One—Individual scientists in cooperation with officials of research institutions should accept responsibility for ensuring the integrity of the research process." (p. 13). Both individual scientists and universities have been remiss in promoting integrity in science; this is a most important recommendation for change. "Recommendation Two—Scientists and research institutions should integrate into their curricula educational programs that foster faculty and student awareness of . . . integrity in the research process." (p. 13) Education of both students and research workers is urgently needed in the area of scientific integrity, again as noted by the major lapses in integrity in the cases described above. In addition,[3] some federal agencies, such as the Office of Research Integrity, should improve their rules on how misconduct allegations are handled, particularly allegations of plagiarism. Especially for younger people in science, such as graduate students, post-doctoral fellows, and beginning assistant professors, who have limited social power in their organizations, plagiarism is a serious offense which should be addressed rather than dismissed as a mere authorship dispute.

Finally, everyone associated with the scientific endeavor should set as a goal improving the scientific integrity environment. Although the percentage of scientific misconduct cases may be low in comparison to the total amount of scientific research conducted, many cases of misconduct are very important to society. Whistleblowers now seem to be the main line of defense, and they need help.

Summary

Using only a few cases of whistleblowing with regard to scientific misconduct, an attempt has been made to provide evidence that whistleblowing is a decidedly unpleasant task which is fraught with many difficulties, twists, and turns.[49–50] Although there has been a call for a Whistleblower Bill of Rights,[51] such a set of legally binding rights seems a long distance in the future.[52] But things are changing. There is now a National Center for Whistleblowers,[53] and the Cavallo Foundation has established an award for reporting misdeeds publicly.[54] There are a variety of laws protecting whistleblowing.[55–56] Yet, recovery from the emotional trauma and stress of whistleblowing still seems to be largely a private, individual matter. There is some unorganized communication between whistleblowers. Such communication is useful particularly when people who have just taken a stand contact older, more experienced whistleblowers for information and advice. Many whistleblowers find comfort in reorganizing their lives and starting a new activity. Perhaps this article might encourage whistleblowers to unite in some kind of organization to provide information and advice for new whistleblowers who seem to be appearing all too frequently.

References and Notes

*I want to thank Miss Tonia van Staveren, a graduate student at the University of Illinois, for bringing the quality of life issue forcefully to my attention in a recent dissertation proposal.

†The quality of life of whistleblowers has not been measured as described above. I will refer to an informal, limited survey of my interaction with and knowledge about some of the more widely known whistleblowers.[15]

**In fact, quality of life surveys of whistleblowers would be an interesting and, I believe, a worthwhile project to undertake.

‡If interested in WISE, contact either Dr. Carolyn Phinney, 313-971-8111, carolyn phinney@ibm.net or the author at 217-333-4143, rlsprague@uiuc.edu.

***One may want to contact one of these three attorneys, one on the east coast, Midwest, and west coast, who have experience in this area. The attorneys are: Mr. Michael Ronemus, 800-252-7072, mronemus@snet.net; Mr. Phil Green, 313-665-4036, greenfirm@aol.com; Dr. Eugene Dong, 415-494-3561, genedong@leland.stanford.edu.

¹Sprague, R. L. (in press) Whistleblowing from a personal perspective. *Forum.*

²Bok, S. (1988) Whistleblowing and professional responsibility. In: Callahan. J. C., ed. *Ethical Issues in Professional Life.* Cambridge University Press, New York: 331–344.

³Glazer, M. & Glazer, P.(1986) Whistleblowing, *Psychology Today,* August, 37–39, 42–43.

[4]Sprague, R. L. (1992) *Scientific misconduct: Recent cases and regulations.* Paper presented at the Department of Psychology colloquium, Reno, NV.

[5]Sprague, R. L. (1993) Whistleblowing: A very unpleasant avocation, *Ethics & Behavior* **3:**103–133.

[6]Greenberg, D. S. (1990) The politics of plagiarism, *The Medical Post,* September 25, 11.

[7]Glazer, M. P. & Glazer, P. M. (1989) *The Whistleblowers,* Basic Books, New York.

[8]Boisjoly, R. M. (1987) *The Challenger disaster: Moral responsibility and the working engineer,* Speech at MIT, Cambridge.

[9]Senate Subcommittee on Science, Technology, and Space (1986) *Hearings before the Subcommittee,* U. S. Government Printing Office, Washington, DC.

[10]Vaughan, D. (1996) *The Challenger Launch Decision: Risky Technology, Culture, and Deviance at NASA.* University of Chicago Press, Chicago, IL.

[11]Boisjoly, R. (1998) Commentary on "How to Blow the Whistle and Still Have a Career Afterwards" (C. K. Gunsalus), *Science and Engineering Ethics* **4:**71–74.

[12]Spurgeon, D. (1994) University censured over research accounting, *Nature* **370:** 320.

[13]Fellowships and Awards (1989) Association for the Advancement of Science, *Chronicle of Higher Education,* January 4, A8.

[14]Teich, A. H. & Frankel, M. S., eds. (1992) *Good Science and Responsible Scientists,* American Association for the Advancement of Science, Washington, DC.

[15]Hoke, F. (1995) Veteran whistleblowers advise other would-be 'ethical resisters' to carefully weigh personal consequences before taking action, *The Scientist,* May 15, 1, 15.

[16]Taubes, G. (1995) Plagiarism suit wins: Experts hope it won't set a trend, *Science* **268:** 1125.

[17]Frasure-Smith, N., Lesperance, F. & Talajic, M. (1993) Depression following myocardial infarction. *Journal of the American Medical Association* **270:** 1819–1825.

[18]Engel, G. (1977) The need for a new medical model: A challenge for biomedicine, *Science* **196:** 129–136.

[19]Diener, E. & Diener, C. (1996) Most people are happy, *Psychological Science* **7:** 181–185.

[20]Sprague, R. L. (1977) Overview of psychopharmacology for the United States. In: Mittler P, ed., *Research to Practice in Mental Retardation—Biomedical Aspects,* **3:** 199–202.

[21]Hill, B., Balow, E. & Bruininks, R. (1985) A national study of prescribed drugs in institutions and community residential facilities for mentally retarded people, *Psychopharmacology Bulletin* **21:** 279–284.

[22]Sprague, R. L. & Galliher, L. (1988) Litigation about psychotropic medication. In: Gadow, K. D. & Poling, A. D., eds. *Pharmacotherapy and Mental Retardation;* pp. 297–312.

[23]Holden, C. (1986) NIMH review of fraud charge moves slowly, *Science* **234:** 1488–1489.

[24]Brand, D. & Nash, J. M. (1987) "It was too good to be true." *Time* June 1, 59.

[25]Greenberg, D. (1987) Publish or perish—or fake it. *U.S. News & World Report* June 8, 72–73.

[26]Gorin, N. (1988) The facts were fiction. *60 Minutes,* Columbia Broadcasting System January 17.

[27]Sprague, R. L. (1987) I trusted the research system. *The Scientist,* December 14, 11–12.

[28]Committee on Science, Space, and Technology (1989) *Maintaining the Integrity of Scientific Research,* U. S. Government Printing Office, Washington, DC.

[29]Bell, R. (1992) *Impure Science: Fraud, Compromise and Political Influence in Scientific Research.* Wiley, New York.

[30]Ferguson, D. G., Cullari, S. & Gadow, K. D. (1987) Comments on the 'Coldwater' studies, *Journal of Mental Deficiency Research* **31:** 219–220.

[31]Poling, A. (1992) The consequences of fraud. In: Miller D J & Hersen M, eds. *Research Fraud in the Behavioral and Biomedical Sciences,* pp. 140–157.

[32]Greenberg, D. S. (1990) Squalor in academe: Plagiarist gets promoted, victim is out of her job, *Science & Government Report,* May 1, pp. 1, 5–7.

[33]Wilford, J. N. (1990) Ex-colleagues turn combatants, *New York Times,* May 22, C7.

[34]Greenberg, D. S. (1990) Copyright-suit winner faces misconduct charges, *Science & Government Report,* November 1, 4, 6.

[35]Greenberg, D. S. (1991) Medical society rapped for electing copyright violator, *Science & Government Report,* December 1, 3.

[36]Greenberg, D. S. (1991) And now a "Policy to Protect Misconduct in Research," *Science & Government Report,* June 15, 5.

[37]Greenberg, D. S. (1991) Science's Maginot mentality on misconduct, *Journal of NIH Research,* August, 32–33

[38]Jaschik, S. (1990) Critics charge Yeshiva U. tried to get a former professor to alter testimony to Congress on academic misconduct, *Chronicle of Higher Education,* May 9, A20, A22.

[39]Heidi S. Weissmann v. Leonard M. Freeman. 684 *Fed Sup,* 1248.

[40]Levy, D. (1994) A settlement is won but a career is lost, *USA Today,* March 30, 5D.

[41]Anderson, C. (1993) Michigan gets an expensive lesson, *Science* **262:** 23.

[42]Phinney, C. (1991) *Truth and Consequences: A Psychologist's Perspective on Scientific Misconduct and Whistleblowing,* Paper presented at the meeting of the American Chemical Society, August 27, New York City.

[43]Hilts, P. J. (1997) University forced to pay $1.6 million to researcher, *New York Times,* August 10, 10.

[44]Guidelines developed on whistleblowers protection, (1995) *ORI Newsletter* 3:1–2.

[45]NIH revitalization act: Whistleblower protection and commission on research integrity, (1993) *Professional Ethics Report,* Summer, 1–3.

[46]Price, A. R. (1996) Federal action against plagiarism in research, *Journal of Information Ethics* **5:** 34–51.

[47]Hoke, F. (1995) Novel application of federal law to scientific fraud worries universities and reinvigorates whistleblowers, *The Scientist,* September 4, 1, 4–5.

[48]Panel on Scientific Responsibility and the Conduct of Research (1992) *Responsible science: Ensuring the Integrity of the Research Process (Vol. I),* National Academy Press, Washington, DC.

[49]Glazer, M. (1988) Ten whistleblowers and how they fared. In: Callahan, J. C., ed. *Ethical Issues in Professional Life.* Cambridge University Press, New York: 322–331.

[50]Westrum, R. (1989). Talks with whistle-blowers. *Social Psychology of Science,* August, 7–8.

[51]Devine, T. (1995) To ensure accountability, a whistleblower's bill of rights, *The Scientist,* May 15, 11.

[52]Goodman, B. (1996). Scientific whistleblowers stress that the media are a last resort, *The Scientist,* March 18, 1, 4.

[53]Lee, G. (1994) Whistle-blower clears the air, *Washington Post,* March 1, The Federal Page.

[54]Yates, R. E. (1995) Whistleblowers pay dearly for heroics. *Chicago Tribune,* July 23, 7–1, 7–2.

[55]Kohn, T. S. & Kohn, M. (1986) An overview of federal and state whistleblower protections, *Antioch Law Journal* **4:** 99–152.

[56]Poon, P. (1995) Legal protection for the scientific whistleblower, *Journal of Law, Medicine & Ethics* **23:** 88–9.

Fostering Responsible Conduct in Science and Engineering Research: Current University Policies and Actions

Nicholas H. Steneck

Introduction

Modern universities are commonly seen as serving three main functions. They educate students. They foster research. Through education, research, and other activities, they serve society.

As both the place where future researchers are trained and the place where much of the nation's research is conducted, universities are vital to science and engineering. A century or two ago, science and engineering were not dependent on universities and higher education. Today they are. Were universities to abdicate their roles in science and engineering, society would have to invent new institutions to train future scientists and engineers and to conduct much of the research that has become vital to the future of society.

The role that universities play in science and engineering encompasses both privileges and responsibilities. Much of the financial and social support that universities enjoy today is based on their capacity to contribute to science and engineering. The support for science and engineering is, in turn, accompanied by a great deal of autonomy, accepting the premise that as professionals, scientists and engineers should be given intellectual or academic freedom. These are the privileges. In return, society assumes that university scientists and engineers will act in ways that serve the best interests of society, however those interests are defined.

This paper describes and analyzes some of the actions universities are taking to foster responsible conduct in science and engineering research, beginning with the most passive steps, those that simply seek to establish normative rules, and progressing through three degrees of proactive policies: monitoring research, promoting discussion, and undertaking institutional reform. Throughout, the term "responsibility" is taken in its most challenging sense. It is assumed, following the stated policies of many universities, that the sought-after goal is setting high standards, not minimum standards. That is to say, "responsibility" is taken to imply more than simply following the letter of the law or not engaging in blatant misconduct (plagiarizing, falsifying data, conflicts of interest, and so on). Responsibility is taken to imply discharging the duties or meeting the obligations of

Nicholas H. Steneck, "Fostering Responsible Conduct in Science and Engineering Research," in *Responsible Science: Ensuring the Integrity of the Research Process*, vol. II, National Academy of Sciences, (Washington: National Academy Press, 1993) 3–25.

a professional in an exemplary way. It is this broad understanding of responsibility, rather than the narrow sense of avoiding fraud or misconduct, that is the main focus of this report, as applied to science and engineering research at universities.

Although this report focuses on science and engineering, it is important to note that there is very little about science and engineering research that is truly unique, other than its subject matter and its particular research methods. Humanists engage in funded research projects; they collect, interpret, and publish data; and they train graduate students and postdoctoral fellows. Accordingly, it is not possible when discussing university policies and actions designed to foster responsible conduct in science and engineering research to focus exclusively or even mostly on actions and policies directed to scientists and engineers. The context of university policy and action is much broader than this. However, broader policies, when combined with policies and actions that do focus more on science and engineering, can potentially do a great deal to foster responsible conduct in science and engineering research. Some of that potential is now being realized on university campuses across the country. The ways in which it is being realized form the subject of this report.

Normative Rules

The least burdensome, but not necessarily the most effective, way to foster responsible conduct in science and engineering research is to establish and publicize responsible behavior. Most professional organizations, including those for science and engineering, have published materials relating to professional conduct, such as Sigma Xi's influential *Honor in Science*[1] or the National Institutes of Health's widely used *Guidelines for the Conduct of Research*.[2] These materials have bearing on science and engineering research on university campuses and are commonly used (formally and informally) by universities for establishing standards for responsible behavior.

Universities have not been as eager as professional societies and the federal government to adopt comprehensive normative rules for responsible conduct in research.[3] Most do have general codes of conduct that apply broadly to faculty, administrators, staff, and/or students. However, their expectations for researchers are more commonly set out within the context of administrative policies dealing with specific problems, such as fraud or misconduct in research, conflict of interest, intellectual property rights, human and animal use in experimentation, computer use, and so on. Piece by piece, these polices provide normative rules that cover most of the major concerns regarding responsible conduct in science and engineering research.

Misconduct Policies

In response to increasing concern over cases of research misconduct and spurred on by Public Health Service requirements in 1985,[4] major research universities have adopted procedures for investigating allegations of misconduct. Although differing in detail, most follow a common format. First, the importance of integrity, the rarity of misconduct, and the need to maintain high standards are stressed. Then, definitions of fraud or misconduct, reaching conclusions, and, when called for, meting out punishment are discussed.

The normative portions of these policies are found in the definitions of misconduct. Some are very short—a sentence with a few examples: "The word *fraud* means serious misconduct with intent to deceive, for example, faking data, plagiarism, or misappropriation of ideas."[5]

Others include more extensive inventories of unacceptable behavior. The University of Michigan misconduct policy gives definitions for:

- Falsification of data,
- Plagiarism,
- Abuse of confidentiality,
- Dishonesty in publication,
- Deliberate violation of regulations,
- Property violations, and
- Failure to report observed fraud.[6]

A similar list is given under "Definition of Academic Misconduct" in the University of Maryland misconduct policy:

- Falsification of data,
- Plagiarism,
- Improprieties of authorship,
- Misappropriation of the ideas of others,
- Violation of generally accepted research practices,
- Material failure to comply with federal requirements affecting research, and
- Inappropriate behavior in relation to misconduct.[7]

Variations of these and other lists, along with explanations and examples, are found in most university policies for dealing with misconduct in research.

The bounds established for unacceptable behavior by inference provide normative guidelines for acceptable behavior. For example, the Maryland misconduct policy defines "improprieties of authorship" as:

> Improper assignment of credit, such as excluding others; misrepresentation of the same material as original in more than one publication; inclusion of individuals as authors who have not made a definite contribution to the work published; or submission of multi-authored publications without the concurrence of all authors.[8]

This statement could easily be rewritten as a set of normative rules for responsible behavior in research: researchers should properly assign credit to others for the work they have done; present original material in only one publication; include in publications only the names of those who have contributed to research;

and include the names of coauthors in publications only after seeking permission to do so. In this way, the reactive misconduct policies in place in the major research universities can become proactive statements of expected or normative behavior in research.

CONFLICT-OF-INTEREST POLICIES

Normative statements about research can also be found in conflict-of-interest policies. Again, as with the misconduct policies, the primary intent is to clarify what should not be done, but by inference or logical extension, proper conduct is also defined. The form of conflict-of-interest policies is not as uniform as that of misconduct policies, thus making it more difficult to identify the normative statements about research conduct. Nonetheless, these policies do provide another source of information that is applicable to scientific and engineering research.

Researchers at Ohio State University can receive guidance on honoring confidences gained during research if they know that their university's conflict-of-interest policy refers them to the State of Ohio government code of ethics, which states that:

> No present or former public official or employee shall disclose or use, without appropriate authorization, any information acquired by him in the course of his official duties which is confidential because of statutory provisions, or which has been clearly designated to him as confidential when such confidential designation is warranted because of the status of the proceedings or the circumstances under which the information was received and preserving its confidentiality is necessary to the proper conduct of government business.[9]

If "university business" is construed as "government business," then researchers should understand that information given in confidence, such as information received when reviewing manuscripts for publication and grant requests for peer review, cannot be disclosed or used for personal gain. The State of Ohio statutes thus provide normative rules for handling manuscripts, shared data, student theses, and the like: researchers should honor confidences and not use or disclose information received in confidence without getting permission to do so.

Researchers at Pennsylvania State University can find normative rules for directing graduate students and postdoctoral fellows in their institution's conflict-of-interest policy, which states that it is wrong to direct students into research activities that are designed primarily to serve personal interests rather than to further their [the students'] scholarly achievement."[10] While not easy to apply in difficult cases, i.e., when there is a genuine conflict between the obligations to a grantor and to those hired under the grant, one normative rule that applies to such situations is again made clear: researchers who serve as mentors to students assume obligations to those students and should not compromise these obligations for personal gain or career advancement.

In the same vein, a set of questions set out in a Johns Hopkins University School of Medicine conflict-of-interest policy statement provides, again by inference, a fairly sophisticated set of guidelines to help researchers sort out responsibilities:

> Does the secondary commitment detract from the ability of a faculty member to discharge his primary obligations to The Johns Hopkins University School of Medicine? To what extent is the opportunity for outside commitment offered because of the University affiliation and thus, to what extent should the financial rewards be shared with the University?[11]

The normative rules inferred in these questions and the subsequent explanations help clarify for researchers how they should sort out their obligations when they have responsibilities to more than one constituency.

MISCELLANEOUS RESEARCH POLICIES AND OTHER DOCUMENTS

Similar guidance can be found in other research policies and documents relating to the conduct of research on university campuses. At the University of Michigan, the Division of Research Development and Administration provides researchers with a document that describes, summarizes, or contains verbatim policies and procedures relating to:

- conflict of interest,
- the responsibilities of project directors,
- account and grant administration,
- export control restrictions,
- the transfer of university equipment,
- restrictions on lobbying, and
- biosafety monitoring.

The latter refers to policies relating to human subjects research review, animal research, radiation safety, biological research review (recombinant DNA research), and occupational safety and environmental health.[12] Subsequent forms and/or policy statements issued by the human- and animals-use committees, the radiation safety committee, and so on provide further guidance on responsible conduct in research, as, for example, questions and guidance on the humane use of animals (discussed below under monitoring).

The normative rules scattered throughout university policies and documents relating to science and engineering research are an important first step for promoting responsible conduct. In defining what is illegal, unethical, and irresponsible, they suggest what is legal, ethical, and responsible. They also provide guidance on fiscal responsibility, safety, the responsible use of human subjects, the humane treatment of animals, the use of computers, the handling of data, and other matters. Therefore, even those universities that do not have comprehensive codes of ethics for science and engineering research, which is the majority, do provide researchers with guidelines for responsible conduct. If these "guidelines" are combined with the various federal regulations and professional statements about professional conduct in research, the total package does provide fundamental rules for determining what is responsible and irresponsible in the conduct of research.

As basic as this first step might seem, it is without question needed. There are researchers who do not know what is meant by plagiarism or the ownership of ideas. There are researchers who believe that words and phrases can be borrowed from someone else's publications without attribution as long as original ideas are not plagiarized.[13] There are researchers who believe that they "own" not only the data generated in their laboratories but also the ideas. Practicing researchers do not always understand the basic normative rules that help to determine responsible conduct in research. Students and beginning researchers may have less understanding. Publications such as Sigma Xi's *Honor in Science*, the codes of conduct published by professional societies, and the research policies of universities are thus useful documents for raising consciousness and establishing a knowledge base for fostering responsibility in research.

The effectiveness of normative rules in fostering responsibility is, however, limited. First, as disjointed and piecemeal as they are on most campuses, they do not make it easy for researchers to comprehend and consider all the responsibilities raised by modern science and engineering. As conditions exist on many campuses, the burden for integrating rules and resolving contradictions is often left to the individual. Given all of the other pressures on modern-day researchers, it may not be reasonable to expect them to read through three, four, or more policies to find out what they should or should not be doing.

In addition, simply stating how researchers *should act* in no way guarantees that they *will act* in this way. This is particularly true if the normative rules aim at unrealistically high standards. Researchers today are rarely able to meet all of their obligations in an exemplary way. More commonly obligations exceed the time available to meet them. Increasing competition for research funds means that more hours must be spent writing and submitting grant applications. More time spent on applications means less time working in the laboratory, advising or teaching students, and reviewing manuscripts. Corners have to be cut. What are needed, therefore, in addition to normative rules for ideal behavior, are guidebooks for how to survive in the increasingly competitive world of academic science and engineering research.

Policy statements about normative or ideal conduct become useful when they are explained, elaborated upon, and illustrated with examples. They also become useful when they deal with the difficult rather than the obvious. There seems to be little doubt that most researchers do not, and know that they should not, manufacture data or forge experimental results. It may be less clear, however, how results should be presented in grant applications, when "enough data" are needed to give confidence that a project will succeed but "enough work" remains to be done to justify getting the grant. How "preliminary" should "preliminary research" be?

To the extent that most normative rules leave many questions unanswered, they fall short of the fostering that is needed to render science and engineering research as responsible as it could be. They do provide important general rules. They also satisfy legal requirements and soothe consciences. But this approach to fostering responsible conduct in research may not be effective, particularly if the rules are not accompanied by other actions. Given the pressures on researchers today, they often are not only busy but also cynical. When their laboratory space and salaries depend on the research dollars generated and their promotions on the number of articles published, they can have a hard time believing the normative rules are anything more than guidelines for staying out of trouble. If this is the case, the sense of responsibility that researchers have will be minimal at best. Recognition of this fact has prompted universities to take additional steps to foster responsible conduct in research.

Monitoring Research

Universities today routinely monitor their research programs, among other reasons because they are required to do so. They must ensure fiscal responsibility. They must supervise the use and treatment of animals and human subjects. They must comply with environmental and workplace regulations. And they must enforce their own policies regulating such activities as classified and proprietary research. Monitoring is the second way universities foster responsible conduct in science and engineering research. It is an active rather than a passive way to foster responsibility.

At the University of Michigan, one monitoring process for research is triggered by an internal form that must be completed by all researchers prior to submitting projects for support (internal or external). The form lists 13 areas of concern that must be checked "yes" or "no."[14] If "yes" is checked for an area, subsequent information or action is required. For the more important areas, such as the use of human subjects, vertebrate animals, and radioactive materials, the researcher is referred to a series of special peer-review committees for approval. These committees review the applications both for their compliance with specific laws and regulations and, in some cases, for problems that could raise questions about responsibility.

For example, researchers using vertebrate animals in research are required to submit an additional form to the University Committee on the Use and Care of Animals. This form asks researchers to explain why they must use animals in their research, why they cannot use "lower" animals or fewer animals, and why the amount of pain inflicted, if any, cannot be reduced. They are also required to identify the person in charge of the animals during experimentation, to give the latter's qualifications, and to indicate how the work will be supervised. The form on which this information is recorded contains explanations of each of the questions, which, in essence, provide brief lessons in the responsible use of animals in research. If the answers given on the forms are not satisfactory or if they raise questions about the use of animals, the researcher is asked to appear before the Use and Care Committee to discuss the project. In this way, researchers are encouraged to think about and justify their responsibilities when they use animals in research and, simultaneously, their use of animals is monitored.

The same procedure is followed for the use of human subjects at Michigan, with the university having a total of twelve peer committees to review grant requests prior to submission.

Again, detailed questions are asked that compel researchers to think about their responsibilities before they begin their work. Medical researchers must tell whether they are using subjects that are:

- Children (age < 18),
- Pregnant women,
- Fetuses,
- Mentally incompetent,
- [Of] questionable state of mental competence or consciousness,
- [A result of] human in vitro fertilization,
- Prisoners or other institutionalized persons, or
- Others who are likely to be vulnerable.[15]

If they are, they must provide a "rationale for and justify their [each subject's] involvement."[16] Providing the rationale again compels researchers to think about their responsibilities. If a rationale is unclear or unsatisfactory, then the researcher must discuss the research with colleagues on a review committee. The human subjects committees also require justifications for the use of human subjects, explanations of the likely benefits to the subjects from the research, and a description of the steps that have been taken to minimize risks—requirements that again compel researchers to think about their responsibilities and, in gray areas, to discuss their responsibilities with colleagues.

Similar monitoring of responsibility in science and engineering research takes place in other ways on most university campuses. Researchers and universities are required by law to monitor the use of radioactive materials, some biological materials, and hazardous chemicals. Most universities also now routinely require researchers to file conflict-of-interest statements and property rights statements with every grant application or on some regular basis. The monitoring inherent in these requirements forces researchers to think about their responsibilities in ways that might not otherwise occur to them and to think about relationships and obligations that might otherwise be ignored.

Responsibility is also routinely monitored through peer review for promotions or annual reviews for salary increases. These reviews provide faculty with opportunities to monitor the work of their colleagues, looking, for example, for the possibility of duplicate publication of the same material, misattribution of authorship, or the sloppy use/misuse of data. Similarly, student evaluations are routinely used to determine how well faculty are discharging their duties as teachers. Such evaluations are not used, but could be adapted, to determine how well faculty discharge their duties as research mentors.

Asking researchers in advance how they will exercise responsibility is intrusive. It requires an investment of time to answer questions for no apparent reason. Moreover, in subtle ways it represents a shift in burden. Rather than presuming that researchers act responsibly and then raising questions when there is reason to believe someone has acted irresponsibly, asking researchers to discuss their research conduct in advance or to be subjected to constant scrutiny during research places a burden on them to demonstrate that they will act or are acting responsibly. In other words, monitoring presumes guilt rather than assuming innocence. It is also compulsory rather than voluntary. It requires that certain standards be met rather than making responsibility a matter of personal initiative. As such, monitoring does not find a comfortable home in professional communities that are accustomed to openness and trust.

Why, for example, should researchers be required to demonstrate in advance how they will comply with rules, regulations, and standards for responsible behavior, if those rules, regulations, and standards are clearly spelled out? We do not require the same researchers to file forms before leaving for work in the morning explaining that they will travel in a licensed car using seat belts and driving at safe, legal speeds. We presume that they know the laws and will obey them, intervening only when there is reason to believe that the law is not being obeyed. Similarly, for science and engineering to develop freely and in a collegial atmosphere, some degree of responsibility must be assumed. If every aspect of research were subject to monitoring, either in advance or in process, the burdens of time and cost could rapidly overwhelm the research enterprise.

For these reasons, it is unlikely that universities will or should use monitoring to any great extent to ensure that research is undertaken responsibly. At the present time, active monitoring is undertaken only when it is required, e.g., in the use of animals, human subjects, dangerous chemicals, conflict of interest, and so on. If used sparingly, primarily as a tool to get researchers to think about particular issues such as the use of animals in research, monitoring can be an effective device for fostering responsible conduct in science and engineering research. If overused, monitoring and the enforcement of compulsory rules of behavior will rapidly become a burden that can destroy the freedom and collegiality that are essential to the vitality of science and engineering research in particular and all academic life in general.

Promoting Discussion

If universities do not directly check responsibility, through monitoring, how else can responsibility be fostered? A third approach to encouraging responsibility is to ensure that researchers at least are aware of the normative rules for undertaking research by bringing the rules to their attention and promoting discussion. At the University of Michigan Medical School all faculty receive and have the obligation to read *Guidelines for the Responsible Conduct of Research* (1989) . . . . This document is also distributed to all Department administrators for subsequent distribution to all postdoctoral fellows, graduate students and research technical staff.[17]

If reading and being informed are all that are required for ensuring responsibility, then this simple policy will go a long way toward fostering responsible conduct in science and engineering research.

Increasing numbers of research universities have chosen to be more aggressive in bringing the responsibilities of researchers to their attention. Their approaches vary, depending on where within administrative structures initiatives derive and how they are most conveniently implemented. However, the goal of each is basically the same: to foster discussion.

Harvard University provides a good example of a top-down approach to promoting discussions of professional ethics, including research ethics. The former president of Harvard University, Derek Bok, has long been a proponent of fostering discussions of ethics in the university setting.[18] He was instrumental in raising funds to establish two major professional ethics programs at Harvard, one in the Kennedy School of Government, the other a separate Program in Ethics and the Professions. The latter fosters scholarly research on professional ethics and serves as a resource for other units seeking to take steps to foster professional responsibility.[19] These and other influences have prompted the medical faculty to revise their rules for research conduct and to join with others in sponsoring symposia on research ethics.[20] The result will undoubtedly be an increased level of discussion of the importance of and special problems pertaining to research conduct. How much impact this will have on students and faculty remains to be seen.

The University of Colorado, Boulder, has taken a different approach to fostering discussions of professional responsibility in research. The Regents of the University of Colorado system vested authority for dealing with research misconduct in a series of standing committees. Besides conducting investigations of "suspected or alleged misconduct," these committees are charged by the regents to "promote exemplary ethical standards for research and scholarship."[21] The Boulder campus decided to form one joint Standing Committee on Research Misconduct and included "Education of Academic Community" in its charge. The written definition of this task reads:

Deans, directors, chairs and graduate advisors shall be reminded annually of *University of Colorado Administrative Policy on Research Misconduct and Authorship* and their responsibility to inform all faculty, students, and staff of (1) the need for integrity in research performance and (2) the role of the Standing Committee in considering allegations of research misconduct.[22]

In practice, the committee has adopted a much more ambitious role in fostering responsible conduct in research.

Under the leadership of Alan Greenberg, associate professor of mechanical engineering, the Boulder campus's Standing Committee on Research Misconduct is playing down its policing duties in favor of a more positive image. The committee plans to send a short, personal letter to all faculty members describing its goals and expressing a desire for dialogue. The letters are being sent to faculty because they are seen as the key to a responsible research environment. Later, through faculty and appropriate administrative units, the committee hopes to expand its reach to graduate education. In each case, the committee's main goal will be to make researchers (and future researchers) aware of and responsive to the existing normative rules for exercising responsibility in research. The committee is not seeking to write new rules; it is simply trying to make researchers more aware of the rules that are already in existence.[23]

The impetus for more discussion at Colorado comes from within. A supportive administration and an ambitious committee have determined that researchers should and hopefully will spend more time talking about their responsibilities as researchers. At other universities, there is more discussion today than a few years ago, in part as the result of an outside influence—the National Institutes of Health's new requirement for the inclusion of some material on "the responsible conduct of research" in institutional training programs. The requirement states that

> all competing National Research Service Award institutional training grant applications must include a description of the formal or informal activities related to the instruction about the responsible conduct of research that will be incorporated into the proposed research training program.[24]

Those universities that have training grants or are anticipating applying for them are now in the process of planning "formal and informal activities" that will meet this objective.[25]

One way to satisfy the new NIH requirement is to foster discussions about responsibility in research settings. Several years ago, Floyd Bloom of the Scripps Clinic and Research Foundation decided this was precisely what he needed in his laboratory and began planning special sessions to discuss problems that had arisen or could arise in the course of research. The special sessions were well received. Three have been turned into video tapes that are now circulated to others with similar needs.[26] If other universities follow this lead, the new NIH training grant requirement should at a minimum serve to promote discussions of the normative rules for responsible conduct in science and engineering research. If the rules are rigorously enforced, the impact could be even greater.[27]

In evaluating the role of discussion in fostering responsibility, an important distinction needs to be made. "Responsibility" is both an academic subject and a matter of practical importance. As an academic subject, "responsibility" can be studied, researched, discussed, and written about in the same way as any other academic subject. There is more than enough that is controversial in the consideration of conflict of interest, the ownership of ideas, the responsible use of humans or animals for experimental purposes, or any other aspect of research to engage scholars who specialize in research ethics in discussion for years to come. However, "responsibility" is also a matter of practical importance. Every day, in small and large ways, individuals who engage in science and engineering research must decide for themselves what it means "to be responsible" and then act. For them, responsibility is not a matter of intellectual curiosity but of practical necessity.

At the present time, there is no lack of academic or scholarly discussions of research ethics, both in general and as applied to science and engineering.[28] The major science and engineering journals routinely publish articles and editorials on the responsibilities of researchers. Most major scientific and engineering meetings have had sessions devoted to the responsibilities of researchers. Scholars who study the social, ethical, and professional side of science and engineering publish articles on responsibility in research. Science educators discuss ways to foster responsibility through science education. The researcher who wants to become better educated on responsibility in science and engineering has no lack of material to consult. The problem that exists today, if there is a problem, is getting this material to researchers who barely have time to keep abreast of developments in their own fields.

It therefore seems logical to assume, for convenience if for no other reason, that the discussion of responsibility in science and engineering research should begin in the settings in which that research is undertaken, with mentors and their advisees talking about their work, the way it is being undertaken, and its consequences. It is in these settings that the norms of professional conduct are set and passed on. The discussions can be informal and personal. They can also be enriched by adding some organization and involving others, who bring different perspectives to bear on difficult problems. However they are planned or undertaken, the important point is that discussions of responsibility in research should begin in the laboratory and in the classroom. They should, however, not end there.

There are at least two problems that arise if the discussion of responsibility is left exclusively to research settings. First, relying on discussions in research settings to address problems of responsibility is not efficient. To get different points of view on difficult problems it is usually necessary to involve philosophers, social scientists, lawyers, theologians, and others who are removed from the problems and can bring special expertise to bear on them. Generally the number of "outsiders" who are prepared to discuss issues relating to responsibility in science and engineering research is limited. To ask them to come to every science and engineering laboratory or department on a campus is not realistic.

A second problem is that research settings may not be conducive to the discussion of some difficult problems that arise in these settings. Junior researchers or graduate students who feel their work is not being fairly cited in a publication may not feel comfortable discussing authorship with their mentors. Students who disagree with a mentor's way of interpreting data may have qualms about raising this issue in a laboratory meeting. Ideally, of course, discussions should be open to any questions or points of view, but settings in which there are problems associated with responsibility are not ideal.

For these and other reasons, other, more generic settings need to be provided for discussions of responsibility in science and engineering research on university campuses. Departmental and university forums allow opportunities for researchers to consider and talk about their responsibilities with colleagues in other fields. Lecture series are a useful device for raising consciousness. Orientation programs for new graduate students, postdoctoral fellows, and even faculty can provide information and along with that the message that responsibility in research is taken seriously at the university. There are many ways to promote discussion of issues associated with responsible conduct in science and engineering research. The more ways a university tries to promote discussion, the stronger the message it sends about its commitment to responsibility.

Undertaking Institutional Reform

As efforts to promote discussion have grown, new institutional arrangements have emerged for their support and coordination. The strategies employed differ significantly from campus to campus. Their goals are basically the same: to provide opportunities for the consideration of professional responsibility and related issues within the normal context of education and university life.[29]

It is impossible in this paper to discuss all of the different ways in which the professional responsibility of scientists and engineers is being addressed through institutional reform. Changes have been suggested for the entire spectrum of science education, from elementary schooling to postdoctoral studies, clinical training, and even continuing education. This section provides a few examples, focusing on advanced undergraduate education, graduate education, and two campuswide programs.

UNDERGRADUATE EDUCATION

Beginning in the late 1960s and early 1970s, hundreds of courses were instituted at the undergraduate level to address what became known as STS (science, technology, and society) studies. In the 1980s, some of these courses added material dealing with professional responsibility.[30] To provide additional support, a significant number of universities (over 100) developed STS programs. STS programs were and remain particularly popular at schools that train large numbers of scientists and engineers, such as MIT, the Illinois Institute of Technology, and Rensselaer Polytechnic Institute, to name only a few.[31] For some students, the discussion of professional responsibility fostered by undergraduate STS programs begins their introduction to the norms of professional life as scientists and engineers. For others, it may be not only their first but also their last formal contact with these issues.

A few schools have gone beyond the single-course/program approach and attempted to change completely the way undergraduates are educated. In 1986, the University of Minnesota College of Agriculture received a two-year grant from the Kellogg Foundation to formulate a curriculum that would provide students with "enhanced learning opportunities in leadership, communication, problem identification and solution, teamwork skills, interdisciplinary approaches, nutritional issues, environmental awareness, societal values and international perspectives." The Kellogg funds were used to provide students with opportunities for discussion, personal interaction, and case-based learning throughout the curriculum. As with all such programs, the long-term effects will be difficult to measure. Short-term, Project Sunrise's directors are pleased enough with the results to heartily recommend their approach to others.[32]

Research, per se, is generally not a major component of undergraduate education. Some undergraduates have research experiences, but they usually do not start thinking seriously about research until graduate school and their first independent work as researchers. Nonetheless, attitudes and knowledge gained during the undergraduate years can play a major role in determining the future responsibility of scientists and engineers. Attitudes about personal and social responsibility gained during undergraduate years can be transferred to graduate work and the laboratory. Knowledge about professional life and its role in society can provide a framework for questioning and seeking solutions when potential problems arise in the research environment. Just as basic mathematics, chemistry, physics, or biology can be essential for careers in science and engineering, so too basic knowledge about the social and values dimensions of science and engineering can be essential ingredients for being a responsible scientist or engineer. For many scientists and engineers, the only opportunity they have to gain such knowledge comes during their undergraduate years. This is particularly true for engineers, who can more easily engage in research without pursuing graduate studies.

GRADUATE EDUCATION

Graduate education (including professional and postdoctoral studies) provides a second setting for formal instruction on professional responsibility, either in general or as related specifically to science and engineering research. As noted above, it is during these years that scientists and engineers begin to think seriously about research.[33] It is also during these years that they have increasing opportunities to consider questions of responsibility. At the present time, most instruction on responsibility at the graduate level takes place informally through discussions in laboratory settings and between mentors and their students (see "Promoting Discussion," above). A few schools have instituted special programs, recognizing that graduate education provides an ideal atmosphere for more formal instruction on responsibility.

The University of Texas Health Science Center requires that all entering graduate students take a 17-week course titled "Philosophical Issues in Science." The course meets weekly for one hour, at lunchtime. To encourage participation, the Dean of the Graduate School of Biomedical Sciences, William Butcher, provides a free lunch and some course materials. The course covers a wide range of topics, from the history and philosophy of science to discussions of research techniques, honesty in science, animal and human experimentation, and laboratory safety. As currently taught by Stanley Reiser, M.D.-Ph.D., it continues to draw support, both from students and administration.[34]

Adding formal instruction on responsibility and related issues at the graduate level is problematic. It is at this level that educational paths start to diverge and specialize dramatically. For the most part students are no longer in large, common classes. Their programs are full, their time limited, and their needs more focused on particular problems. For these and other reasons, there has not been a parallel STS movement at the graduate level. Still, if the Texas experience is at all indicative, there clearly is room for some instruction in common about responsibility and related problems at the graduate level.

CAMPUSWIDE PROGRAMS

The promotion of the activities discussed in this section and previous sections can be accomplished more effectively if there is some coordination. It is for this reason that a few campuses have sought to establish campuswide programs aimed at one or more aspects of the problems and issues associated with professional responsibility.

Emory University has recently established its Center for Ethics and Public Policy and the Professions under the directorship of Robert DeHaan, professor of anatomy and cell biology. Similar programs have been or are being established on a number of campuses to encourage and support the discussion of professional ethics.[35] The Emory center has formulated a set of guidelines for responsible conduct in scholarship, since the center is now fully operational, which will include major sections on scientific research. It is also planning major educational initiatives, working through a series of subcommittees of the center's main Steering Committee. One of the educational initiatives will likely be targeted at graduate education. Other initiatives will target specific audiences or problems, such as a program ("AIDS Training Network") designed to help physicians and researchers consider professional problems raised by the AIDS epidemic. Overall, the Emory center is focused squarely on fostering responsibility, based on the assumption that future scientists, physicians, and other professionals (Emory does not have a school of engineering) should have read and thought about their responsibilities before they become and as they are becoming professionals. The reforms anticipated will be campuswide.[36]

The Poynter Center for the Study of Ethics and American Institutions at Indiana University has for a number of years taken an active campus and national role in promoting discussions of professional ethics. In line with similar centers, it has sponsored courses; encouraged curricular innovation, both on its own campus and other campuses; and organized a number of national symposia. Its director, David Smith, is also the prime organizer of the new Association for Practical and Professional Ethics. The Poynter Center has recently begun a major new initiative, "Catalyst: Indiana University's Program on Ethics in Research," which is seeking to "increase awareness about research ethics issues among students and faculty, through discussion and through the introduction of course units on research ethics. . . ."[37] The impact is intended to be campuswide, introducing the discussion of research ethics issues into as many different forums and settings as possible, but with some direction and coordination from a single program.

Observations and Conclusions

The examples given in this report leave little doubt that universities are seeking to foster responsible conduct in research. The ways vary considerably, from simply publishing rules for appropriate and inappropriate conduct to bringing the discussion of responsibility into research settings, changing courses of study, and instituting campuswide programs. The variations in turn reflect differing commitments and opinions on need. There are those who believe that there is very little that universities can do to foster responsible conduct among scientists, engineers, or any of the other professionals they train or hire. There are others who believe that universities not only can make a difference but also have an obligation to do so. To test whether this range of opinion exists, all one has to do is raise the question of making more room for ethics in the curriculum at a meeting of science or engineering faculty on any university campus.

Those who favor minimal involvement tend to believe that responsibility is learned early in life and outside the classroom, not in university settings. Norms such as honesty, integrity, and reliability, it is argued, are applicable to life in general and are therefore fostered (or not fostered) well before individuals make decisions to become researchers. For those individuals who do eventually become researchers, their sense of responsibility (of morality) adopted early in life may be all that matters when they become scientists and engineers—an assessment that leads some to conclude that responsible researchers are "born," or at least trained early, if not "made."

While it may be true that early education can guide scientists or engineers through some sticky professional problems, it certainly will not help them resolve problems that involve genuine ethical dilemmas. What should a researcher do if she believes she can see a pattern in data being collected but is not sure? What should an engineer do if he is asked to work on a project that might be injurious to the environment or put large numbers of persons out of work? What should clinical researchers or physicians do if they are concerned about the dangers of AIDS research? How should priorities be sorted out when an unread thesis, an unreviewed journal article manuscript, and an unwritten research proposal are all sitting on a scientist's or engineer's desk demanding attention and the time for that attention is limited? Even those who honestly want to act responsibly to follow cherished principles are at times put in situations where principles and general attitudes about responsibility give no clear answers.

Pressures on researchers are real. Data must be interpreted, written up, and published. Names must be included or not included on journal articles. Experimental results are property that someone owns. The ownership of ideas is important; it has a bearing on promotion, and ideas can sometimes be sold for profit. Conflicts of interest exist. Future scientists and engineers must be trained. Public and private interests do compete. Researchers have responsibilities to more than one constituency. Superiors do not always make responsible decisions. The modern practice of science and engineering is complex. It is unlikely that anyone can intuitively know how to act or will instinctively want to act responsibly in every situation. Therefore, even if it is true that basic moral character is set before students come to universities and that basic moral character is what determines whether scientists, engineers, and other researchers act responsibly in research settings, there is still much that universities can do to remind and clarify for researchers what it means to be "responsible."

How much universities will ultimately do to foster responsible conduct in science and engineering research will, no doubt, remain proportional to perceived needs. As long as the present public concern continues about fraud in science, conflicts of interest by researchers, the questionable "good" of some projects, the high cost of research, and other problems, it is likely that universities will seek to do more to foster responsibility. Moreover, whether universities believe so or not, there can be no doubt that the public believes that universities have obligations to foster responsibility, including in science and engineering research.

The stance universities take on their obligations to foster responsibility will, in turn, ultimately determine how much is done. This fact became apparent in talking with colleagues on different campuses, some of whom had active programs on their campuses to foster responsible conduct in research and others who had tried to develop such programs but failed. Where there was a supportive atmosphere, programs, courses, discussions, and so on flourished. Where supportive atmospheres have been lacking, some very well intentioned efforts have failed.

What are the ingredients of a supportive atmosphere? Ideally, an administration that is willing to devote some of its time, attention, and support to activities that will foster responsible conduct in science, engineering, and scholarship in general, plus a faculty that has the willingness to devote some of its time and energies to students, campus service, and discussion of the role of science and engineering in modern society. Where either one of these ingredients has been lacking, steps to foster responsibility have been slow in coming. The best-intentioned faculty have a difficult time making changes without administration support. Administrators cannot make changes without the support of faculty, unless they have been able to raise large amounts of money to make changes.

The atmosphere present on any one campus is, of course, the product of many influences.[39] The size of research budgets has a great deal to do with how much time researchers have to devote to students, to service, and to thinking about anything other than how to get the next grant. The type of research undertaken can influence the way groups of researchers act. The pressure or incentives for advancement, some of which are internal, others external, influence how researchers spend their time. For administrators, research is only one of their concerns. They have to listen to many voices and respond to many calls for action, some of which are louder than others. In sum, the amount that can be done to foster responsible conduct in science and engineering research is dependent on many factors, not all of which can be controlled or predicted with any certainty.

Granting that there is uncertainty, it is nonetheless instructive, encouraging, and exciting to learn of and think about the variety of actions that faculties and administrators on university campuses are taking to ensure that science and engineering research will remain responsible activities in the future. Their efforts surely will not be irrelevant to the role science and engineering play in American society in the decades that lie ahead.

Notes

[1]Sigma Xi, 1986, *Honor in Science,* Second edition, Sigma Xi, New Haven, Conn.

[2]National Institutes of Health (NIH), 1990, *Guidelines for the Conduct of Research at the National Institutes of Health,* NIH, Bethesda, Md.

[3]There are exceptions to this generalization. For example, Harvard University has a general set of guidelines that gives brief normative rules under the headings "Supervision of Research Trainees"; "Data Gathering, Storage, Retention"; "Authorship"; "Publication Practices"; and "Laboratory Guidelines." See Harvard University Faculty of Medicine, 1988, *Guidelines for Investigators in Scientific Research,* Harvard University, Cambridge, Mass. Additional guidance can usually be found in handbooks on administrative procedures published by the offices that oversee research (for an example, see n. 12 below).

[4]U.S. Department of Health and Human Services, 1985, *Interim Public Health Service Policies and Procedures for Dealing with Possible Misconduct in Science,* PHS, Washington, D.C.; following directives in the Health Research Extension Act of 1985 (42 U.S.C. section 289B), which require that each entity receiving a grant submit with its application assurances that (1) it has established procedures for handling allegations of misconduct, and (2) it will report any allegation to PHS.

[5]California Institute of Technology, 1989, *Policy on Research Fraud,* California Institute of Technology, Pasadena.

[6]University of Michigan, 1986, *Interim Policy Statement on the Integrity of Scholarship and Investigating Allegations of Misconduct in the Pursuit of Scholarship and Research,* University of Michigan, Ann Arbor; based on the earlier report by the Task Force on the Integrity of Scholarship, 1984, *Maintaining the Integrity of Scholarship,* University of Michigan, Ann Arbor.

[7]University of Maryland at Baltimore and the University of Maryland, Baltimore County, 1989, *Policies and Procedures Related to Allegations or Other Evidence of Academic Misconduct,* University of Maryland, Baltimore, pp. 2–4. Variations of these lists and brief discussions of misconduct can be found in: University of California, Los Angeles (UCLA) School of Medicine, 1988, *Policy and Procedures for Review of Alleged Unethical Research Practices,* UCLA, Los Angeles; University of Chicago, 1986, *Report of the Provost's Committee on Academic Fraud,* University of Chicago, Chicago; University of Colorado, 1988, *Administrative Policy Statement: Misconduct in Research and Authorship,* University of Colorado, Boulder; University of Minnesota, 1989, *Policies and Procedures for Dealing with Fraud in Research, Interim Administrative Policy,* University of Minnesota, Rochester; and University of North Carolina (UNC), 1989, *Policy and Procedures on Ethics in Research,* UNC, Chapel Hill.

[8]University of Maryland, *Policies and Procedures,* 1989, p. 2.

[9]State of Ohio, "The Ohio Revised Code, Chapter 102: Public Officers—Ethics," p. 7, as referred to in Scott, M. H., 1984, "Ethical Standards," a memorandum, Ohio State University, Columbus, Ohio.

[10]Pennsylvania State University, 1989, *Policy on Conflict of Interest,* Pennsylvania State University, College Park.

[11]Johns Hopkins University School of Medicine, 1984, *Conflict of Commitment Guidelines for Full-Time Faculty,* Johns Hopkins University, Baltimore, pp. 6, 8.

[12]University of Michigan, 1990, *Administration of Sponsored Projects,* Division of Research Development and Administration, University of Michigan, Ann Arbor (revised annually). Not mentioned on this list, but also relevant, would be rules on computer use and the treatment of employees. To one extent or another, all major research universities have similar sets of rules. See, for example, Stanford University, 1990, *Research Policy Handbook,* Stanford University, Palo Alto, Calif. The handbook is "comprised of selected policy statements and guidelines which support the research enterprise at Stanford."

[13]It is interesting to note that some university policies on one or another aspect of responsible conduct are generously borrowed from the policies already adopted at other universities without giving attribution. The bounds between undisputed plagiarism and the "acceptable borrowing" of words, phrases, and introductory and descriptive materials are not as easily drawn as some imagine.

[14]The 13 areas are use of human subjects; use of vertebrate animals; use of radioactive materials; carcinogens; recombinant DNA; biological hazards; proprietary materials; classified research; other restrictions on openness of research; subcontracting; potential conflict of interest; work off university property; and study of another country. See University of Michigan, n.d., *Proposal Approval Form,* University of Michigan, Ann Arbor.

[15]University of Michigan Medical School, n.d., *Application to the Institutional Review Board (IRB) for Approval of Research Involving Human Subjects,* University of Michigan, Ann Arbor.

[16]University of Michigan, *Application to the IRB,* n.d.

[17]University of Michigan Medical School, 1989, *Program in Principles of Scientific Integrity for National Research Service Award (NRSA) Applicants,* University of Michigan, Ann Arbor; and University of Michigan Medical School, 1989, *Guidelines for the Responsible Conduct of Research,* University of Michigan, Ann Arbor.

[18]Bok, D., 1982, *Beyond the Ivory Tower: Social Responsibilities of the Modern Research University,* Harvard University, Cambridge, Mass; see especially chaps. 6 and 7.

[19]Interview, Dennis Thompson, director, Program in Ethics and the Professions, Harvard University, November 1990.

[20]Interview, Morton Litt, Office of Research Issues, Harvard University Medical School, November 1990.

[21]University of Colorado, n.d., *Administrative Policy Statement: Misconduct in Research and Authorship,* University of Colorado, Boulder.

[22]University of Colorado, Boulder, 1990, "Operating Rules and Procedures of the Standing Committee on Research Misconduct," October 1.

[23]Interview, Alan Greenberg, Mechanical Engineering, University of Colorado, Boulder, November 1990.

[24]National Institutes of Health (NIH) and Alcohol, Drug Abuse, and Mental Health Administration (ADAMHA), 1989, "Requirement for programs on the responsible conduct of research in National Research Service Award institutional training programs," *NIH Guide for Grants and Contracts* 18(December 22):1. The requirement was effective July 1, 1990.

[25]The deadline for the first applications affected by this rule was January 10, 1991. It will therefore be some months before the initial impact of the new requirement can be reviewed. For the NIH's initial thoughts on compliance, see Department of Health and Human Services (DHHS), 1990, *PHS Workshop: Education and Training of Scientists in the Responsible Conduct of Research,* March 8–9, Public Health Service, Washington, D.C.

[26]Based on presentation given by Floyd Bloom at the workshop described in DHHS, *PHS Workshop,* 1990, and on subsequent telephone conversations.

[27]Universities have also taken action in response to the NIH requirements for dealing with misconduct in research (see n. 5 above). However, this requirement simply calls for rules to deal with misconduct and therefore does not emphasize fostering responsible conduct.

[28]For example, programs such as the recent symposium titled "Ethical Issues in Research," sponsored by the FIDIA Research Foundation, Georgetown University, April 29–30, 1991.

[29]The institutional reforms discussed below generally have foci that are much broader than science and engineering per se. However, fostering responsibility in sciences and engineering research certainly finds a home under the broader umbrellas of these reforms.

[30]For a description of one such course recently developed at Florida State University, see Gilmer, P. J., and M. Rashotte, 1989/1990, "Marshalling the resources of a large state university for an interdisciplinary 'science, technology, and society' course," *Journal of College Science Teaching* (December/January):150–156.

[31]For a summary of the development of STS studies, focusing particularly on research, see Hollander, R., and N. Steneck, 1990, "Science- and engineering-related ethics and values studies: characteristics of an emerging field of research," *Science, Technology, and Human Values* 15(January):84–104.

[32]University of Minnesota College of Agriculture, 1990, *Project Sunrise Third Annual Report: July 1989–June 1990,* University of Minnesota; and conversations with Mark L. Brenner, associate dean, University of Minnesota Graduate School.

[33]It is recognized that there are differences between science and engineering. Generally, engineers get more deeply into their subjects during their undergraduate years than do scientists.

[34]Presentation given by R. William Butcher at the workshop described in DHHS, *PHS Workshop,* 1990, and subsequent conversations with Stanley J. Reiser.

[35]Other broad programs have been or are being established at Indiana University, Dartmouth College, Wayne State University, Harvard University, and Princeton University, to mention only a few. Special discipline- or profession-based programs (e.g., medical ethics or engineering ethics) exist on many campuses.

[36]Interview, Robert DeHaan, Department of Anatomy and Cell Biology, Emory University, November 1990, and a brief conversation with Billy E. Frye, vice president for academic affairs and provost, Emory University.

[37]Conversations with David Smith, director, Poynter Center, Indiana University, and from descriptions of the Catalyst Program.

[38]One influence that is not specifically related to science and engineering research but that may have a bearing on how much respect policies relating to responsibility in research receive is the gender bias that is found in many of these policies. Some still exclusively use male pronouns. Equally insensitive is the practice of noting in a footnote that "Masculine parts of speech are hereafter presumed to include the feminine" (Harvard University Faculty of Medicine, 1990, *Policy on Conflicts of Interest and Commitment,* Harvard University, Cambridge, Mass.; see also University of Michigan, 1989, Guidelines). The lack of sensitivity to inclusivity is one more factor that bears on atmosphere and helps or undermines efforts to foster responsibility.

Misconduct in Science—
Incidence and Significance

Estimates reported in government summaries, research studies, and anecdotal accounts of cases of confirmed misconduct in science in the United States range between 40 and 100 cases during the period from 1980 to 1990.[1] The range reflects differences in the definitions of misconduct in science, uncertainties about the basis for "confirmed" cases, the time lag between the occurrence and disclosure of some cases, and potential overlap between government summaries (which are anonymous) and cases identified by name in the research literature.

When measured against the denominator of the number of research awards or research investigators, the range of misconduct-in-science cases cited above is small.[2] Furthermore, less than half of the allegations of misconduct received by government agencies have resulted in confirmed findings of misconduct in science. For example, after examining 174 case files of misconduct in science in the period from March 1989 through March 1991, the Office of Scientific Integrity in the Public Health Service found evidence of misconduct in fewer than 20 cases, although 56 investigations, mostly conducted by universities, were still under way (Wheeler, 1991).

However, even infrequent incidents of misconduct in science raise serious questions among scientists, research sponsors, and the public about the integrity of the research process and the stewardship of federal research funds.

Incidence of Misconduct in Science—
Published Evidence and Information

The incidence of misconduct in science and the significance of several confirmed cases have been topics of extensive discussion. Measures of the incidence of misconduct in science include (1) the number of allegations and confirmations of misconduct-in-science cases recorded and reviewed by government agencies and research institutions and (2) data and information presented in analyses, surveys, other studies, and anecdotal reports.

Some observers have suggested that incidents of misconduct in science are underreported. It may be difficult for co-workers and junior scientists, for example, graduate students and postdoctoral fellows, to make allegations of misconduct in science because of lack of supporting evidence and/or fear of retribution. The significant professional discrimination and economic loss experienced by

"Misconduct in Science," report of the Panel on Scientific Responsibility and Conduct of Research, in *Responsible Science: Ensuring the Integrity of the Research Process*, vol. I, National Academy of Sciences, (Washington: National Academy Press, 1993) 80–97.

whistleblowers as a result of reporting misconduct are well known and may deter others from disclosing wrongdoing in the research environment.

GOVERNMENT STATISTICS ON MISCONDUCT IN SCIENCE

Owing to differing perspectives on the role of government and research institutions in addressing misconduct in science, and to discrepancies in the number of allegations received by government offices, the number of open cases, and the cases of misconduct in science confirmed by research institutions or government agencies, many questions remain to be answered. These areas of uncertainty and disagreement inhibit the resolution of issues such as identifying the specific practices that fit legal definitions of misconduct in science; agreeing on standards for the evidence necessary to substantiate a finding of misconduct in science; clarifying the extent to which investigating panels can or should consider the intentions of the accused person in reaching a finding of misconduct in science; assessing the ability of research institutions and government agencies to discharge their responsibilities effectively and handle misconduct investigations appropriately; determining the frequency with which misconduct occurs; achieving consensus on the penalties that are likely to be imposed by diverse institutions for similar types of offenses; and evaluating the utility of allocating substantial amounts of public and private resources to handle allegations, only a few of which may result in confirmed findings of misconduct. The absence of publicly available summaries of the investigation and adjudication of incidents of misconduct in science inhibits scholarly efforts to examine how prevalent misconduct in science is and to evaluate the effectiveness of governmental and institutional treatment and prevention programs.

As a result, analyses of and policies related to misconduct in science are often influenced by information derived from a small number of cases that have received extensive publicity. The panel has not seen evidence that would help determine whether these highly publicized cases are representative of the broader sample of allegations or confirmed incidents of misconduct in science. One trend should be emphasized, however. The highly publicized cases often involve charges of falsification and fabrication of data, but the large majority of cases of confirmed misconduct in science have involved plagiarism (NSF, 1991a; Wheeler, 1991). Possible explanations for this trend are that plagiarism is more clearly identifiable by the complainants and more easily proved by those who investigate the complaint.

Five semiannual reports prepared by the National Science Foundation's Office of Inspector General (NSF 1989c; 1990a,b; 1991a,c) and a 1991 annual report prepared by the Office of Scientific Integrity Review of the Department of Health and Human Services (DHHS, 1991b) are the first systematic governmental efforts to analyze characteristics of a specific set of cases of misconduct in science. Although the treatment of some individual cases reported in these summaries has been the subject of debate and controversy, the panel commends these analyses as initial efforts and suggests that they receive professional review and revisions, if warranted.

National Science Foundation. The National Science Foundation's (NSF's) Office of Inspector General (OIG) received 41 allegations of misconduct in science in FY 1990 and reviewed another group of 6 allegations received by NSF prior to 1990 (NSF, 1990b).[3] From this group of 47 allegations, OIG closed 21 cases by the end of FY 1990. In three cases NSF made findings of misconduct in science; in another four cases, NSF accepted institutional findings of misconduct in science. NSF officials caution that, in their view, future cases may result in a larger percentage of confirmed findings of misconduct because many of the open cases raise complicated issues that require more time to resolve.[4]

The panel matched the 41 allegations reviewed by NSF in FY 1990 against the definitions of misconduct in science used by NSF at that time (Table 4.1).

The NSF's Office of the Director recommended the most serious penalty (debarment for 5 years) in a case involving charges of repeated incidents of sexual harassment, sexual assault, and threats of professional and academic blackmail by a co-principal investigator on NSF-funded research (NSF, 1990b, p. 21). Following an investigation that involved extensive interviews and affidavits, NSF's OIG determined that "no federal criminal statutes were violated . . . [but that] the pattern and effect of the co-principal investigator's actions constituted a serious deviation from accepted research practices" (NSF, 1990b, p. 21). NSF's OIG further determined that these incidents were "an integral part of this individual's

TABLE 4.1
Allegations of Misconduct in Science Reviewed in FY 1990
by the National Science Foundation

Category	Number of Allegations
Fabrication or falsification	9
Plagiarism	20
Other deviant research practices	8[a]
Violations of other research conduct regulations	1[b]
Violations of other legal requirements governing research	4[c]
TOTAL	41[d]

NOTE: The table represents the categories assigned by the panel to the allegations themselves. NSF's OIG does not necessarily endorse these categories, nor does it necessarily regard all these cases as exemplifying misconduct in science.
[a]Allegations of deviant practices included unauthorized use of research preparations, failure to identify original authors of proposal, tampering with others' experiments, discrimination by a reviewer or research investigator, and exploitation of a subordinate.
[b]Alleged violation of recombinant DNA regulations.
[c]Alleged violations included financial conflict of interests under award by an investigator or reviewer, NSF staff mishandling of proposal or award, and violation of a sanction against a principal investigator.
[d]Some allegations involved more than one form of misconduct.
SOURCE: Based on data from Office of Inspector General, National Science Foundation (personal communications on December 27, 1990, and February 22, 1991).

performance as a researcher and research mentor and represented a serious deviation from accepted research practices" (p. 27). However, reports of this particular case have caused some scientists to express concern that the scope of the definition of misconduct in science may be inappropriately broadened into areas designated by the panel as "other misconduct," such as sexual harassment.

Department of Health and Human Services. In FY 1989 and FY 1990, following the creation of the Office of Scientific Integrity (OSI), the Department of Health and Human Services (DHHS) received a total of 155 allegations of misconduct in science, many of which had been under review from earlier years by various offices within the Public Health Service (PHS).[5] In April 1991, OSI reported that since its formation it had closed about 110 cases, most of which did not result in findings of misconduct in science.

The Office of Scientific Integrity Review (OSIR), in the office of the assistant secretary for health, reviewed 21 reports of investigations of misconduct in science in the period from March 1989 to December 1990, some of which involved multiple charges.[6] The cases reviewed by OSIR had been forwarded to that office by OSI and had completed both an inquiry and investigation stage. Findings of misconduct in science, engaged in by 16 individuals, were made in 15 of the reports of investigations reviewed by OSIR. The OSIR's summary of findings is given in Table 4.2.

The OSIR recommended debarment in six cases, the most extreme administrative sanction available short of referral to the Justice Department for criminal prosecution. Actions to recover PHS grant funds were undertaken in two cases.

CONSEQUENCES OF CONFIRMED MISCONDUCT

Confirmed findings of misconduct in science can result in governmental penalties, such as dismissal or debarment, whereby individuals or institutions can be prohibited from receiving government grants or contracts on a temporary or

TABLE 4.2
Findings of Misconduct in Science in Cases Reviewed by the Office of Scientific Integrity Review, Department of Health and Human Services, March 1989 to December 1990

Type of Allegation	Findings of Misconduct (15 investigations)
Fabrication or falsification	6
Plagiarism	5
Other deviant research practices	7
TOTAL	18[a]

[a]The total of findings of misconduct is larger than the number of investigations because some cases had multiple findings.
SOURCE: Department of Health and Human Services (1991b).

permanent basis (42 C.F.R. 50). An individual who presents false information to the government in any form, including a research proposal, employment application, research report, or publication, may be subject to prosecution under the False Claims Act (18 U.S.C. 1001). At least one case of criminal prosecution against a research scientist, for example, rested on evidence that the scientist had provided false research information in research proposals and progress reports to a sponsoring agency.[7] Similar prosecutions have occurred in connection with some pharmaceutical firms or contract laboratories that provided false test data in connection with licensing or government testing requirements (O'Reilly, 1990).

Government regulations on misconduct in science provide a separate mechanism through which individuals and institutions can be subjected to government penalties and criminal prosecution if they misrepresent information from research that is supported by federal funds, even if the information is not presented directly to government officials. Research institutions and scientific investigators who apply for and receive federal funds are thus expected to comply with high standards of honesty and integrity in the performance of their research activities.

GOVERNMENT DEFINITIONS OF MISCONDUCT IN SCIENCE—
AMBIGUITY IN CATEGORIES

The PHS's misconduct-in-science regulations apply to research sponsored by all PHS agencies, including the National Institutes of Health, the Alcohol, Drug Abuse, and Mental Health Administration, the Centers for Disease Control, the Food and Drug Administration, and the Agency for Health Care Policy and Research. The PHS defines misconduct in science as "fabrication, falsification, plagiarism, or other practices that seriously deviate from those that are commonly accepted within the scientific community for proposing, conducting, or reporting research. It does not include honest error or honest differences in interpretations or judgments of data" (DHHS, 1989a, p. 32447).[8]

The PHS's definition does not further define fabrication, falsification, plagiarism, or other serious deviations from commonly accepted research practices. The ambiguous scope of this last category is a topic of major concern to the research community because of the perception that it could be applied inappropriately in cases of disputed scientific judgment.

The first annual report of the DHHS's OSIR suggests the types of alleged misconduct in science that might fall within the scope of this category (DHHS, 1991b):

- Misuse by a journal referee of privileged information contained in a manuscript,
- Fabrication of entries or misrepresentation of the publication status of manuscripts referenced in a research bibliography,
- Failure to perform research supported by a PHS grant while stating in progress reports that active progress has been made,
- Improper reporting of the status of subjects in clinical research (e.g., reporting the same subjects as controls in one study and as experimental subjects in another),

- Preparation and publication of a book chapter listing co-authors who were unaware of being named as co-authors,
- Selective reporting of primary data,
- Unauthorized use of data from another investigator's laboratory,
- Engaging in inappropriate authorship practices on a publication and failure to acknowledge that data used in a grant application were developed by another scientist, and
- Inappropriate data analysis and use of faulty statistical methodology.

The panel points out that most of the behaviors described above, such as the fabrication of bibliographic material or falsely reporting research progress, are behaviors that fall within the panel's definition of misconduct in science proposed in Chapter 1.

The NSF's definition (NSF, 1991b) is broader than that used by the PHS[9] and extends to nonresearch activities supported by the agency, such as science education. NSF also includes in its definition of misconduct in science acts of retaliation against any person who provides information about suspected misconduct and who has not acted in bad faith.

The panel believes that behaviors such as repeated incidents of sexual harassment, sexual assault, or professional intimidation should be regarded as other misconduct, not as misconduct in science, because these actions (1) do not require expert knowledge to resolve complaints and (2) should be governed by mechanisms that apply to all institutional members, not just those who receive government research awards. Practices such as inappropriate authorship, in the panel's view, should be regarded as questionable research practices, because they do not fit within the rationale for misconduct in science as defined by the panel in Chapter 1.

The investigation of questionable research practices as incidents of alleged misconduct in science, in the absence of consensus about the nature, acceptability, and damage that questionable practices cause, can do serious harm to individuals and to the research enterprise. Institutional or regulatory efforts to determine "correct" research methods or analytical practices, without sustained participation by the research community, could encourage orthodoxy and rigidity in research practice and cause scientists to avoid novel or unconventional research paradigms.[10]

REPORTS FROM LOCAL INSTITUTIONAL OFFICIALS

Investigatory Reports. Government regulations currently require local institutions to notify the sponsoring agency if they intend to initiate an investigation of an allegation of misconduct in science. The institutions are also required to submit a report of the investigation when it is completed. These reports, in the aggregate, may provide a future source of evidence regarding the frequency with which misconduct-in-science cases are handled by local institutions.

Although some investigatory reports have been released on an ad hoc basis, research scientists generally do not have access to comprehensive summaries of the investigatory reports prepared or reviewed by government agencies. The absence of such summaries impedes informed analysis of misconduct in science and inhibits the exchange of information and experience among institutions about factors that can contribute to or prevent misconduct in science.

Other Institutional Reports. The perspectives and experiences of institutional officials in handling allegations of misconduct in science are likely in the future to be important sources of information about the incidence of misconduct. This body of experience is largely undocumented, and most institutions do not maintain accessible records on their misconduct cases because of concerns about individual privacy and confidentiality, as well as concerns about possible institutional embarrassment, loss of prestige, and lawsuits.

The DHHS's regulations now require grantee institutions to provide annual reports of aggregate information on allegations, inquiries, and investigations, along with annual assurances that the institutions have an appropriate administrative process for handling allegations of misconduct in science (DHHS, 1989a). The institutional reports filed in early 1991 were not available for this study. These institutional summaries could eventually provide an additional source of evidence regarding how frequently misconduct in science addressed at the local level involves biomedical or behavioral research. If the reports incorporate standard terms of reference, are prepared in a manner that facilitates analysis and interpretation, and are accessible to research scientists, they could provide a basis for making independent judgments about the effectiveness of research institutions in handling allegations of misconduct in science. The NSF's regulations do not require an annual report from grantee institutions.

INTERNATIONAL STUDIES

Cases of misconduct in science have been reported and confirmed in other countries. The editor of the *British Medical Journal* reported in 1988 that in the 1980s at least five cases of misconduct by scientists had been documented in Britain and five cases had been publicly disclosed in Australia (Lock, 1988b, 1990). As a result of a "nonsystematic" survey of British medical institutions, scientists, physicians, and editors of medical journals, Lock cited at least another 40 unreported cases.

There has been at least one prominent case of misconduct in science in India recently (Jayaraman, 1991). Several cases of misconduct in science and academic plagiarism have been recorded in Germany (Foelsing, 1984; Eisenhut, 1990).

ANALYSES, SURVEYS, AND OTHER REPORTS

Hundreds of articles on misconduct in science have been published in the popular and scholarly literature over the past decade. The study panel's own working bibliography included over 1,100 such items.

Although highly publicized reports about individual misconduct cases have appeared with some frequency, systematic efforts to analyze data on cases of misconduct in science have not attracted significant interest or support within the research community until very recently. Research studies have been hampered by the absence of information and statistical data, lack of rigorous definitions of misconduct in science, the heterogeneous and decentralized nature of the research environment, the complexity of misconduct cases, and the confidential and increasingly litigious nature of misconduct cases (U.S. Congress, 1990b; AAAS-ABA, 1989).

As a result, only a small number of confirmed misconduct cases have been the subject of scholarly examination. The results of these studies are acknowledged by their authors to be subject to statistical bias; the sample, which is drawn primarily from public records, may or may not be representative of the larger pool of cases or allegations. Preliminary studies have focused primarily on questions of range, prevalence, incidence, and frequency of misconduct in science. There has been little effort to identify patterns of misconduct or questionable practices in science. Beyond speculation, very little is known about the etiology, dynamics, and consequences of misconduct in science. The relationship of misconduct in science to factors in the contemporary research environment, such as the size of research teams, financial incentives, or collaborative research efforts, has not been systematically evaluated and is not known.

Woolf Analysis. Patricia Woolf of Princeton University, a member of this panel, has analyzed incidents of alleged misconduct publicly reported from 1950 to 1987 (Woolf, 1981, 1986, 1988a).

Woolf examined 26 cases of misconduct identified as having occurred or been detected in the period from 1980 to 1987, the majority of which (22 cases) were in biomedical research. Her analysis indicated that 11 of the institutions associated with the 26 cases were prestigious schools and hospitals, ranked in the top 20 in the Cole and Lipton (1977) evaluation of reputation. Woolf found that a "notable percentage" of the individuals accused of misconduct were from highly regarded institutions: "seven graduated from the top twenty schools" (Woolf, 1988a, p. 79), as ranked by reputation, an important finding that deserves further analysis. She also suggested that because cases of misconduct are often handled locally, the total number of cases is likely to be larger than reported in the public record (Woolf, 1988a).

The types of alleged misconduct reported in the cases analyzed by Woolf, some of which involved more than one type, included plagiarism (4 cases); falsification, fabrication, and forgery of data (12 cases); and misrepresentation and other misconduct (12 cases). She suggested that "plagiarism is almost certainly under-represented in this survey, as it appears to be handled locally and without publicity whenever possible" (Woolf, 1988a, p. 83).

Woolf identified several important caveats, noted below, that still apply to all systematic efforts to analyze the characteristics and demography of misconduct in science (Woolf, 1988a, p. 76):

- *Small number of instances.* There are not enough publicly known cases to draw statistically sound conclusions or make significant generalizations, and those that are available are a biased sample of the population of actual cases.
- *Blurred categories.* It is not possible in all cases to cleanly separate misconduct in science from falsification in drug trials or laboratory tests. Similarly, one person may indulge in plagiarism, fabrication, and falsification.
- *Incomplete information.* Some information about reported instances is not yet available.
- *Variety of sources.* The sources of information (for Woolf's analysis) include public accounts, such as newspaper reports, as well as original documents and interview material. They are not all equally reliable with regard to dates and other minor details.
- *Unclear resolution.* Disputed cases that have nevertheless been "settled" are included (in Woolf's analysis). In some highly publicized cases of alleged misconduct in science, the accused scientist has *not* admitted, and may have specifically denied, misconduct in science.

OSIR Analysis. The DHHS's OSIR prepared a first annual report in early 1991 that analyzed data associated with investigations of misconduct in science reviewed by that office in the period March 1989 through December 1990 (DHHS, 1991b). The report examined misconduct investigations carried out by research institutions and by the OSI.

Seniority of Subjects of Misconduct Cases in Woolf and OSIR Analyses. Both Woolf and the OSIR examined the rank of individuals who have been the subjects of misconduct-in-science cases. Although some have speculated that junior scientists might be more likely to engage in misconduct in science, both Woolf's analysis and the OSIR's analysis suggest that misconduct in science "did not occur primarily among junior scientists or trainees" (DHHS, 1991b, p. 7). Their preliminary studies suggest that the incident of misconduct is likely to be greater among senior scientists (Table 4.3), a finding that deserves further analysis.

Detection of Misconduct in Science in Woolf and OSIR Analyses. Woolf and the OSIR examined processes used to detect incidents of confirmed or suspected misconduct in science and also analyzed the status of individuals who disclosed these incidents (Tables 4.4 and 4.5). Their analyses indicate that existing channels within the peer review process and research institutions do provide information about misconduct in science. Initial reports were often made by supervisors, collaborators, or subordinates who were in direct contact with the individual suspected of misconduct. These findings contradict opinions that checks such as peer review, replication of research, and journal reviews do not help identify instances of misconduct.

However, the panel notes that supervisors, colleagues, and subordinate personnel may report misconduct in science at their peril. The honesty of individuals who hold positions of respect or prestige cannot be easily questioned. It can be particularly deleterious for junior or temporary personnel to make allegations of misconduct by their superiors. Students, research fellows, and technicians can jeopardize current positions, imperil progress on their research projects, and sacrifice future recommendations from their research supervisors by making allegations of misconduct by their co-workers.

TABLE 4.3
Academic Ranks of Subjects in Confirmed Cases of Misconduct in Science

Rank	Number of Subjects	
	1980–1987[a]	1989–1990[b]
Full or associate professor, or senior scientist/laboratory chief	13	7
Assistant professor	2	4
Research associate/fellow	3	3
Various posts held	5	na
No academic appointment/technicians	2	2
Unknown	1	na
	26	16

[a]Data from Woolf (1988a).
[b]Department of Health and Human Services (1991b).

The Acadia Institute Survey. One provocative study of university officers' experience with misconduct in science is a 1988 survey of 392 deans of graduate studies from institutions affiliated with the Council of Graduate Schools (CGS).[11, 12] The survey was conducted with support from NSF and the American Association for the Advancement of Science. Approximately 75 percent (294) of the graduate deans responded to the survey.

The Acadia Institute survey data indicate that 40 percent (118) of the responding graduate deans had received reports of *possible* faculty misconduct in science during the previous 5 years. Two percent (6) had received more than five reports. These figures suggest that graduate deans have a significant chance of becoming involved in handling an allegation of misconduct in science.

The survey shows that about 190 allegations of misconduct in science were addressed by CGS institutions over the 5-year period (1983 to 1988) reported in the survey. It is not known whether any or all of these allegations were separately submitted to government offices concerned with misconduct in science during this time period, although overlap is likely.

The Acadia Institute survey also suggests, not surprisingly, that allegations of misconduct in science are associated with institutions that receive significant amounts of external research funding. As noted in the NSF's OIG summary report of the Acadia Institute survey: "Of the institutions receiving more than $50 million in external research funding annually, 69 percent [36] had been notified of possible faculty misconduct. Among institutions receiving less than $5 million, only 19 percent [14] had been so notified" (NSF, 1990d, pp. 2–3).

When asked about cases of *verified* misconduct by their faculties during the previous 5 years, 20 percent (59) of all the responding graduate deans indicated such instances. Among universities with over $50 million per year in external

TABLE 4.4
Primary Sources of Detection of Alleged Misconduct (1980 to 1987)

Factor	Number of Cases
Admission	2
Co-worker or former co-worker reported:	
Laboratory suspicions, irregular procedures	13
Misuse of funds	1
Inability to replicate or continue work	8
Institutional review board raised questions	1
Scientists at other institutions reported suspicions	
(including inability to replicate work)	6
Editorial peer review	3
Promotion review of publications	1
Formal audit	1
Protest by original author (plagiarism)	3
Unknown	2

NOTE: Some instances were or seem to have been suspected or detected at about the same time by more than one factor. From the available record it is difficult to make a clear distinction between factors that enabled detection of misconduct in science and those used to demonstrate or prove it.
SOURCE: Data from Woolf (1988a).

TABLE 4.5
Status of Individual Bringing Allegations

Status	Number of Cases
Supervisor (e.g., department chair, laboratory chief)	4
Colleague (scientific associate of about	
the same seniority or status)	4
Collaborator	4
Junior scientific associate	2
Graduate student or postdoctoral trainee	5
Laboratory technician	3
Chair of a department at another institution	1
Self (self-report of misconduct by the subject)	1

SOURCE: Department of Health and Human Services (1991b).

funding (about 55 institutions fell within this category in 1988), 41 percent (20) had some verified misconduct, according to responses of graduate deans participating in the Acadia Institute survey. The actual number of cases associated with these percentages, which is small, is consistent with the panel's observation that the total number of confirmed cases of misconduct in science is very small.

Nevertheless, reports indicating that prestigious research institutions consistently receive, and confirm, allegations of misconduct in science are disturbing.

Other Reports—Bechtel and Pearson. Bechtel and Pearson (1985) examined both the question of prevalence of misconduct in science and the concept of deviant behavior by scientists as part of a larger exploration of "elite occupational deviance" that included white collar crime. The authors reviewed 12 cases of misconduct in science, drawn from reports in the popular and scientific press in the 1970s and early 1980s. They found that available evidence was inadequate to support accurate generalizations about how widespread misconduct in science might be. As to the causes of deviant behavior, the authors concluded that "in the debate between those who favor individualistic explanations based on psychological notions of emotional disturbance, and the critics of big science who blame the increased pressures for promotion, tenure, and recognition through publications, one tends to see greater merit in the latter" (p. 244). They suggested that further systematic examination is required to determine the appropriate balance between individual and structural sources of deviant behavior.

Sigma Xi Study. As part of a broader survey it conducted in 1988, Sigma Xi, the honor society for scientific researchers in North America, asked its members to respond to the following statement: "Excluding gross stupidities and/or minor slip ups that can be charitably dismissed (but not condoned), I have direct knowledge of fraud (e.g., falsifying data, misreporting results, plagiarism) on the part of a professional scientist."[13]

Respondents were asked to rank their agreement or disagreement with the statement on a five-point scale. The survey was mailed to 9,998 members of the society; about 38 percent responded (which indicates a possible source of bias).

Although 19 percent of the Sigma Xi respondents indicated that they had direct knowledge of fraud by a scientist, it is not certain from the survey whether direct knowledge meant personal experience with or simply awareness of scientific fraud. It is also possible that some respondents were referring to identical cases, and respondents may have reported knowledge of cases gained secondhand. Furthermore, it is not clear what information can be gained by having respondents rank "direct knowledge" on a five-point scale of agreement and disagreement.

Additional Information. Estimates about the incidence of misconduct in science have ranged from editorial statements that the scientific literature is "99.9999 percent pure" to reader surveys published in scientific journals indicating that significant numbers of the respondents have had direct experience with misconduct of some sort in science.[14] The broad variance in these estimates has not resolved uncertainties about the frequency with which individuals or institutions actually encounter incidents of misconduct in science.

In March 1990, the NSF's OIG reported that, based on a comprehensive review of the results from past surveys that attempted to measure the incidence of misconduct in science, "the full extent of misconduct is not yet known" (NSF, 1990d, p. 9). The NSF reports found that only a few quantitative studies have examined the extent of misconduct in science and that prior survey efforts had poor response rates, asked substantively different questions, and employed varying definitions of misconduct. These efforts have not yielded a database that would provide an appropriate foundation for findings and conclusions about the extent of misconduct in science and engineering.[15]

Findings and Conclusions

The panel found that existing data are inadequate to draw accurate conclusions about the incidence of misconduct in science or of questionable research practices. The panel points out that the number of confirmed cases of misconduct in science is low compared to the level of research activity in the United States. However, as with all forms of misconduct, underreporting may be significant; federal agencies have only recently imposed procedural and reporting requirements that may yield larger numbers of reported cases. The possibility of underreporting can neither be dismissed nor confirmed at this time. More research is necessary to determine the full extent of misconduct in science.

Regardless of the incidence, the panel emphasizes that even infrequent cases of misconduct in science are serious matters. The number of confirmed incidents of misconduct in science, together with the possibility of underreporting and the results presented in some preliminary studies, indicate that misconduct in science is a problem that cannot be ignored. The consequences of even infrequent cases of misconduct in science require that attention be given to appropriate methods of treatment and prevention.

Notes

[1]Reports of cases involving findings of misconduct in science were provided to the panel by DHHS and NSF. These reports indicate a total of 15 cases of findings of misconduct in science by DHHS in the period from March 1989 to December 1990 and 3 cases of findings of misconduct in science by NSF in the period from July 1989 to September 1990. See NSF (1990b) and DHHS (1991b). Information was also provided in a personal communication from Donald Buzzelli, staff associate, OIG, NSF, February 1, 1991.

Congressional testimony by and telephone interviews with NIH and ADAMHA officials indicated that in the period from 1980 to 1987, roughly 17 misconduct cases handled by these agencies resulted in institutional findings of research misconduct, some of which are included in the Woolf analysis discussed below. During this same period, NSF made findings of misconduct in science in seven cases. See the testimony of Katherine Bick and Mary Miers in U.S. Congress (1989a); see also Woolf (1988a).

The report by Woolf (1988a) identified 40 publicly reported cases of alleged misconduct in science in the period from 1950 to 1987, many of which involved confirmed findings of misconduct. Another two dozen or so cases of alleged misconduct in science were reported in congressional hearings in the 1980s. Some of the cases discussed in congressional hearings and in the Woolf analysis are included in the NSF and DHHS reports mentioned above. Some cases discussed in congressional hearings are still open, and the remainder have been closed without an institutional finding of misconduct in science.

The estimate of confirmed cases of misconduct in science does not include cases in which research institutions have made findings of misconduct, unless these cases are included in the Woolf analysis or the congressional hearings mentioned above. During the time of this study, there were no central records for institutional reports on misconduct in science that would indicate the frequency with which these organizations found allegations to have merit.

Finally, several authors have reviewed selected cases of misconduct in science, both contemporary and historical. The most popular accounts are a book by Broad and Wade (1982), who cite 34 cases of "known or suspected cases of scientific fraud" ranging from "ancient Greece to the present day"; a book by Klotz (1985); and one by Kohn (1986), who cites 24 cases of "known or suspected misconduct." These texts, and the government reports, congressional hearings, and Woolf analysis cited above, discuss many of the same cases.

[2]The preamble to the PHS's 1989 regulations for scientific misconduct notes that "reported instances of scientific misconduct appear to represent only a small fraction of the total number of research and research training awards funded by the PHS" (DHHS, 1989a, p. 32446). The preamble to the NSF's 1987 misconduct regulations states that "NSF has received relatively few allegations of misconduct or fraud occurring in NSF-supported research or . . . proposals" (NSF, 1987, p. 24466).

Furthermore, according to the National Library of Medicine, during the 10-year period from 1977 to 1986, about 2.8 million articles were published in the world's biomedical literature. The number of articles retracted because of the discovery of fraud or falsification of data was 41, less than 0.002 percent of the total. See Holton (1988), p. 457.

[3]Analyses of the NSF's experience are complicated by the fact that different offices have held authority for handling research misconduct cases. Prior to the creation of the OIG in March 1989, this authority was assigned to the NSF's Division of Audit and Oversight. The OIG "inherited" approximately 19 case files, and it received 6 new allegations of research misconduct during FY 1989. NSF officials reported in 1987 that NSF had examined 12 charges of research misconduct, 7 of which were found to be warranted, of which 3 were considered minor violations. See Woolf (1988a).

[4]Personal communication, OIG, NSF, February 1, 1991.

[5]Personal communication, Jules Hallum, director, OSI, February 27, 1991.

[6]Four of these investigations were conducted by the PHS. Sixteen were conducted by outside, primarily grantee, institutions. One additional investigation was an intramural case within the PHS.

[7]See the documentation regarding the case of psychologist Stephen Breuning as detailed in the DHHS's Report and Recommendations of a Panel to Investigate Allegations of Scientific Misconduct under Grants MH-32206 and MH-37449, April 20, 1987.

[8]The definition excludes violations of regulations that govern human or animal experimentation, financial or other record-keeping requirements, or the use of toxic or hazardous substances. It applies to individuals or institutions that apply for as well as those that receive extramural research, research-training, or research-related grants or cooperative agreements under the PHS, and to all intramural PHS research. In the proposed rule, the PHS's definition of misconduct included a second clause referring to "material failure to comply with federal requirements that uniquely relate to the conduct of research." This clause was eliminated in the misconduct definition adopted in the final rule (DHHS, 1989a) to avoid duplicate reporting of violations of research regulations involving animal and human subjects, since these areas are covered by existing regulations and policies.

[9]In the commentary accompanying its final rule, NSF (1987) noted that several letters on the proposed rule had commented that the proposed definition was too vague or over-reaching. The NSF's 1987 definition originally included two clauses in addition to those in the PHS misconduct definition: "material failure to comply with federal requirements for protection of researchers, human subjects, or the public or for ensuring the welfare of laboratory animals" and "failure to meet other material legal requirements governing research" (NSF, 1987, p. 24468). These categories were removed in 1991 when the regulations were amended.

[10]In a "Dear Colleague Letter on Misconduct" issued on August 16, 1991, the NSF's OIG stated, "The definition is not intended to elevate ordinary disputes in research to the level of misconduct and does not contemplate that NSF will act as an arbitrator of mere personality clashes or technical disputes between researchers."

[11]K. Louis, J. Swazey, and M. Anderson, *University Policies and Ethical Issues in Research and Graduate Education: Results of a Survey of Graduate School Deans*, preliminary report (Bar Harbor, Me.: Acadia Institute, November 1988). The survey was published as Swazey et al. (1989).

[12]It should be noted that the survey instrument used by the Acadia Institute did not define "research misconduct," but instead left that term open to the interpretation of the respondents. In some parts of the survey, "plagiarism" was distinguished from "research misconduct."

[13]Sigma Xi (1989), as summarized in NSF (1990d), pp. 4–5.

[14]Cited in Woolf (1988a), p. 71. She quotes an editorial by Koshland (1987) for the first figure and a survey by St. James-Roberts (1976b) for the latter.

[15]See Tangney (1987) and Davis (1989). See also St. James-Roberts (1976a). The reader survey reported in St. James-Roberts (1976b) received 204 questionnaire replies. Ninety-two percent of the respondents reported direct or indirect experience with "intentional bias" in research findings. The source of knowledge of bias was primarily from direct contact (52 percent). Forty percent reported secondary sources (information from colleagues, scientific grapevine, media) as the basis for their knowledge.

See also *Industrial Chemist* (1987a,b). The editors expressed surprise at the high level of responses: 28.4 percent of the 290 respondents indicated that they faked a research result often or occasionally.

References

American Association for the Advancement of Science-American Bar Association (AAAS-ABA) National Conference of Lawyers and Scientists. 1989. *Project on Scientific Fraud and Misconduct.* Reports on workshops one (September 18–20, 1987), two (September 23–25, 1988), and three (February 17–18, 1989). Three volumes. AAAS, Washington, D.C.

Bechtel, H. K., Jr. and W. Pearson, Jr. 1985. "Deviant scientists and scientific deviance." *Deviant Behavior* 6:237–252.

Broad, W. and Wade, N. 1982. *Betrayers of the Truth: Fraud and Deceit in the Halls of Science.* Simon and Schuster, New York.

Davis, M. S. 1989. *The Perceived Seriousness and Incidence of Ethical Misconduct in Academic Science,* Unpublished Ph.D. thesis. Ohio State University, Columbus.

Department of Health and Human Services (DHHS). 1989a. "Responsibilities of PHS awardee and applicant institutions for dealing with and reporting possible misconduct in science: final rule." *Federal Register* 54(August 8):32446–32451.

Department of Health and Human Services (DHHS). 1991b. *First Annual Report: Scientific Misconduct Investigations Reviewed by Office of Scientific Integrity Review, March 1989–December 1990*. Office of Scientific Integrity Review, Washington, D.C.

Eisenhut, L. P. 1990. "Universität prüft Anschuldigungen gegen Professorin." *Kolner Stadtanzeiger* (October 24).

Foelsing, A. 1984. *Der Mogelfaktor*. Hamburg, pp. 20–21.

Holton, G. 1988. *Thematic Origins of Scientific Thought: Kepler to Einstein*. Revised edition. Harvard University Press, Cambridge, Mass.

Industrial Chemist. 1987a. "Do you ever fake a research result?" February.

Industrial Chemist. 1987b. "Error and fraud in the lab." May, p. 84.

Jayaraman, K. S. 1991. "Gupta faces suspension." *Nature* 349(February 21):645.

Klotz, I. M. 1985. *Diamond Dealers and Feather Merchants: Tales from the Sciences*. Birkhauser, Boston.

Kohn, A. 1986. *False Prophets: Fraud and Error in Science and Medicine*. Basil Blackwell, New York.

Koshland, D. E. 1987. "Fraud in science." *Science* 235(January 9):141.

Lock, S. 1988b. "Scientific misconduct." *British Medical Journal* 297(September 24): 1531–1535.

Lock, S. 1990. "Medical misconduct: A survey in Britain." In *Ethics and Policy in Scientific Publication*, Bailar et al. (eds.). Council of Biology Editors, Bethesda, Md.

National Science Foundation (NSF), 1987. "Misconduct in science and engineering research: final regulations." *Federal Register* 52(July 1):24466–24470.

National Science Foundation (NSF). 1989c. *Semiannual Report to the Congress*. Number 1. Office of Inspector General, NSF, Washington, D.C.

National Science Foundation (NSF). 1990a. *Semiannual Report to the Congress*. Number 2. Office of Inspector General, NSF, Washington, D.C.

National Science Foundation (NSF). 1990b. *Semiannual Report to the Congress*. Number 3. Office of Inspector General, NSF, Washington, D.C.

National Science Foundation (NSF). 1990d. *Survey Data on the Extent of Misconduct in Science and Engineering*. OIG-90-3214. Office of Inspector General, NSF, Washington, D.C.

National Science Foundation (NSF). 1991a. *Semiannual Report to the Congress*. Number 4. Office of Inspector General, NSF, Washington, D.C.

National Science Foundation (NSF). 1991b. "Misconduct in science and engineering: final rule." *Federal Register* 56(May 14):22286–90.

National Science Foundation (NSF). 1991c. *Semiannual Report to the Congress*. Number 5. Office of Inspector General, NSF, Washington, D.C.

O'Reilly, J. T. 1990. "More gold and more fleece: improving the legal sanctions against medical research fraud." *Administrative Law Review* 42(Summer):393–422.

St. James-Roberts, I. 1976a. "Are researchers trustworthy?" *New Scientist* 72(September 2):481–83.

St. James-Roberts, I. 1976b. "Cheating in science." *New Scientist* 72(November 25):466–69.

Swazey, J. P., K. S. Louis, and M. S. Anderson. 1989. "University policies and ethical issues in research and graduate education: highlights of the CGS deans' survey." *CGS Communicator* 22(March):1–3, 7–8.

Tangney, J. P. 1987. "Fraud will out—or will it?" *New Scientist* (August 6):62–63.

U.S. Congress. 1989a. *Fraud in NIH Grant Programs.* House of Representatives, Committee on Energy and Commerce, Subcommittee on Oversight and Investigations. 100th Cong. 2nd sess., April 12. Serial No. 100–189. U.S. Government Printing Office, Washington, D.C.

U.S. Congress. 1990b. *Maintaining the Integrity of Scientific Research.* House of Representatives, Committee on Science, Space, and Technology, Subcommittee on Investigations and Oversight. 101st Cong., 1st sess., June 28. No. 73. U.S. Government Printing Office, Washington, D.C.

Wheeler, D. 1991. "U.S. has barred grants to 6 scientists in past 2 years." *Chronicle of Higher Education* (July 3).

Woolf, P. K. 1981. "Fraud in science: how much, how serious?" *Hastings Center Report* 11(October):9–14.

Woolf, P. K. 1986. "Pressure to publish and fraud in science." *Annals of Internal Medicine* 104(2):254–56.

Woolf, P. K. 1988a. "Deception in scientific research." *Jurimetrics Journal* 29(Fall):67–95.

Chapter 8
Conflicts, Funding, and Ownership

8.1   INTRODUCTION

In the previous chapter, we explored the range of misconduct in science. We took for granted that all forms of misconduct are wrong. We also exposed some of the reasons that scientists still engage in misconduct, both intentionally and negligently. Only by seeking a better understanding of these motivations will scientists be able to continue to improve their capacities to recognize, avoid, and resolve ethical difficulties in the conduct and reporting of research.

In the present chapter, we turn to the discussion of a series of perplexing ethical issues related to funding research. Research is expensive, and like everything else it is becoming more expensive each year. Early in the twentieth century, universities funded much of the research of their own scientists. More recently, the government has funded research. Now private corporations are footing the bill more and more. For example, pharmaceutical companies, among others, now have their own research laboratories that are quite independent of university labs. We saw in section 3.5 that the growing number of private laboratories funded by industry raises ethical concerns about the protection of human subjects, since private research need not observe federal requirements such as undergoing IRB oversight. A distinct set of ethical concerns has grown up around funding: Who pays for research? How do they pay? Who owns the subsequent data generated? Who owns any patents or copyrights generated? How are funding decisions made? These are some of the questions that will occupy us in this chapter. We begin with the topic of conflict of interest.

8.2   CONFLICT OF INTEREST

We do not always act for the sake of our own benefit. We sometimes act in ways that are directed to the benefit of others, and we thereby promote others' interests. In some cases when we do this, we also manage to secure some benefit for ourselves; in other cases, we sacrifice our own interests for the sake of someone else. Sometimes we do so because those others are related to us in special ways: We sacrifice for the sake of our children or parents, for example. Parents scrimp and save to put their children through college, and children often bear part of the cost of caring for elderly parents. Other times, we try to set aside our own interests because we are paid to do so, as when a lawyer represents a client. Good lawyers strive to ignore any personal feelings they might have toward their clients and represent those clients' interests to the best of their ability. Lawyers advise their clients regarding the best approach to legal issues, but in the end they are obligated to do as the clients think best (or else terminate the professional relationship).

Scientists are in somewhat the same position as lawyers: They are paid to represent another's interests. In the case of scientists, however, the "client" is not another person, but science itself, or in some cases, the scientific community. Science has interests of its own: Science aims to discover the truth about the world. That is a large aim, composed of many smaller aims. Science can be divided into a range of disciplines: the natural sciences, the social sciences, and the behavioral sciences, for example. The natural sciences, in turn, are typically divided into biology, chemistry, and physics, and each of these sciences has sub-divisions and sub-fields. These large divisions are themselves divisible into disciplines and sub-disciplines. Presumably all of these divisions share the aim of discovering part of the truth about the world. Scientists have developed a set of subordinate aims that help them reach this goal, and these aims are built into the range of practices and institutions commonly referred to as "the scientific method." The scientific method, of course, has evolved over time, as scientific practices have come and gone. As mentioned in Chapter 7, the standards for implementing the scientific method may differ from one discipline to the next. For example, standards of acceptable statistical manipulation are not constant throughout all disciplines. Scientists are paid to discover the truth about the world, and thereby to serve the interests of science.

The responsibility of serving interests other than one's own creates the possibility of conflict of interest. A **conflict of interest** arises when one aims to promote another's interests, and those interests conflict with one's own interests. Suppose a lawyer has a client who wishes to sue Company B. Suppose also that the lawyer has a large stake in Company B—perhaps she is a company director or owns considerable stock in Company B or has some other financial interest in the company. The lawyer has a conflict of interest. Her professional obligation to the client requires (if she agrees to represent him) that she present the best lawsuit she can on his behalf and that she win as large an award as possible against Company B. On the other hand, her own personal interest lies in Company B's success, both in business generally and in the client's lawsuit in particular. And so she has a personal reason not to do her best work on the lawsuit. These conflicting motivations—a professional one that leads the lawyer to want the lawsuit to succeed, and a personal one that makes her want the lawsuit to fail—constitute a conflict of interest. Perhaps the first and greatest obligation in this case is to be honest from the beginning—explaining the conflict of interest so that the client can make an informed decision about the lawyer. In any case, of course, lawyers have the option to refuse a case, but that option rarely becomes obligatory. The recommendation to be forthcoming about any conflicts of interest is one that we will continue to endorse throughout this chapter.

Scientists are human beings with their own interests, and these interests can come into conflict with the interests of others. It can happen that scientists' personal interests in career, reputation, income, and so forth conflict with their professional obligations to discover the truth about the world. The scientific method is a long and laborious process. With today's complex institutions, including university, corporate, and government labs, as well as the elaborate process of peer review and evaluation, reporting the truth about the world may take even longer and be more laborious than in decades past. It can be tempting to cut corners in this process for the sake of financial or other personal gain. Given the large amounts of money that have been poured into various areas of research in the past 25 years, these temptations can be strong. At the root of these temptations is a conflict of interest: The individual researcher's interests threaten to compromise his or her ability to pursue the interests of science.

A conflict of interest is not to be confused with a **conflict of obligation.** The latter sort of conflict—also known as the "two hats" problem, which was discussed in Chapters 3 and 4 —arises when an individual occupies two roles whose obligations come into conflict.

8.3   ETHICAL ISSUES IN CONFLICTS OF INTEREST

The conventional wisdom surrounding conflicts of interest is that they are bad and always to be avoided. Professionals who find themselves in conflicts of interest are unreliable and not to be trusted, since it is unclear whose interests they will be motivated to serve—their own or their clients'. We often hear how it is important to avoid even the *appearance* of a conflict, since the perception of conflict can influence trust as much as an actual conflict. In section 9.4 we discuss the obligations that scientists have when reporting the results of their findings to the public. The public is occasionally misinformed about the nature of scientific investigation, and this sort of misinformation can have wide-ranging consequences; in light of these potentially serious consequences, scientists have a responsibility to take special care when reporting their results to the public. In similar fashion, scientists may have special obligations to avoid the appearance of a conflict of interest, because that appearance may erode public confidence in researchers. This lack of confidence could sap public support for the scientific enterprise, resulting in fewer public funds for research, a dearth of willing subjects, or simply less tolerance for scientists who wish to share public resources in their quest for the truth. It might seem best to eschew even the appearance of a conflict of interest, because the objectivity of science depends on the strict neutrality of scientific researchers and their capacity to remain reliable reporters of the truth about the world. When scientists become beholden to interests outside of the scientific enterprise—whether such interests be personal, corporate, or governmental—they risk losing their status as the impartial arbiters of the truth.

Recently, however, attitudes toward conflict of interest have begun to shift. At the root of this transition is the idea that conflicts of interest are *inevitable,* that professionals are always conflicted. Consider again the situation of lawyers (as Larry May does in the article included in this chapter). Lawyers are paid to represent their clients' interests. They are conflicted from the moment a client walks in: Lawyers have a personal interest in making money, whereas the client's interest is to pay as little as possible to accomplish a legal project.

A similar point applies to scientists. Scientists are professionals, possessing advanced degrees and special training, and they are paid to do research, among other things. They have interests in personal advancement, promotions, raises, and so forth, and the dominant consideration in these matters is published results. Scientists therefore have a personal interest in publishing as much and as quickly as they can. These personal interests may cause scientists to engage in any number of dubious practices: publishing findings based upon questionable data, publishing the "smallest publishable unit" so that they can generate numerous publications from the same data set, or rushing their work into print prematurely, to name a very few. The interests of science, in contrast, generally require that research be done slowly and carefully, in order that the conclusions be as well-supported as they can be. The interests of science also call for full disclosure (which requires avoiding "smallest possible units") so that findings can be shared with the scientific community in an attempt to further scientific knowledge. Typically, scientists trade off here: They devote as much time and resources as necessary to yield statistically significant data, which they report fully and responsibly. But the temptation to cut corners—to engage in irresponsible research or publishing practices for the sake of personal advancement and gain—is always present. In light of these tensions between personal advancement and the advancement of science, scientific researchers always find themselves in conflicts of interest, even apart from the potential conflicts that arise from funding, an issue we will discuss below.

What should we conclude about conflicts of interest, given that they are in some ways inevitable? It is worth asking why we might think that conflicts of interest are unethical. The original worry about conflicts of interest is that they render the judgment of professionals unreliable: We worry whether the conflicted people are judging on a professional basis or on the basis of some personal or other non-professional interest. Conflicts of interest are not by themselves failures of professional obligation, but they seem to make the conflicted people less likely to fulfill their obligations by presenting a conflicting or competing source of motivation. It is, of course, unethical to pursue one's own interests at the expense of one's professional obligations. The lawyer who overbills his client is wrong, as is the scientist who fabricates data in order to advance her own career. Notice that in such cases it is the person's *actions* that are wrong; finding yourself in a conflict of interest is not by itself unethical.

This is, we believe, a primary source of ethical concern about conflicts of interest. Such conflicts open the door to wrongdoing by providing a source of motivation that conflicts with one's professional responsibilities. Some people will give into temptation and do what is wrong. Conflicts of interest are, we might

say, the occasions of certain kinds of unethical action. If we could avoid all conflicts of interest, then we might be able to avoid at least some wrongdoing and
unethical behavior.

If conflicts of interest are inevitable, what explains the widespread perception that they are inherently unethical? The concerns here are justified, but
they are likely concerns about trust and not about the conflicts themselves. Conflicts of interest have the potential to undermine the trust needed for successful
professional relationships. A lawyer with a reputation for overbilling clients will
not earn clients' trust. The client who does not trust his lawyer severely compromises the lawyer's ability to serve the client's interests. The physician who exhibits more concern with running a business than with caring for patients may
lose his patients' trust, and the loss of that trust may compromise his capacity to
treat his patients successfully. Similarly, when researchers have gross conflicts of
interest, the public trust in scientific research may be undermined. Researchers
must foster all of the relationships we discussed in section 1.4, and earning trust
in those relationships is a crucial condition of popular acceptance and support
of scientific research.

What is the proper policy for handling conflicts of interest? Consider an
example. If research demonstrating the value of computers as educational tools
in the classroom is paid for by Microsoft, that is something that those who read
the results should know. Even if the research is impeccable, it promotes trust
and confidence in the research to have such potential conflicts of interest reported up front. Every piece of information relevant to assessing the scope and
kinds of conflicts of interest should be reported in published research. This information includes not only the source and amount of funding for the research,
but also a summary of the terms on which funding is granted and accepted, the
source of subjects and criteria for inclusion in the subject population, the source
and nature of research protocols employed, and any interests the researchers
might have in the use of the published results. Many scientific journals already
require the disclosure of the source (and sometimes amount) of funding for research. Readers may also wish to know if a researcher is in the employ of a corporation that stands to gain from the researcher's findings. Failure to disclose this
type of conflict of interest can be construed as a deceptive practice and undermine trust.

Notice two points about our analysis. First, we have suggested that conflicts
of interest are endemic to any professional enterprise, including scientific research. It is impossible to avoid all conflicts of interest. That does not show, however, that all conflicts of interest are of the same kind. It is one thing for a
pharmaceutical company to pay a researcher to provide an objective report on
the safety of a new drug; it is quite another for the company to pay the researcher
to report favorably, regardless of the actual findings. The former, while perhaps
involving a conflict of interest, is not by itself in conflict with the researcher's
professional obligations. But the latter certainly does conflict with the researcher's
obligation to discover the truth, in this case about the safety of the drug.

Second, although we have said that conflicts of interest provide occasions for unethical action, that does not mean that *every* conflict of interest leads to unethical action. Is it possible for research into the effects of smoking that is sponsored by a tobacco company to report the truth? Certainly it is. Is it possible for a scientist not to compromise her professional obligations for the sake of personal advancement? Yes, and we believe that this is the rule rather than the exception in scientific research.

The upshot is that the mere existence of a conflict of interest is of little or no ethical import beyond its potential to undermine trust. The reason for this conclusion is that conflicts of interest are inevitable, and so by themselves are neither good nor bad. We should be more interested in determining the kind and scope of the conflict, as well as how likely it is that a researcher's judgment might be rendered unreliable by the conflict. If all of this is right, then our thinking about conflicts of interest needs to be redirected and refocused. Rather than merely identifying a conflict of interest and condemning it, we ought to inquire about what exactly the conflict is, what interests actually conflict, how seriously the conflict is likely to impinge on the research in question, and how materially biased researchers are likely to be in the conflict. If we know all that, then we will be in a better position to assess how reliable the researcher's judgment is likely to be in that context. Of course, if we then suspected a case of misconduct, we might have a better idea where to look for it.

These considerations suggest that our policy toward conflicts of interest should be not one of strict avoidance, which may be impossible, but instead toward full disclosure. In the example cited earlier, a lawyer may be asked to represent a client who is suing a business in which the lawyer happens to hold a financial interest, thereby creating a conflict of interest. The lawyer should not ignore this conflict of interest, but instead be honest with the potential client, laying out the basis of the conflict. The potential client then has the appropriate information to make the decision about whether to hire this particular lawyer. In exercising full disclosure, rather than being deceptive, the lawyer has done her first duty to her client.

A policy of full disclosure will not end research misconduct, but it can help disarm conflicts of interest. By disclosing as many sources of motivation as feasible, researchers will alert others to their conflicts of interest and provide a basis for assessing the reliability of their research.

8.4   FUNDING OF RESEARCH

Basic and applied research is expensive, and researchers already devote considerable energy toward securing funding for their projects in government, academy, and industry. In light of the large amount of money flowing from various government funding agencies and corporations into scientific research, it is worth looking into the ethical issues, other than conflict of interest, that surround the funding of scientific research.

The main source of ethical interest in the area of funding scientific research concerns who decides how research dollars will be spent and how those individuals make those decisions. Many funding agencies decide which grant proposals to fund using procedures similar to those used by journals and publishers for deciding which articles and books to publish. Those procedures involve peer review, or evaluation by experts in the field. Researchers frequently comment on and evaluate each others' proposals and results, and consequently those who are well-known and respected in a particular area can exercise considerable influence over the decision of what research receives funding.

Peer review at its best involves a large number of researchers in the evaluation process, since one goal of peer review in funding agencies is to allow the scientific community to set its own course. When more members of that community contribute to decisions about funding, those decisions are more representative of the scientific community as a whole.

Unfortunately, peer review at funding agencies does not always attain this level of performance. Occasionally, a group of like-minded researchers will make funding decisions that have little to do with the merits of the proposal or the best interests of science. In some cases, projects are funded based upon the interests of non-scientists, such as the public or politicians, who have embraced a particular scientific question. Projects have been funded not because of their scientific merit, but because the questions that they are considering are topical or popular. As a result, researchers who are working on other important research may have a harder time receiving funding. In other cases, even in science, "it's not what you know but who you know." That is, it sometimes happens that funding decisions are made on the basis of personal connections—for instance, the principal investigator might be a former student of the head of the peer review panel—rather than on whether the proposal is among the best received by the funding agency. If the agency is a federal one, this kind of cronyism may be illegal and in violation of the procedural guidelines established by the agency's enabling legislation. It is in any case unethical, in virtue of the fact that it frustrates the goals internal to good science by directing scarce resources toward less promising research.

Intramural funding also gives rise to ethical concern, because when the funding for research comes from within the researcher's home institution, the funding may be contingent on a range of non-scientific concerns. For example, suppose a bio-technology company was funding research into the splicing of "nice" genes into mice. Researchers have discovered that by swapping genes between species of mice, they can make one species as social and friendly as the other species is known to be. Although this is an important scientific discovery, company managers may insist that these discoveries be directed toward some profitable venture. Rather than spending company time and money generating "nice" mice, why not generate "thin" mice, who can eat and eat and never gain any weight? The market for gene therapy that makes people "nicer" may not be significant, but the market for gene therapy that enables people to take in unlimited calories and never gain any weight would be enormous. In many cases, this drive for profit raises no particular ethical concerns. Indeed, private companies have developed countless new medications and products by insisting that their labs produce marketable items. At the same time, as industry funds a larger share of scientific research, the scientific community must be careful not to shortchange basic research for the sake of corporate profit.

In addition, funding decisions may raise questions concerning justice. For example, pharmaceutical companies prefer to spend research and development funds on drugs that they expect to be profitable. A drug for the treatment of prostate cancer, which affects millions of men, is likely to receive more funding than a drug that treats Ewing's Sarcoma, which is a comparatively rare form of bone cancer. The potential for profit from drugs is limited by the size and characteristics of the patient population. To consider a different case, tuberculosis is an infectious disease with a high global mortality rate. Because the patient population for this disease consists mainly of the poor and indigent, drug manufacturers may prefer to develop drugs like Viagra, whose target audience is relatively wealthy. Although they make good business sense and maximize the companies' profits, it is not clear that these decisions serve the interests of justice. Those who suffer from rare diseases and disorders deserve as much of a chance at successful treatment as those who are afflicted by more common ailments. The poor deserve treatment just as the rich do.

These concerns about peer review and the subversion of scientific goals for the sake of some corporate or organizational goal extrinsic to science are not unique to funding agencies. They are, however, important points to keep in mind when thinking about the ethics of funding research.

8.5   OWNERSHIP OF DATA AND RESULTS

A controversial area of scientific research concerns who owns the data generated by scientific research. Researchers need to store data for a variety of reasons. Raw data provide crucial support for the conclusions of a research project, and if anyone challenges those conclusions—be it another scientist or the original researcher seeking to double check the work—having the data permits a repeat analysis. In addition, the data may provide a resource for other work, by the same researcher or others who may gain access to it. The original data may also provide evidence should any concerns of misconduct arise regarding the project. Thus, scientists are well-advised to store their data. We recognize that this recommendation will impose costs: Storage space costs money, as do the paper, computer disks, and other storage media. Moreover, the existence of stored data will mean that people can access those data, which can raise concerns about privacy, if for example courts can subpoena data. We have addressed some of these concerns in section 4.6.

The presence of data raises ethical problems concerning ownership. Who owns all of this data? At least five parties might claim ownership:

1. The researcher has a claim to own the data in virtue of designing and implementing the experimental protocols that generated the data.
2. The funding agency may claim to own it because they paid for it.
3. The host institution where the research was actually performed (if this is different from the funding agency) may claim the data because it stores the data and employs the researcher.
4. The human subjects, if any, may claim to own the data, as it is information about them and so in a sense theirs.
5. The lab assistants and collaborators in the research may claim the data as their own, in view of the fact that they actually performed some of the labor that generated the data.

We believe that each of these claims may have merit. It may well be that in some cases one party and in other cases a different party ought to own the data. We will distinguish two issues concerning ownership and discuss them separately.

First, we should consider the actual possession and disposition of the physical media on which data are recorded. Recently, the types of media on which data are stored have become more varied: In addition to paper, data are now stored on video and audio tape, microfilm, computer floppy disks, hard disks, CD-ROMs, magneto-optical disks, digital tape, and other forms of electronic storage. These electronic storage devices must all be physically stored, and whoever possesses these media in some sense possesses the data on them. The storage of data is a significant expense: Scientific research in the U.S. alone generates hundreds of tons of data-storage media, and a considerable portion of the data on these media has never been analyzed. In general, researchers must be responsible for the safe disposition and storage of their data. The length of time for which data should be kept, as well as the kinds of data collected, ought to be standardized for each discipline. This standardization would allow researchers within a discipline to have uniform expectations about what data they could access and to share the burden of storing data fairly across the discipline. In this sense of ownership, researchers and their home institutions would generally preserve (at least some of) the physical media on which data are stored, according to the appropriate guidelines of the researcher's particular scientific discipline.

Second, we must discuss the more difficult questions concerning access to the data. Another important sense of "owning" the data involves controlling access to the data, including its publication. It might seem as if scientists should have access to all of each others' data: The spirit of open inquiry embedded in the scientific method seems to foster this notion. To some extent, the NIH plan to create an on-line journal, *E-biomed*, might serve this purpose. That journal will make the results of all NIH-sponsored research available at no cost to anyone on the internet. But ethical concerns immediately arise when we recall that much data provided in human subjects research is private and confidential, and so should not be made available in detail to others, a point that was made in section 4.6. The question of access to data is not simple after all.

The situation is complicated by the growing use of private and corporate funds for research. These private funding sources frequently demand control over access to the data, including when and how the data are published. This state of affairs is cause for concern when research funded by such organizations is only *selectively* published, that is, published when the news is good from the perspective of the funding agency. A recent study reported that 98 percent of new drug studies that received funding from the drug's manufacturer were positive, compared to only 79 percent of studies that received no industry support. (If those numbers seem high, recall that Phase I clinical trials of new drugs or therapies take place only after animal and computer models indicate that the ratio of expected benefit to risk is favorable, and that Phase II and III studies take place only after Phase I clinical trials have demonstrated the safety and likely efficacy of the experimental treatment.) That difference, if accurate, suggests either that the corporate-supported research is extraordinarily lucky in its discovery of favorable results or that a range of negative results are being suppressed. The latter seems more likely and is supported by anecdotal evidence from a range of researchers. Had the researchers funded by those sources retained control over the right to publish their data, the comparison might have been more fair.

Such selective reporting of data may constitute trimming, as we discussed in section 7.2. This sort of misconduct might be easier to detect if data were made public, an effort that is supported by the NIH and its proposal for an on-line journal. In general, the spirit of open inquiry encourages scientists to share their data openly. Provided that issues of privacy and confidentiality are addressed with respect to data concerning human subjects, the public availability of raw data may encourage reproducibility and perhaps deter research misconduct. This spirit of openness may conflict, however, with the proprietary impulse to protect one's intellectual property, as we now discuss.

8.6   PATENTS, COPYRIGHTS, AND INTELLECTUAL PROPERTY

Prior to 1980, when the U.S. Congress passed the Bayh-Dole Act, university-based scientific research that received any federal funding was ineligible for patent or copyright protection. The view at the time was that it was unfair to allow researchers and universities to profit from the inventions and products that taxpayers had subsidized. The Bayh-Dole Act, which aimed to spark innovation and creativity in the face of increased competition from Japan and Europe, allowed researchers to patent their inventions and copyright their original work. The Federal Technology Transfer Acts of 1986 and 1989 expanded protections on what has come to be known as intellectual property.

The term 'intellectual property' captures a category of possession that differs from ordinary property in several ways. Unlike a piece of real estate or an automobile, intellectual property is intangible. Information, text, graphics, logos, and the ideas for inventions are all examples of intellectual property. Furthermore, intellectual property is capable of being shared with others without diminishing its value to its owner or indeed its owner's ability to use it. For example, a new technique used in hypnosis can be used again and again, by many people, without the creator of the technique losing the ability to use this technique. The owner of intellectual property may, however, wish to control this sharing in some instances. If every psychologist used this technique, with equally positive results, then the originator of the technique would not derive as great a benefit from its creation as she would if she had some means of protecting its use. Intellectual property now receives a range of legal protections in the U.S., including patent, copyright, trademark, and trade-secret protection.

Patents are legal protections for inventions and are granted by a branch of the U.S. government. They permit the holder of the patent to control the production of an invention for a fixed term of seventeen years. An invention must meet certain criteria in order to be awarded a patent, including thresholds of usefulness, originality, and non-obviousness. A copyright, in contrast, protects not inventions but the written, graphic, or musical expression of ideas. It permits the holder to control the reproduction and distribution of an original work. Copyrights also grant to their holders the right to demand compensation for the reproduction of their work, usually in the form of royalties.

A trademark registers ownership of a name, design, or logo that a company uses to distinguish itself and its products from those of other companies. A trade secret is information that is crucial to a company's business or manufacturing practice that is not known to anyone else. Ownership of a trade secret depends on two claims: The claimant must show that the information has been deliberately withheld from others and that the information is crucial to the business practice. Unlike a patent, trade secrets need not be original or non-obvious, and they need not be useful to anyone but the owner of the trade secret. In general, scientific researchers have pursued stricter protections of patents and copyrights rather than those of trademarks and trade secrets.

These legal rights granted under a range of U.S. laws are based on a variety of ethical principles. First, intellectual property rights are in some ways like any other property rights. We generally acknowledge the effort and labor that go into making something by granting ownership and property rights to those who make the things, unless the labor is contracted for and the worker is paid instead. By extension, when someone creates something intangible, we may treat it as a kind of property and consider its originator the owner. This rationale for property rights is known as the "desert approach": The creator of a piece of property deserves protection in virtue of having created the item. This rationale emerges from a libertarian conception of ownership, as we discussed in section 2.4. An alternative justification for property rights—and one that seems to be the foundation of many legal protections of those rights—relies on utilitarian considerations, such as the claim that society will be better off and people with ideas will be more creative when property rights are protected. Both accounts afford the owner of a piece of property certain moral claims to the protection of that property, and these moral claims have provided the basis for our legal protections of property rights. They also provide some of the justification for principles prohibiting plagiarism, misappropriation, and other forms of theft, as we described in Chapter 7.

This simple picture of ownership can become extremely complicated, however, once we take into account the circumstances of modern scientific research and technology. For one thing, it is the exception now rather than the rule that an individual alone, with no outside funding or support, creates an invention or copyrighted material through scientific research. Rather, projects in biomedical engineering, industrial agriculture, pharmaceuticals, and a whole host of industries involve hundreds of researchers working under the auspices of both public and private institutions and in both corporate and academic environments. Often a project will have both public and private funding. Under those circumstances, who owns the invention or work? Who is entitled to claim the intellectual property?

Once again, several answers are plausible:

1. The researcher(s) who originally designed, implemented, and tested the invention or work have a claim to the intellectual property on the ground that it was the result of their intellectual work.
2. The funding agency may claim ownership, in virtue of having contracted for the labor of the researchers involved in the project. This claim is analogous to the claim of a car manufacturer to own the new cars its workers build: the workers build them, but they are paid for their work and do not own the products.
3. The host institution where the research was performed may claim ownership on the ground that it is the institution, not the funding agency, that employs the researchers responsible for producing the intellectual property in question.

Each of these claims has some initial plausibility. In fact, it is possible to share ownership of intellectual property, and this is frequently done. As always, it is best for researchers to be aware of these issues and to negotiate them in advance with funding agencies, home institutions, and others who might lay claim to the intellectual property that may emerge from their research.

A distinct set of ethical concerns arises when we ask what may be owned. If you invent a new device for removing gallstones, then you may obviously apply for a patent. But what if you create a new gene or a new living cell line? Is it possible or ethical to patent life? Utilitarian reasoning does not seem to decide the question of whether human gene sequences should be open to patents: Some consequences of patenting genes might be harmful, especially if one could patent an entire sequence and so effectively own a human being (which would constitute slavery). Others, though, seem beneficial, as when a company patents a sequence that could, through gene therapy, eliminate a genetic disease such as Huntington's Disease. In general, science and technology can be put to good or bad uses, and it does not seem that denying patents to human gene sequences will change this fact. A Kantian might claim that patenting human genes would immorally treat people as property. It is less clear what other ethical perspectives have to contribute to this debate.

Ethical questions surrounding ownership arise when we consider the possibility of owning something that has never been owned before, such as a gene sequence. This particular question has yet to be resolved; our on-going sensitivity to this kind of question will be important as technology offers new possibilities of ownership and the application of legal protections to claims of ownership.

8.7   SUMMARY

Conflicts of interest are endemic to all professional activities, including scientific research. Researchers will always be tempted to compromise the scientific method, which is time-consuming and resource intensive, for the sake of personal gain, whether in the form of money, promotion, reputation, publication, or some other reward. The existence of conflicts of interest cannot by itself be a source of ethical concern. Rather, we have tried to suggest, conflicts of interest are worrisome because they provide the occasion for unethical behavior. Where the temptation to engage in misconduct is particularly strong—if a researcher's concerns about promotion are pressing, or if a large amount of funding is at stake—a researcher's judgment may be compromised. As a result, the results of research under those circumstances may be suspect. The best policy seems to be full disclosure. Researchers should disclose especially the source of funding for research, as this is a common source of conflicts of interest. Such disclosure will also promote the trust that conflicts of interest threaten.

Concerns about ownership are rife in scientific research, and they are not always easy to resolve. Since so many people may have at least apparent claims of ownership, including subjects, researchers, technicians, funding agencies, and home institutions, it is worthwhile to sort out ownership claims as far as possible in advance. Ownership may involve both the physical possession of data and controlling access to it. In addition to concerns about the ownership of data, a complete treatment of the ethics of ownership in scientific research must examine the ownership of useful or marketable results. These typically take two forms, patented inventions and copyrighted information. Both forms of intellectual property protection may be useful to scientific researchers.

8.8   CASE STUDIES

Case 8.1: Dr. Ericson is a reviewer of grant proposals for an NIH panel. One of the proposals that he reads contains some pilot data that catch his attention. The proposal itself is unlikely to be funded: The methodology appears to be unsound in some respects, and the project is overly ambitious for the results that the applicant anticipates. Dr. Ericson sees, however, that those data support the conclusions of his own research in the same area. How can Dr. Ericson make use of that data? Who owns that information? What are the issues concerning conflict of interest? How might Dr. Ericson's professional responsibilities as a reviewer conflict with his responsibilities as a scientist?

Case 8.2: Ms. Rao and Ms. Lin are administrators at a pharmaceutical corporation. They are members of the budgeting team for funding research and development of new drugs. The team is considering proposals for research into two new drugs: Monofil, which may promote the growth of hair in balding men, and Nixomal, which has promise as a treatment for malaria. Ms. Rao has been defending Monofil and recommends it, while Ms. Lin advocates the support of Nixomal. What sorts of considerations might they use to support their views? How should funds be dedicated to research on different diseases? Should it depend on the size of the patient population or their ability to pay? Why should private companies develop drugs that they expect will generate little profit? Are they being unreasonable in striving to maintain profitability?

REFERENCES AND FURTHER READING

M. Baram, "Trade Secrets: What Price Loyalty?," in *Moral Issues in Business,* 2nd edition, ed. V. Barry, Belmont, CA: Wadsworth, 1983.

D. Gergen, "The 7 Percent Solution: Funding Basic Scientific Research Is Vital to America's Future," *US News and World Report,* 19 May, 1997: 79.

Dorothy Nelkin, *Science as Intellectual Property,* New York: Macmillan, 1984.

V. Weil and J. Snapper, eds., *Owning Scientific and Technical Information,* New Brunswick, NJ: Rutgers University Press, 1989.

Conflict of Interest

Larry May

> The splitting of the self would, at least, have the finality of destroying its presumptuousness.
> —Jean-François Lyotard, *The Differend*

Conflicts of interest are to be avoided, so the prevailing wisdom has it, because the professional's objective judgment is compromised. When a professional has a conflict of interest, the professional's self is divided, with one part of the self

Larry May, "Conflict of Interest," in *Professional Ethics and Social Responsibility,* ed. Daniel B. Wuste (Lanham: Rowman & Littlefield, 1994) 67–82. Reprinted by permission of the publisher.

pulled toward serving the interests of one's client, and the other part of the self pulled toward personal gain (or some other interest) at the expense of serving the client's interests. *Black's Law Dictionary* defines such conflicts in terms of "a clash between public interest and the private pecuniary interest of the individual concerned."[1] Most codes of professional conduct urge people to avoid conflicts of interest in order to be more integrated professionals, and to be more likely to avoid the violation of their professional duties. Generally, the conflict of interest literature is in agreement with the codes. For example, in their monograph, *Conflicts of Interest in Engineering,* Wells, Jones, and Davis write that "[m]ost conflicts of interest can be avoided. We can take care not to put ourselves in a position where contrary influences or divided interests might undermine our ability to do what we are supposed to do."[2]

In this paper I will draw on some very recent work in postmodern social theory[3] that challenges the view that conflicts within the self are to be avoided or minimized. The postmodern approach to the world is generally to celebrate conflicts, to think of them as part of what constitutes the self. The self is just the diversity of conflicting interests that are constantly operating over the course of a life, if indeed there is such a thing as a stable and coherent concept of a single self at all. While some postmodernists think of the self as an incoherent notion, a view that I do not endorse, postmodernism has important insights nonetheless, which moral philosophers would do well to take seriously.

Postmodernism contains at least two divergent strains. Some postmodernists think of the self as a fiction, or even as an incoherent notion. Jacques Derrida is the best-known defender of such a view. Derrida and his followers have largely eschewed talk of morality and politics, opting instead for a version of nihilism. But there is another postmodern strain that is highly critical of the modernist conception of the self, but which still thinks that there is enough coherence to the self to provide a basis for moral and political obligation. Jean-François Lyotard is the best example of a postmodernist of this sort. In what follows I will follow the latter rather than the former strain in postmodern social theory.

Most modernist discussions of conflicts of interest merely assume that they are bad things to be avoided, especially when they adversely affect the independent judgment of the professional. But there are some exceptions. Charles Wolfram, for instance, begins his handbook, *Modern Legal Ethics,* by noting that

> conflicts of interest are part of the world around us, always have been and inevitably must be. . . . In a sense, every representation begins with a lawyer-client conflict. If the representation is for a fee, the lawyer's economic interest will be to maximize the amount of the fee and the client's will be to minimize it.[4]

I wish to argue that we will seriously misunderstand the moral difficulties of conflicts of interest if we do not realize the extent to which some conflicts of interest are "inevitable" or at least not necessarily problematic in professional settings.

The inevitability of some conflicts of interest in professional settings should not lead us to think that all conflicts are morally permissible. And, indeed, I will attempt to explain which conflicts can and should be avoided. But the thesis of this essay is that conflicts of interest per se are not morally problematic. What makes some conflicts of interest morally problematic is that they involve deception or they infringe client autonomy, but not all conflicts of interest are of this sort and hence not all conflicts are morally problematic. In presenting this thesis I will consider and reject the standard accounts of what is wrong with conflicts of interest. Let us first turn to some cases that will begin to illustrate why the extreme view, namely, that all conflicts of interest are morally problematic and should be rejected.

Real Estate Brokers—Constant Conflicts?

Quite recently my wife and I had the unhappy task of selling one house and buying another. I was struck by the fact that the real estate brokers with whom we worked in buying our St. Louis home were involved in what would standardly be called a conflict of interest. Most of such a broker's work involves showing houses to prospective buyers and advising the buyer whether to place a bid on a certain piece of property and at what price. Some real estate brokers who claim to work for the buyer will actually be paid by the seller. Assuming a zero-sum game, every decrease in price offered by the buyer clashes with the pecuniary interests of the buyer's broker, since the broker's commission is determined as a percentage of the selling price. There is indeed a conflict of interest here since there will surely be situations where it is in the buyer's best interest to offer a lower price or back out of a sale, whereas it is clearly in the personal interest of the buyer's broker to advise the buyer to accept a higher-price counteroffer and go through with the sale. Yet, these brokers see nothing wrong in these situations. My view is that their claims should not be lightly dismissed.

The identity of a real estate broker is conflicted. On the one hand, due to the sheer time they spend with buyers, guiding them through house after house, they clearly work for, or at least with, the buyers. But on the other hand, it is quite clear that their business and personal interests coincide with the seller's interests. As long as real estate brokers are paid by the seller, it is in a sense inevitable that there will be a conflict of interest between the broker's personal interests and the interests of their buyer-clients. The brokers I met, however, continued to talk as if they worked for the buyers. Nevertheless, it was clear that they did not take an adversarial role toward the seller, nor did they have any desire to do so. It was as if they assumed that everyone knew, or at least should have known, that the brokers had personal interests in being paid as high a commission as possible, and that this common knowledge meant that it was not problematic to maintain nonadversarial relations with both parties. Such an arrangement places brokers into a different category than some other professionals.

Real estate brokers who work with buyers could reasonably claim that their main professional duty is to facilitate housing market transactions, rather than to serve in an adversarial process in which they "represent" one person's interests against another person's interests. If facilitation and cooperation are indeed the goals they seek to serve, and if it is assumed that both buyer and seller have an interest in houses being sold rather than not, then the broker's interest in his or her own greater monetary gain is not necessarily, even though it is traditionally thought to be, in conflict with their buyer client's interests. In a sense, real estate brokers can take a communitarian rather than contractarian view of the world, and this may at least partially explain why they are less troubled by their potential or actual conflicts of interest. The problem is that many real estate brokers continue to talk as if, and often claim explicitly that, they do "represent" the interests of the buyer. Because of this fact, these professionals remain entangled in very problematic conflicts of interest.

There is a sense in which many other professionals are caught in conflicts of interest from the beginning of their relationships with their clients. Lawyers, doctors, engineers, accountants, etc., generally do not work for free and are, therefore, as Charles Wolfram points out, already in a conflict of interest the minute they begin work for a client, since their interest in making a larger income clashes with the client's interest in paying as little as possible to solve their legal, medical, safety or financial problems. More important though, many professional lawyers, doctors, engineers, accountants, etc., work for large organizations and corporations. Their salaries are not paid directly by a client, and so their relationship to their clients is often one that involves a conflict of interest since the interest in serving the organization or corporation, which pays the professional, is often at odds with serving the interests of the client. This is evident, for instance, where doctors work for health maintenance organizations that put pressure on them to minimize expensive diagnostic testing, even though such testing may be in the interests of their patients.

In addition, engineers, for instance, are not only supposed to serve their clients' interests but also the larger societal interest in public safety. This latter interest often comes into conflict with the former interest, when, for example, an engineer is urged by her company to use the least costly, and weaker, material in a product even though public safety would dictate a stronger and more costly material. Similarly, lawyers like to forget that they are supposed to be serving the interest of justice, a paramount societal interest, while also serving their client's interests. Yet, they are paid by those whose interests are often at odds with the societal interests these professionals are supposed to be serving, as is true when criminal lawyers are told by their clients of the location of missing bodies, for instance. If I am right about there being rampant conflicts of interest in most professions, should we advise our students not to become professionals at all, so as not to risk entering into morally problematic behavior?

There are several strategies that could be employed to avoid these difficulties. The American Bar Association's code of professional responsibility stipulates that lawyers only need to concern themselves with conflicts that have a "reasonable probability" of interfering "with a lawyer's professional judgment"[5] by compromising the lawyer's chief professional duties of loyalty and confidentiality.

Michael Davis sees the ABA standard as a way to capture what it is about some conflicts of interest that is morally problematic.[6] We could formulate a general rule; namely, that professionals should only be concerned with those conflicts of interest that are likely to have a material effect on their professional judgments. But even if the inherent ambiguity of the word "material" is overlooked, would such a strategy substantially limit the cases of conflict of interest that professionals should worry about?

Such a strategy runs into the following difficulty: one's professional judgment can be materially affected by almost any personal monetary incentive. If real estate brokers working for buyers are being paid by the sellers, then their professional judgment is always at risk of being clouded and they are always in such a compromised position that, from the perspective of the way that conflicts have been viewed, they should not continue in their profession. And yet, it is worth considering whether or not there is any insight to be gained from the moral intuitions of these brokers, which clearly tells them that they are not being morally compromised.

Lawyers have long recognized that not all conflicts of interest are morally problematic. Not only has their code distinguished between conflicts that are likely to affect professional judgment and conflicts that are not, but the judges who interpret the lawyers' obligations have recognized that in many cases the informed consent of the client to a conflict relieves the conflict of interest of its morally problematic character.[7] In the following sections, we will build on this insight in conjunction with some insights gained from the standpoint of postmodernism.

Postmodernism and the Interests of the Self

My view is that what makes conflicts morally problematic is not merely that judgments are compromised, but in addition, that the professionals continue to assert that they are able to serve the interests of their clients unambiguously, even though they know, or should know, that their judgments are likely to be clouded. As I will argue, it is the deceptiveness or the infringement of client autonomy that is morally problematic, not merely the compromised judgment. The alternative I advocate, informed by the postmodern perspective, is to accept rather than decry such potential conflicts, worrying only about the possible deceptions or infringements of client autonomy that might result. Instead of engaging in the often futile attempt to eliminate conflicts, I follow Lyotard who calls for a "metalepsis," a change in the "level of one's take." From my own perspective, the change in the way we respond to conflicts should allow clients to become fully informed about them through a full and open disclosure of the conflict of interest.

Professionals should only feel the need to avoid a conflict of interest if those who have been made aware of these conflicts, and who are likely to be adversely affected by the judgments rendered in such conflict situations, are not willing to accept or for some other reason cannot consent to the situation. In such cases, the professional should either remove the cause of the conflict or terminate his or her relationship with the person whose interests the professional is supposed to serve. Otherwise, the chief professional duty will be that of full and open disclosure of potential and actual conflicts (along with a correspondingly diminished fiduciary duty—to be explained later), rather than the more strenuous and sometimes impossible task of eliminating or evading all possible or actual conflicts.

From a postmodern perspective, selves are always multiply interested and they are also often involved in conflicts concerning those multiple interests. Lawyers, for example, are so often involved in various conflicts of interest that they should discontinue the practice of advertising themselves as persons who act only in the interest of a client. And the American ideal of professional life, which is modeled on the way the lawyers in our society have conceived of themselves, should no longer glorify the single-minded pursuer of a client or patient's interest. Rather, there should be a great deal more honesty in the way that professionals present themselves to their clients and patients.

Lyotard and other postmodern theorists argue that modernists make the mistake of assuming that the self can be objective and unconflicted in its judgments, and that the self can blind itself to, or remove, all of its egoistic motivations.[8] For Lyotard and other postmodernists, the self is always seen as "in progress,"[9] pulled toward several different poles at once. It is never fixed or settled, and if one were to take away all of the various poles, or interests, to which it is attracted or repelled the self would be lost altogether. Similarly, if one were to try to make of the self something that is not drawn in several directions at once, the lack of tension would often destroy the self.[10] It is characteristic of the modern point of view, which Lyotard wholeheartedly rejects, to think that the self or mind can attain an objective, universal, and hence unconflicted standpoint.

The postmodernist's target is well presented by Wells, Jones, and Davis when they write:

> A conflict of interest is like dirt in a sensitive gauge. For the same reason rational persons want reliable gauges, they want those upon whose judgment they rely to avoid conflict of interest (insofar as practical) . . . though conflicts of interest cannot always be avoided, they can always be escaped. We can end the association, divest ourselves of the interest, or otherwise get beyond the influence that might otherwise compromise our judgment.[11]

The postmodernist would deny that the self is indeed like "a sensitive gauge," which, with the proper care, can be kept clean insofar as it is unconflicted.

Lyotard uses the term "differend" to refer to an impasse or unresolveable conflict that often characterizes social interactions.[12] Occasionally, a self is able to communicate with another self in such a way that conflicts are resolved. But in most cases, it is "not possible to evade the differend by anticipating it."[13] While Lyotard's analysis of differends is meant to concern all forms of conflict that would involve some sort of stated claim by two parties, I find it especially useful in understanding why conflicts of interest are often inevitable and, contrary to prevailing sentiment, why they are not things which professionals can or should always avoid.

Lyotard, as is characterisitic of postmodern thinkers, seriously considers the proposal that since we have such intractable problems with conflicts of interest, we should dispense with the idea of professional obligations and duties altogether in such cases. He writes:

> Instead, obligation should be described as a scandal for the one who is obligated: deprived of the "free" use of oneself, abandoned by one's narcissistic image, opposed in this, inhibited in that, worried over not being able to be oneself without further ado. But these are phenomenological or psychoanalytic descriptions of a dispossessed or cloven consciousness. . . . They maintain the self even in the very acknowledgement of its dispersion.[14]

Lyotard does not follow the nihilistic postmodernists. While he does propose that we give up our "nostalgia for the self"—that is, our nostalgia for an unconflicted self that knows its obligations absolutely—he nonetheless urges that we retain the notion of obligation, although it is a more time-bound notion of obligation.

Lyotard argues that we should reject modernist conceptions of universal moral obligation.[15] But he also contends that obligations are like the rules of a language game, binding on those who choose to play the game. This fits nicely with the notion of professional duties sometimes envisioned in codes of professional conduct.[16] Professionals take on special duties by agreeing to project themselves into the world as having unique expertise.[17] But there is no reason to think that these duties should involve unrealistic self-sacrifice on the professional's part. In keeping with Lyotard's brand of postmodernism, I will argue for a revised understanding of the fiduciary relationship between professional and client. First, let me say a bit more about the core problem in conflict-of-interest cases, deceptiveness, and the infringement of client autonomy.

Deception and Client Autonomy

Michael Davis correctly states the major moral difficulty with conflicts of interest when he writes:

> if a lawyer does not at least warn his client of the conflict, he does more than weaken a guarantee worth preserving. He presents himself as having a judgment more reliable than in fact it is. He invites a trust the invitation itself betrays.[18]

As I shall argue in this section, Davis is largely correct, but for the wrong reasons. Davis goes wrong, as do most modern theorists, in believing that there is a type of professional judgment that is trustworthy and reliable in that it is uninfluenced by the material considerations of one's other interests.

Lawyers have perpetuated the view that professionals can and should be expected to serve absolutely the interests of their clients. Wolfram states the point well when he says:

> Whatever may be the models that obtain in other legal cultures, the client-lawyer relationship in the United States is founded on the lawyer's *virtually total* loyalty to the client and the client's interests. . . . The entrenched lawyerly conception is that the client-lawyer relationship is the embodiment of centuries of established and stable tradition.[19]

Other professionals have come to model themselves on the Anglo-American law profession.

The idea that professionals should serve "virtually total[ly]" the interests of their clients is at best unrealistic and at worst deceptive. It is unrealistic, as we will see, because it asks lawyers to blind themselves to their own interests in ways that are nearly impossible to meet, and because it ignores the fact that there is often no objectively right way to conceive of someone's interests. It is deceptive because it creates false expectations on the part of the clients, expectations of loyalty that, when thwarted, lead clients to a position where they lose control over their cases. The clients unknowingly render themselves vulnerable to possible abuses of trust that they would otherwise remain vigilantly on guard against. Lawyers betray the trust they have solicited when they act as if they are capable of rendering judgments in behalf of their clients' interests that are unaffected by their other interests.

There are many factors that intrude upon a professional's judgment, rendering the notion of a "virtually total loyalty" in serving the client's interest itself quite suspicious. Consider again the case of lawyers. Lawyers who are in private practice must be constantly concerned about paying the rent—indeed many lawyers find themselves spending so much time getting, keeping, and billing clients that they come to regard the practice of law as a type of business. Yet rarely is this the picture of lawyers that lawyers themselves present to the public. In addition, the lawyers I have known are also highly ambitious individuals who often see the pursuit of a particular client's case as a means of furthering their own careers. Furthermore, lawyers also have political agendas. As Wolfram and others have pointed out "even in pro bono representations, the ideological or altruistic motives that induce a lawyer to offer legal services" can often obscure the pursuit of the client's interests.[20] All of these factors make it unrealistic to think that lawyers can offer "virtually total loyalty" to their client's interests, a loyalty lawyers nonetheless continue to claim to be the hallmark of their profession.

It is an infringement of client autonomy for professionals to deny clients the knowledge they need to decide whether to entrust themselves to a particular professional. It is deceptive of professionals to present themselves as capable of rendering objective judgments when they are aware of conflicts that will make it even more likely than normal that their "objective" judgments are compromised. This is why some conflicts of interest are morally problematic. But if a professional is quite open about the interests that he or she has, or is likely to have, that are at odds with the client's interest, and secures from the client an understanding and consent to the lawyer's continued service under these circumstances, conflicts of interest are no more troubling, from the moral point of view, than other cases of consensual client services.

It may be objected that in order for possible conflicts to be disclosed my proposal calls for professionals to be able to identify what all of their interests are, a feat sometimes not feasible. On my view, professionals need to be, or to become, self-reflective concerning their interests. But this is no more troublesome for my view than it is for any other view of conflicts of interest. The traditional view, for instance, which calls for professionals to *avoid* all conflicts of interest surely must also call for professionals to be, or to become, aware of what their interests are that may conflict with the client's interests. My view is no worse off than the traditional view.

It may be further objected that I have misidentified the morally suspicious feature of conflicts of interest. Some might claim that the difficulty with all conflicts of interest is that they create temptation for wrongdoing. There are two things to be said about such a view. First, my postmodern orientation leads me to think that at least some conflicts of interest are not occasions for wrongdoing at all, but manifestations of the perfectly legitimate situation where one has multiple and conflicting motivations. Second, wrongdoing occurs, when it does, because of a presumed promise that all the professional's other interests have been subordinated to the client's interests. But when professionals stop claiming that they can subordinate all of their other interests, the basis of the wrongdoing also begins to disappear. Disclosed conflicts that are consented to are not temptations for wrongdoing because the client has waived the right that would otherwise be the basis of a claim of wrongdoing based on the conflict of interest.

From the standpoint of deceptiveness and client autonomy, real estate brokers are better off than lawyers. Real estate brokers make it quite well known that they are working toward the consummation of real estate sales and that their income depends on securing higher rather than lower prices for these pieces of real estate. While they sometimes claim to represent the interests of the buyer, and in this sense perpetuate a deception, they do not claim to serve these interests absolutely. Those who are in the market for real estate are made much more aware of the conflicted nature of the brokers that they encounter than is true of those who find themselves in need of legal counsel. In contrast to the case of real estate brokers, lawyers make it very difficult for clients to see the possible ways in which the client's interests will not necessarily be served. In this way, lawyers infringe client autonomy especially when they continue to assert so strongly that they are uniquely situated to devote themselves to the client's interests.

Next consider a different kind of case taken from engineering. A mechanical engineer is asked to give an informal opinion about a matter that the company he works for is planning to bring before the product standards committee of his profession at large. This engineer helps his work associates draft a letter of

inquiry, which is then submitted to his profession's product standards committee for review. As it turns out, this very engineer serves on the relevant product
standards committee and is assigned the task of responding to the inquiry (which
he had helped draft) in behalf of the professional committee. The engineer gives
a ruling that is favorable to the drafters of the inquiry, who also happen to be his
associates at the company for which he works. A competing company is placed
in a disadvantageous position as a result of the ruling and eventually goes into
bankruptcy. Needless to say, the ruling also works to the advantage of the engineer's own company. In 1982, the U.S. Supreme Court reviewed a similar case,
and held that the professional association had acted wrongly in allowing the engineer to review an inquiry that he himself had helped to draft.[21]

Since it is true that professional engineers must staff such committees as the
professional product standards committee discussed above, and since most engineers are employed by private organizations that will need to get rulings from
such committees, it will inevitably happen that conflicts of interest manifest
themselves in such contexts. It is my view that there is nothing initially wrong
with the engineer in question consulting with his work associates and also draft-
ing a response to the inquiry made by his work associates. Surely it is a mistake
to think that professionals must never assume roles that will possibly conflict
with other roles they *may* play. In the case at issue, the engineer needed to inform
the professional organization as well as the parties who would possibly be affected by the professional organization's ruling.

The postmodern perspective I am advocating in this paper finds it odd indeed
to think that all, or even most, conflicts of interest should be avoided. If, for instance, engineers avoided such conflicts as those described above, their professional lives and the world in which they live would become tremendously
impoverished. Engineers could only serve on those professional standards committees that would never hear cases brought by the companies these engineers
work for. Or, perhaps, such committees could not be staffed at all by engineers
working in the private sector, even though it is just these engineers who are most
likely to retain a day-to-day understanding of the likely problems of the products
in question. In other professions, perhaps including real estate brokerage, avoiding conflicts of interest might mean that the very profession itself would disappear.

Deception and infringement of client autonomy are the key moral problems
when personal interest conflicts with client interest. If the engineer in the case discussed above had informed all relevant parties that he had a special, work-related
interest in the outcome of the product standard review he was preparing, and if
these people had consented to let him continue to serve them, and to notify others who might come to rely on the report, then the writing of this report would
have posed no special moral problems. As it was, though, the people who relied
on the report did not have sufficient knowledge of the writer's interests to be able
to assess it properly; their autonomy was infringed through the lack of such disclosure. They were put into a vulnerable position that they would otherwise have
wanted to guard against. In what follows, I attempt to set out a new model for

understanding the fiduciary duties that have traditionally been seen as the basis for requiring professionals to avoid potential and actual conflicts of interest.

Fiduciary Duties and Professional Responsibility

In law and other professional contexts, there is thought to be a fiduciary relationship between professional and client. *Black's Law Dictionary* defines "fiduciary" as follows:

> The term is derived from the Roman law, and means (as a noun) a person holding the character of a trustee, or a character analogous to that of a trustee, in respect to the trust and confidence involved in it and the scrupulous good faith and candor which it requires.[22]

A "fiduciary relation" establishes a situation where various professionals "in equity and good conscience" are "bound to act in good faith and with due regard to interests of one reposing the confidence."[23] When professionals are viewed as fiduciaries, they are thought to be bound to act as if their interests were those of their clients and hence to sacrifice their own interests for the sake of their client's interests.

It is instructive to contrast this situation with that of the standard way that two parties are viewed if they are not in a fiduciary relationship. In his book, *The Critical Legal Studies Movement*, Roberto Unger rightly points out that in law, nonfiduciary relations are ones in which neither party is thought to owe anything to the other: "the other party's interests can be treated as of no account as long as the rightholder remains within his zone of discretionary action."[24] The contrast between normal commercial relations and fiduciary relations is quite striking—surely there is a middle position that would more appropriately apply to conflict-of-interest cases. Like Unger, in this section I will strive for a view of fiduciary relations that takes account of the reality of professional life.

Unger proposes a fiduciary standard that "requires each party to give some force to the other party's interests, though less than to his own."[25] This proposal is a compromise between the overly minimalistic notion of simple contractual obligation that some might apply to professional-client relationships, and the unrealistic selflessness of the legal model of fiduciary duty. Unger goes too far here. Surely, it is not too much to require professionals to place the interests of their clients at least on a par with their most strongly held personal interests. The special status afforded professionals calls for some serious attempt to serve the client's interest. In order to give proper care to the client, the client's interest must be given serious weight, and this means that it should be at least *equal to* the professional's most strongly held personal interests.

Those who have voluntarily placed themselves into positions of trust concerning the interests of others must give careful consideration to those interests. But it is simply a mistake to demand selfless service to the client's interest. Since "virtually total loyalty" is not a realistic possibility in professional life, the chief duty of professionals cannot be absolute service to their client's interests. Hence, the chief professional duty concerning conflicts of interest should be merely the duty of full disclosure, along with the duty to withdraw from serving the client if the client finds the disclosed conflict objectionable. It is too much to expect professionals to have a duty to be totally loyal or to place the interests of their clients significantly above their own interests. As I have indicated, the perpetuation of the myth that professionals have these more strenuous duties is both unrealistic and deceptive.

It is important to note that many of the most serious harms that occur in conflict-of-interest cases result because one party becomes less vigilant on the assumption that another party is serving absolutely the first party's interests. When the professional raises expectations of total loyalty and trustworthiness, then it would indeed implicate the professional in whatever harms result from the diminished vigilance of the client. This is also true of those expectations raised by the profession of which a given professional is a member. But as with other collective responsibilities, an individual can diminish or extinguish his or her personal responsibility by taking steps to overcome the expectations raised by the profession at large. By explicitly stating the interests the professional has that are likely to conflict with the interests of the client, the professional at least partially distances himself or herself from the expectations of objectivity that the rest of the profession may raise. This heightens the vigilance of the client and makes it less likely that the client will be harmed.

Professional responsibility is not merely a matter of conforming to the fiduciary duties one has, even if we understand these duties in the way in which I have suggested. Rather, it is important that elements of shame exist alongside of the guilt that is associated with the direct violation of a professional duty. Even when a professional has done all he or she can do to avoid harm to a client, professionals should deeply regret whatever harms nonetheless occur, and when those harms result from actions taken by the profession as a whole, shame is often not at all misplaced.[26] But the appropriateness of such shame should not lead us to think that professionals have a *duty* to serve absolutely the interests of their clients, such that they should feel guilt whenever they let personal interest interfere with the pursuit of the client's interest. As I have argued, such guilt is appropriate only in certain cases involving deception or infringement of client autonomy.

I have tried to provide a new basis for understanding what is morally problematic about some conflicts of interest in professional life. In arguing that the deceptiveness and infringement of client autonomy of certain conflicts of interest is their undoing, I have indicated a straightforward strategy for rendering many conflicts of interest morally unproblematic; namely, full and open disclosure of potential conflicts by the professional. In general, professionals have for too long mistakenly thought that they can and should avoid all conflicts of interest, as if it were possible for the professional thereby to provide objective judgments and absolutely loyal service for the client. I have provided a challenge to this assumption that has drawn heavily on a postmodern perspective of social and personal conflicts. But, at least in this case, reliance on some postmodern ideas has not thrown us into a moral abyss,[27] but has rather clarified the picture of a certain part of the moral landscape we call professional life.[28]

Notes

[1]*Black's Law Dictionary,* fifth edition (St. Paul, Minn.: West Publishing Co., 1979): 271.

[2]Paula Wells, Hardy Jones, and Michael Davis, *Conflicts of Interest in Engineering* (Dubuque, Iowa: Kendall/Hunt Publishing Co., 1986): 21.

[3]By "postmodern social theory" I mean roughly what Lyotard means by "the postmodern perspective" on social bonds. Among other things, Lyotard says that there are irreconcilable voices in society, but that "the self does not amount to much" in trying to resolve these conflicts. He writes: "Consensus is an outmoded and suspect value. But justice as a value is neither outmoded nor suspect. We must thus arrive at an idea and practice of justice that is not linked to that of consensus." Lyotard, *The Postmodern Condition,* trans. Geoff Bennington and Brian Massumi (Minneapolis: University of Minnesota Press, 1984): 15, 66.

[4]Charles Wolfram, *Modern Legal Ethics* (St. Paul, Minn.: West Publishing Co., 1986): 312–13.

[5]See Canon 5 of the American Bar Association's *Code of Professional Responsibility and Code of Judicial Conduct,* 1976; and see Wolfram, *Modern Legal Ethics,* 316, 324.

[6]Michael Davis, "Conflict of Interest," *Business and Professional Ethics Journal,* vol. 1, no. 4, (Summer 1982): 17–27.

[7]Wolfram, *Modern Legal Ethics,* 337–49.

[8]See Iris Young's excellent book, *Justice and the Politics of Difference* (Princeton: Princeton University Press, 1990).

[9]Jean-François Lyotard, *Peregrinations: Law, Form, Event* (New York: Columbia University Press, 1988): 6.

[10]Lyotard, *Peregrinations,* 5.

[11]Wells, Jones, and Davis, *Conflicts of Interest,* 20–21.

[12]Lyotard, *The Differend,* trans. George Van Den Abbeele (Minneapolis: University of Minnesota Press, 1989): 9, 13.

[13]Ibid., 19.

[14]Ibid., 109–10.

[15]Ibid., 127.

[16]Dorothy Emmet ably argues for the conclusion that professional codes are matters of role morality and not universal morality. See her book, *Rules, Roles and Relations* (Boston: Beacon Press, 1966): 158–63.

[17]For a more detailed analysis of the moral basis of a professional's duties, especially concerning negligence, see Chapter 5 of my book, *Sharing Responsibility* (Chicago: University of Chicago Press, 1992).

[18]Davis, "Conflict of Interest," 21.

[19]Wolfram, *Modern Legal Ethics,* 146. Emphasis added.

[20]Ibid., 313.

[21]See *American Society of Mechanical Engineers v. Hydrolevel Corporation* (72 L Ed 2d 330) 1982. For an extended discussion of this case see my essay "Professional Action and the Liabilities of Professional Associations: ASME v. Hydrolevel Corp.," *Business and*

Professional Ethics Journal, vol. 2, no. 1 (Fall 1982): 1–14. Also see Wells, Jones, and Davis, *Conflicts of Interest,* 1–24.

[22]*Black's Law Dictionary,* 563.

[23]*Black's Law Dictionary,* 564.

[24]Roberto Mangabeira Unger, *The Critical Legal Studies Movement* (Cambridge, Mass.: Harvard University Press, 1983): 83.

[25]Unger, *Critical Legal Studies,* 83.

[26]See my paper "Metaphysical Guilt and Moral Taint" in *Collective Responsibility,* ed. Stacey Hoffman and Larry May (Savage, Md.: Rowman and Littlefield Publishers, 1991).

[27]See Edith Wyschogrod's *Saints and Postmodernism* (Chicago: University of Chicago Press, 1990), for another attempt at arguing that postmodernism can be conceived as a nonrelativistic standpoint. Also see my review of Wyschogrod's book in *Ethics,* July 1992.

[28]I am grateful to Roger Gibson, Paul Gomberg, Dan Wueste, Bill McBride, Marilyn Friedman, and Bruce Russell for helpful comments on earlier versions of this paper.

General Overview of the Intellectual Property System

Rochelle Cooper Dreyfuss

We are a people increasingly dependent upon innovation. Its fruits support our standard of living and its profits contribute substantially to our prosperity. The central role that invention plays in our economy demands close examination of those factors which influence its creation, distribution, and use. This [essay] looks at one of these mechanisms: the laws of intellectual property that enable individuals to appropriate new knowledge for their own private benefit. The question of rights to information can be explored from a variety of viewpoints, and while the bulk of this volume takes a largely philosophical and ethical perspective, this paper has the more immediate aim of setting out some of the controversies that are currently working their way through courts and legislatures. By developing a taxonomy of the issues occupying the attention of the legal profession, I hope to provide the reader with a framework for understanding the intellectual property system. The framework will help expose the real-world stakes that are involved in the theoretical inquiries found in these pages.

Rochelle Cooper Dreyfuss, "General overview of the intellectual property system," in *Owning Scientific and Technical Information,* ed. V. Weil and J. Snapper (New Brunswick: Rutgers University Press, 1989), pp. 17–40. Reprinted by permission of the publisher.

I have put aside technical questions dealing with the application of the intellectual property statutes to particular cases,[1] and procedural matters common to the administration of the legal system as a whole,[2] in order to concentrate on those problems which best demonstrate how the philosophical issues discussed here come into play in the legal arena. The remaining legal problems are then divided into three categories: 1) questions that require for their resolution an understanding of (if not an agreement upon) the justifications for creating such exclusive rights as patents and copyrights; 2) issues that involve balancing the need for fashioning exclusive rights with other important social concerns; and 3) problems that require explicit investigation into alternative legal strategies for furthering specific goals.[3] Although these categories are not watertight, this breakdown will be useful in delineating the consequences of particular arguments.

The Question of Justifications

One feature of intellectual property that makes it different from some kinds of tangible property is that it can usually be shared. That is, once an invention is perfected, or a manuscript completed, the creator's ability to use it for its intended purpose—to read a research report, or to employ a machine—is usually not diminished by the use made of that same invention by others. Because this distinction between tangible and intangible property is fundamental to the structure of intellectual property law, it is important that its ramifications be fully explored. To do so, compare my ownership of a watch (tangible property) with my invention of a new method for brewing coffee (intellectual property) and ask the question whether each can comfortably be shared.

As to the watch, the answer is usually no. I purchased it in order to ensure my awareness of the time, and this function would be severely impaired if I sometimes had to give the watch over to another. But with a method for brewing coffee, the answer could be yes. Suppose that I invented it to decrease my caffeine intake without significantly sacrificing the flavor of my coffee. My enjoyment of the benefits it produces is in no way reduced when others also use this technology. So long as I can use the technique myself, I drink good coffee and I am spared caffeine. Indeed, society would be better off if everyone knew of my invention: coffee drinkers would be healthier and health care costs would be diminished.

Exclusive rights in intellectual property are, in short, similar in many ways to monopolies in other goods. They have the potential to raise prices, lower output, and produce deadweight social loss as those who could profitably use the innovation (were it priced competitively) forgo purchasing it at the monopolist's price. One could therefore imagine a system of laws that required me to share my invention with the world. Or, less drastically, one could posit a legal regime that held that I may attempt to keep my technique a secret, but if someone manages to learn my method, even against my will, I am powerless to prevent that party from using it. This rule would, in effect, say that if someone reverse engineered the technique (that is, deduced it from an embodiment of the invention, for example, by borrowing my coffeepot and taking it apart) or uncovered it in some more intrusive manner (such as bribing my husband or installing a hidden camera in my kitchen), the public benefit of increased utilization of the discovery should be thought to outweigh my desire to decide for myself with whom I wished to share it. In other words, the legal system should not be structured to enable me to keep my invention as my own exclusive property.

Notice that it would not be so easy to make the same argument with regard to the watch. Sharing my watch will make me late for appointments and class, which will annoy my friends, my business associates, and my students. Since the increased utility to others in having use of the watch is not likely to outweigh my lost utility in forgoing use, there is little public benefit associated with "de-exclusifying" the watch. Thus, there is no point to a legal rule that permits an improper taking—a misappropriation—of it. To the contrary, I should be allowed to count on the legal system to help me keep my watch as my exclusive possession, and in fact the law provides two such remedies: a civil (tort) action to allow me to retrieve my watch, and criminalization of certain interferences with my enjoyment of it.[4]

Since the effect of exclusive possession of intellectual property (*exclusivity*) appears to be a social disutility, the imposition of a private-rights system must be justified, and the justification must be based on some ground other than the practical necessity that supports the laws of tangible property. A variety of rationalizations have been put forward (Machlup 1958). . . . The *natural rights theory*, for example, holds that the creator has a moral right to capture the benefits of whatever he has invented. Various arguments appear in the literature to support this theory. It is often argued that the right attaches to creators because they have found a previously unused resource, or because they have added their labor to the stock of knowledge. To reap the benefits thus produced, the creator must be able to charge others for the use of his innovation, and this he cannot do unless he has the legal right to exclude those who do not pay.

The *profit-incentive argument* similarly turns on the need to provide a mechanism for financial remuneration. This theory, however, relies on a utilitarian argument. While an inventor's anticipated private enjoyment of his innovation might encourage him to produce, further incentives are thought necessary to provide society with the optimal amount of innovative activity. Market mechanisms will generate an appropriate reward if the innovator is given the right to exclude others, at least for a time. Although he could sell products incorporating his innovation without this right, he would compete at a disadvantage. Since those who copy the invention will not themselves have spent time and money developing it, they will be able to offer the invention to the public at a lower price. Although the public would benefit from the price reduction offered by these free riders, the inventor will make fewer (if any) sales, he will not be able to recoup his costs, and he will lack the financial incentive to continue to innovate.

Other justifications stem from noneconomic premises. The *exchange-for-secrecy rationale* states that without a legal right to prevent others from copying his invention, the creator may be tempted to keep it a secret. If he does, others may unknowingly duplicate the effort that went into creating it. If, in contrast, the inventor can rely on legal rules to prevent those who learn the secret from themselves exploiting it, or to seek compensation from those who do learn and use it, then the inventor will be willing to disseminate the invention more widely and disclose its details to others. This disclosure will, in turn, enable others to use the ideas the invention embodies to extend the frontiers of knowledge. Even though the public will pay more for a particular invention because the creator owns an exclusive right, the extra cost is less of a burden than not having the secret revealed at all.[5]

The *quality-control principle* looks at the exclusive right not so much as an element in encouraging invention or disclosure, but more as a method for protecting the innovation once it is released. By giving the holder power to control how the invention is used, exclusive rights enable him to maintain its integrity. He can, for example, use this right to prevent others from distorting or mutilating his work, thereby diluting its quality.

The *prospecting theory* shares some of these quality-promotion elements. It argues that one value in a system of exclusive rights is that it concentrates research. Like a miner who owns his mining claim, the holder of an exclusive right has the incentive to develop fully his ideas. And since anyone else who wants to pursue work in that field necessarily approaches him first, the holder comes to possess comprehensive knowledge of how the field is unfolding and can help maintain an "orderly market" in its further development (Kitch 1977).

At the heart of many pivotal disputes in intellectual property law are questions as to whether exclusivity is justified in a particular case, and if so, on what theory. How these questions are resolved determines whether a particular endeavor will receive legal protection at all[6] and whether it will receive that protection under the patent system,[7] the copyright laws,[8] or some other state or federal regime.[9] In the end, the choice of justification shapes both the rights of creative individuals and the quality (and quantity) of the product that passes to the public.

The centrality of the justification issue to the structure of intellectual property law can be demonstrated by looking at how the legal system handles novel claims to protection. The emerging right of publicity provides one such illustration. Until recently, it was quite clear that anyone was free to tell the story of another person's life. Legal protection, to the extent that it was available at all, protected only the right to privacy. Thus, if the plaintiffs interest was in withholding intimate details about his life, he could (at least sometimes) invoke the protection of the court.[10] However, once information about a person became publicly accessible, it was permissible for anyone to use it for any purpose, including commercial benefit. Thus, so long as information was gleaned from purely public sources, unauthorized biographies as well as sociological and historical studies were not actionable; similarly, plays, movies, and television shows could be made of the lives of interesting persons without their permission.

Within the last few years, however, a new strand of analysis has appeared. The claim has now been made that there is an interest apart from privacy that is infringed by these works: that even the public aspects of a person's story are his property and that the law should protect his exclusive right to utilize that property.[11] Although no full-blown attempt to claim exclusivity in a life story has yet to reach the courts,[12] Estate of Presley v. Russen,[13] which concerned the right to impersonate the late Elvis Presley, provides a vehicle for considering how such a claim will be evaluated.[14]

Clearly, there is a public interest in facilitating impersonations. They enable older generations to relive earlier experiences and share their culture with younger audiences. Impersonation is, in addition, a fascinating art form of its own. Should, then, the public be given free access to Presley's act? The answer depends on which rationale is used to justify the right to exclusivity, for the theories point in contrary directions. If, for example, exclusive rights are thought necessary to promote disclosure of secrets, then the Presley estate should lose. Presley is, after all, dead, and has no further secrets—no new songs or performing ideas—to reveal. The profit-incentive rationale leads to the same conclusion. It could be argued that as long as the impersonator makes clear that he is not providing the audience with the genuine Elvis Presley, the money that he makes cannot be counted as part of the incentive that motivated Presley to produce.[15]

At the same time, however, the estate wins on any of the other theories. Since the impersonator repeats activity that originated with Presley, the estate, as the representative of his interests, could make a substantial moral claim to any natural right Presley had to his act. Furthermore, the impersonations have an impact on the public perception of Presley. The argument that it is desirable to appoint a caretaker to regulate the market for the creator's product and protect its integrity would seem to apply with full force to impersonation.

The choice of justifications affects not only whether an exclusive right is created, as in the above illustration, but its contours as well. For example, if the right of publicity is considered property, then it may seem obvious that it should be treated for inheritance purposes just like any other property.[16] Thus, the owner of the right should be able to dispose of it by will, and if he fails to do so, it should pass to his heirs under the laws of intestacy.

However, close inspection of the justifications supporting exclusivity reveals that another solution may make more sense. Perhaps the right to exclusivity should be recognized during the creator's lifetime, but it should be extinguished upon his death. As applied to the Presley case, the argument under the profit-incentive rationale is as follows: While he is alive, the entertainer and the copyist are in competition with one another. Although the impersonator may not offer precisely the same experience as Presley, he does offer a similar product at a lower price. If a part of the audience is willing to accept the substitution, Presley's profit is diminished. To establish appropriate monetary incentives, the right of publicity must be recognized. After death, however, the creator loses the ability to create, so an incentive is not needed, and the right could be terminated.[17]

Because of its structural implications, the choice of justification also plays a crucial role in many cases involving long recognized exclusive rights, such as federal copyrights and patents. Although these rights are based on article 1, section 8, clause 8 of the Constitution, which directs Congress "to promote the progress of science and useful arts, by securing for limited times to authors and inventors the exclusive right to their respective writings and discoveries," the Constitution does not adopt any particular rationale for believing that progress will be promoted through exclusivity. Thus, in a sense, the issue of justification is somewhat open even in the case of federal rights. It is, however, probably fair to say that the Supreme Court has read the profit-incentive theory into the law,[18] and this view has, in turn, shaped the extent to which creators can avail themselves of federal law to oversee the quality of their product or further their prospecting interests in continuing to regulate exploitation of their innovations.

The Copyright Act, for example, creates a series of restrictions on the author's right to control, including the first-sale doctrine (which allows the copyright holder to control only the first sale of any copy of his work),[19] the principle of fair use (which tolerates certain unauthorized, uncompensated uses of a copyrighted work),[20] and compulsory licenses (which permit certain unauthorized uses at nonmarket prices).[21] These limitations stem in part from legislative judgments that financial considerations are of paramount concern, and that the number of profit-making opportunities created by the law should be no greater than those which will stimulate the optimum amount of innovative activity. Apart from doubts about whether Congress was sufficiently generous to innovators,[22] these doctrines can also be criticized for ignoring the rationales that are directed at protecting the creative environment, and for depriving creators of control over the integrity, impact, and public perception of their work.[23] Indeed, even the limited duration of copyright is problematic in this regard, as the debate over colorization of old motion pictures demonstrates.[24]

Some states do not disregard the other justifications for exclusive rights. Thus, the unfettered right of a buyer to dispose of an original "copy" of a work of fine art has been modified in several states by statutes that enable artists to protect their works from mutilation and destruction.[25] Similarly, state contract, tort, and trade secrecy laws do, in some circumstances, further the objectives underlying the nonpecuniary rationales.[26] Surprisingly, even state unfair competition laws, which are largely designed to protect the efficient conduct of the marketplace, sometimes fill the interstices created by the financial emphasis of federal law. By permitting the creator to prevent others from making changes in his product, these laws allow him to maintain the quality of the material that becomes part of the public domain.

But when there are state laws that establish wider rights, innovators must deal with another, more subtle, question concerning justifications: does the adoption of one theory of protection exclude the application of the other rationales?

The exchange-for-secrecy rationale is, for example, somewhat inconsistent with a regime of trade secrecy that helps inventors keep their discoveries to themselves. Accordingly, it is not surprising that for a time the Supreme Court thought the national interest required preemption—invalidation—of state laws providing exclusivity to innovations that are not protected under federal law. In Sears, Roebuck & Co. v. Stiffel Co., for example, the Court held that "to allow a State by use of its law of unfair competition to prevent the copying of an article . . . would be to permit the State to block off from the public something which federal law has said belongs to the public."[27]

But since the high-water mark of preemption in the 1960s, the Court has substantially retreated from this position and has, in more recent years, sometimes allowed states to offer protection in circumstances not covered by federal law.[28] In part, the trend toward greater flexibility has itself stemmed from the perceived need to provide a profit to motivate research. In Kewanee Oil Co. v. Bicron Corp.,[29] for instance, the Court permitted a state to protect through its trade secrecy law an invention that could have been, but was not, patented. Although the Court recognized that enforcing the trade secrecy law conflicted with an exchange-for-secrets rationale, it reasoned that a state may legitimately decide to use the profit motive to encourage innovation and offer a mechanism of exclusivity to augment the patent law.

Recent cases, however, hint that even nonpecuniary rationales may yet capture the Court's imagination. For instance, the Court accepted a quality-control justification for allowing President Ford to utilize copyright law to determine the time when his memoirs became publicly available.[30] Although the Court recognized that its decision would impinge on the public's access to a work of great national interest, it reasoned that if an author were unable to block the publication of his unfinished works, there would be nothing to prevent the dissemination of inaccurate, unpolished material, and this, too, would work against the public weal. If this trend toward recognizing multiple justifications for exclusivity continues to flourish, the artists' rights provisions, which have not yet been tested in the Supreme Court, may survive preemption challenges. Moreover, nonpecuniary justifications could eventually draw the attention of Congress, paving the way to federal protection expressly premised on concerns for the creative environment.[31]

The Question of Balancing

Debates over the application of doctrines that limit the creator's ability to protect his work stem from more than a dispute over the appropriate justification for exclusivity. Even if a particular objective were universally accepted, questions would remain concerning the extent to which the agreed goal should be compromised in favor of other social interests.

The limitations in copyright law mentioned above are examples of provisions meant to balance the creator's needs against the public's interest in access to his work. The Copyright Act recognizes, for example, that there may be circumstances in which society benefits by use of a work, but that it would be difficult (if not impossible) to secure the author's permission to put his work to that use (Gordon 1982). To ensure public access for these important purposes, the act encroaches on the creator's interests and allows others to utilize the work without his authorization. In these circumstances, the author's remuneration is either determined by nonmarket forces, as in the case of compulsory licenses, or relinquished entirely.

The fair use doctrine is an example of the latter solution. Its application was at issue in Maxtone-Graham v. Burtchaell,[32] a case involving the right of an opponent of abortion to use excerpts from interviews given, at high personal cost, by women who had undergone abortions and wished to preserve the right of others to make similar choices in the future. Even on a a theory of quality control (or exchange for secrecy), the Second Circuit was correct in holding that the quotations were a fair use of these works. Although the decision allowed Burtchaell to use the interviews to support a cause that the interviewer and interviewees opposed, the right to quote is essential if the public is to discuss intelligently the contributions that the creator made and to build upon them to further extend the frontiers of knowledge.[33] Permitting Maxtone-Graham to withhold permission to use these interviews would, in effect, allow her to prescribe the terms of the debate on an important social issue.

Because the national agenda is always in flux, the strategy for mediating between private and public concerns must be reexamined whenever new interests emerge or old interests acquire new importance. Consider, for instance, the question of protecting ideas and facts, an issue that has become prominent as technology and information services have become increasingly significant components of the gross national product. Because free use of facts and ideas has always been considered a public necessity, the law limits patents to applications of ideas and copyrights to original expression of ideas or facts. In that way, the ideas that underlie a patented innovation are available to other inventors, and the ideas and facts expressed in a copyrighted work can be utilized by other authors. If, however, the information and technology industries are to continue to thrive, it may be necessary to rethink this traditional regime.

The tension between encouraging the development of new ideas, or works with high factual content, and safeguarding the public's right to discuss freely ideas and facts is nicely demonstrated in the conflicting opinions of the Second Circuit and the Supreme Court in Harper & Row Publishers, Inc. v. Nation Enterprises,[34] the case involving the *Nation's* unauthorized publication of a portion of President Ford's memoirs before its official publication date. The Second Circuit reasoned that if the copyright on these memoirs were to prevent discussion of such issues as Richard Nixon's pardon, there would be little public benefit in encouraging President Ford to write. Accordingly, it grafted a public-figure exception onto the copyright law and held the work largely uncopyrightable. The Supreme Court, on the other hand, recognized that if the Ford memoirs were freely available, then future presidents would not have the financial incentive to set down their recollections. It therefore reversed the Second Circuit and refused to find Ford's status a bar to the copyrightability of his work.

The arguments heard in the Ford case are also made in regard to the protectability of those works which form the backbone of the information industry, such as computerized data bases. The prevailing approach in these cases has been to decide whether a work is copyrightable by looking at the degree of creativity it embodies. As a result, the more closely a work reflects actual facts, the less likely it is to be protected.[35] This focus on inventiveness neatly protects public access to the factual content of the material, but it largely ignores the real issue of how to stimulate the effort of collecting. Without the labor, the public would not, after all, have the facts so conveniently arrayed and available for use.

State law has, once again, sometimes stepped into the breach by finding that the sale of another's work without the author's permission is an unfair method of competing even when the work is not copyrightable. For example, the New York State Court of Appeals found, as a matter of state law, that the sale of opera music recorded from a radio telecast of the Metropolitan Opera was a misappropriation of material that belonged to the Met. Although sound recordings were not at the time of the case covered by copyright law, the court thought it necessary to protect the Met against activity that threatened its capacity to stage further productions.[36]

These state-based rights are, however, of fairly limited significance. They are available only in states that recognize them. Furthermore, they are, as has been shown, vulnerable to preemption claims, and sometimes tend to turn on distinctive features that may not be found in the entire class of cases raising similar concerns. If development of the information industry is considered vital, systematic federal legislation may be needed, even if that protection requires some intrusion into the public access interest.[37]

Similar arguments apply to patent law. As with the fact/expression dichotomy of copyrights, patent law's distinction between protectable applications and non-protectable ideas is easier to describe than implement. Excessive sympathy with the public-access aspect of the problem may, in the end, provide insufficient stimulation to basic research, especially in fields like computer programming, where the applications of the work are not easily separated from the ideas contained.[38]

The notion that changes in the national agenda require readjusting the balance between proprietary and public interests is also evident in the controversy over the "Nine No-Nos" of patent licensing. For some time a fixture of the Justice Department's antitrust policy, the No-Nos were a list of licensing practices (such as resale price maintenance, tie-outs[39] and tie-ins[40]) that were, in the government's view, anticompetitive (Lipsky 1981). Although the department explained the restrictions imposed by the No-Nos as necessary to prevent the patentee from extending his patent grant beyond its terms—to restrain the patentee from capturing more than the benefit conferred by his invention—this rigid approach has recently come into disfavor (Rule 1986).

Theorists now argue that the No-Nos went far beyond the quantum of regulation required by antitrust policy. These thinkers claim that it is not likely that anyone (including the licensee or his customers) would pay more for the invention than it is worth, no matter how the patentee structured the transaction. Accordingly, except in rare circumstances, it is not possible for the patentee to extract from the public more than the value that the invention created. Under this analysis, the effect of the No-Nos is to shortchange the patentee and prevent him from fully exploiting his patent rights. Although the invention may then be cheaper to its consumers, the No-Nos reduce the financial incentive available to stimulate innovative activity. Since the department now considers innovation an important national goal, and because it believes that innovation is best fostered by allowing inventors to exploit their works fully, it has greatly relaxed and almost abolished the No-Nos (Andewelt 1985).[41]

Whether this is the final word on the licensing issue remains to be seen. As patent rights become more valuable, patentees may be able to use their dominant and unique positions to discourage challengers and suppress newer inventions. If the result is a net loss in progressiveness, the balance between patent rights and antitrust limitations may have to be examined once again.

The rights of innovators must also be weighed against newly emerging public interests. Compatibility is one such concern, for it has become increasingly evident that access alone is not always enough to put innovations to their best use. . . . The distinction between access, on the one hand, and access plus compatibility, on the other, is illustrated by my search for a personal computer for my home. In theory, any computer on the market should be of interest to me. In fact, however, I will look at only one subclass, and that is comprised of computers that are compatible with the computer in my office at New York University (NYU). Only if I buy a computer for home that runs the word-processing program that I use at school will I be able to work at home on files I create in my office. The same concern arises when I purchase software, printers, and other peripheral equipment. And the interest is not mine alone, for every manufacturer wishing to compete for my computer, software, and peripherals business is concerned with making products compatible with the computer that NYU purchased for my office.

Patent and copyright laws have traditionally safeguarded the interest in compatible products through their deposit and specification requirements. The Copyright Act requires the copyright holder to deposit copies of his work in order to obtain the right to sue for infringement;[42] the Patent Act requires the patentee to reveal in a publicly available specification all the information necessary to duplicate his invention.[43] During the term of protection, these provisions guarantee that sufficient information is revealed so that others can manufacture products compatible with the innovator's invention. After the term of protection has expired, they ensure that competitors know enough to compete effectively.

The current enthusiasm for stimulating innovation has, however, led to a relaxation of these rules for new technologies. The Semiconductor Chip Protection

Act of 1984,[44] for example, allows the inventor of an integrated circuit to obtain exclusive rights to his design without entirely revealing the elements that make the design operative.[45] Similarly, the Copyright Office now permits software producers to withhold selected portions of their programs from their deposit copies.[46] Although these rules could be challenged on the ground that they undervalue compatibility concerns, analogous claims against trade secret holders have so far met with little success.[47] To date, the accepted view is that disclosure is not necessary to maintain vigorous competition, but new technologies and a greater appreciation of the benefits of compatibility may lead to different results in the future.

The environment is another nascent focus of public interest. In recent years, a series of right-to-know laws have been enacted at both state and federal levels so that the impact of innovative activity on health and safety can be monitored. The federal Occupational Safety and Health Administration demands, for example, that chemical manufacturers label containers of hazardous chemicals with the chemicals' identity. Employees, their representatives, and health professionals have a right to further vital—and secret—data about these chemicals in specific circumstances.[48] Some states have gone even further. New Jersey requires employers to prepare environmental surveys indicating the hazardous chemicals that are found in the workplace. These surveys are submitted to various governmental authorities, and are available in part to employees.[49] Although these statutes offer partial protection for trade secrets (by, for instance, requiring persons receiving information to sign confidentiality agreements), it is clear that secrecy is severely compromised by any regulation that requires circulation of trade secrets to parties who are beyond the control of the inventor.

Disasters such as Union Carbide's in Bhopal, India, have focused the public's attention on the need for more information about activities that occur in its midst. But despite the appealing nature of the claims that have led to this legislation, "de-exclusifying" protectable intellectual property may have the unintended consequence of diminishing the opportunities for recouping the costs of invention. These enactments are too recent to have been extensively tested in the courts,[50] and insufficient time has elapsed in which to observe their impact on inventive behavior. It will be interesting to see where the nation ultimately strikes the balance between the new social policies furthered by these laws and the accelerating concern for stimulating creativity.

Alternative Schemes

It has been pointed out that the current regime of intellectual property laws is not immutable, and that alternative schemes for protecting innovators could be adopted. The problems noted thus far perhaps hint that the legal system should be actively engaged in the enterprise of searching for better ways to promote innovation.

There are two directions from which to approach the problem. One possibility is to tinker with the current system. That is, once a particular difficulty is detected, the legislature could simply alter the statute to eliminate the problem.[51] This solution has, of course, been followed to a large extent. For instance, three years ago Congress extended the patent term for drugs subject to delays due to regulatory activities,[52] and has considered similar action for agrochemical products and animal drugs.[53] A provision that would bring copyright law into closer alignment with the European quality-control vision of authors' rights is under active contemplation,[54] and the Reagan administration advanced initiatives to clarify the rights of patent licensors.[55] Future problems could (and, indeed, will) be solved in the same manner. For example, should a patentee develop a socially important invention (such as a cure for cancer—or a better technique for brewing coffee) that she refuses to exploit, Congress would undoubtedly quickly import the compulsory license strategy of copyright law into the patent system and enact a statute permitting others to use the invention upon payment of a fee set by the government.

A more drastic approach to the problems surrounding the current legal regime would be to abandon the old system and start afresh. The United States could, for example, move to a patronage system whereby innovators were subsidized by government, social organizations, or other wealthy entities. James Madison at one time suggested that the government determine the social value of every new invention and award an amount proportional to that value to the inventor. A bounty system has also been proposed that would allow the government to purchase innovations and dedicate them to the public. If the government chose not to buy, then the inventor would be given protection from free riders through a system akin to the present one (Jewkes, Sawers, and Stillerman 1969; Scherer 1980; National Academy of Sciences 1962).

To some extent, these ideas are currently being implemented. Government grants and tax write-offs are forms of patronage, and government purchase orders are a variation on the bounty theme. Relying exclusively on these alternatives would, however, introduce a series of new problems. Unlike the market mechanism at the heart of the current system of intellectual property protection, these schemes require someone to make ex ante evaluations that can be difficult and are sometimes dangerous. Patronage systems, for instance, single out certain inventors to receive financial backing, and so require someone to prejudge the abilities of the applicant pool. As experiences with government funding have demonstrated, maverick thinkers who are not affiliated with well-accepted organizations tend to be ignored in these processes. In countries where subsidies are funneled only to those who adhere to particular political philosophies, the results for science have been alarming.[56] Although bounty systems are somewhat less vulnerable to politicization, they also require evaluations of the benefits of the invention. An inventor who takes an unconventional approach is still unlikely to enjoy a reward under such a system.[57]

Congress has occasionally tried to capture the benefits of both tinkering with the old and starting anew. The Semiconductor Chip Protection Act represents one such attempt. A special law enacted to meet the needs of a single technology, the Chip Act is a fascinating experiment in intellectual property legislation. In some respects, such as its use of a market mechanism to reward invention, the act closely resembles copyright and patent law. In other ways, however, Congress has written on a clean slate. Concepts such as fair use have largely been scrapped; instead, the act secures the public's right of access by allowing others to examine and copy protected chips for the purpose of pushing the technology forward.[58] At the same time, the act safeguards proprietary rights by relaxing the requirement of patent law that the application fully reveal all the secrets in the invention. Other special features of the Chip Act—such as a change in the term of protection, protection for those who violate exclusive rights innocently, and a new originality standard—also represent attempts to develop novel solutions that are highly responsive to the needs of the semiconductor industry.

But while this specialized scheme may be a tremendous advantage to integrated-circuit producers, developments of this type present many new challenges to the legal system. The primary one is determining which technologies merit this special attention. It has been forcefully suggested that the computer industry should also receive tailored protection because it suffers many of the same problems that led Congress to enact the Chip Act. But other fields have similar difficulties with existing law. Industrial designers, for instance, are also hampered by many of the concerns that motivated the Chip Act.[59] Other fields, such as microbiology and superconductivity, present new problems that cry out for unique solutions. By providing a new option for Congress to consider, the Chip Act may have done no more than introduce yet another kind of tension into the system.

And if the law continues to move toward more specialized measures, other problems will come into focus. Fine-tuned legislation requires a wait-and-see period during which the needs of the new technology are given time to crystallize. In the interim, the prospect of—and the contours of—the new legislation may be unclear, and innovations that occur before the new scheme is announced may become even more vulnerable to copyists. The advantage given free riders during the time before new legislation is enacted may, in fact, lead to the undoing of the first innovators. Because of these uncertainties, inventors and their financial backers may prefer in the future to concentrate their efforts on those technologies which are subject to laws that are better defined. As a result of Congress's increased willingness to think about novel legislation, research could, paradoxically, end up moving away from those fields where the claim for specialized legislation is especially strong.

Even more serious are the international implications of these schemes. As the world becomes smaller—or as inventors depend more on world markets to recoup their costs—international protection becomes increasingly important. In recognition of the need to assure its citizens protection in important markets, the United States has entered various international, regional, and bilateral treaties.[60] But while these treaties facilitate acquisition of patents and copyrights in signatory countries, they do not apply to alternative protection schemes. Thus, every time the United States (or a foreign country) heeds the cries of a new industry and enacts specialized legislation, new international agreements have to be forged. The experience of the Chip Act is that international accommodation is a slow process. Even after the act was several years old, not a single foreign country had adopted a measure that the United States considered as protective as its own.[61]

In the final analysis, it may turn out that the benefits of starting afresh, considerable though they may be, are radically outweighed by the short-term burdens endured during the period when protection is uncertain, and by the costs incurred in the international arena. The law is a conservative enterprise, and this is especially true when the issue it addresses is the creation of interests that are intended to motivate future performance.

Empirical Research

A puzzling feature of all of this is that many of the controversies described here could be better understood (if not resolved) by empirical research. Did Elvis Presley count on being able to exploit his persona after his death? Are ex-presidents—or scientists—motivated by financial considerations? Do people rely on trade secrecy when patent protection is available? Would products be more convenient if compatibility concerns were more vigorously protected? I conclude this essay with a few brief thoughts as to why such data, at least in the form of surveys, are not forthcoming.[62]

Probably the most significant problem is that these studies are difficult to conduct in a manner that lends itself to unambiguous interpretation. As it turns out, the answers obtained on surveys depend very much on who responds to the questions. Is the patent system critical to research and development? It is not surprising that large firms usually claim it is not. Since these firms are vertically integrated—they control research and development as well as production and distribution—they have at their disposal a variety of tactics for exploiting their inventions, many of which do not rely on patent rights. Small firms, on the other hand, lack the capacity to produce or distribute their inventions themselves. To earn financial return on their discoveries, they must rely on licensing. Although patent rights are not required to obtain royalties for the use of an invention, the amount of royalties will depend on the benefit that the licensee expects to obtain. Without patent protection, small firms cannot reveal enough information to potential licensees to negotiate for the best price for the use of their inventions. Thus, small, nonintegrated firms would tend to report that patent rights are significant to their research decisions (Dreyfuss 1986).

Surveys will be imperfect even if they are corrected for structural problems. Questions that require people to predict how they will behave if the legal regime were different demand imagination and a sophisticated understanding of both the current and the proposed legal rules. Many of the potential targets of surveys lack a firm grip on the details of the regime under which they are now operating; they are unlikely to spend a great deal of time learning about theoretical possibilities. Some authors have little understanding of what it is that motivates their publisher to buy, rather than steal, their work. Many non-lawyers can barely credit the notion that the patent (or copyright) system could be abolished. Parties who have had experience with the current system (such as lawyers, litigants, or witnesses) have a different perspective from those who have not seen the system in operation. Research and development managers have a different view from the patent lawyers, the bench scientists, or the advertising executives employed by their own firms.

Finally, this is an area where, by definition, secrecy is important. Surveys attempting to measure the extent to which trade secrecy is relied upon are notoriously unsuccessful because most firms regard *whether* they rely on trade secrecy as itself a secret. Similarly, firms are extremely reluctant to reveal the extent to which they believe their rights are being infringed. They are afraid that if the numbers appear too high, others may believe that the validity of the underlying claims is in doubt. The direction of future research, how the fruits of creativity will be exploited, the problems anticipated with existing law, are similarly all sensitive items of information that firms hesitate to disclose.

The national agenda will continue to shift as new discoveries are made and public policies emerge and recede in importance. Perhaps the future will also bring better methods for dealing with factual uncertainty. In the meantime, the structure of intellectual property law and the balance that it strikes between public and private rights will depend upon the proficiency with which we wield the analytical tools currently at our disposal.

Notes

[1]See, for example, Hodosh v. Block Drug Co., Inc., 786 F.2d 1136 (Fed. Cir.) considering whether an ancient Chinese folk medicine text is prior art within the meaning of the Patent Act. 35 U.S.C. sec. 102[b], *cert. denied* 107 S.Ct. 106 [1986]; Past Pluto Productions Corp. v. Dana, 627 F. Supp. 1435 (S.D.N.Y. 1986) (deciding that Statue of Liberty hats lack sufficient originality to qualify for copyright protection as a derivative work under the Copyright Act. 17 U.S.C. sec. 103).

[2]See, for example, Dennison Mfg. Co. v. Panduit Corp., 475 U.S. 809 (1986) (discussing the scope of appellate court review of trial court patentability decisions): Young v. U.S. ex rel Vuitton et Fils S. A. 107 S.Ct. 2124 (1987) (holding improper the appointment of an interested attorney to prosecute contempts of trademark injunctions).

[3]Nonetheless, this breakdown is useful for delineating the consequences of particular arguments.

[4]This is not to say that there may not be other, nonutilitarian, justifications for private tangible property rights.

[5]An example may be helpful here. Say that I wish to exploit my coffee-brewing technique. Because of its popularity, I will have to open two coffee-brewing factories if I am to satisfy demand. But since I can be at only one place at a time, I can run the second factory only if I am willing to tell my secret to a foreman. Whether I open two factories or only one factory will depend on my legal rights to the secret. If I can rely on the law to prevent

the foreman from double-crossing me and opening a rival factory, then I will reveal the secret and open two factories. If, on the other hand, I have no legal recourse against the foreman, then the only way to prevent him from going into competition with me will be to withhold the secret. I will, accordingly, open only one factory, leaving substantial un-satisfied demand.

Crucial to understanding this theory is recognizing that no legal rule is required to maintain a *real* secret. Patent law and trade secrecy law come into play only when something is no longer a real secret. Thus, they virtually always operate to prevent peo-ple who actually do know the innovation from practicing it without permission (and usu-ally payment).

[6]It could be argued that innovations inimical to health and welfare should not be pro-tected so that further developments are discouraged. Such a claim has recently been made with regard to the patenting of multicellular organisms; see Schneider (1987). This issue is discussed in Diamond v. Chakrabarty, 447 U.S. 303 (1980).

[7]Federal law creates three kinds of patents. The inventor of a "new and useful process, ma-chine, manufacture, or composition of matter" is eligible for a utility patent, which cre-ates rights against those who would make, use, or sell the invention without permission (35 U.S.C. secs. 101, 271). The design patent provides similar protection for the inventor of a "new, original, and ornamental design for an article of manufacture" (sec. 171). A plant patent allows one who discovers and asexually reproduces a "distinct and new va-riety of plant" to exclude "others from asexually reproducing the plant or selling or using the plant so reproduced" (sec. 161). Patents create exclusivity for only a limited time, gen-erally seventeen years (sec. 154).

[8]A copyright protects "original works of authorship fixed in any tangible medium of ex-pression" against unauthorized reproduction, distribution, public performance, or display. The copyright holder is, in addition, given the right to exclude others from preparing de-rivative works (such as translations) based upon the original work (17 U.S.C. secs. 101, 106). Like patents, the term of copyright protection is limited, generally to the life of the author plus the fifty years following his death (sec. 302[a]).

[9]State trade secrecy and unfair competition laws create exclusive rights by providing remedies against those who discover a secret innovation improperly (for example, through bribery or espionage) or compete unfairly (for example, by using the inventor's trade-marks to convey incorrectly to others that the product they are selling is that of the in-ventor). In theory, these rights extend indefinitely; in practice, however, the protection generally dissipates as others independently invent or reverse engineer the secret. Fur-thermore, unfair competition claims cannot usually be asserted after the trademark holder has ceased doing business.

[10]For example, in Froelich v. Adair, 213 Kan. 357, 516 P.2d 993 (1973), a detective was held liable for bribing a hospital orderly to obtain hair combings from a patient's brush, the court reasoning that the plaintiff had a right to prevent others from intruding into his personal affairs.

[11]Thus, in his seminal work, Prosser considered the right of publicity to be an aspect of privacy (see Prosser 1971), this analysis was carried over into the *Restatement of Torts* by the American Law Institute (1976, sec. 652A). Various commentators have, however, begun to realize that privacy, which protects information from being revealed, and publicity, which protects the right to exploit information that has been revealed, are quite distinct from one another; see, for example, Kwall (1983). Indeed, even the *Restatement* contains hints that the two rights are only tenuously connected; see American Law Institute (1976, sec. 652A, comment b).

[12]There are, however, clear indications that sooner or later the attempt will be made. The Baby M case on surrogate motherhood has, for example, spawned a satellite controversy

over whether Baby M can (through her guardian) prevent the natural mother from telling her story for profit without paying royalties to her; see Hanley (1987). Similarly, Elizabeth Taylor threatened litigation to prevent the American Broadcasting Corporation from making a docudrama of her life (see Lewin 1982, quoting the actress as saying, "I am my own commodity. I am my own industry."). See also Salinger v. Random House, 811 F.2d 90 (2d Cir.) (discussing whether a biographer can, consistent with the copyright laws, use material found in a library to write a convincing and lively account of a reclusive author's life), *cert. denied*, 108 S.Ct. 213 (1987).

[13]513 F. Supp. 1339 (D. N.J. 1981).

[14]Numerous other impersonation cases have also been litigated, including claims by Bela Lugosi, the estate of the Marx Brothers, Jacqueline Onassis, Cher, and Woody Allen. Many of these are described in Allen v. National Video, Inc., 610 F. Supp. 612 (S.D. N.Y. 1985). See also Apple Corps Ltd. v. Leber, 229 U.S.P.Q. 1015 (Cal. App. Dep't. Super. Ct. 1986) (discussing *Beatlemania*, as an infringement of the Beatles' publicity rights).

[15]It is useful to compare this case with Zacchini v. Scripps-Howard Broadcasting Co., 433 U.S. 562 (1977), where the Supreme Court upheld a right-of-publicity claim. In that case, however, the defendant had filmed the plaintiff's entire act and showed it on television, thus arguably exhausting the demand for the plaintiff's product. In contrast, the demand for the "real thing" is not likely to be satisfied with an impersonator.

[16]See, for example, Tennessee ex rel. Elvis Presley Int'l. Memorial Found'n. v. Crowell, 733 S.W. 2d 89 (Tenn. Ct. App. 1987). Accepting a property rather than a privacy rationale for the right of publicity, this court looked to the justifications for creating exclusivity in order to determine whether the right should descend to Presley's heirs.

[17]Although it is true that after his death the creator's heirs may find their ability to sell remembrances of him (such as records) impaired by the offerings of the copyists, it is not likely that an innovator would count heavily on this return in deciding whether to innovate. Thus, the marginal motivational value of the return after death may not compensate the public for forgoing the posthumous performances of copyists.

Similar arguments could be made under some of the other theories. The State of Florida, for example, has accepted a rather sophisticated argument. It recognizes the possibility that a creator may be motivated by the desire to provide for his spouse and children. Thus, Florida has enacted a statute providing a right of publicity that endures during the life of the creator, and also during the lifetimes of his spouse and children. When they die, the right is extinguished. See, for example, Southeast Bank v. Lawrence, 66 N.Y. 2d 910, 498 N.Y.S. 2d 775, 489 N.E. 744 (N.Y. Ct. App. 1985).

[18]See, for example, Harper & Row, Publishers, Inc. v. Nation Enterprises, 471 U.S. 539, 546 (1985) (stating that "the rights conferred by copyright are designed to assure contributors to the store of knowledge a fair return for their labors"); Twentieth Century Music Corp. v. Aiken, 422 U.S. 151, 156 (1975); and Mazer v. Stein, 347 U.S. 201, 219 (1954) (speaking of the "economic philosophy behind the clause empowering Congress to grant patents and copyrights").

[19]17 U.S.C. sec. 109(a). Since federal law defines *copy* to include the original embodiment of a work (17 U.S.C. sec. 101), the first-sale doctrine arguably permits the owner of a painting to deface it, the owner of a bronze sculpture to melt it, or the owner of an original manuscript to burn it. It also permits the owner to rent his copy to those who would otherwise purchase it from the copyright owner; cf. Columbia Pictures Industries, Inc. v. Redd Home, Inc., 749 F.2d 154 (3d Cir. 1984) (enjoining videotape rentals, but only when they can be classified as public performances).

[20]17 U.S.C. sec. 107 permits such use "for purposes such as criticism, comment, news reporting, teaching, scholarship or research." The statue provides a series of factors to decide whether a particular use is fair. These include the purpose of the use (whether it is

commercial or not-for-profit), the nature of the work (such as whether it is factual), the substantiality of the use, and the effect of the use on the market for the work.

[21]The act specifies which uses are subject to compulsory licenses. These include retransmissions of copyrighted works by cable systems (17 U.S.C. sec. 111), and placement of records in jukeboxes (17 U.S.C. sec. 116). Royalties are set by the Copyright Royalty Tribunal, an administrative body created by the act (see secs. 801–803). Although the tribunal attempts to determine market rates, it is possible that the rates they set are lower than the amount that would have been charged had the owner been free to refuse to negotiate with the user.

[22]This was, in part, the issue in Sony Corp. v. Universal City Studios, Inc., 464 U.S. 417 (1984), which presented the question whether motion picture producers have the right to royalties when their work is videotaped from public broadcasts.

[23]See, for example, Shostakovich v. Twentieth Century-Fox Film Corp., 196 Misc. 67, 80 N.Y.S. 2d 575 (1948), *aff'd,* 275 A.D. 692, 87 N.Y.S. 2d 430 (1949) (refusing to enjoin the showing of anticommunist film using the works of Dmitri Shostakovich and other Soviet composers despite the claim that association of their music with an anti-Soviet theme injured their reputations). Cf. Henry Holt & Co., Inc. v. Liggett & Myers Tobacco Co., 23 F. Supp. 302 (E.D. Pa. 1938) (scientific paper quoted by cigarette company in a way that implied the author was hired to find cigarettes safe).

[24]See Bennetts (1986) describing Frank Capra's effort to prevent computer colorization of his classic black-and-white film, *It's a Wonderful Life,* after its copyright expired. Anyone familiar with the commercial jingle for Quaker Puffed Wheat (and Rice) that begins "This is the cereal that's shot from guns" who has tried to listen to Tchaikovsky's *1812 Overture* has suffered the experience of having an exciting work permanently ruined. Similarly, Strauss's "Blue Danube Waltz" loses its magic to those familiar with the advertisement of the Rival Dog Food Company "Give me Rival Dog Food, arf arf arf arf").

[25]See, for example, the California Art Preservation Act, Cal. Civ. Code secs. 987–989 (Deering Supp. 1986); Mass. Gen. Laws Ann. chap. 231, sec. 85S (West Supp. 1985); N.Y. Arts and Cultural Affairs Law, secs. 11.01, 14.03 (McKinney Supp. 1986).

[26]For a comprehensive discussion of state laws that promote nonpecuniary objectives, see Strauss (1960). In some circumstances, federal trademark law may also further some of the objectives underlying these rationales (15 U.S.C. sec. 1125[a]), which declares it a civil wrong to describe or represent falsely goods or services in interstate commerce.

[27]376 U.S. 225, 231–232 (1964). See also Compco Corp. v. Day-Brite Lighting, Inc., 376 U.S. 234 (1964), and Lear, Inc. v. Adkins, 395 U.S. 653 (1969).

[28]See, for example, Aronson v. Quick Point Pencil Co., 440 U.S. 257 (1979) (requiring Quick Point to honor a contract requiring it to pay Aronson for use of an unpatentable design for a key ring). See also Goldstein v. California, 412 U.S. 546 (1973) (upholding a California statute protecting phonograph records despite the failure of copyright law to cover this subject matter).

[29]416 U.S. 470 (1974).

[30]Harper & Row Publishers, Inc. v. Nation Enterprises, 471 U.S. 539, 555 (1985).

[31]However, as other rationales become better incorporated into federal law, state protections premised on similar considerations may become more vulnerable to preemption claims.

[32]803 F. 2d 1253 (2d Cir. 1986), *cert. denied,* 107 S. Ct. 2201 (1987).

[33]See also Rosemont v. Random House, Inc. 366 F.2d 303 (2d Cir. 1966), *cert. denied,* 385 U.S. 1009 (1967); and Time, Inc. v. Bernard Geis Assoc., 293 F. Supp. 130 (S.D. N.Y. 1968).

[34]723 F.2d 195, 204 (2d Cir. 1983) (holding Ford's memoirs uncopyrightable), *rev'd,* 471 U.S. 539, 545–546 (1985) (upholding the copyrightability of the memoirs).

[35]See Financial Information, Inc. v. Moody's Investors Services, Inc., 808 F.2d 204 (2d Cir. 1986) (daily bond cards describing daily trading information on municipal bonds not copyrightable); Eckes v. Card Prices Update, 736 F.2d 859 (2d Cir. 1984) (book listing all baseball cards manufactured 1909–1979 and their probable market prices held copyrightable); and Hoeling v. Universal City Studios, Inc., 618 F.2d 972 (2d Cir.), *cert. denied*, 449 U.S. 841 (1980) (research on burning of *Hindenberg*, including original theories on why incident occurred, not protectable).

[36]Metropolitan Opera Ass'n., Inc. v. Wagner-Nichols Recorder Corp., 199 Misc. 786, 101 N.Y. 2d 483, *aff'd*, 279 App. Div. 632, 107 N.Y. 2d 795 (1950). See generally Gorman (1963).

[37]Novel copyright theories have also, on occasion, proved successful, but these, too, turn on fact patterns that may not be shared across the spectrum of cases requiring protection. West Publishing co. v. Mead Data Central, Inc., 799 F.2d 1219 (8th Cir. 1986), *cert. denied*, 107 S.Ct. 962 (1987), is an example of a case in which a novel copyright theory worked. West, which publishes the decisions of most United States courts in hard copy and maintains a computerized data base of these same decisions, sued a firm running a rival computer data base. Although the cases themselves were in the public domain and were, therefore, not copyrightable, the Eighth Circuit strained to find a way to protect West, the original compiler. It therefore allowed Mead Data free use of the decisions, but enjoined it from noting the page numbers on which the cases appeared in West's publications. But since courts and legal publishers require citation to West page numbers (see, for example, *A Uniform System of Citation* [14th ed., 1986]), the decision protected West's market for hard copies of the decisions.

[38]Cf. Diamond v. Diehr, 430 U.S. 175 (1981) (upholding patent on an industrial process that incorporated a computer program) with Parker v. Flook, 437 U.S. 584 (1978) (invalidating a patent on a computer program that was part of an industrial process).

[39]Tie-outs restrict the licensee's right to sell products that compete with the patented product.

[40]Tie-ins require licensees to buy from the patentee products used with or in the patented invention.

[41]In addition to commenting on the No-Nos, Andewelt, who was speaking in his capacity as Antitrust Division deputy director of operations, expressed doubts over the department's longstanding opposition to patent protection for computer programs and its traditional hostility to trade secrecy laws.

Of course, the patentee and his licensee may together conspire to reduce the public welfare, but that problem can be handled with more finely tuned regulations than the No-Nos. See generally Baxter (1966).

[42]17 U.S.C. secs. 407, 408, 411.

[43]35 U.S.C. sec. 112. In cases in which the invention cannot be adequately described, deposit can also be required for patents (35 U.S.C. sec. 114).

[44]17 U.S.C. secs. 901–914 (Supp. II 1984).

[45]Under 37 C.F.R. sec. 211.5, the applicant is permitted to preserve his trade secrets by withholding two to five layers of his chip design and blocking out sensitive portions of the ones that are revealed, so long as a major portion of the chip is revealed in the deposit.

[46]See 37 C.F.R. sec. 202.20(c)(vii)(permitting deposit of only "identifying portions of the program," generally the first and last twenty-five pages).

[47]See Berkey Photo v. Eastman Kodak Co., 603 F.2d 263, 281 (2d Cir. 1979) (refusing to require Kodak to disclose details of its 110 camera to film manufacturers) *cert. denied*, 444 U.S. 1093 (1980); see also ILC Peripherals Leasing Corp. v. IBM Corp., 458 F. Supp. 423, 436–437 (N.D. Cal. 1978)(holding that IBM is under no duty to disclose interface

information to producers of peripherals), *aff'd sub nom.* Memorex Corp. v. IBM Corp., 636 F.2d 1188 (9th Cir. 1980).

[48]See 29 C.F.R. sec. 1910.1200.

[49]N.J. Stat. Ann. sec. 34: 5A-1-42.

[50]But see Dow Chem. Co. v. United States, 476 U.S. 227 (1986) (sustaining, as against a trade secrecy challenge, the Environmental Protection Agency's right to overfly chemical plants to ascertain compliance with environmental regulations); Ruckelshaus v. Monsanto Co., 467 U.S. 986 (1984) (upholding data-sharing provisions of the Federal Insecticide, Fungicide and Rodenticide Act against trade secrecy challenge); and New Jersey Chamber of Commerce v. Hughey, 774 F.2d 587 (3d Cir. 1985) (sustaining New Jersey's right-to-know law).

[51]In some circumstances, courts can also be called upon to reinterpret a statute to meet newly perceived problems. Other difficulties may be ameliorate through the actions of the government agency charged with administering the law. For example, the Copyright Office has recently promulgated a rule describing the circumstances in which it believes the copyright in a colorized motion picture should be recognized; see 52 Fed. Reg.23691 (1987) (to be codified at 37 C.F.R. sec. 202.20(c)(2)(ii).

[52]See Public Law No. 98-417, codified at 35 U.S.C. sec. 156.

[53]See H.R. 5536, 99th Cong., 2d sess., 1986, and H.R. 2482, 99th Cong., 2d sess., 1986.

[54]See H.R. 1623 100th Cong., 1st sess., 1987.

[55]See H.R. 4585 and H.R. 4808, 99th Cong., 2d sess., 1986.

[56]See, for example, Medvedev (1969) (describing how Soviet horticultural research was affected by genetic theories that were more congenial to communism than was neo-Mendelism).

[57]To some extent, this is a problem under existing intellectual property laws as well. If the invention is so advanced that it cannot be appreciated during the term of protection, the inventor will not be able to use the grant of exclusivity to capture the benefit that his invention will eventually generate. In addition, mavericks sometimes have difficulty convincing the Patent Office that their inventions work and are therefore eligible for patent protection; see Smith (1984) (describing an inventor's efforts to patent a generator that seemingly violates the second law of thermodynamics).

[58]17 U.S.C. sec. 906 permits another to reproduce a protected work without permission if the purpose is "teaching, analyzing, or evaluating the concepts or techniques" embodied in the work.

[59]Indeed, a bill protecting the design of useful objects has already been offered in Congress; see H.R. 379, 100th Cong., 1st sess., 1987.

[60]See, for example, the International Convention for the Protection of Industrial Property (the Paris Convention), 20 March, 1883, 25 Stat. 1372, T.S. No. 37; as revised at Brussels, 14 December, 1900; at Washington, 2 June, 1911, 36 Stat. 1645, T.S. No. 579; at the Hague, 6 November, 1925, 47 Stat. 1978, T.S. No. 834, 74 L.N.T.S. 289; at London, 2 June 1934, 53 Stat. 1748, T.S. No. 941, 192 L.N.T.S. 17; at Lisbon, 31 October, 1958, [1962] 1 U.S.T. 1, T.I.A.S. No. 4931; and at Stockholm, 14 July, 1967, [1970] 2 U.S.T. 1583, T.I.A.S. No. 6923; the Universal Copyright Convention Rev., 24 July, 1971, 25 U.S.T. 1341, T.I.A.S. No. 6839.

[61]See S. Rept. 100-66, 100th Cong., 1st sess., 1987; see also, Assistant Secretary and Commissioner of Patents and Trademarks, *Report on the Operation of the Int'l. Transitional Provisions of the Semiconductor Chip Protection Act of 1984* (7 November, 1986).

[62]One could, of course, imagine other forms of research in this area. For example, the vitality of research and development in countries with very different protection schemes

could be compared with each other; cf. Fox (1986) (comparing antitrust policy in the United States Europe). I do not address the larger issue of what kinds of research should or could be undertaken. See also Griliches (1987).

References

American Law Institute. 1976. *Restatement (Second) of Torts.* St. Paul, Minn.: American Law Institute, sec. 652A.

Andewelt, R. 1985. "Antitrust Perspective on Intellectual Property Protection." *Patent, Trademark, and Copyright Journal* 30 (25 July): 319.

Assistant Secretary and Commissioner of Patents and Trademarks. 1986. *Report on the Operation of the Int'l. Transitional Provisions of the Semiconductor Chip Protection Act of 1984* (7 November).

Baxter, W. 1966. "Legal Restrictions on Exploitation of the Patent Monopoly: An Economic Analysis." *Yale Law Journal* 76: 267.

Bennetts, L. 1986. " 'Colorizing' Film Classics: A Boom or a Bane?" *New York Times,* 5 August 1986, p. A-1, col. 3.

Dreyfuss, R. 1986. "Dethroning *Lear:* Licensee Estoppel and the Incentive to Innovate." *Virginia Law Review* 72: 677, 726–729.

Fox, E. 1986. "Monopolization and Dominance in the United States and the European Community: Efficiency, Opportunity, and Fairness." *Notre Dame Law Review* 61: 981.

Gordon, W. 1982. "Fair Use as Market Failure: A Structural and Economic Analysis of the *Betamax* Case and Its Predecessors." *Columbia Law Review* 82: 1600.

Gorman, R. 1963. "Copyright Protection for the Collection and Representation of Facts." *Harvard Law Review* 76: 1569.

Griliches, Z. 1987. "R&D and Productivity: Measurement Issues and Econometric Results." *Science* 237 (3 July): 31.

Hanley, R. 1987. "Fight Erupts on Baby M Book and Film Rights." *New York Times,* 26 March 1987, p. A-1, col. 2.

Jewkes, J., D. Sawers, and R. Stillerman. 1969. *The Sources of Invention.* 2d ed. New York: W. W. Norton, pp. 189–192.

Kitch, E. W. 1977. "The Nature and Function of the Patent System." *Journal of Law and Economics* 20: 265, 276–279.

Kwall, R. 1983. "Is Independence Day Dawning for the Right of Publicity?" *U. C. Davis Law Review* 17: 191.

Lewin, T. 1982. "Whose Life Is It Anyway? Legally, It's Hard to Tell." *New York Times,* 21 November 1982, sec. 2, p. 1, col. 6.

Lipsky, A. B. 1981. "Current Antitrust Division Views on Patent Licensing Practices." *Antitrust Law Journal* 50: 515.

Machlup, F. 1958. *An Economic Review of the Patent System: Study No. 15 of the Subcommittee on Patents, Trademarks, and Copyrights. Senate Committee on the Judiciary.* 85th Cong., 2d sess., 22–25.

Medvedev, Z. 1969. *The Rise and Fall of T. D. Lysenko.* New York: Columbia University Press.

National Academy of Sciences. 1962. *The Role of Patents in Research.* National Academy of Sciences-National Research Council, pp. 22–23, 44, 48–49, 57.

Noyce, R. 1977. "Microelectronics." *Scientific American* 237: 63.

Prosser, W. 1971. *Handbook of the Law of Torts.* 4th ed. St. Paul, Minn.: West Publishing, sec. 117, p. 807.

Rule, C. 1986. "The Antitrust Implications of International Licensing: Analyzing Patent and Know-How Licenses." *Trade Regulation Reports* (Commerce Clearing House) 5 (21 October), par. 50, p. 482.

Scherer, F. 1980. *Industrial Market Structure and Economic Performance.* 2d ed. Boston: Houghton Mifflin, pp. 457–458.

Schneider, K. 1987. "Science Debates Using Tools to Redesign Life." *New York Times,* 8 June 1987, p. A-1, col. 2.

Smith, R. 1984. "An Endless Siege of Implausible Inventions." *Science* 226 (16 November): 817.

Strauss, W. 1960. *The Moral Right of the Author: Study No. 4 of the Subcommittee on Patents, Trademarks, and Copyrights, Senate Committee on the Judiciary.* 86th Cong., 1st sess., p. 141.

Wolfe, T. 1983, "The Tinkerings of Robert Noyce." *Esquire* 99 (December): 346.

Chapter 9
Eliminating Bias
and Promoting Objectivity

9.1 INTRODUCTION

In Chapter 1 we quoted the Federal Policy Register, which defines research as "a systematic investigation, including research development, testing, and evaluation, designed to develop or contribute to the generalizable knowledge." Research produces knowledge, and knowledge is our grasp of the truth about the world. Learning the truth about the world is an internal goal of scientific research, as we noted in Chapter 7, and it explains the importance of objectivity in research.

The concept of **objectivity** is different in different contexts. Here, we will take for granted that an objective pursuit, such as research at its best, is concerned more with the nature of the object of study than with features of the knowing subject (namely, the researcher). In any instance of human knowledge, we may distinguish between the person who has knowledge—the knowing subject—and the thing that is known—the known object. Objectivity is an attitude in the subject that reflects an interest in learning the truth about the object of knowledge. Learning the truth must be one's paramount concern, and it requires carefulness, diligence, and perseverance in the pursuit of that truth. We often suppose that the truth about the world does not depend on us. It is not a matter of personal preference, for example, what the gravitational constant is, or what percentage of the population has a fear of spiders. We might wish that certain facts about the world were different, but objectivity requires that we learn them—and report them—as they are. In other words, regardless of our desires or other states as knowing subjects, we are objective only when we strive above all to know and report about things as they really are.

We may contrast this idea of objectivity with more subjective concerns, such as tastes, hobbies, or personal preferences. Whether roller coasters are fun, for instance, is a question that we usually leave up to each individual. Similarly, a taste for a certain kind of wine or for Chinese food is not a matter for objective research, since we ordinarily believe that these are matters of individual taste and preference. Notice that in these cases, the desires and preferences of the subjects determine their actions, and that is the sense of calling these concerns "subjective." We do not usually claim that there is a truth about the world concerning whether chocolate ice cream is better than vanilla.

Now it is possible that no hard-and-fast distinction exists between objective and subjective pursuits. Sociologists and philosophers of science have recently called our attention to various ways that scientists' ambitions, desires, preferences, and training all contribute to their (and our) notions of objectivity and to what should count as a good scientific theory. Some of these critiques attack the traditional notion of objectivity—the idea that we can know an object from an objective and impartial standpoint outside of our historically, economically, and socially conditioned individual standpoint—and argue instead that scientific theories are all social constructions. Some theories are dominant for a time, these views maintain, due mainly to the prestige and power of their advocates. Yet no theory ultimately grasps the truth about the world as it is in itself, because all knowledge employs the concepts and ideas characteristic of some particular culture at some particular time. In this constructivist view, knowledge claims reflect the power and prestige of the person claiming knowledge, and thus what we take to be the truth is relative to features of ourselves, including our goals, training, prejudices, and so forth.

Although this sort of view has made important strides and provides illuminating analyses of actual scientific practices, the vast majority of scientists still recognize a distinction between objectivity and subjectivity. Constructivism may help us recognize underlying prejudices or biases, but most scientists still believe that it is possible to learn the truth about the world as it is in itself. In short, they reject the idea that knowledge is relative to one's social setting. If they are right, then they accept certain responsibilities, as researchers, to discover the truth about the world and to contribute to the generalizable knowledge. The present chapter explores these responsibilities to promote objectivity and eliminate bias.

9.2   BIAS IN SCIENTIFIC INQUIRY

The quest for objectivity in research begins with a general concern for learning the truth. This concern imposes on researchers a number of responsibilities. They must, for example, design their experiments and research methodologies so that their research is likely to reveal the truth they seek. They must record data accurately and employ standard techniques of analysis correctly. They must report those data and analyses honestly, even when the results do not support a favored theory. Researchers must above all take responsibility for their work by publishing their research and answering any resulting criticism from the scientific community.

At every stage of research, errors are possible. A lab assistant may record a digit from a readout as a '7' instead of a '9'. An experimenter might misplace a stack of questionnaires from a psychology experiment and so omit crucial data. During analysis, a researcher might mistakenly program her computer with the wrong formula, input incorrect data, or input one batch of data twice. Any of these errors might a have an impact on the results, thus causing the research to deviate from the truth. Since a goal of research is to learn the truth, researchers must do their best both to avoid errors and to refrain from falsifying and fabricating data, as discussed in section 7.2. Although errors are unintentional, the impact that errors can have on the scientific record can be just as grave as other forms of misconduct.

The responsibility that researchers have to avoid errors is fairly straightforward: They must aim not to make mistakes. The notion of bias is somewhat different from that of error. An error is an isolated instance of failure to record or report the truth, including mistakes that might affect an entire data set. Sometimes an error is an honest mistake, one that a researcher could not have helped. Instances of honest mistakes should be admitted promptly and corrected. In other cases, researchers err through negligence, as when carelessness leads one to record or report data or results incorrectly. Such cases of negligence, where the researcher should have known better, often constitute a kind of research misconduct, a point also discussed in section 7.2.

Bias, in contrast, is a systematic failure of some kind that threatens an entire data set, experimental design, or theory. As we use the term bias, it includes not only a prejudice that researchers might bring to their work—such as a conviction that a particular theory *must* be correct, independent of what the evidence shows—but also flaws in experimental method or analysis. Unlike other types of errors, bias stems from a *mistaken mindset* on the part of the researcher. Other types of errors, such as mistakes in calculation or falsification of data stem from imprecision or malice on the part of the researcher, but bias involves neither a lack of precision nor blatantly malicious intentions. Many biased researchers are convinced that their methodology will yield the truth about their field of inquiry. What these researchers do not realize is that their failure to be objective may infect their results. This failure to be objective may manifest itself at different stages in the experimental process: where a hypothesis is formed or where data is collected or analyzed.

Bias might emerge when a sociologist takes a survey of beliefs about advertising. If the questions on the survey are phrased carelessly and reflect the researcher's own beliefs about advertising, then the data are less likely to reflect the subjects' actual beliefs. Rather, the data will be colored by the researcher's own beliefs and prejudices. For example, research subjects may respond differently to the question "Do you find that television commercials affect your decision to buy products in the grocery store?" than to the question, "Have you ever found yourself purchasing a product that you ordinarily would not have purchased, because of the pressure of television commercials that control your buying habits?" The language in the first question may be less biased and more neutral. The language in the second question may betray a subtle distrust of advertisements and a suspicion that they are coercive in some way. As a result, the researcher who uses the second question likely will fail to learn what the subjects' actual beliefs are, and the data will be biased as a result of the poor survey design. This sort of error counts as bias by virtue of its systematic impact on experimental results, due to the researcher's failure to be objective about the field of inquiry.

Another example of bias in scientific research involves the theory of N-rays. After James Clerk Maxwell did his ground-breaking work on electromagnetism in the mid-1800s, physicists explored the electromagnetic spectrum, discovering various wavelengths that we now call X-rays, microwave, and ultraviolet, among others. In the rush to find other forms of electromagnetic radiation, French physicist René Blondlot reported the discovery of "N-rays" in 1903. These rays, detectable only by the unaided human eye, were rendered visible by the flash of an electric spark in various media (gas, electric fields, etc.). In the three years following Blondlot's "discovery" of N-rays, more than 300 papers were published on the phenomenon, mainly in French science journals, many by reputable and respected scientists.

N-rays, however, do not exist. An American scientist, R.W. Wood, called their existence into question by means of a clever experiment. N-rays could be split, according to Blondlot, by a prism, just like visible light. Wood invited Blondlot to his lab and asked him to observe several experimental trials of splitting N-rays. Blondlot reported observing the splitting, even after Wood had removed the prism. The theory of N-rays was discredited by Wood's results, and physicists soon turned their attention to other matters. Today, we generally account for this kind of result in terms of an "observer effect": Researchers expecting or desiring to observe some phenomenon will sometimes seem to observe what is not in fact present. Blondlot and the other discoverers of N-rays had deceived themselves. They saw what they wanted to see. As a result, their theory was biased by their expectations.

A commitment to objectivity in research imposes a responsibility on scientists to avoid all kinds of bias. It would be easy to write off Blondlot's work as carelessness or foolishness; he was, however, neither careless nor foolish but instead was one of the most respected physicists in France. He was self-deceived, and his research was biased by his commitment to his own theory. This demonstrates the need for suspension of judgment pending careful analysis of the evidence. This comment points to the general solution for bias, namely the scientific method. From thoughtful devising of hypotheses to careful experimental design and implementation to rigorous analysis of data to cautious drawing of conclusions, the scientific method has at every step objectivity as one of its primary goals. This general antidote to bias will have particular applications in various disciplines: The requirements imposed by the scientific method in social psychology may differ from those imposed in molecular biology, for instance. However, even though the specific means by which the scientific method is employed in different disciplines may change, the intention to employ the scientific method in a quest for objective knowledge about the world remains the same.

We have already addressed some ethical concerns related to **statistical analysis.** For example, in Chapter 3 we considered the importance of randomization to the accuracy of human subjects research. Inadequate randomization of subjects into control and study groups may affect the reliability of the data generated. Randomization represents one of the most reliable means of ensuring that populations are accurately represented in the study. In this way bias, including both researcher prejudice and unrepresentative sampling, may be averted.

In Chapter 7 we also looked at issues concerning statistics and the analysis of data generally. In this book, we cannot consider the entire range of issues pertaining to data analysis. The field is too vast, and each discipline and sub-discipline within the natural and social sciences has distinctive methodologies and modes of quantitative analysis. A detailed discussion of statistics lies beyond the scope of our discussion. We may, however, stress several general points concerning statistical methods and their uses within scientific research.

Researchers frequently seek statistical correlations. A researcher might seek a correlation between smoking and lung cancer, between phosphate concentration in streams and algae blossoms, or between household income and political affiliation. Whenever researchers seek a correlation, they plot a curve relating an independent variable to a dependent one. For different values of the independent variable, they record the corresponding value of the dependent variable. This data can be plotted on a graph, and a curve may be fit to demonstrate a correlation between the two variables. The curve is rarely a perfect fit, and various algorithms allow the fitting of a curve to the data. The question at this point concerns so-called 'outliers', the data points that do not fall neatly on the correlating curve. How should we treat them? Are they evidence against the correlation? Are they insignificant deviations, perhaps due to the margin of error of the experimental apparatus?

The treatment of outliers may allow for bias to creep into data analysis. Responsible researchers, as we indicated in section 7.2, report outliers in a manner consistent with the standards of their particular discipline, and they explain the significance, if any, of those outliers to the reported correlations. "Trimming" is the elimination of outliers without appropriate justification, in an attempt to create a data set that supports a given hypothesis more strongly than the actual set does. To the extent that they adopt some systematic treatment of outliers, including an assessment of the margin of error, researchers should report that treatment and its rationale. Bias can arise in at least two ways in this context. First, the selection of curve-fitting algorithm may be biased. One's discipline may have a standard curve-fitting routine, but that may be a poor choice for a given experiment, or the discipline as a whole may be using a biased algorithm. Standards do change from time to time, and they change in order to provide more accurate and objective results.

Second, even if one's method of fitting a curve is adequate, one might still misinterpret the significance of outliers. How far from the curve must an outlier be in order to count as a significant deviation from the correlation? We have no general way to answer this question. What in one domain counts as a disconfirming instance of the correlation is in another domain insignificant. The lack of a satisfactory general answer to this question opens the door to bias. If researchers make systematic mistakes in determining the significance of outliers, they will introduce a kind of bias into their results. Once again, the clear solutions are to adhere as closely as possible to the standard statistical methodologies of one's discipline, to report all data, and to state clearly the rationale for treating outliers as one has.

Consider the case of an organic chemist who fails sufficiently to rinse out glassware from a previous trial, resulting in a set of data points that are not consistent with the remaining data. The chemist should recognize these points as outliers, because their integration into the data set will detract from an objective understanding of the results. However, a thorough-going investigation of his methodology will likely yield the cause of the outliers. The researcher's responsibility at this point is to report all of the data that he accumulated, then offer a justification for omitting the outliers from the final data set. Admission of a small error on the part of the researcher is a more responsible act than merely eliminating data points without giving an explanation for their elimination.

Another potential source of bias arises with observation. Virtually all scientific research involves one kind of observation or another. Even questionnaires in the social sciences count as a kind of observation, because those questionnaires are the method by which researchers are "observing" data. An integral part of the scientific method, observation is the use of researchers' senses to record information generated by an experiment. Observation yields the data that subsequently may be analyzed and reported as the results of research. The ideal scientific observer is one who is detached and able to record dispassionately and disinterestedly exactly what happens. Unfortunately, no real scientists are ideal.

The phenomenon of **selective observation** is a species of wishful thinking. Wishful thinking, of course, is believing what one wishes were true rather than what is in fact the case. When researchers approach their scientific observations convinced that they know in advance what they will observe, they sometimes observe what is not in fact the case (as noted above, this is also known as the observer effect). The case of Blondlot's N-rays discussed above provides a classic example.

The possibility of this kind of bias also recommends an attitude of healthy skepticism and dispassion. Only if one is overeager to find a particular experimental result is one likely to be biased in this way. Careful experimental observation uses many observers and attempts to see what is there. Philosophers of science have argued that all observation is "theory-laden," meaning that we always bring assumptions and expectations to our empirical observations. Perfectly objective, uninformed perspectives are impossible, but it can still be a worthwhile goal for researchers to be conscious of their expectations and the potential effects of selective observation. Everyone should approach observation with a skeptical wonder concerning whether what one expects to find is *really* there. Such an attitude is a useful preventative to many kinds of bias, not just those resulting from selective observation.

A third source of bias in scientific research is **errors of reasoning.** Researchers must be on guard concerning the conclusions and the quality of inferences they draw from their data. Once again, the scope of this book does not permit a complete examination of all of the logical fallacies and other errors of reasoning, but a few examples will suffice to indicate how bias may creep into research through errors of reasoning.

A classic fallacy is the *post-hoc* fallacy. Named for a portion of a Latin phrase, "post hoc, ergo propter hoc," meaning "after this, therefore because of this," this is the fallacy of inferring a causal connection from a mere correlation. A correlation discovers a connection between two events, especially that they occur in a certain order; however, the occurrence of event A before event B does not prove that A caused B. For instance, ancient Egyptians prayed to a species of bird that arrived just before the spring floods along the Nile. They believed that, since the birds arrived before the floods, they caused the floods. We now know, of course, that the migratory patterns of birds and the flooding of rivers are both seasonal events caused by changing temperatures and precipitation patterns. Researchers need to be careful about inferring causal claims from the mere correlations they discover.

Another example of an error in reasoning is the fallacy of oversimplification. One might have discovered *a* cause of some kind of event and yet not have the entire story. In many cases, the causes of a particular event are numerous and complex. To say that segregation is the cause of racism or greed caused the Great Depression—even if it is true that segregation and greed are important causal factors of the phenomena in question—is surely an oversimplification of complex social and historical phenomena. Scientific research is precisely research into the causes of things, and therefore researchers need to be cautious about the inferences they draw from their data. Any systematic error in reasoning will introduce a kind of bias into the results of research.

9.3   STUDY DESIGN AND OBJECTIVITY

In sections 3.2 , 3.3, and 3.4 we discussed the ethical aspects of study design, and some of those aspects concerned objectivity. Although the focus of this chapter is different from that of Chapter 3, many of the previously discussed points are relevant to the present topic. In Chapter 3 we explored the ethical aspects of study design, and we highlighted researchers' ethical responsibilities. In the present chapter, we are interested in objectivity and the responsibilities that scientists have as a result of making objectivity one of their goals. It has been a consistent theme of this book that ethical science is good science. That principle receives support when we discover that many of the responsibilities of ethical research are obligations to make research as objective as possible. We can illustrate the principle by considering four dimensions of objectivity: sampling, controls, blinding, and ethics.

First, recall the discussion of sampling. Researchers always work with a sample of a population or substance. Objectivity demands that this sample be representative of the population from which it is drawn. The reason for this demand is that researchers seek generalizable knowledge concerning an entire population, and a suitably representative sample will be the only means of discovering that knowledge. The most objective way to achieve this goal is to use the census method of sampling and use the entire population. In most instances of research, however, this method is not feasible. Conclusions about the effects of advertising on the buying habits of the American public are not drawn from surveys of the entire American population. In this, and in other research on large populations, smaller samples must be employed.

In chemistry and physics, of course, a "representative sample" of a substance will ideally be as pure as possible. Here the avoidance of bias amounts to the elimination of impurities in a sample. But in other areas—especially in disciplines that deal with human and animal subjects—a representative sample will include a relatively small number of individuals drawn from a larger population of diverse individuals. To avoid bias in this kind of sampling, convenience samples should be avoided. Convenience sampling is the selection of subjects from some convenient group, without concern for the degree to which the sample is representative of the larger population. An example from section 3.2 considered the problems that arise when a convenience sample is used.

The obligation to design research studies in such a way that they rely on unbiased samples is a demand of objective science, but it also fulfills an ethical obligation, at least when the subjects of research are human or animal subjects. In human or animal subjects research, the researcher has an obligation to minimize the risk to subjects. To the extent that researchers use biased samples, their results are less likely to be objective or to yield generalizable knowledge. Hence, the subjects have been put at risk needlessly, which is unethical. In November 1996, *The Wall Street Journal* ran a front-page story describing a major drug company's use of homeless alcoholics as research subjects. These individuals had been paid between $125 and $250 a day to take drugs in Phase I clinical trials. The article pointed out that the sample that had been recruited for the studies in question was a biased sample comprising persons who had reason to be willing to undergo multiple medical tests, take an experimental drug with little hope of direct benefit, and live on-site at a clinic. Ethical questions arise when vulnerable populations, such as homeless alcoholics, are the subjects of research. However, questions of bias also emerge from this study: How objective are the results from a Phase I clinical trial that used individuals who were primarily alcoholics? Could the fact that most of the subjects used a great deal of alcohol prior to enrolling in the study affect the study results? These aspects of the research likely compromised not only its ethical justification but also its usefulness to the wider population.

Second, research is more objective when it uses satisfactory controls to isolate the phenomenon under study. In human subjects and animal research, the use of satisfactory controls frequently requires randomization into both treatment and control arms. Control groups may use a placebo, an alternative therapy or treatment, or sometimes no treatment at all. The researcher then distributes subjects into the different arms of the study, some to the treatment arm, some to the control arm (or other arms, if any). As in the case of sampling, how this distribution is accomplished may have an impact on the objectivity of the results. If subjects are sorted according to some property—sex, weight, height, etc.—and distributed into the arms of the study on the basis of that property, then the results may be biased. Even if the subject pool itself is not biased, biased stratification may undermine the objectivity of the research. For example, if human subjects are part of a study testing the affects of caffeine on test-taking, randomizing the subjects by weight may undermine the validity of the study. Common sense dictates that the same amount of caffeine will have more profound effects on smaller persons, and will have less noticeable effects on larger persons. Researchers should be careful that their method of stratification does not bias the results of the study. If instead the distribution of subjects is randomized according to stratification which does not import any biases, then it is more likely that the results will be representative of the larger population. And since representative results are thereby generalizable, randomization serves the goal of objectivity in research.

Third, blinded experiments provide an important way to protect the objectivity of research and eliminate bias. Blinding is the practice of concealing information about an experimental trial. A single-blinded trial may leave the subjects ignorant of which arm of the study they occupy, the control arm or the treatment arm. This can prevent subject biases, including the placebo effect. A double-blinded trial, in which both subjects and researchers are ignorant of the distribution of subjects, controls for both subject and researcher bias. This kind of precaution can preclude observer effects and selective observation. Blinded experiments can also be performed in research that does not involve human or animal subjects, when experimental samples are identified using numbers rather than descriptive labels. If researchers are ignorant about whether they are observing an actual trial or a control, then their biases or expectations are less likely to impact their observations.

Finally, ethical science is good science, in part *because ethical science is more objective science*. Research uses subjects, be the subjects humans, animals, or natural resources, and it is important that research not abuse these subjects. Abuse can take the form of failure to respect individual subjects, but it can also take the form of using subjects to no good purpose. Research generally involves putting subjects at some risk, sometimes grave risk. If that risk is pointless because of poor study design that is unlikely to produce generalizable knowledge, then subjects have been abused. In other words, a flawed study design that fails to be objective is unethical. Flawed research is a waste of time and other resources.

The wastefulness of a biased study is a source of ethical concern. The fact that failure of objectivity in study design is unethical underscores the idea that objective science coincides with ethical science.

9.4   PUBLIC REPORTING OF SCIENTIFIC RESULTS

The primary means by which scientists communicate their results to each other is the scientific journal. Journals typically maintain high standards of rigor for the articles they publish, and the results published in journals are subject to scrutiny for their study design, methodology, reproducibility of results, and quality of analysis. The general public does not often read these journals, and even well-educated people would have difficulty following the discussions in many scientific articles. Yet the public has an interest in scientific research and its results, for a number of reasons. First, if members of the public were used as research subjects, it stands to reason that they should be among those who may have a claim to the results of the research, as we pointed out in section 8.5. One way for the subjects to assert their right to the results of the research—if they in fact have such a right—is to read the results of the study. A second reason that the public has an interest in scientific research is that resources, such as environmental or other natural resources, may have been used in the data-collection or analysis phase. If natural resources were not used, perhaps scientists received public or governmental funding for their research. In either case, the public has an interest in determining whether these resources or funds were well-used. Finally, the public may have an interest in scientific research because the results of scientific research may prove beneficial to the public. Study results about health, nutrition, child rearing, and the environment make headlines. The public is interested in the findings of researchers because what science learns today may have a direct effect on the lives of the public tomorrow. For all of these reasons, researchers have certain responsibilities with respect to informing the public once their research projects have been completed and how best to keep the public informed.

Some researchers adopt the attitude that if people wish to learn about science then they can read the scientific journals. They contend that scientists have enough to do in the course of their research, teaching, or other duties, and that they have neither the time nor the obligation to satisfy public curiosity about their activities. Such researchers resist the suggestion that they have social responsibilities beyond the responsibility to pursue the truths of science. This attitude tends to ignore the above-mentioned considerations about the public's legitimate interest in learning the results of scientific research and in having those results presented in a fashion that is readily comprehensible to the average citizen. Scientists ought to respect this interest and accept that it may occasionally place additional demands on them beyond the specific responsibilities of their research.

An additional issue related to interactions between scientific researchers and the public arises when we consider the impact of research on the public. An awareness that scientific research has consequences for the public should bring researchers to realize that they are—at least partly—responsible for those consequences. This is the case regardless of whether those consequences are beneficial or harmful. Scientists cannot responsibly take on research projects without reflecting on the impact that these projects might have on the public. Science of all sorts has public consequences; even basic research may ultimately have practical applications.

The discussion of whether the risks of a research program are worth the potential benefits is one in which the public may reasonably demand to participate. The Office of Protection from Research Risks (OPRR), a branch of the National Institutes of Health, acted in accordance with this demand in October of 1996 when they issued a "Dear Colleague" letter to the Institutional Officials and IRBs that oversee research on persons in emergency situations. This work includes research on stroke and accident victims who are reasonably expected to benefit directly from the research but are unable to give informed consent to experimental treatments because of the immediacy of their medical situation.

OPRR recommended several ethical safeguards for the research subjects in emergency research. One of these safeguards is the recommendation that prior to the inception of emergency research projects, members of the community from which the research subjects are taken should be consulted regarding the risks, benefits, and course of the research. After the completion of the project, the researchers should again consult with the community regarding their results. OPRR recognized that since this kind of research has obvious and vital effects on the public, the public has a right to participate in a dialogue regarding the scope and impact of the research. For the public dialogue to be an informed one, the public must be educated about scientific methodology, the value of both basic and applied research in these areas, and researchers' commitment to ethical safeguards of human research subjects. The fact that the community should be consulted about the aims and progress of emergency research is only one example of researchers' taking responsibility for the consequences of their research and acknowledging an obligation to make those consequences as beneficial as possible to society.

The responsibilities that researchers have to the public may extend beyond informing the public about the nature of their research to respecting the public's assessment of research practices. Researchers have an obligation to promote benefit in undertaking their research. If research activities do more harm than good, might researchers have an obligation to *not* investigate certain questions? Certain research questions might produce such harmful consequences that society would be better off not knowing the answers. It has been claimed, for instance, that researchers ought not look too closely at correlations between the increase in abortion rates and the drop in crime rates that occurred in the U.S. following the Supreme Court's decision in Roe v. Wade. Many scientists will resist the idea that they ought to censor their research activities, but to some extent—as mentioned in Chapter 8—this happens through funding agencies. The general point to be made here is that the questions that researchers choose to investigate can themselves be a matter of ethical scrutiny, and this point may be particularly pressing when the public is likely to be affected by the results of the research.

Once researchers recognize their responsibility to keep the public informed, they may ask how best to fulfill that responsibility. The results of research, initially published in scientific journals, are often later reported in the mainstream press. Researchers cannot always guarantee the completeness or scientific integrity of these reports and may be responsible to follow these reports with further information. Insofar as researchers take seriously their responsibility to keep the public informed, they will seek to educate the public regarding the nature, significance, and content of their research and its results.

Scientists who wish to address the general public directly use either professional news media or other journalists concerned with science to report their findings. Each mode has its advantages and disadvantages. Media coverage takes many different forms, including press conferences, press releases, reviews of scientific journals or books, interviews, and reports from scientific conferences. The news media have large audiences, and researchers who communicate their results and theories through the news can potentially reach a broad section of the public. Time and energy spent informing the public can thus be used efficiently. On the other hand, relatively few scientific matters are sufficiently significant to attract the attention of the mainstream news media. Less well-known researchers or those working on less well-known matters may not be seen as newsworthy. Moreover, the news media's attention span is short, and scientific complexities can be lost when compressed to a sound bite. The use of the news media can actually be a source of misunderstanding, as well as information, for the public. Scientists and the media must strive for accuracy and avoid oversimplification in presenting scientific discoveries to the public. Responsible researchers should attempt to demonstrate the same integrity in disseminating their results as they demonstrated in collecting the data. Researchers who meticulously perform experiments, only to allow the results of the experiments to be misreported, have not upheld the scientific and ethical responsibilities of their profession.

Science journalism—in the form of books, magazines, columns, and special reporting on science—is another outlet through which scientists can inform the public regarding their research. The generally longer format of these publications allows for a more complete treatment of complex or abstract theories, a real advantage over the news media. However, these specialized forms of journalism have smaller audiences. These smaller audiences often comprise those members of the public most interested in science, so researchers using these outlets are performing a significant public service.

A real danger of science reporting is that results are sometimes reported before they have been confirmed. Controversial stories can make an impact even when the data behind them are mistaken, and retractions usually do not receive nearly the same coverage. Refer to section 1.3 for a significant example.

Such cases support the idea that great caution needs to be taken when reporting scientific findings and that the media need to follow up on their science reporting when errors are discovered.

A similar problem is the overenthusiastic reporting of medical advances in the very early stages of development, thereby causing false hope and expectations on the part of the public. As an example, an enzyme that is instrumental in the progression of heart disease may be isolated years before the development of a medication that makes use of this important piece of basic science. Despite this, the press may report a "Heart-Attack Breakthrough!" and thereby cause false hope on behalf of the general population. Scientists may not wish to take time from their research activities to explain the true scope and limitations of their research, or to repeat that this so-called "breakthrough" may not have real medical application for years to come. However, responsible scientists should recognize that their obligations as ethical researchers extend into the data dissemination stage, and in some cases, well beyond.

9.5   SUMMARY

Scientific research is the enterprise of systematic inquiry into the world for the sake of producing generalizable knowledge. When scientists reject relativism and the idea that knowledge and truth are relative to a researcher's social setting, they commit themselves to objectivity. Objectivity coupled with social responsibility will require many researchers to seek an appropriate public forum for the dissemination of their results.

When researchers aim to learn the truth about the world, it is obviously important for them to avoid errors. The need to avoid error counsels a degree of carefulness in performing research and making observations. Equally important is the avoidance of bias, which is a mistaken mindset that systematically threatens to yield false results. Bias may manifest itself in the collection of data and observations, in faulty statistical analysis, and in fallacious reasoning. Scientists who are committed to objectivity must be wary of all of these potential sources of bias.

A common way to prevent bias is the use of well-designed experiments and studies. Careful selection of sample populations, for instance, can prevent one kind of bias. The incorporation of control groups in a study to isolate the causal relationship under examination can help ensure generalizable results, provided the subjects are distributed appropriately into the control and study arms. Blinded experimental trials can be especially effective in preventing researcher and subject biases from corrupting results. All of these elements of study design foster both the goals of good science and the goals of ethical science. Objectivity is both an ethical demand and a means to excellence in scientific research.

When researchers have fulfilled their responsibilities to perform careful and unbiased research, they are sometimes called upon to present their work in a public forum. The news media report widely on scientific achievements of special importance or wide impact. Science journalism reports on controversial or intriguing developments to a smaller audience that is more informed on scientific issues. Researchers' social responsibilities may also require them to reconsider a line of inquiry, depending on the social impact of the research. Since scientists should confront the social ramifications of their work, they may also need to engage the public before and during their research, as well as after. In every case, researchers must try to see that their work is communicated clearly and correctly to the public and that any errors (whether on the part of the reporter or the researcher) are promptly and noticeably corrected. Objectivity demands nothing less.

9.6   CASE STUDIES

Case 9.1: Terry is a graduate student working in a research group conducting research in high-energy particle physics. Their work involves the use of "bubble chambers," large tanks filled with liquid and placed in a magnetic field into which the high-energy particles travel. Occasionally, a particle will strike a molecule of the liquid, and the magnetic field will deflect the resulting particles along various paths depending on the particles' mass, energy, and other properties. These paths leave bubble tracks in the tank, and the tracks are recorded by cameras. Terry's director believes that he has discovered a new kind of particle, based on an unusual track in the bubble chamber. Terry is skeptical: The path is faint and does not appear on many photographs; it may be a defect in the film or printing equipment. Should Terry raise these concerns about a potential observer effect in this case? How? Would the approach be different if Terry were a colleague rather than a student? How so?

Case 9.2: Dr. Kim's 9-year research project yields some dramatic results: Daily consumption of a compound that he synthesized in his lab prevents lung cancer in mice that are exposed to cigarette smoke. His findings are published in an esteemed scientific journal, and the non-scientific press quickly learns of Dr. Kim's remarkable success. His office and lab phones are soon ringing day and night, as reporters from newspapers, television, and radio all try to learn what they can about his findings and their implications for the public. What are Dr. Kim's responsibilities at this point? If Dr. Kim learns that a newspaper has erroneously claimed that he has "cured" lung cancer that already exists, and not merely prevented lung cancer from occurring, what should he do? What are the limits to what Dr. Kim should reasonably be expected to do in such circumstances?

REFERENCES AND FURTHER READING

Joseph Ben-David, *The Scientist's Role in Society*, Upper Saddle River, NJ: Prentice-Hall, 1971.

Laurie P. Cohen, "Stuck for Money: To Screen New Drugs for Safety, Lilly Pays Homeless Alcoholics," *The Wall Street Journal*, November 14, 1996, pp. A1 and A10.

"Informed Consent Requirements in Emergency Research," *OPRR Reports* Number 97-01, October 31, 1996.

Henry Kyburg, *Theory and Measurement*, Cambridge: Cambridge University Press, 1984.

M. Scriven, "The exact role of value judgments in science," in *Ethical Issues in Scientific Research*, ed. E. Erwin, S. Gendin, and L. Kleiman, Hamden: Garland Publishing, 1994.

Frank von Hippel, *Citizen Scientist*, New York: American Institute of Physics, 1991.

Self-Deception and Gullibility

William Broad and Nicholas Wade

In 1669 the distinguished English physicist Robert Hooke made a wonderful discovery. He obtained the long-sought proof of Copernicus' heliocentric theory of the solar system by demonstrating stellar parallax—a perceived difference in position of a star due to the earth's motion around the sun. One of the first to use a telescope for this purpose, Hooke observed the star Gamma Draconis and soon reported to the Royal Society that he had found what he was looking for: the star had a parallax of almost thirty seconds of arc. Here at last was impeccable experimental proof of the Copernican theory.

This heartening triumph of empirical science was only momentarily dashed when the Frenchman Jean Picard announced he had observed the star Alpha Lyrae by the same method but had failed to find any parallax at all. A few years later England's first Astronomer Royal, the brilliant observer John Flamsteed, reported that the Pole Star had a parallax of at least forty seconds.

Hooke and Flamsteed, outstanding scientists of their day, are leading lights in the history of science. But they fell victim to an effect that to this day has continued to trap many lesser scientists in its treacherous coils. It is the phenomenon of experimenter expectancy, or seeing what you want to see. There is indeed a stellar parallax, but because of the vast distance of all stars from earth, the parallax is extremely small—about one second of arc. It cannot be detected by the relatively crude telescopes used by Hooke and Flamsteed.[1]

Self-deception is a problem of pervasive importance in science. The most rigorous training in objective observation is often a feeble defense against the desire to obtain a particular result. Time and again, an experimenter's expectation of what he will see has shaped the data he recorded, to the detriment of the truth. This unconscious shaping of results can come about in numerous subtle ways.

William Broad and Nicholas Wade, "Self-Deception and Gullibility," in *Betrayers of the Truth* (New York: Simon and Schuster, 1982) 107–125. Reprinted by permission of the publisher.

Nor is it a phenomenon that affects only individuals. Sometimes a whole community of researchers falls prey to a common delusion, as in the extraordinary case of the French physicists and N-rays, or—some would add—American psychologists and ape sign language.

Expectancy leads to self-deception, and self-deception leads to the propensity to be deceived by others. The great scientific hoaxes, such as the Beringer case and the Piltdown man discussed in this chapter, demonstrate the extremes of gullibility to which some scientists may be led by their desire to believe. Indeed, professional magicians claim that scientists, because of their confidence in their own objectivity, are easier to deceive than other people.

Self-deception and outright fraud differ in volition—one is unwitting, the other deliberate. Yet it is perhaps more accurate to think of them as two extremes of a spectrum, the center of which is occupied by a range of actions in which the experimenter's motives are ambiguous, even to himself. Many measurements that scientists take in the laboratory admit judgment factors to enter in. An experimenter may delay a little in pressing a stopwatch, perhaps to compensate for some extraneous factor. He can tell himself he is rejecting for technical reasons a result that gives the "wrong" answer; after a number of such rejections, the proportion of "right" answers in the acceptable experiments may acquire a statistical significance that previously was lacking. Naturally it is only the "acceptable" experiments that get published. In effect, the experimenter has selected his data to prove his point, in a way that is in part a deliberate manipulation but which also falls short of conscious fraud.

The "double-blind" experiment—in which neither doctor nor patients know who is receiving a test drug and who a placebo—has become standard practice in clinical research because of the powerful effects of the doctor's expectancy, to say nothing of the patients'. But the habit of "blinding" the experimenter has not become as universal in science as perhaps it should. A dramatic demonstration of experimenter expectancy has been provided in a series of studies by Harvard psychologist Robert Rosenthal. In one of his experiments he gave psychology students two groups of rats to study. The "maze-bright" group of rats, the students were told, had been specially bred for its intelligence in running mazes. The "maze-dull" group were genetically stupid rats. The students were told to test the maze-running abilities of the two groups. Sure enough, they found that the maze-bright rats did significantly better than the maze-dull rats. In fact there was no difference between the maze-bright and maze-dull animals: all were the standard strain of laboratory rats. The difference lay only in the students' expectancies of each group. Yet the students translated this difference in their expectancies into the data they reported.[2]

Perhaps some of the students consciously invented data to accord with the results they thought they should be getting. With others, the manipulation was unconscious and much more subtle. Just how it was done is rather hard to explain. Perhaps the students handled more gently the rats they expected to perform better, and the treatment enhanced the rats' performance. Perhaps in timing the run through the maze the students would unconsciously press the button on the stopwatch a fraction too early for the maze-bright rats and a fraction too late for the maze-dull animals. Whatever the exact mechanism, the researchers' expectations had shaped the result of the experiment without their knowledge.

The phenomenon is not just a pitfall for laboratory scientists. Consider the situation of a teacher administering IQ tests to a class. If he has prior expectations about the children's intelligence, are these likely to shape the results he gets? The answer is yes, they do. In an experiment similar to that performed on the psychology students, Rosenthal told teachers at an elementary school that he had identified certain children with a test that predicted academic blooming. Unknown to the teachers, the test was just a standard IQ test, and the children identified as "bloomers" were chosen at random. At the end of the school year, the children were retested, by the teachers this time, with the same test. In the first grade, those who had been identified to the teachers as academic bloomers gained fifteen IQ points more than did the other children. The "bloomers" in the second grade gained ten points more than the controls. Teachers' expectancies made no or little difference in the upper grades. In the lower grades, comments Rosenthal, "the children have not yet acquired those reputations that become so difficult to change in the later grades and which give teachers in subsequent grades the expectancies for the pupil's performance. With every successive grade it would be more difficult to change the child's reputation."[3]

A particularly fertile ground for scientific self-deception lies in the field of animal-to-man communication. Time and again, the researcher's expectation has been projected onto the animal and reflected back to the researcher without his recognizing the source. The most famous case of this sort is that of Clever Hans, a remarkable horse that could apparently add and substract and even solve problems that were presented to it. He has acquired immortality because his equine spirit returns from time to time to haunt the laboratories of experimental psychologists, announcing its presence with ghostly laughter that its victims are almost always the last to hear.

Hans's trainer, a retired German schoolteacher named Wilhelm Von Osten, sincerely believed that he had taught Hans the ability to count. The horse would tap out numbers with his hoof, stopping when he had reached the right answer. He would count not just for his master but for others as well. The phenomenon was investigated by a psychologist, Oskar Pfungst, who discovered that Von Osten and others were unconsciously cuing the equine prodigy. As the horse reached the number of hoof taps corresponding to the correct answer, Von Osten would involuntarily jerk his head. Perceiving this unconscious cue, Hans would stop tapping. Pfungst found that the horse could detect head movements as slight as one-fifth of a millimeter. Pfungst himself played the part of the horse and found that twenty-three out of twenty-five questioners unwittingly cued him when to stop tapping.

Pfungst's celebrated investigation of the Clever Hans phenomenon was published in English in 1911, but his definitive account did not prevent others from falling into the same trap as Von Osten. Man's age-old desire to communicate with other species could not so easily be suppressed. By 1937 there were more than seventy "thinking" animals, including cats and dogs as well as horses. In the 1950's the fashion turned to dolphins. Then came an altogether new twist in the dialogue between man and animals. The early attempts to teach speech to chimpanzees had faltered because of the animals' extreme physical difficulty in forming human sounds. Much greater progress was made when Allen and Beatrice Gardner of the University of Nevada taught American Sign Language to their chimpanzee Washoe.

Washoe and her imitators readily acquired large vocabularies of the sign language and, even more significantly, would string the signs together in what appeared to be sentences. Particularly evocative was the apes' reported use of the signs in apposite novel combinations. Washoe was said to have spontaneously made the signs for "drink" and "fruit" on seeing a watermelon. Gorilla Koko reportedly described a zebra as a "white tiger." By the 1970's the signing apes had become a flourishing subfield of psychological research.

Then came a serious crisis in the form of an ape named Nim Chimpsky, in honor of the well-known linguist Noam Chomsky. Nim's trainer, psychologist Herbert Terrace, found he learned signs just like the other chimps, and started using them in strings. But were the strings of signs proper sentences or just a routine that the crafty ape had learned would induce some appropriate action in its human entourage? Certain features in Nim's linguistic development threw Terrace into a crisis of doubt. Unlike children of his age, Nim suddenly plateaued in his rate of acquisition of new vocabulary. Unlike children, he rarely initiated conversation. He would string signs together, but his sentences were lacking in syntactic rigor: Nim's longest recorded utterance was the sixteen-sign declarative pronouncement, "Give orange me give eat orange me eat orange give me eat orange give me you."

Terrace was eventually forced to decide that Chimpsky, and indeed the other pointing pongids, were not using the signs in a way characteristic of true language. Rather, they were probably making monkeys out of their teachers by imitating or Clever Hansing them. Nim's linguistic behavior was more like that of a highly intelligent, trained dog than of the human children he so much resembled in other ways.

The critics began to move in on the field. "We find the ape 'language' researchers replete with personalities who believe themselves to be acting according to the most exalted motivations and sophisticated manners, but in reality have involved themselves in the most rudimentary circus-like performances," wrote Jean Umiker-Sebeok and Thomas Sebeok.[4] At a conference in 1980, Sebeok was even more forthright: "In my opinion, the alleged language experiments with apes divide into three groups: one, outright fraud; two, self-deception; three, those conducted by Terrace. The largest class by far is the middle one."[5] The battle is not yet over, but the momentum at present lies with the critics. Should they prove correct, the whole field of ape language research will slide rapidly into disrepute, and the ghost of Clever Hans will once again enjoy the last laugh.

Researchers' propensity for self-delusion is particularly strong when other species enter the scene as vehicles for human imaginings and projections. But scientists are capable of deluding themselves without any help from other species. The most remarkable known case of a collective self-deception is one that affected the community of French physicists in the early 1900's. In 1903 the distinguished French physicist René Blondlot announced he had discovered a new kind of rays, which he named N-rays, after the University of Nancy, where he worked.

In the course of trying to polarize X rays, discovered by Röntgen eight years earlier, Blondlot found evidence of a new kind of emanation from the X-ray source. It made itself apparent by increasing the brightness of an electric spark jumping between a pair of pointed wires. The increase in brightness had to be judged by eye, a notoriously subjective method of detection. But that seemed to matter little in view of the fact that other physicists were soon able to repeat and extend Blondlot's findings.

A colleague at the University of Nancy discovered that N-rays were emitted not just by X-ray sources but also by the nervous system of the human body. A Sorbonne physicist noticed that N-rays emanated from Broca's area, the part of the brain that governs speech, while a person was talking. N-rays were discovered in gases, magnetic fields, and chemicals. Soon the pursuit of N-rays had become a minor industry among French scientists. Leading French physicists commended Blondlot for his discovery. The French Academy of Sciences bestowed its valuable Leconte prize on him in 1904. The effects of N-rays "were observed by at least forty people and analyzed in some 300 papers by 100 scientists and medical doctors between 1903 and 1906," notes an historian of the episode.[6]

N-rays do not exist. The researchers who reported seeing them were the victims of self-deception. What was the reason for this collective delusion? An important clue may be found in the reaction to an article written in 1904 by the American physicist R. W. Wood. During a visit to Blondlot's laboratory, Wood correctly divined that something peculiar was happening. At one point Blondlot darkened the laboratory to demonstrate an experiment in which N-rays were separated into different wavelengths after passing through a prism. Wood surreptitiously removed the prism before the experiment began, but even with the centerpiece of his apparatus sitting in his visitor's pocket, Blondlot obtained the expected results. Wood wrote a devastating account of his visit in an English scientific journal. Science is supposed to transcend national boundaries, but Wood's critique did not. Scientists outside France immediately lost interest in N-rays, but French scientists continued for several years to support Blondlot.

"The most astonishing facet of the episode," notes the French scientist Jean Rostand, "is the extraordinarily great number of people who were taken in. These people were not pseudo-scientists, charlatans, dreamers, or mystifiers; far from it, they were true men of science, disinterested, honorable, used to laboratory procedure, people with level heads and sound common sense. This is borne out by their subsequent achievements as Professors, Consultants and Lecturers. Jean Bacquerel, Gilbert Ballet, André Broca, Zimmern, Bordier—all of them have made their contribution to science."[7]

The reason why the best French physicists of their day continued to support Blondlot after Wood's critique was perhaps the same as the reason for which they uncritically accepted Blondlot's findings in the first place. It all had to do with a sentiment that is supposed to be wholly foreign to science: national pride. By 1900 the French had come to feel that their international reputation in science was on the decline, particularly with respect to the Germans. The discovery of N-rays came just at the right time to soothe the self-doubts of the rigid French scientific hierarchy. Hence the Academy of Sciences, faced after the Wood exposé with almost unanimous criticism from abroad and strong skepticism at home, chose nonetheless to rally round Blondlot rather than ascertain the truth. The members of the academy's Leconte prize committee, which included the Nancy-born Henri Poincaré, chose Blondlot over the other leading candidate, Pierre Curie, who had shared the Nobel prize the year before.

Most historians and scientists who have written about the N-ray affair describe it as pathological, irrational, or otherwise deviant. One historian who is not part of this consensus is Mary Jo Nye. To seek an understanding of the episode, she chose to examine "not the structure of Blondlot's psyche, but rather the structure of Blondlot's scientific community, its organization, aims and aspirations around 1900." Her conclusion, in brief, is that the episode arose from at most an exaggeration of the usual patterns of behavior among scientific communities. The N-ray affair, she says, "was not 'pathological,' much less 'irrational' or 'pseudo-scientific.' The scientists involved in the investigations and debate were influenced in a normal, if sometimes exaggerated, way by traditional reductionist scientific aims, by personal competitive drives, and by institutional, regional, and national loyalties."[8]

That a whole community of scientists can be led astray by nonrational factors is a phenomenon that bears some pondering. To dismiss it as "pathological" is merely to affix a label. In fact the N-ray affair displays in extreme form several themes endemic to the scientific process. One is the unreliability of human observers. The fact is that all human observers, however well trained, have a strong tendency to see what they expect to see. Even when subjectively assessed qualities such as the brightness of a spark are replaced by instruments such as counters or print-outs, observer effects still enter in. Careful studies of how people read measuring devices has brought to light the "digit preference phenomenon" in which certain numbers are unconsciously preferred over others.[9]

Theoretical expectation is one factor that may distort a scientist's observation. The desire for fame and recognition may prevent such distortions from being corrected. In the case of N-rays, a nexus of personal, regional, and national ties combined to carry French physicists far away from the ideal modes of scientific inquiry, and not only that, but to persist in gross error for long after it had been publicly pointed out.

Do scientists take adequate steps to protect themselves from experimental pitfalls of this nature? "Blinded" studies, in which the researcher recording the data does not know what the answer is supposed to be, are a useful precaution but are not sufficient to rule out self-deception. So pervasive are the coils of self-deception in the biological sciences that a foolproof methodology is hard to devise. Theodore X. Barber compiled a manual of pitfalls in experimental research with human subjects, which he concluded with the following poignant postscript: "Before this text was mailed to the publisher, it was read critically by nine young researchers or graduate students. After completing the text, three of the readers felt that, since there were so many problems in experimental research, it may be wiser to forsake experimentation in general (and laboratory experiments in particular) and to limit our knowledge-seeking attempts to other methods, for example, to naturalistic field studies or to participant observation."[10]

The bedrock of science is observation and experiment, the empirical procedures that make it different from other kinds of knowledge. Yet observation turns out to be most fallible when it is most needed: when an experimenter's objectivity falters. Take the case of the eighteenth-century savant Johann Jacob Scheuchzer, who set out to find evidence that mankind at the time of Noah had been caught up in a terrible flood. Find it he did, and Scheuchzer hailed the skeletal remains of his flood man as *Homo diluvii testis*. Examination years later showed the fossil to be a giant amphibian, long ago extinct.

Twentieth-century science has not escaped the danger to which Scheuchzer fell victim. When the American astronomer Adriaan van Maanen announced in 1916 that he had observed rotations in spiral nebulae, the result was accepted because it confirmed a prevailing belief that the nebulae were nearby objects. Later work by Edwin Hubble, van Maanen's colleague at the Mount Wilson Observatory, showed that, to the contrary, the spiral nebulae are galaxies at an immense distance from our own, and that they do not rotate in the manner described by van Maanen. What made van Maanen's eyes deceive him?

The standard explanation, promulgated in such publications as the *Dictionary of Scientific Biography*, is that "the changes he was attempting to measure were at the very limits of precision of his equipment and techniques."[11] But random error of the sort suggested cannot explain the fact that van Maanen over the course of a decade reported many nebulae to be rotating in the same direction (unwinding rather than winding up). The subjectivity of scientific observers has prompted a historian of the van Maanen affair, Norriss Hetherington, to comment that "today science holds the position of queen of the intellectual disciplines. . . . The decline of the dominance of theology followed from historical studies that revealed the human nature and thus the human status of theology. Historical and sociological studies that begin to investigate a possible human element of science similarly threaten to topple the current queen."[12]

Self-deception is so potent a human capability that scientists, supposedly trained to be the most objective of observers, are in fact peculiarly vulnerable to deliberate deception by others. The reason may be that their training in the importance of objectivity leads them to ignore, belittle, or suppress in themselves the very nonrational factors that the hoaxster relies on. The triumph of preconceived ideas over common sense has seldom been more complete than in the case of Dr. Johann Bartholomew Adam Beringer.

A physician and learned dilettante of eighteenth-century Germany, Beringer taught at the University of Würzburg and was adviser and chief physician to the prince-bishop. Not content with his status as a mere healer and academician, he threw himself into the study of "things dug from the earth," and began a collection of natural rarities such as figured stones, as fossils were then called. The collection assumed a remarkable character in 1725, when three Würzburg youths brought him the first of a series of extraordinary stones they had dug up from nearby Mount Eivelstadt.[13]

This new series of figured stones was a treasure trove of insects, frogs, toads, birds, scorpions, snails, and other creatures. As the youths brought further objects of their excavations to the eager Beringer, the subject matter of the fossils became distinctly unusual. "Here were leaves, flowers, plants, and whole herbs, some with and some without roots and flowers," wrote Beringer in a book of 1726 describing the amazing discovery. "Here were clear depictions of the sun and moon, of stars, and of comets with their fiery tails. And lastly, as the supreme prodigy commanding the reverent admiration of myself and of my fellow examiners, were magnificent tablets engraved in Latin, Arabic, and Hebrew characters with the ineffable name of Jehovah."

Shortly after the publication of his book, historical accounts relate, Beringer discovered on Mount Eivelstadt the most unusual fossil of all, one that carried his own name.

An official inqury was held, at Beringer's request, to discover who was responsible for perpetrating the hoax. One of the young diggers turned out to be in the employ of two of Beringer's rivals, J. Ignatz Roderick, professor of geography, algebra, and analysis at the University of Würzburg, and the Honorable Georg von Eckhart, privy councillor and librarian to the court and to the university. Their motive had been to make Beringer a laughingstock because "he was so arrogant."

What also emerged at the inquiry was that the hoaxsters, apparently fearful that things might go too far, had tried to open Beringer's eyes to the prank before the publication of his book. They started a rumor that the stones were fakes, and when that didn't work they had him told directly. Beringer could not be persuaded that the whole thing was a massive piece of fakery; he went ahead and published his book.

Even within Beringer's lifetime, the legend of the "lying stones" began to gain momentum. By 1804, James Parkinson in his book *Organic Remains of a Former*

World mentioned the debacle and drew out a lesson: "It plainly demonstrates, that learning may not be sufficient to prevent an unsuspecting man, from becoming the dupe of excessive credulity. It is worthy of being mentioned, on another account: the quantity of censure and ridicule, to which its author was exposed, served, not only to render his contemporaries less liable to imposition; but also more cautious in indulging in unsupported hypotheses."[14]

Parkinson was not the only observer to comment on the salutary effect of hoaxes in promoting skepticism. In 1830, in his book *Reflections on the Decline of Science in England,* Charles Babbage remarked: "The only excuse which has been made for them is when they have been practised on scientific academies which had reached the period of dotage." By way of example he noted how the editors of a French encyclopedia had credulously copied the description of a fictitious animal that a certain Gioeni claimed to have discovered in Sicily and had named after himself, *Gioenia sicula.*[15]

When hoaxes go awry, it is often for want of occasion, not of gullibility on the part of the intended victims, as in the case of the Orgueil meteorite, a shower of stones that fell near the village of Orgueil, France, on the night of May 14, 1864. A few weeks earlier, Louis Pasteur had started a furious debate in France by delivering the famous lecture before the French Academy in which he derided the long-standing theory of spontaneous generation, which held that life-forms can develop from inanimate matter. Noticing that the material of the Orgueil meteorite became pasty when exposed to water, a hoaxster molded some seeds and particles of coal into a sample of the meteorite and waited for them to be discovered by Pasteur's opponents. The hoaxster's motive was presumably to let them adduce the seeds as evidence for life spontaneously generating in outer space, whereupon he would pull the rug out from under them by announcing the hoax.

What went wrong with the scheme was that the doctored fragment was never examined during the debate. Though other pieces of the meteorite were intensively studied at the time, the hoaxster's carefully prepared fragment lay unexamined in a glass display jar at the Musée d'Histoire at Montauban, France, for ninety-eight years. When its turn at last came, in 1964, the incentive for belief had disappeared, and the forgery was immediately recognized as such.[16]

Had the fragment been studied at the time, the hoax would doubtless have been successful. When the conditions are right, there is no limit to human gullibility, as was proved by the remarkable incident of the Piltdown man.

British national pride in the early years of the twentieth century suffered from a matter of serious disquiet. The Empire was at its height, the serenity of the Victorian era was still aglow, and to educated Englishmen it was almost self-evident that England had once been the cradle, as it was now the governess, of world civilization. How then to explain that striking evidence of early man—not just skeletal remains but Paleolithic cave paintings and tools as well—was coming to light in France and Germany but not in Britain? The dilemma was exacerbated in 1907 with the discovery near Heidelberg, Germany, of a massive, early human jawbone. It seemed depressing proof that the first man had been a German.

The discovery of the Piltdown man was made by Charles Dawson, a lawyer who maintained a quiet practice in the south of England and dabbled in geology. A tireless amateur collector of fossils, Dawson noticed a promising-looking gravel pit on Piltdown Common, near Lewes in Sussex. He asked a laborer digging there to bring him any flints he might find. Several years later, in 1908, the laborer brought him a fragment of bone that Dawson recognized as part of a thick human skull. Over the next three years further bits of the skull appeared.

In 1912 Dawson wrote to his old friend Arthur Smith Woodward, a world authority on fossil fishes at the geology department of the British Museum of Natural History, saying he had something that would top the German fossil found at Heidelberg. Woodward made several visits with Dawson to the Piltdown gravel pit. On one of these expeditions, Dawson's digging tool struck at the bottom of the pit and out flew part of a lower jaw. Close examination led Woodward and Dawson to believe that it belonged to the skull they had already reconstructed.

In great excitement, Smith Woodward took everything back to the British Museum, where he put the jaw and cranium together, filling in missing parts with modeling clay and his imagination. The result was truly remarkable. The assembled skull became the "dawn man" of Piltdown. Kept secret until December 1912, it was unveiled before a full house at the Geological Society in London, where it created a sensation. Some skeptics suggested that the human skull and apelike jaw did not belong together; others pointed out that two characteristically abraded molar teeth were not enough to prove the jaw was human. But these objections were ignored, and the find was accepted as a great and genuine discovery.[17]

The talk in clubs and pubs could note with satisfaction the new proof that the earliest man was indeed British. The Piltdown skull was also of scientific interest because it seemed to be the "missing link," the transitional form between ape and man that was postulated by Darwin's still controversial theory of evolution. Subsequent excavations at the gravel pit were not disappointing. A whole series of new fossils emerged. The clinching evidence came from a pit a few miles away—the discovery a few years later of a second Piltdown man.

Yet some were troubled by the Piltdown finds, among them a young zoologist at the British Museum, Martin A. C. Hinton. After a visit to the site in 1913, Hinton concluded that the whole thing was a hoax. He decided to smoke out the tricksters by planting clearly fraudulent fossils and watching the reactions. He took an ape tooth from the collection at the museum and filed it down to match the model canine tooth that Smith Woodward had fashioned out of clay. Hinton had the obvious forgery placed in the pit by an accomplice and sat back to wait for it to be discovered and the entire Piltdown collection to be exposed.

The tooth was discovered, but nothing else went right with Hinton's plan. All involved with the "discovery" seemed delighted and soon notified the nation about the new find. Hinton was astonished that his scientific colleagues could be taken in by so transparent a fake, and he suffered the additional mortification of seeing Charles Dawson, whom he suspected to be the culprit, acquiring kudos for his handiwork. He decided to try again, only this time with something so outrageous that the whole country would laugh the discoverers to scorn.

In a box in the British Museum he found a leg bone from an extinct species of elephant. He proceeded to carve it into an extremely appropriate tool for the earliest Englishman—a Pleistocene cricket bat. He took the bat to Piltdown, buried it, and waited for the laughter.

It was a long wait. When the bat was unearthed, Smith Woodward was delighted. He pronounced it a supremely important example of the work of Paleolithic man, for nothing like it had ever been found before. Smith Woodward and Dawson published a detailed, serious description of the artifact in a professional journal but stopped short of calling it an actual cricket bat.[18] Hinton was astonished that none of the scientists thought of trying to whittle a bit of bone, fossil or fresh, with a flint edge. If they had, they would have discovered it was impossible to imitate the cuts on the cricket bat. "The acceptance of this rubbish completely defeated the hoaxsters," notes a historian of the Piltdown episode.[19] "They just gave up, and abandoned all attempts to expose the whole business and get it demolished in laughter and ridicule." Perhaps Hinton and friends should have considered planting a bone on which the name Smith Woodward had been carved.

Piltdown man retained its scientific luster until the mid-1920's and the discovery of humanlike fossils in Africa. These indicated a very different pattern of human evolution to that suggested by the Piltdown skull. Instead of a human cranium with an apelike jaw, the African fossils were just the reverse—they had humanlike jaws with apelike skulls. Piltdown became first an anomaly, then an embarrassment. It slipped from sight until modern techniques of dating showed in the early 1950's that the skull and its famous jaw were fakes: an ape jaw, with filed-down molars, and a human skull had each been suitably stained to give the appearance of great age.

Circumstantial evidence pointed to the skull's discoverer, Dawson, as the culprit. But many have doubted that he could have been the instigator; although he was best placed to salt the gravel pit, he probably lacked access to the necessary fossil collections as well as the scientific expertise to assemble fossils of the right age for the Piltdown gravel. Indeed, the real mystery is not who did it but how a whole generation of scientists could have been taken in by so transparent a prank. The fakery was not expert. The tools were poorly carved and the teeth crudely filed. "The evidences of artificial abrasion immediately sprang to the eye. Indeed so obvious did they seem it may well be asked—how was it that they had escaped notice before," remarked anthropologist Le Gros Clark.[20]

The question is one that the victims always ask in retrospect yet seldom learn to anticipate. A group of scientists particularly plagued by tricksters and charlatans are parapsychologists, researchers who apply the scientific method to the study of telepathy, extrasensory perception, and other paranormal phenomena. Because parapsychology is widely regarded as a fringe subject not properly part of science, its practitioners have striven to be more than usually rigorous in following correct scientific methodology.

The founder of parapsychology, J. B. Rhine, made great strides in putting the discipline on a firm scientific footing. As a mark of its growing scientific acceptability, the Parapsychological Association in 1971 was admitted to the American Association for the Advancement of Science. The field seemed to be making solid headway toward the goal of scientific acceptability. Noting this progress with satisfaction, Rhine in 1974 commented on the decline of fraudulent investigators: "As time has passed our progress has aided us in avoiding the admission of such risky personnel even for a short term. As a result, the last twenty years have seen little of this cruder type of chicanery. Best of all, we have reached a stage at which we can actually look for and to a degree choose the people we want in the field." Rhine also warned against the danger of relying on automatic data recording as a means of avoiding the pitfalls of subjective measurement: "Apparatus can sometimes also be used as a screen to conceal the trickery it was intended to prevent," he noted.[21]

Less than three months after his article had appeared, Rhine's Institute for Parapsychology in Durham, North Carolina, was rocked by a scandal that involved Walter J. Levy, a brilliant young protégé whom Rhine had planned to designate his successor as director of the institute.

Levy had developed a highly successful experiment for demonstrating psychic ability in rats: through psychokinetic powers, the animals could apparently influence an electric generator to activate electrodes implanted in the pleasure centers of the brain. For more than a year the experiment had given positive results, and Rhine urged Levy to have it repeated in other labs. The work, however, quickly took a turn for the worse; results fell back to the chance level.

At this point one of the junior experimenters noticed that Levy was paying more than usual attention to the equipment. He and others decided to check out their suspicions by observing their senior colleague from a concealed position. They saw Levy manipulating the experimental apparatus so as to make it yield positive results. To Rhine's credit, he published an article recounting the whole episode.[22] "Right from the start the necessity of trusting the experimenter's personal accuracy or honesty must be avoided as far as possible," he concluded.

Most parapsychologists have training in a conventional scientific discipline, and they bring their scientific training to bear on the study of the paranormal. The competence with which the study is conducted is probably a measure of that training. But if so, scientists have not shown themselves to be highly successful in dealing with the unexpected problems of the occult world. Their subjects, those who claim occult powers, have invariably followed one of two patterns when put under systematic observation: either their powers "fade" or they are exposed as tricksters. That background might lead parapsychologists to approach new claimants with a certain degree of skepticism. But when the Israeli mentalist Uri Geller toured the United States demonstrating his psychic powers, the parapsychologists gave an enormous boost to his claims by confirming them in the laboratory.

Harold Puthoff and Russell Targ, two laser physicists at the Stanford Research Institute, wrote a scientific article corroborating Geller's ability to guess the number on a die concealed in a metal box. The article was accepted and published by *Nature*, a leading scientific journal.[23] Other scientists, such as the English physicist John Taylor of London University, endorsed Geller's psychic abilities. It fell to a professional magician, not a scientist or a parapsychologist, to explain to the public what was behind the Geller phenomenon. James Randi, of Rumson, New Jersey, showed audiences that he could duplicate all Geller's feats, but by simple conjury. "Any magician will tell you that scientists are the easiest persons in the world to fool," says mathematical columnist Martin Gardner.[24] Geller, note two students of deception, "prefers scientists as witnesses and will not perform before expert magicians, and for good reason. Scientists, by the very nature of their intellectual and social training, are among the easiest persons for a conjuror to deceive. . . ."[25]

For an extreme example of gullibility among some of America's best physicists and engineers, consider the remarkable case of the Shroud of Turin Research Project, a group of scientists devoted to studying a relic that believers say is the true burial cloth of Christ. Members of the group work at the Los Alamos National Laboratory, where America's nuclear weapons are designed, and at other military research centers. "The great majority of them are, or until recently were, engaged in the design, manufacture, or testing of weapons, from simple explosives to atomic bombs to high-energy 'killer' lasers," notes an admiring article.[26]

In their spare time the scientists study the Shroud of Turin with the most modern scientific instruments. Though careful not to say it is genuine, they say they cannot prove it is a fake, leaving the strong impression that it is the real thing. They add that there are features of the shroud that cannot be explained by modern technology; its image, of a full-length crucified man, was not painted, they say, because there is no sign of pigment. It is a reverse image, like a photographic negative, and encodes three-dimensional information. From what they tell reporters, they seem to favor a short intense burst of light, presumably from inside the body, as the cause of the image.

But consider some brief facts about the Shroud of Turin: (i) it first came to light in about 1350, at a time when medieval Europe was swamped with purported Holy Land relics of all kinds; (ii) the bishop of Troyes, France, in whose diocese it first appeared, "discovered the fraud and how the said cloth had been cunningly painted, the truth being attested by the artist who had painted it," according to a letter written to the Pope in 1389 by one of the bishop's successors; (iii) traces of two medieval pigments have been discovered in particles lifted off the shroud.[27] The negative image with its three-dimensional encoded information is simply the result of an artist trying to paint an image as it might be expected to register on a cloth covering a dead body. He put in shading to indicate the body's contours, and used so dilute a pigment that even modern tests mostly fail to reveal it. How did a group of the nation's elite bomb designers get so far along the road of persuading themselves (and numerous reporters) that they had a miracle on their hands?

"In entering upon any scientific pursuit," said the nineteenth-century astronomer John Herschel, "one of the student's first endeavours ought to be to prepare his mind for the reception of truth, by dismissing, or at least loosening, his hold on all such crude and hastily adopted notions respecting the objects and relations he is about to examine, as may tend to embarrass or mislead him." Good advice but hard to follow, as the long and continuing history of self-deception and gullibility in science repeatedly shows.

The frequency of scientific self-deception and hoaxes takes on special significance when it is remembered that the skeptical frame of mind is supposedly an essential part of the scientist's approach to the world. The scientific method is widely assumed to be a powerful and self-correcting device for understanding the world as it is and making sense of nature. What is the scientific method, and what are the flaws that make this adamantine armor so strangely vulnerable to the unexpected?

Notes

[1] It is interesting to note that historians espousing the conventional ideology of science have tried to save appearances by assuming that Hooke and Flamsteed were observing another phenomenon, known as stellar aberration, which they innocently mistook for the stellar parallax. This explanation will not wash. Stellar aberration is an apparent displacement similar to which a raindrop seen from a moving car seems to fall slantwise instead of straight down. It was discovered in 1725 by James Bradley in the very course of trying to repeat Hooke's observation of the stellar parallax. Bradley himself specifically stated that Hooke's data could not be measurements of stellar aberration. Hooke's observations were "really very far from being either exact or agreeable to the phenomena," Bradley reported. "It seems that Hooke found what he expected to find," notes Norriss Hetherington of the University of California, Berkeley, in an account of this episode ("Questions About the Purported Objectivity of Science," unpublished MS).

[2] Robert Rosenthal, *Experimenter Effects in Behavioral Research* (Appleton-Century-Crofts, New York, 1966), pp. 158–179.

[3] *Ibid.*, pp. 411–413.

[4] Jean Umiker-Sebeok and Thomas A. Sebeok, "Clever Hans and Smart Simians," *Anthropos*, 76, 89–166, 1981.

[5] Nicholas Wade, "Does Man Alone Have Language? Apes Reply in Riddles, and a Horse Says Neigh," *Science*, 208, 1349–1351, 1980.

[6] Mary Jo Nye, "N-rays: An Episode in the History and Psychology of Science," *Historical Studies in the Physical Sciences*, 11:1, 125–156, 1980.

[7] Jean Rostand, *Error and Deception in Science* (Basic Books, New York, 1980), p. 28.

[8] Nye, *op. cit.*, p. 155.

[9] Rosenthal, *op. cit.*, pp. 3–26.

[10] Theodore Xenophon Barber, *Pitfalls in Human Research* (Pergamon Press, New York, 1973), p. 88.

[11] Richard Berendzen and Carol Shamieh, "Maanen, Adriann van," *Dictionary of Scientific Biography* (Charles Scribner's Sons, New York, 1973), pp. 582–583.

[12] Norriss S. Hetherington, "Questions About the Purported Objectivity of Science," unpublished MS.

[13]Melvin E. Jahn and Daniel J. Woolf, *The Lying Stones of Dr. Johann Bartholomew Adam Beringer* (University of California Press, Berkeley, 1963).

[14]*Ibid.*

[15]Charles Babbage, *Reflections on the Decline of Science in England* (Augustus M. Kelley, New York, 1970).

[16]Edward Anders *et al.*, "Contaminated Meteorite," *Science,* 146, 1157–1161, 1964.

[17]J. S. Weiner, *The Piltdown Forgery* (Oxford University Press, London, 1955).

[18]Charles Dawson and Arthur Smith Woodward, "On a Bone Implement from Piltdown," *Quarterly Journal of the Geological Society,* 71, 144–149, 1915.

[19]L. Harrison Matthews, "Piltdown Man: The Missing Links," *New Scientist,* a ten-part series, beginning April 30, 1981, pp. 280–282.

[20]Quoted in Stephen J. Gould, *The Panda's Thumb* (W. W. Norton, New York, 1980), p. 112.

[21]J. B. Rhine, "Security Versus Deception in Parapsychology," *Journal of Parapyschology,* 38, 99–121, 1974.

[22]J. B. Rhine, "A New Case of Experimenter Unreliability," *Journal of Parapyschology,* 38, 215–225, 1974.

[23]Russell Targ and Harold Puthoff, "Information Transmission Under Conditions of Sensory Shielding," *Nature,* 251, 602–607, 1974.

[24]Martin Gardner, "Magic and Paraphysics," *Technology Review,* June 1976, pp. 43–51.

[25]Umiker-Sebeok and Sebeok, *op. cit.*

[26]Cullen Murphy, "Shreds of Evidence," *Harper's,* November 1981, pp. 42–65.

[27]Walter C. McCrone, "Microscopical Study of the Turin 'Shroud,' " *The Microscope,* 29, 1, 1981.

Scientific Autonomy, Scientific Responsibility

William Maker

Science's right to a relatively high degree of freedom from external interference in its operations has been long recognized and consistently defended as fundamentally valuable.[1] The autonomy of science is traditionally regarded as one of modernity's unproblematic achievements, and a society's granting of this autonomy is commonly perceived as an indicator of its maturity and civility.

William Maker, "Scientific Autonomy, Scientific Responsibility," in *Professional Ethics and Social Responsibility,* ed. Daniel E. Wueste (Lanham: Rowman & Littlefield, 1994) 219–241. Used with permission from the publisher.

Attempts to compromise it, whether on religious grounds, as with Galileo and Darwin, or political grounds, as in the case of Lysenkoism, are uniformly denounced as dangerous assaults on truth, objectivity, and the well-being of the human condition. In the words of the biologist Robert L. Sinsheimer:

> If one believes that the highest purpose available to humanity is the acquisition of knowledge (and in particular of scientific knowledge, knowledge of the natural universe) then one will regard any attempt to limit or direct the search for knowledge as deplorable—or worse.[2]

I shall argue here that science's continued claim to autonomy is based on an increasingly outdated perception of how science functions in society. The contemporary reality of scientific activity cannot provide an unqualified justification for science's traditional freedom from social interference. As scientific knowledge has become increasing essential to the functioning and the well-being of society, science has become increasingly dependent on public and private support.[3] Scientific knowledge itself is now a valuable commodity and its production has come under the control of particular interests in a variety of ways that compromise science's traditional independence from such interests and undercut its claim to autonomy from social regulation. By way of illustrating this situation I will indicate how the traditional professional ethos of science, crucial to maintaining scientific autonomy, has been challenged and sometimes disregarded in contemporary scientific practice. . . . Concluding that a return to the conditions that could legitimate autonomy is unlikely, I shall contend that we need to rethink the nature of science's relation to society and its social responsibility.

The Legitimacy of Scientific Autonomy

First, what is the traditional understanding of the conditions legitimating scientific autonomy?

The right to scientific autonomy, like all rights, is not unconditional. Rights are always accompanied by responsibilities. The traditional understanding of the legitimacy of scientific autonomy recognizes that the scientific community has certain basic obligations whose fulfillment is needed to justify science's self-regulation.[4] According to this traditional view, there is an implicit social contract between science and society.[5] Society grants science considerable autonomy not afforded to comparable institutions because it is believed that science serves a socially valuable end of a special sort, and because science's autonomy is seen as essential to attaining that end.[6] What does science provide for society that earns it a right to autonomy?

The goal of science is objective truth, knowledge of the workings of nature that is *universal* in scope and validity: science accounts for phenomena accessible (in principle) to all in a manner all can agree upon. The pursuit of such universal knowledge is seen as deserving society's support both because it is

inherently valuable in its own right and because the application of this knowledge can serve particular public and private interests.[7] Although scientific knowledge has proven utility, defenders of science's autonomy insist that scientists'
first and overriding concern must be with attaining knowledge irrespective of a
calculation of its possible utility, not only because such knowledge is inherently
valuable, but in order that the practical fruits of this knowledge can be harvested:
Truth is an end in itself and must be seen and sought as such in order to ensure
that it may be a means to other ends.[8]

Thus society's support of science and the special autonomy it grants to it are
conditioned upon science fulfilling its responsibility of promoting the end of
universal truth. According to Bernard Barber, "only the pursuit of truth for its
own sake can develop and maintain the standards which are necessary to ensure the objectivity and the value of research, pure or applied."[9] Of course, science is not the only institution that serves society. How does science differ from
other institutions such that it is accorded a special autonomy?

Other institutions that receive a considerable measure of public support, (e.g.,
the military) and that markedly affect society (e.g., banking) are subject to external
supervision and control in the name of the public good. We do not allow the experts in these disciplines the same measure of unregulated authority, inside and
outside their fields, that we accord to scientific experts.[10] We treat other special
disciplines differently in part because we believe that by their very nature they
are always in danger of becoming captive to particular interests that may conflict with the common interest society expects them to serve. This insistence on
public regulation extends even to the discipline most closely related to science,
technology. (I will comment on why this is the case below.) In contrast to these
other institutions science is, for the most part, free from external regulation in the
name of the public interest, not because its practitioners are more virtuous, but
because we believe that it has internal, institutionally maintained procedures
that keep it from falling prey to influences that would cause it to deviate from
the public interest. What is it about science that is supposed to justify this difference in treatment? Why is science, in spite of its importance for, support by,
and influence on society, not in need of democratic supervision and regulation?
The story goes like this:

In seeking universal truth science aims to uncover natural phenomena that are
objective in the sense of being accessible, in principle, to all knowers, regardless
of the particular differences of circumstance and background that distinguish
us one from another in a variety of ways and shape the plurality of our divergent
individual interests. Science is thought to be unique in its ability to adopt universal means in order to discover universal truths that transcend social, cultural,
and political differences, just those differences that the system of checks and bal-
ances in democratic society is supposed to control. But science need not be subjected to such balancing or regulation. We are assured that neither a scientist's
economic, national, political, racial, religious, or cultural background, nor her
personal beliefs can—in the long run—enter in a substantive fashion into what

come to be recognized as accepted scientific procedures and results.[11] Believing that other fields do not possess the independent, objective criteria of judgment that make this universality possible, we regard them with suspicion; we fear that, to one degree or another, they will allow a subjective influence into their judgments. Consequently, we either deny them the unmediated *public* authority—the right to speak for all—that we accord science, or, if a measure of such public authority is accorded, it is under strict external supervision in the name of the common good. An early advocate of scientific autonomy, Galileo, drew quite forcefully the key distinction between science and other fields upon which according autonomy and authority to science alone is based:

> If this point of which we dispute were some point of law, or other part of the studies called the humanities, wherein there is neither truth nor falsehood, we might give sufficient credit to the acuteness of wit, readiness of answers, and the greater accomplishments of writers, and hope that he who is most proficient in these will make his reason more probable and plausible. But the conclusions of natural science are true and necessary and the judgement [arbitrio] of man has nothing to do with them.[12]

In Galileo's vision, science alone transcends the merely human level of judgment, where irresolvable disputes abound, even though science too is undertaken by humans.

So it is not simply that science has universal truth as its aim. The same might be said for religion, philosophy, history, or the arts. What marks the difference in the accord and treatment we give to science as opposed to these other disciplines is our conviction that science alone has the successful means to arrive at demonstrably universal truths. In matters of nature we take the view that only one self-selected community of experts ought to determine, without external supervision or intervention, how truth is established, what this truth is, and who may speak in its name, and we socially recognize the pronouncements of this autonomous community as public truths. (Witness the uproar at attempts to present an alternative, religious, view in science classes.) Such special status is not accorded to any religious, philosophical, or artistic group, not because these topics have no public significance, but in large measure because (in social agreement with Galileo) we do not believe that any such group can rightly claim to be able to speak for all. While our recognition of freedom of speech and assembly allows such groups autonomy, they lack the public authority of science. (Or when one of them does speak in the public name—as in the case of the National Endowment for the Arts—they do so under public supervision and scrutiny and without the public conviction that this group of experts has a final say.)

The same Galilean epistemology underlies the different treatment accorded to the technological disciplines: there is a perceived distinction drawn between attaining scientific knowledge and applying it. Attainment is solely a matter for the experts selected by their community of peers to determine, whereas by contrast the application rightly concerns us all. The former is a matter of truth that can only be determined by experts; the latter importantly involves opinions or value judgments in which all affected parties are entitled to a say. Defenders of scientific autonomy consistently draw this distinction and point out that science deserves and requires social autonomy, while technology does not.[13]

According to the traditional view, the fact that science alone possesses the means to transcend particular private interests and biases and attain universal knowledge not only justifies but also *requires* science's autonomy from social regulation in the name of the common good. What the nature of the common good is, is open to diverse interpretations; it's a matter of opinion, not a demonstrable universal Truth. This view holds that, strictly speaking, there is no universal common good, only particular, varying perceptions of it, and thus such particular perceptions must be excluded from the universal domain of science. If science is to be able to serve its socially valuable universal ends, we are told, it must be autonomous from *all* forms of external influence, both private and public.

So the pursuit of scientific truth cannot be particularized, in the sense of making the substantive content of scientific procedures and their results subservient to beliefs, whether those of some particular individual or of some particular culture, political system, or society. External particular influences of all sorts must be excluded from science and the only means to do this lies in science's internally established and maintained procedures for assessing truth claims.

Insofar as this view is correct, science's primary social responsibility ought not to be determined from outside of science. The key point is that science's basic social responsibility is not something other than furthering its own ends: science best serves society by defining and pursuing its own goals. Scientific autonomy is a social good.

> The scientific community has, in essence, bargained for substantial autonomy by claiming the inherent efficiency and, indeed, necessity of an unregulated scientific enterprise, and by promising practical contributions to economic progress in return for funding without intervention. Its bargaining strength comes from belief in the intrinsic value of knowledge, and from the promise of its contribution to the public good. Underlying the negotiation is the implicit threat that society will lose out on the benefits of science if excessive intervention accompanies government support. If the acquisition of basic knowledge is restrained by externally imposed limits, it is society which will bear the costs.[14]

The Ethics of Science

What is the traditional ethic connected with this view of science? In his classic 1942 study, "The Normative Structure of Science," the sociologist of science Robert K. Merton analyzed an uncodified scientific ethic that he found operative in the scientific community.[15] Basic to this ethic is the scientist's self-understanding of science's autonomy and its correlative commitment to an end which is valuable for its own sake. In Merton's words, scientists see themselves "as independent of society" and they also see science as autonomous in the positive sense of being "a self-validating enterprise which is in society but not of it." Rooted in this vision of scientific autonomy (and of the transcendent value of science associated with it) is a scientific ethic defined by four "institutional imperatives": universalism, communism, disinterestedness, and organized skepticism. These imperatives follow from science's goal of objective knowledge and the techniques employed to attain that goal, but according to Merton they are followed not merely because they are efficient means to science's end but also because they are seen to be inherently ethical: "they are believed right and good. They are moral as well as technical prescriptions."[16] The philosopher of science Israel Scheffler agrees with this perception of the scientific endeavor as an inherently moral enterprise; he traces this feature of science precisely to its commitment to objective truth. Scientific procedures "embodied in and transmitted by the institutions of science" ensure that our subjective beliefs are submitted to independent controls; it is not the authority of individuals but "independent and impartial criteria" that are determinative.[17]

This insistence on subjecting all claims to "preestablished impersonal criteria" is what Merton describes as the first, core component of the scientific ethos, the imperative of universalism. It calls upon the scientist to transcend all particularistic features of "race, nationality, religion, class and personal qualities."[18] And this feature of science endows it with a value that transcends the utility of the knowledge it produces; its unswerving commitment to objectivity gives it a "moral import" in that it is a model of "responsible belief."[19] The commitment to universal knowledge is reflected in two of the other imperatives Merton designates—communism and disinterestedness—and a brief consideration of them will disclose how they bear on science's autonomy.

By "communism" Merton refers to the openness of communication and the sharing of scientific discoveries. "Communalism" may be a less confusing term. This is not a feature of science reflecting a high-minded altruism or generosity on the part of scientists; indeed the competition for priority of recognition is extensive and does not compromise the sharing of results. Rather, communalism is an institutional feature of scientific practice that is integral to the attainment of universal knowledge, as is the imperative of distinterestedness. I shall later contend that communalism (the nonprivatization of scientific knowledge and the communal process of its validation) and disinterestedness (the renunciation of personal self-seeking or self-aggrandizement in the name of truth, where this is certified by peer accountability) are increasingly threatened and compromised by the commodification of science, so their relation to the universal goal integral to scientific autonomy needs to be carefully delineated.

Remember that science's attainment of universal knowledge hinges on the impartiality of the criteria against which particular subjective claims are judged. It is said that impartiality—objectivity—of judgment is not a feature of the personality or authority or particular beliefs of individual scientists; it pertains—in practice—to institutional features: to practices shared in common and communally supervised. Before a scientific claim is recognized as valid it must be subjected to the judgment of the community; results must be replicable in order to ensure that the individual producer of scientific knowledge has not made a merely subjective, particular claim.[20] William Lowrance stresses the necessity of peer accountability as a guarantee of the integrity of scientific work. He notes that scientists always act in particular contexts as particular individuals whose actions are influenced by a variety of value judgments. These influences are inescapable; the only effective control on them lies in "proceeding by the internal quality control norms of one's particular scientific community."[21] And according to Lowrance, part of science's responsibility to society involves maintaining scientific integrity by sharing information and adhering to standards established and enforced by the community.[22] Thus peer review is at the core of the scientific claim to offer universal knowledge. According to Merton, it is this internal feature of scientists policing one another that grounds the claim that scientists are, in fact, disinterested when they pursue knowledge. "The translation of the norm of disinterestedness into practice is effectively supported by the ultimate accountability of scientists to their compeers."[23] Thus, results must be shared.

The significance of communalism for the maintenance of science's claim to offer objective, universal knowledge should perhaps be stressed. It is a feature of scientific autonomy that the scientific community recognizes no criteria for science save those endorsed by the community. Thus the *effective determination* of what counts as the *operative* standards of objective judgment and their application falls to the community and to the community alone. Now, we may adopt the philosophical view that the scientific community has, by and large, endorsed criteria which, as a matter of fact, *are* objective and whose objectivity can be determined independently of the judgment of the scientific community. Or we may adopt the view that what we mean by "objective criteria" is whatever criteria the scientific community endorses. Which of these philosophical positions we endorse is irrelevant as long as we recognize two facts of scientific practice: (1) the traditional endorsement, by the scientific community, of communalism, especially as it involves peer review, is an essential feature of what grounds science's claim to offer objective knowledge; and (2) that, in actuality, it is just those more specific standards of objectivity endorsed by the community that are effective in scientific practice.[24] In short, whatever our philosophical views are about the ultimate nature of scientific objectivity, in practice it falls to the community of scientists, operating as an autonomous community, to determine and apply its procedures and standards.

Scientific results are also the product of the whole community of science in another way. The communal character of scientific knowledge also pertains to the fact that any individual's ability to carry on research is tied to access to the results of others.[25] In the words of Isaac Newton, "If I have seen so far it is because I stood on the shoulders of giants." Merton links these features of openness in observing that scientific achievement is "essentially cooperative and selectively cumulative."[26] The need to share discoveries both in order to pursue research and to test its results is completely compatible with the competitive character of science, as Merton observes and as the events related in James D. Watson's *The Double Helix* amply illustrate. What is private property is the priority of discovery. "The products of competition are communized, and esteem accrues to the producer." Communalism, then, is really "the imperative of the communication of findings" and it is antithetical with secrecy.[27]

Merton also sees the willingness to share results as a feature of the distinctively moral character of science. The imperative of openness is not followed solely because it is a technical necessity; there is "a moral compulsion for sharing the results of science." "Even though it serves no ulterior motive, the suppression of scientific discovery is condemned."[28] While Merton does not further analyze communalism's link with the moral dimension of science, I would suggest that it is an important feature of science's claim to be acting, without external supervision, in and for a common good. Science establishes that it is in pursuit of a universal end, and not particular, private ends, and that it is acting for the good of all, by openly communicating and sharing its findings. Communalism is also part of what distinguishes science from technology, according to Merton, for technology is recognized as private property while scientific knowledge is not.[29]

This unqualified image of an autonomous science, in but not of society, effectively free from all interests save an interest in universal knowledge, is no longer defensible. At least two avenues of criticism can be brought to bear on it, one internal and theoretical, the other external and practical. The first, which I shall only mention in passing, would consist in reiterating the criticisms of the very possibility of universal objective knowledge that have been commonplace, if controversial, in anglophone philosophy of science since Kuhn. The contention here is that one can establish in principle that all knowledge is relative to contexts and shaped by interests. The second, external and practical critique of the image of autonomous science, which I shall pursue, is independent of the first. It is based on two sets of empirical observations. The first questions the traditional claim that the pursuit of scientific knowledge can be meaningfully disentangled from its application. The second contends that science has for all intents and purposes become a business. Taken together they point to the conclusion that scientific practice has come under the control and supervision of particular public and private interests that in many instances conflict with the interest in universal knowledge. This conflict is not a matter of how such knowledge, once attained, is used, but concerns the very processes by which the scientific community is supposed to ensure the "scientific"—universal—character of its knowledge.

Traditionally, the character of the particular socioeconomic context in which scientific knowledge is produced has been regarded, along with all particular features of context, as an external matter, pertaining to the "context of discovery" and not the "context of justification." Insofar as scientific procedures are properly followed, how the research happens to be funded is a matter of indifference as regards the scientific character of the results. Whether the bill is being paid by

a private corporation interested in profit, or a public university, or a national research institute may well make some difference in overall direction (in the kind
of research undertaken, and in what uses are made of the results) but the scientific—universal—character of the knowledge will not be affected. This autonomy of science from economic interests presupposes two (related) conditions
that have gradually but steadily changed since the middle of this century. The
change in these conditions bears markedly on the notion of scientific autonomy.
What I have in mind is (1) the continued erosion of a meaningful distinction between science and technology or between basic or pure science and applied science and (2) the steady transformation of scientific knowledge itself into a
valuable commodity, like technology. The former consideration is relevant to the
issue of scientific autonomy since, as noted above, defenders of science's autonomy usually pre-suppose that a far-reaching and meaningful distinction can
(still) be drawn between science, as the search for truth guided only by the interest in truth (focusing exclusively on theoretical concerns), and its application
(focusing on practical concerns), where the consideration of other ends and other
interests becomes effective and where social regulation is appropriate.[30] Because
of space limitations I shall not pursue this issue here, except to note that many
critics of the distinction have contended that today science and technology are
intimately and inseparably interconnected and interdependent. Some have further concluded that because of this interpenetration science is properly described
as a form of action guided by a variety of interests (and open to public regulation as all modes of action are) rather than as a mode of contemplative thought
serving only the interest in truth (where it would be deserving of autonomy on
grounds of the freedom of thought and speech.)[31]

A Conflict of Ethics

What I shall focus on is the challenge to scientific autonomy presented by the fact
that, in virtue of its utility, scientific knowledge itself has become a valuable commodity. According to Dorothy Nelkin:

> [T]he knowledge generated by research is growing in economic and policy impor-
> tance. . . . In the past, commercial interests looked primarily to the goods and services
> produced through applied research; today, more fundamental knowledge is recog-
> nized as having intrinsic value.[32]

Because knowledge itself now has this kind of value, the activity of its pursuit
has come under the influence, or the control, of those, publicly and privately,
who have an interest in its usefulness and marketability. They bear the costs of
research, and are convinced of their right to control the process of production and
the product itself. Why should this be seen as threatening science's claim to be
serving universal truth and thus its right to social autonomy? What I shall contend is that as the scientific enterprise is becoming increasingly commodified, a

rival set of values and a rival ethics—those of the marketplace—are coming into conflict with the traditional values and the traditional ethics of science. In some instances the conflict is such that, when the market ethic prevails, science's ability to serve its universal end is compromised.

*   *   *

What is the nature and extent of commodification and what are its effects? First, commodification pertains to the fact that knowledge is regarded as proprietary, belonging to or strictly controlled by either the individual scientific entrepreneur (itself a new and still relatively rare phenomenon), or those who employ her. Second, commodification pertains to the fact that the process of the production of scientific knowledge comes under the control of those who are paying for it. Defined in this fashion, commodification is not restricted to what occurs in the private sphere, but also pertains to the government, one of the most important employers of scientists and financiers of scientific research. (That much publicly funded research is directly or indirectly available for private exploitation, that businesses and universities are increasingly engaging in joint research ventures—a phenomenon with its own potentially insidious implications—points to the need to define commodification broadly.)

The extent of commodification is broad. For a variety of reasons, chief among them the costs of doing research, the self-supporting scientist who answers to no one but himself and his peers, is a thing of the past. The majority (two-thirds) of scientists today work under contract for, or are employed by, industries or consulting firms. And even those doing work for government agencies or at universities are only relatively insulated from the effects of commodification.[33] What are these effects as they pertain to the ethics of science?

If knowledge is proprietary, and commercially valuable, by the ethic of the marketplace I am under no obligation whatsoever to share it freely, since doing so would run counter to my interest in selling it for a profit. Correlatively, if this knowledge not only has an exchange value but also a use value of a certain sort, there may be an interest—for example, in national security—for severely restricting access to it. But according to the traditional imperative of communalism, I am doubly obligated to share freely the results of my work, as a moral obligation pertaining to science's claim to be acting in the name of and for the sake of all; and as a technical obligation, since the sharing of knowledge with the community is the basis for all scientific work. How has this imperative been questioned or compromised in recent years as a result of commodification? I will mention a few examples to illustrate the situation.

In some instances it is scientists themselves who have become secretive in order to protect their valuable property. The fields of genetic research and molecular biology have recently emerged as having considerable commercial potential. According to one estimate the industrial market for genetic research—

"biocommerce"—alone has been set at $40 billion.[34] These fields exemplify what may become a wider phenomenon insofar as other sciences come to offer knowledge that has market value.

Donald Kennedy, in investigating the commercialization of biomedical research at universities, discovered that some scientists have now refused to divulge detailed information about their research at scientific meetings because they consider it to be potentially marketable.[35] Scientists at the University of California, San Diego, and the nearby Salk Institute and Scripps Clinic and Research Foundation, became involved in a dispute about who had developed a new method for identifying proteins after it was discovered that one group had been negotiating with Johnson and Johnson about commercial application of the method. In the words of one of the scientists involved: "There used to be a good, healthy exchange of ideas and information among researchers at UCSD, the Salk Institute, and the Scripps Clinic. Now we are locking our doors."[36] In a lecture on the question of whether utility and quality can coexist, Kennedy observed that "Scientists who once shared prepublication information freely and exchanged cell lines without hesitation are now much more reluctant to do so. . . . The fragile network of informal communication that characterizes every especially active field is liable to rupture."[37]

In some instances scientists themselves invoke the ethic of openness, only to find their claims challenged by those who have funded the work and claim the right of ownership to protect their investment. Scientific whistleblowers have had numerous conflicts with their employers because of efforts to reveal important findings pertaining to the common good. Thomas Mancuso conducted research on radiation effects on a contract for the Department of Energy. For ten years he discovered no significant threats to workers exposed at the Hanford plant, and his contract was regularly renewed. When it subsequently appeared that his newer findings suggested a more significant cancer risk, his contract was terminated; the Department of Energy tried to confiscate his Hanford data and denied him access to other data he had assembled.[38] Employed by a consulting firm hired by Consolidated Edison to do an environmental impact study, research biologist Morris Baslow concluded that his employer's study was faulty, because it had ignored data he had developed, and that plant discharge was damaging river wildlife. The firm disputed his findings and left them out of its final report. Baslow tried and failed to get his company to let him present his findings to the Environmental Protection Agency. He informed the EPA anyway, and was fired, taking his data with him. The firm claimed he had stolen their property.[39]

Extension of control over scientific work and its products occurs not only in the private sector. Scientists have long been accustomed to restrictions, for reasons of national security, on sharing information and results of research when it pertains to a variety of technical devices relating to military hardware. But in recent years the government imposition of control in the name of secrecy has extended beyond technical devices to scientific knowledge itself. In 1980 the MIT mathematician Leon Adelman applied for a grant from the National Science Foundation for work in computer mathematics, an area that has a bearing on cryptography. The NSF sent his grant to the National Security Agency for review because of its potential implications for military intelligence. Adelman received his grant but was disturbed to discover that his work could end up being classified, unpublishable and not available for public use.[40] According to Dorothy Nelkin, what is new and disturbing here—and this is not the only case—is the move to extend government control beyond areas directly funded by national security agencies and to institute control not only over things but ideas.[41]

These examples illustrate, first, a clash of interests: particular market interests in pursuing and attaining salable commodities or a governmental interest in controlling valuable information versus an interest in pursuing and attaining universal knowledge. Scientists seeking government funding may discover that some agency's perception of the national interest conflicts with the renunciation of secrecy and of withholding information central to the scientific interest in attaining and disseminating knowledge. What may be done in the best interest of producing and realizing the value of a certain commodity may not be in the best interest of furthering knowledge for its own sake. The California biologists discovered that their traditional interest in sharing information with fellow scientists for the common good of science conflicted with an economic interest to preserve for themselves the market value of something they had produced. The whistleblowing scientists discovered that those who fund research are likely to claim, on broadly recognized market principles, that they are the only ones who determine their own best interests, including what is to be done with the products they have paid for. That is, after all, the freedom of the market.

In addition, these examples illustrate a clash of ethics. Scientists have traditionally perceived a higher obligation to the universal end of truth. Consequently, they have committed themselves to the imperatives of disinterestedness (asking only for recognition and honor) and communalism (sharing what they produce) in order to attain that end. But the contemporary economic reality of the market is predicated not just upon different but upon antithetical, radically particularistic values. Its ethic is precisely an ethic of particularity rather than universality. The market exists as a sphere to *pursue* one's particular private interest, not to renounce it, and it serves that particular end not through free sharing but rather by regarding everything as private property that no one else has any legitimate claim to and that is only available to others for a price the owner may (or may not) agree to. What this clash suggests is that, ethically speaking, scientists may face an unresolvable dilemma, given the reality of the present economic system. Who in our world has any choice but to participate in the market in some fashion? And given the enormous costs of research, an individual desirous of pursuing scientific research has no choice but to accommodate themselves to the market. What I am suggesting is that if scientists are breaking the social contract upon which their claim to autonomy is based (by accommodating interests that are antithetical to the universal interest in truth and cooperating in the privatization of knowledge that had been regarded as belonging to everyone), they are not doing so willingly. Given the inescapability of the market and the pervasiveness of its ethic of self-seeking, can we blame the genetic researchers for wanting to profit from their discoveries? Can we blame those who invest in and fund research for insisting that the knowledge produced is their property, to do with as they see fit, even if that means altering or suppressing it? Alternatively, given scientific tradition, can we blame the whistleblowers who feel that an obligation to science's universal ends overrides their obligation to their employers?

The seriousness of what is at stake here goes beyond ethics to the practice of science itself. Can science avoid accommodating itself to the market, or to governmental interests? Given the enormous costs of training and research, will any science be done except that which the funders see as valuable for their own ends? Can science recapture its self-determining status? And now that scientific knowledge itself and not merely technology is a valuable commodity and the process of its production is brought under market controls and market principles, can science continue to maintain its claim—and its social responsibility—to serve universal ends? If it cannot—if science becomes thoroughly penetrated by the market—is it still deserving of social autonomy?

I think that the emerging subservience of science to the market, owing to its costs and the commercial value of its product, threatens the quality and integrity of science itself, in two ways. . . . First, insofar as secrecy and proprietary ownership of knowledge become more common, science is threatened in the long run since its cumulative growth presupposes (or has in the past) the sharing of information. The less scientists or their employers are willing to communicate, the more difficult it is for any scientists to do their work. This very fact could function as a corrective on excessive secrecy.

Second, if scientists or their employers are no longer willing to share information for the purposes of peer review, because data or methods are (or may be) commercially valuable and not to be given away, then the quality—or the nature—of the product will be altered. Remember that it is peer review and peer review alone, according to defenders of scientific autonomy, which ensures the quality of scientific knowledge. Peer review is the sole effective guarantee of the objective, universal character of scientific knowledge.[42] It is the control on the subjective, and possibly self-seeking, interests of the individual scientist. If it is bypassed or avoided, if those in control of the process of producing scientific knowledge are not peers, but capitalists or bureaucrats, how can the claim that scientific—universal—knowledge is being offered be sustained? And if it cannot be sustained, then the claim that science deserves autonomy in virtue of this production is compromised.

There is an obvious reply to this and I will address it immediately. The rejoinder reminds us that science has been granted autonomy both because universal knowledge is intrinsically valuable and because it has utility. The reply says that we can substitute the latter as a control for the former and lose nothing. May it not be the case that science is still offering universal knowledge (and is still deserving of its social autonomy) even if the imperatives of openness and sharing are eliminated, because, even under market control, useful knowledge will still be produced? Won't the necessary utility of the knowledge be indicative of its universality? Now the traditional claim for scientific autonomy recognizes the utility of scientific knowledge, but holds that truth—as exclusively determined by the autonomous community of scientific peers—must be the basis for utility: scientists alone can determine what is the truth, and when they are allowed to do so utility will follow. So the traditional view is that if you compromise autonomy you will sacrifice utility. The reply I am sketching says something else, for it holds that science's autonomy from particular private interests—market interests—may be safely compromised without compromising science's claim to offer universal knowledge.

It may be that, as a result of the commodification of science, we are witnessing a transformation in the standards by which "scientific" knowledge is defined. Perhaps there is a shift underway, in the direction of technological or utilitarian standards that do not require the communal procedures that necessitate sharing and the renunciation of secrecy. If this is so, then the proof of scientific knowledge would not be determined by judgment of the scientific community, but by its use, or more precisely by its marketability. In any case, the question at hand is whether utility as determined by the market provides the "independent, impartial criteria" that are the *universal* criteria needed to justify scientific autonomy from social regulation. I would suggest not. Notions of utility, with perhaps a few exceptions so general as to be unhelpful, are varying. They depend on different value judgments and perceptions of ends, and they are *appropriately* particular in a democratic society. While "utility," *otherwise unspecified*, may be in some sense a universal end, in practice it must always be defined in a particular, varying fashion (unless, of course, some particular group in society is in the position to impose its definition of utility on the rest of us.) Beyond this, the more specific problem with a market definition of utility, to put it quite baldly, is that it does not recognize a manifold variety of notions of what is useful, but only those notions of utility that can command ready cash. So a science subservient to direction by those concerned with market utility would be a science in the interest of a few, not of all. (Not to be forgotten in this regard is how susceptible to manipulation by the market are our notions of what is desirable and useful.)

If it is the case that science cannot escape market direction, and thus that it has sacrificed a right to social autonomy as a consequence of its no longer being independent of special particular interests, what is to be done? If science has a social responsibility to serve universal ends, can this be in any way assured? Given the importance of science to everyone in society, a counterbalance to the subservience of science to market interests would seem to be called for. If we cannot agree as a society on any single set of interests, science's aim of fulfilling a universal interest may best be accommodated by opening it up to a plurality of interests, including those not mediated by the market. In calling for such a democratization of science in the name of once again aligning science with a universal end, this view assumes that the recapture of science's autonomy from the market through a return to earlier circumstances or by governmental intervention is unlikely. The market system has led us forever beyond the former and has, at least temporarily, captured the latter.

Thus, ensuring that nonmarket interests have a voice in the scientific enterprise would require something other than simply more governmental regulation in the traditional format. We are all painfully aware of the cozy relationship governmentally managed regulators establish with those they are ostensibly watching. (For example, the Bush administration consistently pushed, on economic grounds, for a loosening of controls on the release of genetically novel organisms.[43]) Democratization would require the participation of outsiders not representing the interests of public or private big science, for the problem is just that those institutions are increasingly captive to certain special interests; scientific autonomy as traditionally understood has already been compromised. If we cannot expect that those whose task it is to represent the public interest will in fact do so, if something like a coherent notion of *the* public interest has become problematic, then what is needed is the creation of mechanisms that ensure the systematic representation of those interests that currently have no voice in the business of science. Additionally, the effectiveness of this democratization would require allowing nonscientists to play a role in science. This last compromise of the traditional ideal of scientific self-regulation is needed in order to counterbalance the already prevailing influence of nonscientists from industry or the government whose special interests are increasingly efficacious in science today (not to mention the increasingly commercial interests of the scientific community itself). Some things that might be done:

Increased pressure by public interest groups modeled on consumer activists (such as Science for the People) needs to be brought to bear on big industrial science (and on its partner, the government). The involvement of such countervailing special interests should concern not just obvious matters such as possible hazards of dangerous research, but the whole spectrum of research, including its direction. Concern for public safety may be a foot in the door, leading to the raising of other concerns. (The model of the Cambridge, Mass., City Council's intervention in genetic research at Harvard and MIT indicates that local involvement that includes nonscientists can work to the satisfaction of both parties.) Intervention might be approached on a market-exchange basis, rooted in the perception that, while business has a right to profit, scientific matters are of vital and legitimate public concern, not least of all because of the risks involved. More specifically, industrial science (as well as the government) should be persuaded to set aside some percentage of its profits for projects that are not of immediate and obvious market value.

Universities need to take their traditional obligations as institutions that serve public interests much more seriously. Practically, it is in the university context that research "for its own sake" can best be undertaken. As I have argued, in the contemporary context, this does not mean renouncing outside funding and the influence and interests of those funders, but insisting that there be a balancing of interests, by way of a setting aside of a percentage of funds—again—for commercially nonviabie research and for research that is more obviously directed to "small" interests. (For example, research directed specifically to what is called "sustainable" or "alternative" agriculture.[44])

The possible success of such democratization would rest finally, I think, on a change in the nature of the prevailing market ideology. As Lester Thurow has argued, what reigns now is the traditional competitive Friedmanesque view of individual entrepreneurs who are and who must remain opposed to any form of public involvement in their operations. Thurow contends that this model is outdated and that the U.S. economy is threatened by the greater success of cooperative models (in Japan and Germany) where capitalism is seen more as a cooperative group enterprise and where a public role in business operations is seen as good business.[45] Unless the market can be more generally democratized along such lines, the democratization of science also seems unlikely. Science as we have traditionally understood it may be the victim not of irrationality or indifference but rather of the rival claim to universal rationality presented by the market.

Notes

[1]Science has "a leading place if not . . . the first rank in the scale of cultural values." Robert K. Merton, "The Normative Structure of Science" in Robert K. Merton, *The Sociology of Science: Theoretical and Empirical Investigations*, ed. Norman W. Storer (Chicago: University of Chicago Press, 1973), 268. Discussing a survey of 800 scientists, Dorothy Nelkin reports that "seventy-seven percent agreed that 'The pursuit of science is best organized when as much freedom as possible is granted to all scientists.'" The study also suggests that certain attitudes are characteristic of scientists: " 'A pure scientist must not deny himself a discovery by worrying about social consequences.' 'I would insist that no area of investigation be closed because someone feels that society is incapable of handling it.' Wide consensus on the importance of autonomy has meant significant federal patronage of science with minimal public control." Dorothy Nelkin, "Threats and Promises: Negotiating the Control of Research," in *Limits of Scientific Inquiry*, ed. Gerald Holton and Robert S. Morison (New York: W. W. Norton, 1978), 192. According to physicist Gerald Holton "calls for any explicit limits [to scientific research] go against long-standing traditions of academic and research freedoms as still understood by most scientists. They contradict the predominant philosophical base of science as an infinitely open system. . . ." Gerald Holton, "From the Endless Frontier to the Ideology of Limits," in *Limits of Scientific Inquiry*, ed. Holton and Morison, 229 (hereafter, the Holton and Morison collection is cited as *Limits of Inquiry*).

[2]Robert L. Sinsheimer, "The Presumptions of Science," in *Limits of Inquiry*, 23.

[3]"Society *invests* in the training, professional development, and general work of technical communities. It invests heavily: including research facilities and instruments, information

banks, communication systems, and other aspects of infrastructure, as well as R&D grants and contracts, substantial public subsidy of one form or another goes to virtually every college, university, medical center, field station and research facility in the United States. . . . The situation is similar in most other countries. For the most part the technical professions are left free to govern themselves, control admission to memberships, direct their own research, enforce quality of work, and advise on allocation of public and semipublic funds." William W. Lowrance, *Modern Science and Human Values* (Oxford: Oxford University Press, 1985), 81–82.

[4]Lowrance sees science as having two sorts of social obligations. The first involves maintaining its integrity as a self-governing institution (and this importantly involves peer accountability and the sharing of information) and the second is service to society. Ibid., 82.

[5]See Harvey Brooks, "The Problem of Research Priorities," in *Limits of Inquiry*, 177. For a detailed discussion of the history of scientific autonomy in post-World War II USA see Nelkin, "Threats and Promises."

[6]"Probably the strongest reason for championing the hallowed ideal of scientific freedom is, quite pragmatically, that it gets scientific results." Lowrance, *Modern Science and Human Values*, 102. *Science, The Endless Frontier,* by Vannevar Bush (reprinted 1960, National Science Foundation, U.S. Government Printing Office), details how science has had its autonomy delegated to it by society in the post-World War II years; it articulates the contract. "It is likely indeed that scientists today enjoy greater freedom of inquiry than ever before in history, in terms of both public support through use of tax funds and reasonableness of government restriction." Peter Barton Hurt, "Public Criticism of Health Science Policy," in *Limits of Inquiry*, 157.

[7]Francis Bacon was among the first of the moderns to envision modern science as combining the separate ends of theoretical and practical knowledge: "now these two directions—the one active, the other contemplative—are one and the same thing; and what in operation is most useful, that in knowledge is most true." *Novum Organum*, bk. 2, aphorism 4. According to historian of science Loren Graham, "The greatest value of science is not what it does for scientists, but what it does in both intellectual and material terms for society. . . ." Loren Graham, "Concerns About Science and Attempts to Regulate Inquiry," in *Limits of Inquiry*, 19. The physicist Gerald Holton holds that "the 'old credo' of science" has "immense power and usefulness" and has helped to "fashion two activities of great strength. The first is concerned with " 'pure' or 'basic' science rather than public need. It is the product of a largely autonomous self-governing system, not directed by the calculus of risk and benefits. If there are other affected interests, most often these are placed at a distance and the scientists are insulated from them. The hope for social utility as a by-product of one's discipline-oriented research may be in the background. But the ruling motto is that 'truth must set its own agenda.' "The "second mode of current excellence" involves applying "the basic scientific findings to a multitude of public needs. . . ." Holton, "From the Endless Frontier," 231.

[8]". . . the scientific and technical enterprise needs a certain measure of internal autonomy in order to pursue the most pragmatic goals. This is true because the ends we can pursue are constrained by the possibilities presented to us by nature, and in the words of Charles Fried we cannot affirm 'truth as a constraint on the pursuit of the useful, while denying truth any power to set its own agenda.' " "Even in the most applied research activity, once the search is underway, utility is bracketed and reality must be the goal, lest the desired utility itself never be reached." Harvey Brooks, "The Problem of Research Priorities," in *Limits of Inquiry*, 177.

[9]Bernard Barber, *Science and the Social Order* (New York: Collier Books, 1962), 41.

[10]According to Don Price science is "the only institution for which tax funds are appropriated almost on faith, and under concordats which protect the autonomy . . . of the

laboratory." Don Price, "The Scientific Establishment," *Science*, 134 (August 18, 1961): 1099. The medical and legal professions might seem to be counterexamples: like science they are of considerable social significance and are largely self-regulating. What distinguishes medicine and law from science is that they are still for the most part private enterprises undertaken by individual practioners for the sake of individual clients. According to William Lowrance, physicians are subjected to "elaborate societal and peer controls." Lowrance, *Modern Science and Human Values*, 61.

[11]For a discussion of the "discomfort and irritation" of scientists when, in a public forum, laypersons demand that they identify their "political base" or "source of support," see Nelkin, "Threats and Promises," at 204.

[12]*Dialogue on the Great World Systems*, in the Salisbury translation, ed. G. de Santillana (Chicago: University of Chicago Press, 1953), 63.

[13]"For the most part, it is conceded that scientists cannot determine social goals, and politicians or the public should not determine scientific methods or tactics, nor influence conclusions. The problem is how to reach agreement on what constitutes ends and what constitutes means, where the line between strategy and tactics in science is to be drawn." Harvey Brooks, "The Problem of Research Priorities," 178.

This conventional distinction reflects two related features pertaining to science's accorded autonomy: Universal truth is not merely worthwhile as such but inherently value neutral in the following sense: those who pursue it do so in such a way that interests other than an interest in truth cannot enter into the results and, once attained, this truth (again as universal) is neutral as regards any possible application and as regards the particular direction such application might take. Insulated in these ways from interested value judgments in a way in which technology is not, autonomy from social regulation for science is seen as justified. Defenders of scientific autonomy traditionally make this distinction. See Nelkin, "Threats and Promises," 201; Holton "From the Endless Frontier," 231; Brooks, "The Problem of Research Priorities," 177.

[14]Nelkin, "Threats and Promises," 193. "There is still a large category of research where regulation of science should not be permitted. This autonomy of science should be defended not as a privilege for an elite, nor as an absolute right, but as a need of society itself." Graham, "Concerns about Science," 2.

[15]Merton, "The Normative Structure of Science," 267–78.

[16]Ibid., 270. This suggests that modern science has preserved a distinctive feature of premodern science: the notion that the pursuit of truth is morally beneficial to the pursuer, irrespective of any utility. See Hans Jonas, "The Practical Uses of Theory," in *Philosophy and Technology*, ed. Mitchum and Mackey (New York: The Free Press, 1983), 335–46.

[17]Israel Scheffler, *Science and Subjectivity* (Indianapolis: Hackett Publishing Co., 1982), 2, 1.

[18]Merton, "The Normative Structure of Science," 270.

[19]Scheffler, *Science and Subjectivity*, 2, 1, 4. This vision of science as possessing a moral dimension because of its service to objective truth has distinctively Kantian overtones in that it locates the core of moral behavior in our rational ability to perceive and conform to the universal. At the heart of Merton's and Scheffler's sense that scientific activity is a kind of moral action is the notion that there is something independent of us, of the merely subjective, something universal and universally accessible, with which we need to accord our thoughts and actions, in order to correct or curb what, as merely subjective, may deviate from the norm of truth. Morality lies in just such accordance, and science, functioning impartially to provide access to this universal is thus inherently moral, even if the universal truths it aims for are not themselves moral laws (and even if these truths should, on occasion, not be useful). In fact, the moral character of scientific activity may well be enhanced in our age where there is considerable skepticism about the possibility of universal moral laws. See Max Weber, "Science as Vocation," in *From Max Weber:*

Essays in Sociology, trans. and ed. Hans Gerth and C. Wright Mills (New York: Oxford University Press, 1946). The irony, of course, is that science appears to have attained this level of moral character precisely through the methodological provisions that restrict it from searching for moral universals.

[20]According to Harvey Brooks, "[t]here appears to be ample empirical evidence from recent research by sociologists of science to indicate that . . . 'objective' criteria of scientific choice do exist. . . ." He thus "assume[s] that peer review does indeed select the 'best science' and that [there are] more or less universalistic criteria of scientific merit which any competent group of scientists will agree upon, at least in application to concrete proposals." Brooks, "The Problem of Research Priorities," 178.

[21]Lowrance, *Modern Science and Human Values,* 74.

[22]Ibid., 82.

[23]Merton, "The Normative Structure of Science," 276.

[24]Lowrance stresses the importance of following the community. See Lowrance, *Modern Science and Human Values,* 74.

[25]Merton, "The Normative Structure of Science," 273.

[26]Ibid., 275.

[27]Ibid., 274.

[28]Ibid.

[29]Ibid., 275.

[30]While this is a common defense of autonomy, one could take a completely pragmatic view and still defend scientific autonomy. I will argue below that this will not succeed.

[31]See especially Hans Jonas, "Freedom of Scientific Inquiry and the Public Interest," *The Hastings Center Report* 6 (August 1976): 15–17; Sissela Bok, "Freedom and Risk" in *Limits of Inquiry;* and Ian Hacking, *Representing and Intervening* (Cambridge: Cambridge University Press, 1983).

[32]Dorothy Nelkin, *Science as Intellectual Property* (New York: Macmillan, 1984), 2.

[33]Richard Levin and Richard Lewontin, "The Commoditization of Science" in *The Dialectical Biologist* (Cambridge, Mass.: Harvard University Press, 1985), 203. Nelkin, *Science as Intellectual Property,* 61.

[34]Nelkin, *Science at Intellectual Property,* 20.

[35]Ibid., 25.

[36]Ibid., 11.

[37]Ibid., 12.

[38]Ibid., 57–58.

[39]Ibid., 58–60.

[40]Ibid., 71–72.

[41]Ibid., 72.

[42]There is some question as to whether peer review alone, independently of the moral integrity of the participants, can yield its desired and promised results. See John Hardwig, "The Role of Trust in Knowledge," *The Journal of Philosophy* 88:12 (December 1991): 693–708.

[43]Jack Kloppenburg, Jr., "Alternative Agriculture and the New BioTechnologies," *Science as Culture* 2:13 (1991), 492.

[44]See Kloppenburg, "Alternative Agriculture," 482–506.

[45]Lester Thurow, *Head to Head: The Coming Economic Battle Among Japan, Europe, and America* (New York: Morrow, 1992).

Index to Text